History of the Conquest of England

CW00670303

By

Augustin Thierry

BIOGRAPHICAL NOTICE OF M. AUGUSTIN THIERRY.

L'histoire aura son Homere comme la poesie.—Chateaubriand, Preface des Etudes Historiques.

Si j'avais à recommencer ma route, je prendrais celle qui m'a conduit où je suis. Aveugle et souffrant, sans espoir et presque sans relache, je puis rendre ce temoignage, qui de ma part ne sera pas suspect: il y a au monde quelque chose qui vaut mieux que les jouissances materielles, mieux que la fortune, mieux que la santé elle-même; c'est le devouement à la science—Augustin Thierry, Dix ans d'Etudes Historiques, Preface,.

Of all the superior men I ever met, few have left so deep an impression upon my mind as M. Augustin Thierry.

I had long been acquainted with the mighty labours that have rendered him one of the leading representatives of the modern school of history; I had a vivid recollection of the enthusiasm that pervaded all the forms of our colleges, when, in utter disgust as we were with the meagre, monotonous, and mendacious narratives of Velly, or Millot, or Anquetil, we all at once saw new, grand, and comprehensive views unfolded before our dazzled and delighted eyes, by M. Augustin Thierry. I had long known that after having endowed his country with two masterpieces of literature, in which the erudition of a Benedictine is combined with the glowing style of a poet, M. Augustin Thierry had purchased with the loss of sight, worn out over old texts and manuscripts, the honour of having been one of the first to raise the standard of historical reform, and to teach France the true sources of her national origin. I knew also that, after this, as if to put the inflexible champion of learning to the utmost proof, fate had been pleased to accumulate for him affliction upon affliction; that having deprived him of sight, it next deprived him of movement; that having extinguished the light of those penetrating eyes, it had paralyzed his once robust limbs; that having for ever shut out from him the view of those monuments of the past, whose examination and study had constituted his joy, his happiness, his very life, it had not even left to his hand, mutilated with severest suffering, the power to hold a pen. But I knew, also, that M. Augustin Thierry had come victorious out of this fearful struggle; that never had his great mind striven with more vivid brilliancy than after he had, to use his own expression, become friends with darkness; that never had his march over the difficult ground of history been made with firmer and more assured step than when he was guided on his way by the brightness of the inward light alone; I knew that the author of the Recits des Temps Merovingiens had never been more lucid, more graphic, more graceful, and at the same time more vigorous in his style, than when it had become necessary for him to commit to other hands the transcription on paper of the works cast and elaborated in that powerful brain, as in a burning furnace.

I knew all this, and it was this that made me eager to witness a spectacle, to my mind the finest of all, the spectacle of a great soul struggling with physical pain, conquering it, prostrating it, reducing it to impotence, and deriving from a loftier sentiment than the world-pride of Epictetus the power and the right to say to it: "Pain, thou art but a word!"

The happiness I so desired I obtained; and as it is impossible for me, within the limits of this sketch, to analyze as I could wish, works, that after all are in every one's hands, I will at least endeavour, ere I succinctly relate the noble life of M. Augustin Thierry, to convey to the reader the impressions made upon my mind in a visit recently paid to the historian, in the company of a lady and two other friends.

On reaching the eminence which overlooks the charming valley of Montmorency, not far from the Hermitage immortalized by Jean Jacques, you perceive to the left a narrow winding road bordered with villas in the Italian style. About half way down this road, on the right, our carriage drew up at a little gate, the threshold of which we passed full of the respectful emotion, ever created by the thought of great talent dignified by a great calamity; for here, in the summer months, dwells Augustin Thierry; hither he comes with the return of spring, to seek strength from the fresh, pure air of the valley, enabling him to continue his labours. We found ourselves in an elegant garden: before us was a lawn varied with flower beds, and beyond it a sloping shrubbery. On the right were a green-house and a summer-house; in front of the latter, lay at full length a handsome Newfoundland dog, which, raising its head, gave us a look of welcome with its mild, well-natured eyes. To the left, on the opposite side of the lawn, rose a rectangular house, white, simple, and in good taste, consisting of two stories, the lower windows opening into the garden. The façade was adorned with a Canova Venus, a Bacchus, a head of Paris, and another of Helen, standing in niches in the wall. Before the door I observed a Bath chair, painted green; this was the carriage in which the illustrious invalid took the air.

Entering a small apartment on the ground floor, furnished with simple elegance, we were received by a lady attired in black; still young, of small stature, graceful manners, and an intellectual but pensive countenance. It was Madame Augustin Thierry, wife of the historian; she who has so appreciated the beauty and happiness of associating her name with a great name, her life with a life of glory and of suffering, of quitting the vain pleasures of the world to devote herself wholly to the noblest part in the drama of life that can be assigned to a woman, the part of a guardian angel, of a providence on earth for a great soul imprisoned in a suffering body. Even had I not known that Madame Augustin Thierry is endowed with faculties that qualify her to take a direct and active part in all the labours of her husband, even had I not read the pieces, so remarkable for thought and for expression, that, proceeding from her pen, have appeared in the Revue des Deux Mondes, under the title of Philippe de Morvelle, the destiny that she has adopted would suffice in my eyes to manifest that hers is a noble heart, a noble spirit.

Having been introduced to Madame Augustin Thierry by the lady under whose auspices we had come, I sat down in a corner of the apartment, and, while the reflections I have just expressed were passing through my mind, looked over a small round table, nearly covered with books, which stood at my side; upon the books lay some embroidery-work just commenced; here was a bronze sphynx paper-weight, and there, in the middle of the table, a vase filled with flowers in their early bloom.

Ere long, we were joined by M. Augustin Thierry's brother, M. Amédée Thierry, a man of middle height, grave in speech as in countenance, wherein we may read the profound depression of his fraternal heart. On his arrival the conversation became more general; but, for my own part, I scarcely listened to it, absorbed as I was in expectation of him whom I was about to see, and in endeavours to picture to myself, beforehand, the extent to which evil is able to attain the soul through the medium of the body.

At length I heard the sound of approaching steps; a door on my right opened, and a domestic appeared, carrying on his back a man, blind, paralyzed, incapable of movement. We all rose: my heart was penetrated with emotion, at the sight of a being so powerful in intellect, so powerless in body; the domestic in his every motion exhibited a respectful solicitude that sensibly affected me; he seemed thoroughly to appreciate the value of him he bore. He bent gently back towards an arm chair, in which he deposited his charge, enveloping the lower part of the motionless frame with a wrapper. This done, in an instant the scene changed, and I at once recalled a passage in the Essai sur la litterature Anglaise, where M. de Chateaubriand describes the visit of a contemporary to Milton. "The author of 'Paradise Lost,' attired in a black doublet, reclined in an arm-chair; his head was uncovered, his silver hair fell upon his shoulders, and his fine dark eyes shone bright in their blindness upon his pallid face." It was the same head, with the exception of the white hair, that I now saw before me; the same face, more youthful and vigorous, the noblest blind face that can be conceived. The head was firmly set upon broad shoulders; glossy hair, of the deepest black, carefully parted over an expansive forehead, ell in curls beside each temple; beneath their arched brows opened the dark eyes; but for the vagueness of their direction, I should have imagined them animated with sight; the nose was of the purest Greek form; the mouth, with lips fine, delicate, and expressive, seemed endowed with all the sensibility of which the eyes had been deprived; the finely turned chin had a slight dimple at its extremity; there was in the contour of the face, and in the general expression of the physiognomy, a remarkable combination of energy, subtleness, and sedate tranquillity; the tones of his voice were clear, well poised, and distinct, though, from his feeble health, not sonorous, his bearing was, in the highest degree, elegant; the lower portion of the frame, as I have said, was paralyzed, but the movement of the bust and of the arms was free; the hands, of which only the forefinger and thumb appeared capable of action, were gloved.

When the name of the lady who had introduced us was announced to him, the handsome blind man smiled, and like the smile of Chactas in Renè, "that smile of the mouth, unaccompanied by the smile of the eyes, partook of the mysterious and of the celestial." The lady approached him, and Thierry kissed, with a chivalrous air, the fair hand placed in his own.

Conversation once fairly begun, that fine head seemed as it were radiant in the light of the intellect still finer within. I have been in the company of many persons who have the reputation of good talkers, and who do talk admirably, but I have perhaps never heard anything comparable with the colloquial language of M. Angustin Thierry, in facility, perspicuity, elegance. It is, doubtless, the habit of dictation, that has given so much of style to his conversation; but whatever the cause, it may indeed be said of him, that without any effort, without any affectation whatever, he really speaks like a book.

One of our party, M. Ampère, was preparing to depart for the East; he had no sooner mentioned the circumstance, than M. Augustin Thierry discoursed to us of the East, in what, for thought and language, was an absolute poem; this blind man knows everything, recollects everything; that which he has not seen with the eyes of the body, he has seen with the eyes of the spirit. Like Milton, he is acquainted with nearly all the European languages. One of his friends told me, that he has sometimes heard him in the evening, seated in his garden, beneath the pale rays of the setting sun, singing, with his feeble voice, a love song in modern Greek; and at such moments, added my informant, 'he seemed to me finer than Homer, or than the unknown Klepht, who himself, perhaps also blind, had composed the verses he was reciting.'

Throughout the conversation, to which I was a silent and attentive listener, I could detect in M. Augustin Thierry not the slightest trace of selfishness, not the least self-reference; on the contrary, he who had been so cruelly tried by fate, spoke of the sufferings and infirmities of others with the most unaffected and touching commiseration. And thus, from day to day, does this martyr to science intrepidly pursue the task he has imposed upon himself; at times only, when his pains are most racking, he is heard to murmur: "Oh, that I were only blind!" Except in such moments of depression, which are short and far between, and discernible only by his most intimate associates, M. Augustin Thierry seems more a stranger to his own condition than are those who surround and listen to him; science, history, poetry, anecdotes, reminiscences of his youth—he applies to these and all other subjects the same full, rich, elegant, nervous, noble diction; every shade of thought is reflected on his lips. At times, when an idea of a more peculiarly grave and lofty character arises in his mind, you can discern a movement in the muscles of the eye; those blind eyes, the dark pupil of which stands out in bold relief from the cornea, open wide; the thought within seems essaying to make its way through the opacity of the ball, and, after vain efforts to effect this, returns within, descends to the lips, which receiving it, give it forth, not only in language, but with the expression of the look; from time to time, the blind man passes his poor weak hand over those, in every sense, so speaking lips, as if cherishing the precious organ, enriched for him with all the faculties that the other organs have lost. The two hours we spent with him seemed not a moment.

M. Augustin Thierry was born at Blois, on the 20th May, 1795, of poor and humble parents. He passed through his studies with distinguished success at the college of his native town, and judging from the first production of his youth, impressed with a singular energy and even enthusiasm, he must have been endowed by nature with an extreme sensibility, with an imagination highly vivid, and of such vigorous organization as must have necessitated enormous, pitiless toil to quell it. He himself relates, in the preface to his Recits des Temps Merovingiens, how the author of Les Martyrs, whom we find, as it were, a great lighthouse at the entrance to every new idea of our age, became, in a great degree, the primum mobile of his future vocation; how, one day, when alone in one of the school-rooms, reading, for the first time, Les Martyrs, and having come, in the sixth book, to the so dramatic picture of the battle of the Franks and the Romans in the marshes of Batavia, the young student suddenly felt within him, as it were, a revelation of historical truth falsified by the classic historians and restored by the powerful instinct of a great poet; how, seized with enthusiasm, he rose from his seat, and made the apartment resound, as he marched up and down its length, shouting the war-song of the terrible Franks of M. de Chateaubriand: "Pharamond, Pharamond, we have fought with the sword! &c." and, lastly, how the memory of this electric impression remained stamped upon his mind in indelible characters.

In 1811, on quitting his college, M. Augustin Thierry entered the normal school; after passing two years there, he was appointed professor in a provincial college; the invasion of 1814 brought him to Paris. He was at this time in all the ardour of early youth; versed in the most various studies, he had as yet no particular predilection for any distinct branch of science, and his political ideas, though fervent, partook of the vagueness and confusion which characterized the period. He has himself described the condition of his mind at this time: "With a hatred of military despotism, part of the reaction of the general mind against the imperial regime, I combined a profound aversion for revolutionary tyranny, and, without any decided preference for one form of government over another, a certain distaste for the English constitution, or rather for the odious and absurd aping of it which at this period prevailed in France. I yearned for a future, I knew not exactly what; for a liberty whose definition, if I gave it any at all, assumed something of this form: a government with the greatest possible amount of individual guarantees, and the least possible amount of administrative action."

There was living at this time a celebrated political economist, then, indeed, obscure, but whom it has since been sought to elevate into a god. The daring scope of his views at first led away the ardent mind of the youthful Augustin, who, quitting the university, devoted himself with all the fervency of his nature to the study of the loftiest social problems, and attached himself to St. Simon in the capacity of secretary, and of disciple. It is unnecessary to say that at this period St. Simon had propounded no idea of constructing anything at all resembling a new religion. This was a notion which occurred to him much later, if, indeed, it be not altogether a posthumous crotchet, gratuitously attributed to him by his successors. However this may have been, though limited to questions of an entirely social, industrial, or political character, this co-operation of M. Augustin Thierry in the labours of a man, whose eminent qualities as a political economist and thinker are incontestable, was of short duration; the gloomy, narrow, and despotic tendencies of sectarianism could not but jar upon a mind essentially endowed with explicitness, precision, and independence; the disciple often rebelled against the views of the master, and, besides, he felt more and more attracted towards a sphere of studies more positive in their nature. M. Augustin Thierry left St. Simon in 1817, and joined the Censeur Europeén, which, under the editorship of MM. Comte and Dunoyer, enjoyed the reputation of the most important and most high-minded of the liberal journals of the period.

The new school of history had not at this time raised its head; Velly, Garnier, Millot, Anquetil, reigned sovereign supreme. The general aspect of our own history, more especially that of the first eight centuries, was utterly disfigured; in that dull and arid nomenclature of faits et gestes royaux, the Sicambrian Chlodowig is presented to us in flowing wig and laced ruffles, the leudes of Charlemagne in the guise of the courtiers of the Œil de Bæuf, Fredegonde in fontanges, and Hermangarde in hoopedpetticoat and red-heeled shoes. "These men," observes M. de Chateaubriand, "carried in their heads the fixed form of a solemn monarchy, ever the same, from first to last, marching sedately onwards with three orders and a parliament of grave persons in black robes and powdered hair." No historian had thought of moving out of this beaten track, when M. Thierry, having occasion to seek, in the history of the past, materials for the polemics of the day, first descended into the arena, and young, ardent, unconscious of his vocation and of his destiny, entered upon that grand struggle, the result of which was to be the establishment of new doctrines and new principles.

In his youthful fervour and the excess of his popular enthusiasm, M. Augustin began with rushing beyond the bounds of truth into the regions of paradox. And this was to be expected. Aristocracy, assailed and decimated under Louis XI., gagged and beaten down by Richelieu and Louis XIV., dishonoured under Louis XV., beheaded by the Convention, led in a string by Napoleon, sought once more to raise its head under the Restoration; it would, perhaps, to a certain extent, have attained its object, had it been better served, and more especially had it been less compromised by the majority of those who constituted themselves its organs. Listening to its political champions, you would have supposed that it desired to pass a sponge over four centuries of progressive decay: it did not content itself with assailing accomplished facts, it denied them; and feeble, weak, obscured, lost as it was in the grand social unity, the result of '89, instead of quietly settling down in its position, and seeking, in self-renovation, an element of strength and duration, it aimed at nothing less than the annihilation of the past, the confiscation of history. In the nineteenth century, an eloquent voice ventured to say, in the very teeth of new France— "Enfranchised race, slaves wrested from our grasp, tributary people, new people, leave was granted you to be free, but not to be noble; for us, all is of right, for you, all is of favour." Pretensions of this sort, wholly based upon the old right of conquest, naturally brought into the field of history a plebeian, proud of his plebeian birth, and ready to oppose pride to pride. When, a century before, the Comte de Boulainvilliers sought to construct an historical system of his own, by deducing false consequences from the false proposition already generally scouted, of the distinction of conquerors and conquered in Gaul, a man of the people, the abbé Dubos, stood forward to combat fallacy with fallacy; in reply to a book which abused the fact of conquest, he wrote a very learned work to prove that there had been no conquest at all; that there had been an alliance between the two races and nothing more; that, five centuries later, in the tenth century, in consequence of the dismemberment of the sovereignty, and the conversion of offices into seigneuries, a dominant caste had intrusively interposed itself between kings and people; and that it was feudalism and not the Frankish invasion which had enslaved Gaul.

In reproducing the aristocratic theories of M. de Boulainvilliers, M. de Montlosier encountered at the very outset an antagonist much less accommodating than the Abbé Dubos. Far from denying the fact of conquest, M. Augustin Thierry proudly accepted it, as a premises on which to found his claims in favour of the conquered; not content with establishing the original iniquity of the fact and its fatal consequences at the period, he traced its progress through fourteen ages, subsisting ever and everywhere, and denounced it as the source not merely of evils past, but of all present difficulties. Gravely adopting the assertions of M. de Montlosier, and his imaginary division of the France of 1815 into Gauls and Franks, combating menace with menace, and paradox with paradox, he in his turn exclaimed: "We think we are one nation, yet we are two nations in the same land; two nations, hostile in their recollections of the past, irreconcilable in their projects for the future. The genius of the conquest has made its mock of nature and of time, it still hovers over this unhappy country. It is under its influence that the distinctions of castes have succeeded to those of blood, those of orders to those of castes, those of titles to those of orders." Hurried on in this manner, by the necessities of polemics, beyond the bounds of the true, it continued the fight in the void. Once engaged in supplying France with the reason and solution of all things in this permanent fact of conquest, he undertook to follow it out of France, and to combat it wherever, as he conceived, he should find it. He commenced by giving in the Censeur a sketch of the revolutions of England from the Norman invasion to the death of Charles I., and not content with metamorphosing the Cavaliers and Roundheads into Normans and Saxons, he carried the theory of the conquest, and subjection of the one race by the other, even beyond the reign of Charles II.

He has himself given an account of these exaggerations and gropings in the dark of a young and great mind feeling its way; he has told us, with the frankness which belongs to a superior man, that he soon saw he was carrying too far this, in itself, so true and fecund principle of the distinction of races, that he was falsifying history by applying to epochs entirely different forms entirely identical. But he has also described how to his aberrations as a journalist, who had at first lost his way, as it were, in the past, he owed the sentiment of his true vocation, how from the very day when he first touched upon the great problem of the Germanic invasions and the dismemberment of the Roman empire, he was drawn to it by an irresistible attraction; how, upon his first glance at history he said to himself; I will be an historian: and how deeply he became impressed with the essentiality of regulating and maturing by study the passion that had risen within him.

When the Censeur Europeen succumbed beneath the blows of a censorship altogether different from its own, M. Augustin Thierry, already more especially devoted to the labours of pure erudition, contributed to the Courrier Français a series of letters in which, sketching an outline of one of his future works, he expounded his plan of a reform in the manner of studying and writing history. The exigencies of daily polemics closing this arena to him, M. Thierry, who had hitherto divided his attention between the history of the past and the business of the present, sequestered himself from the world and its politics, and engaged in a pertinacious study of facts, reading, analysing, comparing, and extracting the marrow out of every book and every manuscript that could throw a light upon his investigations. Still under the influence of the grand problem of the Germanic invasions which had struck his imagination at the outset, he digested all the documents calculated to throw light upon it, to fathom it, to solve it; and from step to step, his ideas progressively matured and developed, by five years of solitary labours, resulted at length in two works, alike admirable in their matter and their manner, and which our epoch, so encumbered with futile and absurd productions, may well regard as memorable and glorious to it, destined as they are to a permanent existence among the proudest annals of learning. The first edition of the Histoire de la Conquête de l'Angleterre par les Normands appeared in the spring of 1825; the first edition of the Lettres sur l'Histoire de France about the close of 1827; a second edition, entirely revised and recast, was published in the following year.

The reader is aware of the immense sensation produced by the former of these works, the so cherished production of an historian of twenty-six. The author was enjoying all the triumph of success when he, too late, perceived that his eyes had failed under his intense labours, and that his strength was giving way. After a journey into Switzerland, he visited Provence, accompanied by his learned friend M. Fauriel, and on his return to Paris, in 1826, found his health somewhat improved, but his sight still declining. Almost blind, he resumed his labours; a young man, obscure at this period, but whose name was destined to take a brilliant position in literature, Armand Carrel, joined him, as secretary, and by his friendly earnestness of purpose rendered the necessity of reading with the eyes of others less painful to Thierry: relieved by this co-operation, he at one time formed, with M. Mignet, the project of writing in concert a great national history, but, after some experiments which seemed to show the futility of the attempt, the project was abandoned.

His next publication was the Letters sur l'Histoire de France, shortly after the appearance of which, in the spring of 1830, the Institute elected him a member of the Academie des Inscriptiones et Belles Lettres. He was ere long assailed by the most acute pains, and by a nervous malady of the gravest character. He had once more to renounce his beloved studies and to quit Paris. He lived, from 1831 to 1836, between Vesoul, with his brother the prefect of Haute-Saône, and the baths of Luxeuil. It was at the latter place that, in 1831, he became acquainted with and married the lady who was to alleviate his sufferings, by aiding him on his way through the evil days of premature old age. In the intervals of repose granted him by his maladies, he resumed with fresh ardour his task of historian. He first occupied himself with the revision of his Histoire de la Conquête de l'Angleterre, and then with selecting and correcting the various productions of his youth, which he collected into a volume, published in 1834, under the title of Dix Ans d'Etudes Historiques. Still full of the desire to complete his history of the Germanic invasions, he commenced in the Revue des Deux Mondes a series of letters, giving an exact and perfect picture of the civil, political, and religious life of the French of the sixth century.

These elegant, animated, and at the same time substantial productions, published in the next year under the title of Recits des Temps Merovingiens, obtained for their author the prize of 400l., founded by Baron Gobert, and awarded by the Academie Française. Almost at the same moment—in the autumn of 1835—M. Guizot recalled him to Paris, for the purpose of entrusting to him the superintendence of a great undertaking, honourable alike to the historian who conceived it and the historian who directed it. It was nothing less than to extract from the archives of every town and parish of France all the materials directly or indirectly bearing upon the history of the Third estate, so as to form a collection rivalling the great Benedictine compilations devoted to the nobility and the clergy, and to supply future genius with all the materials for a gigantic work, hitherto declared impossible—a general and complete history, namely, of the French nation. Should this splendid monument be ever constructed, on its base must be prominently inscribed the names of Francis Guizot and Augustin Thierry.

An illustrious philosopher, whose untimely death Germany still deplores, Edward Gans, writes thus:—

"It is Thierry who has triumphantly demonstrated the fallacy of those historical systems which see all France in a number of Frankish tribes; which, passing over in silence the element imported from the south, forget that up to the beginning of the thirteenth century the limits of the Frankish empire did not extend beyond the Isère, and that in the tongue of oc and no, the tongue of ouy and nenny, was likened to the barking of a dog; in a word, it is Thierry who has taught us to appreciate the true signification of what is called the fourteen centuries of the French monarchy."

I will add, that it is M. Augustin Thierry who, by his efforts to restore to proper names, under the two first races, their true orthography, has succeeded in fixing the moment of the metamorphosis of Franks into French; and it is M. Thierry who has demolished to its foundations the historical axiom inscribed at the head of the charter of 1814—namely, the pretended enfranchisement of the communes by Louis le Gros. He has created in our annals a glorious trace that will never be effaced; no historian, ancient or modern, has exhibited, in a higher degree than he, that human sense which is the very soul of history, I mean that comprehensive sensibility, synthetic without losing aught of the true, which leads a writer to attach himself to the destiny of a whole people as to the destiny of an individual; following this people, step by step, through ages, with an interest as earnest, emotions as vivid, as though he were following the steps of a friend engaged in a perilous enterprise; no one, in a word, has better realized than M. Thierry this conception of the ideal in history enunciated by himself: "La narration complete épuisant les textes, rassemblant les details epars, recueillant jusqu'aux moindres indices des faits, et des caractères, et de tout cela formant un corps, auquel vient le souffle de vie, par l'union de la science et de l'art."

INTRODUCTION.

The principal states of modern Europe have at present attained a high degree of territorial unity, and the habit of living under one same government and in the bosom of one same civilization, seems to have introduced among the population of each state an entire community of manners, language, and patriotism. Yet there is perhaps not one of them which does not still present to the inquirer living traces of the diversity of the races of men which, in the progress of time, have combined to form that population. This variety of races is displayed under different aspects. Here a complete separation of idioms, local traditions, political sentiments, and a sort of instinctive hostility, distinguish from the great national mass the population of particular districts, of limited extent; there a simple difference of idiom, or even of accent, marks, though more faintly, the limit of the settlements formed by peoples of diverse origin, and long separated by deep-seated animosities. The further we go back from the time in which we live, the more distinct do these varieties become; we clearly perceive the existence of several peoples in the geographical circumscription which bears the name of one alone: instead of varying provincial dialects, we find complete and regular languages; and that which in the light of the present seems merely defective civilization and protracted resistance to progress, assumes, in the past, the aspect of original manners and patriotic adherence to ancient institutions. In this way, facts themselves of no social importance, retain great historical value. It is a falsification of history to introduce into it a philosophical contempt for all that does not enter into the uniformity of existing civilization, or to regard as alone worthy of honourable mention the peoples with whose name the chances of events have connected the idea and the destiny of that civilization.

The populations of the European continent and its islands have come at various periods into juxtaposition, usurping the one from the other, territories already occupied, and arrested only in their progress, at the point where natural obstacles, or resistance more powerful than their attack, the result of some extraordinary combination of the conquered, absolutely compelled them to stop. Thus the conquered of various epochs have become, so to speak, ranged in layers of populations, in the different directions taken by the great migration of peoples. In this movement of successive invasions, the most ancient races, reduced to a few families, have deserted the plains and flown to the mountains, where they have maintained a poor but independent existence; while the invaders, invaded in their turn, have become serfs of the soil in the plains they occupied, from want of a vacant asylum in the impregnable recesses already possessed by those whom themselves had driven there.

The conquest of England by William duke of Normandy, in the year 1066, is the last territorial conquest that has been operated in the western portion of Europe. The conquests effected there since that period have been political conquests, quite different from those of the barbarians, who transferred themselves and their families to the conquered territory, and apportioned it out among themselves, leaving to the conquered merely life, and this on condition of their doing all the work and keeping quiet. This invasion having taken place at a period nearer to our own than those of the populations which, in the fifth century, dismembered the Roman empire, we possess numerous documents elucidating well nigh every fact connected with its history, and which are even complete enough to give us a just idea of what a conquest in the middle ages was, how it was executed, and how maintained, what description of spoliations and sufferings it inflicted on the vanquished, and what means were employed by the latter to react against their invaders. Such a picture carefully traced in all its details, and set off in fitting colours, has an historical interest more general than might at first seem to belong to the limits of time and place within which itself is circumscribed, for almost every people in Europe has, in its actual existence, something derived from the conquests of the middle ages. It is to these conquests that the majority of them owe their geographical limits, the name they bear, and, in great measure, their internal constitution, that is to say, their distribution into orders and classes.

The higher and lower classes who, at the present day, keep so distrustful an eye upon one another, or actually struggle for systems of ideas and of government, are in many countries the lineal representatives of the peoples conquering and the peoples conquered of an anterior epoch. Thus the sword of the conquest, in renewing the face of Europe and the distribution of its inhabitants, has left its ancient impress upon each nation created by the admixture of various races. The race of the invaders, when it ceased to be a separate nation, remained a privileged class. It formed a military nobility, which, to avoid gradual extinction, recruiting its numbers from time to time from the more ambitious, adventurous, and turbulent of the inferior ranks, domineered over the laborious and peaceful masses below them, so long as the military government derived from the conquest endured. The invaded race, despoiled of property in the soil, of command, and of liberty, not living by the sword but by the compulsory labour of their hands, dwelling not in castles but in towns, formed a separate society beside the military association of the conquerors. Whether it retained, within the walls of its towns, the remains of Roman civilization, or whether, aided by only a slight vestige of that civilization, it had commenced a new civilization of its own, this class raised its head in proportion as the feudal organization of the nobles by descent or political affiliation, declined.

Hitherto the historians of the modern peoples, in relating these great events, have transported the ideas, the manners, and the political position of their own time to past ages. The chroniclers of the feudal period placed the barons and peerage of Philip-Augustus in the court of Charlemagne, and confounded the savage government and brute force of the conquest with the more regular rule and more fixed usages of the feudal establishment. The historians of the monarchical era, who have constituted themselves exclusively the historians of the prince, have proceeded on even narrower and more singular ideas; they modelled the Germanic royalty of the first conquerors of the Roman empire, and the feudal royalty of the 12th century, upon the vast and powerful royalties of the 17th. In the history of France, the various invasions of Gaul, the numerous populations, different in origin and manners, settled upon its territory, the division of the soil into several countries, because there were several peoples, and lastly, the union, which it required six hundred years to effect, of all these countries under one sceptre; these are facts wholly neglected by the writers in question. The historians formed by the 18th century are, in like manner, absorbed in the philosophy of their period. Witnesses of the progress of the middle classes, and organs of their wants as against the legislation and the opinions of the middle ages, they have not calmly viewed or correctly described the old times in which the classes they championed scarce enjoyed civil existence. Full of a disdain inspired by abstract right and reason, they treated facts as nought: a process which may be very well with the view of operating a revolution in men's minds and in the state, but by no means proper in the composition of history. Yet we must not be surprised at all this; whatever superiority of mind a man may possess, he cannot overpass the horizon of his century; each new epoch gives to history new points of view and a special form.

In the present day, however, it is no longer permissible to write history for the profit of one single idea; our age will not sanction it; it requires to be told everything, to have portrayed and explained to it the existence of nations at various epochs; and that each past century shall have assigned to it its true place, its colour, and its signification. This is what I have endeavoured to do with the great event of which I have undertaken to write the history. I have consulted none but original texts and documents, either for the details of the various circumstances narrated, or for the characters of the persons and populations that figure in them. I have drawn so largely upon these texts, that, I flatter myself, little is left in them for other writers. The national traditions of the less known populations and old popular ballads, have supplied me with infinite indications of the mode of existence, the feelings, and the ideas of men at the period and in the places whither I transport the reader.

As to the narrative, I have adhered as closely as possible to the language of the ancient historians, contemporaries of the facts related, or but little removed from them in point of time. When I have been obliged to supply their inadequacy by general considerations, I have sought to give authority to these by citing the original passages on which I had relied in my deductions. Lastly, I have throughout preserved the narrative form, so that the reader might not abruptly pass from an old tradition to a modern commentary, or my work present the incongruous aspect of fragments of chronicles intermingled with dissertations. I thought, besides, that if I applied myself rather to relate than to lecture, even in the exposition of general facts and results, I might communicate a sort of historical life to the masses of men as well as to the individual personages, and that thus the political career of nations might offer somewhat of that human interest which is aroused by an unaffected account of the mutations of fortune and adventures of an individual.

I propose, then, to exhibit, in the fullest detail, the national struggle which followed the conquest of England by the Normans established in Gaul; to reproduce every particular afforded by history of the hostile relations of two peoples violently placed together upon the same soil; to follow them throughout their long wars and their obstinate segregation, up to the period when, by the intermixture of their races, manners, wants, languages, there was formed one sole nation, one common language, one uniform legislation. The scene of this great drama is England, Scotland. Ireland, and also France, by reason of the numerous relations which the successors of the Conqueror had, since the invasion, with that portion of the European continent. On the French side of the Channel, as well as on the other, their enterprises have modified the political and social existence of many populations whose history is almost completely unknown. The obscurity in which these populations have become involved does not arise from any unworthiness on their part to have had historians, equally with other populations; most of them, on the contrary, are remarkable for an originality of character which distinguishes them in the most marked manner from the great nations into which they have been absorbed, and in resistance to a fusion with which they have displayed a political activity, the moving cause of many great events that have hitherto been erroneously attributed to the ambition of particular individuals, or to other accidental causes. The research into the history of these populations may contribute to solve the problem, hitherto undecided, of the varieties of the human race in Europe, and of the great primitive races whence these varieties derive.

Under this philosophical point of view, and independent of the picturesque interest which I have endeavoured to create, I hoped to aid the progress of science by constructing, if I may use the expression, the history of the Welsh, of the Irish of pure race, of the Scots, both those of the primitive and those of the mixed race, of the continental Bretons and Normans, and more especially of the numerous population then, as now, inhabiting Southern Gaul, between the Loire, the Rhone, and the two seas. Without assigning to the great facts of history less importance than they merit, I have applied myself with peculiar interest to the local events relating to these hitherto neglected populations, and while necessarily relating their revolutions in a summary manner, I have done this with that sort of sympathy, with that sentiment of pleasure, which one experiences in repairing an injustice. The establishment of the great modern states has been mainly the work of force; the new societies have been formed out of the wrecks of the old societies violently destroyed, and in this labour of recomposition, large masses of men have lost, amid heavy sufferings, their liberty, and even their name as a people, replaced by a foreign name. Such a movement of destruction was, I am aware, inevitable. However violent and illegitimate it may have been in its origin, its result has been the civilization of Europe. But while we render to this civilization its due homage, while we view with glowing admiration the noble destiny it is preparing for the human race, we may regard with a certain tender regret the downfal of other civilizations that might one day have also grown and fructified for the world, had fortune favoured them.

This brief explanation was necessary to prevent that feeling of surprise which the reader might otherwise have felt upon finding in this work, the history not merely of one, but of several conquests, written in a method the very reverse of that hitherto employed by modern historians. All of these, following what seemed to them the natural path, go from the conquerors to the conquered; they take their stand in the camp where there is triumph, rather than in that where there is defeat, and exhibit the conquest as accomplished the moment that the victor has proclaimed himself master, taking no more heed than he to the ulterior resistance which his policy has afterwards defeated. Thus, for all those who, until recently, have written the history of England, there are no Saxons after the battle of Hastings and the coronation of William the Bastard; a romance writer, a man of genius, was the first to teach the modern English that their ancestors of the eleventh century were not all utterly defeated and crushed in one single day.

A great people is not so promptly subjugated as the official acts of those who govern it by the law of the strongest would appear to indicate. The resuscitation of the Greek nation proves how great a misconception it is to take the history of kings, or even that of conquering peoples, for that of the whole country over which they rule. Patriotic regret lives on in the depth of a nation's heart, long after the desire to raise its fallen condition has become hopeless. This sentiment of patriotism, when it is no longer adequate to the creation of armies, still creates bands of guerillas, of political highwaymen in the forest or on the mountain, and venerates as martyrs those who die in the field or on the gibbet, in its cause. Such is what recent investigations have taught us with reference to the Greek nation, and what I have myself discovered with respect to the Anglo-Saxon race, in tracing out its history where no one previously had sought it, in the popular legends, traditions, and ballads. The resemblance between the state of the Greeks under the Turks and that of the English of Saxon race under the Normans, not only in the material features of the subjugation, but in the peculiar form assumed by the national spirit amidst the sufferings of its oppression, in the moral instincts and superstitious opinions arising out of it, in the manner of hating those whom it would fain, but could not, conquer, and of loving those who still struggled on while the mass of their countrymen had bent the neck—all this is well worthy of remark. It is a resemblance in the investigation of which much light may be thrown upon the moral study of man.

To keep in view the distinction of races in England after the conquest, does not merely communicate importance to facts before unperceived or neglected: it gives an entirely new aspect and signification to events celebrated in themselves, but hitherto incorrectly elucidated. The protracted quarrel between Henry II. and archbishop Becket is one of these events; a version of that affair, entirely differing from the account previously most accredited, will be found in the present work. If, in relating the struggle between these famous personages, the philosophic historians have taken part against the weaker and more unfortunate of the two, it is from not having viewed the struggle under its true aspect, from not having been thoroughly acquainted with all the elements of which the mutual hate of the antagonists was composed. They have wholly laid aside, in reference to a man assassinated with the most odious circumstances, all those principles of justice and philanthropy which they so energetically profess. Six hundred years after his murder, they have assailed his memory with the fiercest malignity; and yet there is nothing in common between the cause of the enemies of Thomas Becket, in the twelfth century, and that of philosophy in the eighteenth. Henry II. was no citizen king, no champion of religious independence, no systematic antagonist of papal domination; there was nothing of the sort, as will be seen, in his inveterate hostility to a man against whom he was the first to solicit the assistance of the pope.

If the grave circumstances which marked the dispute of the fifth king of Norman race with the first archbishop of English race since the conquest, are to be attributed, more than to any other cause, to the still living animosity between conqueror and conquered, another fact, equally important, the great civil war under John and Henry III. was also a quarrel of races rather than of government. Its real motive was the fear, well or ill founded, which the barons of Norman origin entertained, of experiencing a conquest, in their turn, on the part of other foreigners called into England by the kings, and of being despoiled of their territories and of the ruling power by Poitevins, Aquitans, and Provençals, as, a century and a half before, they themselves had dispossessed the Saxons. It was this material, personal interest, and no lofty desire to found political institutions, that made the barons and knights of England rise up against their kings. If this great aristocratic movement was sustained by popular favour, it was because the alarm of a second conquest, and the indignation against those who sought to bring it about, were common to the poor and to the rich, to the Saxon and to the Norman.

A close examination of all the political phenomena that accompanied the conquests of the middle ages, and of the part taken in them by religion, have led me to a new manner of considering the progress of papal power and of catholic unity. Hitherto historians have represented this power as extending itself solely by metaphysical influence, as conquering by persuasion, whereas it is certain that its conquests, like all other conquests, have been effected by the ordinary means, by material means. The popes may not have headed military expeditions in person, but they have been partners in almost all the great invasions and in the fortune of the conquerors, even in that of conquerors still pagans. It was the destruction of the independent churches effected throughout Christian Europe concurrently with that of the free nations, which gave reality to the title of universal, assumed by the Roman church long before there was anything to warrant the assumption. From the fifth century up to the thirteenth, there was not a single conquest which did not profit the court of Rome quite as much as it profited those who effected it with sword and lance. A consideration of the history of the middle ages under this hitherto unnoticed aspect has given me, for the various national churches which the Roman church stigmatized as heretical or schismatic, the same sort of interest and sympathy which I expressed just now for the nations themselves. Like the nations, the national churches have succumbed to powers that had no sort of right over them; the independence they claimed for their doctrines and their government was a part of the moral liberty consecrated by Christianity.

Ere I conclude, I would say a few words as to the plan and composition of this work. Pursuant to its title, it will be found to contain a complete narrative of all the details relating to the Norman conquest, placed between two other briefer narratives—one, of the facts preceding and preparing that conquest; the other, of those which flowed from it as necessary consequences. Before introducing the personages who figure in the great drama of the conquest, I was desirous of making the reader acquainted with the ground on which its various scenes were to take place. For this purpose, I have carried him with me from England to the Continent, from the Continent to England. I have explained the origin, the internal and external situation, the first relations of the population of England with that of Normandy, and by what chances these relations became so complicated as necessarily to involve hostility and invasion. The success of the Norman invasion crowned by the battle of Hastings, produced a conquest, the progress, settlement and direct results of which form several distinctly marked epochs.

The first epoch is that of territorial usurpation: it commences with the battle of Hastings, on the 14th of October, 1066, and embracing the successive progress of the conquerors from east to west and from south to north, terminates in 1070, when every centre of resistance had been broken up, and every powerful native who survived had submitted or abandoned the country. The second epoch, that of political usurpation, begins where the first ends; it comprehends the series of efforts made by the Conqueror to disorganize and denationalize the conquered population. It terminates in 1076 with the execution of the last chief of Saxon race, and the decree degrading the last bishop of that race. During the third epoch, the Conqueror is engaged in subjecting to regular order the violent results of the conquest, and in converting the forcible possession of lands by his soldiers into legal if not legitimate property; this epoch terminates in 1086, by a comprehensive review of all the conquerors in possession of estates, who, renewing to the king in a body the oath of fealty, figure for the first time as an established nation, and no longer as merely an army in the field. The fourth epoch is occupied with the intestine quarrels of the conquering nation, and with its civil wars, whether for the possession of the conquered territory or for the right of rule there. This period, more extended than the preceding, terminates in 1152, with the extinction of all the pretenders to the throne of England, except one, Henry, son of Geoffroy, earl of Anjou, and of the empress Matilda, niece of the Conqueror. Lastly, in the fifth epoch, the Normans of England and of the continent, having no intestine dissensions wherein to expend their activity and their strength, either go forth from their two centres of action to conquer and colonize abroad, or extend their supremacy without themselves moving. Henry II. and his successor Richard I. are the representatives of this epoch, filled with wars upon the continent, and with new territorial or political conquests. It terminates, in the earlier part of the thirteenth century, by a reaction against the Anglo-Norman power, a reaction so violent that

Normandy itself, the native land of the kings, lords, and chivalry of England, is severed for ever from the country to which it had given its conquerors.

With these various epochs correspond successive changes in the lot of the Anglo-Saxon nation; it first loses the property in the soil; next, its ancient political and religious organization; then, favoured by the divisions of its masters, and siding with the kings against their revolted vassals, it obtains concessions which give it a momentary hope of once more becoming a people, and it even essays a vain attempt to enfranchise itself by force. Lastly, overwhelmed by the extinction of parties in the Norman population, it ceases to play any political part, loses its national character in public acts and in history, and falls altogether into the condition of an inferior class. Its subsequent revolts, extremely rare of occurrence, are simply referred to by the contemporary writers as quarrels between the poor and the rich; and it is the account of an outbreak of this nature, which took place at London in 1196, under the conduct of a person evidently or Saxon race, that concludes the circumstantial narrative of the facts relating to the conquest.

Having brought the history of the Norman conquest up to this point, I have carried on, in a more summary form, that of the populations of various race which figure in the main body of the work. The resistance they opposed to the more powerful nations, their defeat, the establishment of the conquerors among them, the revolutions they essayed and accomplished, the events, political or military, over which they exercised an influence, the fusion of people, languages, and manners, and the exact period of this fusion, all this I have endeavoured clearly to exhibit and to demonstrate. This last portion of the work, where a special article is devoted to each race of men, begins with the continental populations which have since become French. Next come those, now called English, each in its rank; the Welsh, whose spirit of nationality is so tenacious that it has survived a territorial conquest; the Scots, who have never undergone any such conquest, and who have struggled with such vast energy against a political conquest; the Irish, who had better have become serfs, like the Anglo-Saxons, than have preserved a precarious liberty at the expense of peace, of individual and family happiness, and of the civilization of their country; lastly, the population of England herself, of Norman or Saxon origin, where these national differences become a distinction of classes, less and less marked, as time progressed.

I have only now to mention one other historical innovation, of no less importance than the rest; the retaining the orthography of the Saxon, Norman, and other names, so as to keep constantly marked out the distinction of races, and to secure that local colouring, which is one of the conditions, not merely of historic interest, but of historic truth. I have, in like manner, taken care not to apply to one period the language, forms, or titles of another. In a word, I have essayed thoroughly to reintegrate political facts, details of manners, official forms, languages, and names; so as, by restoring to each period comprised in my narrative its external aspect, its original features, its reality, to communicate to this portion of history the certitude and fixity which are the distinguishing characteristics of the positive sciences.

HISTORY OF THE CONQUEST OF ENGLAND BY THE NORMANS.

BOOK I. FROM THE ESTABLISHMENT OF THE BRITONS TO THE NINTH CENTURY.

B.C 55—A.D 787

Ancient populations of Britain—Picts and Scots—Social state of the Britons—Their form of government—Attacks from without—Internal discords—The Saxons called in as auxiliaries of the Britons; become their enemies—Conquests of the Saxons in Britain—Emigration of the Angles—Conquests of the Angles—Anglo-Saxon colonies—Settlement of Britons in Gaul—Political state of Gaul—Influence of the Gaulish bishops; their friendship towards the Franks—Conversion and baptism of Chlodowig, king of the Franks—Successes of the Franks; their conquests—State of the Britons in Gaul; their quarrels with the Gaulish clergy; their wars with the Franks—Heresy of Britain—Character of pope Gregory—His desire to convert the Anglo-Saxons—Roman missionaries sent into Britain—Conversion of an Anglo-Saxon king—Plan of ecclesiastical organization—Ambition of bishop Augustin; Religious belief of the Welsh—Conferences of Augustin with the Welsh clergy—His vengeance upon them—Return of the Anglo-Saxons to paganism—Fresh successes of the Romish priests—Essays at conversion in Northumberland—Conversion of Northumberland—Anglo Saxon church—Attempts of the Romish clergy against the church of Ireland—Religious zeal of the Irish—Catholic devotion of the Anglo-Saxons—Rupture of the Anglo-Saxons from the Romish church—Respective limits of the various populations of Britain—Remnant of the British race—Feelings of the historian with regard to the conquered peoples.

Ancient tradition informs us that the great island which now bears the name of the united kingdom of England and Scotland, was primitively called the Country of the Green Hills, then the Island of Honey, and thirdly, the Island of Bryt or Prydyn; the Latinization of the latter term produced the name Britain. From the most remote antiquity, the isle of Prydyn, or Britain, was regarded, by those who visited it, as divided from east to west, into two large unequal portions, of which the Firth of Forth, and the Clyde, constituted the common limit. The northern division was called Alben (Albyn, Alban, Latinè Albania), that is to say, the region of mountains; the other portion, towards the west was named Kymru, towards the east and south Loegwr. These two denominations were not, like the first, derived from the nature of the country, but from the appellation of two distinct nations, who conjointly occupied nearly the whole extent of Southern Britain, the Kymrys and the Lloëgrwys, or, according to the Latin orthography, the Cambrians and the Logrians.

The nation of the Cambrians boasted the higher antiquity; it had come in a mass from the eastern extremities of Europe, across the German ocean. A portion of the emigrants had landed on the coast of Gaul; the remainder, disembarking on the opposite shores of the straits (Fretum Gallicum, Fretum Morinorum), had colonized Britain, which, say the Cambrian traditions, had previously no other inhabitants than bears and wild cattle, and where, consequently, the colonists established themselves as original occupants of the soil, without opposition, without war, without violence. The claim is honourable, but scarcely historical; the great probability is that the Cambrian emigrants found in the island men of another origin and of a different language from their own, whom they dispossessed of the territory. This probability is rendered almost matter of fact, by the existence of many names of places altogether foreign to the Cambrian language, and by ruins of an unascertained period, which popular tradition assigns to an extinct race of hunters who employed foxes and wild cats, instead of dogs in the chase. This aboriginal population of Britain was driven back towards the west and north by the gradual invasion of the foreigners who landed on the eastern shores.

A portion of the fugitives passed the sea to the large island called by its inhabitants Erin (Latiné, Iierne, Inverna, Iiernia, Hibernia), and to the other western islands, peopled, according to all appearance, by men of the same race and language with the British aborigines. Those who retreated into North Britain, found an impregnable asylum in the lofty mountains which extend from the banks of the Clyde to the extremity of the island, and maintained their position here under the name of Gael or Galls (more correctly, Gadhels, Gwyddils), which they still retain. The wreck of this dispossessed race, augmented, at different periods, by bands of emigrants from Erin, constituted the population of Alben, or the highlands of Britain, a population foreign to that of the plains of the south, and its natural enemy, from the hereditary resentment growing out of the recollection of conquest. The epoch at which these movements of population took place is uncertain; it was at a later period, but equally unascertained, that, according to the British annals, the men called Logrians landed on the south of the island.

These, according to the same annals, emigrated from the south-western coasts of Gaul, and derived their origin from the primitive race of the Cambrians, with whom they could readily converse. To make way for these new comers, the previous colonists voluntarily, says the old tradition, but more probably on compulsion, retired to the shores of the western ocean, which then exclusively assumed the name of Cambria, while the Logrians gave their own appellation to the southern and eastern coasts of the island, over which they diffused themselves. After the establishment of this second colony, there came a third band of emigrants, issuing from the same primitive race, and speaking the same language, or, at all events, a dialect very slightly differing from it. The district which they had previously occupied was the portion of western Gaul comprehended between the Seine and the Loire; these, like the Logrians, obtained lands in Britain with very little difficulty. It is to them that the ancient annals and the national poems especially assign the name of Brython or Briton, which, among foreigners, served to designate generally all the inhabitants of the island. The precise site on which they settled is not known; but the most probable opinion places them to the north of the Cambrians and Logrians, on the frontier of the Gaelic population, between the Firth of Forth and that of Solway.

These nations of common origin were visited at intervals, either pacifically, or in a hostile manner, by various foreign tribes. A band from that portion of the Gaulish territory now called Flanders, compelled permanently to quit their native country, in consequence of a great inundation, passed the sea in sail-less vessels, and landed on the Isle of Wight and the adjacent coast, first as guests, and then as invaders. The Coranians (Corraniaid, latiné, Coritani), men of Teutonic descent, emigrating from a country which the British annals designate the Land of Marshes, sailed up the gulf formed by the mouth of the Humber, and established themselves on the banks of that river and along the eastern coast, thus separating into two portions the territory of the Logrians. Lastly, Roman legions, led by Julius Cæsar, disembarked on the eastern point of the district now called Kent. They encountered a determined resistance at the hands of the Logrian-Britons, entrenched behind their war-chariots; but, ere long, thanks to the treachery of the tribes of foreign race, and more especially the Coranians, the Romans, penetrating into the interior of the island, gradually achieved the conquest of the two countries of Logria and Cambria. The British annals call them Caisariaid, Cæsarians, and enumerate them among the invading peoples who made but a temporary stay in Britain: "After having oppressed the land during four hundred years," say these annals, "and having exacted from it the yearly tribute of three thousand pounds of silver, they departed hence for Rome, in order to repel the invasion of the black horde. They left behind them only their wives and young children, who all became Cambrians."

During this sojourn of four centuries, the Romans extended their conquests and their domination over the whole southern portion of the island, up to the foot of the northern mountains which had served as a rampart for the aboriginal population against the Cambrians. The Roman invasion stopped at the same limit with the British invasion; and the Gael remained a free people throughout the period that their former conquerors were groaning under a foreign yoke. They more than once drove back the imperial eagles; and their ancient aversion for the inhabitants of Southern Britain grew stronger and stronger amidst the wars which they had to maintain against the Roman governors. The pillage of the coloniæ and municipia, adorned with sumptuous palaces and gorgeous temples, increased, by a new feature, this national hostility. Every spring, the men of Alben, or Caledonia, passed the Clyde in boats of osier covered with leather: becoming formidable to the Romans, they obliged the latter to construct, on the limits of their conquest, two immense walls, furnished with towers, and extending from one sea to the other. These irruptions, which grew more and more frequent, acquired a terrible celebrity for the people of Alben, under the designation of Scots and Picts, the only terms employed by the Latin writers, who appear to have been unacquainted with the appellation, Gael.

The former of these two names appertained to the inhabitants of the island of Erin, which the Romans called indifferently Hibernia or Scotia. The close relationship between the British highlanders and the men of Hibernia, with the frequent emigrations from the one country to the other, had produced this community of name. In northern Britain itself, the term Scots was applied to the inhabitants of the coasts and of the great archipelago of the north-west, and that of Picts to the eastern population on the shores of the German ocean. The respective territories of these two peoples, or distinct branches of one population, were separated by the Grampian hills, at the foot of which, Gallawg (Galgacus), the leading chieftain of the Northern Forests (Calyddon), had valiantly combated the imperial legions. The manner of life of the Scots wholly differed from that of the Picts; the former, dwellers on the mountains, were hunters or wandering shepherds; the latter, enjoying a more level surface, and more fixedly established, occupied themselves in agriculture, and constructed solid abodes, the ruins of which still bear their name. When these two peoples were not actually leagued together for an irruption into the south, even a friendly understanding ceased at times to exist between them; but on every occasion that presented itself of assailing the common enemy, the two chiefs, one of whom resided at the mouth of the Tay, the other among the lakes of Argyleshire, became brothers, and set up their standards side by side. The southern Britons and the Roman colonists in their fear and their hate, made no distinction between the Scots and the Picts.

Upon the departure of the legions, recalled to defend Rome against the invading Goths, the Britons ceased to recognise the authority of the foreign governors who had been left in charge of their provinces and towns. The form, and even the name of these administrators perished; and in their place arose once more the ancient authority of the chiefs of tribe, which had been abolished by the Romans. Old genealogies, carefully preserved by the national poets, ascertained those who were entitled to claim the dignity of chief of a district or family; for these words were synonymous in the language of the ancient Britons among whom the ties of family relationship constituted the basis of the social state. With them, people of the lowest condition committed to memory the whole line of their descent, with a care which, among other nations, was peculiar, in such matters, to the wealthy and exalted. Every Briton, poor as well as rich, had to establish his genealogy, ere he could be admitted to the full enjoyment of his civil rights, or of any property in the district of which he was a native; for each district belonged in original ownership to one particular primitive family, and no man could legally possess any portion of its soil unless he were by descent a member of that primitive family, become, by gradual extension, a tribe.

Above this singular social order, of which the result was a federation of petty sovereignties, some elective, some hereditary, the Britons, delivered from the Roman authority, raised, for the first time, a high national sovereignty: they created a chief of chiefs, (Penteyrn,) a king of the country, as their annals express it, whom they made elective. This new institution, which seemed destined to give the people more union and more strength against external aggressions, became, on the contrary, a cause of divisions, of weakness, and, ere long, of subjection. The two great populations who shared the southern portion of the island, respectively asserted the exclusive right of furnishing candidates for the monarchy. The seat of this central royalty was in the Logrian territory, in the ancient municipal town, called by the Britons Lon-din, the town of ships, (Llundain, latinè, Londinium.) The Cambrians, jealous of this advantage, maintained that the royal authority belonged of right to their race, as the most ancient, as that which had received the others on the soil of Britain. To justify this claim, they carried back the origin of the power they sought, far beyond the time of the Roman conquests, attributing its institution to a certain Prydyn, son of Aodd, a Cambrian, who, according to their account, had combined the whole island under one monarchical government, and decreed that this government should for ever remain vested in his nation. With what fable this fable was met by the southern and eastern peoples, is not known; but this is certain, that the dispute grew fiercer and fiercer, until at last this rivalry of self-love had lighted up civil war throughout south Britain. The intervention of the tribes of foreign origin, ever hostile to the two great branches of the British population, encouraged its discords and nourished the intestine war. Under a succession of chiefs, called national, but regularly disowned as such by a portion of the nation, no army was levied to replace the Roman legions which had guarded the frontiers against the invasions of the Gaelish tribes.

Accordingly, amidst the disorders which thus afflicted South Britain, the Picts and Scots broke down the two great Roman walls, and passed into south Britain, at the same time that other enemies, not less formidable, burst upon the country from the sea. These were pirates come forth from the coasts and islands along the German ocean, to pillage and then return home laden with booty. When the great ships of Roman construction were forced by tempests back to port, the light vessels of these men of the sea dashed boldly on at full sail, and suddenly attacking the tall ships amid the terror and confusion of the storm, seldom failed to capture them. Several British tribes made singly great efforts against the enemy, and in a number of engagements defeated their aggressors, both of German and of Gallic race. The inhabitants of the southern coasts, who had frequent communication with the continent, solicited foreign aid; once or twice Roman troops, coming over from Gaul, fought for the Britons, and assisted them in repairing the great walls of Hadrian and Severus. But, ere long, the Romans themselves were driven from Gaul, by three invasions of barbarians from the south, the east, and the north, and by the national insurrection of the maritime districts of the west. The legions fell back upon Italy, and from that time forth the Britons had no succour to expect from the empire.

At this period, the dignity of supreme chief of all Britain was in the hands of one Guorteyrn, a Logrian. On several occasions he assembled around him all the chiefs of the British tribes, in order to take, in concert with them, measures for the defence of the country against the northern invasions. But little union prevailed in these deliberations, and, justly or not, Guorteyrn had many enemies, more especially among the western people, who seldom assented to anything proposed by the Logrian. The latter, in virtue of his royal preeminence, and by the counsel of several tribes, though without the consent of the Cambrians, suddenly adopted the resolution of introducing into Britain a population of foreign soldiers, who, in consideration of pecuniary subsidies and grants of land, should, in the service of the Britons, carry on the war against the Picts and Scots. At about the epoch when this decision was formed, a decision which the Cambrians denounced as base and cowardly, chance directed to the shores of Britain three German piratical ships, commanded by two brothers, called Henghist and Horsa, who landed in Kent, on the same promontory where the legions of Rome had formerly disembarked.

It would appear that the three vessels had come to Britain on this occasion on a mission, not of piracy, but of trade. They were of the nation of the Jutes, or, more correctly, Iutes, a nation forming part of a great league of peoples spread over the marshy coasts of the ocean, north of the Elbe, and all designating themselves by the general name of Saxons, or men with the long knives. Other confederations of the same kind had been already formed among the Teutonic tribes, either for the better defence of all from the Romans, or in order the more advantageously to assume the offensive against them. Such had been the league of the Alamans, or men of men, and that of the Franks, or men rude in fight. On landing, the Saxon chiefs, Henghist and Horsa, received from the British king, Guorteyrn, a proposition to enrol them and an army of their countrymen in his service. There seemed nothing strange in this to men with whom war was a business. They at once promised a considerable body of troops in exchange for the little island of Thanet, formed on the coast of Kent, on one side by the sea, and on the other by a river with two arms. Seventeen vessels speedily brought over from the north the new military colony, which divided out its new settlement, and organized itself there according to its national customs, under the command of the two brothers, he promoters of the enterprise. It received from its hosts, the Britons, all the necessaries of life; it fought well and truly for them on several occasions, advancing against the Picts and Scots its standard of the White Horse, emblem of the name of its two leaders; each time, the mountain bands, strong in numbers, but ill armed with long, brittle pikes, fled before the great axes, the national weapon of the Saxon confederation. These exploits created throughout Britain infinite rejoicing and warm friendship for the Saxons.

"Having overthrown our enemies," says an ancient poet, "they celebrated with us the festival of victory: we vied with one another how best to show to them our gratitude and our loving welcome! but woe to the day when we loved them! Woe to Guorteyrn and his craven councillors."

In effect, the good understanding was of no long duration between those who made war and those for whom it was made; the former soon demanded more land, more provisions, and more money than had been stipulated, and menaced, in the event of refusal, to pay themselves by pillage and usurpation.

To render these threats more effective, they called to their aid fresh bands of adventurers, either belonging to their own nation or to other peoples of the Saxon confederation. The emigration continuing, the lands assigned by the Britons no longer sufficed; the bounds agreed upon were violated, and ere long a numerous German population collected upon the coast of Kent. The natives, who at once needed its aid and feared it, treated with it on the footing of nation with nation. On either side there were frequent embassies and fresh treaties, broken almost as soon as concluded. At length, the last ties were broken: the Saxons formed an alliance with the Picts; they sent messengers inviting them to descend in arms towards the south; and themselves, favoured by this diversion, advanced into the interior of Britain from east to west, driving the British population before them, or forcing it to submit. The latter, indeed, did not give way to them unresistingly; they once even drove them back to the seacoast, and compelled them to re-embark; but they soon returned with increased numbers, and with a fiercer determination subdued the country for many miles on the right bank of the Thames, and did not again quit the conquered lands. One of the two brothers who commanded them was killed in battle; the other, from a mere military chief, became the ruler of a province; and his province, or, to use the customary language, his kingdom, was called the kingdom of the men of Kent; in the Saxon language, Kent-wara-rike.

Twenty-two years after the first landing of the Germans, another Saxon chief, named Œlla, came with three vessels to the south coast of Kent, and, driving the Britons back towards the north-west, established a second colony, which received the name of the kingdom of the South Saxons, (Suth-seaxna-rice.) Eighteen years afterwards, a certain Kerdic, followed by the most powerful army that had yet passed the ocean to seek lands in Britain, disembarked on the southern coast, to the west of the south Saxons, and founded a third kingdom, under the name of West Saxony, (West-seaxna-rice, more briefly, West-seax.) The chiefs who succeeded Kerdic gradually extended their conquests to the vicinity of the Severn: this was the ancient frontier of the Cambrian population; the invaders did not find this population disposed to give place to them; it maintained against them an obstinate struggle, during which other emigrants, landing on the eastern coast, obtained possession of the left bank of the Thames, and the great city of Londin, or London. They called the territory in which they established themselves East Saxony, (East-seaxna-rice, East-seax.) All these acquisitions were made at the expense of Logria and of the race of Logrian-Britons, who had invited the Saxons to come and dwell beside them.

From the moment that the city of London was taken, and the coasts of Logria became Saxon, the kings and chiefs selected to oppose the conquerors were all of the Cambrian race. Such was the famous Arthur. He defeated the Saxons in numerous battles; but, despite the services he rendered to his people, he had enemies among them, as had been the case with Guorteyrn. The title of king obliged him to draw his sword against the Britons almost as often as against the foreigner, and he was mortally wounded in a battle with his own nephew. He was removed to an island formed by several streams, near Afallach, (Insula Avallonia,) now Glastonbury, south of the bay into which the Severn discharges itself. He there died of his wounds, but as it was at the time that the western Saxons invaded this territory, amid the tumult of invasion, no one exactly knew the circumstances of the death of Arthur, or the spot where he was buried. This ignorance surrounded his name with a mysterious celebrity: long after he was no more, his followers still looked for him; the need they felt of the great war chief, who had conquered the Germans, nourished the vain hope of one day seeing him return. This hope was not abandoned; and for many centuries the nation, which had loved Arthur, did not despair of his recovery and return.

The emigration of the inhabitants of the marshes of the Elbe and the neighbouring islands, gave the desire for a similar emigration to nations situated further east, near the shores of the Baltic sea, and who were then called Anghels, or Angles, (Engla, Anglen.) After having experimented with petty partial incursions upon the north-east coast of Britain, the entire population of the Angles put itself in motion, under the conduct of a military chief, named Ida, and his twelve sons. Their numerous vessels came to anchor between the mouths of the Forth and the Tweed. The better to succeed against the Britons of these districts, they formed an alliance with the Picts, and the confederate troops advanced from east to west, striking such terror into the natives, that the king of the Angles received from them the appellation of the flame-man, (Flamddwyn.) Despite his ferocity and his valour, Ida encountered, at the foot of the mountains in which the Clyde takes its rise, a population that resisted him. "The flame-man has come against us," says a contemporaneous British poet; "he asks us in a loud voice: 'Will you give me hostages? are you ready?' Owen, brandishing his lance, replied: 'No, we will not give thee hostages; no, we are not ready.' Urien, chief of the land, then cried: 'Children of one race, united by one cause, let us, having raised our standard on the mountains, rush into the plain; let us throw ourselves upon the flame-man, and combine in the same slaughter, him, his army, and his auxiliaries.' "

This same Urien, at the head of the northern Britons, descendants of the ancient emigrants from Armorican Gaul, gained several victories over the confederated invaders. The chief of the Germans perished on the banks of the Clyde; but in a decisive battle, in which the combatants on one side were the Picts and Angles, on the other the men of the valley of the Clyde, the men of the banks of the Forth and of Deifr and Brynich. (or Bryneich and Deywr, or Dewyr,) that is to say, of the mountainous country north of the Humber, the British cause was lost. Here perished a great number of chiefs wearing the collar of gold, a token of elevated command among the Britons. Aneurin, one of the most celebrated bards, fought in the first ranks, and survived this signal defeat, which he sang in a poem that has come down to us.

The victors spread themselves over the whole of the eastern country, between the Forth and the Humber. Those of the conquered to whom the foreign yoke was insupportable, took refuge in the south, in the country of the Cambrians, which then, as now, was called Wales. The conquering Germans gave no new names to the northern country; they retained the ancient geographical denominations, and themselves made use of them to distinguish their different colonies, according to their place of settlement. They called themselves, for example, men of the north of the Humber, (Northan-hymbra-menn, latinè, Nord-anhymbri, Northumbri,) men of Deifr, men of

Brynich, or, according to the Latin orthography, Northumbrians, Deirians, Bernicians. The territorial designation of the Angles, (East-engla-land, East Englas, latiné, Orientales Angli, East Anglia,) was only given to a small portion of the eastern coast, where men of that nation, before the general emigration, had founded a colony, few in number, but capable of maintaining itself against the hostility of the natives, by the aid of the East-Saxons, north of whom they dwelt.

The ancient population of the Coranians, established for several centuries south of the Humber, and whom so long a sojourn among the Britons had not reconciled with them, readily joined the Anglo-Saxon invaders as they had formerly joined the Romans. In their alliance with the conquerors, their national appellation disappeared from the district they inhabited; but the name of their allies did not take its place; both were lost, and the country between the Humber and the Thames was thenceforward called the country of Merk (Myrcan, Myrena-rice,) or Mercia, perhaps from the nature of the soil, chiefly marshy, perhaps from the vicinity of the free Britons of whom this kingdom formed the frontier or march, as the Germans called it. It was Angles from the territories of Deira and Bernicia, or from the eastern coast, who, under this name, founded the eighth and last Germanic colony in Britain. The limits of the people of Mercia, (Myrena-menn,) a mixture of Coranians and Angles, were not at first at all definite; this people progressively extended its territory towards the west at the expense of the Cambrians, and towards the south at the expense of the Saxons themselves, with whom they did not feel themselves united by community of origin, so closely as the Saxons were among themselves.

Of these eight colonies, principalities, states, or kingdoms, call them what you will, founded in Britain within the space of a century, by the conquests of the Saxons and Angles, none possessed any territory on the coast of the western sea, except the western Saxons, who, however, did not extend north of the Bristol Channel. The western coasts, almost throughout their extent, from the mouth of the Clyde to the Land's-End, remained in the hands of the native race, and more peculiarly of the Cambrian-Britons. The irregular form of these coasts, isolated from the great mass of this still free population, the tribes who dwelt towards the south, beyond the Bristol Channel, and towards the north beyond the Solway Firth; but between these two opposite points was a long tract of compact land, though more or less contracted, according to the projection of the coast into the ocean. This mountainous and unfertile territory was the abode of the Cambrians, (Gwylt Wallia,) who there offered a poor, but secure asylum to emigrants from every corner of Britain, to all who, as the ancient historians expressed it, preferred suffering with independence, to a beautiful country under foreign servitude. Others crossed the ocean to seek in Gaul a country which their ancestors had peopled at the same time with Britain, and where still dwelt men of their race, and speaking their language.

Many vessels full of fugitive Britons landed in succession on the western point of Armorica, in the districts which, under the Romans, and even before them, had been called territories of the Osismians, of the Curiosolites, and of the Venetes. By the consent of the ancient inhabitants, who recognised in them brothers by descent, the new-comers diffused themselves over all the northern coast, as far as the Rance, and towards the south-east, as far as the lower stream of the Vilaine. On this peninsula they founded a separate state, whose limits frequently varied, but beyond which the cities of Rennes and Nantes remained down to the middle of the ninth century. The increasing population of this western nook of land, the immense number of people of Celtic race and language who thus found themselves agglomerated together, preserved it from the irruption of the Roman tongue, which, under forms more or less corrupt, gradually spread throughout Gaul. The name of Brittany was given to these coasts, and superseded the various names of the indigenous populations, while the island which, for so many centuries, had borne this appellation, lost it, and, adopting that of its conquerors, began to be called the land of the Saxons and Angles, or, in one word, England, (Engel-seaxna-land, Engla-land.)

At the time when the men of Britain, flying before the Anglo-Saxons, settled on the point of land called the Horn of Gaul, other expatriated Saxons fixed their abode on a more northern point of the coast of Gaul, near the town whose ancient name was changed into that of Bayeux. At the same time, also, the Germanic league, whose members, for two centuries, had borne the name of Franks, that is to say, undaunted, descended, in several bands, from the mouths of the Rhine and the Meuse, upon the central lands of Gaul. Two other nations of Teutonic race had already thoroughly invaded and fixed their abode in the provinces of the south, between the Loire and the two seas. The western Goths or Visigoths occupied the country west of the Rhone; the Burgundiones that to the east. The establishment of these two barbarous nations had not taken place without violence and ravage; they had usurped a portion of the possessions of each native family; but the love of repose, and a certain spirit of justice which distinguished them among all the Germans, had speedily softened their manners; they contracted relationships with the conquered, whom their laws treated with impartiality, and gradually came to be regarded by them as simply friends and neighbours. The Goths for the most part adopted the Roman manners, which they found generally in use among the civilized inhabitants of Gaul; their laws were, in great measure, mere extracts from the imperial code; they prided themselves in a taste for the arts, and affected the polished elegance of Rome.

The Franks, on the contrary, filled the north of Gaul with terror and devastation; strangers to the manners and arts of the Roman cities and colonies, they ravaged them with indifference and even with a sort of pleasure. Being pagans, no religious sympathy tempered their savage humour. Sparing neither sex nor age, say the ancient historians, destroying churches as readily as private houses, they gradually advanced towards the south, invading the whole extent of Gaul; while the Goths and Burgundians, impelled by a similar ambition, but with less barbarous manners— sometimes at peace with each other, more often at war—essayed to make progress in the opposite direction. In the then weak condition of the central provinces, still united, but only in name, to the Roman empire, and utterly disgusted with that empire, which, in the words of an ancient Gaulish poet, made them feel the weight of its shadow, there was reason to suppose that the inhabitants of these provinces, incapable of resisting the conquering nations who pressed upon them on three sides, would come to terms with the least ferocious of them; in a word, that the whole of Gaul would submit either to the Goths or to the Burgundians, Christians like itself, to escape the grasp of the Franks. Such would have been its true policy; but those who disposed of its fate decided otherwise.

These were the bishops of the Gaulish cities, to whom the decrees of the Roman emperors assigned high administrative authority, and who, by favour of the disorders caused by the invasion of the barbarians, had found means illegally to aggrandize this already exorbitant power. The bishops, who at that time all bore the title of popes or fathers, were the plenipotentiaries of the Gaulish cities, either with the empire, becoming more and more distant, or with the Germans, each day approaching nearer. Their diplomatic negotiations were conducted altogether at their own will and discretion, and, whether from habit or fear, no one ever thought of saying them nay; for their power was backed by the sanguinary executive laws of the empire in its decline.

Sons of Rome, and strictly bound by the imperial ordinances to recognise as their patron and common head the bishop of the eternal city, to do nothing without his consent, to receive his decrees as laws, and his policy for their rule of conduct, to model their own faith upon his, and thus, by the unity of religion, to contribute to the unity of empire, the bishops of the Gaulish provinces, when the imperial power ceased to have any compulsory action upon them, and when they had become altogether independent of it, did not enter upon a new path. From instinct or from calculation, they still laboured, as we are told by one of their own body, to retain under the authority of Rome, by the tie of religious faith, the countries where that political subjection was broken. Their aversion or their good-will towards the emigrant peoples of Germany was not measured by the degree of barbarism and ferocity of those nations, but by their supposed aptitude to receive the Catholic faith, the only faith that Rome had ever professed. Now this aptitude was calculated to be far greater in a people still pagan, than in schismatic Christians, wittingly and willingly separated from the Roman communion, such as the Goths and Burgundians, who professed the faith of Christ, according to the doctrine of Arius. But the Franks were strangers to any Christian belief, and this consideration sufficed to turn the hearts of the Gaulish bishops towards them, and to make them all, as a nearly contemporary author expresses it, desire the domination of the Franks with a desire of love.

The portion of the Gaulish territory occupied by the Frank tribes extended at this period from the Rhine to the Somme, and the tribe most advanced into the west and south was that of the Merowings or children of Merowig, so called from the name of one of their ancient chiefs, renowned for his bravery, and respected by the whole tribe as a common ancestor.

At the head of the children of Merowig was a young man, named Chlodowig, who combined with the warlike ardour of his predecessors a greater degree of reflection and skill. The bishops of the portion of Gaul still subject to the empire, partly as a precaution for the future, partly out of their hatred to the Arian powers, entered, of their own motion, into relations with this formidable neighbour; sending to him frequent messages, replete with flattering expressions. Many of them visited him in his camp, which, in their Roman politeness, they dignified with the name of Aula Regia, or royal court. The king of the Franks was at first very insensible to their adulations, which in no degree kept him from pillaging the churches and treasures of the clergy: but a precious vase, taken by the Franks from the cathedral of Reims, placed the barbarian chief in relations of interest, and ere long, of friendship, with a prelate more able or more successful than the rest. Under the auspices of Remigius or Remi, bishop of Reims, events seemed themselves to concur in promoting the grand plan of the high Gaulish clergy. First, by a chance, too fortunate to have been wholly fortuitous, the king, whom they desired to convert to the Roman faith, married the only orthodox princess then existing among the Teutonic families; and the love of the faithful wife, as the historians of the time express it, gradually softened the heart of the infidel husband. In a battle with some Germans who sought to follow the Franks into Gaul and to conquer their part also, Chlodowig, whose soldiers were giving way, invoked the god of Chlothilda (such was the name of his wife), and promised to believe in him, if he conquered: he conquered, and kept his word.

The example of the chief, the presents of Chlothilda and of the bishops, and perhaps the charm of novelty, brought about the conversion of a number of Frank warriors, as many, indeed, according to the historians, as three thousand. The baptism took place at Reims; and all the splendour that could still be furnished by the arts of the Romans, which were soon to perish in Gaul in the hands of the barbarians, was displayed in profusion to adorn this triumph of the Catholic faith. The vestibule of the cathedral was decorated with tapestry and garlands; veils of various colours softened the glare of day; the most exquisite perfumes burnt abundantly in vases of gold and silver. The bishop of Reims advanced to the baptistry in pontifical robes, leading by the hand the Frankish king who was about to become his spiritual son: "Father," said the latter, marvelling at so much pomp, "is not this that kingdom of heaven which you promised me?"

Messengers speedily conveyed to the pope of Rome intelligence of the baptism of the king of the Franks; whereupon letters of congratulation and friendship were addressed from the eternal city to the king who thus bowed his head beneath her yoke: and he, in return, sent rich presents, as tributes of filial submission, to the blessed apostle Peter, the protector of the new Rome. From the time that king Chlodowig was declared son of the Roman church, his conquests spread in Gaul, almost without effusion of blood. All the cities of the north-west, to the Loire and to the territory of the British emigrants, opened their gates to his soldiers. The garrisons of these cities passed over to the service of the German king, and among his skin-clad warriors retained the arms and banners of Rome. Ere long, the limits of the territory or kingdom of the Franks were extended towards the southeast, and, at the instigation of those who had converted him, the neophyte entered, sword in hand, the lands conquered by the Burgundians.

The Burgundians were Arians, that is, they did not believe that the second person of the Trinity was co-substantial with the first; but, despite this difference of doctrine, they in no way persecuted the priests and bishops who, in their cities, professed the creed adopted by the church of Rome. The bishops, little grateful for this toleration, corresponded with the Franks, encouraging them to invasion, and sought to avail themselves of the dread of this invasion to persuade the king of the Burgundians to embrace the Roman faith, which they described to be the only true, evangelical, and orthodox faith. The king, named Gondebald, although a barbarian, and their master, opposed them with great gentleness; while they addressed him in a tone of menace and arrogance, calling him madman, apostate, and rebel to the law of God. "Nay, not so," he answered, mildly; "I obey the law of God; but I cannot, like you, believe in three gods. Besides, if your faith be the better one, why do not your brother bishops prove it so, by preventing the king of the Franks from marching upon us to destroy us?"

The entrance of the Franks was the only answer to this embarrassing question: they signalized their passage by murder and fire; they tore up the vines and fruit-trees, pillaged the convents, carried away the sacred vessels, and broke them up without the slightest scruple. The king of the Burgundians, reduced to extremity, submitted to the conquerors, who imposed a tribute on him and all his cities, made him swear to be for the future their ally and soldier, and returned to the north of the Loire, with an immense booty. The orthodox clergy declared this sanguinary expedition to be a pious, illustrious, and holy enterprise for the true faith. "But," said the aged king, "can faith co-exist with coveting other men's goods, and thirsting for their blood?"

The victory of the Franks over the Burgundians again brought all the cities on the banks of the Rhone and Sâone under the sway of the Roman church and of the palace of San Giovanni di Latran, where thus, bit by bit, was gathered together the heritage of the ancient Capitol. Six years afterwards, under similar auspices, began the war against the Visigoths. Chlodowig assembled his warriors in a circle, in a large field, and said to them:—"I like not that these Goths, who are Arians, should occupy the best part of Gaul; let us go against them, with the aid of God, and drive them away; let us subject their territory to our power: we shall do well in this, for the land is very good." The proposition pleased the Franks, who adopted it with acclamations, and joyously proceeded on their march towards the good land of the south. The terror of their approach, say the old historians, resounded far before them; the mind of the inhabitants of the south of Gaul was so agitated, that in many places men imagined terrible signs and prognostics, announcing all the horrors of invasion. At Toulouse, it was said, a fountain of blood burst forth in the centre of the town, and flowed for an entire day. But amidst the public consternation, one class of men was impatiently calculating the days of the march of the barbarian troops. Quintianus, the orthodox bishop of Rodez, was detected intriguing for the enemy, and he was not the only member of the high clergy guilty of these machinations.

The Franks passed the Loire; and ten miles from the city of Poitiers, a bloody battle took place, in which the ancient inhabitants of southern Gaul, the Gallo-Roman population of Aquitaine and Arvernia (Arvernia, Alvernia, Alvernh, Auvergne), aided the Goths in defence of the country. But their cause did not prevail against the conquering ardour of the Franks, powerfully assisted by the fanaticism of the orthodox Gauls; Alarik, king of the Goths, was killed fighting; and the Arvernians in this defeat lost the principal personages of their nation, whom they entitled senators, in imitation of the Romans. Few cities were taken by assault; the surrender of the majority was the result of treachery. All whose consciences had been troubled by the Arian domination, revenged themselves by inflicting every possible injury upon their ancient rulers. The Goths, unable to retain the country, abandoned Aquitaine, and passed into Spain, or took refuge in the fortresses on the Mediterranean; the victorious bands, in whose ranks were combined, under the orders of the converted king, pertinacious pagans and orthodox fanatics, marched to the foot of the Pyrenees, pillaging the cities, devastating the rural districts, and carrying away the inhabitants into slavery. Wherever the victorious chief encamped, the orthodox prelates besieged his tent. Germerius, bishop of Toulouse, who abode twenty days with him, eating at his table, received a present of five hundred coins and gold crosses, and silver chalices and patines, three gilt crowns, and three robes of fine linen, taken from the Arian churches. Another bishop, who was unable to come himself, wrote thus to the king of the Franks: "Thou shinest in power and majesty; and when thou fightest, to us is the victory."

Such was the domination which, extending from the Rhine to the Pyrenees, at length completely surrounded on all sides the western nook of land in which the Britons had taken refuge. Frankish governors established themselves in the cities of Nantes and Rennes. These cities paid tribute to the king of the Franks; but the Britons refused to pay it, and alone dared the attempt to save their narrow country from the destiny of Gaul. This enterprise was all the more perilous to them, that their Christianity, the fruit of the preaching of missionaries from the churches of the East, differed in some points from the doctrines and practices of the Romish church. These, Christians for several centuries past, and perhaps the most fervent Christians in the world, had come into Gaul, accompanied by priests and monks of greater knowledge than those of the isolated province where they fixed their abode. They purified the still very imperfect faith of the ancient inhabitants of this country; they even extended their gratuitous preaching into the surrounding territories: and, as their missionaries sought no gain, not accepting money or even maintenance from any one, they were everywhere well received. The citizens of Rennes chose an emigrant Briton as their bishop, and the Bretons instituted bishops in many cities of their new country, where there had been none before. They founded this religious constitution as they had founded their civil constitution, without asking permission or advice from any foreign power.

The chiefs of the Breton church held no intercourse with the prelates of Frankish Gaul, and did not attend the Gaulish councils convoked by the rescripts of the Frank kings. This conduct soon drew upon them the animosity of the other clergy. The archbishop of Tours, who claimed the spiritual superintendence of the whole extent of country which the Roman emperors had named the third Lyonnese (Lugdunensis tertia), summoned the clergy of Brittany, as inhabiting his ancient diocese, to recognise him as metropolitan, and receive his commands. The Bretons did not consider that the imperial circumscription of the Gaulish territories imposed upon them the slightest obligation to subject to the authority of a foreigner the national church, which they had transplanted from beyond seas; moreover, it was not their custom to attach the archiepiscopal supremacy to the possession of a particular see, but to decree it to the most worthy among their bishops. Their religious hierarchy, vague and fluctuating at the popular will, was not rooted in the soil, or graduated in territorial divisions, like those which the emperors instituted when they converted Christianity into a means of government. Accordingly, the ambitious pretensions of the prelate of Tours seemed wholly futile to the Bretons, who paid no heed whatever to it; the Gaulish bishops excommunicated them. They were equally unmoved at this, feeling no regret at being deprived of the communion with strangers, from whom they had themselves separated.

In punishment of its political and religious independence, this small nation underwent frequent and formidable invasions on the part of the powerful conquerors of Gaul. The Frank kings, having assembled around them, in high council, the governors of their provinces, whom they called grafs, (grav, græf, geref, gerefa, overseer, prefect) and the Gauls counts (comites), the count of the Breton frontier was questioned as to the religious faith of the Bretons: "They do not believe in the true dogmas," answered the Frank captain; "they do not walk in the straight path." Thereupon war was voted against them by acclamation; an army, collected in Germany and in the north of Gaul, descended towards the mouth of the Loire; priests and monks quitted their books and threw aside the long robe, to accompany, sword in hand and baldric on shoulder, the soldiers, whose laughter they excited by their awkwardness. After the first victory, the conqueror issued from his camp, on the river Ellé or Blavet, manifestos respecting the tonsure of the priests and the lives of the monks of Brittany; enjoining them, under pain of corporal punishment, to adhere in future to the rules of the Romish church.

All the differences of opinion and practice between the orthodox church and the Bretons of Gaul, were common to them with the men of the same race who continued to inhabit the island of Britain. The most important point of this schism was the refusal to believe in the original degradation of our nature, and in the damnation of children dying unbaptized. The Britons thought that, in order to become better, man has no need of a supernatural grace gratuitously to enlighten him, but that, by his own will and reason, he may raise himself to moral well being. This doctrine had been professed, from time immemorial, in the poems of the Celtic bards; a

Christian priest, born in Breton, and known by the name of Pelagius, introduced it into the churches of the East, and created a great sensation by his opposition to the dogma of the culpability of all men, through the fault of their first father. Denounced to the imperial authority as the enemy of the Catholic doctrines, he was banished the Roman world, and sentences of proscription were hurled against his disciples. The inhabitants of the island of Britain, already separated from the empire, escaped these persecutions, and might indulge in peace their belief that no man is born guilty; they were simply visited from time to time by orthodox missionaries, who endeavoured to bring them over, by persuasion, to the doctrines of the Romish church.

In the early period of the Saxon invasion, there came into Britain two Gaulish preachers, Lupus, bishop of Troyes, and Germanus, bishop of Auxerre: these men combated the Pelagians, not with logical arguments, but with citations and texts. "How can it be pretended," said they, "that man is born without original sin, when it is written: "We are born in sin?"

This sort of proof was not without its effect upon simple minds, and Germanus of Auxerre succeeded in raising up in Britain that which the orthodox termed the honour of the Divine grace. It must be admitted in praise of this person, that an ardent conviction and a charitable zeal were the only motives of his preaching, and that he had a brother's love towards those whom he essayed to convert. He gave proof of this by himself marching at the head of his proselytes against the conquering Saxons, whom he drove back with the cry of Hallelujah, repeated thrice by his whole troop: unhappily, it was not thus that the missionaries, deputed by the Romish church, treated the British population established in Wales.

At the time when the Anglo-Saxons had completed the conquest of the finest portion of the island of Britain, the dignity of bishop or pope of Rome was held by a personage skilfully zealous for the propagation of the catholic faith and the aggrandizement of the new Roman empire, which was establishing itself on the primacy of the see of St. Peter. This pope, Gregory, successfully laboured to concentrate more and more strictly, around the metropolis of the west, the bonds of the episcopal hierarchy created by the policy of the emperors. The Frank kings, orthodox chiefs of armies still semi-pagan, were the faithful allies of pope Gregory; and their power, dreaded from afar, gave support and sanction to his pontifical decrees. When he thought fit to impose upon the bishops of Gaul some new law of subordination towards himself or his chosen vicars, he addressed his ordinance to the glorious personages, Hildebert, Theodorik, or Theodebert, charging them to enforce its execution by their royal power, and to punish recusants. Preposterous flattery, the epithets of most illustrious, most pious, most Christian, and the donation of certain relics, "which, worn round the neck in battle, will protect the wearer from all danger," were, on the part of the Roman pontiff, the easy payment of the good offices of the barbarian king.

A similar alliance with the conquerors of Britain, for the benefit of the orthodox faith and of the pontifical supremacy, was an early object of the zeal and ambition of pope Gregory; he formed the design of converting the Anglo Saxons to the doctrines of catholicism, and of applying their domination, as that of the Franks, to the aggrandizement of his spiritual power, which was unrecognised by the British Christians. These, defeated and dispossessed, gave no uneasiness to the Roman pontiff in his projects; they were deficient neither in faith nor in zeal, but, between them and their pagan enemies, any compact was impossible. Resentment of foreign usurpation, and anxiety to provide for the national defence, absorbed all their thoughts; they had neither leisure nor inclination to negotiate with their conquerors pacific relations, which might subsequently create a title of legitimacy for the Anglo-Saxon conquest.

Pope Gregory thus found the field open to him; and, to pave the way for his enterprise, he sought in the slave markets of various places youths of Anglo-Saxon race, of seventeen or eighteen years of age. These his agents bought and placed in monasteries, imposing upon them the task of making themselves acquainted with the doctrines of the catholic faith, so as to be able to teach them in their native language. It would seem that these missionaries on compulsion did not answer the purpose of their masters, for pope Gregory, soon laying aside his fantastic expedient, resolved to intrust the conversion of the Anglo-Saxons to Romans of tried faith and solid learning. The chief of this mission was named Augustin; he was, ere his departure, consecrated bishop of England. His companions followed him, full of zeal, as far as the city of Aix in Provence; but here they conceived alarm at their enterprise, and desired to retrace their steps. Augustin returned alone, to seek from Gregory, in the name of the mission, permission to withdraw from this perilous journey, the result of which, he said, was extremely precarious among a people of an unknown tongue. But the pope would not consent. "It is too late to retreat," he said; "you must accomplish your enterprise without listening to the ill-disposed; were it possible, I myself would willingly labour with you in this good work." The missionaries belonged to a convent founded by pope Gregory on his own estate, in the very house where he was born; all had sworn obedience to him as to their spiritual father: they therefore obeyed, and went first to Chalons, where dwelt Theodorik, son of Hildebert, king of half the eastern portion of the country conquered by the Franks. They next repaired to Metz, where, over the other half, reigned Theodebert, also son of Hildebert.

The Romans presented to these two kings letters full of panegyrical expressions, calculated to excite their good will, by flattering their vanity to the highest degree. Pope Gregory knew that the Franks were at war with the Saxons of Germany, their neighbours on the north, and, availing himself of this circumstance, he did not hesitate to describe the Anglo-Saxons beyond seas, whom these monks were on their way to convert, as subjects of the Franks: "I have felt," he wrote to the two sons of Hildebert, "that you would ardently desire the happy conversion of your subjects to the faith which you yourselves profess, you, their lords and kings; this conviction has induced me to send Augustin, the bearer of these presents, with other servants of God, to labour there under your auspices."

The mission had also letters for the grandmother of the two young kings, the widow of Sighebert, father of Hildebert, a woman of lofty ambition and rare ability in intrigue, who, in the name of her two grandsons, governed one half of Gaul. She was of the nation of the Goths, then driven by the Frank invasion beyond the Pyrenees. Before her marriage, her name had been Brune, which in the Germanic language signified brilliant; but the Frank king, who espoused her, desiring, say the historians of the time, to augment and adorn her name, called her Brunehilde, that is to say, brilliant girl, (Brunehaut, latinè, Brunechildis.) From an Arian she became a catholic, received the unction of the sacred oil, and thenceforward displayed great zeal for her new belief; the bishops vied with each other in praising the purity of her faith, and, in consideration of her pious works, omitted to cast a single glance at her personal immoralities or her political crimes. "You, whose zeal is so ardent, whose works are so pious, whose excellent soul is strong in the fear of the Almighty God," wrote pope Gregory to this queen, "we pray you to aid us in a great work. The English nation has manifested to us a desire to receive the faith of Christ, and we would satisfy its desire." The Frank kings and their grandmother were in no degree anxious to verify the truth of this ardent desire of the Anglo-Saxon people, or to reconcile it with the evident repugnance and terror of the missionaries: they welcomed the mission, and defrayed its expenses on its way towards the sea. The chief of the western Franks, although at war with his relations of the east, received the Romans as graciously as they, and assisted them with men of the Frank nation to act as interpreters between them and the Saxons, who spoke almost the same language.

By a fortunate chance, it happened that the most powerful of the Anglo-Saxon chiefs, Ethelbert, king of Kent, had just married a woman of Frank origin, who professed the Catholic religion. This news raised the courage of the companions of Augustin, and they landed with confidence on the promontory of Thanet, already famous for the disembarkation of the ancient Romans, and of the two brothers who had opened to the Saxons the way into Britain. The Frank interpreters repaired to Ethelbert, and announced to him men who had come from afar to bring him joyful tidings, the offer of an endless happiness in heaven, an eternal kingdom with the true and living God, if he would believe in their words. The Saxon king at first gave no positive answer, and ordered that the strangers should remain in the isle of Thanet, until he had deliberated upon what course to adopt with regard to them. We may well suppose that the Christian wife of the pagan king did not remain inactive at this important juncture, and that all the effusions of domestic tenderness were employed to render Ethelbert favourable to the missionaries. He consented to hold a conference with them; but not having wholly overcome his distrust, he could not bring himself to receive them in his palace, or even in his royal city, but visited them in their island, where, further, he required that the interview should take place in the open air, to prevent the effect of any witchcraft which these strangers might employ against him. The Romans proceeded to the conference with studied display, in a double rank, preceded by a large silver cross, and a picture representing Christ; they explained the object of their journey, and made their propositions.

"These are fine words and fine promises," answered the pagan king; "but as this is all new to me, I cannot at once put faith in it, and abandon for it the belief which I, with my whole nation, profess. However, since you have come so far to communicate to us what you yourselves seem to think good and true, I will not ill treat you; I will furnish you with provisions and lodging, and will leave you free to make known your doctrine, and to convert to it whom you can."

The monks repaired to the capital city, which was called the city of the men of Kent, in Saxon, Kentwara-Byrig (Cantware-byrig, Canterbury); they entered it in procession, bearing their cross and their picture, and chanting litanies. They had soon made some proselytes; a church built by the Britons in honour of St. Martin, and deserted since the Saxon conquest, served them for the celebration of mass. They struck the imaginations of men by great austerities; they even performed miracles, and the sight of their prodigies gained the heart of king Ethelbert, who at first had seemed to apprehend sorcery on their part. When the chief of Kent had received baptism, the new religion became the road to royal favour, and numbers accordingly rushed into that path, though king Ethelbert, as the historians tell us, constrained no man. As a pledge of his faith, he gave houses and lands to his spiritual fathers; such in all countries was the first payment which the converters of the barbarians demanded. "I supplicate thy grandeur and munificence," said the priest to the royal neophyte, "to give me some land and all its revenues, not for myself, but for Christ, and to confer these upon me by solemn grant, to the end that thou in return mayst receive numerous possessions in this world, and a still greater number in the world to come." The king answered: "I confirm to thee in full property without reserve, all this domain, in order that this land be to thee a country, and that in future thou cease to be a stranger among us."

Augustin assumed the title of bishop of Kent, (Kent-ware, Cant-wara, latinè, Cantuarii.) The mission extended its labours beyond this territory, and by the influence of example, obtained some success among the eastern Saxons, whose chief, Sighebert, was a relation of Ethelbert. Pope Gregory learned with infinite joy the result of the preaching which had rendered a portion of the conquerors of Britain Christians and Catholics; the latter point, indeed, was the great feature with him, for his attachment to the creed of Nicea and to the doctrines of Saint Augustin rendered him the mortal enemy of all that savoured of schism or heresy; in his purism of orthodoxy, he went so far as to refuse the host to heretics dying in vindication of the faith of Jesus Christ. "The harvest is great," wrote Augustin to him, "but the husbandmen are few." Upon this intelligence, a second deputation of missionaries departed from Rome with letters addressed to the bishop of Gaul, and a sort of diplomatic note for Augustin, the grand plenipotentiary of the Roman church in Britain. The note addressed to Melitus and to Laurentius, chiefs of the new mission, was conceived in these terms:

"Gregory, the servant of the servants of God, to his most beloved brother, the abbot Melitus.

"We have been in a state of great anxiety since the departure of our congregation, which you have taken with you, because we have heard nothing of the successful progress of your journey.

"When the Almighty God shall bring you to the presence of that most reverend man, our brother, bishop Augustin, say to him that I have long been cogitating upon the matter of the English people, and the result is this; the fanes of the idols which are amongst that people ought by no means to be demolished, but the idols that are in them ought to be destroyed, the temples, meanwhile, sprinkled with holy water, altars constructed, and relics of the saints deposited. If these temples are well constructed, it is necessary that they be changed from the worship of demons to the service of the true God; so that whilst the people do not see their temples destroyed, they may lay aside the error of their hearts, and, recognising the true God, adore Him in those very places to which they have been in the habit of resorting.

"In the same manner, let this be done: as these people have been in the habit of slaying many cattle in the sacrifices to their demons, so for their sakes ought there to be some solemnity, the object of it only being changed. Then upon a dedication, or upon the nativity of some of the holy martyrs, whose relics are in the churches, let it be permitted to make arbours with the branches of trees, around what once were but heathen temples. Then celebrate such solemnities with religious feasts, so that the people will not immolate animals to the devil, but slay them and partake of them, with thanks and praises to God, for that abundance which has been bestowed upon them by Him who is the giver of all things; and thus whilst exterior joys are permitted to them, they may with the greater facility be attached to those joys that are of the spirit. For be it remembered, that it is not possible at once to deprive those whose minds are hardened, of all things. He who tries to reach the highest place, does so gradually, and step by step, and is never elevated by leaps. When our Lord made himself known to the people of Israel in Egypt, He still reserved for his own use the sacrifices which it had been accustomed to tender to the demon, and he even commanded them to immolate animals in His honour; so that as their hearts changed they would lose one portion of the sacrifice; that whilst the animals were immolated, as they had been immolated, yet being offered to God, and not to idols, the sacrifices may no longer be the same."

Together with these instructions, Melitus and Laurentius delivered to Augustin, the ornament of the pallium, which, according to the ceremonial the Romish church had borrowed from the Roman empire, was the living and official emblem of the power to command given to bishops. They at the same time brought a plan of an ecclesiastical constitution, prepared beforehand at Rome to be applied to the provinces of England, as the domain of the spiritual conquest became extended over them. According to this project, Augustin was to appoint twelve bishops, and to fix in London, when that city should become Christian, the metropolitan see, upon which the twelve other bishoprics should be dependent. In like manner, as soon as the great northern city, called in Latin Eboracum, and in Saxon Eoforwic, Everwic, (York), should have received Christianity, Augustin was to institute there a bishop, who, in his turn receiving the pallium, should become the metropolitan of twelve others. The latter metropolitan, though dependent upon Augustin during his life, was under the successors of Augustin to be subject only to Rome.

Regarding these arrangements solely under their material aspect, we may fancy we see the revival under other forms of the partition of provinces conquered or to be conquered, which in anterior ages so often occupied the Roman senate. The see of the first archbishop of the Saxons was not established at London, as the papal instructions had ordered; and either to conciliate the new Christian king of Kent, or in order to watch him more closely, and to be nearer at hand to oppose in him any return of old habits, Augustin fixed his abode in the city of Canterbury, in the very palace of Ethelbert, the king himself retiring to Reculver. Another Roman missionary was fixed as a simple bishop in London, the capital of the eastern Saxons; and Rofeskester, now Rochester, became the seat of a second bishopric. The metropolitan and his two suffragans had the reputation of performing miracles, and the fame of their marvellous works soon spread even into Gaul. Pope Gregory skilfully made use of this intelligence to re-animate in the hearts of the Frank kings the love and fear of Rome; but, while fully availing himself of the renown of Augustin, it was not without umbrage that he saw this renown augment, and his subaltern agent viewed by men as another apostle. There exists an ambiguous letter, wherein the pope, not venturing to express his whole opinion on this matter, appears to caution the apostle of the Saxons not to forget his rank and his duty, and to recommend him quietly to modify the exercise of his supernatural powers.

"On learning," says Gregory, "the great marvels that our God has been pleased to operate by your hands, in the eyes of the nation he has elected, I rejoiced thereat, because external prodigies efficaciously serve to give souls an inclination towards internal grace: but you yourself must take good heed, that amidst these prodigies your spirit be not inflated and become presumptuous; beware least that which outwardly raises you in consideration and honour, should inwardly become unto you a cause of fall, by the allurements of vain glory." These counsels were not without their meaning; the ambitious character of Augustin had already manifested itself in a sufficiently evident manner: unsatisfied with his dignity of metropolitan of the English, he coveted a more flattering and more assured supremacy over nations long since Christian. In one of his despatches to Rome, there was, among other things, this brief and peremptory question: "How am I to deal with the bishops of Gaul and the bishops of the Britons?" "As to the bishops of Gaul," answered Gregory, somewhat alarmed at the question, "I have not given thee, and I do not give thee any authority over them: the prelate of Arles has received the pallium from me; I cannot take his power from him; it is he who is the chief and judge of the Gauls; and as for thee, thou art forbidden to put the reaping-hook of judgment in the corn-field of another. As for the bishops of the Briton-race, I confide them all to thee; teach the ignorant, strengthen the weak, and chastise evil doers."

The enormous difference which the Roman pontiff thought proper to establish between the Gauls, whom he protected against the pretensions of Augustin, and the Cambrians, whom he abandoned to him, will be understood, when we call to mind that the Cambrians were schismatics. This unfortunate remnant of a great nation, restricted to a mere corner of their ancient country, had lost all, says one of their old poets, but their name, their language, and their God. They believed in one God in three persons, a rewarder and avenger, but not punishing, as the Romish church maintained, the sins of the father in his posterity; granting his grace to whomsoever practised justice, and not damning children who die before they have possibly committed a single sin. To these disagreements as to dogma, the result of the Pelagian or semi-Pelagian opinions retained by the Britons, were added other differences relating to points of discipline and arising from local customs, or from the oriental traditions which the British church, a daughter of the churches of the east, followed in preference. The form of the clerical tonsure and that of the monastic habit were not the same in Britain as in Italy and Gaul; they did not in Britain celebrate the festival of Easter precisely at the period fixed by the decrees of the popes. Although very rigid, the rules of the British monasteries were in this way peculiar, that very few of the monks took orders, either of priesthood or clerkship, and that all the rest, simple laymen, laboured with their hands the whole day, exercising some art or trade for their own support and that of the community. The Cambrians had bishops; but these bishops were, most of their time, without any fixed see: they lived sometimes in one town, sometimes in another, true overseers; and their archbishop, in the same way, lived now at Kerleon (Caër-Lleon) on the Usk, now at Menew, (Mynyw, latine Menevia) since named Saint David's; this archbishop, independent of all foreign authority, did not receive the pallium, or solicit it. These were crimes in the eyes of the Roman clergy, who desired that all should bow beneath the supremacy of their church, and fully sufficed to warrant pope Gregory, according to his view of the matter, in not recognising any of the bishops of Cambria as a religious authority, and in handing them over to the guardianship and correction of one of his missionaries.

Augustin, by an express message, conveyed to the clergy of the conquered Britons the order to acknowledge him archbishop of the whole island, under pain of incurring the anger of the Romish church, and that of the Anglo-Saxon kings. For the purpose of demonstrating to the Cambrian priests and monks the legitimacy of his pretensions, he invited them to a conference on the banks of the Severn, the boundary of their territory and that of the conquerors. The assembly was held in the open air, under a large oak. Here Augustin called upon the Britons to reform their religious practices according to the discipline of Rome, to join the Catholic unity, to give obedience to himself, and to employ themselves, under his direction, in the conversion of the Anglo-Saxons. In aid of his harangue, he produced a counterfeit blind man, a Saxon by birth, and pretended to restore him to sight; but neither the eloquence of the Roman nor his miracle could awe the Cambrians, and make them abjure their ancient spirit of independence. Augustin was not discouraged; he appointed a second interview, to which repaired, with a complaisance which proved their good faith, seven bishops of British race and many monks, chiefly from a large monastery called Bangor, situated in North Wales, on the banks of the Dee.

On their approach, the Roman did not deign to rise from his seat; and this token of pride at once wounded them. "We will never admit the pretended rights of Roman ambition," said their spokesman, Dimothus, "any more than those of Saxon tyranny. In the bond of love and charity, we are all subjects and servants to the church of God, yea, to the pope of Rome, and every good Christian, to help them forward, both in deed and in word, to be the children of God; but for the submission of obedience, we owe that only to God, and, after God, to our venerable head, the bishop of Kerleon on Use. Besides, we would ask why those who glorify themselves upon having converted the Saxons, have never reprimanded them for their acts of violence towards us and their spoliation of us?"

The only answer made by Augustin was a formal summons to the Welsh priests to acknowledge him as archbishop, and to aid him in converting the Germans of the island of Britain. The Welshmen unanimously replied that they would not unite in friendship with the invaders of their country, until these had restored all which they had unjustly wrested from them: "And as for the man," added they, "who does not rise and pay us respect when he is only our equal, how much greater the contempt he would manifest for us, if we admitted him superior." "Well, then," exclaimed the missionary, in a threatening tone, "since you will not have peace with your brethren, you shall have to endure war with your foes; since you refuse to join me in teaching the way of life to the Saxons, ere long, by a just judgment of God, you shall have to suffer from the Saxons the bitter pains of death."

And, in effect, but a short time had elapsed when the king of an Anglo-Saxon tribe, still pagan, marched from the north country to the very spot where the conference had been held The monks of Bangor, bearing in mind the menace of Augustin, quitted their convent in the utmost terror, and fled to the army which the chief of the Welsh province of Powis assembled. This army was defeated, and in the rout the victorious king perceived a body of men singularly clad, without arms, and all kneeling. He was told that these were the people of the great monastery, and that they were praying for the safety of their countrymen. "If they cry to their God for my enemies," said the Saxon, "they are fighting against me, though without arms;" and he had them all massacred, to the number of two hundred. The monastery of Bangor, whose chief had been the spokesman in the fatal interview with Augustin, was razed to the ground; "and it was thus," say the ecclesiastical authors, "that the prediction of the holy pontiff was accomplished, and those perfidious men who had slighted his counsels in aid of their eternal salvation, punished with death in this world." It was a national tradition among the Welsh, that the chief of the new Anglo-Saxon church caused this invasion, and pointed out the monastery of Bangor to the pagans of Northumberland. It is impossible to affirm anything positive on this point; but the coincidence of time rendered the imputation so grave as to make the friends of the Romish church desirous of destroying all traces of that coincidence. In almost all the manuscripts of the sole historian of these events, they inserted the statement that Augustin was dead when the defeat of the Britons and the massacre of the monks of Bangor took place. Augustin was, indeed, old at this period; but he lived at least a year after the military execution which he had so exactly predicted.

On his death, Laurentius, a Roman, like himself, took the title of archbishop; Melitus and Justus were still bishops, the one of London, the other of Rochester. The first had converted to Christianity Sighebert, a relation of Ethelbert, who, in the novelty of his conversion, manifested infinite zeal, and surrounded his growing clergy with honours and authority. But this state of things was not of long duration: this fervent king was succeeded by princes indifferent or even opposed to the new worship; and when the two sons of Sighebert (familiarly termed Sibert, or Sib) had committed their father to the tomb, they returned to paganism, and abolished all the laws directed against the old national religion. Being, however, of gentle disposition, they at first did not persecute either bishop Melitus or the small number of true believers who continued to listen to him; they even attended the Christian church, to pass the time, or perhaps with a sort of inward doubting.

One day that the Roman was administering the communion of the Eucharist to his faithful, the two young chiefs said to him: "Why dost thou not offer to us, as well as to the others, some of that white bread which thou didst use to give our father Sib?" "If," answered the bishop, "you will wash in the fountain of salvation, wherein your father was washed, you shall, like him, share this wholesome bread." "We will not enter the fountain; we have no need of it; but still we desire to refresh ourselves with that bread." They several times renewed this singular request; the Roman on each occasion repeated that he could not accede to it; and they, imputing his refusal simply to ill will, became irritated, and said: "Since thou wilt not please us in so easy a matter, thou shalt quit our country."

And they drove him and all his companions from London. The exiles went into Kent, to Laurentius and Justus, whom they found also discouraged by the indifference manifested towards them by the successor of Ethelbert. They all resolved to pass into Gaul. Melitus and Justus departed together; but Laurentius, on the point of following them, determined to make one last effort to turn the mind of the king of Kent, still wavering and uncertain, he believed, as to the religion of his ancestors. The last night that he was to pass among the Saxons, he had his bed set up in the church of Saint Peter, built at Canterbury by the old king; and in the morning he issued from it, bruised, wounded, and bleeding. In this state he presented himself before Edbald, son of Ethelbert. "See," he cried, "what the apostle Peter hath done unto me in punishment of my having for a moment thought of quitting his flock." The Saxon king was struck by this spectacle, and trembled lest he himself should incur the hostility of the holy apostle, who so severely chastised his friends. He invited Laurentius to remain, recalled Justus, and promised to employ all his authority in reconverting those who, following his example, had fallen into apostasy. Thanks to the aid of the temporal arm, the faith of Christ arose once more, never again to be extinguished, on both banks of the Thames. Melitus was the successor of Laurentius in the archiepiscopal see; Justus succeeded Melitus; and the king of Kent, Edbald, who had been on the point of driving them all away, was complimented by the sovereign pontiff upon the purity of his belief and the perfection of his Christian works.

A few years after these events, a sister of Edbald, Ethelberge, was married to the pagan chief of the country north of the Humber. The bride left Kent, accompanied by a priest of Roman birth, named Paulinus, who was beforehand consecrated archbishop of York, according to the plan of pope Gregory, and in the hope that the faithful wife would convert the infidel husband. The king of Northumberland, named Edwin, allowed his wife Ethelberge to practise the Christian religion under the auspices of the man she had brought with her, whose black hair and brown thin face astonished the light-haired inhabitants of the country. When the wife of Edwin became a mother, Paulinus gravely announced to the Anglo-Saxon king that he had obtained for her the blessing of child-bearing without pain, on condition that the child should be baptized in the name of Christ. In the effusion of his paternal joy, the pagan consented to all his wife desired; but, on his part, he would not hear of any proposition of baptism, though he allowed free speech to those who desired to convert him, argued with them, and sometimes embarrassed them.

In order to attract him, if possible, towards celestial things by the bait of worldly goods, there came from Rome a letter addressed by pope Boniface "to the glorious Edwin:" "I send you," wrote the pontiff, "the benediction of your protector, the blessed Peter, prince of the apostles, that is to say, a linen shirt ornamented with gold embroidery, and a mantle of fine wool of Ancona." Ethelberge, in the same way, received as a pledge of the blessing of the apostle Peter, a gilt ivory comb and a silver mirror. These gifts were accepted, but they did not decide king Edwin, whose reflective mind could only be gained over by a strong moral impression.

The life of the Saxon had been marked by an extraordinary adventure, of which he thought he had kept the secret wholly to himself; but it had probably escaped him amidst the endearments of wedded life. In his youth, before he became king, he had incurred a great peril; surprised by enemies, who sought his life, he had fallen into their hands. In the prison where he languished, without hope of safety, his heated imagination had, in a dream, brought before him an unknown personage, who approached him with a grave air, and said: "What wouldst thou promise to him who would and could save thee?" "Aught that it shall ever be in my power to perform," answered the Saxon. "Well," replied the unknown, "if he who can save thee only required of thee to live according to his counsels, wouldst thou follow them?" Edwin swore it, and the apparition, stretching forth his hand, and putting it on his head, said, "When such a sign shall again present itself to thee, recal this moment and our conversation." Edwin escaped his danger by some happy chance, but the memory of his dream remained engraven on his mind.

One day that he was alone in his apartment, the door suddenly opened, and he saw enter a personage, who advanced gravely forward like the man in his dream, and who, without pronouncing a single word, placed his hand upon his head. It was Paulinus, to whom, according to the ecclesiastical historians, the Holy Spirit had revealed the infallible means of overcoming the king's obstinacy. The victory was complete; the Saxon, struck with utter amazement, fell with his face to the ground, whence the Roman, now his master, graciously raised him. Edwin promised to be a Christian: but firm in his good sense, he promised for himself alone, saying that the men of the country should themselves decide what to do. Paulinus asked him to convoke the great national council, called in the Saxon language, wittena-ghemote, the assembly of the sages, summoned around the German kings on all important occasions, and at which were present the magistrates, the rich landed proprietors, the warriors of high grade, and the priests of the gods. King Edwin explained to this assembly the reasons of his change of faith; and addressing all present, one after another, he asked them what they thought of this new doctrine.

To this question, the chief of the pagan high priests, Coifi, thus replied:—"Your majesty sees, and can judge of that religion, which is now expounded to us; whilst I can truly declare to you, that which I most assuredly know, namely, that there is no advantage in the religion to which we hitherto have adhered. There is no one, for instance, who has been more devout in the worship of our gods than myself, and yet, there are many who receive greater benefits from you, who are possessed of more dignified offices, and who are far more prosperous in all their undertakings than myself. If our gods could be of any avail, assuredly they would have assisted him who paid the most court to them. It follows from this, that if, upon a due examination, you shall find that the new doctrines that are preached to you are better and superior to the old, then you are bound, in common with us all, not to delay the adoption of them."

A chief of the warriors then arose, and spoke thus:—"The life of man," said he, "on this earth, in comparison to that space of time which is unknown to us, is like to that which may happen when you with your nobles and attendants are seated at supper, in the winter season, and when a fire is lighted in the midst, and the room is filled with the genial heat, whilst the whirlwind rages, the rain beats, and the snow falls outside, and a sparrow flutters quickly in at one door, and flies as hastily out at the other. During the brief period that it is within the room, the chill of winter does not touch it; but in an instant the serenity it has enjoyed in its flight has disappeared—and as you look upon it, it has flashed from the darkness of winter at one door, into the darkness of winter in which it disappears at the other—such, too, is the brief measure of human existence. We know not what went before, and we are utterly ignorant as to what shall follow. If the new doctrine can make you more certain as to this, then it is one, in my opinion, that ought to be adopted by us."

After the other chiefs had spoken, and the Roman had explained his dogmas, the assembly, voting as in sanction of national laws, solemnly renounced the worship of the ancient gods. But when the missionary proposed to destroy the images of those gods, none among the new Christians felt himself firmly enough convinced to brave the perils of such a profanation; none save the high priest, who demanded of the king arms and a full-horse, that he might thus violate the rule of his order, which prohibited priests to assume warlike habits, or to ride on anything but a mare. Then, girt with a sword, and brandishing a pike, he galloped to the temple, and in sight of all the people, who thought him mad, he struck the walls and images with his lance. A wooden house was raised wherein king Edwin and a great number of men were baptized. Paulinus having thus really achieved the archbishopric of which he bore the title, traversed the countries of Deire and Bernicia, and baptized in the waters of the Swale and the Glen those who hastened to obey the decree of the assembly of sages.

The political influence of the great kingdom of Northamberland drew towards Christianity the population of the East-Angles, or eastern English, dwelling south of the Humber, and north of the eastern Saxons. This people had already heard some discourses of the Roman bishops of the south; but the two religions were still so equally balanced, that the chief of the country, Redwald, had two altars in the same temple, one to Christ and the other to the Teutonic gods, whom he invoked alternately. Thirty years after the conversion of the people on the banks of the Humber, a woman of that country converted the chief of the kingdom of Mercia, which then extended from the Humber to the Thames. The Anglo-Saxons who latest retained their ancient worship, were those of the southern coasts; they did not renounce it until the end of the seventh century.

Eight Roman monks were successively archbishops of Canterbury, before that dignity, instituted for the Saxons, was attained by a man of Saxon race, Berhtwald, or Brithwald. The successors of Augustin did not renounce the hope of constraining the clergy of Cambria to yield to their authority. They overwhelmed the Welsh priests with summonings and messages; they even extended their ambitious pretensions over the priests of Erin, as independent as the Britons of all foreign supremacy, and so zealous for the Christian faith, that their country was surnamed the Isle of Saints. But this merit of holiness, without complete subjection to the power of the Romish church, was as nothing in the eyes of the members of that church who had established their spiritual dominion over the portion of Britain conquered by the Anglo-Saxons. They sent messages full of pride and acerbity to the inhabitants of Erin: "We, the deputies of the apostolic see in the western regions, of late foolishly credited the reputation of your island for holiness; but we now fully regard you as no better than the Britons. The journey of Columban into Gaul, and that of a certain Dagaman into Britain, have fully convinced us of this, for among other things, this Dagaman passed by the places we inhabit, and not only refused to eat at our table, but even to take his meals in the same house with us."

This journey into Gaul, cited in proof of the ill doctrines and perversity of the Christians of Hibernia, had in it circumstances which deserve mention. Columban, or more correctly Colum, an Irishman by birth, and a missionary by inspiration, filled with a desire to seek adventures and perils for the sake of the Christian faith, had put to sea with twelve chosen companions. He passed into Britain, and thence into Gaul; then proceeding to the eastern frontier of that country, by which German paganism was rushing in or threatening to do so, he resolved to establish a place of prayer and preaching. After having traversed the vast forests of the Vosges, he selected as a residence the ruins of a Roman fortress, called Luxovium, now Luxeuil, in the centre of which was a spring of mineral waters and magnificent baths, adorned with marble basins and statues. These ruins furnished Columban and his companions with materials for building a house and an oratory, and the monastery founded by them was established according to the rule of the convents of Ireland. The reputation for sanctity of these cenobites from beyond sea, soon attracted numerous disciples, and the visits of powerful personages. Theodorik, the Frank king, in whose country they were, came to recommend himself to their prayers.

Columban, with a freedom which no member of the Gallo-Frankish clergy had permitted himself, severely remonstrated with the visitor upon the wicked life he led, instead of espousing a lawful wife, with concubines and mistresses. These reproaches displeased the king less than they did the king's grandmother, that Brunechild whose piety pope Gregory had so lauded, and who, the more absolutely to govern her grandson, dissuaded him from, and gave him a distaste for marriage. At the instigation of this woman, as cunning as she was ambitious, the Frank lords and the bishops themselves laboured, by malignant observations, to indispose Theodorik towards the chief of the foreign monks. He was accused of being of but doubtful orthodoxy, of creating a schism in the Gaulish church, of following an unwonted rule, by which no lay visitor was admitted into the interior of the monastery. After a scene of violence, in which the king, coming to Luxeuil, penetrated into the refectory, and in which Columban asserted his rule with inflexible courage, the Irishman was ordered to retrace the same road he had come. An escort of soldiers, under the order of count Theudoald and bishop Suffronius, conducted him to Besançon, from Besançon to Autun, from Autun to Nevers, and thence by the Loire to Nantes, where he embarked for Ireland. But his adventurous destiny and his ardent zeal took him back to Gaul, whence he crossed the Helvetian Alps into Italy, where he died. Such was the man from whose conduct the bishops of Saxon Britain judged that the Christianity of the inhabitants of Hibernia was of a suspicious nature, and that it had need to be purified and reformed by them.

The same church which expelled the censurer of the Frank kings from Gaul, gave to the Anglo-Saxon kings consecrated crosses for standards, when they went to exterminate the ancient Christians of Britain. The latter, in their national poems, attribute much of their disasters to a foreign conspiracy, and to monks whom they call unjust. In their conviction of the ill-will of the Romish church towards them, they daily became more confirmed in their determination to reject her dogmas and her empire; they preferred addressing themselves, as they repeatedly did, to the church of Constantinople, for counsel in theological difficulties. The most renowned of their ancient sages, Cattawg, at once bard and Christian priest, curses, in his political effusions, the negligent shepherd who does not guard the flock of God against the wolves of Rome.

But the ministers and envoys of the pontifical court, thanks to the religious dependence in which they held the powerful Anglo-Saxon kings, gradually, by means of terror, subdued the free spirit of the British churches. In the eighth century, a bishop of North Cambria celebrated the festival of Easter on the day prescribed by the catholic councils; the other bishops arose against this change; and, on the rumour of this dispute, the Anglo-Saxons made an irruption into the southern provinces where the opposition was manifested. To obviate foreign war and the desolation of his country, a Welsh chief attempted to sanction, by his civil authority, the alteration of the ancient religious customs; the public mind was so irritated at this, that the chieftain was killed in a revolt. However, the national pride soon declined, and weariness of a struggle constantly renewing, brought a large portion of the Welsh clergy to the centre of catholicism. The religious subjection of the country was thus gradually effected; but it was never so complete as that of England.

The kings of the Saxons and of the Angles had for the city of Rome and the see of St. Peter, a veneration which they frequently testified by rich offerings, and even by annual tributes, under the name of Rome-money or Church-money. The successors of the ancient leaders of adventurers Henghist, Horsa, Kerdic, Ælla and Ida, taught by the Roman clergy to assume the peaceful symbols of the royal dignity, and to bear, instead of the hatchets of their ancestors, staves with gilt ornaments, ceased to place the exercises of war in the first rank. Their ambition now was to see around them, not like their fathers, troops of warriors, but numerous converts under the rule of Saint Benedict, the most in favour with the pope. They themselves in many cases cut off their long hair to devote themselves to seclusion, and, if the need of an active life detained them amidst public affairs, they reckoned the consecration of a monastery as one of the great days of their reign. This event was celebrated with all the pomp of national solemnities; the chiefs, bishops, warriors, sages of the people, were assembled, and the king sat in the midst of them surrounded by his family. When the newly built walls had been sprinkled with holy water, and consecrated in the names of the blessed apostles Peter or Paul, the Saxon king arose and said aloud:—

"Thanks be given unto God Most High, that I have been enabled to do somewhat in honour of Christ and the holy apostles. All you here present be witnesses and guarantees of the donation, made by me to the monks of this place, of the lands, waters, meres, weirs, and fens hereafter set forth. I will that they have and hold them, in full and royal manner, so that no tax be levied upon them, and that the monastery be subject to no power on earth, save the holy see of Rome; for it is here that those among us who cannot go to Rome, shall visit Saint Peter. Let those who succeed me, whether my son, my brothers, or any other person, inviolably maintain this donation, if they would participate in eternal life, if they would be saved from eternal fire: whosoever shall abridge any part of it, may the porter of heaven abridge his share of heaven; whosoever shall add to it, may the porter of heaven add to his share of heaven." The king then took the roll of parchment on which was set forth the deed of donation, and drew a cross upon it; after him, his wife, his sons, his brothers, his sisters, the bishops, the public officers, and all persons of high rank, successively subscribed the same sign, repeating the form: "I confirm it by my mouth and by the cross of Christ."

This good understanding between the Anglo-Saxons and the court of Rome, or rather the absolute submission of the former to the latter, which gradually converted its religious primacy into political suzerainty, was not of very long duration. The illusion upon the imagination wore off, the dependence was more and more felt. While some kings bowed their head before the representative of the apostle who opened and shut the doors of heaven, there were others who repudiated the infliction of the law of the foreigner, disguised under the name of the Catholic faith. In this struggle, the members of the Saxon clergy, the spiritual sons of the Romish church, at first ranged themselves on her side and defended her power; but afterwards, themselves drawn into the current of national opinion, they claimed to owe to papacy only the duties of respect which the British Christians had offered to render it in the time of Augustin, and which it had so harshly disdained. The English people then became to the court of Rome, what the Cambrians had been at the time of their schism; by a conduct less religious than politic, it accordingly united itself with their national enemies; it excited foreign ambition against them, as it had excited their own ambition against the indigenous Britons. It promised, in the name of Saint Peter, their country and their goods, with absolution from all sin, to whomsoever would march against them; and to recover the tribute at first paid voluntarily, and then refused by slackened zeal or patriotic economy, it engaged in an enterprise, the aim of which was the subjection of the nation.

The detail of these later events and their consequences will occupy the greater portion of this history, devoted, as its title indicates, to the narrative of the fall of the Anglo-Saxon people. But we have not yet regularly attained this point; the reader's attention must still be directed to the victorious Germanic race and the conquered Celtic race; he must view the white standard of the Saxons and of the Angles gradually driving the red standard of the Kymri back towards the west. The Anglo-Saxon frontiers, continually enlarging in the west, after being extended on the north to the Forth and the Clyde, were again contracted in this direction at the close of the seventh century. The Picts and the Scots, attacked by Egfrith, king of Northumberland, skilfully drew him into the gorges of their mountains, defeated him, and after their victory advanced south of the Forth as far as the Tweed, the banks of which they then made the limits of their territory. This limit, which the inhabitants of the south never afterwards altered, marked from that day the new point of separation between the two parts of Britain. The tribes of Anglian race who inhabited the plain between the Forth and the Tweed became by this change embodied with the population of Picts and Scots, or Scotch, the name which this mixed population soon took, and from which was formed the modern name of the country.

At the other extremity of the island, the men of Cornwall, isolated as they were, long struggled for independence, aided occasionally by the Britons of Armorica. In the end, they became tributaries of the western Saxons; but this was never the case with the people of Wales: "Never," exclaim their old poets, "no, never shall the Kymri pay tribute; they will fight till death for the possession of the lands, bathed by the Wye." It was, in fact, the banks of that river which stayed the progress of Saxon domination; the last chieftain by whom it was extended was a king of Mercia, named Offa. He passed the Severn by the chain of mountains which, as it were the Apennines of southern Briton, had hitherto protected the last asylum of the conquered. Almost fifty miles beyond these mountains, on the west, Offa, instead of these natural boundaries, constructed a long rampart and trench, which extended from south to north, from the Wye to the valleys through which runs the Dee. Here was permanently fixed the frontier of the two races of men who, with unequal shares, conjointly inhabited the south of the island of Britain, from the Tweed to Cape Cornwall.

North of the bay into which the Dee discharges itself, the country inclosed between the mountains and the sea had already, for half a century, been subjugated by the English, and depopulated of the ancient Britons. The fugitives from these countries had reached the great asylum of Wales, or rather, the corner of land, bristling with mountains, which is washed by the sea at the bay of Solway. Here they for a long period preserved a sort of savage liberty, distinguished from the English race, in the language of that race, by the name of Cambrians; a name that remained attached to the country which was their asylum. Beyond the plains of Galloway, in the deep valleys of the Clyde (Ystrad-Clwyd), small British tribes, who, favoured by the locality, had maintained their freedom among the Angles, maintained it likewise among the Scots and Picts, when these had conquered all the lowlands of Scotland to Annandale and the Tweed. This last remnant of the pure race of Britons had for their capital and fortress the town, built upon a rock, which is now called Dumbarton, (Dun-briton, the town of the Britons.) So far down as the tenth century, we find traces of their independent existence; but after that period, they ceased to be designated by their ancient national name, either because they were all at once annihilated by some war, or because they had insensibly become incorporated with the mass of the population which surrounded them on all sides.

Thus disappeared from the island of Britain, with the exception of the remnant left in the small and sterile province of Wales, the Celtic race of Cambrians, Logrians, and Britons especially so called, partly direct emigrants from the eastern extremity of Europe, and partly colonists who had come into Britain, after an intermediate stay of various duration, on the western coast of Gaul. This poor wreck of a great nation had the glory of defending the possession of their last corner of territory against the efforts of an enemy immensely superior in numbers and wealth; often defeated, they were never subjugated, and, from century to century, they bore deep within their hearts the immovable conviction of a mysterious eternity reserved for their name and their language. From the very outset of their national defeats, this eternity was announced to them by the Welsh bards; and each time that, in the progress of years, a new foreign invader traversed the mountains of Cambria, let his victories have been as complete as they might, he still heard this cry from the vanquished: "Do thy worst: thou canst not destroy our name or our language." Chance, valour, and more particularly the nature of the country, composed of rocks, lakes, and sands, vindicated the daringly sanguine prediction; but in itself, it must be ever regarded as a remarkable proof of energy and imagination in the petty people who unhesitatingly acted upon it as a national article of faith.

The ancient Britons lived and breathed in poetry: the expression may seem extravagant, but it is not so in reality; for, in their political maxims, preserved to our own times, they place the poet-musician beside the agriculturist and the artist, as one of the three pillars of social existence. Their poets had but one theme: the destiny of their country, its misfortunes and its hopes. The nation, a poet in its turn, caught up and adopted their fictions with earnest enthusiasm, giving the wildest construction to their simplest expressions: that which in the bard was merely a patriotic wish, became to the excited imagination of the hearers a national promise; his expectations were for them prophecies; his very silence was a confirmation of their dreamiest speculations. That he sang not the death of Arthur, was a proof that Arthur still lived; and when the harper, without any particular meaning, sounded a melancholy strain, the auditors at once spontaneously applied to the vague melody the name of some spot become mournful to the nation, as the scene of a battle lost, of some triumph of the foreign aggressor. These memories of the past, these hopes of the future, embellished, in the eyes of the later Cambrians, their land of rocks and marshes. Though poor, they were gay and sociable; they bore misery lightly, as a transient suffering, and awaited, with untiring patience, the grand political revolution which was to give back to them all they had lost, to render them, as one of their bards expresses it, the crown of Britain.

Centuries after centuries passed away; yet, notwithstanding the predictions of the poets, the land of the ancient Britons did not come back again to the hands of their descendants. If the foreign oppressor was vanquished, it was not by the nation justly entitled to this retributive victory; his defeat and his subjection in no degree benefited the refugees of Wales. The narrative of the reverses of the Anglo-Saxons, invaded and subjugated in their turn by a people from beyond seas, will occupy the following pages. And here this race, hitherto victorious over all those that had preceded it in Britain, will excite a species of interest to which it had not previously given rise; for its cause will become the good cause, the cause of the suffering and oppressed. If distance of time ever weakens the impression produced in former ages by contemporary calamities, it is when the want of vivid memorials throws the veil of oblivion more or less completely over the sufferings of those who have so long since passed away. But in presence of the old documents wherein these sufferings are described with a minuteness and a naiveté which seem actually to bring before us the men of remote ages, a sentiment of gentle pity awakens in our hearts, and blending with the impartiality of the historian, softens him, without in the least impairing his determination to be honest and just.

BOOK II. FROM THE FIRST LANDING OF THE DANES IN ENGLAND TO THE END OF THEIR DOMINATION.

787—1048.

First landing of the Danish pirates—Their character; their conquests in England—Invasion of Ragnar Lodbrog; his death-song—Descent of the Danes in the south—Destruction of the monasteries—Termination of the kingdom of East Anglia—Invasion of the kingdom of Wessex—Resistance of Alfred—Flight of king Alfred—His return; he attacks the Danes, and concludes peace with them—Successive combinations of the English territory under a sole

For more than a century and a half, almost the entire of southern Britain had borne the name of England, and in the language of its German-descended possessors, that of Briton or Welsh, had meant serf or tributary, when a body of men, of unknown race, entered, in three vessels, a port on the eastern coast. In order to learn whence they came and what they wanted, the Saxon magistrate of the place proceeded to the shore where they had landed; the strangers suffered him to approach; then surrounding him and his escort, they fell upon them, killed them, and, having pillaged the town, returned with the booty to their ships and departed.

Such was the first appearance in England of the northern pirates, variously called Danes or Normans, according as they came from the islands of the Baltic sea or the coast of Norway.

They descended from the same primitive race with the Anglo-Saxons and the Franks; their language had roots identical with the idioms of these two nations: but this token of an ancient fraternity did not preserve from their hostile incursions, either Saxon Britain, or Frankish Gaul, nor even the territory beyond the Rhine, then exclusively inhabited by Germanic tribes. The conversion of the southern Teutons to the Christian faith had broken all bond of fraternity between them and the Teutons of the north. In the ninth century the man of the north still gloried in the title of son of Odin, and treated as bastards and apostates the Germans who had become children of the church: he made no distinction between them and the conquered populations whose religion they had adopted. Franks or Gauls, Lombards or Latins, all were equally odious to the man who had remained faithful to the ancient divinities of Germany. A sort of religious and patriotic fanaticism was thus combined in the Scandinavian with the fiery impulsiveness of their character, and an insatiable thirst for gain. They shed with joy the blood of the priests, were especially delighted at pillaging the churches, and stabled their horses in the chapels of the palaces. When they had devastated and burned some district of the Christian territory: "We have sung them the mass of lances," said they, mockingly; "it commenced early in the morning, and lasted until night."

In three days, with an east wind, the fleets of Denmark and Norway, two-sailed vessels, reached the south of Britain. The soldiers of each fleet obeyed in general one chief, whose vessel was distinguished from the rest by some particular ornament. The same chief commanded when the pirates, having landed, marched in troops, on foot or on horseback. He was called by the German title, rendered in the southern languages by the word king: but he was king only on the sea and in the battle-field; for, in the hour of the banquet the whole troop sat in a circle, and the horns, filled with beer, passed from hand to hand without any distinction of first man or last. The sea-king was everywhere faithfully followed and zealously obeyed, because he was always renowned as the bravest of the brave, as one who had never slept under a smoke-dried roof, who had never emptied a cup seated in the chimney-corner.

He could guide his vessel as the good horseman his steed, and to the ascendancy of courage and skill were added, for him, the influence created by superstition; he was initiated in the science of the runes; he knew the mystic characters which, engraved upon swords, secured the victory, and those which, inscribed on the poop and on the oars, preserved vessels from shipwreck. All equal under such a chief, bearing lightly their voluntary submission and the weight of their mailed armour, which they promised themselves soon to exchange for an equal weight of gold, the Danish pirates pursued the road of the swans, as their ancient national poetry expressed it. Sometimes they coasted along the shore, and laid wait for the enemy in the straits, the bays, and smaller anchorages, which procured them the surname of Vikings or children of the creeks; sometimes they dashed in pursuit of their prey across the ocean. The violent storms of the north seas dispersed and shattered their frail vessels; all did not rejoin their chieftain's ship at the rallying signal, but those who survived their shipwrecked companions were none the less confident, none the more depressed; they laughed at the winds and waves that had failed to harm them: "The strength of the tempest," they sang, "aids the arm of the rower; the storm is our servant; it throws us where we desired to go."

The first great army of Danish and Norman corsairs that visited England, landed upon the coast of Cornwall, the natives of which district, reduced by the English to the condition of tributaries, joined the enemies of their conquerors, either in the hope of gaining a certain degree of liberty, or simply to satisfy their passion of national vengeance. The Northmen were repulsed, and the Britons of Cornwall remained under the yoke of the Saxons; but shortly afterwards, other fleets, steering to the eastern coast, brought Danes in such vast numbers, that no force could prevent their penetrating to the heart of England. They ascended the course of the great rivers, until they had found a commodious station; here they quitted their vessels, moored them or laid them up dry, spread over the country, everywhere seized beasts of burden, and from mariners became men and horses, as the chroniclers of the time express it. They at first contented themselves with pillaging and then retiring, leaving behind them on the coasts a few military posts and small entrenched camps, to protect their next return; but soon changing their tactics, they established themselves fixedly, as masters of the soil and of the inhabitants, and drove back the English race of the north-east towards the south-west, as the latter had driven back the ancient British population of the Gaulish sea towards the other sea.

The sea kings who connected their names with the events of this great invasion are, Ragnar-Lodbrog and his three sons, Hubbo, Iugvar, and Afden. Son of a Norwegian and of the daughter of a king of one of the Danish isles, Ragnar had obtained, either fairly or by force, the crown of all these islands; but fortune becoming unfavourable to him, he lost his territorial possessions, and then equipping several vessels and assembling a troop of pirates, turned sea king. His first expeditions were in the Baltic and upon the coasts of Friesland and Saxony; he next made numerous descents in Brittany and Gaul, ever successful in his enterprises, which procured for him great wealth and great renown. After thirty years of successes, obtained with a simple fleet of barks, Ragnar, whose views had enlarged, resolved to essay his skill in a more scientific navigation, and had two vessels constructed, which surpassed in dimensions anything that had been hitherto seen in the north. Vainly did his wife Aslauga, with that cautious good sense which, among the Scandinavian women, passed as the gift of prophecy, urge upon him the perils to which this innovation exposed him; he would not listen to her, and embarked, followed by several hundred men. England was the object of this novel expedition. The pirates gaily cut the cables which held their two vessels, and, as they themselves expressed it in their poetical language, gave the rein to their great sea-horses.

All went well with the sea king and his companions so long as they were on the open sea; it was when they approached the coast that their difficulties commenced. Their large ships, unskilfully steered, struck upon shoals, whence vessels of Danish construction would easily have extricated themselves, and the wrecked crews were obliged to throw themselves upon the land, destitute of every means of retreat. The coast on which they thus disembarked against their will was that of Northumberland; they advanced in good order, ravaging and pillaging according to their custom, the same as though they were not in a hopeless position. On hearing of their devastations, Œlla, the king of the country, marched and attacked them with superior forces; the combat was furious, though very unequal; and Ragnar, enveloped in a mantle his wife had given him on his departure, penetrated the enemy's ranks four times. But, nearly all his companions having perished, he himself was taken alive by the Saxons. King Œlla proved cruel to his prisoner; not content with putting him to death, he inflicted unwonted tortures upon him. Lodbrog was shut up in a dungeon, filled, say the chroniclers, with vipers and venomous serpents. The death song of this famous sea king became celebrated as one of the chefs-d'œuvre of Scandinavian poetry. It was attributed, upon very slight foundation, to the hero himself; but whoever the author may have been, the production bears the vivid impress of the warlike and religious fanaticism which in the ninth century rendered the Danish and Norman Wikings so formidable.

"We struck with our swords, in the time when, yet young, I went towards the east, to prepare the repast of blood for the wolves, and in that great combat wherein I sent the people of Helsinghie in crowds to the palace of Odin. Thence our vessels bore us to the mouth of the Vistula, where our lances pierced the cuirasses, and our swords broke the bucklers.

"We struck with our swords, on the day when I saw hundreds of men prostrate on the sand, near a promontory of England; a dew of blood dropped from our swords; the arrows whistled as they went seeking the helmets; it was for me a pleasure equal to that of holding a beautiful girl in my arms.

"We struck with our swords, the day when I laid low that young man, so proud of his long hair, who in the morning had been wooing the young girls and the widows. What is the lot of a brave man, but to fall among the first? He who is never wounded, leads a wearisome life; man must attack man or resist him, in the great game of battle.

"We struck with our swords; and now I feel that men are the slaves of destiny, and obey the decrees of the spirits who preside over their birth. Never did I think that death would come to me through this Œlla, when I urged my vessels so far across the waves, and gave such banquets to the wild beasts. But I smile with pleasure when I reflect that a place is reserved for me in the halls of Odin, and that soon, seated there at the great banquet table, we shall drink flowing draughts of beer, in our cups of horn.

"We struck with our swords. If the sons of Aslanga knew the anguish I suffer, if they knew that venomous serpents wind themselves around me and cover me with bites, they would all shudder, and would rush to the combat; for the mother whom I have left them has given them valiant hearts. A viper now tears open my breast, and penetrates to my heart; I am conquered; but soon, I hope, the lance of one of my sons will pierce the side of Œlla.

"We struck with our swords in fifty and one combats; I doubt whether among men there is a king more famous than I. From my youth I have shed blood, and desired an end like this. The goddesses sent by Odin to meet me, call to me and invite me; I go, seated among the foremost, to drink beer with the gods. The hours of my life are passing away; I shall die laughing."

This lofty appeal to vengeance and to the warlike passions, first sung in a funeral ceremony, passed from mouth to mouth wherever Ragnar-Lodbrog had admirers; not only his sons, his relations, his friends, but a crowd of adventurers and young men from every northern kingdom responded to it. In less than a year, and without any hostile intelligence reaching England, eight sea kings and twenty ïarls or chiefs of secondary rank, confederating together, united their vessels and their soldiers. This was the largest fleet that had ever left Denmark on a distant expedition. Its destination was Northumberland, but a mistake of the pilots carried it more to the south, towards the coast of East Anglia.

Incapable of repelling such a great army, the people of the country gave the Danes a pacific reception, of which the latter availed themselves to collect provisions and horses, while awaiting reinforcements beyond seas; on the arrival of these, deeming themselves sure of success, they marched upon York, the capital of Northumberland, devastating and burning everything on their way. The two chiefs of this kingdom, Osbert and Œlla, concentrated their forces under the walls of the city for a decisive battle. The Saxons at first had the advantage; but dashing on prematurely in pursuit of the enemy, the latter, perceiving their disorder, turned upon them, and completely defeated them. Osbert was killed while fighting, and, by a singular destiny, Œlla, falling alive into the hands of the sons of Lodbrog, expiated by unheard of tortures, the tortures he had inflicted on their father.

Vengeance thus consummated, another passion, that of power, took possession of the confederate chiefs. Masters of a portion of the country north of the Humber, and assured by messengers of the submission of the rest, the sons of Ragnar-Lodbrog resolved to retain this conquest. They garrisoned York and the principal towns, distributed lands among their companions, and opened an asylum to people of every condition who chose to come from the Scandinavian provinces to augment the new colony. Thus Northumberland ceased to be a Saxon kingdom; it became the rallying point of the Danes, for the conquest of the south of England. After three years preparation, the great invasion commenced. The army, led by its eight kings, descended the Humber as far as the heights of Lindsay, and there landing, marched in a direct line from north to south, pillaging the towns, massacreing the inhabitants, and, with fanatic rage, taking especial delight in burning the churches and monasteries.

The Danish vanguard was approaching Croyland, a celebrated monastery, the name of which will often figure in these pages, when it met a small Saxon army, which, by dint of courage and good order, held it in check for a whole day. It was a levy en masse of all the people of the neighbourhood, commanded by their lords and by a monk called brother Toli, who, before taking the vows, had borne arms. Three Danish kings were slain in the battle; but, on the coming up of the others, the Saxons, overwhelmed by numbers, were nearly all killed in defending their posts. Some of the fugitives hastened to the monastery to announce that all was lost, and that the pagans were approaching. It was the hour of matins, and all the monks were assembled in the choir. The abbot, a man of advanced age, addressed them thus: "Let all those among you who are young and robust retire to a place of safety, carrying with them the relics of the saints, our books, our charters, and everything that we have of value. I will remain here with the old men and the children, and perhaps by the mercy of God the enemy will take pity on our weakness."

All the able-bodied men of the community, to the number of thirty, departed, and having loaded a boat with the relics, sacred vases, and other valuables, took refuge in the neighbouring marshes. There remained in the choir only the abbot, a few infirm old men, two of whom were upwards of an hundred years old, and some children, whom their parents, according to the devotional custom of the period, were bringing up under the monastic habit. They continued to chant the psalms at all the regular hours; when that of the mass arrived, the abbot placed himself at the altar in his sacerdotal robes. All present received the communion, and almost at the same moment the Danes entered the church. The chief who marched at their head killed with his own hand the abbot at the foot of the altar, and the soldiers seized the monks, young and old, whom terror had dispersed. They tortured them, one by one, to make them reveal where their treasure was concealed, and on their refusing to answer, cut off their heads. As the prior fell dead, one of the children, ten years of age, who was greatly attached to him, fell on his body, embracing him, weeping, and asking to die with him. His voice and face struck one of the Danish chiefs; moved with pity, he drew the child out of the crowd, and taking off his frock, and throwing over him a Danish cassock, said: "Come with me, and quit not my side for a moment." He thus saved him from the massacre, but no others were spared. After having vainly sought the treasure of the abbey, the Danes broke open the marble tombs in the church, and, furious at not finding any riches in them, scattered the bones, and set fire to the church. They then proceeded eastward, to the monastery of Peterborough.

This monastery, one of the chefs-d'œuvre of the architecture of the period, had, according to the Saxon style, massive walls pierced with small semi-circular windows, which rendered it the more easy to defend. The Danes found the doors closed, and were received with arrows and stones by the monks and the country people who had shut themselves up with them: in the first assault, one of the sons of Lodbrog, whose name the chroniclers do not mention, was mortally wounded; but, after two attacks, the Danes entered by storm, and Hubbo, to revenge his brother, killed, with his own hand, all the monks, to the number of eighty-four. The apartments were pillaged, the sepulchres burst open, and the library used to feed the fire applied to the building: the conflagration lasted fifteen whole days.

During a night march of the army towards Huntingdon, the boy whom a Danish chief had saved at Croyland, escaped, and regained the ruins of his late abode. He found the thirty monks returned, and employed in extinguishing the fire, which still burned. He recounted to them the massacre with every detail; and all, full of grief, proceeded to seek the bodies of their brethren. After several days labour, they found that of the abbot, headless and crushed by a beam; the rest were afterwards discovered, and buried near the church in one grave.

These disasters occurred partly in the territory of Mercia, and partly in that of East Anglia, or Eastern English. The king of the latter country, Edmund, speedily paid the penalty of the indifference with which, three years before, he had witnessed the invasion of Northumbria; surprised by the Danes in his royal residence, he was led a prisoner before the sons of Lodbrog, who haughtily commanded him to acknowledge himself their vassal. Edmund pertinaciously refused; whereupon the Danes, having bound him to a tree, essayed upon him their skill in archery. They aimed at the arms and legs, without touching the body, and at length terminated this barbarous sport by striking off the head of the Saxon king with an axe. He was a man of little merit or reputation, but his death procured for him the greatest renown then attainable, that of holiness and martyrdom. Common opinion, in the middle ages, sanctified the memory of any one who had perished by the hand of the pagans; but here something else was in operation, a peculiar feature of the Anglo-Saxon character, the tendency to surround patriotic sufferers with a religious halo, and to regard as martyrs those who had died defending the national cause, or persecuted by its enemies.

East-Anglia, entirely subjected, became, like Northumberland, a Danish kingdom, and a point of emigration with the adventurers of the north. The Saxon king was replaced by a sea king, called Godrun, and the indigenous population, reduced to a state of demi-servitude, lost all property in their territory, and in future cultivated it for the foreigners. This conquest involved in great danger the kingdom of Mercia, which, already encroached upon in its eastern portion, had the Danes upon two of its frontiers. The ancient kingdoms of Eastsex, Kent, and Suth-sex, had no longer an independent existence; for more than a century past they had all three been annexed to that of West-sex (Wessex), or of the western Saxons. Thus the struggle was between two Danish kingdoms and two Saxon kingdoms. The kings of Mercia and Wessex, hitherto rivals and enemies, leagued together in defence of that portion of England which remained free; but despite their utmost efforts, the whole of the territory north of the Thames was overrun; Mercia became a Danish province; and of the eight kingdoms originally founded by the Saxons and the Angles, but one alone remained, that of Wessex, which at this time extended from the mouth of the Thames to the Bristol Channel.

In the year 871, Ethelred, son of Ethelwolf, king of Wessex, was mortally wounded in a battle with the Danes, who had passed the Thames and invaded his territory. He left several children; but the national election fell upon his brother Alfred, a young man of two and twenty, whose courage and military skill inspired the Saxons with the most vivid hopes. Alfred twice succeeded, by arms or negotiation, in relieving his kingdom from the presence of the Danes; he repulsed several attempts to invade his southern provinces by sea, and for seven years maintained the boundary line of the Thames. It is probable that no other Danish army would ever have overpassed that boundary, had the king of Wessex and his people been thoroughly united; but there existed between them germs of discord of a very singular nature.

King Alfred was more learned than any of his subjects; while quite a youth he had visited the southern countries of Europe, and had closely observed their manners; he was conversant with the learned languages, and with most of the writings of antiquity. This superior knowledge created in the Saxon king a certain degree of contempt for the nation he governed. He had small respect for the information or intelligence of the great national council, the Assembly of Wise Men. Full of the ideas of absolute power, that so frequently recur in the Roman writers, he had an ardent desire for political reforms, and framed infinite plans, better in themselves, we may perhaps concede, than the ancient Anglo-Saxon practices they were destined to replace, but wanting in that essential requisite, the sanction of a people who neither understood nor desired these changes. Tradition has vaguely preserved some severe features of Alfred's government; and long after his death, men used to speak of the excessive rigour he applied to the punishment of prevaricators and other evil judges. Although this severity had for its object the good of the Anglo-Saxon nation, it was far from agreeable to a people, who at that time more highly valued the life of a free man than regularity in the administration of public affairs.

Besides, this rigour of king Alfred towards the great, was not accompanied by affability towards the small; he defended these, but he did not like them; their petitions and their appeals were distasteful to him, and his house was closed against them.

"If any needed his aid," says a contemporary writer, "whether in a case of personal necessity, or against the oppression of the powerful, he disdained to give audience to their plaint; he gave no support to the weak, regarding them as of no consideration whatever."

Thus, when, seven years after his election, this learned king, unconsciously odious, having to repel a formidable invasion of the Danes, summoned his people to defend the land, he was fearfully astonished to find them indisposed to obey him, and even careless about the common peril. It was in vain that he sent to each town and hamlet his war messenger, bearing an arrow and a naked sword, and that he published this ancient national proclamation, to which hitherto no Saxon, capable of bearing arms, had refused obedience: "Let each man that is not a nothing, whether in the town or country, leave his house and come." Very few men on this occasion accepted the invitation; and Alfred accordingly found himself almost alone, surrounded solely by the small circle of private friends who admired his learning, and whom he sometimes affected to tears by reciting his works to them.

Favoured by this indifference of the nation towards the chief whom itself had chosen, the enemy made rapid progress. Alfred, abandoned by his people, in turn abandoned them, and quitting, says an ancient historian, his warriors, his captains, and all his people, fled to save his life. Concealing himself as he went, in the woods and on the moors, he reached, on the limits of the Cornish Britons, the confluence of the rivers Tone and Parret. Here, in a peninsula surrounded by marshes, the Saxon king sought refuge, under a feigned name, in the hut of a fisherman, compelled himself to bake the bread which his indigent host permitted him to share with his family. Very few of the people knew what had become of him, and the Danish army entered his kingdom without opposition. Many of the inhabitants embarked from the western coasts to seek an asylum in Gaul, or in Erin, called by the Saxons, Ireland; the remainder submitted to pay tribute, and to cultivate the land for the Danes. It was not long ere they found the ills of conquest a thousand times worse than those of Alfred's rule, which in the hour of suffering had appeared to them insupportable, and they regretted their former condition and the despotism of a king chosen from among themselves.

On his part, calamity suggested to Alfred new thoughts, and he earnestly meditated the means of saving his people, and of regaining their favour. Fortified in his island against hostile surprise by entrenchments of wood and earth, he led there the wild and rugged life reserved in all conquered countries for those of the conquered who will not submit to slavery, the life of a brigand in the woods and marshes and mountain gorges. At the head of his friends, formed into bands, he pillaged for their support the Danes, enriched with Saxon spoils, or failing these, the Saxons who obeyed them and acknowledged them as masters. All whom the Danish yoke burdened, all who had become guilty of high treason to the men in power, by defending against them their goods, their wives, or their daughters, came to range themselves under the orders of the unknown chief who refused to share the general servitude. After a systematic warfare of stratagems, surprises, and nocturnal combats, the partisan leader resolved to avow himself, to make an appeal to the whole western country, and openly to attack, under the Anglo-Saxon standard, the Danish head-quarters, at Ethandun, on the borders of Wiltshire and Somersetshire, close to a forest called Selwood, or the Great Forest. Before giving the decisive signal, Alfred determined to make a personal observation of the Danish position; he entered their camp disguised as a harper, and with his Saxon songs entertained the Danish army, whose language differed very little from his own; he visited every part of the encampment, and on his return to his own quarters despatched messengers throughout the surrounding country, appointing as the rendezvous for all Saxons who would arm and fight under his command, a place called Egberthes-stane (Egbert's-stone), on the eastern edge of Selwood, and a few miles from the enemy's camp.

During three consecutive days, armed men from all quarters arrived at the spot indicated, singly or in small bands. Each new comer was hailed by the name of brother, and received with cordial and tumultuous joy. Some rumours of the movement reached the camp of the Danes; they discerned around them symptoms of agitation; but, as every Saxon was true to his cause, their information on the subject was extremely vague, and not knowing precisely where the insurrection would commence, they took no further steps than doubling their outposts. It was not long ere they saw the White Horse, the banner of Wessex, bearing down upon them. Alfred attacked their redoubts at Ethandun in the weakest point, carried them, drove out all the Danes, and, as the Saxon chronicles expresses it, remained master of the carnage, (Wœl-stow.)

Once dispersed, the Danes did not again rally, and Godrun, their king, did that which was a frequent occurrence with people of his nation under circumstances of peril: he promised that if the conquerors would relinquish their pursuit of him, he and his people would be baptised, and retire to their territories in East Anglia, and henceforth live there in peace. The Saxon king, who was not in a position to carry matters to extremity, accepted the proposal; Godrun, with his captains, swore on a bracelet consecrated to their gods that they would in all good faith receive baptism. King Alfred officiated as spiritual father to the Danish chief, who, putting the neophytical white robe over his armour, departed with the wreck of his army for the land whence he had come, and where he engaged for the future to remain. The limits of the two populations were fixed by a definitive treaty, sworn to, as its preamble set forth, by Alfred, king; Godrun, king; all the Anglo-Saxon wise-men, and all the Danish people. These limits were, on the south, the course of the Thames as far as the Lea, which discharges its waters into the greater stream not far from London; on the north and east, the Ouse and the great highroad constructed by the Britons and renewed by the Romans, called by the Saxons Wetlenga-street, the way of the sons of Wetla.

The Danes settled in the towns of Mercia, and in the country north of the Humber, did not consider themselves bound by the agreement between Alfred and Godrun, and the war accordingly still proceeded on the northern frontier of Wessex. The ancient kingdoms of Sussex (Suthsex, Suth-Seaxna-land) and Kent, delivered by him from foreign servitude, unanimously proclaimed Alfred their liberator and their king. Not a single voice was raised against him, either in his own country, where his former unpopularity had been effaced by his recent services, or in those which his predecessors had by conquest subjected to their sway. All those portions of England which were not occupied by the Danes, thenceforth formed one single state; and thus for ever disappeared the ancient division of the English people into various peoples, corresponding in number to the bands of emigrants which had incessantly come from the islands and coasts of Germany. The flood of Danish invasion had permanently thrown down the line of fortresses which had before separated kingdom from kingdom, and isolation, frequently hostile, was now replaced by the union ever produced by common misfortunes and common hopes.

When the general division of Anglo-Saxon England into kingdoms was abolished, the other territorial divisions assumed an importance which they had not previously possessed.

It is from this period that historians begin to make mention of skires, scires, shires, or portions of kingdoms, and of hundreds and tithings, local circumscriptions, indeed, as old in England as the establishment of the Saxons and Angles, but of which little notice was taken, while there prevailed above them a more extended political circumscription. The custom of reckoning families as simple units, and then aggregating them in tens or hundreds, to form districts and hundreds, is found amongst all peoples of Teutonic origin. If this institution plays a principal part in the laws which bear the name of Alfred, it is not that he invented it, but, on the contrary, because, finding it deeply rooted in the soil of England, and well nigh uniformly diffused throughout all the kingdoms he peacefully annexed to that of Wessex, it was essential for him to make it the great basis of his regulations for the establishment of public order. He himself instituted neither tythings nor hundreds, nor the municipal officers called tything-men and hundred-men, nor even that form of procedure which, modified by the action of time, resulted in trial by jury. All these things existed among the Saxons and Angles prior to their emigration.

The king of Wessex, after his second accession to the throne, acquired such celebrity as a brave, and more especially as a wise man, that we scarce meet in history with any trace of that unpopularity under which he at first laboured. Without relaxing in his earnest care to maintain the independence he had achieved for his people, Alfred found leisure for the studies he still loved, but now without preferring them to the men for whom he destined their fruit. There have come down to us from his pen, productions in verse and in prose, remarkable for their wealth of imagination, and for that luxurious imagery which constitutes the distinctive character of the old German literature.

The remainder of Alfred's life was occupied in these labours, and in war. The oath sworn to him by the Danes of East Anglia, first on the bracelet of Odin, and then on the cross of Christ, was broken by them at the first appearance of a fleet of pirates on their coasts. They saluted the new comers as brothers, and the combined influence of the recollections thus awakened, and of national sympathy, induced them to quit the fields they were cultivating, and to detach from the smoke-discoloured beam, where it had been peacefully suspended, the weighty battle-axe, or the club bristling with iron spikes, which they called the Morghen stürna (star of the morning). Very soon afterwards, in their case violating no treaty, the Danes of the Humber marched towards the south, to join, with the men of East Anglia, the army of the famous seaking, Hasting, who adopting, as the southern poets expressed it, the ocean for his home, passed his life in sailing from Denmark to the Orcades, from the Orcades to Gaul, from Gaul to Ireland, from Ireland to England.

Hasting found the English, under king Alfred, well prepared to receive him as an enemy, and not as a master. He was defeated in several engagements; a portion of his routed army took refuge among the Northumbrian Danes; another body became incorporated with the Danes of East Anglia; such of them as had realised any booty by their sea and land expeditions, became citizens in the towns, and farmers in the country districts; the poorer sort repaired to their ships, and followed their indefatigable chief to new enterprises. They crossed the English channel and ascended the Seine. Hasting, standing at the prow of his own vessel, was wont to collect the other vessels of his corsair-fleet by the sound of an ivory horn, which hung from his neck, and which the inhabitants of Gaul called the thunder. On the instant that this dreaded blast was heard in the distance, the Gaulish serf quitted the field on which he was employing his compulsory labours, and fled, with his little property, to the depths of the neighbouring forests; while his master, the noble Frank, filled with equal terror, raised the drawbridge of his stronghold, hastened to the donjon to examine the state of the armoury, and buried the money-tribute he had been levying from the surrounding district.

On the death of the good king Alfred, his son Edward, who had distinguished himself in the war against Hasting, was elected by the Anglo-Saxon chieftains and wise men to succeed him. Ethelwald, a son of Ethelred, Alfred's elder brother and predecessor, was daring enough to protest, in the name of his hereditary rights, against the national choice. This pretension was not only rejected; it was regarded as an outrage upon the laws of the land, and the great council pronounced the banishment of the offender, who, instead of obeying the sentence thus legally passed upon him, threw himself, with some partisans, into the town of Wimborne, on the south-western coast, swearing that he would either maintain his position there or die. But he did not keep his oath: on the approach of the English army, he fled without a blow, and, taking refuge with the Northumbrian Danes, turned pagan and pirate. The Danes having, some time after, made him leader of an expedition against his countrymen, Ethelwald invaded the Anglo-Saxon territory, but was defeated and killed in the first encounter. Hereupon king Edward assumed the offensive against the Danes, expelled them from the eastern coast, from the mouth of the Thames to Boston Wash, and shut them up in their northern provinces by a line of fortresses, erected along the banks of the Humber. His successor, Ethelstan, passed that river, took York, and compelled the inhabitants of Scandinavian race to swear, in the customary form, that they would do all that he should command them to do. One of the Danish chiefs was honourably received in the palace of the Saxon king, and admitted to his table; but, four days of this peaceful life sufficed to disgust him: he fled to the sea-coast, and embarked in a pirate ship, as incapable as a fish, says an ancient historian, of living out of water.

The English army advanced to the Tweed, and Northumberland was annexed to the territories of Ethelstan, who was thus the first king that ever reigned over all England. In the ardour of this triumph, the Anglo-Saxons overpassed their ancient northern limit, and perturbated by an invasion the descendants of the Picts and Scots, and the tribe of ancient Britons who inhabited the valley of the Clyde. An offensive league was immediately formed between these nations, and the Danes arriving from beyond seas to deliver their countrymen from the domination of the men of the south. Olaf, son of Sithrik, last Danish king of Northumberland, was named generalissimo of this confederation, which comprised within its ranks the men of the Baltic, the Danes of the Orcades, the Galls or Gael of the Hebrides, armed with the long two-handed sword which they called glay-more or the great sword, the Galls of the Grampians, and the Cambrians of Dumbarton and Galloway (latinè Galwidia), bearing long, slight pikes. The two armies met north of the Humber, at a place called in Saxon Brunanburgh, or the town of fountains (Bamborough). Victory declared for the English, who compelled the wreck of the confederates to make a painful retreat to their ships, their islands, and their mountains. The conquerors named this day the Day of the Great Fight, and celebrated it in national songs, fragments of which have come down to us.

"The king Ethelstan, chief of chiefs, he who bestows the collar of honour on the brave, and his brother, the noble Edmund, fought at Brunanburgh with the edge of the sword. They clove the wall of the bucklers, they threw down the warriors of renown, the race of the Scots, and the men of the ships.

"Olaf fled with the petty remnant of his people, and wept upon the waters. The foreigner speaks not of this battle, seated at his fire-side, with his family; for their relations fell in it, and their friends returned not from it. The kings of the north, in their council-halls, will lament that their warriors ventured to play the game of carnage with the sons of Edward.

"King Ethelstan and his brother Edmund returned to the land of Wessex. They left behind them the raven feasting on corses, the black raven with the pointed beak, and the toad with hoarse voice, and the eagle famishing for flesh, and the voracious kites, and the yellow wolf of the woods.

"Never was there greater carnage in this island, never did more men perish by the edge of the sword, since the day when the Saxons and Angles came from the east across the ocean, and entering Britain, noble war-makers, vanquished the Welsh, and took possession of the country."

Ethelstan made the Cambrians of the south pay dearly for the succour which their northern brethren had afforded to the enemy; he ravaged the territory of the Welsh, and imposed tribute upon them; the king of Aberfraw, as the old instruments express it, paid to the king of London tribute in money, in oxen, in falcons, and in dogs of chace. The Cornish Britons, expelled from the city of Exeter, which hitherto they had inhabited conjointly with the English, were driven beyond the Tamar, which then became, as it still continues, the boundary of Cornwall. Ethelstan subjected to his power, by war or by policy, all the populations of various origin which inhabited the Isle of Britain. He appointed as governor of the Northumbrian Anglo-Danes, a Norwegian, Erik, son of Harold, a veteran pirate, who turned Christian to obtain this command.

On the day of his baptism, he swore to maintain and defend Northumberland against all pirates and pagans, Danes or otherwise; from a sea-king he became a provincial king, a folk-king, as the Scandinavians expressed it. But this too pacific dignity soon ceased to please, and he returned to his ships. After some years' absence, he revisited the Northumbrians, who received him joyfully, and again adopted him as their chief, without the sanction of king Edred, Ethelstan's successor. This king accordingly marched against them, and compelled them to abandon Erik, who, in his turn, in revenge for their desertion, attacked them, by the aid of five pirate-bands from Denmark, the Orcades and the Hebrides. He fell in the first encounter, and with him the five sea-kings his allies. His death, glorious in the eyes of a Scandinavian, was celebrated by the skalds or northern poets, who, paying no heed to the baptism which Erik had received from the English, placed him in a far different paradise from that of the Christians.

"I have dreamt a dream," chants the panegyrist of the pirate; "Methought I was at daybreak in the hall of Walhalla, preparing all things for the reception of the men killed in battles.

"I awakened the heroes from their sleep; I asked them to rise, to arrange the seats and the drinking cups, as for the coming of a king.

" 'What means all this noise?' cried Braghi; 'why are so many men in motion, and why all this ordering of seats?' 'It is because Erik is on his way to us,' replied Odin; 'I await him with joy. Let some go forth to meet him.'

" 'How is it that his coming pleases thee more than the coming of any other king?'—'Because in more battle-fields has his sword been red with blood; because in more places has his ensanguined spear diffused terror.'

" 'I salute thee, Erik, brave warrior! enter; thrice welcome art thou to this abode. Say, what kings accompany thee; how many come with thee from the combat?'

" 'Five kings accompany me,' replied Erik; 'I am the sixth.' "

The territory of the Northumbrians had now lost that title of kingdom which it had hitherto preserved, and was divided out into provinces. The district between the Humber and the Tees was called Yorkshire,—in Saxon, Everwicshire. The rest of the country, as far as the Tweed, retained the general name of Northumbria, Northan-humbra-land, though with several local circumscriptions, such as the land of the Cambrians, Cumbra-land, next to the Solway Firth; the land of the Western Mountains, Westmoringa-land; and lastly, Northumberland proper, along the coast of the eastern sea, between the rivers Tyne and Tweed. The Northumbrian chiefs, in passing under the supreme authority of the Anglo-Saxon kings, retained the Danish title they had borne since the invasion; they continued to be called ïarls, or eorls according to the Saxon orthography of the word. The original signification of the term is no longer known, but the Scandinavians applied it to every description of commander, military or civil, who acted as lieutenant of the supreme chief, the kining or king. By degrees the Anglo-Saxons introduced their new title into their southern and western territories, qualifying by it the magistrates to whom was delegated the government of the larger provinces, formerly called kingdoms, and the supremacy over all the local magistrates, over the administrators of shires, scire-gerefas, shire-reeves, sheriffs, over the administrators of towns, port gerefas, port reeves, and over the ealdermen, aldermen. The latter title, before the introduction of that of eorl, had been the generic appellation of the higher Anglo-Saxon magistracies; it thenceforward descended a step, and was only applied to inferior jurisdictions and to municipal dignitaries.

Most of the new Danish citizens of England turned Christians in order to remove from themselves one marked indication of alienship. Several, in consideration of grants of land, assumed the title and the employment of perpetual defenders of the church, of that church whose edifices, before, they had with such peculiar delight destroyed and burned. Some of them even entered religious orders, and professed a rigid and sombre austerity, a reminiscence under another form, of the rugged, though free, condition of their former life.

In the revolution which combined all England, from the Tweed to Cape Cornwall, in one sole and undivided body politic, the power of the kings, now monarchs, acquired force with extension, and became, for each of the populations thus united together, more oppressive than the ancient sway of its own peculiar kings had been. The association of the Anglo-Danish provinces with the Anglo-Saxon provinces necessarily involved the latter to a certain extent in the strict and distrustful system which weighed upon the former, as peopled with foreigners who were subjects against their will. The same kings, exercising concurrently in the north the right of conquest, in the south that of legitimate sovereignty, soon yielded to the tendency to confound these two characters of their power, and to make but a very slight distinction between the Anglo-Dane and the Anglo-Saxon, the foreigner and the native, the subjugated and the subject. They began to entertain an exaggerated idea of themselves and of their power; they surrounded themselves with a pomp hitherto unknown; they ceased to be popular like their predecessors, who, invoking the people as councillor in all things, ever found the people ready to do that which itself had counselled. Their conduct created new sources of weakness for England. Great as she henceforth seemed to be, under chiefs whose titles of honour occupied several lines, she was in reality less capable of resisting an external enemy than at the period when, with few provinces, but these governed alike without display and without despotism, she saw inscribed at the head of her national laws these simple words:—"I, Alfred, king of the West Saxons."

The Danish inhabitants of England, unwilling subjects of kings of foreign race, had their eyes constantly directed towards the sea, in the hope that some favourable breeze would bring them liberators and leaders from their old country. They had not long to wait; in the reign of Ethelred, son of Edgard, the descents of the Northmen upon Britain, which had never been wholly discontinued, suddenly assumed a very menacing character. Seven war-ships appeared off the coast of Kent, and their crews pillaged the isle of Thanet; three more vessels, sailing from the south, ravaged the vicinity of Southampton, while other pirate troops landed on the eastern coast, and took up positions on several points. The alarm extended itself to London: Ethelred immediately convoked the great national council; but, under this supine and ostentatious monarch, the assembly was composed of bishops and courtiers more disposed to flatter the prince and encourage his indolence, than to give him sound advice. Conforming to the king's aversion for anything like prompt or energetic measures, they thought they could get rid of the Danes by offering them a sum equivalent to the gain which these pirates had calculated upon realizing by their invasion of England.

There existed, under the name of Dane-money, Dane-gheld, an impost of twelvepence upon every hide of land throughout the country, levied from time to time for the payment of the troops who guarded the coasts against the Scandinavian corsairs. This money the council proposed to give the new invaders, in the shape of a tribute: the offer was accepted, and the first payment, amounting to £10,000, received, on condition of their forthwith quitting England. They departed accordingly, but only to return in greater numbers, for the purpose of obtaining a larger sum. Their fleet sailed up the Humber, devastating both banks. The Saxon inhabitants of the adjacent provinces ran in arms to give the enemy battle; but on the eve of combat, three of their leaders, Danes by origin, betrayed them, and passed over to the foe. Every Northumbrian Dane abandoned his new faith and his new fidelity, and made close friendship and alliance with the pagan pirates from the Baltic.

The breezes of spring wafted up the Thame a fleet of eighty war-ships, commanded by two kings, Olaf of Norway, and Swen of Denmark, the latter of whom, after having received baptism, had returned to the worship of Odin. The two kings, in token of possession, having planted one lance on the shore of the Thames, and thrown another into the current of the first river they crossed after landing, marched, says an old historian, escorted by their wonted leaders, fire and sword. Ethelred, whose consciousness of his unpopularity made him fear to assemble an army, once more proposed to give money to the enemy, on condition of their retiring in peace; they demanded eighty thousand pounds, which the king immediately paid them, satisfied with their promises and with the conversion of a Danish chief, who received in Winchester cathedral, amid vast ceremony, that baptism which one of the Danes present on the occasion contemptuously declared that he had already received twenty times, without the slightest effect.

The truce granted by the invaders was far from being a peaceful truce; in the vicinity of their cantonments they outraged the women and slew the men. Their insolence and their excesses raising the indignation of the natives to the highest point, brought about, ere long, one of those acts of national vengeance which it is alike difficult to condemn or to justify, because a noble instinct, the hatred of oppression, is mixed up in them with the indulgence of atrocious passions. In pursuance of a vast conspiracy, formed under the eyes and with the connivance of the royal magistrates and officers, all the Danes of the late invasion, men, women, and children, were, in the same hour of the same day, attacked and killed in their quarters, by their hosts and neighbours. This massacre, which excited general attention, and the odious circumstances of which afterwards served as a pretext for the enemies of the English nation, took place on St. Brice's day, in the year 1003. It did not extend to the northern and eastern provinces, where the Danes, longer established, and become cultivators or citizens, formed the majority of the population; but all the recent invaders, with very few exceptions, perished, and among them a sister of the king of Denmark. To avenge this massacre, and to punish what he called the treason of the English people, king Swen assembled an army far more numerous than the first, and in which, if we are to credit the ancient historians, there was not a single slave, or even freed man, nor an old man, every soldier in it being noble, or a free man, the son of a free man, and in the full vigour of life.

This army embarked in tall ships, each of which had a distinctive badge designating its commander. Some had at the prow figures of lions, bulls, dolphins, men, in gilt copper; others bore at their mast-head birds spreading their wings and turning with the wind; the sides of the ships were painted in various colours, and the bucklers of polished steel were suspended along them in rows. The king's own ship had the elongated form of a serpent, the prow forming its head, the twisted stern its tail; it was on this account called the Great Dragon. On landing in England, the Danes, falling into battalions, unfurled a mystic standard, termed by them the Raven. It was a flag of white silk, in the centre of which appeared the black figure of a raven, with open beak and outspread wings; three of king Swen's sisters had worked it in one night, accompanying their labour with magic songs and gestures. This banner, which, according to the superstitious ideas of the Scandinavians, was a certain pledge of victory, augmented the ardour and confidence of the invaders. In every place they visited on their way, writes an old historian, they gaily ate the repast unwillingly prepared for them, and on departing, slew the host and burned his house.

They seized all the horses they could find, and, according to the tactics of their predecessors, converting themselves into cavalry, rapidly traversed the country, and, presenting themselves in directions where they were wholly unexpected, surprised castles and towns, one after another. In a very short time they had conquered all the south-eastern provinces, from the mouth of the Ouse to Spithead. King Ethelred, who was never prepared to fight, could devise no other expedient than to purchase truces of a few days each, for various sums of money—a temporizing policy, which compelled him to burden the people with constantly increasing taxes. Thus the English who had the good fortune to escape being pillaged by the Danes, could not avoid the oppressive exactions of their own king; so that, under the one form if not under the other, they were sure to be stripped of all they possessed.

While the administrators of England thus made their dastardly bargains with the foreign foe at the expense of the people, there was one man found who, a rich and powerful magnate of the land, preferred death to giving a sanction to such conduct by his own example. This was the archbishop of Canterbury, Elfeg. A prisoner of the Danes, on the capture of his metropolitan city, and dragged among their baggage from encampment to encampment, he remained day after day in chains, without even uttering the word ransom. The Danes, first breaking this silence, offered to restore their captive to liberty on condition of his paying them three thousand gold pieces, and counselling king Ethelred to give them four times that amount in addition. "I have no money of my own," replied the archbishop; "and I will not deprive my ecclesiastical territory of one penny on my account; neither will I counsel my sovereign aught that is contrary to the honour of my country." The Danes, more eager for money than for the archbishop's blood, pressed their demand. "You urge me in vain," replied Elfeg; "I am not one who will furnish Christian flesh for pagan teeth to tear, and it were doing so to give up to you that which my poor people have been saving for their sustenance."

The Danes at length lost all patience, and one day that they had been drinking copiously of wine just brought them from the south, they bethought themselves of trying the archbishop, by way of pastime. He was led bound, and seated upon a miserable horse, to the centre of the encampment, which served alike for the council-chamber, the judgment-seat, and the banqueting-hall; here the chiefs and the more distinguished warriors were seated in a circle, on great stones; close by was a heap of the bones, the jaws and horns of the oxen consumed at the recent repast. As soon as the Saxon prelate was in the midst of the circle, a great cry arose from all around: "Gold, bishop, gold, or we will cause thee play a game shall make thee noted through the world." Elfeg calmly replied: "I offer you the gold of wisdom, that you renounce your superstitions and be converts to the true God; if you heed not this counsel, know that you shall perish as Sodom, and shall take no root in this land." At these words, which they regarded as a menace to themselves and an insult to their religion, the mock judges rose furiously from their seats, and rushing upon the archbishop, beat him to the earth with the backs of their hatchets; several of them then ran to the heap of bones, and taking up some of the largest, rained a deluge of blows upon the prostrate Saxon. The archbishop, having fruitlessly endeavoured to kneel, in order to offer up a last prayer, fell forward in a senseless condition; his sufferings were terminated by the barbarous compassion of a soldier, whom he had converted and baptised on the previous day, and who now split his skull with his axe. The murderers at first intended to throw the corpse into a neighbouring marsh; but the Anglo-Saxons, who honoured Elfeg as a martyr for Christ's and for his country's sake, purchased the body at a heavy cost, and buried it at London.

Meantime king Ethelred practised without any scruple that which the archbishop of Canterbury, at the sacrifice of his life, had refused to counsel him to do. One day his collectors of taxes levied the tribute for the Danes; next day the Danes themselves came and exacted the tribute over again, on their own account. On their departure, the royal agents again presented themselves, and treated the wretched people more harshly than before, reproaching them as traitors and as purveyors for the enemy. The real purveyor for the Danes, Ethelred, at length exhausted the patience of the people who had made him king for the common defence. Hard to bear as foreign domination might be, it was deemed better to undergo it at once, than to await, amid constant suffering, under a king alike without valour and without virtue, the moment when, instead of subjection, there would be slavery. Several of the midland provinces submitted spontaneously to the Danes; Oxford and Winchester soon afterwards opened their gates, and Swen, advancing through the western countries as far as the Bristol Channel, assumed, without opposition, the title of king of all England. Terrorstruck at finding himself thus forsaken, Ethelred fled to the Isle of Wight, and thence passed over into Gaul, to seek an asylum with his wife's brother, the chief of one of the western provinces, adjoining the mouth of the Seine.

In wedding a foreigner, Ethelred had conceived the hope of obtaining from the powerful relations of his wife aid against the Danes; but he was deceived in this expectation. The union, which was to have procured defenders for England, had only the effect of bringing over from Gaul infinite solicitors for employment, greedy seekers of money and dignities. When the invasion came, it was found that all the towns which the weak monarch had entrusted to these foreigners were the first surrendered to the Danes. By a singular chance, the Gaulish prince whose alliance the king of England had sought as a support in the struggle against the power of Scandinavia, was himself of Scandinavian origin, the son of an old pirate chief who had conquered the Gaulish province he afterwards bequeathed as an inheritance to his posterity, had established in it his corsair comrades, and had, in common with them, formed of it a state which, after their own national appellation, he called Normandy, or the land of the Northmen.

Normandy on the south adjoined Brittany, a state founded, as we have seen, by refugees from Britain; and on the east, the extensive country from which it had been severed, northern Gaul, which, since the settlement in it of the Franks, had borne the new name of France. The descendants of these German emigrants were still, after a lapse of five centuries, separated from the indigenous Gauls, less by manners and ideas than by social condition. It was in this profoundly marked difference between their social condition, and in the terms which served to express it, that the distinction between the races was most clearly indicated. In the tenth century, to designate civil liberty, there was, in the spoken language of France, but one word, frankise or franchise, according to the various dialects, and Franc signified at once free, powerful, and rich.

The mere invasion of the children of Merowig and the conversion of their kings to Catholicism, would not, perhaps, have sufficed to establish at this point the predominance of the conquering population. In less than three centuries after their settlement in Gaul, these terrible invaders had almost become Gauls; the regal descendants of Chlodowig, as inoffensive as their ancestors had been fierce and formidable, limited their ambition to a good table, and to riding about in an easy waggon, drawn by trained oxen. But at this period there existed between the Rhine and the Forest of Ardennes, in the territory called by the Franks Oster-rike, or Eastern-kingdom, a population in whom the Teutonic character had better resisted the influence of southern manners. Coming last to the conquest of Gaul, and excluded from the rich provinces and great cities of the south, it was filled with a desire to obtain a portion of that more valuable territory, and even to supplant in their possessions the Franks of Neoster-rike, or Western Kingdom. This daring project, long pursued with various success, became accomplished in the eighth century, when, under the outward form of a ministerial revolution, there was a regular invasion of the Neustrian Franks by the Austrasian Franks. A fresh division of lands took place throughout well nigh all Gaul; a second race of kings arose, strangers to the first, and the conquest, in its renewal, assumed a more durable character.

And this was not all; the warlike activity of the Franks, aroused by this powerful impulse, carried them in every direction beyond their ancient limits; they effected conquests towards the Danube and the Elbe, beyond the Pyrenees and the Alps. Masters of Gaul and of both banks of the Rhine, of the ancient territory of the Saxon confederation, and of a portion of the Slavonian provinces, of almost all Italy, and of the north of Spain, the second prince of the new dynasty, Karl, surnamed the Great—Charlemagne—exchanged his title of king for that of emperor or Cæsar, which had disappeared from the west for more than three centuries past. He was a man of indefatigable activity, and endowed with that administrative genius which embraces in its grasp the pettiest details alike with the great whole, and which, most remarkably, reappears from time to time, almost identically the same, at epochs the most differing from each other. But with all its resources, this genius, wanting the action of ages, could not fuse into a single body so many nations of various origin, manners, and language; under the outward semblance of union the natural isolation still subsisted, and to keep the empire from dissolution in its very cradle, the great emperor had to be in constant action on every point. So long as he himself lived, the peoples of the western continent, strangers to each other, remained aggregated under his vast domination; but this factitious union began to disappear when the Frank Cæsar had gone down, in imperial robes, to his tomb in the cathedral of Aix-la-Chapelle.

Soon, a spontaneous movement of revolt agitated, almost at the same moment, the whole of these unconsentingly associated nations. Gaul aimed at separation from Germany, Italy at separation from both. Each of these great masses of men, in its movement, drew with it the portion of the conquering people which dwelt in its bosom, as mistress of the soil, invested with titles of power and honour, Latin or German. Frank drew the sword against Frank, brother against brother, father against son. Three of the grandsons of Charlemagne fought against each other, in the centre of Gaul; one at the head of an army of Gauls and Gallo-Franks, another followed by Italians, the third commanding an army of Teutons and Slaves. This domestic dissension of the royal descendants of the Frankish Cæsar was but a reflection of the quarrel between these nations, and it was this circumstance which rendered it so protracted and so pertinacious. The kings made and unmade ten divisions of that empire which the peoples desired altogether to dissolve; they exchanged oaths in the German and in the Romane tongue, which they almost immediately violated, compelled to discord by the turbulence of the masses, whom no treaty could satisfy.

It was amidst this disorder, at a time when civil war raged from one end of the vast empire of the Franks to the other, that the Danish or Norman Vikings (Norman was the national designation by which they were known in Gaul,) afflicted the country with incessant invasions. Their mode of conducting war was entirely novel in its character, and such as to disconcert even the best framed measures of defence. Their fleets of large boats, impelled both by sail and by oar, entered the mouths of rivers, and ascending them sometimes up to their source, landed alternately on either bank, bands of intrepid and well-disciplined depredators. Whenever a bridge or other obstacle impeded the navigation, the crews drew their vessels on shore, and, placing them on rollers, conveyed them beyond the obstacle. From the greater they passed into the smaller rivers, and from one of these into another, seizing upon all the more considerable islands, which they fortified as winter quarters, depositing there, under huts constructed in rows, their booty and their captives.

Making their attacks thus by surprise, and, whenever they were prepared for, retreating with the utmost rapidity, they devastated whole districts to such an extent that, to use the expression of a contemporary writer, "where they had passed, no dog remained to bark." Castles and fortified places were the sole refuge against them; but at this first epoch of their irruptions, very few of these existed, and even the walls of the old Roman towns were falling into decay. While the rich seigneurs flanked their manor-houses with turreted towers, and surrounded them with deep ditches, the inhabitants of the plains emigrated in crowds from their villages to the neighbouring forest, where they encamped in huts defended by palisades and felled trees. Ill protected by the kings, dukes, and counts of the land, who often entered into treaties with the enemy on their own account, at the expense of the peasantry, the latter sometimes became inspired with the courage of despair, and, armed merely with clubs, would encounter the axes of the Normans. In other cases, finding all resistance vain, depressed and demoralized, they renounced their baptismal vow to propitiate the pagan conqueror, and in token of initiation into the worship of the northern gods, ate of the flesh of a horse sacrificed at their altars. This apostasy was very general in the quarters most exposed to the disembarkation of the pirates, who even recruited their ranks from among the very people that had lost all by their ravages; we are, indeed, assured by ancient historians, that the famous sea-king, Hasting, was the son of a labourer near Troyes.

Nearly a century elapsed between the first and the second descent of the Normans upon Gaul, in which interval was accomplished, amid calamities of every description, the dismemberment of the empire founded by Karl the Great. Not only had there been detached from the Gaulish territory, lands whose natural limits had anciently separated them from it, but, in the very heart of that territory itself, there had taken place a division, based upon geographical congruities, upon local traditions, upon differences of language or dialects. Brittany, which, independent under the first Frankish dynasty, had been subjected by the second, commenced the movement, and, in the first half of the ninth century, became once more a separate state. She had her national princes, free from all foreign suzerainty, and even her conqueror-princes, who took from the grandson of Charlemagne the towns of Rennes, Vannes, and Nantes. Fifty years later, the ancient kingdom of the Visigoths, the district between the Loire, the Rhone, and the Pyrenees, after having long, and with various success, struggled against the Frank domination, became, under the name of Aquitaine or Guienne, a distinct sovereignty; whilst, on the other side of the Rhone, a new sovereignty was formed of Provence and the southern part of the ancient kingdom of the Burgundians. At the same time, the provinces along the Rhone, whither the flood of Germanic invasions had brought the Teutonic idiom, raised a political barrier between themselves and the countries where the Roman dialect prevailed. In the intermediate space left by these new states, that between the Loire, the Meuse, the Scheldt, and the Breton frontier, was compressed the kingdom of the Gallo-Franks, or France. Its extent exactly corresponded with that of the Neoster-rike, or a Neustrithe of the ancient Franks; but the latter name was now only applied to the westernmost seacoast, in the same way that its correlative, Oster-rike, or Austrasia, formerly extending over the whole of Germany, became insensibly limited to districts towards the Danube.

This new kingdom of France, the genuine cradle of modern France, contained a mixed population, German under one aspect, Gaulish or Roman under another; and foreigners applied to it different names according to the different point of view under which they regarded it. The Italians, the Spaniards, the English, and the Scandinavian nations called the people of Gaul Franks; but the Germans, who asserted this noble appellation for themselves, denied it to their western neighbours, whom they termed Wallons or Welches. In the country itself there prevailed another distinction: the landed proprietor in dwelling amidst his vassals and coloni, solely occupied in war or the chace, and who thus lived conformably with the manners of the ancient Franks, assumed the title of frank-man, or that of baron, both taken from the language of conquest. Those who had no manor-house, and who inhabited towns (villæ), hamlets, or villages, in masses, after the Roman fashion, derived from this circumstance a special designation: they were called villeins or manans (manentes). There were villeins reputed free, and villeins serfs of the glebe; but the freedom of the former, constantly menaced and even invaded by the lord, was feeble and precarious. Such was the kingdom of France, as to its extent and as to the different classes of men who inhabited it, when it underwent that grand invasion of the northern pirates which was to terminate the long series of such expeditions by a territorial dismemberment. For the cause of this famous event, we must turn to the history of the north.

About the close of the ninth century, Harold Harfagher (Harold with the beautiful hair), king of one portion of Norway, extended, by force of arms, his power over the remainder, and made of the whole country one sole kingdom. This destruction of a number of petty states previously free, did not take place without resistance; not only was the ground disputed inch by inch, but, after the conquest was completed, many of the inhabitants preferred expatriation and a wandering life on the sea, to the domination of a foreign ruler. These exiles infested the northern seas, ravaged the coasts and islands, and constantly laboured to excite their countrymen to insurrection. Political interest thus rendered the conqueror of Norway the most determined enemy of the pirates. With a numerous fleet he pursued them along the coasts of his own kingdom, and even to the Orcades and Hebrides, sinking their vessels, and destroying the stations they had formed in many of the islands of the northern seas. He, moreover, by the severest laws, prohibited the practice of piracy and of every species of armed exaction throughout his states.

It was an immemorial custom of the Vikings to exercise upon every coast, without distinction, a privilege which they termed strandhug, or impressment of provisions. When a vessel found its stores drawing to an end, the pirate-crew landed at the first place where they perceived a flock insecurely guarded, and seizing upon the animals, killed them, cut them up, and carried them off without payment, or, at best, with a payment quite below the value of the goods. The strandhug was thus the scourage and terror of the country districts which lay along the sea-coast or the banks of rivers, and all the more so that it was at times exercised by men not professional pirates, but to whom power and wealth gave impunity.

There was at the court of king Harold, among the ïrals or chieftains of the first rank, a certain Rognvald, whom the king greatly loved, and who had served him zealously in all his expeditions. Rognvald had several sons, all of them noted for their valour; of these, the most renowned was Rolf, or, by a sort of euphony common to many of the Teutonic names, Roll. He was so tall that, unable to make use of the small horses of his country, he always marched on foot, a circumstance which procured him the appellation of Gang-Roll, Roll the Walker. One day that the son of Rognvald, with his companions, was on his return from a cruise in the Baltic, before landing in Norway, he shortened sail off the coast of Wighen, and there, whether from actual want of provisions, or simply availing himself of a favourable opportunity, he exercised strandhug. Chance brought king Harold into the vicinity at the particular juncture; the peasants laid their complaints before him, and at once, without heeding the position of the offender, the monarch summoned a Thing, or great council of justice, to try Roll according to law. Ere the accused appeared before the assembly, which would in all probability sentence him to banishment, his mother hastened to the king, and implored for pardon; but Harold was inexorable. Hereupon this woman, inspired by anger, the result of maternal tenderness, proceeded to improvise, as frequently occurred with the Scandinavians when they were highly excited. Addressing herself to the king, she said to him, in verse: "Thou expellest from the country and treatest as an enemy a man of noble race; listen, then, to what I tell thee, it is dangerous to attack the wolf; when once he is angered, let the herd in the forest beware."

Despite these somewhat vague menaces, the sentence was pronounced; and Roll, finding himself banished for life, collected some vessels, and sailed towards the Hebrides. These islands had been adopted as an asylum by a portion of the Norwegians who emigrated after the conquests of Harold; and all these men were of high birth and great military reputation. The new comer entered into association with them for the purposes of piracy, and his vessels added to theirs formed a numerous fleet, which it was agreed should act under the orders, not of one sole chieftain, but of the confederates generally, Roll having no other pre-eminence than that of his personal merits and his name.

Sailing from the Hebrides, the fleet doubled the extreme point of Scotland, and proceeding towards the south-east, entered the Scheldt; but as Gaul in that direction, naturally poor and already devastated on several occasions, offered very little to take, the pirates soon put to sea again. Going further south, they sailed up the Seine as far as Jumièges, five leagues from Rouen. It was just at this period that the limits of the kingdom of France had been definitely fixed between the Loire and the Meuse. To the protracted territorial revolutions which had lacerated that kingdom, there had succeeded a political revolution, the object of which, realized a century later, was the expulsion of the second dynasty of the Frank kings. The king of the French, a descendant of Karl the Great, and bearing his name, the only resemblance between them, was disputing the crown with a competitor whose ancestors had never worn that crown. By turns conquerors and conquered, the king of ancient race and the king by election were masters alternately; but neither the one nor the other was powerful enough to protect the country against foreign invasion; all the forces of the kingdom were engaged, on either side, in maintaining the civil war; no army, accordingly, presented itself to stay the pirates, or prevent them from pillaging and devastating both banks of the Seine.

The report of their ravages soon reached Rouen, and filled that city with terror. The inhabitants did not expect any succour, and despaired of being able to defend their walls, already in ruins from former invasions. Amidst the universal dismay, the archbishop of Rouen, a man of prudence and firmness, took upon himself to save the city, by capitulating with the enemy before the first attack. Without being deterred by the hatred often so cruelly testified by the pagans of the north towards the Christian clergy, the archbishop repaired to the camp, near Jumièges, and spoke to the Norman chief through the medium of an interpreter. He talked and did so well, promised so much, gave so much, says an old chronicler, that he concluded a truce with Roll and his companions, guaranteeing them admission to the city, and receiving from them, in return, an assurance that no violence should be committed by them. It was near the church of St. Morin, at one of the gates of the Seine, that the Norwegians peaceably landed. Having moored their vessels, all the chiefs went through the city in different directions; they attentively examined the ramparts, the quays, the fountains, and finding everything to their taste, resolved to make it the citadel and head quarters of their new establishment.

After thus entering upon possession, the Norman chiefs, with their principal troops, continued to ascend the Seine. At the point where that river receives the waters of the Eure, they established a fortified camp, in order to await the arrival of a French army which was then on its march against them. King Carl, or Charles, as it was called in the Romane language, finding himself for the moment sole master of the kingdom, had resolved, by a great effort, to repel the new invasion: his troops, led by one Raghenold, or Regnauld, who bore the title of duke of France, took up a position on the right bank of the Eure, at some distance from the Norman camp. Among the counts who had hoisted their banners at the command of the king, to oppose the pagans, was a converted pagan, the famous sea-king, Hasting. Twenty years before, weary of a life of adventure, he had made his peace with the kingdom of France, accepting the county of Chartres.

In the council of war, held by the French, Hasting, consulted in his turn, advised a parley with the enemy before risking a battle; although this advice was regarded with suspicion by many lords of the army, it prevailed; and Hasting departed with two persons who knew the Danish language, to communicate with the Normans.

The three envoys followed the course of the Eure, until they came opposite the spot where the confederates had raised their intrenchments. There, stopping and raising his voice so as to be heard on the opposite bank, the count de Chartres cried: "What, ho! brave warriors, what is the name of your lord?" "We have no lord," replied the Normans, "we are all equal." "For what purpose come you into this country? what seek you here?" "To drive out the inhabitants, or subject them to our power, and make for ourselves a country. But who art thou who speakest our language so readily?" The count replied: "Have you not heard of Hasting, the famous pirate, who scoured the seas with so many vessels, and did so much injury to this kingdom?" "Aye," replied the Normans, "we have heard of him. Hasting began well, but he has made a bad ending." "Will you submit to king Charles, who offers you fiefs and honours, on condition of faith and service?" "By no means; we will submit to no one, and all that we acquire by our arms we will assert the dominion of; go and tell this, if thou wilt, to the king, whose messenger thou art."

On his return to the camp, Hasting delivered this answer, and in the consultation which followed, advised them not to attempt to force the pagan intrenchments. "'Tis the counsel of a traitor," cried a lord, named Rolland; and several others repeated the cry. The old sea-king, either from indignation, or because he felt himself not entirely without reproach, immediately quitted the army, and even abandoned his county of Chartres, going none knew whither. But his predictions were verified: on attacking the intrenched camp, the troops were totally defeated, and the duke of France perished by the hand of a fisherman of Rouen, who served in the Norwegian army.

Free to navigate the Seine at will, Roll and his companions ascended it to Paris, and laid siege to that city, but without being able to make themselves masters of it. One of the principal chiefs having been taken prisoner by the besieged, in order to redeem him, they concluded a year's truce with king Charles, during which time they ravaged the northern provinces, which had ceased to be French. On the expiration of the truce, they returned in all haste to Rouen, from which city they proceeded to surprise Bayeux, which they took by assault, killing the count and many of the inhabitants. This count, Beranger, had a daughter of great beauty, named Popa, who, in the division of the booty, fell to the share of Roll, and whom the Scandinavian wedded, according to the rites of his religion and the law of his country.

Evreux and several other neighbouring towns next fell into the hands of the Normans, who thus extended their dominion over the greater part of the territory to which the old name of Neustria was given. Guided by a certain political good sense, they ceased to be cruel when they no longer encountered resistance, and contented themselves with a tribute regularly levied upon the towns and country districts. The same good sense induced them to create a supreme chief, invested with permanent authority; the choice of the confederates fell upon Roll, "whom they made their king," says an old chronicler; but this title, which was perhaps merely given him in the language of the north, was ere long replaced by the French title of duke or count. Pagan as he was, the new duke made himself popular with the native inhabitants. After having cursed him as a pirate, they loved him as a protector, whose power secured them at once from new attacks by sea, and from the miseries caused in the rest of the land by civil war.

Having become a territorial power, the Normans carried on a better sustained, and, so to speak, more methodical war upon the French. They leagued themselves with other Scandinavians, probably Danes by origin, who occupied the mouth of the Loire, and agreed simultaneously to pillage the whole territory between that river and the Seine. The devastation extended into Burgundy and Auvergne. Paris, attacked a second time, resisted successfully, as did Chartres, Dijon, and other strong places; but many unfortified towns were destroyed or sacked. At last, in the year 912, sixteen years after the occupation of Rouen, the French, of all conditions, harassed by these continual hostilities, began to complain, and to demand that the war should be put an end to, at whatever price; the bishops, the counts, and the barons, remonstrated with the king; the citizens and peasants implored mercy as he passed. An old author has preserved the expression of the popular murmurs: "What do we see in all places? Churches burnt, people killed; by the fault of the king and his weakness, the Normans do as they please in the kingdom; from Blois to Senlis there is not an acre of corn, and no man dares labour either in the fields or in the vineyards. Unless the war be finished, we shall have dearth and dearness." King Charles, who was surnamed the Simple, or the Fool, and to whom history has continued the former of these names, had sufficient good sense on this occasion to listen to the voice of the people; perhaps, also, in yielding to it, he thought to achieve a stroke of policy, and, by the alliance of the Normans, to secure himself against the powerful intrigues which tended to dethrone him. He convoked his barons and bishops in a grand council, and, according to the formula of the time, demanded of them aid and advice. All counselled him to conclude a truce, and to negotiate for peace.

The man best adapted successfully to conduct this negotiation was the archbishop of Rouen, who, notwithstanding the difference of religion, exercised the same kind of influence over Roll that the bishops of the fifth century had obtained over the conquerors of the Roman empire. His relations with the other bishops and with the lords of France had not been interrupted; perhaps he was even present at their consultations; but present or absent, he willingly undertook to convey and to support their offers of peace. The archbishop went to the son of Rognvald, and said to him—"King Charles offers you his daughter Gisla in marriage, with the hereditary seigneury of all the country situated between the river Epte and the borders of Brittany, if you consent to become Christian, and to live in peace with the kingdom."

The Norman this time did not answer. "We will obey no one:" other ideas, another ambition than that of an adventurer, had come to him, since he had governed no longer a mere band of pirates but a vast territory. Christianity, without which he could not rank as the equal of the great lords of France, had ceased to be repugnant to him; and the habit of living amidst Christians had extinguished the fanaticism of most of his companions. With regard to the marriage, he thought himself free to contract a new one, and, becoming a Christian, to dismiss the wife whom he had married with pagan ceremonies. "The words of the king are good," said he to the archbishop; "but the land he offers me is insufficient; it is uncultivated and impoverished; my people would not derive from it the means of living in peace." The archbishop returned to the king, who charged him to offer Flanders in his name, although he had in reality no other right over that kingdom than that of a disputed claim; but Roll did not accept this new proposal, replying that

Flanders was a poor country, muddy, and full of swamps. Then, not knowing what else to give, Charles the Simple sent word to the Norman chief that, if he would, he should have in fief Brittany, conjointly with Neustria: this offer was of the same kind with the preceding, for Brittany was a free state, the suzerainty of the kings of France only extending there to the county of Rennes, taken from the French by the Breton princes half a century before. But Roll heeded little this; he did not perceive that they only gave him an old quarrel to fight out, and the arrangement was accepted.

In order to ratify the treaty in the most solemn manner, the king of France and the chief of the Normans repaired to the village of St. Clair-sur-Epte. Each was accompanied by a numerous train; the French pitched their tents on the one bank of the river, and the Normans on the other. At the hour fixed for the interview, Roll approached the king, and, remaining standing, placed his hands between those of the monarch, pronouncing the formula:—

"Henceforth I am your vassal and your man, and I swear faithfully to protect your life, your limbs, and royal honour." Then the king and the barons gave to the Norman chief the title of count, and swore to protect his life, his limbs, his honour, and all the territory set forth in the treaty of peace.

The ceremony seemed at an end, and the new count was about to retire, when the Frenchmen said to him: "It is fitting that he who receives such a gift as this, should kneel before the king and kiss his foot." But the Norman answered: "Never will I bend the knee before any man, or kiss the foot of any man." The lords insisted on this formality, a last remnant of the etiquette formerly observed in the court of the Frank emperors; whereupon Roll, with an affected simplicity, signed to one of his men to come and kiss the king's foot for him. The Norwegian soldier, stooping without bending the knee, took the king's foot, and lifted it so high to put it to his mouth, that the king fell upon his back. Little accustomed to the niceties of ceremony, the pirates burst into a shout of laughter; there was a momentary tumult, but this absurd incident produced no serious result.

Two clauses of the treaty remained to be fulfilled, the conversion of the new count or duke of Normandy, and his marriage with the daughter of the king; it was arranged that this double ceremony should take place at Rouen, and many of the high barons of France repaired thither as an escort to the bride. After a brief lesson, the son of Rognvald received baptism at the hands of the archbishop, to whose counsels he listened with the greatest docility. On quitting the baptismal font, the neophyte inquired the names of the most celebrated churches and of the most revered saints in his new country. The archbishop repeated to him the names of six churches and three saints, the Virgin, Saint Michael and Saint Peter. "And who is the most powerful protector?" asked the duke. "Saint Denis," answered the archbishop. "Well, before dividing my land among my companions, I will give a part of it to God, to Saint Mary, and to the other saints whom you have named." And during the seven days he wore the white habit of the newly baptised, he gave each day an estate to one of the seven churches that had been indicated to him. Then, having resumed his ordinary dress, he occupied himself with political affairs and with the grand partition of Normandy among the Norwegian emigrants.

The country was divided out by the cord, say the old chroniclers: such was the mode of mensuration used in Scandinavia. All the lands, whether desert or cultivated, except those of the churches, were shared out afresh, without any attention to the rights of the natives. The companions of Roll, chiefs or soldiers, became, according to their rank, seigneurs of the towns and rural districts, sovereign proprietors, great or small, of domains. The former proprietors were compelled to accommodate themselves to the will of the new comers, to give place to them if they so required, or to hold of them their own domain under lease or in vassalage. Thus the serfs of the country changed masters, and many freemen became serfs of the glebe. New geographical denominations even resulted from this repartition of territorial property, and usage thenceforth attached to many of the domains the names of the Scandinavian warriors to whose portion they had fallen. Although the condition of the craftsmen and peasants of Normandy differed little from what it was in France, the hope of a more complete security, and the movement of social life which generally accompanies a rising empire, induced many artizans and labourers to emigrate and establish themselves under the government of duke Roll. His name, which the French pronounced Rou, became widely popular; he was deemed the greatest enemy of robbers, and the most vigorous justiciary of his time.

Although the majority of the Norwegians, following the example of their chief, had eagerly accepted baptism, it appears that a certain number of them refused it, and resolved to preserve the customs of their ancestors. These dissentients united together to form a kind of separate colony, and settled in the environs of Bayeux. They were, perhaps, attracted thither by the manners and language of the inhabitants of Bayeux, who, Saxons by origin, still spoke in the tenth century a German dialect. In this district of Normandy, the Norwegian idiom, differing but little from the popular language, became fused with it, and purified it, in a measure, so as to render it intelligible to the Danes and the other Scandinavians. When, after several generations, the repugnance of the Norman barons of Bessin and the Cotentin for Christianity had yielded to the force of example, the impress of the Scandinavian character was still found among them in a striking degree. They were remarkable among the other lords and knights of Normandy for their extreme turbulence, and for an almost permanent hostility to the government of the dukes; some of them even long bore pagan devices on their shields, and opposed the old war cry of the Scandinavians, Thor aide! to that of Dieu aide! the cry of Normandy.

Peace was not of long duration between the French and the Normans, and the latter skilfully profited by circumstances to extend their dominion towards the east, almost to the point where the river Oise joins the Seine; on the north, their territory was bounded by the little river Bresle, and by that of Coësnon on the south-west. The inhabitants of this district were all called Normans by the French, and by foreigners, with the exception of the Danes and the Norwegians, who only gave this name, honourable in their eyes, to that portion of the population which was really of Norman race and language. This, the least numerous portion, stood, with regard to the mass, whether native or emigrant, of the other parts of Gaul, on the same footing as the sons of the Franks with regard to the sons of the Gauls. In Normandy, the mere qualification of Norman was from the first a title of nobility: it was the sign of liberty and of power, of the right to levy taxes from the citizens and serfs of the country.

All the Normans, by name and by race, were equal in civil rights, though not equal in military grades and political dignities. No man among them was taxed without his own consent, or subject to toll for his goods by land or by water: all enjoyed the right of hunting and fishing to the exclusion of the villeins and peasants, terms which, in point of fact, comprehended the whole mass of the native population. Although the court of the dukes of Normandy was organized almost wholly upon the model of that of the kings of France, the higher clergy did not at first form a part of it, on account of their French origin; at a later period, when a great number of men of Norwegian or Danish race had assumed the ecclesiastical habit, a certain distinction in rank and privileges continued to subsist, even in the monasteries, between them and the other ecclesiastics.

This distinction, still more oppressive in the political and civil order, soon raised against it the ancient population of the country. In less than a century after the establishment of the new state, of which it was the oppressed portion, this population conceived the idea of destroying the inequality of races, so that the country of Normandy should contain only one nation, as it bore but one name. It was under the reign of Rikhart or Richard II., third successor of Roll, that this great project manifested itself. In all the districts of Normandy, the inhabitants of the villages and hamlets began, in the evening, after the hour of labour, to assemble and talk together of the miseries of their condition; these groups of politicians were composed of twenty, thirty, or an hundred persons, and often the assembly formed into a circle to listen to some orator who animated them by violent speeches against the lords of the country, counts, viscounts, barons, and knights. Ancient chronicles in verse present to us, in a manner vivid and powerful, if not authentic, the substance of these harangues.

"The lords do nothing but evil; we cannot obtain either reason or justice from them; they have all, they take all, eat all, and make us live in poverty and suffering. Every day is with us a day of pain; we gain nought by our labours, there are so many dues and services. Why do we allow ourselves to be thus treated? Let us place ourselves beyond their power; we are men like they, we have the same limbs, the same height, the same power of endurance, and we are an hundred to one. Let us swear to defend each other; let us be firmly knit together, and no man shall be lord over us; and we shall be free from tolls and taxes, free to fell trees, to take game and fish, and do as we will in all things, in the wood, in the meadow, on the water."

These appeals to natural right, and to the power of the greater number, did not fail to produce an effect, and many people of the hamlets mutually swore to keep together, and to aid each other against all comers. A vast association for common defence spread over the whole country, comprehending, if not the entire mass, at all events the agricultural class of the indigenous population. The associates were divided into various circles, which the original historian designates by the term conventicula; there was at least one for every county, and each chose two members to form the superior circle or central assembly. The business of this assembly was to prepare and organize throughout the country the means of resistance or insurrection; it sent from district to district, and from village to village, eloquent and persuasive persons, to gain over new associates, to register their names, and to receive their oaths.

Affairs had arrived at this point, and no open rebellion had yet broken out, when the news reached the court of Normandy that throughout the country the villeins were holding councils and forming themselves into a sworn association. There was great alarm among the lords, thus threatened with losing at one blow their rights and their revenues. Duke Richard, who was then too young to act for himself, sent for his uncle Raoul, count of Evreux, in whom he placed full confidence. "Sire," said the count, "rest in peace, and let me deal with these peasants; do not yourself stir, but send me all the knights and men-at-arms at your disposal."

In order to surprise the chiefs of the association, count Raoul sent able spies in every direction, whom he specially charged to discover the place and hour at which the central assembly was to be held; upon their reports he marched his troops, and arrested in one day all the deputies of the inferior circles, some while sitting, others while they were receiving in the villages the oaths of the associates. Whether from passion or calculation, the count treated his prisoners with extreme cruelty. Without any trial, without the slightest inquiry, he inflicted upon them mutilations or atrocious tortures; of some he put out the eyes, of others he cut off the hands or feet; some had their legs burned, others were impaled alive, or had melted lead poured over them. The unfortunate men who survived these tortures were sent back to their families, and on the way paraded through the villages, to spread terror around. And in effect, fear prevailed over the love of liberty in the hearts of the Norman peasants; the great association was broken up; no more secret assemblies were held, and a mournful resignation succeeded, for several centuries, to the momentary enthusiasm.

At the period of this memorable attempt, the difference of language which had at first separated the nobles and commons of Normandy scarcely existed; it was by his genealogy that the man of Scandinavian origin was distinguished from the Gallo-Frank. Even at Rouen, and in the palace of the successors of Roll, no other language was spoken at the commencement of the eleventh century than Romane or French. The town of Bayeux alone was still an exception, and its dialect, a mixture of Saxon and Norwegian was easily understood by the Scandinavians. Accordingly, when fresh emigrants came from the north to visit their Norman relations, and seek from them a portion of land, it was around Bayeux that they established themselves in preference. So again, it was there, if we are to credit ancient chronicles, that the Norman dukes sent their children to learn to speak Danish. The Danes and the Norwegians maintained relations of alliance and affection with Normandy so long as they found in the resemblance of language the token of an ancient national fraternity. Several times, during the quarrels which the first dukes had to sustain against the French, powerful succours were sent them from Norway and Denmark, and, Christians as they were, they were aided by kings who still remained pagans; but when the use of the Romane language became universal in Normandy, the Scandinavians ceased to look upon the Normans as natural allies; they even ceased to give them the name of Normans, and called them Frenchmen, Romans, or Welskes, in common with the other inhabitants of Gaul.

These ties of relationship and friendship were already greatly relaxed in the first years of the eleventh century, when the king of England, Ethelred, married the sister of this same Richard, fourth duke of Normandy, whom we have just mentioned. It is probable, indeed, that if the branch of Scandinavian population established in Gaul had not been at this time entirely detached from its northern trunk, the Saxon king would not have conceived the hope of being supported by the grandson of Roll against the power of the northern kings. The little readiness shown by the Norman Richard to assist his brother-in-law, did not arise from any scruple or moral repugnance, but because Richard did not see in this intervention anything favourable to his own interest, which he was skilful in discerning and ardent in pursuing, consistently with the character which already distinguished the inhabitants of Normandy.

Whilst Ethelred in exile was receiving the hospitality of his brother-in-law, the English, under the dominion of the foreigner, regretted, as in the time of the flight of Alfred and the first Danish conquest, the sway of him whom they had deserted in disgust; Swen, whom, in the year 1014, they had allowed to assume the title of king of England, died in that same year, so suddenly as to occasion his death being attributed to an impulse of patriotic indignation. The Danish soldiers, stationed in the towns or in their vessels at the mouths of the rivers, chose as successor to their late chief, his son Knut, who was then on a mission to the country along the Humber with the tributes and hostages from the English of the south. The latter, encouraged by his absence, sent a messenger to the exile in Normandy, telling him, in the name of the English nation, that they would again accept him as king, if he would promise to govern better.

In answer to this message, Ethelred sent his son Edward, charging him to salute, in his name, the whole English people, and to take a public oath that for the future he would fulfil his duties as a sovereign with fidelity, would amend whatever was not liked, and forget everything that had been done or said against his person. The friendship sworn between the nation and the king was confirmed on both sides by mutual pledges, and the Wittenagemote pronounced a sentence of perpetual outlawry against any Dane who should style himself king of England.

Ethelred again assumed his emblems of honour; it is not exactly known over what extent of territory he reigned, for the Danish garrisons, although driven from some towns, still retained many others, and even the city of London remained in their hands. Perhaps the great road called Wetlingastreet, served, for the second time, as a line of demarcation between the free provinces and the provinces subject to foreign domination. King Knut, son of Swen, dissatisfied with the portion which the Anglo-Saxons obliged him to accept, returned from the north; and landing near Sandwich, in a fit of rage, cut off on the sea-shore the hands and noses of all the hostages his father had received. This futile cruelty was the signal for a fresh war, which Ethelred, for the future faithful to his promises, courageously maintained with various success. Upon his death, the English chose for king, not one of his legitimate children, who remained in Normandy, but his natural son, Edmund, surnamed Iron Sides, who had given great proofs of courage and skill. By his energetic conduct, Edmund raised the fortunes of the English nation; he took London from the Danes, and fought five great battles with them.

After one of these battles, fought on the southern boundary of Warwickshire, and lost by the Danes, one of their captains, named Ulf, separated from his men in the rout, and flying to save his life, entered a wood, with the paths of which he was unacquainted. Having wandered about it all night, at daybreak he met a young peasant driving a herd of oxen. Ulf saluted him, and asked his name. "I am called Godwin, son of Ulf-noth," answered the herdsman; "and you, if I mistake not, are one of the Danish army?" The Dane, obliged to declare himself, begged the young man to tell him at what distance he was from the vessels stationed in the Severn or the adjacent rivers, and by what road it would be possible for him to reach them. "The Dane must be mad," answered Godwin, "who looks for his preservation at the hands of a Saxon." Ulf intreated the herdsman to leave his herd, and to guide him on his way, joining to his entreaties the promises most calculated to tempt a poor and simple man. "The way is long," said the young herdsman, "and it will be dangerous to guide you. The peasants, emboldened by our victory of yesterday, are armed throughout the country; they would show no mercy either to your guide or to yourself." The chief drew a gold ring from his finger and presented it to the young Saxon, who took it, looked at it with curiosity, and after a moment's reflection, returned it, saying: "I will not take it, but I will give you my aid." They passed the day in the cottage of Godwin's father, and when night came, as they departed, the old peasant said to the Dane: "Know that it is my only son who trusts to your good faith; there will be no safety for him among his countrymen from the moment that he has served you as a guide; present him, therefore, to your king, that he may take him into his service." Ulf promised to do far more than this, and he kept his word; on his arrival at the Danish camp, he seated the peasant's son in his tent, upon a seat raised as high as his own, treating him as his own son. He obtained for him from king Knut military rank, and ultimately the Saxon herdsman attained the dignity of governor of a province in that part of England occupied by the Danes. This man, who from the condition of a cowherd was raised by the protection of foreigners to the highest dignities of his country, was, by a singular destiny, to contribute more than any other man to the downfal of the foreign domination. His name will soon figure among the great names of this history, when, perhaps, there will be some interest in calling to mind the origin and singularity of his fortune.

The victories of the Anglo-Saxons over the Danes led to an armistice and a truce which was solemnly sworn to, in the presence of the two armies, by the kings, Edmund and Knut; they mutually exchanged the name of brother, and by common consent fixed the limit of their respective kingdom at the Thames. On the death of Edmund, the Danish king passed this boundary, which was to have been inviolable; he had secretly gained over several interested or ambitious chieftains, and the terror caused by his invasion gave success to their intrigues. After a brief resistance, the Anglo-Saxons of the southern and western provinces submitted, and acknowledged the son of Swen as king of all England. Knut swore in return to be just and benevolent, and with his bare hand touched the hands of the principal chiefs, in token of sincerity.

Despite these promises and the facility with which he had gained the crown, Knut was at first suspicious and cruel. All those who had been remarkable for their attachment to the ancient liberty of the country and the Anglo-Saxon royalty, some even of those who had betrayed this cause for that of the foreign power, were banished from England or put to death. "Whoever will bring me the head of an enemy," said the Danish king, with the ferocity of a pirate, "shall be dearer to me than a brother." The relations of the two last kings, Ethelred and Edmund, were proscribed in a body; the sons of Ethelred were then at the court of Normandy; but those of Edmund, who had remained in England, did not escape persecution. Not venturing to put them to death before the eyes of the English people, Knut sent them to Scandinavia, and carefully insinuated to the petty king to whose care he confided them, what were his intentions respecting them; but the latter feigned not to understand him, and allowed his prisoners to escape into Germany. Thence, for greater security, they went to the court of the king of Hungary, who now began to figure among the Christian powers. They were received with honour, and one of them afterwards married a cousin of the emperor of the Germans.

Richard, duke of Normandy, seeing the impossibility of establishing his nephews on the throne of England, and wishing to have the benefit of a close alliance with that country, adopted an entirely personal policy; he negotiated with the Danish king to the prejudice of the sons of Ethelred. By a singular but skilfully conceived arrangement, he proposed that Knut should marry the mother of these two children, who, as we have seen, was his sister: she had received at her baptism the name of Emme or Emma, but on her arrival in England the Saxons had changed this foreign name into that of Alfghive, signifying present from the genii. Flattered at the idea of becoming once more the wife of a king, Emma consented to this second union, and left it doubtful, say the old historians, which had acted with most dishonour, she or her brother. She soon became the mother of a new son, to whom the power of his father promised a fortune very different from that of the children of Ethelred, and, in the intoxication of her ambition, she forgot and slighted her first-born, who, on their part, kept out of their native land, gradually forgot its manners and even its language; they contracted in exile foreign habits and friendships: an event of little importance in itself, but which had fatal consequences.

Secured in his power by a possession of several years, and by a marriage which made him, in a measure, less foreign to the English nation, king Knut gradually became gentler; a new character was developed in him; his ideas of government were as elevated as his epoch and situation were capable of; he had even the desire to be impartial between the English and the Danes. Without at all diminishing the enormous taxes which the conquest had imposed on England, he employed them partly in purchasing of his countrymen their return to Denmark, and thus rendering less sensible the division of the inhabitants of England into two races, races hostile and of unequal condition. Of all the armed Danes who had accompanied him, he only retained a chosen troop of a few thousand men, who formed his guard, and who were called Thingamanna, that is to say, men of the palace. The son of an apostate to Christianity, he proved a zealous Christian, rebuilding the churches that his father and himself had burned, and magnificently endowing the abbeys and monasteries. From a desire to please the national feelings of the Anglo-Saxons, he raised a chapel over the grave of Edmund, king of East Anglia, who, for a century and a half past, had been venerated as a martyr of the faith and of patriotism; the same motive led him to erect at Canterbury a monument to the archbishop Elfeg, a victim, like king Edmund, to the cruelty of the Danes: he wished, further, to have the body of this saint, which had been buried at London, removed hither, and the inhabitants of that city having refused to deliver it up, the Danish king, suddenly resuming, for an act of devotion, the habits of the conqueror and pirate, had the coffin forcibly carried off by the troops, between two lines of whom, with drawn swords, it was conveyed to the Thames, and there placed in a ship of war, having for its figure-head the upper part of an enormous dragon, richly gilt.

During the time of the partition of England into independent kingdoms, several of the Anglo-Saxon kings, especially those of Wessex and Mercia, had, at different periods, established certain payments in favour of the Romish church. The object of these purely gratuitous gifts was to procure a better reception and aid, in case of need, for the English pilgrims who visited Rome, to support a school there for youths of that nation, and to go towards the expense of the lights in the tombs of St. Peter and St. Paul. The payment of these dues, which in the Saxon language were called Rom-feoh, Rom-skeat, Rome-money, Rome-tax, more or less regular, according to the degree of zeal of the kings and people, was entirely suspended in the ninth century by the Danish invasions. Wishing to expiate, in some degree, the evil which his country had done to the church, and to surpass in munificence all the Anglo-Saxon kings, Knut revived this institution, giving it a greater extent, and subjected England to a perpetual tribute, called Peter's pence (Rom-feth). This tax, paid at the rate of a penny of the money of the time, for each inhabited house, was, in the terms of the royal ordinances, to be levied every year, to the praise and glory of God, on the day of the feast of the prince of the apostles.

The pecuniary homage of the ancient Saxon kings to the Romish church had not in any way increased the religious dependence of England. This dependence and the power of the church were then of an essentially spiritual nature; but in the course of the ninth century, in consequence of the revolutions which took place in Italy, the supremacy of the court of Rome assumed quite a new character. Several towns, which had escaped from the authority of the emperors of Constantinople, or been taken by the Franks from the Lombard kings, had placed themselves under the subjection of the pope, who thus combined the character of temporal sovereign with that of head of the church; the name of Patrimony of Saint Peter ceased from that time to be applied to private domains, separated by great distances, spread through Italy, Sicily, and Gaul, but served to designate a vast and compact territory, possessed or ruled sovereignly, by seigneural title. Pursuant to the fixed and universal law of political development, this new state was not, more than any other, to be without ambition, and its necessary tendency was to abuse, in promotion of its material interests, the moral influence which its chief exercised over the kingdoms of the west. After such a revolution, the transmission of an annual tribute to the pontifical court could not fail to have, at all events in the idea of that court, a meaning wholly different from before. Notions hitherto unheard of began to germinate there; the pope and those about him spoke of the universal suzerainty of Saint Peter over all countries, however distant, which had received the Christian faith from Rome. England was of this number; the re-establishment, therefore, of a tax, though meant merely as a proof of Christian fervour, was perilous for the political independence of that kingdom. No one there, it is true, suspected the consequences which might result from the perpetual obligation of Saint Peter's pence, neither the king, who formed the engagement from religious zeal, or from vanity, nor the people, who had submitted to it without a murmur, as an act of devotion; yet half a century sufficed to develop these consequences, and to enable the court of Rome to treat England as a fief of the apostolic see.

About the year 1030, king Knut resolved to go in person to Rome, to visit the tombs of the apostles, and receive the thanks due to his liberalities; he set out with a numerous retinue, bearing a wallet on his shoulder, and a long staff in his hand. Having accomplished his pilgrimage, and on the point of returning to the north, he addressed to all the English nation a letter, throughout which there prevails a tone of kindliness that contrasts singularly with the education and first acts of royalty of the son of Swen.

"Knut, king of England and Denmark, to all the bishops and primates, and all the English people, greeting. I hereby announce to you that I have been to Rome for the remission of my sins, and the welfare of my kingdoms. I humbly thank the Almighty God for having granted me, once in my life, the grace of visiting in person his very holy apostles Peter and Paul, and all the saints who have their habitation either within the walls, or without the Roman city. I determined upon this journey, because I had learned from the mouths of wise men, that the apostle Peter possesses great power to bind or to loose, and that he keeps the keys of the celestial kingdom; wherefore I thought it useful to solicit specially his favour and patronage with God.

"During the Easter solemnity was held here a great assembly of illustrious persons—namely, pope John, the emperor Kunrad, and all the chief men of the nations, from Mount Gargano to the sea which surrounds us. All received me with great distinction, and honoured me with rich presents: I have received vases of gold and silver, and stuffs and vestments of great price. I have conversed with the emperor, the lord pope, and the other princes, upon the wants of all the people of my kingdoms, English and Danes. I have endeavoured to obtain for my people justice and security in their pilgrimages to Rome, and especially that they may not for the future be delayed on their road by the closing of the mountain passes, or vexed by enormous tolls. I also complained to the lord pope of the immensity of the sums exacted to this day from my archbishops, when, according to custom, they repair to the apostolical court to obtain the pallium. It has been decided that this shall not occur for the future.

"I would also have you know that I have made a vow to Almighty God to regulate my life by the dictates of virtue, and to govern my people with justice. If during the impetuosity of my youth I have done anything contrary to equity, I will for the future, with the help of God, amend this to the best of my power; wherefore, I require and command all my councillors and those to whom I have confided the affairs of my kingdom, to lend themselves to no injustice, either in fear of me, or to favour the powerful. I recommend them, if they prize my friendship and their own lives, to do no harm or violence to any man, rich or poor; let every one in his place enjoy that which he possesses, and not be disturbed in that enjoyment, either in the king's name or in the name of any other person, nor under pretext of levying money for my treasury; for I need no money obtained by unjust means.

"I propose to return to England this summer, and as soon as the preparations for my embarkation shall be completed. I intreat and order you all, bishops and officers of my kingdom of England, by the faith you owe to God and to me, to see that before my return all our debts to God be paid—namely, the plough dues, the tithe of animals born within the year, and the pence due to Saint Peter from every house in town and country; and further, at mid August, the tithe of the harvest, and at Martinmas the first fruit of the seed; and if, on my landing, these dues are not fully paid, the royal power will be exercised upon defaulters, according to the rigour of the law and without any mercy."

It was in the reign of Knut, and favoured by the protracted wars that he prosecuted to reunite the other Scandinavian kingdoms to Denmark, that Godwin, the Saxon peasant, whose singular adventure we have before related, gradually rose to the highest military honours. After a great victory gained over the Norwegians, he obtained the dignity of earl, or political chief of the ancient kingdom of Wessex, now reduced to the state of a province. Many other English zealously served the Danish king in his conquests in Norway and on the shores of the Baltic. He employed the Saxon navy to destroy that of the petty kings of the north, and having dispossessed them, one after the other, he assumed the new title of emperor of the north, by the grace of Christ, king of kings. Despite this intoxication of military glory, however, the national antipathy to the Danish domination did not cease; and on the death of their grea king, as his contemporaries called him, things resumed their course. Nothing remained of the apparent fusion of two races under the same flag; and this empire, raised for a moment above all the kingdoms of the north, was dissolved in the same manner as the vast empire of Charlemagne. The Scandinavian populations expelled their Danish conquerors, and chose national chiefs for themselves. More anciently subjected, the Anglo-Saxons could not all at once regain their liberty in so complete a manner; but they secretly attacked the power of the foreigners, and commenced by intrigues a revolution that was to be terminated by force.

The Danish king died in the year 1035, and left three sons, of whom one only, named Hardeknut, (Harda-knut, Horda-knut, Hartha-knut,) that is, Knut the strong or the brave, was born of the Norman Emma; the others were the children of a first wife. Knut had at his death desired that the son of Emma should be his successor; such a nomination was rarely without influence upon those to whom the German customs gave the right of electing their kings. But Hardeknut was then in Denmark; and the Danes of London, eager to have a chief, that they might be united and powerful against the discontented Saxons, elected as king another son of Knut, named Harold. This election, sanctioned by the majority, met with some opponents, whom the English hastened to join, in order to nourish and envenom the domestic quarrel of their masters. The provinces of the south-west, which, for the whole duration of the conquest, were always the first to rise and the last to submit, proclaimed Hardeknut king, while the Danish soldiers and sailors installed Harold in London. This political schism again divided England into two zones, separated by the Thames. The north was for Harold, the south for the son of Emma; but the struggle carried on in these two names was in reality the struggle between the two great interests of the all-powerful conquerors to the north of the Thames, and the less feeble of the conquered to the south.

Godwin, son of Ulfnoth, was then chief of the vast province of Wessex, and one of the most powerful men in England. Whether he had already conceived the project of using the power he derived from the foreigners for the deliverance of his nation, or felt a personal affection for the younger son of Knut, he favoured the absent claimant, and invited the widow of the late king into the west. She came, accompanied by some Danish troops, and bringing with her part of her husband's treasures. Godwin assumed the office of general in chief and protector of the kingdom in the name and in the absence of the son of Emma. He received, for Hardeknut, the oaths of fidelity of the whole southern population. This ambiguous insurrection, which, under one aspect, appeared the struggle of two pretenders, under another, a war of nation against nation, did not extend north of the Thames. There the mass of the Saxon inhabitants swore, in common with the Danes, fidelity to king Harold; there were only a few individual exceptions, as the refusal of Ethelnoth, an Englishman by birth and archbishop of Canterbury, to consecrate the king elected by the foreigners, and to give him the sceptre and crown of the Anglo-Saxon kings. Harold, according to some historians, crowned himself with his own hand, without any religious ceremony; and renewing in his heart the ancient spirit of his ancestors, he conceived a hatred for Christianity. It was the hour of worship, and when the people were repairing to church, that he selected to send for his hunting dogs, or have his table served.

A fierce war between the south and north of England, between the Saxon population and the Danish population, appeared inevitable. This expectation occasioned a sort of panic among the Anglo-Saxon inhabitants of the left bank of the Thames, who, despite their apparent fidelity to the king recognised by the Danes, feared lest they should be treated as rebels. Many families quitted their houses, and sought shelter in the forests. Whole troops of men, women, and children, with their cattle and goods, proceeded to the marshes, which extended for more than a hundred miles over the four counties of Cambridge, Huntingdon, Northampton, and Lincoln. This district, which appeared a vast lake interspersed with islands, was only inhabited by monks, who owed to the munificence of the ancient kings vast houses built amidst the waters, upon piles and earth brought from a distance. The poor fugitives settled in the willow groves which covered these low and muddy lands. Wanting many of the necessaries of life, and having nothing to do the whole day, they assailed with solicitations, or with visits of simple curiosity, the monks of

Croyland, Peterborough, and other neighbouring abbeys. They went to and fro unceasingly to demand assistance, counsel or prayers; they followed the monks or servants of the convent at every turn, importuning them to pity their lot. In order not to depart from the observance of their rules, the monks shut themselves up in their cells, and deserted the cloister and the church, because the crowd flocked there. Wulf, a hermit, who lived alone in the marshes of Pegland, was so alarmed at finding himself suddenly surrounded by men and noise, that he abandoned his cabin, and fled to seek other deserts.

The war, so desired on one side of the Thames, and so dreaded on the other, did not take place, because the absence of Hardeknut being protracted, the enthusiasm of his Danish partisans subsided, and the English of the south did not think the moment had arrived for them to raise their national standards, not as favourers of a Danish pretender, but as enemies to all the Danes. The Norman woman, whose presence served to give to the insurrection a colour less offensive in the eyes of a foreign power, made peace with this power, and surrendered the treasure of Knut to the rival of her own son. Godwin and the other Saxon chiefs of the west, forced by her desertion to acknowledge Harold as king, swore obedience to him, and Hardeknut was forgotten. At the same time there happened a tragical event, the story of which has only reached us enveloped in much obscurity. A letter from Emma, who was living at London on good terms with king Harold, was sent, it would appear, to the two sons of Ethelred in Normandy; their mother informed them in it that the Anglo-Saxon people appeared disposed to make one of them king, and to shake off the Danish yoke; she invited one of them to come secretly to England, to advise with her and their friends. Whether the letter was genuine or forged, the sons of Ethelred received it with joy, and the younger of the two, Alfred, embarked by the consent of his brother, with a troop of Norman or Boulognese soldiers, which was contrary to the instructions of Emma, if, indeed, the invitation proceeded from her.

The young Alfred landed at Dover, and advanced south of the Thames, where he was likely to encounter less danger and difficulty, because the Danes were not numerous there. Godwin went to meet him, perhaps to ascertain his capacity, and to concert with him some plan for the national deliverance. He found him surrounded by foreigners, who had come in his train to share the high fortune he hoped to find in England, and this sight suddenly converted the favourable disposition of the Saxon chief towards Alfred into hatred. An ancient historian on this occasion puts into the mouth of Godwin a speech to the assembled chiefs, in which he represents to them that Alfred was come escorted by too many Normans; that he had promised to these Normans possessions in England, and that they must not allow this race of foreigners, known throughout the world for their craft and daring, to become masters in the country. Whatever may have been the fact as to this harangue, Alfred was abandoned, if not betrayed by Godwin and the Saxons, who in truth had not summoned him from beyond seas, nor drawn him into the peril in which they left him. Harold's officers, informed of his landing, surprised him with his companions in the town of Guildford, while they were unarmed and dispersed in different houses. They were all seized and bound, without any attempt being made to defend them.

More than six hundred foreigners had followed young Alfred; they were separated from him, and treated with the greatest barbarity; nine of each ten perished in horrible tortures; the tenth alone obtained his life. The son of Ethelred, transferred to the island of Ely, in the heart of the Danish territory, was brought before judges, who condemned him to lose his eyes as a violator of the peace of the country. His mother took no steps to save him from this punishment. She deserted the orphan, says the ancient chronicler; and other historians reproach her with having been an accomplice in his death. The latter assertion may be doubted, though it is a singular circumstance that Emma, on being shortly afterwards banished from England by king Harold, did not repair to Normandy with her own relations and the second son of Ethelred, but sought a foreign asylum in Flanders, whence she addressed herself to the son of Knut in Denmark, intreating him to revenge his maternal brother, the son of Ethelred the Saxon, who, said Emma, had been assassinated by Harold, and betrayed by Godwin.

The treachery of Godwin was the war-cry of the Normans, who in their blind resentment accused the Saxons rather than the Danes of the massacre of their countrymen, victims of a too hazardous enterprise. There are, besides, many versions of this affair, of which not one is supported by sufficient proofs to be regarded as the true one. An historian, among the most worthy of belief, commences his narration in these words: "I am now going to relate what the story-tellers recount of the death of Alfred:" and at the end of his narrative, he adds, "This being the common rumour, I have not omitted it, but as no chronicle mentions it, I affirm it not." What appears, beyond doubt, is the execution of the son of Ethelred, and of several hundred men who had accompanied him from Normandy and France, to excite the Saxons to insurrection; the interview of Godwin with this young man, and more especially, the premeditated treachery of which he is accused by many writers, appear to be fabulous circumstances, superstructed on one genuine fact. However unworthy of belief these fables may be, they are far from being destitute of historical importance, in consequence of the credit they obtained in foreign countries, and the national resentment which they excited against the English people.

On the death of Harold, the Anglo-Saxons, still not bold enough to choose a king of their own race, concurred with the Danes in electing the son of Emma and Knut. The first act of royalty done by Hardeknut was to order the body of his predecessor, Harold, to be disinterred, and after the head had been cut off, to be thrown into the Thames. Some Danish fishermen found the body, and again buried it at London, in the cemetery set apart for their nation, who even in the grave were resolved to be distinguished from the English. Having given this example of vengeance and barbarity against one dead brother, the new king, with a great show of fraternal affliction, commenced an extensive judicial inquiry into the murder of Alfred. He himself being a Dane, no man of Danish race was cited by him to appear before the justice-seat, and Saxons were alone charged with a crime which could only have been useful to their masters. Godwin, whose power and doubtful designs inspired great fears, was the first accused; he presented himself, according to the English law, accompanied by a great number of relations, friends and witnesses, who, with him, swore that he had taken no part, directly or indirectly, in the death of the son of Ethelred. This legal proof was not sufficient with a king of foreign race; and in order to give it value, it was necessary for the Saxon chief to back it with rich presents, the details of which if not wholly fabulous, would lead one to believe that many of the English assisted their countryman to buy off this prosecution, instituted in bad faith. Godwin gave king Hardeknut a vessel adorned with gilt metal and manned with eighty soldiers, each with a gilt helmet, a gilt axe upon his left shoulder, a javelin in his right hand, and on each arm bracelets of gold, weighing six ounces. A Saxon bishop, named Leofwin, accused of having assisted the son of Ulfnoth in his alleged treason, like Godwin, cleared himself by presents.

In general, in his relations with the conquered, Hardeknut showed less cruelty than avarice; his love of money equalled and perhaps exceeded that of the pirates his ancestors. He overwhelmed England with taxes, and more than once his collectors fell victims of the hatred and despair they excited. The citizens of Worcester killed two in the exercise of their functions. As soon as the news of this murder reached the Danish authorities, two chieftains of that nation, Leofrik and Siward, the one governor of Mercia, the other of Northumbria, united their forces and marched against the rebel city, with orders to waste it by fire and steel. The inhabitants abandoned their houses in a body, and took refuge in one of the islands formed by the Severn; they here raised intrenchments, and resisted, until the wearied assailants allowed them to return in peace to their dwellings.

Thus the spirit of independence, which the conquerors called revolt, gradually revived among the sons of the Saxons and the Angles. Misery and insults were not wanting to awaken in their minds regret for their lost liberty. The Dane who bore the title of king of England was not the only oppressor of the natives; under him was a whole nation of foreigners, each of whom did his best towards the evil work. This superior class, of whom the English were subjects and not fellow citizens, did not pay taxes like the English, but, on the contrary, shared the imposts levied by their chief, receiving, at fixed periods, large distributions of money. When the king, in his military reviews or pleasure excursions, used the house of a Dane as his lodging, the Dane was paid, sometimes in money, sometimes with the fat cattle which the Saxon peasant had thus fed for the table of his conquerors. But the house of the Saxon was the inn of the Dane; the foreigner there gratuitously enjoyed fire, food, and bed; he occupied the place of honour as master. The head of the family might not drink without his guest's permission, nor be seated in his presence. The latter could at pleasure insult the wife, the daughter, or the servant of his Saxon, and if he defended or avenged them, he found no asylum; he was pursued and tracked like a wild beast; a price was set on his head as on a wolf's; he became a wolf's head, to adopt the Anglo-Saxon expression; and nothing remained for him but to fly to the forest with the wolves, to become a brigand there, and war against the foreign conquerors, and the natives, who slumbered like cowards beneath the yoke of these foreigners.

These long accumulated sufferings at length produced their fruits; on the death of king Hardeknut, which took place suddenly amidst a marriage feast, before the Danes assembled to elect a new king, a great insurrectionary army was formed under the command of a Saxon named Howne. Unfortunately, the patriotic exploits of this army are now as little known, as the name of its chief is obscure. Godwin and his son, Harald (or Harold, according to the Saxon orthography), now raised the standard of independence of their country, against every Dane, king or claimant, chief or soldier. Beaten back rapidly to the north, driven from town after town, the Danes left the country, and landed, greatly diminished in number, on the shores of their old country. They in their turn related a story of treachery, the romantic circumstances of which are found, equally fabulous, in the history of several nations; they said that Harold, son of Godwin, had invited the chiefs among them to a grand banquet, to which the Saxons came armed, and attacked them unexpectedly.

It was not a surprise of this kind, but open war, which put an end to the dominion of the Scandinavians in England. Godwin's son and Godwin himself, played, at the head of the revolted nation, the most conspicuous part in this national war. At the moment of deliverance, the whole care of public affairs was confided to the son of the cowherd Ulfnoth, who, in saving his country from the hands of the foreigners, had accomplished the extraordinary fortune he had begun by saving a foreigner from the hands of his countrymen. Godwin, had he desired it, might have been named king of the English; few suffrages would have been denied him, but he preferred to direct the attention of the people towards a man unconnected with the recent events, without enviers, without enemies; inoffensive to all from his absence from public affairs, interesting to all by his misfortunes—towards Edward, the second son of Ethelred, the same whose brother he was accused of having betrayed and put to death. By the advice of the chief of Wessex, a great council, assembled at Gillingham, decided that a national message should be sent to Edward in Normandy, to announce to him that the whole people had elected him king, but upon condition that he should bring but few Normans with him.

Edward obeyed, says an ancient chronicle, and came to England with very few men. He was proclaimed king on his arrival, and crowned in the cathedral of Winchester. On giving him the crown and sceptre, the bishop made him a long speech upon the duties of royalty, and the mild and equitable government of his Anglo-Saxon predecessors. As he was unmarried, he selected for his queen the daughter of the powerful and popular man to whom he owed his kingdom. Various evil rumours circulated on the subject of this marriage; it was said that Edward, alarmed at the immense authority of Godwin, had taken him for a father-in-law, to avoid having him for an enemy. Others say that, before procuring the election of the new king, Godwin had exacted from him an oath, by God and his soul, that he would, if elected, marry his daughter. However this may have been, Edward received in marriage a young person of great beauty and learning, modest and of a sweet disposition; she was called Edith, a familiar diminutive for Edswith or Ethelswith. "I have often seen her in my childhood," says a contemporary, "when I went to visit my father, who was employed in the king's palace. If she met me on my return from school, she interrogated me upon my grammar, poetry, or even logic, in which she was well versed; and when she had entangled me in the meshes of some subtle argument, she never failed to bestow upon me three or four crowns by her servant, and to send me to have refreshment in the pantry." Edith was mild and kind to all who approached her; those who disliked the somewhat savage pride of character of her father and brother, praised her for not resembling them, as is poetically expressed in a Latin verse, then much esteemed: "Sicut spina rosam, genuit Godwinus Editham."—"As the thorn produces the rose, so Godwin produced Edith."

The withdrawal of the Danes, and the complete destruction of the rule of the conquest, in awakening patriotic thoughts, had rendered the Anglo-Saxon customs dearer to the people. They desired to restore them in all their pristine purity, freed from all that the mixture of races had added to them of foreign matter. This wish led them to revert to the times which preceded the great Danish invasion, to the reign of Ethelred, whose institutions and laws were sought out with a view to their re-establishment. This restoration took place to the utmost extent possible, and the name of king Edward became connected with it; it was a popular saying that this good king had restored the good laws of his father Ethelred. But, in truth, he was no legislator; he promulgated no new code; the only thing was, that the ordinances of the Danish kings ceased in his reign to be executed. The tax of the conquest, at first granted temporarily under the name of Danegheld, as we have seen above, then levied each year, during thirty years, for the foreign soldiers and sailors, was in this manner abolished, not through the spontaneous benevolence of the new king, but because there were no longer any Danes in England.

That is to say, there were no longer any Danes living in the country as rulers; such had all been expelled; but the English, restored to liberty, did not drive from their habitations the laborious and peaceable Danes who, swearing obedience to the common law, were content with existing simply as cultivators or citizens. The Saxon people did not, by way of reprisals, levy taxes on them, or render their condition worse than their own. In the eastern, and especially in the northern provinces, the children of the Scandinavians continued to exceed in number those of the Anglo-Saxons; these provinces were distinguished from the midland and southern by a remarkable difference of idiom, manners, and local customs, but not the slightest resistance was raised to the government of the Saxon king. Social equality soon drew together and fused the two nations, formerly hostile. This union of all the inhabitants of the English soil, formidable to foreign invaders, stayed their ambitious projects, and no northern king dared to assert in arms the heritage of the sons of Knut. These kings even sent messages of peace and friendship to the peaceable Edward: "We will," said they, "allow you to reign unmolested over your country, and we will content ourselves with the lands which God has given us to rule."

But under this exterior appearance of prosperity and independence, new germs of trouble and ruin were silently developing themselves. King Edward, son of a Norman woman, brought up from infancy in Normandy, had returned almost a foreigner to the country of his ancestors; a foreign language had been that of his youth; he had grown old among other men and other customs than the customs and men of England; his friends, the companions of his pleasures and his sorrows, his nearest relatives, the husband of his sister, were all beyond seas. He had sworn to bring with him but few Normans, and but few, in fact, accompanied him, but many followed him: those who had loved him in his exile, those who had more or less assisted him when he was poor, all hastened to besiege his palace. He could not help receiving them at his fireside and at his table, or even the preferring them to the, to him, strangers from whom he derived his fireside, his table, and his title. The irresistible tendency of early affections so misled him, that he gave all the high dignities and great offices of the country to men born in another land, and who cared not for England. The national fortresses were placed under the guard of Norman warriors; Norman priests obtained bishoprics in England, and became the chaplains, councillors, and intimate confidants of the king.

Many who called themselves cousins to Edward's mother passed the Channel, sure of a good reception. None who solicited a favour in the Norman tongue met with a denial; their language even banished from the palace the national language, which became an object of ridicule with the foreign courtiers; flattery was ever addressed to the king in the favourite idiom. All the ambitious English nobility spoke or stammered in their houses the new court language, as alone worthy of a well born man. They cast aside their long Saxon cloaks, for the short wide-sleeved Norman mantle; they imitated in their writing the lengthened form of the Norman letters; instead of signing their name at the bottom of civil acts, they affixed seals of wax, in the Norman fashion. In short, all the ancient national customs, even in the most trifling things, were abandoned to the lower class.

But the people who had shed their blood that England might be free, and who were not so delighted with the grace and charm of the new customs, deemed that they saw the revival, under another form, of a foreign government. Godwin, although among his countrymen the highest in dignity and the next after the king, fortunately had not forgotten his plebeian origin, and joined the popular party against the Norman favourites. The son of Ulfnoth and his four sons, all brave warriors and greatly beloved by the people, resisted, with erect front, the Norman influence, as they had drawn their swords against the Danish conquerors. In the palace, where their daughter and sister was lady and mistress, they returned with insolence the insolence of the parasites and courtiers from Gaul; they ridiculed their exotic customs, and contemptuously denounced or jested at the weakness of the king, who abandoned to them his confidence and the fortune of the country.

The Normans carefully collected their observations and envenomed them at leisure; they incessantly repeated to Edward that Godwin and his sons grossly insulted him, that their arrogance was unbounded, and that it was easy to discern in them the ambition of reigning in his stead, and the intention to betray him. But while these accusations were current in the king's palace, in the popular meetings the conduct and character of the Saxon chief and his sons were judged far differently. "Is it astonishing," asked the people, "that the author and support of Edward's reign should be indignant at seeing new men from a foreign nation raised above him? and yet never does he utter one harsh word to the man whom he himself created king." The Norman favourites were denounced as infamous informers, fabricators of discord and trouble, and there was ever a prayer, in acclamations, for long life to the great chief, to the chief magnanimous by sea or land. They cursed the fatal marriage of Ethelred with a Norman, that union contracted to save the country from foreign invasion, and from which a fresh invasion was now the result, a new conquest, under the mask of peace and friendship.

The traces and perhaps the original expression of these national maledictions are found in a passage of an ancient historian, in which the singular turn of the ideas and the vivacity of the language seem to reveal the style of the people: "The all-powerful God must have proposed to himself at once two plans of destruction for the English race, and must have framed a sort of military ambuscade against it; for on one hand he let loose the Danish invasion; on the other he created and cemented the Norman alliance, so that, if we escaped the blows aimed at our faces by the Danes, the cunning of the Normans might be at hand to surprise us."

BOOK III. FROM THE INSURRECTION OF THE ENGLISH PEOPLE AGAINST THE NORMAN FAVOURITES OF KING EDWARD, TO THE BATTLE OF HASTINGS.

1048—1066.

Eustache of Boulogne, lands at Dover; his quarrel with the inhabitants—Patriotic resistance of Godwin—Grand armament of king Edward—Proscription of Godwin and his sons—Triumph of the Norman favourites—William, duke of Normandy—His origin and character—His visit to England—His ambitions projects—Landing of Godwin and his sons—Their entry into London—Terror and flight of the Norman favourites—Reconciliation of Godwin with king Edward—Death of Godwin—Death of Siward, chief of Northumberland—Talents and popularity of Harold, son of Godwin—Insurrection of the Northumbrians against Tosti—Banishment of Tosti—Hostility of the Romish church to the English people—Friendship between the Romish church and the duke of Normandy—Harold visits Normandy—He is imprisoned by the count de

Ponthieu—His release—He is received at Ronen by duke William—Request made him by William—Harold's oath upon relics—His return to England—Death of king Edward—Election of Harold—Indignation of the duke of Normandy—Tosti persuades Harold of Norway to make a descent upon England—Message from William to Harold—William's negotiation with the Romish church—Temporal sovereignty of the church at this period—The dispute between William and Harold referred to the pope—Alexander II, decides in favour of William—Convocation of the states of Normandy—William baffles this opposition—Grand military preparations—Enrolment of men from all counties—William seeks to form allies—National animosity between the Normans and Britons—Conan, earl of Brittany, refuses his assistance—He is poisoned—Departure of the Norman fleet—Harold of Norway lands in England—Harold of England attacks the Norwegians—Rout of the Norwegians—Landing of the Norman army at Pevensey—Harold marches against the Normans—He forms an entrenchment seven miles from their camp—Message from William to Harold—Reply of the latter—State of the Anglo-Saxon army—Preparations of the two armies—Attack upon the Anglo-Saxon camp—Victory of the Normans—The body of Harold recognised by his mistress.

Among those who came from Normandy or France, to visit king Edward, was a certain Eustache, who on the other side of the channel bore the title of count de Boulogne. He held the hereditary government, under the suzerainty of the kings of France, of the town of Boulogne and a small territory along the coast, and in token of his dignity of lord of a maritime country, when he was armed for war, wore in his helmet two long plumes of whalebone. Eustache had just married Edward's sister, the widow of another Frenchman named Gualtier de Mantes. The Saxon king's new brother-in-law sojourned with him for some time, with a numerous retinue. He found the palace filled with men born, like himself, in Gaul, and speaking its idiom, so that England appeared to him a conquered country, in which the Normans and French had the right to do anything they pleased. After having rested, on his return home, in the city of Canterbury, the count proceeded towards Dover; at about a mile from the town, he made his escort halt, quitted his travelling palfrey, and mounted the charger which one of his men led in his right hand; he put on his coat of mail, and all his companions did the same. In this menacing attire they entered Dover.

They insolently paraded the town, marking the best houses to pass the night in, and authoritatively established themselves in them. The inhabitants murmured; one of them had the courage to stop on the threshold one of the Frenchmen who was about to take up his quarters in his house. The foreigner drew his sword and wounded the Englishman, who liastily arming with his household, attacked and killed the aggressor. On hearing this, Eustache de Boulogne and his troop left their lodgings, remounted their horses, and besieging the house of the Englishman, murdered him, says the Saxon chronicle, before his own hearth. They then went through the town, sword in hand, striking men and women, and crushing children under the feet of the horses. They had not proceeded far before they met a body of armed citizens; and in the combat which took place, nineteen of the Boulognese were killed. The count fled with the remainder, and not venturing to seek the harbour to embark, he turned back and hastened to Gloucester, where king Edward then resided with his Norman favourites.

The king, say the chronicles, gave his peace to Eustache and his companions. He believed, on the bare word of his brother-in-law, that all the blame lay with the citizens of Dover, and, violently enraged against them, he sent for Godwin, in whose government the town was included. "Go without delay," said Edward, "and chastise, by a military execution, those who attack my relations with arms in their hands, and disturb the peace of the country." Less prompt to decide in favour of a foreigner against his countrymen, Godwin suggested that instead of exercising a blind vengeance upon the whole town, the magistrates should be cited, in legal form, to appear before the king and royal judges, to account for their conduct. "It is not right," said he to the king, "to condemn, without hearing them, men whom it is your duty to protect."

Edward's fury, aggravated by the clamours of his courtiers and favourites, now turned wholly against the English chief, who himself, charged with disobedience and rebellion, was cited to appear before a great council convoked at Gloucester. Godwin at first was little moved by this accusation, thinking the king would soon be calmer, and that the other chiefs would do him justice. But he soon learned that by means of the royal influence and the intrigues of the foreigners, the assembly had been corrupted, and that a sentence of banishment would be pronounced against himself and his sons. Both father and sons hereupon resolved to oppose their popularity to these machinations, and to make an appeal to the English against the foreign courtiers, although it was far from their intention, says the ancient chronicle, to offer any violence to their national king.

Godwin raised a troop of volunteers in the country south of the Thames, the whole extent of which he governed. Harold, his eldest son, assembled a great number of men on the eastern coast, between the Thames and Boston Wash; his second son, Swen or Sweyn, engaged the inhabitants of the Severn and the Welsh frontier in this patriotic confederation. The three armies united near Gloucester, and demanded of the king, by messengers, that count Eustache and his companions, with some other Normans and Boulognese at the court, should be given up to the judgment of the nation. Edward made no answer to these requests, and sent an order to the two great chiefs of the northern and central provinces, Siward and Leofrik, both Danes by birth, to march south-west, with all the forces they could assemble. The inhabitants of Northumbria and Mercia, though they armed at the call of the two chiefs for the defence of the royal authority, did so with little ardour. Siward and Leofrik heard their soldiers murmur that it was an entire miscalculation to suppose that they would shed the blood of their countrymen for any foreign interest, or for Edward's favourites.

Both chieftains saw the force of this; the national distinction between the Anglo-Saxons and the Anglo-Danes had become too slight for the old hatred of the two races to be again worked for the profit of the enemies of the country. The chiefs and warriors of the northern provinces refused positively to cross arms with the insurgents of the south; they proposed an armistice between the king and Godwin, and that their dispute should be investigated before an assembly held at London. Edward was compelled to yield; Godwin, who did not desire war for the sake of war, willingly consented; and on one side and the other, says the Saxon chronicle, they swore the peace of God and perfect friendship. This was the formula of the time, but, on one side at least, these promises were insincere. The king availed himself of the interval before the meeting of the assembly, fixed for the autumnal equinox, to augment the number of his troops, while Godwin retired to the south-western provinces, and his band of volunteers, having neither pay nor quarters, returned to their families. Breaking his word, although indirectly, Edward proclaimed his ban for the levy of an army, south as well as north of the Thames.

This army, say the chroniclers, was the greatest that had been seen under the new reign. The king gave the command of it to his foreign favourites, amongst whom in the first rank, figured a youthful son of his sister Goda and the Frenchman Gualtier de Mantes. Edward quartered his forces in and near London, so that the national council opened in the centre of a camp exposed to the influence of terror and of royal seduction. Godwin and his two sons were cited by this council, deliberating under compulsion, to absolve from their oaths and their attendance the few men who remained with them, and to appear without escort and unarmed. They replied that they were ready to obey the first of these two orders, but that before appearing in the assembly alone and unprotected, they demanded the king's peace and hostages to guarantee their personal safety both coming and going. Twice they repeated this demand, which the military array displayed in London fully justified on their part, and twice they were met by a refusal, and the summons to appear without delay, with twelve compurgators to affirm their innocence on oath. They did not appear, and the great council declaring them contumacious, banished them, granting them only five days of peace to quit England with all their family. Godwin, his wife Ghitha or Edith, and three of his sons, Sweyn, Tosti, and Gurth, proceeded to the eastern coast, whence they embarked for Flanders. Harold and his brother Leofwin went westward, to Brig-stow, now Bristol, and crossed the Irish sea. Before the expiration of the five days, and in contempt of the decree of the assembly, the king sent a troop of horse in pursuit of them, but the commander of the party, who was a Saxon, either could not or would not overtake them.

The property of Godwin and his children was seized and confiscated. His daughter, the king's wife, was deprived of all her possessions in land, goods or money. It was not right, the foreign courtiers ironically said, that while the family of this woman was undergoing the evils of exile, she herself should sleep upon down. The weak-minded Edward went so far as to allow her to be confined in a cloister; the favourites maintained that she was his wife in name only, although she shared his bed, and he himself did not contradict this proposition, upon which his reputation for sanctity was partly founded. The days which followed were days of rejoicing and high fortune for the foreigners, and Normandy furnished more governors than ever to England. The Normans gradually obtained there the same supremacy which the Danes had formerly achieved by the sword. A monk of Jumièges, named Robert, became archbishop of Canterbury; another Norman monk was made bishop of London; Saxon prelates and abbots were deposed, to make room for Frenchmen and pretended relations of king Edward on the mother's side; the governments of Godwin and his sons became the property of men bearing foreign titles. One Eudes was made chief of the four counties of Devon, Somerset, Dorset, and Cornwall, and the son of Gualtier de Mantes, named Raulfe, had charge of Herefordshire and of the fortresses erected against the Welsh.

A new guest from Normandy, the most considerable of all, now came with a numerous train to visit king Edward and the towns and castles of England; this was William, duke of Normandy, bastard son of the last duke Robert, whose violent character had gained for him the surname of Robert the Devil. He was born to Robert by a young girl of Falaise, whom the duke saw one day on his return from hunting, by the side of a brook, washing linen with her companions. Her beauty made a great impression on Robert, who, wishing to have her for a mistress, sent, says the poetical chronicle, one of his most discreet knights to make propositions to the family. The father at first treated the offer with disdain; but on reflection he went to consult one of his brothers, a hermit in the neighbouring forest, a man of great religious reputation, who replied that in all things it was fitting to do the will of the prince; the request was accordingly granted, says the poet, and the night and hour fixed. The name of the young Norman was Arlete, a corruption of the ancient Danish name Herleve; the duke Robert loved her tenderly, and the child he had by her was brought up with as much care as though he had been the son of a lawful wife.

William was only seven years of age when his father was seized with a desire to make a pilgrimage on foot to Jerusalem, to obtain forgiveness for his sins. The Norman barons wished to prevent this, by representing to him that it would be unwell for them to remain without a chief. "By my faith," answered Robert, "I will not leave you without a lord. I have a little bastard, who will grow and be a gallant man, if it please God; and I am certain that he is my son. Receive him, then, as your lord; for I make him my heir, and give him from this time forth the whole duchy of Normandy." The Norman barons did as the duke desired, "because," says the old chronicle, "it suited them to do so." They swore fidelity to the child, placing their hands between his. Duke Robert dying on his pilgrimage, several chiefs, and especially the relations of the ancient dukes, protested against this election, saying that a bastard could not command the sons of Normans. The seigneurs of Bessin and the Cotentin, more turbulent than the rest, and still more proud of the purity of their descent, placed themselves at the head of the malcontents, and raised a numerous army; but they were defeated in a pitched battle at the Val des Dunes, near Caen, with the assistance of the king of France, who maintained the cause of the young duke from personal interest, and in order to exercise some influence over the affairs of the country. William, as he advanced in years, became more and more dear to his partisans; the day on which he for the first time assumed armour, and mounted his first war-horse without using the stirrup, was a day of rejoicing throughout Normandy. From his youth he occupied himself with military matters, and made war on his neighbours of Anjou and Brittany. He was passionately fond of fine horses, and had them brought, say his contemporaries, from Gascony, Auvergne, and Spain, selecting always those which had proper names by which their genealogy was distinguished. The young son of Robert and Arlete was ambitious and vindictive to excess; he impoverished his father's family as much as he could, to enrich and elevate his relations on the mother's side. He often punished in the most cruel manner the jests in which the stain of his birth involved him, whether on the part of foreigners or of his countrymen. One day, while he was attacking the town of Alencon, the besieged cried from the walls: "Hides! hides!" and beat skins of leather, in allusion to the trade of William's tanner grandsire. The bastard immediately cut off the hands and feet of all the prisoners who were in his power, and made his slingers throw the amputated members into the town.

While traversing England, the duke of Normandy might well have thought that he had not quitted his own duchy; Normans officered the fleet he found stationed at Dover; at Canterbury, Norman soldiers formed the garrison of a fortress built on the side of a hill; other Normans came in every place to salute him, attired as captains or prelates. The favourites of Edward respectfully gathered round the chief of their native land, around their natural seigneur, to adopt the language of the period. William appeared in England more a king than Edward himself, and his ambitious mind was not slow in conceiving the hope of becoming such in reality at the death of this prince, so entirely the slave of Norman influence. Such thoughts could not fail to arise in the mind of the son of Robert; and yet, if the testimony of a contemporary is to be believed, he allowed nothing of it to appear, and never mentioned the subject to king Edward, believing that circumstances would adapt themselves to his ambitious purposes. On his side, Edward, whether or not he guessed these projects, and contemplated the one day having his friend for successor, said nothing to him about it, but simply received him with the greatest tenderness; gave him arms, horses, dogs, and falcons, in a word, all sorts of presents and assurances of affection. Entirely absorbed in the remembrance of the country in which he had passed his youth, the king of England thus yielded to an oblivion of his own nation; but this nation did not forget itself, and those who still loved it soon found occasion to draw the king's attention towards them.

In the summer of the year 1052, Godwin set out from Bruges with several vessels, and landed on the coast of Kent. He sent secret messengers to the Saxon garrison of the port of Hastings, in Suth-sex, or, by euphony, Sussex; other emissaries spread themselves north and south. On their solicitation, numbers of men fit to bear arms bound themselves by oath to the cause of the exiled chief, all vowing, says an old historian, to live and die with him. The news of this movement reached the royal fleet, which was cruizing in the eastern sea, under the command of the Normans, Eudes and Raulfe; they went in pursuit of Godwin, who, finding his forces inferior, retreated before them, and took shelter in Pevensey Roads, while a tempest arrested the progress of the hostile ships. He then coasted along the south as far as the Isle of Wight, where his two sons, Harold and Leofwin, joined him from Ireland with a small army.

The father and sons then together began to open communications with the inhabitants of the southern counties. Wherever they touched, the people supplied them with provisions, and bound themselves to their cause by oath, giving hostages for their fidelity; all the royal soldiers, all the royal ships they found in the ports, deserted to them. They sailed towards Sandwich, where they landed without any obstacle, notwithstanding Edward's proclamation, which ordered every inhabitant to stay the progress of the rebel chief. The king was then at London; he commanded all the warriors of the west and north to that city. Few obeyed the order, and those who did, came too late. Godwin's ships freely ascended the Thames, to the suburb of London, then called Southward (Southwark). When the tide went down, they cast anchor, and secret emissaries dispersed among the inhabitants of London, who, following the example of the outports, swore to will whatever the enemies of foreign influence should will. The vessels passed under London bridge without impediment, and landed a body of troops, who drew up on the banks of the river.

Before bending a single bow, the exiles sent a respectful message to king Edward, entreating a revision of the sentence which had been pronounced against them. Edward at first refused; other messengers followed, and meantime Godwin could scarcely restrain the irritation of his friends. On his side, the king found the men who remained under his standard little inclined to draw the sword against their own countrymen. His foreign favourites, who foresaw that peace among the Saxons would be their ruin, urged him to give the signal for battle; but necessity making him wiser than usual, he did not heed the Normans, and consented to abide by the decision of the English chiefs of the two parties. These met under the presidency of Stigand, bishop of East Anglia, and unanimously decided that the king should accept from Godwin and his sons the oath of peace, and hostages, giving them, on his part, equivalent guarantees.

On the first intimation of this reconciliation, the Norman and French courtiers hastily mounted their horses, and fled in every direction—some to a western fortress guarded by the Norman Osbert, surnamed Pentecoste; others to a northern castle, also commanded by a Norman. The Normans, Robert, archbishop of Canterbury, and William, bishop of London, left the city by the eastern gate, followed by some armed men of their nation, who, even while thus retreating, massacred several English children. They reached the coast, and embarked in fishing-boats. In his agitation and haste, the archbishop left in England his most precious effects, and among other things the pallium which he had received from the Roman church, as the ensign of his dignity.

A great council of the wise men was held out of London, and this time they assembled freely. All the chiefs and best men of the country, says the Saxon chronicle, were there. Godwin spoke in his own defence, and justified himself from every accusation before the king and the people; his sons exculpated themselves in the same way. Their sentence of banishment was revoked, and another sentence, unanimously decreed, banished all the Normans from England, as enemies of the public peace, promoters of discord, and calumniators of the English to their king. The youngest son of Godwin, called Ulfnoth, like his ancestor the cowherd of the west, was placed, with a son of Sweyn, in the hands of Edward, as hostages for the peace. Still, even at this moment, influenced by his fatal friendship for the foreigners, the king sent them both to the care of William duke of Normandy. Godwin's daughter left her convent, and returned to inhabit the palace; all the members of this popular family were reinstated in their honours, with one exception, Sweyn, who renounced them of his own will. He had formerly carried off a nun, and had committed a murder in a fit of passion; to satisfy justice, and appease his own remorse, he condemned himself to make a pilgrimage to Jerusalem barefooted. He rigorously accomplished this painful task; but a speedy death was the result.

Bishop Stigand, who had presided over the assembly held for the great reconciliation, replaced the Norman Robert in the archbishopric of Canterbury; and, pending the negotiation for the pallium for himself from the Roman church, he officiated in that which Robert had left on his departure. The Normans, Hugh and Osbert Pentecoste, gave up the keys of the castles they held, and obtained safe conducts to leave England, but on the request of the weak Edward, some exceptions were made to the decree of banishment pronounced against the whole body of foreigners. Raulfe, the son of Gaultier de Mantes, and of the king's sister; Robert, surnamed the Dragon, and his son-in-law, Richard Fitz-Scrob; Onfroy, the equerry of the palace; Onfroy, surnamed Pied-de-Guai, and several others for whom the king entertained a personal friendship, or who had taken little part in the late troubles, obtained the privilege of inhabiting England, and of retaining their offices. William, bishop of London, was also recalled some time after, and re-established in his see. A Fleming, named Herman, remained bishop of Wilton. Godwin opposed with all his might this tolerance, so contrary to the public feelings, but his voice did not prevail, because too many people wished to conciliate the king, and thus succeed to the credit of the foreign courtiers. The result showed which of these were the best politicians, the court people or the austere Godwin.

It is difficult exactly to estimate the degree of the sincerity of king Edward in his return to the national interest, and his reconciliation with the family of Godwin. Surrounded by his countrymen, he perhaps thought himself enslaved, and regarded his obedience to the wishes of the nation that had made him king as a constraint. His ulterior relations with the duke of Normandy, his private conferences with the Normans who remained about his person, are the secrets of this history. All that the chronicles of the time say is, that an apparent friendship existed between the king and his father-in-law, and that, at the same time, Godwin was utterly detested in Normandy. The foreigners whom his return had deprived of their places and honours, those to whom the facile and brilliant career of courtier to the king of England was now closed, never named Godwin without calling him traitor, enemy of his king, murderer of the young Alfred.

This last accusation was the most accredited, and it followed the Saxon chief to the hour of his death. One day, at the table of Edward, he suddenly fell fainting, and upon this incident was founded a story altogether romantic and doubtful, though repeated by several historians. They relate that one of his servants, while pouring him out a cup of wine, stumbled with one foot, but stayed his fall with the other. "Well," said Godwin to the king, smiling, "the brother has come to assist the brother." "Ay," answered Edward, casting a significant look on the Saxon chief, "brother needs brother, and would to God mine still lived!" "O king," exclaimed Godwin, "why is it that, on the slightest recollection of your brother, you always look so angrily on me? If I contributed even indirectly to his death, may the God of heaven grant that this piece of bread may choke me!" Godwin put the bread in his mouth, say the authors who relate this anecdote, and was immediately strangled. The truth is, that his death was not so sudden; that falling from his seat, and carried out by his two sons, Tosti and Gurth, he expired five days after. In general, the account of these events varies, according as the writer is of Norman or English race. "I ever see before me two roads, two opposite versions," says an historian of less than a century later; "I warn my readers of the peril in which I find myself."

Shortly after the death of Godwin, died Sig-ward or Siward, the chief of Northumberland, who had at first followed the royal party against Godwin, but subsequently voted for peace, and the expulsion of the foreign favourites. He was a Dane by birth, and the population of the same origin, whom he ruled, gave him the title of Siward-Digr, Siward the Strong; a rock of granite was long shown, which he had, it was said, split with one blow of an axe. Attacked by dysentery, and feeling his end approach: "Raise me," said he to those who surrounded him; "let me die like a soldier, and not huddled together like a cow; put me on my coat of mail, place my helmet on my head, my shield on my left arm and my gilt axe in my right hand, that I may expire in arms." Siward left one son, named Waltheof, too young as yet to succeed to his government, which was given to Tosti, Godwin's third son. Harold, who was the eldest, succeeded his father in the government of all the country south of the Thames, and transferred to Alfgar, son of Leofrik, governor of Mercia, the administration of the eastern provinces, which he had previously governed.

Harold was now, in power and military talents, the first man of his time; he drove back within their ancient limits the Welsh, who at this time made several incursions into England, encouraged by the incapacity of the Frenchman Raulfe, Edward's nephew, who commanded the foreign garrison at Hereford. Raulfe showed little vigilance in guarding a country which was not his own; or if, in virtue of his power as chief, he called the Saxons to arms, it was to exercise them, against their will, in the warfare of the continent, and make them fight on horseback, contrary to the custom of their nation. The English, embarrassed by their horses, and abandoned by their general, who fled with his Normans at the first peril, could not resist the Welsh; the vicinity of Hereford was occupied, and the town itself pillaged. It was then that Harold came from the south of England; he drove the Cambrians beyond their frontiers, and compelled them to swear that they would never again pass them, and to receive a law that every man of their nation found in arms east of the entrenchment of Offa, should have the right hand cut off. It would appear that the Saxons, on their part, constructed a similar entrenchment, and that the space between the two became a kind of neutral ground for the traders of both nations. The antiquarians imagine that they can still distinguish the traces of this double line of defence, and upon the heights several remains of ancient fortified posts, established by the Britons on the west, and by the English on the east.

Whilst Harold was thus increasing his fame and his popularity with the southern Anglo-Saxons, his brother Tosti was far from acquiring the love of the Anglo-Danes of the north. Tosti, although a Dane by the mother's side, from a false national pride treated those whom he ruled more as subjects than as citizens voluntarily combined together, and made them feel the yoke of a conqueror rather than the authority of a chief. He violated their hereditary customs at will, levied immense taxes, and put to death those who had offended him, without any trial. After several years of oppression, the patience of the Northumbrians became exhausted, and a troop of insurgents, led by two men of distinction in the country, suddenly appeared at the gates of York, the residence of Tosti. The chief fled, but his officers and ministers, Saxons and Danes, were put to death in great numbers.

The insurgents seized the arsenal and the treasure of the province; then, assembling a great council, they declared the son of Godwin deprived of his charge, and outlawed. Morkar, one of the sons of the Alfgar who, on the death of Leofrik his father, had become chief of all Mercia, was elected to succeed Tosti. The son of Alfgar proceeded to York, took the command of the Northumbrian army, and drove Tosti towards the south. The army advanced on the territory of Mercia, as far as the town of Northampton, and many of the inhabitants of the district joined it. Edwin, the brother of Morkar, who held a command on the Welsh frontier, levied, in aid of his brother, some troops in his province, and even a body of Cambrians, induced by the promise of pay, and partly perhaps by the desire to satisfy their national hatred in fighting against Saxons, even though under a Saxon banner.

On the news of this great movement, king Edward sent Harold, with the warriors of the south and east, to meet the insurgents. Family pride wounded in the person of a brother, joined to the natural aversion of the powerful against any energetic act of popular independence, seemed calculated to render Harold a pitiless enemy of the population which had expelled Tosti, and the chief whom it had elected. But the son of Godwin showed himself superior to such vulgar influences, and before drawing the sword on his countrymen, he proposed to the Northumbrians a conference of peace. The latter set forth their grievances, and the grounds of their insurrection. Harold endeavoured to exculpate his brother, and promised in the name of Tosti better conduct for the future, if the people of Northumberland would pardon and again receive him; but the Northumbrians unanimously protested against any reconciliation with him who had so tyrannized over them. "We were born free," said they, "and brought up free; a haughty chief is insupportable to us, for we have learned from our ancestors to live free or to die." They charged Harold himself to bear their answer to the king; Harold, preferring justice and the peace of the country, to the interest of his own brother, went to Edward; and it was he also who, on his return, swore to the Northumbrians, and subscribed with his hand, the peace which the king granted them in sanctioning the expulsion of Tosti and the election of the son of Alfgar. Tosti, enraged with the king and with his countrymen who thus abandoned him, and more especially with his brother, whom he deemed bound to defend him, right or wrong, quitted England, hatred deep in his heart, and took up his residence with the count of Flanders, whose daughter he had married.

Since the kingdom had been freed from the dominion of the Danes, the law instituted by king Knut for the annual tribute called Peter's pence had undergone the same fate with the other laws decreed by a foreign power. The public authority obliged no one to observe it, and Rome only received the voluntary offerings and gifts of individual devotion. Accordingly, the ancient friendship of the Roman church for the English nation rapidly declined. Injurious reflections, couched in mystic language, were made upon this nation and its king in the halls of St. Giovanni Latran; the Saxon bishops were accused of simony, that is, of buying their sees for money, a reproach of which great use was made against others by the court of Rome, and which the court of Rome itself frequently incurred, accustomed as it was, in the language of a contemporary proverb, to sell everything. The archbishop of York, Eldred, underwent the first attack. He went to the eternal city to solicit the pallium, the usual token of the high catholic prelacy, as the purple mantles transmitted by the Cæsars were the signs of royalty with the vassal kings of ancient Rome. The Roman priests refused the archiepiscopal mantle to Eldred; but a Saxon chief who accompanied him threatened, in reprisal, to prevent any money being sent to the apostolic see, and the Romans yielded, retaining in their hearts deep anger at having been constrained to yield, and an eager desire for revenge.

The Norman Robert de Jumièges, expelled by the English patriots from the see of Canterbury, now proceeded to Rome, to complain that the sacred character had been violated in his person; he denounced as an usurper and an intruder, the Saxon Stigand, whom the popular voice had elevated to his place. The pontiff and the Roman cardinals listened favourably to his complaints; they declared it a crime in the Saxon prelate to have assumed the pallium which the Norman had abandoned in his flight; and the complainant returned to Normandy with papal letters which declared him legitimate archbishop of Canterbury. Stigand, the elected of the English, seeing the danger of not being acknowledged at Rome, meanwhile opened negotiations, and addressed to the reigning pope a demand for the pallium; but a circumstance, impossible to foresee, occasioned other embarrassing difficulties to arise out of this demand. At the time it reached the pontifical court, the papacy was in the hands of a man chosen by the principal Roman families, against the will of the king of Germany, who, in virtue of the title of Cæsar, transmitted to him by the Frank emperors, asserted that no sovereign pontiff could be created without his consent.

This pope was Benedict, the tenth of that name: disposed to be indulgent, because his power was insecure and he needed friends, he granted the pallium to archbishop Stigand. But an army advancing from beyond the mountains, soon enforced the election of a new pope, who, having expelled Benedict, assumed, without any scruple, the pontifical ornaments abandoned by the defeated pontiff, degraded him, excommunicated him, and annulled all his acts. Stigand thus found himself once more without a pallium, and charged, in the eye of the papal power, with the crime of usurpation, and with another, and still greater crime, that of having sought the good graces of an excommunicated anti-pope. The journey from Canterbury to Rome was at this time one of great difficulty; Stigand was in no haste to justify himself before the successful rival of Benedict X., and the old ferment of hatred against the English became more violent than ever.

Another incident furnished the Romans with the means of associating in their hatred the desire of vengeance, which the so-called treason of Godwin had excited in many of the Normans, and the ambitious projects of duke William. There was at the court of Normandy a monk named Lanfranc, a Lombard by origin, famous in the Christian world for his knowledge of jurisprudence, and for works devoted to the defence of catholic orthodoxy; this man, whom duke William cherished as one of his most useful councillors, fell into disgrace for having blamed the Norman duke's marriage with Matilda, daughter of Baldwin, count of Flanders, his relation in one of the degrees prohibited by the church. Nicholas II., successor to the anti-pope Benedict, obstinately refused to acknowledge and sanction this union; and it was with him that the Lombard monk, banished from his lord's court, took refuge. But far from complaining of the duke of Normandy, Lanfranc respectfully pleaded before the sovereign pontiff in favour of the marriage, of which he himself had before not approved. By dint of intreaties and great address, he obtained a dispensation in form, and for this signal service was received by the duke with greater friendship than before. He became the soul of his councils and his plenipotentiary at the court of Rome. The respective pretensions of the Romish clergy and of the duke of Normandy over England, the possibility of giving effect to them, now became, it would appear, the object of serious negotiations. An armed invasion was not perhaps yet thought of, but the relationship of William to Edward seemed a great means of success, and, at the same time, an incontestable claim in the eyes of the Romans, who favoured throughout Europe the maxims of hereditary royalty against the practice of election.

For two years internal peace had reigned in England without interruption. The animosity of king Edward to the sons of Godwin disappeared from want of aliment, and from the habit of constantly being with them. Harold, the new chief of this popular family, fully rendered to the king that respect and deferential submission of which he was so tenacious. Some ancient histories tell us that Edward loved and treated him as his own son, but, at all events, he did not feel towards him that aversion mingled with fear with which Godwin had ever inspired him; and he had now no longer any pretext for retaining, as guarantees against the son, the two hostages whom he had received from the father. It will be remembered that these hostages had been confided by the suspicious Edward to the care of the duke of Normandy. They had, for more than ten years, been far from their country, in a sort of captivity. Towards the end of the year 1065, Harold, their brother and their uncle, deeming the moment favourable for obtaining their deliverance, asked permission of the king to go and demand them in his name, and bring them out of exile. Without showing any repugnance to release the hostages, Edward appeared greatly alarmed at the project which Harold had formed of going in person to Normandy. "I will not compel you to stay," said he; "but if you go, it will be without my consent; for your journey will certainly bring some evil upon yourself and upon your country. I know duke William and his crafty mind; he hates you, and will grant you nothing unless he gain greatly by it; the only way safely to obtain the hostages from him were to send some one else."

The brave and confiding Saxon did not adopt this advice; he departed on his journey, as on a party of pleasure, surrounded by gay companions, with his falcon on his wrist and his hounds running before him. He sailed from one of the ports of Sussex. Contrary winds drove his two vessels from their track towards the mouth of the Somme, upon the territory of Guy, count de Ponthieu. It was the custom of this maritime district, as of many others in the middle ages, that every stranger thrown on the coast by tempest, instead of being humanely succoured, was imprisoned and put to ransom. Harold and his companions were subjected to this rigorous law; after being despoiled of all their more valuable property, they were thrown by the lord of the territory into his fortress of Belrain, now Beaurain, near Montreuil.

To escape from the wearisomeness of a protracted captivity, the Saxon declared himself the bearer of a message from the king of England to the duke of Normandy, and sent to require William to obtain his release, that he might come to him. William did not hesitate, and demanded from his neighbour, the count de Ponthieu, the liberty of the captive, at first menacingly, and with no mention of ransom. The count de Ponthieu was deaf to the threats, and only yielded to the offer of a large sum of money and a fine estate upon the river Eaume. Harold proceeded to Rouen, and the bastard of Normandy had the satisfaction of having in his power the son of the greatest enemy of the Normans, one of the chiefs of the national league which had banished from England the friends and relations of William, the upholders of his pretensions to the English crown. Duke William received the Saxon chief with great honours and an appearance of frank cordiality: he told him that the two hostages were free on his request alone, that he could immediately return with them; but that as a courteous guest he ought not to depart so abruptly, but at least remain some days to see the towns and festivals of the country. Harold went from town to town, from castle to castle, and with his young companions took part in all the military sports. The duke created them knights, that is to say, members of the high Norman militia, a kind of warlike brotherhood, into which every rich man who devoted himself to arms, was introduced under the auspices of an associate, who, with great ceremony, gave him a sword, a baldric plated with silver, and a bannered lance. The Saxon warriors received from their godfather in chivalry presents of fine weapons and valuable horses. William then proposed to him, by way of trying their new spurs, to follow him in an expedition he had undertaken against his neighbours of Brittany. Since the treaty of St. Clair-sur-Epte, each new duke of Normandy had attempted to give effect to the claim of suzerainty which Charles the Simple had ceded to Roll; the result had been continual wars and a national enmity between these two states, separated only by the little river Coësnon.

Harold and his friends, foolishly tenacious of acquiring a reputation for courage among the Normans, did for their host, at the expense of the Bretons, deeds of valour which were one day to cost themselves and their country dear. The son of Godwin, robust and active, saved at the passage of Coësnon several soldiers who were perishing in the quicksands. He and William, so long as the war lasted, had but one tent and one table. On their return, they rode side by side, enlivening the way with friendly conversation, which one day the duke turned upon his youthful friendship with king Edward: "Edward and I," said he to the Saxon, "lived under the same roof, like two brothers; he promised me if ever he became king of England, to make me heir to his kingdom; Harold, if thou wouldst aid me in realising this promise, be sure that, if I obtain the kingdom, whatever thou askest thou shalt have." Harold, taken by surprise at the excess of this unexpected confidence, could not help answering it by some vague words of compliance, whereupon William continued: "Since thou consentest to serve me, thou must engage to fortify Dover castle, to dig a well there of fresh water, and deliver it up, when the time comes, to my people; thou must also give thy sister in marriage to one of my barons, and thyself marry my daughter Adeliza; moreover, on thy departure, thou must leave me, as guarantee for thy promise, one of the two hostages thou reclaimest, and I will restore him to thee in England when I come there as king." Harold felt at these words all the peril in which he himself stood, and in which he had unconsciously involved his two young relations. To escape from the more pressing embarrassment, he acquiesced in word to all the demands of the Norman; and he who had twice taken up arms to drive foreigners from his country, promised to deliver to a foreigner the principal fortress of that country, with no intention, indeed, of fulfilling this unworthy engagement, thinking to purchase, by a falsehood, his safety and his repose. William did not pursue the conversation further; but he did not long leave the Saxon at rest on the point.

On arriving at the castle of Bayeux, duke William held his court, and thither convoked the great council of the high barons of Normandy. According to the old histories, on the eve of the day fixed for the assembly, William collected from the churches of the town and neighbourhood all the relics they possessed. Bones taken from their shrines, and the entire bodies of saints were laid, by his order, in a large tub or trough, which was placed, covered with rich cloth of gold, in the council-hall. When the duke was seated on his throne of ceremony, crowned with a worked circlet, holding in his hand a drawn sword, and surrounded by a crowd of Norman lords, amongst whom was the Saxon, two small reliquaries were brought and placed upon the golden cloth which covered and concealed the larger box of relics. William then said: "Harold, I require thee, before this noble assembly, to confirm, by oath, the promises thou hast made to me; namely, to aid me to obtain the kingdom of England after the death of king Edward, to marry my daughter Adeliza, and to send thy sister, that I may wed her to one of my people." The Englishman thus a second time taken by surprise, and not venturing to deny his own words, approached the two reliquaries, extended his hand over them, and swore to execute, as far as lay in his power, his agreement with the duke, if he lived and God aided him. All the assembly repeated, God aid him! Then William made a sign; the cloth of gold was raised, and the bones and sacred bodies revealed which filled the box to the brim, and upon which the son of Godwin had sworn, without suspecting their presence. It is said, that at this sight he shuddered and changed countenance, terrified at having made so formidable an oath. Shortly afterwards Harold departed, taking his nephew with him, but, much against his inclination, leaving his younger brother Ulfnoth in the hands of the duke of Normandy. William accompanied him to the seaside, and made him fresh presents, delighted at having surprised the man the most capable of impeding his projects, into a solemn promise, backed by a terrible oath, to serve and aid him.

When Harold, on his return home, presented himself to king Edward, and recounted all that had passed between himself and duke William, the king became pensive, and said: "Did I not warn thee that I knew this William, and that thy journey would bring great evils upon thyself and upon thy nation? Heaven grant that these evils happen not in my time!" These words and this mournful expression would seem to prove that Edward had really, in the days of his youth and heedlessness, made the rash promise to a foreigner, of a royalty that did not belong to him. It is not known whether, subsequent to his accession, he had by any expressions nourished William's ambitious hopes; but, in default of specific words, his constant friendship for the Norman had, with the latter, supplied the place of positive assurances, and given grounds for believing him still favourable to his views.

Whatever might before have been the secret negotiations of the duke of Normandy with the Roman church, henceforward there was afforded them a fixed basis, a distinct direction. An oath sworn upon relics, however absurd the oath might have been, called, if it were violated, for the vengeance of the church; and in such a case, in the opinion of the period, the church struck legitimately. Whether from a secret presentiment of the perils with which England was threatened by the spirit of ecclesiastical revenge, combined with the ambition of the Normans, or from a vague impression of superstitious terror, a fearful depression came over the English nation. Gloomy reports were spread from mouth to mouth; fears and alarms spread abroad, without any positive cause for alarm; predictions were dug up from the graves of the saints of the old time. One of these prophesied calamities such as the Saxons had never experienced since their departure from the banks of the Elbe; another announced the invasion of a people from France, who would subject the English people, and abase their glory in the dust for ever. All these rumours, hitherto unheeded or unknown, perhaps indeed purposely forged at the time, were now thoroughly credited, and kept every mind in the expectation of some vast and inevitable evil.

The health of king Edward, a man of naturally weak constitution, and who had become more alive, as it would appear, to the destiny of his country, declined rapidly after these events. He could not conceal from himself that his love for foreigners was the sole cause of the peril which terrified England; his mind was thus still more overwhelmed than was even that of the people. In order to drown these thoughts, and perhaps, also, the remorse which beset him, he occupied himself wholly with religious exercises. He made great donations to the churches and monasteries; and his last hours came upon him amidst this mournful and inactive life. Upon his death-bed he was entirely absorbed in his melancholy forebodings; he had frightful visions, and, in his melancholy ecstacies, the menacing passages of the Bible recurred involuntarily, and in a confused manner, to his mind. "The Lord has bent his bow," he would exclaim, "the Lord has prepared his sword; he brandishes it like unto a warrior; his anger is manifested in steel and flame." These words froze with horror those who surrounded the king's bed; but the archbishop of Canterbury, Stigand, could not refrain from a smile of contempt at men who trembled at the dreams of a sick old man.

However weak the mind of the aged Edward, he had the courage, before he expired, to declare to the chiefs who consulted him as to the choice of his successor, that in his opinion the man worthy to reign was Harold, son of Godwin. In pronouncing the name of Harold, under the circumstances, the king showed himself superior to his habitual prejudices, and even to the ambition of advancing his own family; for there was then in England a grandson of Edmund Ironsides, born in Hungary, where his father had taken refuge at the time of the Danish proscriptions. This young man, whose name was Edgar, had neither talent nor acquired glory, and having passed his childhood in a foreign country, could hardly speak the Saxon tongue. Such a candidate could not compete in popularity with the brave and rich Harold, the destroyer of foreign power. Harold was the man most capable of encountering the dangers which seemed to menace the country; and even had the dying king not designated him to the choice of the other chiefs, his name would have been pronounced by every mouth. He was elected the day after the funeral of Edward, and consecrated by archbishop Stigand, whom the Roman church, as we have seen, persisted in not acknowledging. The grandson of the cowherd, Ulfnoth, showed himself, from the day of his accession, just, wise, affable, active for the good of his country, not sparing himself, says an old historian, any fatigue by land or by sea.

Much anxious care was needed on his part to overcome the public discouragement which displayed itself in different ways. The appearance of a comet, visible in England for nearly a month, produced upon every mind an extraordinary impression of wonder and fear. The people collected in the streets and public places of the towns and villages, to contemplate this phenomenon, which they regarded as a confirmation of the national forebodings. A monk of Malmesbury, who studied astronomy, composed upon this comet a sort of poetical declamation, in which were these words: "Thou hast, then, returned at length, thou who wilt cause so many mothers to weep! Many years have I seen thee shine; but thou seemest to me more terrible now, that thou announcest the ruin of my country."

The commencement of the new reign was marked by a complete return to the national customs abandoned under the preceding reign. In the charters of king Harold the ancient Saxon signature replaced the seals lately appended in the Norman fashion. He did not, however, carry reform so far as to deprive of their offices or expel from the country the Normans, whom, despite the law, a compliance with the affections of king Edward had spared. These foreigners continued to enjoy all civil rights, but little grateful for this generosity, they began to intrigue, at home and abroad, for the duke of Normandy. It was a messenger from them who announced to William the death of Edward, and the election of the son of Godwin.

When the duke received this great news, he was in his park, near Rouen, trying some new arrows. All at once he appeared pensive, gave his bow to one of his people, and crossing the Seine, repaired to his palace at Rouen; he stopped in the great hall, and walked to and fro, now seating himself, now rising and changing his seat and position, unable to remain in any one place. None of his people dared to approach him; all remained apart, looking at each other in silence. An officer, admitted to more than ordinary familiarity with William, happening to enter, the others pressed around him to learn from him the cause of the great agitation they remarked in the duke. "I know nothing certain," answered the officer, "but we shall soon learn." Then advancing alone to William: "My lord," he said, "why not communicate your intelligence to us? It is reported in the town that the king of England is dead, and that Harold has seized upon the kingdom, thus breaking his faith to you."—"They report truly," answered the duke; "my anger is touching the death of Edward, and the injury Harold has done me." "Sir," returned the courtier, "chafe not at a thing that may be amended: for Edward's death there is no remedy, but there is one for the wrong that Harold has done; yours is the right: you have good knights; strike boldly; well begun is half done."

A man of Saxon race, and Harold's own brother, that Tosti whom the Northumbrians had expelled, and whom Harold, become king, had refused again to impose upon them, hastened from Flanders to urge William not to allow the perjurer to reign in peace. Tosti boasted to the foreigners that he had more credit and power in England than the king his brother, and promised the possession of the country to whomsoever should unite with him to make its conquest. Too prudent to engage in a great undertaking upon the mere word of an adventurer, William, to test his power, gave him some vessels, with which, instead of landing in England, Tosti sailed to the Baltic, to seek other aid, and to excite the ambition of the northern kings against his country. He had an interview with Swen, king of Denmark, his relation by his mother's side, and called upon him to aid him against his brother and his nation. But the Dane gave a harsh refusal. Tosti withdrew in utter discontent, and went to seek elsewhere a king less tenacious about justice. He found in Norway Harald or Harold, the son of Sigurd, the most valiant of the Scandinavians, the last among them who led the adventurous life whose charm had vanished with the religion of

Odin. In his southern expeditions, Harold had carried on his pursuits alternately by land and by sea; he had by turns been pirate and soldier of fortune, viking and varing, as the language of the north expressed it. He had served in the east under the chiefs of his nation, who for nearly two centuries had possessed a portion of the Slavonian provinces. Then, impelled by curiosity, he had been to Constantinople, where other Scandinavian emigrants, mercenary troops under this same name of varings, in which the conquerors of the Russ towns prided themselves, acted as the imperial guard.

Harold was brother to a king, but he deemed it no derogation to enrol himself in this troop. He kept guard, axe on shoulder, at the gates of the imperial palace, and was employed with the corps to which he belonged in Asia and Africa. Enriched by the booty acquired in these expeditions, he wished to depart, and offered his resignation; finding that it was intended to detain him by force, he escaped by sea, taking with him a young woman of high birth. After this, he cruized as a pirate along the coasts of Sicily, and thus augmented the treasure he carried with him in his ship. He was a poet, like most of the northern corsairs, who in their long voyages, and when their progress was slackened by calms, amused themselves with celebrating, in verse, their successes and their hopes. On his return from the long voyaging in which, as he expressed it in his songs, he had led his vessel afar, the terror of the labourers, his dark vessel, filled with grim warriors, Harold raised an army, and made war upon the king of Norway, in order to dispossess him. He asserted an hereditary claim to the crown of that kingdom; but soon perceiving the difficulty of conquering it, he made peace with his competitor, on the condition of a division; to complete the arrangement, it was agreed that the treasure of the son of Sigurd should be shared between them, as well as the territory of Norway. In order to gain over to his views this man, so famous throughout the north for his wealth and courage, Tosti approached him with honied words. "The world knows well," said he, "that there exists not a warrior worthy to be compared with thee; thou hast only to will it, and England will be thine." The Norwegian allowed himself to be persuaded, and promised to put his fleet to sea, as soon as the annual melting of the ice should set the ocean free.

Pending the departure of his Norwegian ally, Tosti essayed his fortune on the northern coasts of England, with a band of adventurers collected in Friesland, Holland, and Flanders. He pillaged and devastated several villages; but the two great chiefs of the provinces laying along the Humber, Morkar and Edwin, united their forces, and pursuing his vessels, compelled him to seek a retreat on the coast of Scotland. Meantime Harold, son of Godwin, tranquil in the south of England, witnessed the arrival of a messenger from Normandy, who addressed him in these terms: "William, duke of Normandy, reminds thee of the oath which thou didst swear to him, by mouth and by hand, upon good and holy relics." "It is true," answered the Saxon king, "that I swore such an oath to duke William; but I swore it under compulsion. I promised that which did not belong to me, and which I could not perform; for my royalty is not mine, and I cannot divest myself of it, without the consent of the country; nor, without the consent of the country, can I marry a foreign wife. As to my sister, whom the duke claims, to marry her to one of his chiefs, she died this year; would he have me send him her body?" The Norman ambassador took back this answer; and William replied by a second message, couched in terms of gentle remonstrance, intreating the king, if he would not consent to fulfil all the sworn conditions, to execute at least one of them, and to take as a wife the young girl he had promised to marry. Harold again replied that he would not, and to settle the point, married a Saxon wife, the sister of Edwin and Morkar.

Then the last words of rupture were pronounced; William swore that within the year he would come and demand the whole of his debt, and pursue the perjurer to the very places where he thought he had the surest and firmest footing.

As far as publicity could go in the eleventh century, the duke of Normandy published what he called the Saxon's gross dishonesty. The general influence of superstitious ideas prevented indifferent spectators of this dispute from understanding the patriotic conduct of the son of Godwin, and his scrupulous deference to the will of the people who had made him king. The opinion of the majority upon the continent was with William against Harold, with the man who had employed holy things as a snare, and accused of treason the man who refused to commit it. The negotiation commenced with the Romish church by Robert de Jemièges and the monk Lanfranc was actively pursued, from the moment that a deacon of Lisieux had borne beyond the mountains the news of the alleged crime of Harold and the English nation. The duke of Normandy laid an accusation of sacrilege against his enemy before the pontifical court; he demanded that England should be placed under the ban of the church and declared the property of the first occupant, sanctioned by the pope. He founded his demand upon three principal causes of complaint: the murder of young Alfred and his Norman companions, the expulsion of the archbishop Robert from the see of Canterbury, and the perjury of king Harold. He also pretended to have incontestable claims to the royalty, in virtue of his relationship to king Edward, and the intentions which this king had, he said, manifested on his death-bed. He affected the character of a plaintiff awaiting justice, and desiring that his adversary shall be heard. But Harold was summoned in vain to defend himself before the court of Rome. He refused to acknowledge the jurisdiction of that court in the matter, and deputed no ambassador there, too proud to submit the independence of his crown to foreigners, and too sensible to believe in the impartiality of the judges invoked by his enemy.

The consistory of Saint John Latran was at this time governed by a man whose celebrity surpasses that of any other man of the middle ages; Hildebrand, monk of Cluny. created archdeacon of the Romish church by pope Nicholas II. After having reigned several years under the name of this pope, he found himself sufficiently powerful to elect one of his own choice, who took the name of Alexander II.; and to maintain him on his throne, despite the ill will of the imperial court. All the views of this personage, who was gifted with indefatigable activity, tended to transform the religious supremacy of the holy see into an universal sovereignty over the Christian states. This revolution, commenced in the ninth century by the reduction of several towns of central Italy to the obedience or suzerainty of the pope, was continued during the two following centuries. All the cities of Campania, of which the pontiff of Rome was the immediate metropolitan, had passed, voluntarily or by force, under his temporal power; and, strange circumstance, in the first half of the eleventh century, Norman knights, emigrants from their country, had been seen leading the Roman troops to this conquest, under the banner of Saint Peter. At the same epoch, other Normans, pilgrims or adventurers, had taken service under the petty lords of southern Italy; then, like the Saxons with the Britons, they had broken their engagement, seized the fortresses, and established their dominion over the country. This new power, having put an end, if not to the pretensions, at all events to the power of the Greek empire over the towns of Apulia and Calabria, suited the religious intolerance of the court of Rome, and flattered its ambition, in the hope of an authority readily obtained over simple-minded warriors, filled with veneration for the holy see. In fact, several of these new dukes or counts successively declared themselves vassals of the prince of the apostles, and consented to receive a banner of the Roman church, as a feudal investiture of the lands which they themselves had conquered. Thus the church profited by the power of the Norman arms gradually to extend her sovereignty in Italy, and accustomed herself to look upon the Normans as destined to combat in her service, and to do her homage for their conquests.

Such were the singular relations which the chance of events had created, when the complaints and demand of the duke of Normandy reached the court of Rome. His mind full of his favourite idea, the archdeacon Hildebrand thought the moment favourable for attempting on the kingdom of England that which had succeeded in Italy; he applied all his efforts to substitute for the ecclesiastical discussion on the indifference of the English, the simony of their bishops, and the perjury of their king, a formal negotiation for the conquest of the country, at the common cost and for the common profit. Notwithstanding the reality of these purely political projects, the cause of William against Harold was examined in the assembly of cardinals, without any other question being discussed than that of the hereditary right, the sanctity of the oath, and the veneration due to the relics. These did not appear to several of those present sufficient grounds to warrant, on the part of the church, an armed aggression against a Christian people; and when the archdeacon persisted, a murmur arose, and the dissentients told him that it was infamous to authorize and encourage homicide; but he was unmoved at this, and his views prevailed.

In the terms of the sentence which was pronounced by the pope himself, William duke of Normandy was permitted to enter England, to bring that kingdom back to the obedience of the holy see, and to re-establish there for ever the tax of Saint Peter's pence. A bull of excommunication, directed against Harold and all his adherents, was given to William's messenger, and to it was added a banner of the Roman church and a ring containing one of the hairs of Saint Peter, set under a diamond of great price. This was the double emblem of military and ecclesiastical investiture; the consecrated banner which was to consecrate the invasion of England by the duke of Normandy, was the same which, a few years before, the Normans Raoul and William de Montreuil had planted, in the name of the church, on the castles of Campania.

Before the bull, the banner, and the ring had arrived, duke William assembled, in a cabinet council, his most intimate friends, to demand their advice and assistance. His two brothers by the mother's side, Eudes and Robert, one of them bishop of Bayeux, the other count of Mortain; William Fitz-Osbern, seneschal of Normandy, or ducal lieutenant for civil administration, and some high barons, attended the conference. All were of the opinion that it was proper to make a descent upon England, and promised to serve him with body and goods, even to selling or pledging their inheritances. "But this is not all," said they; "you must seek aid and counsel from the body of the inhabitants of this country; for it is right that those who pay the cost should be asked their consent." William, say the chroniclers, then convoked a great assembly of men of every class in Normandy—warriors, churchmen, and merchants, all the richest and most considerable personages of the land. The duke explained his projects to them, and solicited their assistance; the assembly then withdrew, in order to deliberate more free from influence.

In the debate which followed, opinions seemed greatly divided; some wished to aid the duke with vessels, munitions, and money; others protested against any kind of aid, saying that they had already more debts than they could pay. This discussion was not carried on without tumult, and the members of the assembly, risen from their seats and divided into groups, spoke and gesticulated with great noise. In the midst of this confusion, the seneschal of Normandy, William Fitz-Osbern, raised his voice, and said: "Why dispute ye thus? he is your lord, he has need of you; it were better your duty to make your offers, and not to await his request. If you fail him now, and he gain his end, by God he will remember it; prove, then, that you love him, and act accordingly." "Doubtless," cried the opponents, "he is our lord; but is it not enough for us to pay him his dues? We owe him no aid beyond the seas; he has already enough oppressed us with his wars; let him fail in his new enterprise, and our country is undone." After a long discussion, resulting in various opinions, it was determined that Fitz-Osbern, who knew the position of each man present, should be the messenger to excuse the limited offers of the assembly.

The Normans returned to the duke, and Fitz-Osbe n spoke thus: "I do not believe that there are in the whole world people more zealous than these; you know the aids they have given you, the onerous services they have rendered you; well, sire, they will do more, they offer to serve you beyond the sea as they have done here. Forward, then, and spare them in nothing; he who hitherto has only supplied you with two good mounted soldiers, will now supply four." "No! no!" exclaimed the Normans; "we did not charge you with such an answer; we did not say that, and it shall not be so. In things within his own country we will serve him as is due; but we are not bound to assist him to conquer another man's country. Besides, if once we rendered him double service, and followed him across the sea, he would make it a right and a custom for the future; he would burden our children with it; it shall not be, it shall not be!" Groups of ten, twenty, thirty, formed; the tumult was general, and the assembly separated.

Duke William, surprised and enraged beyond measure, dismulated his anger, and had recourse to an artifice, which has scarcely ever failed of its effect when powerful personages have desired to overcome popular resistance. He sent separately for the same men whom he had first convoked in a body; commencing with the richest and most influential, he intreated them to aid him out of pure favour and as a voluntary gift, affirming that he had no intention of making it an ill precedent for the future, or of abusing their own liberality against them; offering even to confirm his verbal assurance by letters sealed with his own great seal. None had the courage to pronounce a refusal to the face of the chief of the country, in an interview with him alone. That which each agreed to do was immediately registered; and the example of the first summoned, decided those who came afterwards. One subscribed for ships, another for armed soldiers, others promised to march in person; priests gave money, merchants merchandize, peasants their goods.

Presently after this, the consecrated banner and the bull authorizing the invasion of England arrived from Rome, which greatly increased the popular ardour; every one brought what he could; mothers sent their sons to enrol their names for the salvation of their souls. William published his ban in the neighbouring countries; he offered good pay and the pillage of England to every able man who would serve him with lance, sword, or cross-bow. A multitude accepted the invitation, coming by every road, far and near, from north and south. They came from Maine and Anjou, from Poitou and Brittany, from France and Flanders, Aquitaine and Burgundy, from the Alps and the banks of the Rhine. All the professional adventurers, all the military vagabonds of Western Europe hastened to Normandy, by long marches; some were knights and chiefs of war, the others simple foot-soldiers and sergeants of arms, as they were then called; some demanded money-pay, others only their passage and all the booty they might make. Some asked for land in England, a domain, a castle, a town; others simply required some rich Saxon in marriage. Every thought, every desire of human avarice presented itself. William rejected no one, says the Norman chronicle, and satisfied every one as well as he could. He gave, beforehand, a bishopric in England to a monk of Fescamp, in return for a vessel and twenty armed men. During the spring and summer, in all the ports of Normandy, workmen of every kind were employed in constructing and fitting up ships; smiths and armourers forged lances, swords, and coats of mail, and porters went to and fro continually, transporting the completed arms from the workshops to the vessels. While these preparations were actively going on, William went to Philip, king of the French, at Saint Germain, and saluting him with the form of deference which his ancestors had often omitted towards the kings of the Frank country: "You are my seigneur," said he; "if it please you aid me, and I, by God's grace, obtain my right over England, I promise to do you homage for it, as though I held it from you." Philip assembled his council of barons, without which he could not decide any important affair, and the barons were of opinion that they ought not in any way to aid William in his conquest. "You know," said they to the king, "how ill the Normans obey you now; it will be still worse when they possess England. Besides, it would cost us a great deal to assist the duke, and if he fail in his enterprise, the English will be our enemies for ever." Thus defeated in his object, duke William withdrew, greatly discontented with king Philip, and addressed the same request to the count of Flanders, his brother-in-law, who also declined to aid him.

Despite the national enmity of the Normans and Bretons, there existed between the dukes of Normandy and the counts of Brittany alliances of relationship, which complicated the relations of the two states without rendering them less hostile. At the time when duke Robert, the father of William, departed on his pilgrimage, he had no nearer relation than the Breton count Allan or Alain, a descendant of Roll by the female side, and it was to him that, on his departure, he confided the charge of his duchy and the guardianship of his son. Count Alain had not long delayed to declare the birth of his pupil doubtful, and to favour the party which wished to deprive him of the succession; but after the defeat of this party at the Val des Dunes, he died, poisoned, according to all appearances, by the friends of the young bastard. His son Conan succeeded him, and still reigned in Brittany at the time of William's great armament for the conquest of England. He was a daring man, dreaded by his neighbours, and whose principal ambition was to injure the duke of Normandy, whom he regarded as an usurper and as the murderer of his father. Finding the latter engaged in a difficult enterprise, Conan thought the moment favourable for declaring war against him, and sent him, by one of his chamberlains, the following message:

"I hear that thou art about to cross the sea, to conquer the kingdom of England. Now duke Robert, whose son thou pretendest to be, on departing for Jerusalem, remitted all his heritage to count Allan, my father, who was his cousin. But thou and thy accomplices poisoned my father: thou hast appropriated to thyself his seigneury, and hast detained it to this day, contrary to all justice, seeing that thou art a bastard. Restore me, then, the duchy of Normandy, which belongs to me, or I will make war upon thee to the last extremity, with all the forces at my disposal."

The Norman historians admit that William was somewhat alarmed at this message, for the slightest diversion might defeat his projects of conquest; but he found means to get rid, without much difficulty, of the enemy who declared himself with such rash boldness. The chamberlain of the count of Brittany, gained over doubtless by bribes, rubbed with poison the mouthpiece of the horn which his master used in the chase, and, to make assurance doubly sure, poisoned also his gloves and the reins of his horse. Conan died a few days after the return of his messenger. Count Eudes, his successor, was careful not to imitate him, or alarm William the Bastard as to the validity of his rights: on the contrary, uniting with him in a friendship, quite new between the Bretons and the Normans, he sent his two sons to aid him against the English. These two young men, Brian and Allan, came to the rendezvous of the Norman troops, accompanied by a body of horse, who gave them the title of Mactierns, whilst the Normans called them counts. Other rich Bretons, not of purely Celtic race, and who bore names of French form, such as Robert de Vitry, Bertrand de Dinand, and Raoul de Gaël, also came to the duke of Normandy to offer him their services. The rendezvous of the vessels and troops was at the mouth of the Dive, a river which empties itself into the ocean, between the Seine and the Orne. For a month, the winds were contrary, and detained the Norman fleet in port. Then a southern breeze carried them as far as the roadstead of Saint Valery, at the mouth of the Somme; there the bad weather recommenced, and it was necessary to wait some days. The fleet anchored, and the troops encamped upon the shore, greatly incommoded by the rain, which did not cease to fall in torrents.

During this delay, some of the vessels, shattered by a violent tempest, sank with their crews; this accident created a great sensation among the troops, fatigued by protracted encamping. In the long leisure of their days, the soldiers passed hours conversing under their tents, exchanging their reflections upon the perils of the voyage and the difficulties of the enterprise. No combat had yet taken place, and, said they, already many men were dead; they reckoned and exaggerated the number of bodies that the sea had thrown on the sand. These conversations abated the ardour of the adventurers, at first so full of zeal; some even broke their engagement and withdrew. To check this tendency so fatal to his projects, duke William had the dead secretly interred, and increased the rations of provisions and strong liquors; but the want of active employment continually brought back the same thoughts of sadness and discouragement. "The man is mad," said the murmuring soldiers, "who seeks to seize the land of another; God is offended with such designs, and proves it by refusing us a favourable wind."

Despite his strength of soul and habitual presence of mind, William was a prey to uneasiness which he could hardly conceal. He was frequently seen to go to the church of Saint Valery, the patron of the place, to remain there a long time in prayer, and each time that he quitted it, to look at the cock which surmounted the bell-tower, and showed the direction of the wind. If it seemed turning towards the south, the duke appeared joyful; but if the wind blew from the north or west, his face and manner became still more depressed. Whether it was an act of sincere faith, or merely to furnish some occupation to his sad and discouraged troops, he took from the church the coffer which contained the relics of the saint, and had it carried in procession with great ceremony through the camp. The whole army joined in prayer. The chiefs made rich offerings; every soldier, to the very lowest, gave his piece of money; and the following night, as if heaven had granted a miracle, the wind changed, and the weather became calm and serene. At daybreak of the 27th September, the sun, hitherto each day enveloped in clouds, appeared in all its splendour. The camp was immediately raised, all the preparations for embarkation executed with great ardour and no less promptitude, and some hours before sunset the entire fleet was ready. Four hundred ships with large sails, and more than a thousand transport vessels, made for the open sea, amid the sound of trumpets and a shout of joy, sent forth from sixty thousand mouths as from one.

The vessel in which William sailed was in the van, bearing at its mast-head the banner sent by the pope, and a cross on its own flag. Its sails were of different colours, and on them in various places were painted the three lions, the arms of Normandy; at the prow was the carved figure of a child, bearing a bow bent, with the arrow ready to quit the string. Lastly, large lanterns suspended from poles, a necessary precaution for a night-passage, were to serve as a beacon to the whole fleet, and to indicate the rallying point. This vessel, a better sailer than the rest, outstripped them during the day, and at night left them far behind. In the morning, the duke sent a sailor to the mast-head to see if the other vessels were coming. "I see only sky and sea," answered the sailor; whereupon they dropped anchor. The duke affected a gay countenance, and, lest fear and anxiety should spread among the crew, he had a copious repast and wines highly spiced given to them. The sailor again ascended, and now said that he saw four vessels; a third time, he exclaimed: "I see a forest of masts and sails."

Whilst this great armament was preparing in Normandy, Harold, king of Norway, faithful to his engagements with the Saxon Tosti, had assembled several hundred ships of war and transports. The fleet remained some time at anchor, and the Norwegian army, pending the signal for departure, encamped upon the coast as the Normans had done at the mouth of the Somme. Vague impressions of discouragement and anxiety were produced by the same causes, but under a still more gloomy aspect, conformable with the pensive imagination of the inhabitants of the north. Several soldiers believed they had had prophetic revelations during their sleep. One of them dreamed that he saw his companions landed on the coast of England, and in presence of the English army; that in front of this army, riding upon a wolf, was a woman of gigantic stature; the wolf held in his jaws a human body, dripping with gore, and when he had devoured it, the woman gave him another. A second soldier dreamed that the fleet sailed, and that a flock of crows, vultures, and other birds of prey were perched upon the masts and sails of the vessels; on an adjacent rock a woman was seated, holding a drawn sword in her hand, and looking at and counting the vessels: "Go," said she to the birds, "go without fear, you shall have enough to eat, and you shall have plenty to choose from, for I go with them." It was remarked, not without terror, that at the moment when Harold placed his foot on the royal boat, the weight of his body pressed it down more than usual.

Despite these threatening presages, the expedition sailed towards the southwest under the command of the king and his son Olaf. Before landing in England, they touched at the Orcades, islands inhabited by men of Scandinavian race, and two chiefs and a bishop joined them. They then coasted along the eastern shore of Scotland, where they met Tosti and his vessels. They sailed thence together, and, on their way, attacked the maritime town of Scarborough. Finding the inhabitants prepared to make an obstinate defence, they took possession of a high rock which commanded the town, and raised there an enormous pile of trunks of trees, branches and stubble, which, firing, they rolled down upon the houses, and then, favoured by the conflagration, forced the gates of the town and pillaged it. Relieved by this first success from their superstitious terrors, they gaily doubled Holderness at the mouth of the Humber; and ascended that river. From the Humber they passed into the Ouse, which runs near York. Tosti, who had the direction of the campaign, wished first of all to regain this capital of his ancient government, in order again to instal himself there. Morkar, his successor, Edwin, Morkar's brother, and young Waltheof, son of Siward, governor of Huntingdonshire, assembled the inhabitants of the surrounding country, and gave battle to the foreigners south of York, upon the banks of the

Humber; conquerors at first, but then obliged to retreat, they shut themselves up in the city, where the Norwegians besieged them. Tosti assumed the title of chief of Northumberland, and issued a proclamation dated from the foreigner's camp: a few weak-minded men acknowledged him, and a small number of adventurers answered his appeal.

While these things were passing in the north, the king of the Anglo-Saxons remained with all his forces on the southern coast, to watch the movements of William, whose invasion, which had been long expected, gave rise to much alarm. Harold had passed the whole summer and autumn upon his guard, between the landing-places nearest to Normandy; but the delay of the expedition occasioned it to be believed that it would now not be made before the winter. Moreover, the danger was greater from the enemy in the north, already masters of a portion of the English territory, than from an enemy who had not yet set foot in England; and the son of Godwin, prompt and daring in his projects, hoped in a few days to expel the Norwegians, and return to his post to receive the Normans. He made rapid marches at the head of his best troops, and arrived by night under the walls of York, just as the inhabitants had agreed to surrender to the allies of Tosti. The Norwegians had not yet made their entry: but, on the word of the inhabitants and the conviction of the impossibility of their retracting that word, they had broken up the lines, and were reposing. On their part, the inhabitants of York had no other idea than that of receiving on the next day Tosti and the king of Norway, who were to hold a great council in the city, to regulate the government of all the province, and distribute, among the foreigners and deserters, the lands of the rebel English.

The unexpected arrival of the Saxon king, who had marched so as to avoid the enemy's outposts, changed the whole face of things. The citizens of York resumed their arms, and the gates of the city were closed and guarded, so that no one could quit it for the camp of the Norwegians. The following day was one of those autumnal days in which the sun is still in all its vigour; the portion of the Norwegian army which left the camp on the Humber to accompany their king to York, not expecting to have enemies to combat, were without their coats of mail, on account of the heat; and of their defensive arms had only retained their helmets and bucklers. At some distance from the town the Norwegians suddenly perceived a great cloud of dust, and in the midst of this cloud something glittering like steel in the sunshine. "Who are these men advancing towards us?" said the king to Tosti. "It can only be," said the Saxon, "Englishmen coming to demand pardon and implore our friendship." The advancing mass growing gradually more distinct, soon appeared a numerous army, ranged in battle order. "The enemy! the enemy!" exclaimed the Norwegians, and they detached three horsemen to bring up in all haste the soldiers who remained behind in the camp and on board the ships. The king unfurled his standard, which he called the ravager of the world! the soldiers drew up around it, in a long narrow line, curved at the extremities. They stood pressed against each other, their lances planted in the ground with the points turned towards the enemy. Harold, son of Sigurd, rode through the ranks on his black charger, singing extempore verses, a fragment of which has been transmitted to us by the northern historians: "Let us fight," said he, "let us advance, though without our cuirasses, to the edges of blue steel; our helmets glitter in the sun; that is enough for brave men."

Before the two armies met, twenty Saxon cavaliers, men and horses clothed in steel, approached the Norwegian lines; one of them, in a loud voice, cried: "Where is Tosti, son of Godwin?"— "Here," answered the son of Godwin himself. "If thou art Tosti," returned the messenger, "thy brother greets thee by me, and offers thee peace, his friendship, and thy ancient honours." "These are fine words, and very different to the insults and hostilities they made me submit to a year ago. But if I accept these offers, what shall be given to the noble king Harold, son of Sigurd, my faithful ally?" "He," answered the messenger, "shall have seven feet of English land, or a little more, for his height passes that of other men." "Say, then, to my brother," answered Tosti, "that he prepare to fight: for none but liars shall ever say that the son of Godwin deserted the son of Sigurd."

The battle immediately began, and at the first shock of the two armies the Norwegian king was killed by an arrow which pierced his throat. Tosti took the command; and then his brother Harold sent a second time to offer him peace and life, for himself and the Norwegians. But all exclaimed that they would rather die than owe aught to the Saxons. At this moment, the men from the ships arrived, armed with cuirasses, but fatigued with their march under a burning sun. Although numerous, they did not sustain the attack of the English, who had already broken the first line of the battle and taken the royal banner. Tosti was killed, with most of the Norwegian chiefs, and, for the third time, Harold offered peace to the conquered. They accepted it; Olaf, the son of the dead king, the bishop and surviving chief of the Orcades, retired, with twenty-three vessels, having sworn friendship to England. The country of the English was thus delivered from a new conquest by the men of the north. But while these enemies withdrew, to return no more, other foes approached, and the same breeze in which the banners of the victorious Saxons waved, also swelled the Norman sails, and urged them on towards the coast of Sussex.

By an unfortunate chance, the vessels which had long been cruizing upon this coast had just returned to port from want of provisions. The troops of William thus landed, without resistance, at Pevensey near Hastings, the 28th of September 1066, three days after the victory of Harold over the Norwegians. The archers landed first; they wore short coats, and their hair was shaved off; then came the cavalry, wearing coats of mail and helmets of polished steel, of a nearly conical form, armed with long and strong lances, and straight double-edged swords. These were followed by the workmen of the army, pioneers, carpenters, and smiths, who brought on shore, piece by piece, three wooden castles, ready prepared beforehand. The duke was the last to land; at the moment his foot touched the sand, he slipped and fell on his face. A murmur arose, and voices exclaimed: "God preserve us! this is a bad sign." But William, rising, said immediately: "Lords, what is't you say? What, are you amazed? I have taken seizin of this land with my hands, and, by the splendour of God, all that it contains is ours." The repartee prevented the effect of the evil presage. The army took the road towards Hastings, and near that place marked out a camp, and raised two of the wooden castles as receptacles for provisions. Bodies of troops overran the neighbouring country, pillaging and burning houses. The English fled from their dwellings, hiding their goods and cattle, and hastened in crowds to the churches and churchyards, which they deemed the surest asylum against enemies, who were Christians like themselves. But, in their thirst for booty, the Normans paid little heed to the sanctity of places, and respected no asylum.

Harold was at York, wounded, and resting from his fatigues, when a messenger arrived in great haste, to inform him that William of Normandy had landed, and planted his banner on the Anglo-Saxon territory. He immediately marched towards the south with his victorious army, publishing, on his way, an order to all the provincial governors to arm their fighting-men, and bring them to

London. The militia of the west came without delay; those of the north were later, on account of the distance; but there was still reason to believe that the king of the English would soon find himself surrounded by the forces of the whole country. One of those Normans who had been made exceptions to the law of exile pronounced against foreigners, and who now played the part of spies and secret agents of the invader, sent word to the duke to be upon his guard, for that in four days the son of Godwin would have an hundred thousand men with him. Harold, too impatient, did not await the expiration of the four days; he could not overcome his desire to close with the foreigners, especially when he learned the ravages of every kind which they were committing round their camp. The hope of sparing his countrymen further evil, and perhaps the desire of attempting against the Normans a sudden and unforeseen attack, like that which had succeeded against the Norwegians, determined him to march to Hastings, with an army four times less numerous than that of the duke of Normandy.

But William's camp was carefully guarded against a surprise, and his outposts extended to a great distance. Some detachments of cavalry falling back, gave notice of the approach of the Saxon king, who, they said, was advancing furiously. Failing in his design of attacking the enemy by surprise, the Saxon was obliged to moderate his impetuosity; he halted at a distance of seven miles from the Norman camp, and suddenly changing his tactics, intrenched himself, to await them behind ditches and palisades. Some spies, who spoke French, were sent to the foreign army to observe its disposition and force. On their return, they related that there were more priests in William's camp than there were fighting men on the English side. They had mistaken for priests all the soldiers of the Norman army who wore shaved beards and short hair. Harold smiled at this report: "They whom you saw in such great numbers," said he, "are not priests, but brave warriors, who will soon show us what they are worth." Some of the Saxon chiefs advised the king to avoid a battle, and to retreat towards London, ravaging the country on his way, to starve out the foreigners. "I!" exclaimed Harold, "I ravage the country which has been confided to my care! By my faith, that were indeed treason, and I prefer taking the chances of battle with the few men I have, my courage, and my good cause."

The Norman duke, whose totally opposite character led him, in every circumstance, to neglect no means that occurred, and to place interest above all personal pride, profited by the unfavourable position in which he saw his adversary, to renew his demands. A monk, called Dom Hugues Maigrot, came, in William's name, to require the Saxon king to do one of three things; either to surrender the crown to the duke of Normandy, or to submit the matter to the arbitration of the pope, or to refer its decision to the chance of a single combat. Harold shortly answered: "I will not resign the crown, I will not refer the matter to the pope, I will not fight a single combat." Not discouraged by these positive refusals, William again sent the Norman monk, to whom he dictated his instructions in the following terms: "Go and say to Harold, that, if he will fulfil his compact with me, I will leave him all the land which is beyond the Humber, and will give his brother Gurth all the land that Godwin held; if he persist in not accepting my offer, thou shalt say to him, before all his people, that he is a perjurer and a liar, that he and all those who support him are excommunicated by the pope, and that I have the papal bull for this."

Dom Hugues Maigrot delivered this message in a solemn tone, and the Norman chronicle says that at the word excommunication the English chiefs looked at each other, as though they stood in the presence of a great danger. One of them spoke: "We ought," said he, "to fight, whatever the danger may be; for it is not here the question of receiving a new lord, as if our king were dead; the matter in hand is very different. The duke of Normandy has given our lands to his barons, his knights, and all his people, most of whom have already rendered him homage for them; they will all have their donations carried into effect if the duke becomes our king, and he will be bound to give them our goods, our wives, and our daughters, for all is promised them beforehand. They come, not only to ruin us, but to ruin our descendants also, to take from us the country of our ancestors; and what shall we do, or where shall we go, when we have no longer any country?" And hereupon the English unanimously took an oath to make neither peace, truce, nor treaty, with the invader, and to drive out the Normans or die in the attempt."

A whole day was employed in these futile messages; it was the eighteenth since the battle fought with the Norwegians near York. Harold's precipitate march had not as yet permitted any additional troops to join him. Edwin and Morkar, the two great northern chieftains, were at London, or on the road to London; none but volunteers came, one by one, or in small bands, citizens armed in haste, monks who quitted their cloisters to obey the call of their country. Among the latter was Leofrik, abbot of the great monastery of Peterborough, near Ely, and the abbot of Hide, near Winchester, who brought with him twelve of his monks, and twenty warriors raised at his expense. The hour of battle appeared at hand; Harold's two young brothers, Gurth and Leofwin, had taken their positions near him; the former endeavoured to persuade him not to be present in the action, but to go to London to seek fresh reinforcements, whilst his friends sustained the attack of the Normans. "Harold," said the young man, "thou canst not deny that, whether on compulsion or willingly, thou hast sworn to duke William an oath upon the relics of saints; why risk a combat with a perjury against thee? For us, who have taken no oath, the war is just, for we defend our country. Leave us, then, to fight the battle; thou shalt aid us if we retreat, and if we die thou wilt revenge us." To these words, so touching in the mouth of a brother, Harold replied that his duty forbad him to remain apart while others risked their lives; too confident in his courage and his good cause, he drew up his troops for the combat.

On the ground, which has ever since borne the name of Battle, the lines of the Anglo-Saxons occupied a long chain of hills, fortified by a rampart of stakes and willow hurdles. In the night of the 13th October, William announced to the Normans that the next day would be the day of battle. Priests and monks who had followed the invading army in great numbers, attracted, like the soldiers, by the hope of booty, met to pray and chaunt litanies, while the warriors prepared their arms. The time which remained to them, after this first care, was employed by them in confessing their sins and receiving the sacrament. In the other army, the night was passed in a very different manner; the Saxons diverted themselves with noisily singing old national songs, and emptying, around their fires, horns filled with beer and wine.

When morning came, in the Norman camp, the bishop of Bayeux, brother, on the mother's side, of duke William, celebrated mass and blessed the troops, armed with a hauberk under his rochet; he then mounted a large white courser, took a baton of command, and drew up the cavalry. The army was divided into three columns of attack; in the first were the men-at-arms from the counties of Boulogne and Ponthieu, with most of the adventurers engaged individually for pay; in the second were the Breton, Manceaux, and Poitevin auxiliaries; William in person commanded the third, composed of the Norman chivalry. In front and on the flanks of each of these bodies were infantry, lightly armed, wearing quilted coats, and armed with long bows or with steel crossbows. The duke was mounted on a Spanish charger, which a rich Norman had brought him on his return from a pilgrimage to St. Iago in Galicia. He wore around his neck the most revered of the relics upon which Harold had sworn, and the standard, blessed by the pope, was carried at his side by a young man, named Toustain le Blanc. At the moment, ere the troops began their march, the duke, raising his voice, thus addressed them:—

"Fight your best, and put every one to death; for if we conquer, we shall all be rich. What I gain, you gain; if I conquer, you conquer; if I take the land, you will share it. Know, however, that I am not come here merely to take that which is my due, but to revenge our whole nation for the felon acts, perjuries, and treason of these English. They put to death the Danes, men, and women, in the night of Saint Brice. They decimated the companions of my relation, Alfred, and put himself to death. On, then, in God's name, and chastise them for all their misdeeds."

The army soon came in sight of the Saxon camp, northwest of Hastings. The priests and monks who accompanied it, retired to a neighbouring hill, to pray and watch the combat. A Norman, named Taillefer, spurred his horse in front of the array, and began the song, famous throughout Gaul, of Charlemagne and Roland. As he sang, he played with his sword, throwing it far into the air, and catching it, as it fell, in his right hand; the Normans repeated the burthen, or shouted, Dieu aide! Dieu aide!

Coming within shot, the archers began to discharge their arrows, and the cross-bowmen their bolts; but most of the shots were rendered useless by the high parapets of the Saxon redoubts. The infantry armed with lances, and the cavalry, advanced to the gates of the redoubts, and endeavoured to force them. The Anglo-Saxons, all on foot around their standard, planted in the ground, and forming behind their palisades a compact and solid mass, received the assailants with heavy blows of their axes, ævissimæ secures, as the historian calls them, one blow of which broke the lances and cut through the coats of mail. The Normans, not being able to penetrate the redoubts, or to tear up the stakes, fell back, fatigued with their useless attack, upon the division commanded by William. The duke then made all his archers advance, and ordered them not to shoot straightforward, but into the air, so that the arrows might fall into the enemy's camp. Many of the English were wounded, most of them in the face, by this manœuvre; Harold himself had his eye pierced with an arrow; but nevertheless, continued to issue his orders and to fight. The attack of the infantry and cavalry again commenced, amid cries of Notre Dame! Dieu aide! Dieu aide! But the Normans were driven back from one of the gates of the camp, to a deep ravine, covered with brushwood and grass, the growth of time, into which they and their horses fell one upon the other, and thus perished in great numbers. There was a moment of terror in the foreign army. The report spread that the duke had been killed, and at this news a retreat commenced. William threw himself before the fugitives and barred their passage, threatening them, and striking them with his lance; then uncovering: "I am here," he exclaimed; "look at me, I still live, and, with the help of God, I will conquer."

The cavalry returned to the redoubts, but they could not force the gates or make a breach; the duke then thought of a stratagem to induce the English to quit their position; he ordered a thousand horse to advance and immediately retreat. The sight of this feigned flight made the Saxons lose their coolness; they all rushed in pursuit, their axes hanging from their necks. At a certain distance, a body previously disposed, joined the fugitives, who turned; and the English, surprised in their disorder, were assailed on every side by blows of lances and swords, from which they could not defend themselves, having both their hands occupied in wielding their great battle-axes. When they had lost their ranks, the redoubts were forced; horse and foot made their way into them, but the combat was still fierce, hand to hand. William had his horse killed under him; Harold and his two brothers fell dead at the foot of their standard, which was torn up and replaced by the banner sent from Rome. The wreck of the English army, without chief and without standard, prolonged the struggle till the end of the day, so late that the combatants of the two parties only recognised each other by their language.

Then, and not till then, did this desperate resistance end. Harold's followers dispersed, many dying upon the roads of their wounds and the fatigue of the combat. The Norman horse pursued them, granting quarter to none. The victors passed the night on the field of battle, and the next day at sunrise, duke William drew up his troops and called over the names of all those who had crossed the sea with him, from the list which had been drawn up before their departure, at St. Valery. Numbers of these lay, dead or dying, beside the conquered. The fortunate survivors had, for the first fruits of their victory, the spoils of the dead enemy. In turning over the bodies, thirteen were found with a monk's habit under their armour; they were the abbot of Hide and his twelve companions: the name of their monastery was the first written in the black book of the conquerors.

The mothers and wives of those who had come from the neighbourhood to fight and die with their king, united to seek together and bury the bodies of their relations. That of king Harold lay for a long time on the field of battle, without any one daring to claim it. At length, Godwin's widow, Ghitha, subduing for the moment her grief, sent a message to duke William, asking his permission to render the last honours to her son. She offered, say the Norman historians, to give the weight of his body in gold. But the duke sternly refused, saying that a man who had been false to his word and to his religion, should have no other sepulchre than the sand of the shore. He relented, however, if we are to believe an old tradition, in favour of the monks of Waltham abbey, which Harold had founded and enriched. Two Saxon monks, Osgod and Ailrik, deputed by the abbot of Waltham, demanded and obtained permission to transport the remains of their benefactor to their church. They sought among the mass of bodies, despoiled of arms and clothes, examining them carefully one after the other, but could not recognise the body of him they sought, so much had his wounds disfigured him. Despairing ever to succeed in their research unaided, they addressed themselves to a woman whom Harold, before he became king, had kept as a mistress, and intreated her to assist them. She was called Edith, and surnamed the Beauty with the swan's neck. She consented to accompany the two monks, and was more successful than they in discovering the corpse of him whom she had loved.

All these events are related by the chroniclers of Anglo-Saxon race, in a tone of despondency which it is difficult to convey. They call the day of the battle a bitter day, a day of death, a day stained with the blood of the brave. "England, what shall I say of thee," exclaims the historian of the church of Ely; "what shall I relate to our descendants? Woe to thee! thou hast lost thy national king, and thou hast fallen into the hands of the foreigner; thy sons have perished miserably, thy councillors and thy chiefs are conquered, dead, or disinherited." Long after the day of this fatal fight, patriotic superstition still saw traces of fresh blood upon the ground where it had taken place; they were visible, it was said, on the heights north-west of Hastings, when a slight rain had moistened the soil. Immediately after his victory, William made a vow to build an abbey on the spot, dedicated to the Holy Trinity and Saint Martin, the patron of the warriors of Gaul. The vow was soon accomplished, and the high altar of the new monastery was raised on the very spot where the standard of king Harold had been planted and torn down. The outer walls were traced around the hill which the bravest of the English had covered with their bodies, and the whole extent of the adjacent land, upon which the famous scenes of the battle had taken place, became the property of this abbey, which was called, in the Norman language, L'Abbaye de la Bataille. Monks from the great convent of Marmoutiers, near Tours, came to settle here and pray for the souls of all who had died on the field.

It is said, that, when the first stones of the edifice were laid, the architects discovered that there would be a deficiency of water; they went, quite disconcerted, to acquaint William with this untoward circumstance: "Work, work away," replied the conqueror, in a jovial tone, "for if God give me life, there shall be more wine among the monks of Battle Abbey than there is water in the best convent of Christendom!"

BOOK IV. FROM THE BATTLE OF HASTINGS TO THE TAKING OF CHESTER, THE LAST CITY CONQUERED BY THE NORMANS.

1066—1070.

Battle of Romney—Taking of Dover—Capitulation of Kent—Election of king Edgar— Defection of Edwin and Morkar—Blockade of London—Proceedings of the citizens— Submission of London—William proclaimed king—The ceremony of the coronation disturbed by conflagration—Division of the spoils among the Normans—Extent of the conquered territory—Sufferings of the conquered—Courageous resistance of three Saxons—Fortresses erected in London—Ancient lists of the conquerors of England—William revisits Normandy— Revolt of Kent—Eustache, count of Boulogne, comes to the assistance of the English—Limits of the territory invaded—Return of king William—He marches into the west—Siege of Exeter— Division of lands in the western provinces—Imprisonment and deposition of Brihtrik— Resistance of the monks of Winchcomb—Their punishment—The English chiefs retire to the north—Conspiracy against the Normans—King Edgar flies into Scotland—State of the Scottish population—Friendship of the kings of Scotland for the men of Teutonic race—William marches into the north—Taking of Oxford, &c.—Taking of York—Archbishop Eldred's malediction upon king William—His despair and death—Weariness of the Normans—Insurrection of the western provinces—Landing of the sons of king Harold—Suppression of the western revolt— State of the northern provinces—March of Robert Comine against Durham—His defeat and death—Alliance between the northern English and the Danes—Arrival of Danish succours in England—The English and Danes besiege and take the city of York—York retaken by the Normans—Devastation of Northumberland—Taking of Durham—Ravages and cruelties exercised by the conquerors—St. John of Beverley intimidates the Norman soldiers— Completion of the conquest in the north—Famine in the conquered districts—Division of houses and lands—French colony in Yorkshire—Distribution of English domains and heiresses—Tosti killed by Osulf in a spirit of national vengeance—Second submission of the English chieftains and of king Edgar—Defeat of Edrik the Saxon—Invasion of Wales—Fresh emigrants from Gaul—Society of gain and loss among the soldiers of the Conquest—Brothers-in-arms—March of William upon Chester—Taking of Chester—Battle near the Ruddlan marshes—Utility of local details.

While the army of the king of the Anglo-Saxons and the army of the invader were in presence of each other, some fresh vessels from Normandy had crossed the Channel to join the main fleet stationed in the bay of Hastings. Those who commanded them, landed, by mistake, several miles further to the north, in a place then called Rumeney, now Romney. The inhabitants received the Normans as enemies, and a combat took place, in which the latter were beaten. William learned their defeat a few days after his own victory, and to save from a similar misfortune the succours he still expected from the opposite shore, he resolved, first of all, to secure the possession of the south-eastern coast. Instead, therefore, of advancing to London, he fell back to Hastings, where he remained some time, to see if his presence alone would not suffice to determine the population of the neighbouring country to voluntary submission. But no one coming to sue for peace, the conqueror again commenced his march with the remains of his army, and some fresh troops which, in the interval, had joined him from Normandy.

He proceeded along the sea coast, from north to south, devastating every thing on his way. At Romney, he avenged, by burning the houses and massacring the inhabitants, the defeat of his soldiers; thence he marched to Dover, the strongest fortress on the whole coast, and of which he had formerly endeavoured to make himself master, without danger and without fighting, by the oath into which he had entrapped Harold. Dover castle, recently completed by the son of Godwin for better purposes, was constructed on a rock bathed by the sea, naturally steep, and which, with great difficulty and labour, had been hewn on every side, so as to make it present the appearance of a vast wall. The details of the siege made by the Normans are not known; all the historians tell us is, that the town of Dover was fired, and that, either from terror or treason, the garrison of the fortress surrendered it. William passed a week at Dover, erecting additional walls and defensive works; then changing the direction of his march, he left the coast, and proceeded towards the capital city.

The Norman army advanced by the great Roman road, which the English called Wtling-street, the same which had figured so often as a common boundary in the divisions of territory between the Saxons and Danes. This road led from Dover to London, through the middle of Kent; the conquerors passed through a portion of this county without any one appearing to dispute their passage; but in a spot where the road, approaching the Thames, ran near a forest, adapted for concealing an ambuscade, a large body of armed Saxons suddenly presented themselves. They were commanded by two priests, Eghelsig, abbot of the monastery of Saint Augustin at Canterbury, and Stigand the archbishop of Canterbury, the same who had crowned king Harold. It is not precisely known what passed at this meeting; whether a combat took place, followed by a treaty between the two armies, or whether the capitulation was concluded before they crossed weapons. The Kentish army, it appears, stipulated for all the inhabitants of the province that they would offer no further resistance, on condition of remaining, after the conquest, as free as they had been before.

In treating thus for themselves alone, and separating their own from the national destiny, the men of Kent (if it be true, indeed, that they concluded this compact) did more harm to the common cause than good to themselves; for no act of the time shows that the foreigner kept faith with them, or distinguished them from the other English, in his laws and oppressive measures. Archbishop Stigand, whether he had taken part in this capitulation, or had fruitlessly opposed it, a conjecture more conformable with his haughty and daring character, quitted the province which thus laid down its arms, and went towards London, where, as yet, no one thought of surrendering. The inhabitants of that great city, and the chiefs assembled there, had resolved to fight a second battle, which, well arranged and well conducted, would, according to all appearance, be more fortunate than the first.

But there was wanting a supreme chief, under whose command the whole strength and will of the country should rally; and the national council, which had to name this chief, was slow in giving a decision, agitated and divided as it was by intrigues and contending claims. Neither of the brothers of the late king, men capable of worthily filling his place, had returned from the battle of Hastings. Harold had left two sons still very young, and little known to the people; it does not appear that they were at this time proposed as candidates for the crown. The claimants most powerful in renown and fortune were Edwin and Morkar, brothers-in-law to Harold, and chiefs of Northumbria and Mercia. They had with them the votes of all the men of the north of England; but the citizens of London, the people of the south, and the party malcontent with the late reign, opposed to them young Edgar, king Edward's nephew, surnamed Etheling, the illustrious, because he was of the ancient royal race. This young man, feeble in character, and of no acquired reputation, had not, a year before, been able to outweigh the popularity of Harold; he counterbalanced now that of the sons of Alfgar, and was supported against them by Stigand himself, and by Eldred, archbishop of York. Of the other bishops, several would accept for a king neither Edgar nor Edgar's competitors, and required the people to submit to the man who came with a bull from the pope and a standard of the church. Some acted thus, from blind obedience to the spiritual power, others from political cowardice; others, again, of foreign origin and gained over by the foreign pretender, played the part for which they had been paid in money or promises. They did not prevail, and the majority of the great national council fixed their choice on the man least able to command in difficult circumstances—the youthful nephew of Edward. He was proclaimed king, after considerable hesitation, during which much precious time was lost in futile disputes. His accession did not combine the divided opinions; Edwin and Morkar, who had promised to head the troops assembled at London, withdrew this promise, and retired to their governments in the north, taking with them the soldiers of those provinces, over whom they were all-influential. They madly thought they could defend the northern provinces apart from the rest of England. Their withdrawal weakened and discouraged those who remained at London with the new king; depression, the fruit of civil discord, took the place of the first impulse of patriotism which had been excited by the foreign invasion. Meantime, the Norman troops were approaching from several directions, overrunning Surrey, Sussex, and Hampshire, pillaging and burning the towns and villages, and massacring the inhabitants, armed or unarmed. Five hundred horse advanced as far as Southwark, engaged a body of Saxons who met them, and burned in their retreat all the houses on the right bank of the Thames. Judging from this that the citizens were prepared to stand on their defence, William, instead of approaching London and besieging it, turned towards the west, and passed the Thames at Wallingford, in Berkshire. He formed a fortified camp in this place, and left troops there to intercept the Saxon succours that might come from the western counties; then proceeding north-east, he himself encamped at Berkhamsted, in Hertfordshire, for the purpose of intercepting all communication between London and the northern counties, and preventing the return of the sons of Alfgar, should they repent their inaction. By these tactics the great Saxon town was entirely hemmed in; numerous bodies of scouts ravaged the environs, and cut off the provisions, without engaging in any decisive battle; more than once, the inhabitants of London came to blows with the Normans; but by degrees, becoming worn out, they were conquered, less by the strength of the enemy, than by the fear of famine, and by the discouraging thought that they were isolated from all succour.

There existed in the city two powers, accord between which it was necessary but very difficult to maintain—the court and the guild, or municipal confraternity of the citizens. The municipality, entirely free, was ruled by its elective magistrates; the court had for its chief the officer designated Staller, or Standard-bearer.

This post, at once civil and military, had just been restored to the person who filled it under Edward; an old soldier, named Ansgar, whose legs were paralyzed with fatigue and wounds, and who was carried on a litter wherever his duty called him. William had met him in 1051, at the court of king Edward. He thought it possible to gain him over to his cause, and sent him, by a secret emissary, his propositions and offers, which were no less than, in case of success, the lieutenancy of the kingdom. We cannot say whether Ansgar was moved by these promises, but he certainly received them with circumspection, and, preserving absolute secrecy with respect to them, adopted a course calculated to relieve him from the peril of having personal correspondence with the enemy. Of his own authority, or in conjunction with the king's council, he assembled the principal citizens of London, and addressing them by the name which the members of the municipal corporation gave each other, said: "Honourable brothers, our resources are nearly exhausted, the city is threatened with assault, and no army comes to its aid. Such is our situation; but when strength is exhausted, when courage can do no more, artifice and stratagem still remain. I advise you to resort to them. The enemy is not yet aware of our miserable position; let us profit by that circumstance, and send them fair words by a man capable of receiving them, who will feign to convey your submission, and, in sign of peace, will lay his hand in theirs, if required."

This counsel, the aptness and merit of which it is difficult to comprehend, pleased the chiefs of the citizens, as coming from an able politician and experienced warrior. They flattered themselves, it would appear, with the hope of obtaining a suspension of hostilities, and protracting the negotiations until the arrival of succours, but the result was quite different. The messenger sent to deceive duke William, returned himself deceived, loaded with presents and devoted to his cause. When he appeared before the principal citizens to give an account of his mission, an anxious crowd followed and pressed behind him. His singularly daring speech consisted of boundless eulogy of the armed pretender, to whom he attributed every royal virtue, and a promise, in his name, of peace, justice, and obedience to the wishes of the English nation. These words, so different from the reports in circulation of the implacable severity of the conqueror of Hastings, far from raising the cry of treachery, were received by the crowd, if not by the magistrates themselves, with joy and confidence. There was, in favour of the peace party—and the duke of Normandy, one of those popular outbursts which nothing can resist, and which are soon followed by futile repentance. People and magistrates unanimously resolved by acclamation to carry, without further delay, the keys of the city to duke William.

The court of the young king Edgar, without army or free communication beyond the walls, was incapable of counteracting the will of the citizens, or of compelling them to incur the chances of a desperate resistance. This government, created in the midst of disorder, and which, notwithstanding its popularity, was in want of the most ordinary resources, found itself necessitated to declare that it no longer existed. The king himself, accompanied by archbishops Stigand and Eldred, and by Wulstan, bishop of Worcester, several chiefs of high rank, and the leading citizens, came to the camp at Berkhamsted, and made their submission, most unhappily for the country. They gave hostages to the duke of Normandy, swore to him the oath of fidelity, and, in return, the duke promised them, on his faith, to be gentle and clement towards them. He then marched to London, and, despite the promise just issued from his lips, allowed his people to devastate everything on the way. Upon the road from Berkhamsted to London, was the rich monastery of Saint Alban, built near the vast ruins of an ancient Roman municipium. On approaching this abbey, William beheld with surprise great trunks of trees disposed so as to intercept the passage, or render it difficult. He sent for the abbot, Frithrik. "Why," asked the conqueror, "hast thou thus cut down thy woods?" "I have done my duty," answered the Saxon monk; "and if all of my order had done the same, as they might and ought to have done, thou wouldst not, perhaps, have advanced thus far into our country." William did not go quite to London, but halting at a distance of some miles, sent forward a numerous detachment of soldiers to construct a fortress for his residence in the heart of the city.

Whilst the works were proceeding in all haste, the council of war held by the Normans, in their camp, discussed the means of promptly completing the conquest, so favourably commenced. William's more intimate friends said that to mitigate the resistance of the provinces still free, their future movements should be preceded by his assuming the title of king of the English. This proposition was, no doubt, most agreeable to the duke of Normandy, but with his usual circumspection, he feigned indifference to it. Although the possession of the crown was the object of his enterprise, it appears that weighty reasons induced him to seem less ambitious than he really was, of a dignity which, raising him above the conquered, would, at the same time, separate his fortune from that of all his companions in arms. William modestly excused himself, and demanded at least some delay, saying that he had not come to England for his own interest alone, but for that of the whole Norman nation; that, besides, if it were the will of God that he should become king, the time to assume the title had not arrived, too many counties and too many men still remaining to be subjected.

The majority of the Norman chiefs were inclined to take these hypocritical scruples literally, and to decide that in reality it was not yet time to create a king, when the captain of one of the auxiliary bands, Aimery de Thouars, to whom the royalty of William would naturally give less umbrage than to the natives of Normandy, energetically rose, and, in the style of a flatterer and mercenary trooper, exclaimed: "It is too modest of you to appeal to warriors, whether or no they will have their lord a king; soldiers have nothing to do with questions of this nature; and besides, our discussions only serve to retard that which, as a matter of feeling, we all so ardently desire." Those Normans who, after William's feigned excuses, might have ventured to concur in them, thought very different after the Poitevin had spoken, fearing to appear less faithful and less devoted than he to their common chief. They therefore unanimously decided that, before carrying the conquest further, duke William should be crowned king of England, by the few Saxons whom he had succeeded in terrifying or corrupting.

The ceremony was fixed for Christmas-day, then close at hand. The archbishop of Canterbury, Stigand, who had sworn the oath of peace to the conqueror, in his camp at Berkhamsted, was invited to attend and crown him, according to ancient custom, in the church of the monastery of the west, called in English, Westmynster, near London. Stigand refused to bestow his blessing on one covered with the blood of men, and an invader of the rights of others. But Eldred, archbishop of York, with greater worldly discretion, seeing, say the old historians, that it was needful to fall in with the times, and not to oppose the will of God, by whom the powers of the world are raised up, consented to fulfil the office. The church of Westminster abbey was prepared and decorated as in the old days, when, by the free vote of the best men of England, the king of their choice presented himself to receive investiture of the power which they had conferred upon him. But this previous election, without which the title of king could only be a vain mockery, the bitter insult of the strongest, did not take place for the duke of Normandy. He left his camp, and walked between two ranks of soldiers to the monastery, where awaited him several timid Saxons, affecting, however, a firm countenance, and an air of freedom, in their dastardly and servile office. Far around, all the approaches to the church, the squares and streets of the then suburban village of Westminster, were guarded by armed cavalry, who, as the Norman narratives have it, were to keep the rebels in check, and watch over the safety of those whose office called them to the interior of the temple. The counts, the barons, and other war-chiefs, in number two hundred and sixty, entered the church with their duke.

When the ceremony opened, Geoffroy, bishop of Coutances, ascending a platform, asked the Normans, in the French language, whether they were all content that their lord should take the title of king of the English; and at the same time, the archbishop of York asked the English, in the Saxon language, whether they accepted the duke of Normandy for their king. Hereupon there arose in the church acclamations so vehement that they resounded beyond the doors, and reached the ears of the cavalry who occupied the neighbouring streets. They took the sound for a cry of alarm, and, according to their secret instructions, hastily set fire to the houses. Several rushed to the church, and at sight of their drawn swords and of the flames, all present dispersed, Normans as well as Saxons; the latter rushed to extinguish the fire, the former to seek plunder amid the tumult and confusion. The ceremony was interrupted by this sudden event, and there only remained hastily to complete it, the duke himself, the archbishop Eldred, and a few priests of the two nations. Tremblingly they received from him whom they called king, and who, according to an ancient narrative, himself trembled in common with them, an oath to treat the Anglo-Saxon people as well as the best king ever elected by that people.

But on the same day London was to learn the value of such an oath in the mouth of a foreign conqueror; an enormous war tribute was imposed on the citizens, and their hostages were imprisoned. William himself, who could not really believe that the benediction of Eldred and the acclamations of a few dastards had made him king of England, in the legal sense of this word, and, consequently, at a loss how to frame his manifestoes, sometimes falsely styled himself king by hereditary succession, and sometimes, in all frankness, king by the edge of the sword. But if he hesitated as to words, he had no hesitation as to deeds, but showed his real position by the attitude of hostility and distrust which he maintained towards the people; he dared not yet establish himself in London, nor inhabit the embattled castle which had been hastily constructed for him. He retired accordingly to Barking, until his engineers had given more solidity to this work, and laid the foundation of two other fortresses, destined to keep in check, says a Norman author, the changeable spirit of a too numerous and too haughty people.

During the period that the king remained at Barking, the two Saxon chiefs, whose fatal withdrawal had caused the subjection of the great city, intimidated by the augmented power which the possession of London and the title of king gave to the invader, came from the north to swear to him the oath which the English chiefs were accustomed to swear to their ancient kings. The submission of Edwin and Morkar did not, however, involve that of the provinces they had governed, and the Norman army did not advance to occupy these provinces; they remained concentrated around London, and upon the southern and eastern coasts nearest Gaul. The partition of the wealth of the invaded territory now almost solely occupied them. Commissioners went over the whole extent of country in which the army had left garrisons; they took an exact inventory of property of every kind, public and private, carefully registering every particular; for the Norman nation, even in those remote times, was already extremely fond of deeds, and documents, and law forms.

A close inquiry was made into the names of all the English partisans of Harold, who had either died in battle, or survived the defeat, or by involuntary delays had been prevented from joining the royal standard. All the property of these three classes of men, lands, revenues, furniture, houses, were confiscated; the children of the first class were declared for ever disinherited; the second class were, in like manner, wholly dispossessed of their estates and property of every kind, and, says one of the Norman writers, were only too grateful for being allowed to retain their lives. Lastly, those who had not taken up arms were also despoiled of all they possessed, for having had the intention of taking up arms; but, by special grace, they were allowed to entertain the hope that after many long years of obedience and devotion to the foreign power, not they, indeed, but their sons might perhaps obtain from their new masters some portion of their paternal heritage. Such was the law of the conquest, according to the unsuspected testimony of a man nearly contemporary with and of the race of the conquerors.

The immense product of this universal spoliation became the pay of those adventurers of every nation who had enrolled under the banner of the duke of Normandy. Their chief, the new king of England, retained, in the first place, for his own share, all the treasure of the ancient kings, the church plate, and all that was most rare and precious in the shops of the merchants. William sent a portion of these riches to pope Alexander with Harold's standard, in exchange for that which had triumphed at Hastings; and all the foreign churches in which psalms had been chanted, and tapers burnt for the success of the invasion, received in recompence crosses, sacred vessels, and cloth of gold. After the king and clergy had taken their share, that of the soldiers was awarded according to their rank and the conditions of their engagement. Those who, at the camp of the Dive, had done homage for lands, then to be conquered, received those of the dispossessed English; the barons and knights had vast domains, castles, villages, and even whole cities; the simple vassals had smaller portions. Some received their pay in money, others had stipulated that they should have a Saxon wife, and William, says the Norman chronicle, gave them in marriage noble dames, great heiresses, whose husbands had fallen in the battle. One only among the knights who had accompanied the conqueror, claimed neither lands, gold, nor wife, and would accept none of the spoils of the conquered. His name was Guilbert Fitz-Richard: he said that he had accompanied his lord to England because such was his duty, but that stolen goods had no attraction for him, and that he would return to Normandy and enjoy his own heritage, a moderate but legitimate heritage, and, contented with his own lot, would rob no one.

The new king employed the last months of the winter of 1066 in making a sort of military progress through the provinces then invaded. It is difficult to determine exactly the number of these provinces, and the extent of country which the foreign troops freely occupied and overran. Yet by carefully examining the accounts of the contemporary writers, we find, at all events, negative proofs that the Normans had not advanced in a north-easterly direction beyond the rivers, the mouths of which form Boston Wash; or towards the south-west, not beyond the high territory which bounds Dorsetshire. The city of Oxford, nearly equi-distant between these two opposite points, upon a straight line drawn from one to the other, had not yet surrendered; but perhaps this ideal frontier had been passed, either to the north or to the south of Oxford. It is equally difficult to deny or to affirm this, or to fix, at any particular moment, the limits of a gradual invasion. The whole extent of country really occupied by William's garrisons and held by him in a more than nominal manner, in virtue of his title of king, were in a short time bristling with citadels and fortresses; all the inhabitants were disarmed, and obliged to swear obedience and fidelity to the new chief imposed on them by the lance and sword. They swore, but in their hearts they did not hold this foreigner legal king of England; in their eyes the true king was young Edgar, fallen and a captive as he was. The monks of Peterborough abbey gave a remarkable proof of this. Having lost their abbot, Leofrik, on his return from the battle of Hastings, they chose, as his successor, their prior, named Brand; and as it was their custom to submit the election of the dignitaries of their monastery to the approval of the supreme chief of the country, they sent Brand to Edgar. According to the chronicle of the monastery, they took this step, because all the inhabitants of the country thought that Edgar would again be king. Information of the fact soon reached William's ears, and his rage was unbounded. "From that day," continues the contemporary narrator, "every evil and every tribulation has fallen upon our house. May God have mercy on it."

The prayer of this monk might well have been repeated by every inhabitant of the conquered provinces, for each had his full share of grief and misery: the men had to undergo indigence and servitude; the women insult and outrage more cruel than death itself. Those who were not taken par mariage were taken par amours, as it was termed in the language of the conquerors, and became the plaything of the foreign soldiers, the least and lowest of whom was lord and master in the houses of the conquered. "Ignoble grooms, base scum of armies," say the old annalists, "did as they pleased with the noblest women, and left them nothing but to weep and wish for death. These licentious knaves were amazed at themselves; they went mad with pride and astonishment at beholding themselves so powerful, at having servants richer than their own fathers had ever been. Whatever they willed, they deemed it fully permissible to do; they shed blood at random, tore the bread from the mouths of the wretched people, and took everything, money, goods, land. . . ."

Such was the fate which extended itself over the men of English race, as the three-lion banner advanced into their country, and waved over their towns. But this destiny, everywhere equally severe, assumed different appearances, according to the diversity of places. The towns were not struck so hard as the country; this town or district was afflicted in a different way from that; around a common centre of misery, if we may thus express ourselves, there were the varied forms and the multiplicity of circumstances which are ever exhibited by the course of human affairs.

The city of Dover, half consumed by fire, was allotted to Eudes, bishop of Bayeux, who could not, say the ancient documents, calculate its exact value, because it was so devastated. He distributed the houses among his soldiers and people; Raoul de Courtespine (Crookthorne), received three, with the field of a poor woman. William Fitz-Geoffroy had three houses, one of which was the ancient Guildhall, near Colchester in Essex; Geoffroy de Mandeville alone had forty manors, or houses surrounded with cultivated land; fourteen Saxon proprietors were dispossessed by Engelry, and thirty, by one Guillaume. A rich Englishman, to secure his safety, placed himself under the power of the Norman Gualtier, who made him his tributary; another Englishman became a serf on the glebe of his own field. The domain of Sutton, in Bedfordshire, that of Burton and the town of Stafford, fell to the lot of Guy de Riencourt. He possessed these lands during his life. But Richard, his son and heir, lost the greater part of them to king Henry I. at dice.

In Suffolk, a Norman chief appropriated the lands of a Saxon lady, named Ediva the fair; the entire city of Norwich was set aside as the private domain of the conqueror; it had paid to the Saxon kings thirty pounds and twenty pence; but William exacted seventy pounds a year, a horse of value, an hundred pence for the queen his wife, and twenty pounds for the salary of the officer who commanded there in his name. A strong citadel was built in the centre of the city, for its inhabitants being men of Danish origin, the conquerors feared that they might demand and receive aid from the Danes, who often cruised on the coast. In Dorchester, instead of an hundred and seventy-two houses that were there in the time of king Edward, eighty-eight alone remained; the rest were a heap of ruins; at Warham, of an hundred and thirteen houses, sixty-two had been destroyed; at Bridport, twenty houses disappeared in the same manner, and the poverty of the inhabitants was such, that more than twenty years after not one had been rebuilt. The Isle of Wight was invaded by William Fitz-Osbern, seneschal of the Norman king, and became a portion of his vast domains in England; he transmitted it to his son, then to his grand-nephew, Baldwin, called in Normandy, Baudoin des Reviers, and in England, Baldwin de l'Isle.

Near Winchester, in Hampshire, was the monastery of Hide, the abbot of which, accompanied by twelve monks and twenty men-at-arms, had gone to the battle of Hastings and fallen there. The revenge which the conqueror exercised on this monastery was mingled with a sort of pleasantry; he divested the domains of the monastery, as ransom in land for the patriotic crime of its thirteen members, of one barony for the abbot's share of the offence, and one knight's fee for each of the twelve monks. Another circumstance that may be mentioned among the joyeusetés of the conquest, is that a dancing girl, named Adeline, is named in the roll of partition of the same county, as having received a fief from Roger, one of the Norman counts.

In Hertfordshire, an Englishman had redeemed his land by a payment of nine ounces of gold; and yet, to avoid a violent ejectment, he was obliged to become the tributary of a soldier named Vigot or Bigot. Three Saxon warriors, Thurnoth, Waltheof and Thurman, associated in a brotherhood of arms, possessed near Saint Albans a manor which they held of the abbot on the terms of defending it with their swords, in case of need. They faithfully fulfilled this office against the Norman invaders; but, overcome by numbers and obliged to fly, they abandoned their domain. It fell to the share of a noble baron, called Roger de Toëny, who had soon to defend his new property against the three expelled Saxons. The latter, who had sought refuge in the neighbouring forests, assembled there a small troop of men, driven out like themselves, and unexpectedly attacking the Normans established on their lands, killed several, and burned their houses.

These facts, taken at random from among a thousand others which it would be wearisome to enumerate, will enable the reader to figure to himself the sad but varied scenes presented by English counties of the south and east, while the Norman king was installing himself in the Tower of London. This fortress, constructed in one of the angles of the city wall, close to the Thames, received the name of the Palatine Tower, a name formed from an old Roman title that William bore in Normandy, conjointly with that of duke or count. Two other fortresses, built westward, and confided to the care of the Normans Baynard and Gilbert de Montfichet, took respectively the name of their keepers. The three-lion banner was planted on William's donjon, and over the two others floated those of Baynard and Montfichet. But these captains had first both sworn to lower their flags and to raise that of the king, their lord, on his first command, preferred in anger or without anger, supported by a great force or a small, for offence committed or without offence committed, as the formal acts set forth. Before making, amid the sound of trumpets, their first entry into their towers, before they garrisoned them with their men, they placed their hands in the hands of the Norman king, and acknowledged themselves his liege-men. In a word, they had promised to undergo as a just and legal decree, their sentence of depossession, if ever they voluntarily took part against their lord and separated their banner from his.

The same oath was sworn to the chief of the conquest by other leaders, who again received from inferior dignitaries a similar oath of fealty and homage. Thus the troops of the conqueror, although scattered and dispersed over the land of the conquered, remained united by a vast chain of duty, and observed the same subordination as when in his ships or behind his fortifications at Hastings. The subaltern owed fealty and service to his military superior, or to him from whom he had received in fief either lands or money. Upon this condition, those who had realized the larger share of the spoil, bestowed a portion of their superfluity upon those who had been less fortunate; the knights received from the barons, men-at-arms from their captains; in their turn these gave to the squires, the squires to the sergeants, the sergeants to the archers and grooms. In a word, the rich gave to the poor; but the poor soon became enriched by the gains of the conquest; and thus, among these classes of combatants, great fluctuations took place, because the chances of war rapidly advanced men from the lowest ranks to the highest.

Men who had crossed the sea in the quilted frocks and with the dark wooden bow of foot soldiers, appeared upon war-horses and girded with the knightly baldric, to the eyes of the new recruits who crossed the sea after them. He who had came over a poor knight, soon had his own banner and his company of men-at-arms, whose rallying cry was his name. The drovers of Normandy and weavers of Flanders, with a little courage and good fortune, soon became in England great men, illustrious barons; and their names, base or obscure on one side of the Channel, were noble and glorious on the other.

"Would you know," says an ancient roll in the French language, "what are the names of the great men who crossed the sea with the conqueror, William the Vigorous? Here are their surnames as we find them written, but without their baptismal names, which are often wanting or are changed; they are, Mandeville and Dandeville; Omfreville and Domfreville; Bouteville and Estouteville; Mohun and Bohun; Biset and Basset; Malin and Malvoisin. . . . " All the other names are in like manner arranged so as to assist the memory, by the rhythm and alliteration. Several of the same kind have been preserved to our days; they were found written upon great pages of vellum, in the archives of churches, and decorated with the title of Book of the Conquerors. In one of these lists, the names are arranged in groups of three: Bastard, Brassard, Baynard; Bigot, Bagot, Talbot; Toret, Trivet, Bouet; Lucy, Lacy, Percy. . . . . Another catalogue of the conquerors of England, long preserved in the treasury of Battle abbey, contained names singularly low and fantastic, as Bonvilain and Boutevilain, Trousselot and Troussebout, L'Engayne and Longue Epée, Œil-de-bœuf and Front-de-bœuf. . . . . . Lastly, several authentic documents designate as Norman knights in England, a Guillaume le charretier, a Hugues le tailleur, a Guillaume le tambour; and among the surnames of the chivalry collected from every corner of Gaul, figure a great many mere names of towns and districts—Saint-Quentin, Saint-Maur, Saint-Denis, Saint-Malo, Tournai, Verdun, Fismes, Chalons, Chaunes, Etampes, Rochefort, La Rochelle, Cahors, Champagne, Gascogne. . . . Such were the men who assumed in England the titles of nobleman and gentleman, and planted it there by force of arms, for themselves and their descendants.

The mere valet of the Norman man-at-arms, his groom, his lance-bearer, became gentleman on the soil of England; they were all at once nobles by the side of the Saxon, once rich and noble himself, but now bending beneath the sword of the foreigner, driven from the home of his ancestors, having nowhere to lay his head. This natural and general nobility of all the conquerors at large, increased in proportion to the personal authority or importance of individuals. After the nobility of the Norman king, came that of the provincial governor, who assumed the title of count or earl; after the nobility of the count came that of his lieutenant, called vice-count or viscount; and then that of the warriors, according to their grade, barons, chevaliers, ecuyers, or sergents, not equally noble, but all nobles by right of their common victory and their foreign birth.

Before marching to conquer the northern and western provinces, William, ever provident, desiring to deposit in a secure place the booty he had realized in the provinces already conquered, considered that his new wealth would be nowhere so safe as in his own country. On the eve of his return to Normandy, he confided the lieutenancy of his royal power to his brother Eudes, and to William Fitz-Osbern. With these two viceroys were joined other lords of note, as coadjutors and councillors: Hugh de Grantmesnil, Hugh de Montfort, Walter Giffard, and William de Garenne (Warrenne.) The new king proceeded to Pevensey, to embark from the same spot on which, six months before, he had landed. Several vessels awaited him there, decorated in token of joy and triumph. A great number of English had repaired thither, by his order, to cross the Channel with him. Among them were king Edgar, archbishop Stigand, Frithrik, abbot of Saint Albans, the two brothers Edwin and Morkar, and Waltheof, son of Siward, who had not arrived in time to fight at Hastings. These men, and several others whom the conqueror also took with him, were to serve as hostages and guarantees for the quiescence of the English; he hoped that, deprived by their absence of its most powerful and most popular chiefs, the nation would be less turbulent, less prompt to insurrection.

In this port, where for the first time he had set foot in England, the conqueror distributed presents of every kind to those of his soldiers who again crossed the sea, in order, says a Norman author, that no one on his return might say that he had not gained by the conquest. William, if we may believe the same author, his chaplain and biographer, brought more gold and silver to Normandy than was contained in all Gaul. The whole population of the town and country districts, from the sea to Rouen, hastened to meet him, and saluted him with cries of enthusiasm. The monasteries and secular clergy rivalled each other in their zealous efforts to entertain the conqueror of the English, and neither monks nor priests remained unrecompensed. William gave them gold in money, sacred vessels, and bullion, with stuffs richly embroidered, which they displayed in the churches, where they excited the admiration of travellers. It would appear that embroidery in gold and silver was an art in which the English women excelled; the commerce of that country, already very extended, brought there also many precious things, unknown in the north of Gaul. A relation of the king of France, named Raoul, came with a numerous suite to the court held by king William during Easter. The French, equally with the Normans, viewed with curiosity and amazement the chased gold and silver plate, and the drinking cups of the Saxons, made of large horns, adorned with metal at the two extremities. They were astonished at the beauty and long hair of the young English hostages or captives of the Norman king. "They remarked," says the contemporary narrator, "these things and many others equally new to them, that they might relate them in their country."

Whilst this display was made on one side the Channel, on the other the insolence of the conquerors was deeply felt by the conquered. The chiefs who governed the subjected provinces outvied each other in oppressing the natives, the people of rank equally with the commons, by exactions, tyranny, and outrage. Bishop Eudes and Fitz-Osbern, inflated with their new power, scorned the complaints of the oppressed people, and refused all remedy; if their soldiers pillaged the houses or violated the wives of the English, they applauded them, and punished the unfortunate sufferers who dared to complain. Excess of suffering drove the people of the eastern coast to attempt the emancipation of themselves from the Normans by the aid of a foreign power. Eustache, count of Boulogne, the same who in the reign of Edward had occasioned such tumult in England, was now at enmity with king William, who kept his son prisoner. Eustache was renowned for his military skill, and, besides, his connexion with king Edward caused the Anglo-Saxons to regard him as a natural ally.

The people of Kent therefore sent a message to Eustache, and promised to assist him to take Dover, if he would make a descent and succour them against the Normans. The count of Boulogne consented, and landed near Dover under favour of a dark night. All the Saxons of the district took up arms: Eudes de Bayeux and Hugh de Montfort, the two governors of the town, had gone beyond the Thames with part of their troops. Had the siege lasted two days, the inhabitants of the neighbouring provinces would have come in great numbers to join the besiegers; but Eustache and his men, prematurely endeavouring to take Dover castle by surprise, met with an unexpected resistance on the part of the Normans, and were discouraged after this one effort. A false report of the approach of Eudes, returning, it was said, with the main body of his troops, struck them with a panic terror. Eustache sounded a retreat; his soldiers hastened in disorder to their vessels, and the Norman garrison, seeing them dispersed, left the town to pursue them. Several fell in their flight from the steep rocks upon which Dover castle stands. The count owed his life solely to the speed of his horse, and the Saxon insurgents returned to their houses through bye-roads. Such was the result of the first attempt made in England to overthrow the Norman dominion. Eustache shortly after made his peace with the duke of Normandy; and, forgetting his allies of a day, solicited the riches and honours which their enemy had to bestow.

In Herefordshire, beyond the great chain of mountains, which had formerly protected the independence of the Britons, and which might still serve as a rampart for that of the English, there dwelt, before the invasion, upon lands which he had received from the munificence of king Edward, a Norman, named Richard Fitz-Scrob. He was one of those whom the Saxons exempted from the sentence of exile pronounced in the year 1052 against all the Normans living in England. In return for this favour, Fitz-Scrob, on William's landing, became chief intriguer for the conquest, established a correspondence with the invaders, and placed himself at the head of some bodies of soldiers, emigrants from Gaul, who, since the time of Edward, had garrisoned several castles near Hereford. He visited them in these castles, and, making frequent sallies, endeavoured to force the neighbouring towns and villages to submit to the conqueror. But the population of the west made an energetic resistance, and, commanded by the young Edrik, son of Alfrik, repulsed the attacks of Fitz-Scrob and his soldiers.

The young Saxon chief had the art to interest in his cause several chiefs of the Welsh tribes, hitherto mortal enemies of the English. Thus the terror of the Normans reconciled for the first time the Cambrians and the Teutons of Britain, and did that which, in former times, the invasions of the northern pagans could not accomplish. Supported by the inhabitants of Wales, Edrik successfully assumed the offensive against Richard Fitz-Scrob and his soldiers, who are called in the chronicles of the time, castellans of Hereford. Three months after the departure of king William for Normandy, he drove them from the territory they occupied, pillaged their encampments, and delivered all the country about the river Lugg. South of this district, upon the coasts of the Bristol channel, and in the north, upon the territories adjoining the mountains, there were, at this period, neither military posts established by the Normans, nor strongholds built or possessed by them. The conquest, if we may so express ourselves, had not yet reached that point; its laws did not prevail there, its king was not acknowledged there, any more than in the north of England from Boston Wash to the Tweed.

In the midland districts the enemy's scouts freely possessed the open country; but many fortified towns had not yet surrendered, and even in the parts where the invasion seemed accomplished, the conquerors were not without alarm; for messengers, sent from the provinces where independence still reigned, went secretly from town to town to rally the friends of the country, and revive the courage which had been depressed by the rapidity of the defeat. Every day, one or more of the men most in credit with the people, disappeared from under the eyes of the foreign authorities; those who, following the first impulse of terror, had repaired to William's camp, and sworn to him the oath of peace and submission, were invited by patriotic addresses to break their compact with the stranger, and to join the party of good and brave men who aimed at restoring the liberty transmitted them by their forefathers.

The news of this agitation and these operations, reaching William in Normandy, obliged him to hasten his return to England. He embarked at Dieppe, on a cold night in the month of December, and, on his arrival, placed in the fortresses of Sussex new governors, selected in Normandy from among the men in whom he most confided. He found in London a fermentation which seemed to presage some approaching movement; fearing that his three castles, with their towers garnished with war-machines, would not suffice to protect him against a popular insurrection, he resolved to avert it, or at least defer the moment, by exercising that craft, that cunning of the fox, which the ancient historians attribute to him, in lulling the patriotic spirit which he despaired of destroying. He celebrated at London, with great pomp, the festival of Christmas, and assembling around him several Saxon chiefs and bishops, overwhelmed them with false caresses; he appeared full of affability, and gave the kiss of welcome to every new comer; whatever was asked, he granted; whatever was counselled, he assented to; and all were the dupes of his artifices.

After having thus gained over a portion of the more important class, king William directed his attention to the people; a proclamation, written in the Saxon language and addressed to the inhabitants of London, was published in his name, and read aloud in the churches and streets. It ran thus: "Learn all what is my will. I fully consent that all of you enjoy your national laws, as in the days of king Edward; every son shall inherit from his father, after his father's death; none of my men shall do you any wrong." Upon this promise, insincere as it was, the effervescence of the people of London was calmed; its solace rendered men's minds less disposed to run the perilous risks of opposing power. Exempt for a moment from the three scourges which the conquest had brought into England, outrages, foreign laws, and expropriation, the inhabitants of the great Saxon city abandoned the cause of those who were suffering elsewhere, and, upon a calculation of gain and loss, resolved to remain quiet. How long they were permitted to enjoy the conqueror's concessions is not known, but meantime they made no objection to his marching from London with his best troops, for the subjugation of the provinces that still remained free.

The Norman king first proceeded to the south-west, and crossing the hills which separate Dorsetshire from Devonshire, marched against Exeter. It was in this city that, after the battle of Hastings, the mother of Harold had taken refuge, and here she had collected the wreck of her treasures, which she devoted to the cause of that country for which her son had died. The citizens of Exeter were numerous and full of patriotic zeal: contemporary history renders to them this testimony, that, young and old, they hated with mortal hate the foreign invader. They fortified their towers and their walls, sent for armed men from all the adjacent districts, and engaged the services of the foreign sailors in their port. They also sent messages to the people of the towns around, inviting their co-operation in resisting the foreign king, with whom, say the chronicles, they had before nothing to do.

The approach of the invading army was heralded to the inhabitants of Exeter from afar, by the intelligence of its ravages; every place through which it passed was utterly devastated. The Normans halted at a place four miles distant, whence William sent to the citizens a summons to submit and to swear to him the oath of fidelity. "We shall not," they replied, "swear the oath of fidelity to the pretended king, or admit him within our walls; but if he thinks proper to receive, by way of tribute, the impost we pay to our kings, we will give it to him." "I require subjects," answered William, "and I am not accustomed to take them on any such conditions." The Norman troops advanced, headed by a battalion of English, who had joined the foreign army, either on compulsion, or from utter want of other means of support, or in the idea of enriching themselves by the pillage of their countrymen. Ere the first assault began, the magistrates and leading citizens of Exeter, in pursuance of some secret negotiation, came to the king, delivered hostages, and demanded peace on terms of surrender. But on their return, the body of citizens, far from fulfilling the engagement thus made, kept the gates closed, and stood to their arms.

William invested the city, and bringing within sight of the ramparts one of the hostages he had received, had his eyes put out. The siege lasted eighteen days; a considerable portion of the Norman army perished; their place was supplied by fresh troops, and the miners laboured to sap the walls; but the determination of the citizens was inflexible. It is quite probable that they would have wearied William out, had not the chiefs again betrayed them. Some historians relate that the inhabitants of Exeter repaired to the foreign camp, in the attitude of suppliants, with their priests bearing missals and sacred vessels in their hands. The Saxon chronicle has merely these words, mournful from their very brevity: "The citizens surrendered the town, because their thanes deceived them."

A great number of women, escaping the outrages which followed upon the surrender of Exeter, took refuge with Harold's mother, first in one of the islands of the Severn, and then in the city of Bath, which had not as yet been taken by the enemy; hence they gained the western coast, and, in default of a more direct route, embarked for Flanders. Fortyeight houses had been destroyed in the siege; the Normans applied their materials to the construction of a fortress, which they called Rougemont, from its site being a hill of red earth. This castle was then confided to the keeping of Baldwin, son of Gilbert Crespin, also called Baldwin de Brionne, who received for his share as conqueror, and for his salary as viscount of Devonshire, twenty houses in Exeter, and an hundred and fifty-nine manors in the county.

During this campaign, a defensive alliance had been formed between the Anglo-Saxons and the ancient Britons of Cornwall. After the taking of Exeter, the two populations thus united were involved in one common ruin, and the territory of both was shared out among the conquerors. One of the first names inscribed on the partition roll was that of the wife of the conqueror, Matilda, daughter of Baldwin, earl of Flanders, whom the Normans called the Queen, a title unknown to the English, who only employed in their language the terms, dame or wife. Matilda obtained as her portion of the conquest, all the lands of a rich Saxon, named Brihtrik. This personage, if we are to credit the chronicles, was not unknown to Matilda; on the contrary, he had formerly, when ambassador from king Edward at her father's court, incurred her deep resentment by refusing to marry her. It was Matilda herself who requested the king her husband to adjudge to her, with all his lands, the Englishman who had slighted her; and she satisfied at once her vengeance and her avarice, by appropriating the lands and by imprisoning their owner in a fortress.

It was probably in continuation of this first invasion of the west, that Somersetshire and Gloucestershire were conquered and apportioned out. Various facts prove that this conquest was not accomplished without resistance. According to the local tradition, the monastery of Winchcombe was at this time deprived of all its possessions, because the monks, ill advised and short sighted men, as an ancient historian calls them, took upon themselves to oppose king

William. Their abbot, Godrik, was removed by the Norman soldiers and imprisoned at Gloucester; and the monastery, become odious to the conquerors, was transferred to Eghelwig, abbot of Evesham, whom the contemporary annalists surname the Circumspect, one of those men whose national treason assumes, to feeble minds, the shape "of the fear of God, and veneration of the king appointed by Him." On the first intelligence of the first defeat of his countrymen, Eghelwig had hastened to swear true faith to the foreigner, "for whom God had declared." When the conquest had extended itself into the western provinces, he solicited a share in the spoil, and, in imitation of his friends the conquerors, expelled several English from their domains; to others, he sold his protection at a heavy price, and then leaving them to be killed by the Normans, entered upon their lands. His character and conduct caused him to be distinguished by king William, who greatly delighted in him; he governed the rebellious monks of Winchcombe entirely to the satisfaction of the Conqueror, until the arrival from beyond seas of a monk named Galand, to whom he remitted the abbey.

The theatre of English independence thus became more and more limited in the west; but the vast regions of the north still offered an asylum, a retreat, and battle-fields to the patriots. Hither repaired those who had no longer home or family, whose brothers were dead, whose daughters dishonoured; those who, in the language of the old annalists, preferred a life of war to slavery. They made their way from one forest or deserted place to another, until they had passed the furthest line of fortresses erected by the advancing Normans, and once beyond this girdle of slavery, found themselves among free Englishmen. Remorse soon brought to them the chiefs who, the first to despair of the common cause, had the first given an example of voluntary submission. They made their escape from the palace in which the Conqueror had detained them captives, under a false show of affection, calling them his dear friends, his special friends, and making use of their presence at his court as a ground of reproach against the nation, which refused to recognise a king thus surrounded by its national chiefs. When Edwin and Morkar departed for the north, the prayers of the poor, say the historians of English race, accompanied them in their flight, and the priests and monks offered up fervent orisons for their safety and success.

On the arrival of the sons of Alfgar in their former governments of Mercia and Northumbria, every indication of a patriotic movement manifested itself from Oxford to the Tweed. No Norman had as yet passed the Humber, and but very few had reached the central parts of Mercia. This province maintained an uninterrupted communication, by its north western frontier, with the Welsh population, who, forgetting their ancient grievances, made common cause with the Saxons against the new invaders. It was rumoured that the English and Welsh chieftains had held several councils together in the mountains, that they had unanimously resolved to deliver their island from Norman domination, and were despatching emissaries in every direction to arouse popular indignation and revolt. The great camp of independence was to be formed beyond the Humber; the city of York was to be its first bulwark, and its last, the lakes and marshes of the north. Large numbers of men had sworn never to sleep beneath the shelter of a roof until they had effected the national deliverance; they lay under the open sky or in tents, whence the Normans contemptuously designated them savages Among them was young Edrik, the son of Alfrik, who had so energetically maintained the Saxon cause in Herefordshire.

It is impossible to say how many projects of national deliverance, well or ill conceived, were formed and destroyed at this period. History scarcely deigns to mention some two or three of the men who preferred war to servitude; the same power which defeated their efforts, effaced the memory of them. One Norman chronicler denounces, with bitter reproaches, a conspiracy, the object of which, he tells us, was to make a sudden attack upon the soldiers of every foreign garrison throughout England, on the first day of Lent, when, according to the devotion of the period, they all repaired to church, bare-footed and unarmed. The historian, while thanking God for the discovery of this abominable machination, regrets that the chiefs of the plot had, by flight, escaped the vengeance of the Great conqueror. Their flight, it appears, was directed to the northern provinces, where they were shortly afterwards joined by another fugitive, young Edgar, the lawful king, according to the political maxims of the period, by the election of the people and the consecration of the church. He proceeded onwards, accompanied by his mother Agatha, his two sisters Margaret and Christina, a chieftain named Merlsweyn, and many other good men, as the Saxon chronicle expresses it; and passed the frontier which, since the defeat of king Egfrith by the Picts and Scots, had separated England from the land of Albyn.

The invasions of the Danish pirates, though extending north as well as south of the Tweed, had not displaced this boundary. The only political result of the domination exercised for a time by the Danes over the mixed population of Picts, Britons, and Saxons, which occupied the territory between the Forth and the Tweed, had been to augment this mixture of races by a new accession of Germanic population. Hence it was, that south of the Forth, and more peculiarly towards the east, the preponderating idiom was a Teutonic dialect, interspersed with Gallic and British words, and more nearly approximating, in its grammatical forms, to the Danish than to the Anglo-Saxon. About the time when this change was gradually operating in the southern districts of Albyn, in the northern a more rapid revolution united into one state and under one authority the Picts of the eastern coast and the Scots of the western mountains, who had hitherto existed as separate nations, each ruled by its own independent chief. Their union was not effected without some violence; for the two peoples, though apparently of the same origin, though speaking a language almost identical, and naturally disposed to act in co-operation against a common adversary, were rivals in time of external peace.

The Scots, hunters of the mountains, and leading a more rugged and more active life than their neighbours of the plain, deemed themselves nobler than the latter, whom they contemptuously designated the bread-eaters. But, notwithstanding this assumed scorn of bread, the chieftains of the Scots were very desirous of extending over the corn-growing plains, the power which they exercised in their mountain land of rocks and lakes. They pursued this object year after year, by art and by arms; but the Pict nation successfully resisted them, until it became enfeebled by the incursions and victories of the Danes. Kenneth Mac-Alpin, king of western Albyn, availing himself of the occasion, descended into the land of the Picts; the bread-eaters were conquered, and the great proportion of them submitted to the authority of Kenneth; the remainder, withdrawing to the extreme north, sought to retain a king of their own nation and their own choice, but they failed in this object; and Kenneth, king of the Scots, became king of all Albyn, which thenceforward bore the name of Scotland. The nation of the Picts lost its name in its incorporation with the Scots; but it does not appear that the fusion was effected on unequal terms, as would, doubtless, have been the case, had the conquerors and the conquered been of different race. The latter had not to undergo any slavery, any political degradation; serfage, the ordinary result of foreign conquest in the middle ages, was not established in Scotland. Ere long there existed north of the Forth but one people, and it early became a fruitless attempt to seek the traces of the idiom which the Picts had spoken in the time of their independence. The kings of the victors, quitting their native mountains, came to dwell with the vanquished at Dunfermline and at Scone. They brought with them the consecrated stone chair in which, according to an ancient custom, they sat at their inauguration, to take the accustomed oath to the people, and to which an ancient national superstition attached the fate of the Scottish race.

At the period of the Norman invasion of England, there remained not the slightest vestige of the original separation of the Scottish Gael into two distinct populations; the only national division observable in the kingdom of Scotland was that between the men who spoke the Gaelic language, called also Erse, i.e. Irish, and the descendants of the Teutonic colonists, whose idiom was alike intelligible to the English, the Danes, and the Germans. This population, the nearest to England, though called Scottish by the English, had much closer affinity with the latter people (from the resemblance of languages and the community of origin) than with the Scots of Gaelic race. These, who combined with a somewhat savage pride, habits of independence derived from their organization in separate clans or tribes, had frequent disputes with the Teutonic population of the southern plains, and even with the kings of Scotland. The latter almost invariably found the southern Scots disposed to aid them in their projects against the liberty of the clans; and thus the instinctive enmity of these two races, fruit of the diversity of origin and language, turned to the profit of royal despotism. This experience, more than once highly profitable to the successors of Kenneth Mac-Alpin, gave them a great affection for the lowlanders of Scotland, and generally for men of English origin; they preferred these strangers to the men who descended from the same ancestry with themselves; they favoured, to their utmost ability, the Scots by name, at the expense of the Scots by race, and received with earnest cordiality every immigrant from England.

It was this political tendency which induced the Scottish king Malcolm, surnamed Kenmore, to receive as welcome and honoured guests the youthful Edgar, his relatives, and his friends. He saluted Edgar as the true and lawful king of the English, and proffered him a secure asylum and succours wherewith to raise his fallen fortunes. He gave to all the expatriated and dispossessed chiefs who accompanied their king, offices and estates, taken despotically, in all probability, from his own British or Gaelic subjects, and he himself espoused Edgar's youngest sister Margaret. This princess was not acquainted with the Gaelic tongue, so that she had frequent occasion for an interpreter when she conversed with the chieftains of the northern and western tribes, and with the bishops of those districts; her interpreter was her husband Malcolm, equally versed in both idioms, though after his reign the kings of Scotland disdained to speak or even to know the language of the ancient Scots, of the people from whom they descended, and from whose name was derived that of the country.

The news of the alliance formed between the Saxons and the king of Scotland, and the hostile assemblages formed in the north of England, determined William not to await an attack, but energetically to assume the offensive. His first military operation in this new expedition was the siege of Oxford. The citizens resisted the foreign king, and insulted him from their ramparts; but a portion of the wall having been sapped, gave way, and the Normans entering by the breach, avenged themselves upon the inhabitants by fire and massacre. Of seven hundred and twenty houses, nearly four hundred were destroyed. The monks of St. Frideswide's abbey, following the example of their brethren of Hide and Winchcomb, took up arms to defend their monastery, and, as a consequence, were all expelled from it after the victory of the Normans. Warwick was next taken, then Leicester, which was utterly destroyed, with its castle and its church; then Derby, one-third of which was in like manner demolished. After the siege and capture of Nottingham, a strong citadel was erected there, and confided to the keeping of the Norman, William Peverel. This William had for his share of the conquest, fifty-five manors in Nottinghamshire, and in the town itself forty-eight houses belonging to English merchants, twelve the property of soldiers, and eight taken from agriculturists. He fixed his own abode in Derbyshire, on a peaked rock, where his castle seemed suspended in the air, as it were the nest of a bird of prey.

From Nottingham the Norman troops proceeded eastward to Lincoln, which they compelled to capitulate and to give hostages. Here, besides seventy-four other houses destroyed, an hundred and ninety-six were demolished to make room for a citadel and other fortifications, with which the foreigners here surrounded themselves more carefully than elsewhere; for in this town, the population of which was of Danish origin, the conquerors, as at Norwich, feared an attack from the transmarine Danes. Among the Lincoln hostages imprisoned in the Norman fortresses as guarantees of the peace of the county, was a young man named Thurgot, of Danish origin, who succeeded in opening his prison, gaining over his keepers with the aid of money. He went secretly to the port of Grimsby, at the mouth of the Humber, to some Norwegian merchants, whose vessel was about to sail. It happened that this vessel had been detained, awaiting certain ambassadors, whom the conqueror had resolved to send into the north, to dissuade the kings of those parts from interesting themselves in the Saxon cause, or lending it any assistance. The Norwegians unhesitatingly received the young fugitive, and concealed him in the hold of their vessel so effectually, that the Norman coast inspectors, who visited it at the moment of departure, suspected nothing. The ambassadors embarked, and when they had lost sight of land, the hostage suddenly appeared, to their great astonishment. They desired the sailors to return, that they might, as they said, restore the fugitive to king William; but the Norwegians answered, mockingly: "The wind is too favourable, the vessel sails well; it were pity to baulk her." The dispute grew so warm, that the two parties came to blows, but the sailors were the strongest; and as the vessel advanced into the open sea, the Normans became more tractable.

On leaving Lincoln, which, by a kind of French euphony, they called Nicole, the invading troops marched upon York; at the spot where the rivers unite whose junction forms the Humber, they met the confederate army of Anglo-Saxons and Welsh. Here, as at the battle of Hastings, by the superiority of their numbers, and by their armour, they drove the enemy from his position, though defended inch by inch. Many of the English perished; the survivors sought refuge within the walls of York; but the conquerors, following close upon them, made a breach in the wall and entered the city, killing all, say the chroniclers, from the child in arms to the old men. The wreck of the patriot army (or as the Norman historians designated it, the army of factious robbers), descended the Humber in boats, and then went northward to Scotland, or the English territory adjoining Scotland. Here the conquered men of York rallied: "Hither retired," says an old chronicler, "Edwin and Morkar, the noble chiefs, and other men of distinction, bishops, priests, men of every rank, sad to find their cause the weakest, but not resigned to slavery.

The conquerors built a citadel in the centre of York, which thus became a Norman fortress, and the bulwark of conquest in the north. Its towers, garrisoned by five hundred men, completely armed, having several thousand squires and soldiers, menaced Northumbria. The invasion, however, was not at this period continued over this country, and it is even doubtful whether Yorkshire was ever occupied in its whole breadth from the ocean to the mountains. The capital, subdued before its territory, was the advanced post of the conquerors, and a perilous post; they worked there night and day to complete their lines of defence; they forced the poor Saxon, who had escaped the massacre, to dig ditches and to repair for the enemy the ruin which the enemy had made. Fearing that they might, in their turn, be besieged, they collected provisions from every quarter, and stored them in the donjon. At this juncture the archbishop of York, Eldred, the same who had officiated at the coronation of the foreign king, came to his metropolis to celebrate a religious solemnity. On his arrival, he sent to his estates near York for provisions for his use. His servants, leading horses and carts laden with wheat and other provisions, were met by chance at one of the gates by the viscount or Norman governor of the city, followed by a great train. "Who are you?" asked the Norman, "and to whom are you taking these things?" "We are," they answered, "the servants of the archbishop, and these things are for the use of his house." The viscount, very indifferent about the archbishop or his house, ordered the armed men who escorted him to take both horses and carts to the citadel of York, and to deposit the provisions in the Norman storehouses.

When the archbishop, the friend of the conquerors, found himself also struck by the conquest, there arose in him a sentiment of indignation which his calm and cautious soul had not before experienced. He immediately proceeded to the king's quarters, and presented himself before him in his pontifical dress, holding his pastoral staff. William rose to offer him, according to the custom of the time, the kiss of peace, but the Saxon prelate drew back, and said: "Listen to me, king William; thou wert a stranger, and yet, God wishing to punish our nation, thou didst obtain, at the cost of much blood, the kingdom of England; then I crowned thee king; I crowned thee and blessed thee with my own hand: but now I cure thee, thee and thy race, because thou hast merited it, in becoming the persecutor of the church of God, and the oppressor of her ministers."

The Norman king listened, without emotion, to the impotent malediction of the old priest, and tranquilly silenced the indignation of his flatterers, who, trembling with rage and drawing their swords, demanded permission to punish the insolence of the Saxon. He allowed Eldred to return in peace and safety to his church of York; but this affair cast deep affliction into the heart of the archbishop, and perhaps remorse for having contributed to the establishment of the foreign domination. The destruction at one blow of his dreams of ambition, and the sad conviction that he himself was not exempt from the insults of the foreigner or from the general servitude, threw him into a slow illness, which gradually undermined his strength. A year after, when the Saxons, who had again rallied, advanced to attack the city of York, Eldred's grief and languor redoubled; and as if he feared, more than death, the presence of those who had remained faithful to their country, he prayed to God, say the chroniclers, to take him from this world, that he might not behold the total ruin of that country, and the destruction of her church.

War was still proceeding in the extremities of England,—agitation was everywhere;—all expected that the fugitives from York would return, by land or by sea, and make some new effort. The irksomeness of this struggle, apparently interminable, began to produce its effect upon the soldiers, and even upon the leaders, of the invading army; many, thinking themselves rich enough, resolved to renounce these fatigues; others considered that the lands of the English were not worth the trouble and danger of obtaining them; others wished to see their wives, who overwhelmed them with messages and intreaties to return to them and their children. King William was greatly alarmed at this increasing tendency; to reanimate the zeal of his troops, he offered more than he had yet given, and promised, when the conquest should be completed, lands, money, and honours in abundance. He caused imputations of cowardice to be diffused with reference to those who might abandon their leader, surrounded by danger in a foreign land. Bitter and not very decent jests were directed against the Norman who were in such haste to recal their protectors and the fathers of their children. But, despite all these manœuvres, Hugh de Grantmesnil, earl of Norfolk, his brother-in-law Onfroy du Tilleul, keeper of the castle of Hastings, and many others departed, leaving their lands and honours, to become, as the courtiers of William expressed it, the slaves of their lascivious ladies, at the expense of their honour as vassals to their lord. Their departure made a deep impression upon the new king; seeing in the future greater difficulties than he had yet encountered, he sent his wife Matilda to Normandy, to remove her from danger, and to give himself entirely to the prosecution of the war. New events soon justified his apprehensions.

One of Harold's two sons, Edmund, came from Ireland, where he and his brother had sought refuge, either after the battle of Hastings or after the taking of Exeter, and brought, to aid the English, sixty-six vessels and a small army. He entered the mouth of the Avon, and laid siege to Bristol; but failing to take it, returned to his vessels, sailed along the south-western coast, and landed in Somersetshire. On his approach, all the inhabitants of the country rose against the Normans, and the insurrection extended to Devonshire and Dorsetshire. The alliance of the Britons of Cornwall with their Saxon neighbours was renewed, and together they attacked the foreign troops who were stationed in this district, under the command of one Dreux de Montaigu. There were sent to reinforce these Normans the English auxiliaries, who had found it easier to join the enemy than to resist them; and, as at the siege of Exeter, they were placed in the front to receive the first attack. They were led by Ednoth, formerly one of Harold's great officers, whom William wished to get rid of by sending him against the insurgents; for it was his policy, says an ancient historian, to set these foreigners against each other, calculating to find his advantage in it, on whatever side victory might fall. Ednoth perished with many of his people; the insurrection remained on foot, and the son of Harold returned to Ireland for his brother and fresh troops.

Edmund and Godwin, sailing together, and doubling the Land's End, entered the mouth of the Tamar, in Devonshire. They imprudently ventured onwards in this territory, where the Normans, quartered in the southern provinces, had assembled all their forces to oppose a barrier to the insurrection of the west. Two chiefs, one of whom was Brian, son of Eudes, the earl or duke of Brittany, attacked them unexpectedly, and destroyed more than two thousand of them, English, Welsh, and Irish. The sons of the last Saxon king again regained their vessels, and set sail, deprived of all hope. To complete the destruction of the insurgents in Dorsetshire and Somersetshire, Geoffroi, bishop of Coutances, marched thither with the garrisons of London, Winchester, and Salisbury. He seized many men, armed, or suspected of having taken up arms, and caused them to be cruelly mutilated.

This defeat, and the retreat of the auxiliaries from Ireland, did not wholly depress the western population. The movement, commenced in the south, had extended over all the frontier of the Welsh territory; the inhabitants of the country around Chester, a country still free from invasion, marched to Shrewsbury, and joining the soldiers of young Edrik Guilda (Wild), whom the Normans called Le Sauvage (the Forester), drove back the foreigners towards the east.

The two chiefs, Brian and William, who had defeated the sons of Harold, and subdued the men of Devon and Cornwall, then marched from the south; and the king himself, leaving Lincoln, advanced with his chosen troops. Near Stafford, at the foot of the mountains, he encountered the main body of the insurgent army, and destroyed it in one engagement. The other Norman captains marched upon Shrewsbury, and this town, with the surrounding country, fell again under the dominion of the foreigner; the inhabitants gave up their arms; a few brave men only, who resolved to retain them, withdrew to the seacoast or to the mountain fastnesses. They continued the war with little advantage, against small parties of the enemy, lying in ambush in the woods and narrow valleys, for the straggling soldier or adventurous scout, or the messenger bearing the orders of the chief; but the high roads, the cities and the villages, were open to the enemy's troops. Terror took the place of hope in the hearts of the conquered; they avoided each other, instead of uniting, and the entire south-western portion of the country was once more silent.

In the north, the city of York was still the extreme limit of the conquest; the Norman soldiers who occupied this city did not seek to advance beyond it; even their excursions in the country south of York were not without danger for them. Hugh Fitz-Baudry, viscount or governor of the city, dared not venture to Selby or to cross the Ouse without a numerous escort. The Norman soldiers were no longer in safety the moment they had quitted their ranks and their arms; for bands of insurgents, who reassembled as fast as they were dispersed, continually harassed the troops on their marches, and even the garrison of York. William Malet, the colleague of Fitz-Baudry in the command of this garrison, went so far as to declare in his despatches that without prompt succours he would not answer for his post. This news, conveyed to king William, caused great alarm. The king himself hastily departed, and on his arrival before York, found the citizens, leagued with the inhabitants of the surrounding districts, besieging the Norman fortress. He attacked them with superior forces, spared no one, say the chroniclers, dispersed those whom he did not kill, and laid the foundations of a second stronghold, of which he confided the works and keeping to his most intimate confident, William Fitz-Osbern, his seneschal and marshal for Normandy and England.

After his departure, the English again rallied, and besieged the two castles; but they were driven back with loss, and the Normans tranquilly completed their new works of defence. Assured of the possession of York, the conqueror resumed the offensive, and endeavoured to extend the limits of the conquest to Durham; he intrusted this perilous expedition to one Robert Comine or De Comines, whom he invested, by anticipation, with the title of earl of Northumberland. His army was not numerous, but his confidence in himself was great, and increased beyond all measure when he found himself nearly at the end of his journey, without having encountered any resistance. He was already in sight of the towers of Durham, which the Normans called the fortress of the northern rebels, when Eghelwin, the Saxon bishop of the city, met him, and advised him to be prudent and to beware of a surprise. "Who would attack me!" answered

Comine. "None of you, I imagine, would dare to do so." The Normans entered Durham, and massacred a few unarmed men, as if to insult and defy the English; the soldiers encamped in the squares, and their chief took up his quarters in the bishop's palace.

When night came, the inhabitants of the banks of the Tyne lighted signal fires on all the hills; they assembled in great numbers, and hastened to Durham. By day-break they were before the gates, which they forced, and the Normans were attacked from every side, in streets with whose turnings they were unacquainted. They sought to rally in the episcopal palace; they erected barricades there, and defended it for some time, shooting their arrows on the Saxons from the roof, until the latter terminated the contest by setting fire to the mansion, which was burned, with all those who were in it. Robert Comine was of the number. He had brought with him twelve hundred horse, completely armed; the number of the foot soldiers and military attendants who accompanied him is not known, but all perished. This terrible defeat made such an impression on the Normans, that a numerous body of troops, sent to avenge the massacre, and who had advanced as far as Elfertun, now Northallerton, half-way between York and Durham, refused, seized with a panic terror, to proceed further. It was reported that they had been struck motionless by a supernatural power, by the power of Saint Cuthbert, whose body reposed at Durham, and who thus protected his last home.

The Northumbrians who gained this great victory were the descendants of Danish colonists, and there had never ceased to exist between them and the population of Denmark relations of reciprocal friendship, the fruit of their common origin. When they found themselves threatened by the Norman invasion, they demanded aid from the Danes, in the name of the ancient brotherhood of their ancestors; and similar solicitations were addressed to the kings of Denmark by the Anglo-Danish inhabitants of York, Lincoln, and Norwich. A crowd of Saxon refugees pleaded the cause of their country with the northern nations, earnestly intreating them to undertake a war against the Normans, who were oppressing a nation of the great Teutonic family, after having killed its king, the near relative of several kings of the north. William, who in his life had never uttered one word of the northern language which his ancestors had spoken, foresaw from the outset this natural alliance of the English with the Danes, and it was this had made him build so many fortresses on the eastern coasts of England. He also several times sent to Swen, king of Denmark, accredited ambassadors, skilful negotiators, bishops of insinuating tongue, with rich presents, to persuade him to remain in peace. But the man of the north would not be seduced, or consent, say the Danish chronicles, to leave the English nation in servitude to a people of foreign race and language. He collected his fleet and his soldiers. Two hundred and forty vessels sailed for Britain, led by Osbiorn, brother of king Swen, and his two sons, Harold and Knut. On hearing of their departure, the English waited with impatience the days which must elapse ere the arrival of these sons of the Baltic, once so terrible to them, and pronounced with tenderness names which their fathers had cursed. They also expected mercenaries from the coasts of ancient Saxony and Friesland; the Saxons who had sought refuge in Scotland also promised aid. Encouraged by their victory, the inhabitants of Northumberland made frequent excursions south of their country, to the encampments of the foreigners. The governor of one of the castles of York was killed in a skirmish of this kind.

It was in the interval between the two festivals of the Virgin Mary in autumn, that the son of king Swen, Osbiorn his brother, and five other Danish chiefs of high rank, landed in England. They boldly attempted a descent on the part of the coast best guarded, the south-east; but successively repulsed from Dover, Sandwich, and Norwich, they returned northwards, and entered the mouth of the Humber, as their ancestors had formerly done, but under quite different auspices. As soon as the news of their approach spread over the surrounding districts, the chiefs of English race in every direction, all the English in a body, left their villages, houses, and fields, to form friendship and alliance with the Danes, and join their ranks. The young king Edgar, Merlsweynn, Gospatrick, Siward Beorn, and many other refugees, hastened from Scotland. There came, also, Waltheof son of Siward, who had escaped, like Edwin and his brother, from the palace of king William; he was still very young, and was remarkable, as his father had been, for his great height and extraordinary vigour of body.

The Saxons forming the advanced guard, the Danes the main body, the patriot army marched upon York, some on horseback, others on foot, says the Saxon chronicle, all filled with hope and joy. Messengers preceded them to inform the citizens that their deliverance was at hand, and ere long the city was invested on every side. On the eighth day of the siege, the Normans who had charge of the two castles, fearing that the neighbouring houses might furnish the assailants with materials for filling up the moats, set fire to them. The flames made rapid progress, and it was by their light that the insurgents and their auxiliaries, aided by the inhabitants, penetrated into the city, and forced the foreigners to shut themselves up in their two citadels, which on the same day were carried by assault. In this decisive combat there perished several thousand men of France, as the English chronicles express it. Waltheof, in ambuscade at one of the gates of the castle, killed with his own axe a score of Normans, who sought to fly. He pursued an hundred knights to a neighbouring wood, and to save himself the trouble of a further chase, set fire to the wood, and with it burned the whole party of fugitives. A Dane, at once warrior and poet, composed on this deed of arms a song, in which he praised the Saxon chief as being brave as Odin, and felicitated him on having supplied the English wolves with an ample repast of Norman corses.

The conquerors gave quarter to the two governors of York, Gilbert de Gand and Guillaume Malet, the wife and children of the latter, and a few others, who were conveyed to the Danish fleet. They destroyed, perhaps imprudently, the fortifications raised by the foreigners, in order to efface all vestige of their passage. Young Edgar, once more king in York, concluded, according to the ancient Saxon custom, a treaty of alliance with the citizens; and thus for a while was revived the national royalty of the Anglo-Saxons. The territory and power of Edgar extended from the Tweed to the Humber; but William, and with him slavery, still reigned over the whole of the south, over the finest counties, the richest and largest towns.

Winter approached; the Danish fleet took up quarters in the mouths of the Humber, Ouse, and Trent. Their army and that of the free Saxons awaited the return of spring to advance towards the south, to drive back the conquerors, and confound king William, as the historians of the period express it.

William was not without alarm; the news of the taking of York and the complete defeat of his people had transported him with rage and vexation; he had vowed not to lay aside his lance until he had killed all the Northumbrians; but moderating his anger, he first essayed stratagem, and sent able messengers to Osbiorn, brother of king Swen, the commander-in-chief of the Danish fleet. He promised this chief to give him secretly a large sum of money, and to allow him freely to take provisions for his army from the whole eastern coast, if, at the end of winter, he would depart without fighting. Tempted by avarice, the Dane was faithless to his mission and a traitor to the allies of his country; to his eternal dishonour, exclaim the chroniclers, he promised to do all that king William desired.

William was not content with this one precaution; after having quietly deprived the free Saxons of their principal support, he directed his attention to the Saxons of the subjected districts, satisfied some of their complaints, checked the elated insolence of his soldiers and agents, conciliated by slight concessions the weak mind of the masses, gave them a few good words, and in return received from them fresh oaths and additional hostages. He then marched upon York, by long marches, with his best troops. The defenders of the city learned at the same time the approach of the Norman cavalry and the departure of the Danish fleet. Abandoned as they were, and deprived of their highest hopes, they still resisted, and were killed by thousands in the breaches of their walls. The fight was long, and the victory dearly purchased. King Edgar was obliged to fly, and all who could escape followed him to Scotland. Malcolm, king of this country, again received him with kindness, and offered an asylum to all of every class, who emigrated from the north of England.

A second time master of York, the Conqueror did not stop there; he continued the rapid march of his troops northwards. They precipitated themselves on the land of Northumbria in the very frenzy of vengeance; they burned the fields under cultivation, as well as the hamlets and towns, and massacred the flocks with the men. This devastation was prosecuted upon a studied and regular plan, in order that the brave men of the north, finding their country uninhabitable, might be compelled to abandon it, and to disperse in other districts. They sought refuge in the mountains of Cumberland, once the asylum of the Cambrians, at the extremities of the eastern coast, in the marshes, and upon the sea, where, respectively, they became robbers and pirates against the foreigner, and were gravely charged in the proclamations of the Conqueror with violating the public peace and with leading a dishonourable life. The Normans entered Durham for the second time; and their slumbers were not disturbed, as those of Robert Comine had been.

Previous to their entering this city, which was for them the key to the whole northern country, the bishop of Durham, Eghelwin, the same who had given Robert Comine the warnings which had proved so futile, had resolved with the principal inhabitants to fly to some place where, says an ancient English poet, neither Norman, nor Burgundian, nor brigand, nor vagabond could reach them. Carrying with them the bones of that Saint Cuthbert whose formidable power the Normans themselves believed they had experienced, they reached a place in the mouth of the Tweed, called Lindisfarn-ey, and more commonly, Holy Island, a peninsula, peopled more with relics than with men, which twice a day, at high tide, was surrounded by the water, and twice also, at ebb tide, again joined the mainland. The great church of Durham, abandoned and left without guardians, became the asylum of the wounded, poor, and sick Saxons, who lay, to the number of several thousand, upon the bare stone, worn out with misery and hunger.

The conquering army, the divisions of which covered a space of an hundred miles, traversed in every direction this territory, now for the first time invaded by them, and the traces of their passage were profoundly marked there. Old historians relate, that from the Humber to the Tyne, not one rood of land remained under cultivation, not a single village inhabited. The monasteries which had escaped the ravages of the Danish pagans, that of Saint Peter on the Wear, and that of Whitby, inhabited by nuns, were profaned and burned. South of the Humber, if we may believe the same narrators, the ravages were not less terrible. They say that, between York and the Eastern sea, every living thing was put to death, man and beast, all except those who sought refuge at Beverly, in the church of Saint John the archbishop. This was a saint of Anglo-Saxon race, and on the approach of the conquerors, a great crowd of men and women hastened with all their valuables to the church dedicated to their sainted countryman, that he, remembering in heaven that he was born a Saxon, might protect them and their property from the fury of the foreigner. The camp of the Normans was then seven miles from Beverly, and a report spread there that this church was the refuge of the rich and the depository of the wealth of the country. Several adventurous scouts hastened, under the command of one Toustain, to be the first at the pillage. They entered Beverly without resistance, marched direct to the cemetery where the terrified crowd had sought shelter, and leaped the walls, without heeding the Anglo-Saxon saint any more than they did those who invoked him. Toustain, the chief of the band, running his eye over the groups of English, saw an old man richly attired and wearing gold bracelets, according to the custom of his nation. He galloped towards him, sword in hand; the terrified old man sought refuge in the church, and Toustain followed him thither; but he had scarcely passed the doors, when his horse slipped on the pavement, and fell, crushing him in its fall. At the sight of their captain half dead, the other Normans turned their horses' heads, and, their imagination deeply struck, hastened in terror to the camp to relate this terrible example of the power of Saint John of Beverly. When the army proceeded on its march, no soldier dared expose himself to the vengeance of the saint, and the territory of his church, if we are to believe the legend, was the only spot which remained covered with dwellings and cultivation amidst the general destruction of the country.

William, pursuing the wreck of the free Saxon forces, advanced to the foot of the great Roman wall, the remains of which still extend east and west from the mouth of the Tyne to the Solway Firth. He then returned to York, whither he had brought from Winchester the gold crown, the gilt sceptre, the mantle lined with fur, and all the other insignia of English royalty; these he displayed with great pomp during the feasts of the Nativity, as if to challenge those who some months before had fought for king Edgar and their country. There no longer remained any one capable of accepting the challenge; a last assembly of patriots on the banks of the Tyne had been dispersed; and such, in the northern provinces, was the end of resistance: the end of liberty, according to the English; of rebellion, according to the Normans.

Upon both banks of the Humber, the cavalry of the foreign king, his counts, his bailiffs, could for the future freely travel on the roads and through the towns. Famine, the faithful companion of conquest, followed their steps; in the year 1067 it had already desolated the counties which had been invaded; in 1070 it extended over all England, manifesting itself in its utmost horrors in the newly conquered districts. The inhabitants of Yorkshire and of the territory further north, after feeding on the flesh of the dead horses left by the Norman army on their way, ate human flesh. More than an hundred thousand persons, of all ages, perished of famine in this district. "It was a frightful spectacle," says an old annalist, "to behold, in the roads and streets, at the doors of houses, human bodies devoured by the worms, for none remained to scatter a little earth over them, all being destroyed by famine or the sword. This distress was felt only by the natives; the foreign soldier lived in plenty; for him, in the heart of his fortresses, there were vast stores of provisions, and more was sent him from abroad, in return for the gold wrung from the English. Moreover, famine aided him entirely to quell the conquered; often, for the remains of the repast of a groom in the Norman army, the Saxon, once illustrious among his countrymen, in order to sustain his miserable life, came to sell himself and his whole family to perpetual slavery. The act of sale was registered upon the blank page of some missal, where may still be found, half effaced, and serving as a theme for the sagacity of the antiquaries, these monuments of the wretchedness of a bygone period.

The territory on both sides of the Humber, devastated as it lay, was partitioned out among the conquerors with the same order which had regulated the division of the southern countries. Several allotments were drawn out of the houses, or rather the ruins of York; for in the two sieges which this city had suffered, it was so devastated that, several centuries afterwards, the foundations of the ancient suburbs were still seen in the open country, more than a mile distant. King William appropriated the greater number of the houses which remained standing; the Norman chiefs shared the rest, with the churches, shops, and even the butchers' stalls, which they then let out. William de Warenne had twenty-eight villages in Yorkshire alone, and William de Percy more than eighty manors. Most of these domains, in the list drawn up fifteen years after, had for their description these simple words: waste-land. A property which, in the time of king Edward, had produced sixty pounds rent, produced less than five in the hands of its foreign possessor, and upon a domain in which two Englishmen of rank had lived at their ease, there were found after the conquest only two wretched serfs, scarce able to render their Norman lord a tenth of the revenue of the ancient free cultivators.

Vast districts of land, north of York, were the portion of the Breton Allan, whom the Normans called Alain, and whom his countrymen in their Celtic tongue surnamed Fergan, that is, the Red. This Alain constructed a strong castle and works of defence, near his principal manor, called Ghilling, on a steep hill which was nearly surrounded on every side by the rapid river Swale. This fortress, says an old narrative, was designed to protect him and his men from the attacks of the disinherited English. Like most of the other captains of the conquering army, he gave a French name to the castle which became his dwelling, calling it Richemont, from its raised situation, commanding the surrounding country.

The entire island, formed by the ocean and the rivers at the easternmost point of Yorkshire, was the share of Dreux Bruere, a captain of Flemish auxiliaries. This man married one of William's relations, and killed her in a fit of passion; but ere tidings of the murder were circulated, he hastened to the king, and asked him to give him money in exchange for his lands, for that he wished to return to Flanders. William gave the Fleming the sum he required, and did not learn until afterwards the reason of his abrupt departure. The island of Holderness then became the property of Eudes de Champagne, who afterwards married the conqueror's maternal sister. When the wife of Eudes had given birth to a son, he told the king that his island was not fertile, that it produced nothing but oats, and begged him to grant him some land capable of producing wheat, wherewith to support the child. King William, say the ancient acts, gave him the entire town of Bytham, in Lincolnshire.

Not far from this island of Holderness, on the banks of the Humber, Gamel Fitz-Quetel, who had come from Meaux in France, with a troop of men of the same town, took a certain portion of land, where he fixed his abode and that of his companions. They, wishing to attach to their new habitation a remembrance of their native town, gave it the name of Meaux, and this name remained for some centuries that of an abbey founded in the same place. Gamel, chief of the Meaux adventurers, and possessor of the principal manor of their little colony, negotiated with the Norman chiefs who occupied the neighbouring lands, in order that their respective possessions might be immutably determined. Several conferences, or parliaments, as they were then called, were held with Basin, Sivard, Franco, and Richard d'Estouteville. All by common accord measured their portions of land and set up marks, "so that," says the old narrative, "their posterity should have nothing to dispute about, and that the peace which existed between them should be transmitted to their heirs."

The great domain of Pontefract, the spot where the Norman troops had forded the river Aire, was the share of Gilbert de Lacy, who, following the example of nearly all the other Norman captains, built a strong castle there. It appears that this Gilbert was the first who with his troops passed the mountains west of York, and invaded the adjoining county of Lancaster, which then formed part of Cheshire. He appropriated to himself, in this county, an immense territory, the chief town of which was Blackburn, and which extended south and east to the borders of Yorkshire. To form this great domain, he expelled, according to an ancient tradition, all the English proprietors from Blackburn, Rochdale, Tollington, and the vicinity. Before the conquest, says the tradition, all these proprietors were free, equal in rights, and independent of each other; but after the Norman invasion, there was in the whole county but one lord.

King William, with his chosen troops, had not advanced beyond Hexham; it was his captains, who, penetrating further, conquered the rest of Northumbria, north and west. The mountainous district of Cumberland was reduced to a Norman county; one Renouf Meschin took possession of it, and the land of marsh and moor, called Westmoreland, was also brought under the power of a foreigner, who divided among his soldiers the rich domains and beautiful women of the county. He gave the three daughters of Simon Thorn, proprietor of the two manors of Elreton and Todewick, one to Onfroy, his squire, another to Raoul Tortesmains, and the third to one Guillaume de Saint Paul. In Northumberland proper, Ivo de Vescy took the town of Alnwick, with the granddaughter and all the inheritance of a Saxon who had fallen at Hastings. Robert de Brus obtained by conquest, say the ancient acts, several hundred manors and the dues of the port of Hartlepool in Durham; as a last instance of these territorial usurpations, Robert d'Omfreville had the forest of Riddesdale, which belonged to Mildred, son of Akman; in token of investiture of this domain, he received from king William the sword which the latter had worn on his entry into Northumberland, and swore upon it that he would use it to free the land of wolves and of the enemies of the conquest.

When the Northumbrians, after having expelled Tosti, brother of Harold, in a national insurrection, had chosen for their chief Morkar, brother of Edwin, Morkar had by their consent placed in the goverment of the country beyond the Tees, young Osulf, son of Edulf. Osulf kept his command up to the time when the Normans passed the Tyne; he was then obliged to fly, like the rest, to the forest and mountain. In his place was appointed a Saxon, named Kopsi, whom the inhabitants of Northumbria had expelled with Tosti, who eagerly desired to be revenged on them, and whom for this reason the new king imposed on them as their chief. Kopsi installed himself in his post under the protection of the foreigners; but after having exercised his office for some time, he was assailed in his house by a body of the disinherited, led by the Osulf whose spoils he had received. He was quietly taking his dinner, expecting no attack, when the Saxons fell upon him, killed him, and immediately dispersed.

Similar instances of daring vengeance, of which the historians cite but a few, must certainly have taken place in many districts; but however numerous they may have been, they could not save England. An immense force, regularly governed, and regularly distributed, mocked the virtuous but impotent efforts of the friends of independence. The patriots themselves, with their great chiefs, whose names alone called forth many men, lost all courage, and again capitulated. Waltheof, Gospatrik, Morkar, and Edwin, made their peace with the conqueror. It was upon the banks of the Tees that this reconciliation, so fatal to the Saxon cause, took place. King William held his camp there, and there he received the oaths of Gospatrik and Waltheof. The former, who was absent and who made his submission by proxy, obtained the government of Northumbria, vacant by the death of Kopsi, with the title of earl. Waltheof placed his bare hand in that of the Norman king, and became earl of the two counties of Huntingdon and Northampton. He married Judith, one of the nieces of his new friend; but as the result will show, the bed of the foreign woman was harder for the Saxon chief than the bare ground upon which he had feared to lay, in keeping faith with his country. Ere long, king Edgar himself came for the second time to abjure his national title and the rights which he held from the people. He was a man of little vigour of soul, who was ever led, in good or evil, by circumstances and by the example of others. He was not more faithful to the Normans than to England, and the wind of resistance once more rising, Edgar again fled to Scotland, amid the imprecations of the foreigners. The English, indulgent in their misery, pardoned his fickleness, and although deserted by him, still loved him: "He was young and handsome," say the ancient chroniclers, "and descended from the true race, the best race of the country."

After the conquest of the north, that of the north-western counties adjoining the Welsh territory appears to have been speedily accomplished. Edrik, surnamed the Forester, no longer stayed the Norman bands who overflowed on every side, and ceased to trouble by his incursions their settlements, hitherto so precarious, near the entrenchment of Offa. Raoul de Mortemer took the young partisan chief prisoner, and, with the sanction of a council of war, deprived him of all his estates, for having, says an ancient history, refused to obey the conquest, although several times summoned to do so. The Norman army, which reduced the population of the Welsh marches, did not stop at Offa's Dyke, but passing that ancient frontier, west of Shrewsbury, penetrated the territory of the Cambrians. This was the commencement of that subjugation of Wales, which, from that time, the conquerors of England prosecuted without intermission. The first Norman fortress raised upon the Welsh territory was built sixteen miles from Shrewsbury, by a chief named Baldwin. The people of the place called it, in the Cambrian language, Tre-Faldwin, the castle of Baldwin; but the name which the Normans retained for it was Mont-Gomery, in compliment to Roger de Montgomery, earl of Shropshire and of all the conquered portion of Wales.

The town of Shrewsbury, fortified with a citadel built upon the site of fifty-one houses, was reserved in the demesne of king William. The taxes were here received for the king's exchequer (so the Normans called that which the Romans had named fiscus). The agents of the conqueror did not demand more tribute than the town had paid in the time of English independence; but an authentic protest of the inhabitants shows the value to them of this apparent moderation. "The English inhabitants of Shrewsbury," runs the passage in Domesday Book, "say that it is hard for them to pay the whole of the tax which they paid in the time of king Edward, and to be taxed for as many houses as then existed; for fifty-one houses have been pulled down for the earl's castle; fifty others are so devastated as to be uninhabitable; forty-three Frenchmen occupy houses which paid taxes in the time of Edward; and, moreover, the earl has given to the abbey he has founded thirty-nine citizens who formerly contributed with the rest."

These monasteries, founded by the Normans in the towns or country districts of England, were peopled with monks who had come over with the foreign troops. Each new band of soldiers was escorted by a new band of tonsured priests, who repaired to the country of the English pour gaaingner, as the phrase ran. In the year 1068, the abbot of St. Riquier in Ponthieu, proceeding to the port of Wissant to embark for England, found there more than an hundred monks of every order, with a crowd of soldiers and merchants, all like himself about to pass the Channel. Benedictines from Seez in Normandy, poor, absolutely destitute, came to establish themselves in a vast habitation given them by Roger de Montgomery, and received for their table the tithe of all the venison killed in Shropshire. Other monks of St. Florent at Saumur emigrated to occupy a church which, by right of conquest, had fallen to the Angevin Guillaume de Brause. In Staffordshire, near Stone-upon-Trent, was a little oratory, where two nuns and a Saxon priest passed their lives praying in honour of the local saint, Wolfed: all three were killed by one Enisant, a soldier of the conquering army, and "this Enisant," says the old legend, "killed the priest and the two nuns, that his sister, who accompanied him, might have their church."

When the conquest grew flourishing, not merely young soldiers and old captains, but whole families, men, women, and children, emigrated from almost every corner of Gaul to seek their fortune in England; this country had become for foreigners, as it were a land newly discovered, which had to be colonised, and which belonged to every comer. "Noël and Celestria, his wife," says an ancient deed, "came in the army of William the Bastard, and received in gift from the same bastard the manor of Elinghall with all its dependencies." According to an old rhyme, the first lord of Coningsby, named William, came from Brittany, with his wife Tiffany, his servant Maufas, and his dog Hardigras. Sworn brotherhoods-in-arms, societies of gain and loss, for life and death, were formed between those who together ran the risks of the invasion. Robert d'Ouilly and Roger d'Ivry sailed to the conquest as leagued brothers, confederated by faith and by oath; they wore dresses and arms alike, and divided, share and share alike, the English lands they conquered; Eudes and Picot, Robert Marmion and Gauthier de Somerville, did the same. Jean de Courcy and Amaury de St. Florent swore their brotherhood-in-arms in the church of Notre Dame at Rouen; they made a vow to serve together, to live and die together, to share together their pay and all that they should gain by their good fortune and their swords. Others, at the moment of departure, relinquished all the property they possessed in their native land, as of little value compared with what they hoped to conquer. Thus Geoffrey de Chaumont, son of Gedoin, viscount of Blois, bestowed upon his niece Denise the lands he had at Blois, Chaumont, and Tours. "He departed for the conquest," says a contemporary history, "and afterwards returned to Chaumont, with an immense treasure, large sums of money, great stores of rare commodities, and the titles of possession of more than one rich domain."

There now only remained to invade the country around Chester, the one great city of England that had not yet heard the tramp of the foreigners' horses. Having passed the winter in the north, king William undertook in person this last expedition; but as he was about to leave York, loud murmurs arose in his army. The reduction of Northumberland had fatigued the conquerors, and they foresaw in the invasion of the shores of the western sea and of the river Dee, still greater fatigues. Exaggerated accounts of the ruggedness of the country and the determined ferocity of the inhabitants, circulated among the soldiers. The maladie du pays was felt by the Angevin and Breton auxiliaries, as, the year before, it had attacked the Normans, and they in their turn loudly complained of the severity of the service, more intolerable, they said, than slavery, and in great numbers demanded leave to return home. William, unable to overcome the pertinacity of those who refused to follow him, feigned to despise them. He promised repose after the victory to those who should remain faithful to him, and great estates as a reward for their labour; he then traversed, by roads until then deemed impracticable for horses, the chain of mountains which extends, north and south, the whole length of England, entered as a conqueror the city of Chester, and, according to his custom, erected a fortress there. He did the same at Stafford; at Salisbury, on his return to the south, he distributed abundant rewards among his soldiers. He then went to his royal castle at Winchester, the strongest in England, and which was his spring palace, as that of Gloucester was his winter palace, and his summer palace the Tower of London, or the abbey of Westminster, near London.

Troops commanded by a Fleming named Gherbaud remained behind to keep and defend the newly conquered province; Gherbaud was the first captain who bore the title of earl of Chester; to support this title and his post, he was exposed to great perils, both from the English and from the Welsh, who long harassed him. He became disgusted with these fatigues, and returned to his own country. Hereupon king William gave the earldom of Chester to Hugh d'Avranches, son of Richard Gosse, surnamed Hugh-le-Loup, and who bore a wolf's head painted on his shield. Hugh-le-Loup and his lieutenants passed the Dee, which formed, at the extremity of Offa's Dyke, the northern limit of the Welsh territory. They conquered Flintshire, which became part of the Norman country of Chester, and built a fortress at Rhuddlan. One of these lieutenants, Robert d'Avranches, changed his name to that of Robert de Rhuddlan, and from an opposite fancy, Robert de Malpas or de Maupas, governor of another castle built upon a steep hill, gave his own name to this place, which still bears it. "They both," says an ancient historian, "made war with ferocity, and shed at pleasure the blood of the Welsh." They fought a sanguinary battle at the marshes of Rhuddlan, a place already marked as calamitous in the memory of the Cambrians, from a great battle they had lost there against the Saxons towards the close of the eighth century. A singular monument of these two national disasters still existed a few years ago in Wales, in the form of a melancholy air, without words of its own, but which was applied to many mournful subjects, and which was called the Air of the Marshes of Rhuddlan.

Old histories relate that when Hugh-le-Loup was installed, with his title of earl, in the county of Chester, he sent to Normandy for one of his old friends, called Nigel or Lenoir, which Lenoir brought with him five brothers, Houdard, Edward, Volmar, Horsuin and Volfar, among whom Hugh distributed lands in his earldom; he gave to Lenoir the town of Halton, near the Mersey, and made him his constable and hereditary marshal, that is to say, that whenever the earl of Chester should go to war, Lenoir and his heirs, in going, were to march at the head of the army, and, in returning, at the extreme rear. They had for their share in the division of the spoils taken from the Welsh all four legged beasts of more than one colour. In time of peace, they exercised high justice in the district of Halton, and received all fines; their followers had the privilege of pre-emption in Chester market before all other persons, except the servants of the earl, when these presented themselves first. Besides these prerogatives, the constable Lenoir obtained for himself and his heirs the highway and street tolls at Chester fairs, the market dues throughout Halton, all animals found straying in that district, and lastly, the right of stallage, or the liberty of selling, free from all tax or toll, every kind of merchandise, except salt and horses.

Houdard, the elder of the five brothers, was to Lenoir much the same that the latter was to earl Hugh; he was hereditary seneschal of the constablery of Halton. Lenoir, his lord, gave him for his service and homage, the lands of Weston and Ashton. He had, as war profit, all the bulls taken from the Welsh, and the best ox, as recompense for the man-at-arms who bore his banner. Edward, the second brother, received from the constable as much land in Weston as an ox could plough in two days; two others, Volmar and Horsuin, received a domain in the village of Runcorn; and the fifth, Volfar, who was a priest, obtained the church of Runcorn.

These singular details are of little interest in themselves; but they may aid the reader in forming an idea of the varied scenes of the conquest, and investing, with their original colours, the facts of greater importance. All these arrangements, all the divisions of possessions and offices which took place in Cheshire between the Norman governor, the first lieutenant of this governor, and the five companions of the lieutenant, give a true and vivid idea of the transactions of the same kind which were taking place, at the same time, throughout England. When, in future, the reader meets with the titles of earl, count, constable, seneschal, when, in the course of this history, he hears of the rights of jurisdiction, of market dues, of tolls, of war and justice profits, let him call to mind Hugh d'Avranches, his friend Lenoir, and the five brothers who accompanied Lenoir; and then, perhaps, he will perceive some reality in these titles and forms, which, considered abstractedly, have only a vague and uncertain meaning. Through the distance of ages, we must make our way to the then living men; we must, as well as we can, realize them living and acting upon the land, where not even the dust of their bones is now to be found; and it is with this design that many local facts, that many now unknown names, have been introduced into this history. The reader must fix his imagination upon these; he must repeople ancient England with her conquerors and her conquered of the eleventh century; he must figure to himself their various situations, interests, and languages; the joy and insolence of the one, the misery and terror of the other; the whole movement which accompanies the deadly war between two great masses of men. For seven hundred years these men have ceased to exist; but what matters this to the imagination? With the imagination there is no past, and even the future is of the present.

BOOK V. FROM THE FORMATION OF THE CAMP OF REFUGE IN THE ISLE OF ELY, TO THE EXECUTION OF THE LAST SAXON CHIEF.

1070—1076.

Deplorable condition of the Anglo-Saxons after their defeat—Emigration to Greece of many Englishmen, who enter the service of the Byzantine court—Many other English withdraw into the forests, and by armed brigandage make their last protest against their conquerors—General terror of England—Camp of refuge—Patriotic contributions of the English church—King William orders the strict visitation of all the monasteries and convents—Spoliation of the churches—Arrival of three pontifical legates—Circulars of the legates—Deposition of Stigand, archbishop of Canterbury—Deprivation of the bishops and abbots of English race—Lanfranc, archbishop of Canterbury—Miserable condition of the English churches—Establishment of the primacy of Canterbury—Submission of the archbishop of York to the see of Canterbury—Introduction of foreign prelates into English bishoprics—Character of the new bishops—The complaints of the English conveyed to Rome—The pope sides with the Normans—Disinterested conduct of Guimond, monk of Saint Leufroy, in Normandy—The saints of English race are assailed by the Normans—Insurrection led by three English prelates—The laws of Edward are confirmed by king William—Futility of this concession—Recommencement of persecution—Paul, an abbot of Norman race—Accession of refugees to the camp of refuge—Death of Edwin—Ivo Taillebois, an Angevin chief—His character—Angevin monks established at Spalding—Herewaid, chief of the Saxon partisans—Anglo-Saxon chivalry—Torauld, a Norman abbot, transferred to the abbey of Peterborough—Fresh alliance between the English and the Danes—Retreat of the Danes—Attack on the camp at Ely by the Normans—Treachery of the monks of Ely—Defeat of the Insurgents—Hereward preserves his independence—His exploits—His marriage—Dishonourable conduct of the Normans towards him—His death—Atrocious cruelties exercised by the Normans upon the insurgents of Ely—The monks of Ely receive the punishment of their treachery—Peace between the Normans and the king of Scotland—Vaulcher, bishop of Durham—Deprivation of Gospatrick; promotion of Waltheof—King William visits Gaul—Revolt of the people of Mans against the Normans—Establishment of the corporation of Mans—Troubles of that corporation—Devastation and submission of Maine—Alliance of Edgar with the king of France—Third submission of king Edgar—English women take refuge in the convents—Marriage concluded contrary to the order of the king—Marriage festival at Norwich—Conspiracy of Normans and English against the king—Preparations to meet it; defeat of the conspirators—Proscription of Raulf de Gael, and sentence upon Roger, earl of Hereford—Ruin of the family of William Fitz-Osbern—Impeachment of Waltheof—His execution—He is honoured as a martyr—Pilgrimage to his tomb—His widow, Judith la Normande—Wulfstan, the last bishop of Anglo-Saxon race—Superstitions founded upon the national turn of mind.

The whole country of the Anglo-Saxons was conquered, from the Tweed to Cape Cornwall, from the English Channel to the Severn, and the conquered population was overrun in every direction by the army of the conquerors. There were no longer any free provinces, no longer masses of men in military organization; there were only a few scattered remains of the defeated armies and garrisons, soldiers who had no chiefs, chiefs without followers. War was now continued against them in the form of individual persecution; the most prominent were tried and condemned with some show of form; the remainder were handed over to the discretion of the foreign soldiers, who made them serfs on their domains, or massacred them, with circumstances which an ancient historian declines to detail, as incredible and monstrous to relate. Those who retained any means of emigration proceeded to the ports of Wales or Scotland, and embarked thence, as the old annals express it, to carry their grief and misery through foreign lands. Denmark, Norway, and the countries where the Teutonic language was spoken, were generally the goal of these emigrations; but English fugitives were also seen journeying to the south, and soliciting an asylum among nations of an entirely different language.

The rumour of the high favour which the Scandinavian guard of the emperors enjoyed at Constantinople, induced a certain number of young men to seek their fortune in that direction. They assembled under the command of Siward, the late chief of Gloucestershire, sailed along the coast of Spain, and landed in Sicily, whence they addressed a proposition to the imperial court, and were, in accordance with it, incorporated in the select troop which, under the German name of Varings, guarded the chamber of the emperors, and had the custody of the keys of the towns in which they were quartered, and at times of that of the public treasure. The Varings, or as the Greeks pronounced it, Varangs, were in general Danes, Swedes, or Germans; they allowed their hair to grow in the northern fashion, and their principal weapon was the great double-bladed axe, which they ordinarily bore on the right shoulder. This body, whose aspect was truly formidable, had for centuries been renowned for their strict discipline and inflexible fidelity. The example of the first Saxons who enrolled themselves in it was followed by others, and ultimately the body of Varings was almost entirely formed of Englishmen, or, as the Greeks, in their still classic idiom called them, of Barbarians from the island of Britain. The Anglo-Saxon tongue, or a dialect compounded of Saxon and Danish, became, to the exclusion of Greek, the official language of these guards of the imperial palace; it was in this language that they received the orders of their chiefs, and that they themselves addressed to the emperor, on high festival days, their felicitations and their homage.

Of the Saxons who could not or would not emigrate, many sought refuge in the forests with their families, and, if they were rich and powerful, with their servants and vassals. The roads along which the Norman convoys passed were infested by their armed bands; they resumed from the conquerors in detail that which the conquerors had taken from them in mass, and thus obtained ransom for their heritages, or revenged by assassination the massacre of their countrymen. These refugees are called brigands by the historians favourable to the conquest, who in their narratives treat them as men wilfully and wickedly armed against lawful order. "Every day," say they, "were committed infinite thefts and homicides, instigated by the innate wickedness of the natives, and the immense riches of this kingdom;" but the natives thought they had a right to recover as best they might these riches of which they had been deprived; and if they became robbers, it was only, in their opinion, to obtain their own property. The order against which they rose, the law which they violated, had no sanction in their eyes; and thus the English word outlaw thenceforth lost in the mouth of the subjugated people its once unfavourable meaning, so much so, that the old tales, the popular legends and romances of the English, have spread a sort of poetic colouring over the person of the proscribed men, and the wandering and free life they led in the greenwood. In these romances, the outlaw is ever the most joyous, the bravest of men; he is king in the forest, and fears not the king of the country.

It was more especially the north country, which had most energetically resisted the invaders, that became the land of these armed wanderers, of this last protest of the conquered. The vast forests of Yorkshire were the abode of a numerous band, who had for their chief a man named Sweyn, son of Sigg. In the midland counties and near London, even under the walls of the Norman castles, there were formed many of these troops, who, rejecting slavery to the last, say the historians of the time, took up their dwelling in the desert. Their encounters with the conquerors were always sanguinary, and whenever they appeared in some inhabited place, it was a pretext for the foreigner to redouble his tyranny; he punished the unarmed for the trouble occasioned him by the armed; and the latter, in their turn, frequently paid formidable visits to those who were pointed out to them as friends of the Normans. Thus the country was kept in a state of perpetual terror. To the danger of perishing by the sword of the foreigner, who thought himself a demigod among brutes, who understood neither prayer nor explanation nor excuse proffered him in the tongue of the conquered, was added that of being regarded as a traitor or lukewarm patriot by the free Saxons, frantic with despair as the Normans were with pride. Thus no man dared to walk alone, even on his own grounds around his own house; the abode of every Englishman who had sworn peace and given hostages to the conqueror was closed and fortified like a town in a state of siege. It was filled with weapons of every description, bows and arrows, axes, maces, poniards, and iron forks; the doors were furnished with bolts and bars. When the hour of rest arrived, at the moment of closing up everything, the head of the family arose and repeated aloud the prayers which were said at sea on the approach of a storm; he concluded thus: "The Lord bless us and help us;" and all present answered Amen. This custom subsisted in England for more than two centuries after the conquest.

In the northern part of Cambridgeshire, there is a vast extent of low and marshy land, intersected in every direction by rivers. All the waters from the centre of England, which do not flow into the Thames or the Trent, empty themselves into these marshes, which in the latter end of autumn overflow, cover the land, and are charged with fogs and vapours. A portion of this damp and swampy country was then, as now, called the Isle of Ely; another the Isle of Thorney, a third the Isle of Croyland. This district, almost a moving bog, impracticable for cavalry and for soldiers heavily armed, had more than once served as a refuge for the Saxons in the time of the Danish conquest; towards the close of the year 1069, it became the rendezvous of several bands of patriots from various quarters, assembling against the Normans. Former chieftains, now dispossessed of their lands, successively repaired hither with their clients, some by land, others by water, by the mouths of the rivers. They here constructed entrenchments of earth and wood, and established an extensive armed station, which took the name of the camp of refuge. The foreigners at first hesitated to attack them amidst their rushes and willows, and thus gave them time to transmit messages in every direction, at home and abroad, to the friends of old England. Become powerful, they undertook a partisan war by land and by sea, or, as the conquerors called it, robbery and piracy.

Every day, to the camp of these "robbers," these "pirates" in the good cause, came some Saxon of rank, layman or priest, bringing with him the last remnant of his fortune or the contribution of his church; among them were Eghelrik, bishop of Lindisfarn, and Sithrik, abbot of a monastery in Devonshire. The Normans charged them with outraging religion and dishonouring the holy church, in abandoning themselves to this infamous career; but these interested reproaches did not stay them. The example of the insurgent prelates encouraged many men, and the ascendancy which they exercised over all minds, for good as for evil, became favourable to the patriotic cause. The churchmen, hitherto lukewarm in that cause, rallied there with zeal. Many of them, it is true, had already nobly devoted themselves to their country's cause, but the mass had applied to the conquerors the apostolic precept of submission to the powers that be. The conquest had, in general, treated them somewhat better than the rest of the nation; all their lands had not been taken; the asylum of their habitations had not been everywhere violated. In the vast halls of the monasteries, whither the Norman spies had not yet penetrated, the Saxon laymen could assemble in great numbers, and, under the pretext of pursuing their religious exercises, could freely converse and conspire. They brought with them the money that had escaped the grasping perquisitions of the conquerors, and deposited it in the treasury of the sanctuary, for the support of the national cause, or the subsistence of their children, should they themselves perish in the struggle. Sometimes the abbot of the monastery removed the gold plates and precious stones with which the Saxon kings had adorned the altars and reliquaries, thus disposing of their gifts for the salvation of the country which they themselves had loved in their lives. Brave and faithful messengers conveyed the produce of these common contributions, through the Norman posts, to the camp of refuge, but these patriotic operations did not long remain secret. King William, by the counsel of William Fitz-Osbern, his seneschal, soon ordered perquisitions in all the convents of England, and removed all the money that the rich English had deposited there, with most of the vases, reliquaries, and precious ornaments. He also took from the churches, where they had been deposited, the charters which contained the false promises of clemency and justice made by the foreign king when his victory was yet uncertain. This vast spoliation took place in the Lent, which, in the ancient calendar, terminated the year 1070; and in the octave of Easter there arrived in England, pursuant to William's application to that effect, three legates from the apostolic see; Ermenfroy, bishop of Sion, and the cardinals John and Peter. The Conqueror founded great designs upon the presence of these representatives of his ally, pope Alexander, and he kept them with him a whole year, honouring them, says an old historian, as though they were angels of God. Amidst the famine which was sweeping off the English by thousands, brilliant festivals were celebrated in the fortified palace of Winchester. There the Roman cardinals, again placing the crown upon the head of the Norman king, effaced the futile malediction which the archbishop of York, Eldred, had fulminated against him.

After these entertainments there was held at Winchester an assembly of all the foreigners, laymen or priests, who had realized a great fortune by the spoliation of the English. The Saxon bishops were summoned to attend, in the name of the authority of the Roman church, by circulars, the haughty style of which was calculated to warn them what the result of this great council, as it was called, would be with regard to them. "The church of Rome," said the envoys, "has the right to superintend the conduct of all Christians; and it more especially behoves her to make inquiry into your deportment and manner of life; you whom she has instructed in the faith of Christ, and to remedy the decline among you of that faith which you hold from her. It is to exercise over you this salutary inspection that we, the ministers of the blessed apostle Peter, and authorized representatives of our lord the pope Alexander, have resolved to hold a council with you, to seek out and uproot the evil things that pullulate in the vineyard of the Lord, and to plant others in their place, profitable to the body and the soul."

The real meaning of these mystic words was, that the new king, in concert with the pope, had resolved to get rid of the whole body of the high clergy of English race; the legates gave a sort of religious colour to this political operation. Such was their mission, and the first prelate whom they struck was the archbishop of Canterbury, Stigand, the same who had marched in arms against the foreigner, and refused to crown him king. But these his actual offences were not mentioned; the decree of ecclesiastical degradation was based upon other causes, upon an honester pretext, as an ancient historian expresses it. The ordination of Stigand was annulled, first because he had assumed the archbishopric of Canterbury in the life-time of archbishop

Robert, exiled by the English people; secondly, because he had celebrated mass in the pallium of the said Robert; and finally, because he had received his own pallium from Benedict, declared antipope and excommunicated by the church.

When the friend of king Harold and of his country had been, in the ecclesiastical language, struck by the axe of correction as a barren tree, his lands were divided between king William, the bishop of Bayeux, the king's brother, and Adeliza, wife of Hugh de Grantmesnil, who, doubtless conciliated by this handsome present, came to inhabit England, and brought her husband back with her. The English bishops, to whom no canonical objection could be found, were none the less struck. Alexander, bishop of Lincoln, Eghelmar, bishop of East Anglia, Eghelrik, bishop of Sussex, and other prelates, with the abbots of the principal monasteries, were deposed nearly at the same time. At the moment of pronouncing sentence upon each, each was compelled to swear upon the gospel that he regarded himself as deprived of his dignity for ever, and that, whoever his successor might be, he would do nothing to disparage him, by protesting against him. The deprived bishops were conducted either to a fortress, or to a monastery, which was to serve as a prison. Those who had formerly been monks, were forcibly re-cloistered in their old monasteries, and it was officially announced that, disgusted with the bustle and noise of the world, they had been anxious to rejoin the companions of their youth.

Several members of the high Saxon clergy found means to escape this fate; archbishop Stigand and the bishop of Lincoln both fled to Scotland; Eghelsig, abbot of Saint Augustin, sailed to Denmark, and remained there, although demanded by the Conqueror, as the king's fugitive. Eghelwin, bishop of Durham, upon the point of leaving also for exile, solemnly cursed the aggressors of his country, and declared them separated from the communion of Christians, in the grave and sombre formula by which this separation was pronounced. But his words fell harmless upon the Norman king: William had priests to gainsay the Saxon priests, as he had swords to break the Saxon swords.

Lanfranc, that monk of Lombard origin whom we have seen playing the part of negotiator at the court of Rome, still lived in Normandy, greatly renowned for his learning as a jurist, and still equally beloved by the pope and the new king. Him the legate of Alexander II. proposed as successor of Stigand in the archbishopric of Canterbury, and William fully approved the choice, in the hope that the ability of Lanfranc would greatly contribute to consolidate the conquest. Queen Matilda and the Norman lords hastened his departure for England, where he was joyfully received by the Normans, who hypocritically celebrated his arrival as that of "an institutor sent from God to reform the evil habits of the English." Lanfranc was named archbishop by the election of the king and his barons, contrary to the ancient custom of the Anglo-Saxon church, where the prelates were elected by the body of the clergy, and the abbots by the monks. This custom was one of those which the conquest could not permit to remain, for all the religious, as well as the civil power, was to pass from the natives to the conquerors.

When archbishop Lanfranc made his first entry into the metropolis transferred to his sway, he was seized with a profound sentiment of sadness on seeing the state to which the Normans had reduced it. The church of Christ at Canterbury was devastated by pillage and conflagration, and the high altar, despoiled of its ornaments, was well nigh buried under a heap of rubbish.

At the feast of Pentecost, a second council was held at Windsor, and Thomas, one of the king's chaplains, was named archbishop of York, in the place of the Saxon Eldred, who had died of grief. Thomas, like Lanfranc, found his metropolitan church destroyed by fire, with its ornaments, charters, titles, and privileges; he found the territory of his diocese ravaged, and the Normans, who inhabited it, so saddened by the spectacle of their own devastations, that they even hesitated to settle on the lands which they had taken. Thomas took possession of all the domains of the church of York, but, whether from disgust or terror, no man, Norman or Saxon, would rent them.

The pope sent his own pallium to Lanfranc, in token of investiture, and loaded him with flatteries. "I long for you," he said, "and am only consoled for your absence by reflecting on the happy fruits which England will derive from your care." It was thus that, viewed from a distance, the hideous operations of the conquest appeared under agreeable colours. The mission of Lanfranc to England, his real and avowed mission, was to make religion subservient to the enslavement of the English, to complete, says an old narrator, the ruin of the conquered nation, by the mutual embraces of royalty and the priesthood. The more effectually to realize this object, the archbishop of Canterbury proposed to the Conqueror a new plan of ecclesiastical constitution, a plan as favourable to the ambition of the prelate as to the stability of the conquest. "It is necessary," said Lanfranc to king William, "that there should be in England but one religious chief, in order that the royalty you have conquered may be maintained in all its integrity. It is necessary that the church of York, the church of the land of rebellion, though ruled by a Norman, should become subject to that of Kent; it is necessary, above all, that the archbishop of York shall not enjoy the prerogative of crowning the kings of England, lest some day, voluntarily, or on compulsion, he lend his ministration to some Saxon or Dane, elected by the revolted English."

The church of Kent or Canterbury was, as we have already seen, the first church founded by the missionaries from Rome among the yet pagan Saxons; upon this priority in point of time had been established the vague idea of a kind of hierarchal pre-eminence, but without any effective supremacy having resulted from it, either for the church of Kent or for those who governed it. The metropolitan see of York had remained its equal, both conjointly exercising the chief superintendence over all the bishoprics of England. It was this order of things that archbishop Lanfranc undertook to reduce to absolute unity; a new thing, say the historians of the period, a thing unheard of before the reign of the Normans. He ransacked the archives for every possible privilege, however ambiguous, of every pope that had so evinced his affection for the church of Canterbury, the eldest daughter of papacy in Britain. He established the axiom that the law should proceed whence the faith had proceeded, and that as Kent was subject to Rome, because from Rome it had received Christianity, so York ought to be hierarchally subject to Kent.

Thomas, the Norman archbishop of York, whose personal independence this policy tended to destroy, was not sufficiently devoted to the cause of the conquest to agree, without opposition, to this new constitution. He requested his colleague Lanfranc to cite some authentic titles in support of his pretensions. This was an embarrassing demand; but Lanfranc eluded it by assuring him that good and valid acts and titles would not be wanting if, unfortunately, they had not all perished four years before in the burning of his church. This evasive answer terminated the dispute, aided, indeed, by certain official warnings, which the indiscreet adversary of king

William's confident received, and which signified to him that if, for the peace and unity of the kingdom, he did not submit to receive the law from his colleague, and to acknowledge that the see of York had never been the equal of the other metropolitan see, he and all his relations would be banished not only from England, but from Normandy. Thomas insisted no further, but did his duty as a faithful son of the conquest; he resigned into the hands of Lanfranc all the power which his predecessors had exercised south of the Humber, and, making a solemn profession of obedience and fidelity, retained only the name of archbishop; for Lanfranc, with the title of primate, concentrated in his own person all its rights. In the language of the conquerors, he became, by the grace of God, father of all the churches; in the language of the conquered, all the churches fell under his yoke and were his tributaries. He expelled whom he chose, replacing them with Normans, Frenchmen, men of Lorraine, men of every country and every race, provided they were not English; and it is to be remarked, that in the general dispossessing of the former prelates of England, those of foreign birth who had been naturalized in the country were spared; for example, Hermann, Guis, and Walter or Gualtier, all three men of Lorraine, who retained the bishoprics of Wells, Sherborne, and Hereford.

Most of the bishoprics and abbeys were employed, as had formerly been the property of the rich, the liberty of the poor, and the beauty of the women, in paying the debts of the conquest. One Remi, formerly a monk at Fecamp, received the bishopric of Lincoln for a vessel and twenty armed men whom he had brought, in 1066, to the rendezvous of the Norman troops. This man and the other prelates come from beyond seas—a spiritual arriere-ban—everywhere expelled the monks who, according to a custom peculiar to England, lived upon the domains of the episcopal churches; and king William thanked them for this, holding, says a contemporary writer, that monks of English race could only bear him ill will. A class of adventurers, priests in name only, poured down upon the prelacies, archdeaconries, and deaneries of England, carrying with them the spirit of violence and rapine, the haughty and domineering manners of the foreign ruler; many of them became noted for their splendid ostentation and their disorderly life—several for their infamous actions. Robert de Limoges, bishop of Lichfield, pillaged the monastery of Coventry; he took the houses and goods of the monks who inhabited it, forced open their caskets and their coffers, and ultimately pulled down their houses, to build with the materials an episcopal palace, the cost of furnishing which was defrayed by melting down the gold and silver ornaments that decorated the church. The same Robert made a decree forbidding the Saxon priests the use of nourishing food and instructive books, fearing, say the historians, lest good eating and learning might render them too strong and too bold against their bishop.

Nearly all the Norman bishops disdained to inhabit the ancient capitals of their dioceses, which were, for the most part, petty towns, and transferred their residences to places better adapted for the luxurious enjoyment of life; it was thus that Coventry, Lincoln, Chester, Salisbury, and Thetford, became episcopal towns. In general, the churchmen introduced by the invasion were a new affliction for England; and their tyranny, which assailed consciences, was even more odious than the brute force of the men of the sword. In some cases, indeed, the Norman abbots also wielded the sword, though only against unarmed monks; more than one English convent was the scene of military executions. In that governed by one Turauld or Torauld, of Fecamp, the abbot was accustomed to cry, "A moi, mes hommes d'armes," whenever his monks resisted him in any point of ecclesiastical discipline. His warlike exploits in this way became so noted, that the Conqueror thought himself called upon to punish him, and, a singular mode of chastisement, sent him to rule the abbey of Peterborough in Northamptonshire, a post dangerous from its vicinity to the Saxon camp of refuge, "but very fit," said William, "for an abbot who is so good a soldier." Delivered from this formidable chief, the monks were none the better off; for in his place they received one Guerin de Lire, who, in the words of an ancient narrative, took the last crown from their purses, to gain for himself the renown of wealth among those who had once seen him poor. This Guerin had the bodies of his predecessors, the abbots of English race, dug up, and threw their bones out of doors.

Whilst these things were going on in England, fame was publishing abroad by the pens of hired priests, or priests who wished to be hired, that William, the powerful, the victorious, the pious, had civilized that country, until then barbarous, and revived Christianity there, until then greatly neglected. The truth, however, was not wholly stifled: the cries of the oppressed reached even to Rome; and in that Roman court, accused by contemporary historians of being so venal, there were some conscientious men who denounced the revolution operating in England, as odious and contrary to the ecclesiastical laws. The degradation in a body of the Saxon bishops and the principal abbots, and the intrusion of Normans into their places, was warmly censured. But the death of Alexander II., and the accession, under the name of Gregory VII., of that archdeacon Hildebrand who, as we have seen, had displayed so much zeal in favour of the invasion, reduced well nigh to silence the impeachers of the new church founded by the Norman conquest. Her canonical legitimacy ceased to be questioned, and two individuals only, Thomas, archbishop of York, and Remi, bishop of Lincoln, were cited before the pontifical court, the one because he was the son of a priest, the other because he had bought the episcopal dignity with money.

Lanfranc accompanied them to Rome, laden with presents for the pope and principal citizens. All three largely distributed the gold of the English in the city of the apostles, and thus acquired great renown. This conduct smoothed all difficulties for them; the affair of the two Norman prelates was privately arranged, and, instead of an investigation into their conduct, there was merely an arranged scene, in which both returned to the pope, in sign of obedience, their ring and pastoral staff; then Lanfranc pleaded their cause, proving that they were useful, nay, very necessary to the new king and to the arrangements of the kingdom; and the pope answered: "Decide the affair as thou thinkest fit; thou art the father of that country; I place the two pastoral rods at thy disposition." Lanfranc took them and returned them to Remi and Thomas; then having himself received from Gregory VII. the confirmation of his title of primate of all England, he departed with his companions.

Thus the churches of the English continued to be handed over without obstacle, and by the consent of the Roman church, to priests of every nation. The prelate of foreign race delivered his homilies to a Saxon auditory in the French language, and because they listened patiently, from fear or apathy, grew elated with the power of his discourse, which, he said, miraculously insinuated itself into the ears of the barbarians. A sort of shame, and the desire to exhibit to the Christian world something different from this ridiculous spectacle, induced William to seek some ecclesiastic whom the opinion of the period extolled, from afar, for the austerity of his monastic life. Such was Guimond, a monk of the abbey of La Croix-Saint-Leufroi, in Normandy; the king invited him to cross the sea, and he at once obeyed the order of his temporal lord. On his arrival, the Conqueror told him that he designed to retain him there, and to raise him to a high ecclesiastical dignity: this is the monk's answer, if we may believe an historian only a few years posterior:

"Many motives lead me to avoid ecclesiastical dignities and power; I will not enumerate them all. I shall only say that I do not conceive how it were possible for me worthily to be the religious chief of men whose manners and language I do not understand, and whose fathers, brothers, and dear friends have died under your sword, or have been disinherited, banished, imprisoned, or cruelly enslaved by you. Search the Holy Scriptures, and see whether any law there permits the pastor of God's flock to be violently imposed on it by the will of an enemy. That which you have forcibly acquired by war, at the cost of the blood of so many men, can you without sin share it with me, with those who, like me, have sworn to despise the outer world, and who, for the love of Christ, have renounced the goods of this world? It is the law of all monks to abstain from rapine, and to accept of no share of any spoil, even as an offering to the altar; for as the Scriptures say, he that offereth in sacrifice the goods of the poor, acteth as one who sacrificeth the son in the presence of the father. When I recal to mind these divine precepts, I feel terrified; your England seems to me a vast prey; and I fear to touch either her or her treasures, as I should fear to touch a burning brasier."

The monk of Saint Leufroi again crossed the sea, and returned to his cloister; but the report soon spread that he had exalted the poverty of the monks above the wealth of the prelates; had, in the very teeth of the king and his barons, denounced the acquisition of England as plunder; and had treated as spoliators and intruders all the bishops and abbots installed in that country against the will of the English. His words displeased many who, not desiring to imitate him, calumniated him, and succeeded, by their intrigues, in driving him from the country. Guimond went to Rome, and thence to Apulia, to one of the towns conquered and possessed by the Normans.

The hatred which the clergy of the conquest bore to the native English extended even to the saints of English race, and in more than one place their tombs were opened and their bones scattered abroad. Whatever had formerly been an object of veneration with the country, was regarded by the new comers as base and despicable. But the violent aversion with which the English saints inspired the Normans was based upon political considerations, apart from their general contempt for all that the conquered people respected. In many instances, religious veneration had been, with the English, but a reflection of patriotism, and among the saints then invoked in England, several had become such for dying by the hands of the enemy, in the time of the Danish invasions; as Elfeg, archbishop of Canterbury, and Edmund, king of East Anglia. Such saints as these would necessarily give umbrage to the new invaders; for their worship kept alive the spirit of revolt, and hallowed old memories of courage and independence. The foreign prelates, accordingly, with archbishop Lanfranc at their head, did not long delay to proclaim that the Saxon saints were not true saints, nor the Saxon martyrs true martyrs.

Guerin de Lire attacked Saint Adhelm; Lanfranc undertook to degrade Saint Elfeg, by lessening the merits of his so fine and so patriotic death. "That which constitutes martyrdom," said the primate, "is the cause and not the death; I see in this saint of yours, merely a man who was killed by the pagans in default of a ransom which he could not pay himself, and with which he would not burden others." Perhaps with analogous views, and to give a new direction to the mind of the English, he seized, throughout England, the copies of the Bible, and corrected them with his own hand, on the pretext that Saxon ignorance had theretofore corrupted the text; but all did not credit this broad assertion, and Lanfranc, notwithstanding his renown for virtue and learning, incurred in his own time the reproach of having falsified the Sacred Books.

Violence done to popular conviction, reasonable or superstitious, often arouses the courage of the oppressed more than the loss even of liberty and property. The insults lavished upon objects of long-established devotion, the sufferings of the bishops, a sort of fanatic hatred to the religious innovations of the conquest, strongly agitated men's minds, and became the mobile of a great conspiracy, which extended over all England. Many priests engaged in it, and three prelates were its chiefs: Frithrik, abbot of Saint Albans; Wulfstan, bishop of Worcester, the only man of English race who retained a bishopric; and Walter, bishop of Hereford, a Fleming, the only foreigner who, a bishop prior to the conquest, had remained faithful to the cause of his adopted country. The name of the young king Edgar was again pronounced; popular songs were circulated in which he was called the beautiful, the brave, the darling of England. The two brothers Edwin and Morkar quitted the court of the Norman for the second time. The city of London, hitherto peaceable and resigned to the foreign yoke, began to be turbulent, and, as the old historians express it, in a language unfortunately somewhat vague, to face king William.

To meet this new peril, William resorted to the means he had more than once found successful, promises and lies. Frithrik and the other insurgent chiefs, invited by him to Berkhamsted, to treat of peace, repaired to that ill-omened place, where, for the first time, Saxon hands had, in sign of subjection, touched the armed hand of the conqueror. They found the king there, with his bosom-friend and councillor the primate Lanfranc. Both affected towards them an air of gentleness and good faith; and there was a long discussion upon their respective and mutual interests, which terminated in an accommodation. All the relics of the church of Saint Alban had been brought to the place of conference; an open missal was laid upon these relics, at the page of the gospel for the day; and king William, placing himself in the position in which he had formerly placed Harold, swore, by the holy relics and by the sacred gospels, inviolably to observe the good and ancient laws which the holy and pious kings of England, and above all, king Edward, had theretofore established. The abbot Frithrik and the other English, satisfied with this concession, repaid William's oath with the oath of fidelity sworn to their ancient kings, and then separated, dissolving the great association they had formed for the deliverance of the country. Bishop Wulfstan was sent into Cheshire to calm the excitement of the people there, and to make a pastoral visitation which no Norman prelate dared undertake.

These good and ancient laws, these laws of king Edward, the mere promise of which sufficed to allay insurrections, were not a particular code or system of written provisions; by these words was understood simply the mild and popular administration which had existed in England in the time of the national kings. During the Danish domination, the English, in their prayers to the Conqueror, demanded, under the name of the laws of Ethelred, the destruction of the odious rule of the conquest; to demand the laws of Edward, under the Norman domination, was to make the same prayer, a futile prayer, which, notwithstanding his promises, the new conqueror could not grant. Even had he honestly maintained all the legal practices of the olden time, and enforced their observance to the letter by his foreign judges, they would not have borne their former fruits. There was an entire error in terms in the demand thus made by the English nation; for it was not the absence of its ancient criminal or civil laws that rendered its situation so disastrous, but the destruction of its independence and of its existence as a nation. Neither William nor his successors ever manifested any particular hatred to the Saxon legislation, civil or criminal; they allowed it to be observed in various points, and the Saxons were none the better for this concession. They left the rates of fines for theft and murder committed upon the English to vary as before the conquest, according to the division of the great provinces; they allowed the Saxon, accused of murder or robbery, to justify himself, as by the old custom, by the ordeal of red hot iron and boiling water; while the Frenchman, accused by a Saxon, appealed to single combat, or if the accused declined the combat, freed himself by oath, according to the law of Normandy. This difference of procedure, operating altogether against the conquered population, did not disappear until a century and a half later, when the decrees of the Roman church had everywhere prohibited the ordeal of fire and water.

Moreover, among the ancient Saxon laws there were some which were especially favourable to the conquest; such as that which rendered the inhabitants of each hundred responsible for every offence committed in the hundred, the perpetrator of which was unknown—a law well adapted, in the hands of the conquerors, to spread terror throughout the country. As to these laws, it was the interest of the Conqueror to maintain them, and as to those which related to their private transactions, their preservation was a matter of indifference to him. He accordingly fulfilled the promise he had made to the Saxon conspirators, without troubling himself as to whether they put a different construction upon that promise. He summoned before him, at London, twelve men from each county, who declared upon oath, to the best of their knowledge and belief, the ancient laws and customs of the country, omitting nothing, and adding nothing. What they said was formed into a sort of code, in the French idiom of the time, the only legal language acknowledged by the government of the conquest. The Norman heralds then went throughout the country, announcing, to the sound of the horn, "the laws which king William granted to all the people of England, the same that king Edward his cousin observed before him."

The laws of Edward were published, but the times of Edward did not return for England, and the chiefs of the patriotic movement were the first to experience the futility of this concession. From the moment their league was dissolved, they were persecuted to extremity by the power they had constrained to treat with them. Bishop Walter fled to Wales; the Norman soldiers were ordered to pursue him into that country, over which the dominion of William did not extend; but the prelate escaped them, favoured by the forests and mountains. King Edgar, perceiving that snares were laid for him, again fled to Scotland. Bishop Wulfstan, a man of feeble mind and character, gave all the securities required from him, and thus found favour with the Conqueror; he offered the abbot of Saint Alban's to obtain pardon for him at the same price; but Frithrik was too proud to accept it on such terms. He assembled all his monks in the great hall, and taking leave of them with emotion: "My brothers, my friends," he said, "this is the hour in which, as the holy Scriptures tell us, we must flee from one city to another before our persecutors." Taking with him provisions and some books, he proceeded to the isle of Ely and the camp of refuge, where he died shortly afterwards.

King William, irritated at this flight of a man whom he thought dangerous, directed all his fury against the monastery of Saint Alban. He seized its domains, cut down its woods, and resolved to destroy it utterly. But the primate Lanfranc severely reproached him for this purpose, and, by dint of persuasion, secured the preservation of the abbey, and permission to place in it an abbot of his own choice. Lanfranc had brought with him to England a young man named Paul, who passed for his son, and upon him he bestowed the vacant abbey. The first administrative act of the new abbot was to demolish the tombs of all his predecessors, whom he denounced as brutes and idiots, because they were of English race. Paul sent over to Normandy for his relations, among whom he distributed the offices and part of the property of his church. "They were all," says an ancient historian, "men without the slightest literary culture, and ignoble in their manners to a degree which it is impossible to describe."

The reader must now turn his attention to the isle of Ely, that land of marsh and rushes, as the chroniclers term it, which was the last refuge of Anglo-Saxon independence. Archbishop Stigand and bishop Eghelwin quitted Scotland for this place. Edwin and Morkar, after having wandered for some time in the forests and country districts, also came there with other chiefs. The king, who had just succeeded by his craft alone in dissolving the conspiracy of the patriot priests, essayed craft once more, ere he employed force against the Saxons of the camp of Ely. Morkar was for the third time the dupe of his false professions; he allowed himself to be persuaded to quit the camp of refuge for the court, but he had scarce set foot beyond the entrenchments raised by his companions than he was seized and put in irons, in a fortress the keeper of which was Roger, the founder and proprietor of the castle of Beaumont in Normandy. Edwin also quitted the isle of Ely, not to submit like his brother, but to attempt his deliverance. For six months he sought aid and collected friends in England, Scotland and Wales; but at the moment when he found himself strong enough to attempt his enterprise, two traitors sold him to the Normans. He defended himself for a long time with twenty knights against greatly superior forces. The final combat took place near the coast of the North Sea, towards which the Saxon chief was retreating, in the hope of finding some means of embarking there; but he was stopped by a brook which the rising tide had swollen. Overcome by numbers, he fell; his enemies cut off his head, and carried it to the Conqueror, who was touched, and wept, say some historians, over the fate of a man whom he loved, and whom he would fain have attached to his fortune.

Such was the lot of Edwin and Morkar, the sons of Alfgar, and brothers-in-law of king Harold, both victims to the cause which they had several times abandoned. Their sister, Lucy, shared the fate of all the Englishwomen who were left without a protector. She was given in marriage to Ivo Taille-Bois, the chief of the Angevin auxiliaries, who received with her all the ancient domains of the family of Alfgar. The bulk of these were situated about Spalding, towards the borders of Cambridgeshire and Lincolnshire, in the marshy country called Holland, near the camp of refuge. Ivo Taille-Bois settled in this place; he became for the farmers of the ancient domain what in the Saxon language was called the hlaford, and, by contraction, the lord of the land. This name ordinarily signified loaf-giver, distributor of bread, and in old England designated the head of a large house, him whose table fed many men. But other ideas, ideas of dominion and servitude, were substituted for this honourable signification, when the men of the conquest received from the natives the title of lords. The foreign lord was a master; the inhabitants of the domain trembled in his presence, and approached with terror his manor or hall, as the Saxons called it; an abode once hospitable, whose door was ever open, whose fire ever lit; but now fortified, walled, embattled, garrisoned with men-at-arms and soldiers, at once a citadel for the master and a prison for the neighbourhood.

"Thus," says a contemporary, "all the inhabitants of the lowlands were careful always to appear with great humility before Ivo Taille-Bois, and never to address him but on one knee; but although they rendered him every possible honour, and paid him all they owed him and more in rents and services, on his part he had for them neither affability nor kindness. On the contrary, he vexed them, tormented them, tortured them, imprisoned them, overwhelmed them with compulsory labour, and by his daily cruelties obliged most of them to sell the little they still possessed, and to seek other countries. By a diabolical instinct, he delighted to do evil for evil's sake; he often set his dogs upon the cattle of the poor people, drove the domestic animals into the marshes, drowned them in the lakes, or mutilated them in various ways, and rendered them incapable of service, by breaking their limbs or their backs."

Some of the English monks of the abbey of Croyland lived near Spalding, in a chapel of ease which the monastery possessed just at the gates of this formidable Angevin. He made them, even more than the rest of the neighbourhood, feel the effects of his destructive mania against all that was Saxon, or that belonged to Saxons. He lamed their horses and cattle, killed their sheep and poultry, overwhelmed their farmers with exactions, and assailed their servants on the roads with sticks or swords. The monks tried the effect of supplications and offers; they made presents to his attendants; "they tried all and suffered all," says the contemporary history; "then, seeing that their efforts were thrown away, and that the malice of the tyrant and his people only increased, they took with them the sacred vessels, their beds and their books, leaving their house in the hands of the all-powerful God, and shaking the dust from their feet against the sons of eternal fire, they returned to Croyland." Ivo Taille-Bois, rejoicing at their departure, promptly sent a messenger to Angers, his native town, requesting to have monks sent him, to whom he offered a good house, large enough for a prior and five monks, amply furnished, and well provided with lands and farms.

The French monks passed the Channel and took possession of the succursal of Croyland. The abbot, who happened to be an Englishman, was bold enough to address a complaint to the king's council against the Angevin chief; but Ivo Taille-Bois was fully acquitted, and even congratulated upon all he had done in the way of pillage, outrage, and murders. "These foreigners mutually supported each other," says the ancient historian; "they formed a close league, one backing the other, as, upon the dragon's back, scale is joined to scale."

There was at this time in Flanders a Saxon named Hereward, long settled in that country, to whom some English emigrants, flying their native land, after having lost all they had possessed there, announced that his father was dead, that his paternal heritage was the property of a Norman, and that his aged mother had suffered and was still suffering infinite indignities and vexations. On hearing this, Hereward departed for England, and arrived without suspicion at the place formerly inhabited by his family; he made himself known to such of his relations and friends as had survived the invasion, induced them to assemble in arms, and at their head attacked the Norman who had insulted his mother and taken possession of his inheritance. Hereward expelled him and took his place; but compelled, for his own safety, not to limit himself to this one exploit, he maintained a partisan warfare in the vicinity of his dwelling, and encountered the governors of the neighbouring fortresses and towns in numerous engagements, wherein he signalized himself by his extraordinary bravery, skill, and personal strength. The report of his great deeds spread over England, and the eyes of the conquered turned towards him with a sentiment of hope; upon his adventures and in his praise, popular songs, now lost, were composed and sung in the streets, in the very ears of the conquerors, with impunity, thanks to their ignorance of the English idiom.

The inheritance regained from the Normans by the Saxon Hereward was situated at Brunn, now Bourn, in the south of Lincolnshire, near the abbey of Croyland, and not far from that of Peterborough and from the isles of Ely and Thorney: the insurgents of these districts did not delay to open a correspondence with the bands commanded by the brave partisan chief. Struck with his renown and his talents, they invited him to join them and to be their captain; and Hereward, yielding to their intreaties, passed over to the camp of refuge with all his companions. Before assuming the command of men, several of whom were members of the high Saxon militia, a sort of brotherhood or corporation in arms, authorized by the ancient laws of the country, he was desirous of joining that body, so as to become, to use the expression of the contemporary authors, a right war-man.

The institution of a superior class among those who devoted themselves to arms, and of ceremonies without which none could be admitted into this military order, had been propagated throughout the rest of Europe by the Germanic tribes who dismembered the Roman empire. This custom existed in Gaul, and in the Romane language of that country a member of this high militia was called cavalier or chevalier, because mounted warriors were then, throughout Gaul, and generally upon the continent, the principal strength of armies. It was not so in England; the perfection of equestrian skill went as nothing in the idea there entertained of a perfect war-man; the two only elements of this idea were youth and strength, and in the Saxon tongue, they called knit, that is to say, young man, him whom the French, the Normans, the southern Gauls, and even the Germans, called horseman.

Notwithstanding this difference, the ceremonies by which a warrior was admitted into the high national militia in England and upon the Continent, were exactly the same; the aspirant had to confess in the evening, watch in a church during the whole night, and in the morning, at the hour of mass, lay his sword upon the altar, receive it again from the hands of the officiating priest, and communicate after receiving it. Every combatant who had gone through these formalities was thenceforward reputed a right war-man, and capable of assuming any grade of command. It was in this manner that a warrior was made a knight in France and throughout Gaul, except in Normandy, where, by a vestige of the Danish customs, the investiture of knighthood took place under forms more military and less religious. The Normans, indeed, had a saying, that he who had had his sword girded on by a priest was not a true knight, but a degenerate burgess. This sneer was applied to the Saxon Hereward, when the knights with whom he had often crossed swords learned that he had gone to the monastery of Peterborough to receive the military baldric from the hands of a Saxon abbot. There was, however, in this, on the part of the Normans, something more than their habitual aversion for the rites which connected the priesthood with chivalry; they were indignant that an English rebel should obtain, in any way whatever, the right to style himself a knight equally with themselves. Their pride of conquerors seems, on this occasion, to have been more deeply wounded than their point of honour, as warriors, was with the religious ceremony; for they themselves afterwards submitted to this ceremony, and accorded to the bishops the right of conferring knighthood.

The monastery of Peterborough was at this time governed by the same Brand who, after his election by the monks of the abbey, had sought from Edgar the confirmation of his title of abbot. A man of a lofty and indomitable spirit, he had not attempted, in any way, to conciliate the favour of king William. In performing for a rebel chief the ceremonial of blessing of arms, he gave a second example of patriotic courage and of contempt for the foreign power. His fate was inevitable, but death removed him from this world ere the Norman soldiers came in the king's name to seize him; it was upon his decease there was sent, as his successor, the Norman Turauld, the fighting monk, who has been already spoken of. Turauld, bringing with him an hundred and sixty well armed soldiers, stopped at Stamford, some leagues from Peterborough, and thence sent scouts to observe the position of the English refugees, and to ascertain the exact obstacles that he should have to encounter in taking possession of the abbey. On their part, the refugees, informed of the approach of the Norman, made a descent upon the monastery, and finding the monks not at all resolved to defend themselves against the abbot and his soldiers, carried away with them all the valuables they could find, crosses, chalices, stuffs, and transported them by water to their quarters, that they might, as they said, have hostages for the fidelity of the convent. The convent was not faithful, and admitted the foreigners without any resistance.

Turauld installed himself as abbot, and appropriated sixty-two hides of the land of his church for the payment or fee of his soldiers. The Angevin Ivo Taille-Bois, viscount of Spalding, soon proposed to his neighbour, the abbot, an expedition against Hereward and the camp of the Saxons. Turauld appeared to receive the proposition with delight, but as his courage was less decided against armed men than against monks, he allowed the Angevin viscount to advance alone to reconnoitre among the forests of willows which served as the Saxon intrenchment, and himself remained at a distance behind, with some Normans of high rank. As Ivo entered the wood on one side, Hereward quitted it on the other, attacked the abbot and his Normans unexpectedly, seized them and kept them in his marshes until they paid a ransom of thirty thousand marks of silver.

Meantime, the Danish fleet, which, after having passed the winter of 1069 in the mouth of the Humber, had returned in the spring without fighting a single battle, and thus occasioned the second capture of York, had arrived in Denmark. Its chiefs, on their return, were ill received by king Swen, whose orders they had disobeyed in allowing themselves to be gained over by William. The indignant king banished his brother Osbiorn, and, himself assuming the command of the fleet, sailed for Britain; he entered the Humber, and on the first rumour of his approach the inhabitants of the surrounding country again rose, came to meet the Danes, and formed an alliance with them. But in this country, so devastated, so intimidated by military executions, there were not sufficient means to undertake an efficacious resistance. The Danish king returned home, while his captains and warriors, continuing their route towards the south, entered Boston Wash, and, by the mouth of the Ouse and the Glen, reached the isle of Ely. The refugees received them as liberators and friends.

As soon as king William was informed of the appearance of the Danish fleet, he sent, in all haste, messages and presents to king Swen in Denmark; and this king, who but just before had punished his brother for having betrayed the Saxons, himself gained over, it is not known how— for many things are obscure in the history of these times—betrayed them in his turn. The Danes at Ely received orders to return home; they were not content with simply obeying the order, but carried off with them part of the treasure of the insurgents, and, among other things, the sacred vessels, crosses, and other ornaments of the abbey of Peterborough. Then, as in 1069, the Norman king assembled all his forces against the deserted Saxons. The camp of refuge was invested by land and by water, and the assailants constructed on every side dykes and causeways over the marshes. Hereward and the other chiefs, among whom were distinguished Siward Beorn, the companion of the flight of king Edgar, resisted bravely for some time. William commenced on the western side, across the waters covered with willows and rushes, a road which was to be three thousand paces long; but his workmen were constantly harassed and disturbed in their labours.

Hereward made attacks so sudden, he employed stratagems so wholly unforeseen, that the Normans, struck with superstitious fear, attributed his success to the aid of the evil one. Thinking to fight him with his own weapons, they had recourse to magic; Ivo Taille-Bois, appointed by the king to superintend the works, sent for a witch, who was to disconcert by her enchantments all the warlike devices of the Saxons. The magician was placed in a wooden tower at the head of the works in progress; but at the moment when the soldiers and pioneers were confidently advancing, Hereward sallied out from the side, and, firing the forest of osiers which covered the marsh, destroyed in the flames the sorceress and most of the soldiers and Norman workmen who were with her.

This was not the only success of the insurgents; despite the superiority in numbers of the enemy, they stayed them by dint of address and activity. For several months, the isle of Ely was entirely blockaded, like a town in a state of siege, and received no provisions from without. There was in the isle a monastery, whose inmates, unable to endure the hunger and misery of the siege, sent to the king's camp and offered to show him a passage, if he would promise to leave them in possession of their property. The offer was accepted, and two Norman lords, Gilbert de Clare and Guillaume de Garenne, plighted their faith for the execution of this treaty. Thanks to the treachery of the monks of Ely, the royal troops penetrated suddenly into the island, killed a thousand English, and closely surrounding the camp of refuge, forced the remainder to lay down their arms. All surrendered with the exception of Hereward, who, with a few followers, daring to the last, retreated by paths into which the Normans did not venture to follow him.

Passing from marsh to marsh, he gained the lowlands of Lincolnshire, where some Saxon fishermen, who carried fish every day to the adjacent Norman station, received him and his companions in their boats, and concealed them under heaps of straw. The boats approached the station as usual; the chief and his soldiers, knowing the fishermen by sight, conceived no alarm or suspicion; they prepared their dinner, and began tranquilly to eat it under their tents. Hereward and his friends rushed, axe in hand, upon the foreigners, who were taken wholly by surprise, and killed a great number of them. The rest fled, quitting their post, and leaving their horses ready saddled, which the English seized.

This daring action was not the last exploit of the great partisan captain. He appeared at various points with his band newly recruited, and lay in ambush for the Normans, to whom he never gave quarter, resolved, says a contemporary author, that his old companions should not die unavenged. He had with him an hundred men, well armed and of inflexible fidelity, among whom were distinguished as the bravest and most devoted, Winter, his brother-in-arms; Gheri, his cousin; Alfrik, Godwin, Leofwin, Torkill, Siward, and another Siward, surnamed the Red. If one of these, says an old poet, met three Normans, he refused not the combat; and as for the chief, he often fought with seven Normans at a time. It appears that the glory of Hereward, so dear to every Saxon heart, gained for him the love of a lady named Alswithe, who had retained her large property, probably because her family had early declared for the new king. She offered her hand to the insurgent chief, in admiration of his courage; he accepted it, and then, dreading his continued exposure to dangerous adventures, she employed all her influence to induce him to live tranquilly, and to make his peace with the Conqueror.

Hereward, who loved her, yielded to her intreaties, and, as the phrase ran, accepted the king's peace. But this peace could only be a truce; despite William's oath, and perhaps by his orders, the Normans soon sought to rid themselves of the formidable Saxon chief. His house was several times attacked; and one day that he was sleeping in the open air after dinner, a troop of armed men, among whom were several Bretons, surprised and surrounded him. He was without his coat of mail, and his only weapons were a sword and a short pike, with which the Saxons were always armed. Suddenly awakened by the noise, he arose, and, unintimidated by their number, exclaimed: "Felon traitors, the king has given me his peace; if you seek my goods or my life, by God, you shall pay for them dearly!"

And at these words, Hereward thrust his lance with such force against a knight who stood facing him, that it pierced his heart through his hauberk. Notwithstanding numerous wounds, he continued to thrust with his pike while it lasted; he then drew his sword; and this weapon breaking on the helmet of one of his enemies, he still fought with the pommel. Fifteen Normans, says the tradition, had already fallen around him, when he received at once four lancethrusts. He had still sufficient strength to remain on his knees, and in this position seizing a buckler which lay beside him, he struck Raoul de Dol, a Breton knight, so fiercely in the face, that he fell back dead; but at the same moment Hereward himself expired. The chief of the troop, named Asselin, cut off his head, swearing by the virtue of God that in his life he had never seen so valiant a man. It was afterwards a popular saying among the Saxons, and even among the Normans, that if there had been four such as he in England, the French would never have entered it, and that had he not died in this manner, one day or another he would have driven them all out.

Thus was destroyed, in the year 1072, the camp of Ely, which had shed a moment's gleaming hope of liberty over five counties. Long after the dispersion of the brave men who had sought refuge in it, there were found in this nook of marshy land traces of their entrenchments and the remains of a wooden fortress, which the local population called Hereward's castle. Many of those who submitted had their hands cut off or their eyes put out, and in this condition, with cruel mockery, the Conqueror set them free; others were imprisoned in fortresses in every part of England. Archbishop Stigand was condemned to perpetual seclusion; Eghelwin, bishop of Durham, accused by the Normans of having stolen the treasures of his church, because he had employed them in maintaining the patriotic cause, was imprisoned at Abingdon, where, a few months after, he died of hunger. Another bishop, Eghelrik, was shut up in Westminster abbey, for having, as the sentence pronounced against him by the foreign judges set forth, broken the public peace and exercised piracy. But the judgment of the English, the popular opinion of his case, were far different; he was praised so long as he lived, and after his death was honoured as a saint. Fathers taught their children to implore his intercession; and a century afterwards, pilgrims still visited his tomb.

The treachery of the monks of Ely soon received its recompence; forty soldiers occupied their convent as a military post, and lived at free quarters. Every morning the butler had to distribute to them provisions and pay in the great hall of the cloister. The monks complained bitterly of the violation of the treaty they had concluded with the king, and were answered that it was necessary to guard the isle of Ely. They then offered seven hundred marks to be exempted from the charge of maintaining the foreign soldiers; and this sum, which they obtained by despoiling their church, was carried to the Norman Picot, the royal viscount at Cambridge. The viscount had the money weighed, and finding that by chance the weight was an ounce short, he formally accused the monks of seeking to defraud the king, and condemned them, by his court, to pay three hundred marks more, as a penalty for the offence. After the payment of the thousand marks, came the royal commissioners, who carried off from the abbey of Ely everything of value, and drew up a survey of the lands of the abbey, for the purpose of dividing it into fiefs. The monks poured forth complaints to which no one listened; they invoked pity for their church, once the most beautiful, they said, among the daughters of Jerusalem, and now suffering and oppressed. But not a tear flowed, not a hand was armed in their cause.

After the entire defeat and dispersion of the refugees of the Isle of Ely, the Norman army and fleet proceeded towards the northern counties, to make a sort of battue there, and prevent the formation of new assemblies. Passing the Tweed, for the first time, they entered the territory of Scotland, to arrest all the English emigrants there, and terrify king Malcolm, who had just before made a hostile incursion into Northumberland. The emigrants escaped their search, and the king of Scotland would not deliver them up to the Normans; but, intimidated by the presence of troops better disciplined and better armed than his own, he came to meet king William in a peaceful attitude, touched his hand in sign of friendship, promised that William's enemies should be his also, and freely acknowledged himself his vassal and liege-man.

William returned, content with having thus deprived the Saxon cause of its last support; on his way back he was received at Durham by bishop Vaulcher, a man of Lorraine, whom the Normans had instituted in the place of Eghelwin, degraded by them, and condemned, as we have seen, to perpetual imprisonment. It appears that the mournful fate of the Saxon prelate had excited throughout the country a violent animosity to the successor elected by the foreigners. Although the city of Durham, standing upon an eminence, was strong by its position, Vaulcher did not consider himself safe there from the enmity of the Northumbrians. At his request, say the chronicles, the king built a citadel upon the topmost height of the place, where the bishop could dwell with his people secure from any attack.

This bishop, after his consecration at Winchester, had been accompanied to York by a numerous escort of Norman knights, and, in this city, the Saxon Gospatrick, who had purchased for a large sum the government of the country beyond the Tyne, came to meet the bishop and conduct him to Durham. This service rendered to the cause of the conquest did not efface from the Conqueror's mind the fact that Gospatrick was an Englishman, and had been a patriot: no obsequiousness could remove that original stain. In the same year, king William deprived the Saxon of the dignity he had purchased, without making him any restitution, and the reason he alleged was, that Gospatrick had fought at the siege of York, and taken part in the insurrection in which Robert de Comine had fallen. Filled with the same grief and the same remorse that had formerly attacked archbishop Eldred, Gospatrick quitted England for ever, and settled in Scotland, where his family long endured, honoured and opulent. The government, or to use the Norman phrase the earldom, of Northumberland was then given to Waltheof, son of Siward, who, like his predecessor, had fought in the Saxon ranks at the siege of York, but whose fatal hour had not yet arrived.

After this series of successful expeditions, king William, finding in England prostrate depression—happy peace the conquerors styled it—ventured upon a new journey to Gaul, whither he was called by intestine disorders and resistance to his authority. The count of Maine, shut up, so to speak, between two much more powerful states, Normandy and Anjou, seemed destined alternately to fall under the suzerainty of the one or the other. But notwithstanding the disadvantage of position and inferiority of forces, the Manceaux often struggled vigorously for the re-establishment of their national independence; so that it was said of them in the eleventh century, that they were of a rugged, haughty, and disobedient temperament. Some years before his invasion of England, William was acknowledged suzerain of Maine by Herbert, count of that country, the great enemy of the Angevin power, and whose nocturnal incursions against the towns and villages of Anjou had procured for him the singular and striking surname of Eveille-Chiens (Wake-dog). As vassals of the duke of Normandy, the Manceaux readily furnished their contingent of horse and archers; but when they found him occupied with the cares and embarrassments of the conquest, they conceived the idea of emancipating themselves from the Norman domination. Nobles, war-men, burgesses, every class of the population, concurred in the patriotic work; the castles guarded by Norman troops were attacked and taken one after another; Turgis de Tracy and Guillaume de la Ferté, who commanded the citadel of Mans, surrendered it, and left the country, with all such of their countrymen as had escaped the popular vengeance.

The impulse given to the people by this insurrection did not cease when Maine had been restored to its national lords; a revolution of a new kind now broke out in the capital town. After having fought for the independence of the country, the citizens of Mans, on their return home, began to find the government of their count harassing and vexatious, and grew angry at many things which they had hitherto tolerated. At the first heavy tax that was imposed upon them, they rose, and binding themselves together by the oath of mutual support, formed what in the language of the time was called a commune.

The bishop of Mans, the nobles of the town, and Geofroi de Mayenne, guardian of the reigning count, were compelled to take the oath of the commune, and to confirm by this oath the new laws published against their own power; but several of the nobles around refused their adhesion, and the citizens, to compel them to it, proceeded to attack their castles and manorhouses. They marched upon these expeditions in parishes, the men of each parish being preceded by its own cross and banner; but despite this religious display, they fought furiously, passionately, cruelly, as ever happens in political troubles. They were reproached with carrying on war during Lent and in Passion week; with too severely and too summarily executing justice on their enemies, hanging some and mutilating others, without any regard to the rank of persons. Hated by nearly all the seigneurs of the country, the commune of Mans, at a period when these institutions were yet rare, obstinately defended its liberty. An act of treachery, which placed Count Geofroi de

Mayenne in possession of the citadel, compelled the citizens to fight in the streets, and to set fire to their own houses, to advance the operations of the siege. They did this with that valorous self-devotion which, half a century later, was displayed so strikingly in the great communes of France.

It was during this struggle between feudal power and civic liberty, that the king of England prepared to invade Maine, and impose his suzerainty upon both of the rival parties. Skilful in profiting by occasion, he ordered the enrolment of all the English who chose to serve him for pay; he calculated that, in the misery to which most of them were reduced, they would be tempted by the booty which the war seemed to promise. Men who had not house or home, the remnant of the partisan bands, and even chieftains who had distinguished themselves in the camp of refuge, assembled under the Norman banner, without ceasing to hate the Normans. They rejoiced at the idea of going to combat men who, though the enemies of king William, seemed to them, by the similarity of language, of the same race with him. Without asking whether it had been willingly or on compulsion that the Manceaux had, seven years before, taken part in the conquest, they marched against them in the train of the Conqueror, as to an act of national vengeance. From their first entry into the country, they gave themselves up, with a sort of frenzy, to every species of devastation and rapine, tearing up the vines, cutting down the trees, burning the villages; in a word, doing to Maine all the evil they would fain have done to Normandy.

The terror caused by their excesses contributed more than the bravery of the Norman knights, or even the presence of king William, to the submission of the country. The fortresses and castles surrendered, for the most part, before the first assault, and the principal citizens of Mans brought the keys of their town to the king in his camp on the banks of the Sarthe. They took the oath of allegiance to him as to their legitimate lord, and in return, William promised them the preservation of their ancient franchises, but it would appear, without consenting to the maintenance of the commune. The army then returned to England, where the Saxon soldiers landed, laden with booty; but these ill acquired riches were fatal to many of them in exciting the envy and cupidity of the Normans.

While these events were taking place, king Edgar went from Scotland to Flanders, to negotiate with the earl of that country, the political rival, although the relation of William, some aid for the Saxon cause, now more hopeless than ever; his efforts meeting with little success, he returned to Scotland, where he was surprised to receive a friendly message from the king of France, Philip, the first of that name. Philip, alarmed at the successes of the Norman king in Maine, had resolved, by assisting the Saxons, to raise up obstacles in his way, which should render him less active on the other side of the Channel; he invited Edgar to come to him, and aid him in his counsels; he promised him a fortress at Montreuil, at once near England, upon which he might thence make a descent, and near Normandy, which he might ravage. Edgar accepted his proposal, and arranged everything for his journey to France. King Malcolm, his brother-in-law, become the liegeman and vassal of William, could not, without breaking his faith, supply the Saxon with soldiers for this enterprise; he contented himself with secretly giving him money, and, as was the custom of the period, distributing arms and clothes among his companions.

Edgar set sail, but had hardly got out of sight of land when his vessels were dispersed and driven on shore by a violent tempest. Some were dashed to pieces on the northern coasts of England,

and their crews became prisoners to the Normans; the others sunk. The king and the principal personages who were with him escaped these two dangers, and returned to Scotland, having lost all, some on foot and the rest poorly mounted, says the contemporary chronicle. After this misfortune, Malcolm advised his brother to struggle no longer against fate, and for a third time to seek peace of the Conqueror. Edgar, allowing himself to be persuaded, sent a message across the Channel to king William, who invited him to join him in Normandy; on his way he traversed all England, escorted by the chiefs and Norman governors of the counties, and entertained in their castles. At the court of Rouen, where he remained eleven years, he lived in the king's palace, wore his uniform, and occupied himself more with dogs and horses than with political interests; but, at the end of these eleven years, he experienced a sentiment of regret, and returned to England to dwell among his countrymen; he afterwards returned once more to Normandy, and passed the remainder as he had passed the former part of his life, in utter irresolution, taking no determinate course, the sport of events, a man without energy and without pride.

The sad destiny of the English seemed to be irretrievably fixed. In the absence of all opposition, the calm of entire hopelessness reigned throughout the land. The foreign merchants fearlessly displayed in the towns and villages, stuffs and weapons fabricated on the continent, which they exchanged for the booty of the conquest. A man might then travel, says the contemporary history, having with him his weight in gold, and get none but good words addressed to him. The Norman soldier, more at ease in the possession of his share of land or money, less disturbed by midnight alarms, less frequently obliged to sleep in his hauberk, became less violent and less malevolent. The conquered themselves had some moments of repose; the English women no longer feared for their chastity: many of them, who had sought refuge in the nunneries, and had taken the veil as a protection against the brutality of the conquerors, becoming weary of this enforced retirement, wished to return to their friends and families. But it was not so easy for the Saxon women to quit the cloister as it had been to enter it. The Norman prelates held the keys of the monasteries, as the Norman barons held those of the towns; and it was deemed necessary for these sovereign masters of the souls and bodies of the English to deliberate, in solemn assembly, upon the question of setting free the Saxon women who had become nuns against their inclination, and solely from necessity. Archbishop Lanfranc presided at this council, at which were present all the bishops nominated by king William, several abbots from Normandy, and other personages of high rank. The opinion of the primate was, that the English women who, to preserve their chastity, had bought the convent as an asylum, ought not to be punished for having obeyed the holy precepts, and that the doors of the cloisters ought to be thrown open for all who so desired. This opinion prevailed in the Norman council, less, perhaps, because it was the most humane, than because it proceeded from the confident and intimate friend of king William; the women who had still a family or a protector regained their liberty.

About the same time, William Fitz-Osbern died a violent death in Flanders, where a love affair had involved him in political intrigues. The eldest of his sons, who bore the same name with himself, inherited his lands in Normandy, and Roger, the youngest, had the domains conquered in England, with the earldom of Hereford. He took upon himself the charge of providing for and portioning his young sister, named Emma, and negotiated a marriage for her with Rault de Gael, a Breton seigneur, who had become earl of Norfolk. For some reason or other, this alliance was displeasing to the king, who sent from Normandy an express order not to conclude it; but the parties paid no heed to this prohibition, and on the day fixed for the ceremony the bride was conducted to Norwich, where was celebrated, says the Saxon chronicler, a marriage that proved fatal to all who were present at it. Bishops and Norman barons were there, Saxons, friends of the Normans, and even several Welshmen, invited by the earl of Hereford; Waltheof, son of Siward, husband of one of the king's nieces, and earl of Huntingdon, Northampton, and Northumberland, prominently figured throughout the affair.

After a sumptuous repast, whereat the wine flowed in abundance, the tongues of the guests became loosened. Roger de Hereford loudly censured the refusal of king William to sanction this union between his sister and the earl of Norfolk; he complained of this as an insult to the memory of his father, the man to whom the Bastard, he said, undoubtedly owed his conquest and his kingdom. The Saxons, who had received from William other and far more cruel outrages, vehemently applauded the invectives of the Norman earl; and all present becoming gradually excited, there arose a tumult of execration against the conqueror of England.

"He is a bastard, a man of low birth," said the Normans; "he may call himself king, but 'tis clearly seen that he is not made for one, and that he is not agreeable in the sight of God." "He poisoned," cried the Bretons, "he poisoned Cona, the brave earl of Brittany, for whom our country still mourns."—"He invaded the noble land of England," exclaimed the Saxons in their turn; "he massacred the legitimate heirs, or obliged them to expatriate themselves." "And those who came in his train or to his assistance," cried the foreigners; "those who raised him higher than any of his predecessors have not been honoured by him as they ought to have been; he is ungrateful to the brave men who have shed their blood in his service. What has he given to us, the conquerors who are covered with wounds? Sterile and devastated tracts of land; and when he sees our fiefs improving, he deprives us of them."—"'Tis true, 'tis true!" tumultuously exclaimed all the guests: "he is odious to all, and his death would gladden the hearts of all."

One of the two Norman earls then arose, and addressing Waltheof: "Brave man," he said, "this is the moment; this is for thee the hour of vengeance and fortune. Join us, and we will re-establish the kingdom of England, in every respect as it was in the time of king Edward. One of us three shall be king, the other two shall command under him, and all the lordships of the kingdom shall be held of us. William is occupied beyond sea with interminable affairs; we are satisfied that he will not again cross the Channel. Now, brave warrior, adopt this plan; 'tis the best for thee, thy family, and thy crushed and fallen nation." New acclamations arose at these words; earls Roger and Raulf, several bishops and abbots, and a great number of Norman barons and Saxon warriors, bound themselves by oath against king William. Waltheof, after a resistance which proved his distaste for this strange association, allowed himself to be persuaded, and joined the conspiracy. Roger de Hereford hastened to his province to collect his friends, and engaged in his cause many of the Welsh of the borders, who joined him, either for pay, or out of hatred to the Conqueror, who menaced their independence. As soon as earl Roger had assembled his forces, he marched towards the east, where the other conspirators awaited him.

But when about to pass the Severn at the bridge of Worcester, he found that formidable preparations had been made to stop him; and ere he could find another passage, the Norman Ours, viscount of Worcester, and bishop Wulfstan, still faithful to king William, directed troops upon various points of the east bank of the river. Eghelwig, the courtier-abbot, who had become the servant of the foreigners against his countrymen, induced the population of Gloucestershire to obey the call of the royal chiefs, rather than the proclamations and promises of the Norman conspirators. They accordingly assembled under the banner of count Gualtier de Lacy against Roger de Here ford and his Welshmen, whose cause did not seem to them so clearly identical with the national cause. Of two parties, both almost equally indifferent to them, they adopted that which appeared to involve the least danger, and served king William, whom they hated more than death. In his absence, the primate Lanfranc, under the title of royal lieutenant, administered affairs; he hastily despatched troops from London and Westminster to the county in which Roger was held in check, and at the same time hurled a sentence of excommunication against him, couched in the following terms:

"Since thou hast departed from the rules of conduct observed by thy father, hast renounced the faith that he all his life preserved towards his lord, and which gained him such great riches, in virtue of my canonical authority I curse thee, excommunicate thee, and exclude thee from the threshold of the church and the society of the faithful."

Lanfranc also wrote to the king in Normandy, to inform him of the revolt, and his hope of soon putting an end to it. "It were with great pleasure," said he, "and as a messenger from God himself, that we should see you again among us. Do not, however, hasten to cross the sea; for it were shame to us were you obliged to come and assist us in destroying a handful of traitors and robbers." The former epithet would seem to have been directed at the Normans who followed earl Roger, and the second at the numerous Saxons in the army of Raulf de Gaël, encamped near Cambridge, or who, encouraged by the presence of this army, began to rise in the maritime towns of the east, and to renew their old negotiations with the Danes.

The king of Denmark once more promised to send troops against king William; but, before the arrival of these succours, the army of the earl of Norfolk was attacked by Eudes, bishop of Bayeux, Geoffroy, bishop of Coutances, and earl William de Warenne, with superior forces. The battle was fought in a place which is called by the ancient historians Fagadon. The Norman and Saxon conspirators were completely defeated, and it is related that the conquerors cut off the right foot of every prisoner, of whatever rank or nation. Raulf de Gaël escaped, and hastened to shut himself up in his citadel of Norwich, whence he soon afterwards sailed to seek assistance from his friends in Brittany, leaving his castle in the charge of his bride and his vassals. The daughter of William Fitz-Osbern made protracted resistance to the attacks of the royal officers, and only capitulated under the pressure of famine. The men-at-arms who defended the fortress submitted, upon condition of having their lives granted them, if they quitted England within forty days. "Glory to God in the highest," wrote the primate Lanfrance to William; "your kingdom is freed from the filthy Bretons." Many of the men of this nation, who had come as auxiliaries or adventurers to the conquest, now involved in the disgrace of Raulf de Gaël, lost the lands they had taken from the English. While the friends of Raulf were thus conquered and dispersed, those of Roger de Hereford were defeated in the west, and their chief made prisoner.

Before returning to England to enjoy this new triumph, king William made a hostile incursion into the territory of his neighbours the Bretons, in pursuit of earl Raulf de Gaël, and under this pretext to attempt the conquest of a portion of the country, the constant aim of the ambition and policy of his ancestors. But after vainly besieging the town of Dol, he retreated before the army of the duke of Brittany, who marched against him, supported by the king of France. Then crossing the Channel, he came to London at Christmas, to preside over the great council of Norman barons, and to judge the authors and accomplices of the late conspiracy. Raulf de Gaël, absent and contumacious, was deprived of all his estates; Roger de Hereford appeared, and was condemned to lose his lands and to pass his life in a fortress. In the depths of his prison, his proud and indomitable spirit often made him brave with insults the king whom he had not been able to dethrone. One day, during Easter, William, according to the custom of the court of Normandy, sent to him, as though he were free, a complete suit of precious stuff, a coat and mantle of silk, and a jacket trimmed with foreign furs. Roger examined these rich vestments with an air of satisfaction; he then had a great fire lighted, and cast them all into it. The king, who did not expect to have his gifts received in this manner, was fiercely angered, and swore, by the splendour of God (his favourite oath), that the man who thus insulted him should never quit his prison.

After having narrated the deplorable story of this son of the most powerful man next to the king, and who had most urgently persuaded William to undertake the conquest, the historian, born in England though of foreign race, touched by the misery of his native land, exclaims with a kind of patriotic enthusiasm: "Where is now this William Fitz-Osbern, viceroy, earl of Hereford, seneschal of Normandy and England? He who was the first and greatest oppressor of the English, who, through ambition and avarice, encouraged the fatal enterprise in which so many thousands of men perished; he fell in his turn, and received his just reward. He who killed so many men with the sword, died by the sword, and after his death, the spirit of discord made his son and his son-in-law revolt against their lord and kinsman. The race of William Fitz-Osbern has been uprooted from England, so that now there is not a corner in which it can set foot."

The royal vengeance extended to all who had been present at the wedding feast at Norwich; and the city itself was assailed with indiscriminating revenge. Infinite oppressions ruined the Saxon inhabitants, and compelled numbers of them to emigrate into Suffolk, around Beccles and Halesworth. Here three Normans, Roger Bigot, Richard de Saint Clair and William de Noyers, seized them, and made serfs of them, although they were too poor to be a beneficial acquisition. Other Saxons, and the Welsh, taken prisoners with arms in their hands, on the banks of the Severn, had their eyes put out and their limbs mutilated, or were hung upon gibbets, by order of the Norman earls, prelates, barons and knights, assembled at the court of the king.

Meanwhile, a fleet of two hundred ships left Denmark, commanded by one of the sons of king Swen, who had again become the friend of the English, and approached the eastern coast; but when the Danes learned what had passed, they dared not fight the Normans, and turned their helms towards Flanders. Waltheof was accused of having invited them over; he denied the charge, but the Norman woman whom he had received in marriage from king William became his denouncer, and bore witness against him. The votes of the assembly or of the court (as it was then called) were divided as to the sentence which should be passed upon the Saxon chief. Some were for death, as for a revolted Englishman, others for perpetual imprisonment, as for a disloyal officer of the king. The discussion lasted for nearly a year, during which time Waltheof was confined in the royal fortress of Winchester. At last his enemies prevailed, and in one of the courts which was held three times a year, sentence of death was pronounced. Contemporary English writers accuse Judith, the niece of the king, married to Waltheof against her will, of having desired and urged the sentence which was to widow her and to set her at liberty.

Moreover, many Normans aspired to the three earldoms possessed by the Saxon chief; and Ivo Taille-Bois, whose lands joined his, and who desired to annex them, was one of the most eager for his destruction. Lastly, the king, to whom Waltheof was no longer useful, rejoiced at a pretext for getting rid of him; if we may believe the old chroniclers, he had long entertained this desire.

Early in the morning, while the people of Winchester still slept, the Normans conducted the Saxon chief beyond the walls of the city. Waltheof walked to execution, attired in his costume as earl, the outer portions of which he distributed among the priests and poor people who followed him, and whom the Normans allowed to approach, on account of their limited number and wholly peaceful aspect. Coming to an eminence at a short distance from the walls, the soldiers stopped, and the Saxon, prostrating himself, with his face to the ground, prayed in under tones for some minutes; the Normans, fearing lest delay should spread the news of the execution through the city, and a rising take place to save Waltheof, said to him impatiently: "Rise, that we may fulfil our orders." As a last request, he asked them to await until he had said the Lord's Prayer, for himself and for them. They consented, and Waltheof, rising from his prostrate attitude, but remaining on his knees, began to say, in a loud voice: "Our Father, which art in heaven," but at the first words of the verse: "and lead us not into temptation," the executioner, whoperhaps saw the early rays of the coming day, would wait no longer, and, suddenly drawing his large sword, decapitated the condemned man with a single blow. His body was thrown into a hole dug between two roads, and hastily covered with earth.

Having been unable to save the life of Waltheof, the Saxons went into mourning for his death, and honoured him with the name of "martyr," which they had just awarded on the same grounds to bishop Eghelwin, who had died of hunger in a Norman dungeon. "They sought," says a contemporary, "to efface his memory from this world, but they did not succeed, for we firmly believe that he is in heaven with the blessed." It was reported among the serfs and towns-people of England, that after fifteen days interment, the body of the last chief of the English race, when removed by the monks of Croyland, had appeared intact and sprinkled with fresh blood. Other miracles, propagated in like manner by patriotic superstition, were operated, it was said, at the tomb of Waltheof, erected, with the king's permission in the chapel of the abbey of which he had been patron. The news of these prodigies affrighted the Norman widow of the decapitated chief. To appease the soul of him she had betrayed, and whose death she had occasioned, she repaired to Croyland to the tomb of Waltheof, and offered a silken cloth, which she placed on the sepulchre. The chronicles of the time relate that an invisible arm repelled her offering, and that men saw the piece of stuff raised and cast to a distance, as if by a violent gust of wind.

Wulfketel, the abbot of Croyland, an Englishman, hastened to make known these miraculous events, by narrating them in the Saxon language from the pulpit of his church. But the Normans did not long permit him to continue his preaching in peace, and he was accused of idolatry before a council held in London. The assembled bishops and earls degraded him from his ecclesiastical dignity, and sent him, as a simple monk, far from his friends, to the abbey of Glastonbury, ruled by a Norman named Toustain, conspicuous among all the abbots of the conquest for his hard and ferocious disposition. This example, however, did not cast down the popular superstition: founded upon national regrets, it disappeared only with those regrets, when the sons of the Saxons had forgotten the old cause for which their ancestors had suffered. But this period did not arrive so speedily as the conquerors desired; and forty years after the death of Waltheof, when the government of the monastery of Croyland had passed through a succession of foreign abbots, under the authority of one Geoffroy, a native of Orleans, miracles again began to be worked at the tomb of the last Saxon chief. People of English race came in crowds to visit his sepulchre, the monks of Norman origin, who occupied the abbey, ridiculing their fervour and abusing them and the object of their worship, calling the latter a felon traitor, justly punished with death.

The widow of Waltheof inherited all his possessions, and even the lands which he had given in full and entire possession to the abbey of Croyland were resumed and given to her. Judith hoped to share this vast inheritance with a husband of her own choice; but she was mistaken; the same power that had disposed of her hand to gain over a Saxon, now proposed to employ it in repaying the services of a Frenchman. Without consulting his niece any more than on the former occasion, king William offered the possessions of Waltheof to one Simon, from the town of Senlis, a brave knight, but lame and ill-formed. Judith expressed an utter contempt for the man and refused the match: the Conqueror, little accustomed to make his policy yield to the fancies of a woman, gave to Simon de Senlis the earldom of Northampton, and the whole inheritance of Waltheof, without his widow, who thus lost the fruit of her treachery. Left alone with two children, she led an obscure and mournful life in a remote corner of England. The Normans despised her because she had become poor; the Saxons abhorred her as an infamous traitor; and the old historians of English race exhibit a degree of joy in relating her years of desolation and sorrow.

The execution of Waltheof completed the prostration of the conquered nation. It would seem that the people had not lost all hope, so long as they saw one of their countrymen invested with great power, even though under foreign authority. After the death of the son of Siward, there was not in England, of all those invested with honours and political functions, one single man born in the country who did not look upon the natives as enemies or brute-beasts. All religious authority had also passed into the hands of men of foreign race, and of the old Saxon prelates there remained only Wulfstan, bishop of Worcester. He was a simple, weak-minded man, incapable of even a daring thought, and who, as we have seen above, after a momentary impulse of patriotic enthusiasm, became heartily reconciled with the conquerors. He had since rendered them important services; he had made pastoral visitations and proclaimed the amnesties of the king in the provinces still in commotion; he had marched in person against Roger de Hereford, on the banks of the Severn: but he was of English race: his day came, as that of others had come.

In the year 1076, Wulfstan was cited before a council of Norman bishops and lords, assembled in the church of Westminster, and presided over by king William and archbishop Lanfranc. The assembly unanimously declared that the Saxon prelate was incapable of exercising the episcopal functions in England, by reason of his not being able to speak French. In virtue of this singular judgment, the king and archbishop ordered the condemned prelate to resign the staff and ring, the ensigns of his dignity. Astonishment and indignation at being so ill rewarded inspired Wulfstan with an energy entirely new to him; he rose, and holding his pastoral staff in his hand, walked straight to the tomb of king Edward, who was buried in this church; there, stopping and addressing the dead man, in the English tongue, he said: "Thou, Edward, gavest me this staff; to thee I return it and confide it." Then turning towards the Normans: "I received this from a better man than any of you; I return it to him, take it from him if you can." As he pronounced these last words, the Saxon energetically struck the tombstone with the end of the pastoral staff. His air and this unexpected action produced on the assembly an impression of utter astonishment, mingled with superstitious fear: the king and the primate did not repeat their demand, and permitted the last English bishop to retain his staff and his office.

The popular imagination converted this affair into a prodigy, and the report spread that the pastoral staff of Wulfstan, when he struck the stone with it, had penetrated deep into it, as into soft earth, and that no one had been able to withdraw it but the Saxon himself, when the foreigners had revoked their sentence. After the death of Wulfstan, who was succeeded in his see by a canon of Bayeux, named Samson, the English honoured him, as they had done Waltheof and Eghelwin, with the title of saint. It was so with almost all those who, eminent for dignity and character, suffered death or persecution for the cause of Anglo-Saxon nationality.

All this seems somewhat strange to us of the present day; for oppressed nations have lost the custom of making saints of their defenders and friends; they have strength of mind enough to preserve the remembrance of those whom they have loved, without surrounding their names with a superstitious glory. But whatever the difference between our patriotic manners and those of the men who have preceded us on the earth, let this difference inspire us neither with anger nor with contempt towards them. The grand thought of human independence was revealed to them as to us; they environed it with their favourite symbols; they assembled around it all that they deemed noblest, and made it religious as we make it poetical. It is the same conviction and the same enthusiasm expressed in a different manner; the same inclination to immortalize those who have devoted their life to the good of their fellow-creatures.

BOOK VI. FROM THE QUARREL BETWEEN KING WILLIAM AND HIS ELDEST SON ROBERT, TO THE LAST VISIT OF WILLIAM TO THE CONTINENT.

1077—1087.

Discords among the victors—Quarrel between William and his son Robert—Robert demands Normandy—He joins his father's enemies—William curses his son—Conspiracy against and murder of Vaulcher—Devastation of Northumberland—Miserable condition of the northern provinces—Anglo-Saxon outlaws—Popular poems in their honour—Ambition of Eudes—His arrest—Results of the Norman conquest—Toustain, abbot of Glastonbury—Saxon monks killed or wounded by his order—Death of Matilda—Severance of interests between the king and the Normans—Domesday book—Levies upon the Normans and English—Equalization of property in the hands of the Normans—Laws of William against hunting—Political reasons for the severity of these laws—Expropriation of the English subsequent to the conquest—Emigration of Normans to Scotland—Descent of the Danes—Preparations for defence—Singular order issued to the English—Motives for the armament of king Knut—Termination of alliance between the English and the Danes—General assembly and review of the Normans—Ordinances of king William—State of the Anglo-Saxon population—Anxiety and mental torments of king William—Establishment of episcopal jurisdiction—Separation of the civil and ecclesiastical tribunals—Conduct of William with reference to the pope—Aspect of the conquered country.

One of the necessary phases of all conquests, great or small, is, that the conquerors quarrel among themselves for the possession and partition of the property of the conquered. The Normans did not escape this necessity. When there were no more rebels to subdue, England became a cause of intestine war to her masters; and it was in the bosom of her new royal family, between the father and his eldest son, that discord first broke out. His son Robert, whom the Normans surnamed in their language, Gamberon or Courte-Heuse, on account of the shortness of his legs, had, before the battle of Hastings, been named by duke William heir to his lands and title. This nomination had taken place, according to custom, with the formal consent of the barons of Normandy, who had all taken the oath to young Robert, as to their future lord. When William had become king, the young man, whose ambition was aroused by his father's successes, required him at least to abdicate in his favour the government of Normandy; but the king refused, willing to keep both his old duchy and his new kingdom. A violent quarrel ensued, in which the two younger brothers, William Rufus and Henry, took part against Robert, under colour of filial affection, but in reality to supplant him, if they could, in the succession which their father had assigned to him.

One day that the king was at Laigle with his sons, William and Henry came to Robert's apartments, in the house of one Roger Chaussiègue, and ascending to the upper rooms began to play at dice, after the manner of the soldiers of that time; then they made a great noise, and threw water upon Robert and his friends, who were in the court-yard below. Irritated by this insult, Robert hastened, sword in hand, to chastise his brothers: there was a great tumult, which the king had some difficulty in appeasing. On the following night, the young man, followed by all his companions, left the town, and proceeded to Rouen, where he attempted to surprise the citadel, but failed in his object. Many of his friends were arrested; he himself escaped, with some others, and, passing the frontier of Normandy, took refuge in La Perche, where Hugh, nephew of Aubert-le-Ribaud, received him in his castles of Sorel and Reymalard.

A reconciliation afterwards took place between the father and son, but it did not last long; for the young men who surrounded the latter began again to stimulate his ambition by every device. "Noble son of a king," said they, "thy father's people must take good care of his treasure, since thou hast not a penny to bestow on thy followers. Why endurest thou to remain so poor, when thy father is so rich? Ask him for a portion of his England, or at least for the duchy of Normandy, which he promised thee before all his barons." Robert, excited by this and similar suggestions, renewed his former request, but the king again refused, and exhorted him. in a paternal tone, to return to his duty, and especially to make choice of better counsellors, wise and grave persons, of mature age, such as archbishop Lanfranc. "Sir king," sharply replied Robert, "I came here to claim my right, and not to listen to sermons; I heard enough of them, and wearisome enough they were, when I was at my grammar. Answer me therefore distinctly, so that I may know what I have to do; for I am firmly resolved not to live on the bread of others, and not to receive the wages of any man."

The king answered angrily, that he would not divest himself of Normandy, where he was born, or share England, which he had acquired by so much labour. "Well," said Robert, "I will go—I will go and serve strangers, and perhaps obtain from them what is refused me in my own country." He departed, and went through Flanders, Lorraine, Germany, then to France and Aquitaine, visiting, says an old historian, dukes, counts, and rich lords of castles, telling them his grievances and demanding their aid; but all he received for the support of his cause he spent upon mountebanks, parasites, debauched women, and soon found himself compelled to beg afresh, or to borrow at enormous usury. Matilda, his mother, sometimes sent him money unknown to the king. William heard of this, and forbad her to send any more; she disobeyed, and the irritated king reproached her, in bitter terms, "with supporting his enemies by the treasure he had placed in her keeping;" he ordered Matilda's messenger, who conveyed the money, to be arrested and to have his eyes put out; but the latter, a Breton, named Samson, escaped, and turned monk, to save at once, says an old chronicle, his soul and his body.

After much journeying, young Robert repaired, under the auspices of Philip, king of France, to the castle of Gerberoy, in Beauvoisis, on the confines of Normandy. He was well received here by Elie, viscount of the castle, and by his colleague; for, says the old narrator, it was the custom at Gerberoy to have two seigneurs equal in power, and to receive fugitives from all countries. There the son of the Conqueror assembled a body of mercenaries; some came to him from France and Normandy; even men-at-arms of king William, and several of those who had been flattering him daily, and living at his table, quitted their posts, and repaired to Gerberoy; and at length he himself, crossing the sea, came in person to besiege the castle where his son had shut himself up.

In a sally made by Robert, he engaged, hand to hand, a knight enveloped in armour, wounded him in the arm, and threw him from his horse; the voice of the wounded man told him that it was his father he had overthrown; he instantly dismounted, aided him to rise and to regain his saddle, and left him free to depart. The Norman chiefs and bishops endeavoured once more to reconcile father and son; but William at first resisted their intreaties. "Why," said he, "do you solicit me in favour of a traitor who has seduced from me my soldiers, those whom I have fed with my bread, and whom I have supplied with the arms they bear?" He, however, ultimately gave in; but the good understanding between father and son was not of long duration; for the third time, Robert withdrew, went into a foreign country, and returned no more during his father's life. The king cursed him on his departure, and the historians of the age attribute to this malediction the misfortunes which filled the life of the eldest son of William the Bastard—misfortunes of which, as we have seen, the conquest of England was the first cause.

From these dissensions, which troubled the repose of the chief of the conquerors, the conquered derived no advantage; and if, in the absence of William, the royal hand itself weighed not upon that people, other hands, those of earls, viscounts, judges, prelates, and abbots, all of foreign race, made it feel their heaviness. Among the most pitiless of these ministers of the conquest, figured the Lorrainese, Vaulcher, bishop of Durham, who, since the execution of Waltheof, had added to his ecclesiastical office the government of the whole country between the Tweed and the Tyne. The friends of the earlbishop loudly vaunted his administration, and praised him for equal skill in repressing the rebellions of the English by the edge of the sword, and in reforming their morals by the power of his discourses. The simple fact was, that Vaulcher harassed his province by insupportable exactions, that he allowed his officers, after him, to levy tributes on their own account, and that he permitted his soldiers also to rob and murder with impunity. Among those whom he put to death without trial was one Liulf, a man beloved by the whole country, who had retired to Durham after having been despoiled by the Normans of all the property he possessed in the south of England. This murder, executed with most atrocious circumstances, put the crowning point to the hatred of the people to the Lorrainese bishop and his agents. The old spirit of Northumberland was aroused, and the inhabitants of that district, so fatal to foreigners, assembled as in the time of Robert Comine.

They held nocturnal conferences, and unanimously agreed to proceed with concealed weapons to the assembly of justice, held from time to time by the bishop, at the county court. This court was held on the banks of the Tyne, near the New Castle, built by the conquerors on the high road to Scotland, at a place called in Saxon Gotes-Heaved, or Goats-Head. The Northumbrians repaired hither in great numbers, as if to address humble and pacific solicitations to their lord. They demanded reparation for the wrongs that had been done them. "I will not redress any of these," said the bishop, "unless you first give me four hundred pounds, good money." The Saxon who, knowing French, spoke in the name of the rest, asked permission to confer with them, and all went apart for a moment, as if to consult together about paying the sum demanded; but suddenly the speaker, who was the chief also of the plot, cried out in the English tongue, "Short reed, good reed, slay ye the bishop!" At this signal, they drew their weapons, threw themselves upon the Lorrainese, killed him, and with him an hundred men of Norman or Flemish race. Two servants only, Englishmen by birth, were spared by the conspirators. The popular rising extended to Durham; the fortress built there by the Normans was attacked; but the garrison, numerous and well provided, resisted the Northumbrians, who, after a siege of four days, became discouraged, and dispersed.

At this new indication of life given by the population of the north, Eudes, bishop of Bayeux, the king's brother, and one of his lieutenants in his absence, promptly marched to Durham, with a numerous army. Without taking the time or the trouble to investigate the circumstances of the insurrection, he promiscuously seized the natives, who, confiding in their innocence, remained in their homes, and beheaded or mutilated them. Others only purchased their life by surrendering all they possessed. Bishop Eudes pillaged the church of Durham, and carried away all that remained of the sacred ornaments that Eghelwin had saved by removing them to Lindisfarn. He renewed throughout Northumberland the ravages made there by his brother in 1070; and it was this second devastation which, added to the first, impressed upon the northern counties of England that aspect of desolation and gloom which they presented for more than a century afterwards. "Thus," says an historian, who lived seventy years later, "thus were cut the nerves of this county, once so flourishing. Those towns, formerly so renowned, now so abased, those lofty towers, which threatened heaven, now in ruins, those pasture fields, once smiling and watered by sparkling rills, now wholly waste, the stranger who sees them, beholds with a sigh, the old inhabitant no longer recognises."

In this county, ruined as it was, the population, half Saxon, half Danish, long preserved its ancient spirit of independence, and of somewhat savage pride. The Norman successors of the Bastard dwelt in full safety in the southern provinces; but it was scarcely without apprehension that they journeyed beyond the Humber; and an historian of the twelfth century tells us that they never visited that part of their kingdom without the escort of an army of veteran soldiers. It was in the north that the tendency to rebel against the social order established by the conquest longest endured; it was the north which, for more than two centuries, furnished those bands of outlaws who were the political successors of the refugees of the camp of Ely, and of the companions of Hereward. History has not understood them; it has passed them over in silence, or else, adopting the legal acts of the time, it has branded them with names which divest them of all interest, with the names of rebels, robbers, and bandits. But let us not be misled by these apparently odious titles; in all countries subjugated by foreigners, they have been given by the victors to the brave men who in small numbers took refuge in the mountains or in the forests, abandoning the towns and cities to those who chose to support slavery. If the Anglo-Saxon nation had not the courage to follow their example, it at least loved those who gave it, and accompanied them with its blessing. While ordinances, drawn up in the French language, required all the inhabitants of the cities and boroughs of England to hunt the outlaw, the man of the forest, as a wolf, to pursue him from hundred to hundred, with hue and cry, the English sang ballads in honour of this enemy to foreign rule, who, as they expressed it, had the earl's purse for his treasure, and the king's deer for his herd. The popular poets celebrated his victories, his combats, his stratagems against the agents of authority. They sang how he had outstripped the men and horses of the viscount, how he had taken the bishop, had put him to a thousand marks ransom, and made him dance a measure in his pontifical robes.

The Norman bishop, Eudes de Bayeux, after his expedition into Northumberland, became famous among his people, as one of the greatest quellers of the English; he was chief of the judges, or grand justiciary of all England, earl of Kent and of Hereford, since the imprisonment of Roger Fitz-Osbern. The reputation he enjoyed inflated him with pride, and the power he exercised in England and in Normandy excited in him the ambition of the greatest power then extant, the papal power. Some Italian soothsayers had predicted that a pope named Eudes should succeed Gregory VII. The bishop of Bayeux, relying upon this prediction, commenced intrigues at Rome, bought a palace there, sent rich presents to those whom the people beyond the Alps still called senators, and loaded the pilgrims of Normandy and England with letters and despatches; he engaged Norman barons and knights, among others Hugh le Loup, earl of Chester, to follow him into Italy, in order to constitute a brilliant escort for him. King William, while still in Normandy, heard of these preparations, which, for some reason or other, displeased him. Not desiring that his brother should become pope, he sailed, and surprised him at sea, off the Isle of Wight. The king immediately assembled the Norman chiefs in that island, and accused before them the bishop of having abused his power of judge and earl; of having, beyond all measure, illtreated the Saxons, to the great danger of the common cause; of having despoiled the churches; and lastly, of having attempted to seduce and take with him, beyond the Alps, the warriors upon whose fidelity rested the safety of the country.

"Consider these grievances," said the king to the assembly, "and tell me how I ought to act towards such a brother." No one dared reply. "Let him then be arrested," continued the king, "and put into safe custody." None present dared lay his hand upon the bishop. Hereupon the king advanced and seized him by his robe. "I am a priest," cried Eudes; "I am the minister of the Lord: the pope alone can judge me." But William, without quitting his hold, answered: "It is not a priest nor prelate I judge; it is my earl, my vassal and false viceroy whom I arrest." The brother of the conqueror of England was taken to Normandy and imprisoned in a fortress, perhaps in the same where still languished Ulfnoth, the brother of king Harold, whose fate was now like his own, after fifteen years of a fortune so different.

The reproaches of the king to the bishop as to his conduct in the north of England, if they are not an invention of the old historian, seem to betray some fears of a fresh rising on the part of those who had killed Robert Comine, retaken York, massacred bishop Vaulcher, and who joyfully hastened to embrace every and any enemy of the Normans that landed on their coasts. Such an apprehension was not entirely futile, for more than one revolt broke out in the neighbourhood of Durham, under the administration of William, successor to the Lorrainese. In the rest of England the conquered showed less energy, or more resignation to their sufferings. Few positive facts as to the nature of their sufferings have come down to us, and those few relate, for the most part, to the miseries of the clergy, the only class of the oppressed men of old England that has found historians. However, what was done to this privileged class may enable us to conjecture to what the other classes, whom religious scruples did not protect, would be subjected; and an incident in the internal rule of an English monastery, under a Norman abbot, in the sixteenth year of the conquest, will aid us in forming an idea of the rule of the conquerors in the cities and provinces under the authority of the earls, viscounts and bailiffs of the foreign king.

The convent of Glastonbury, Somersetshire, after the deposition of Eghelnoth, its Saxon abbot, had been given to Toustain, a monk of Caen. Toustain, according to the custom of other Normans, who had become abbots in England, had begun with lessening the rations given to his monks, in order to render them more manageable; but hunger only irritated them against the power of him whom they loudly termed intruder. The abbot, from national predilections, or out of pure despotism, ordered his Saxon monks to learn to chant the service after the method of a famous musician of Fécamp, and the Saxons, as much through hatred of the Norman music, as from habit, adhered to the Gregorian chant. They received repeated injunctions to renounce it, as well as many other ancient usages; but they resisted, and at length declared, in full chapter, their firm resolution not to change it. The Norman arose in a fury, went out, and immediately returned at the head of a body of soldiers, fully armed.

At this sight the monks fled towards the church, and took refuge in the choir, the door of which they had time to shut. The soldiers attempted to force it, and meanwhile some of them climbed the pillars, and, placing themselves on the rafters at the top of the choir, assailed the monks below with discharges of arrows. The latter, retreating to the high altar, glided behind the shrines or reliquaries, which, serving them as ramparts, received the arrows discharged against them. The great crucifix of the altar soon bristled with these missiles. By and bye the door of the choir yielded to the efforts of the soldiers, and the Saxons, forced in their retreat, were attacked with swords and lances; they defended themselves as best they could with the wooden benches and the metal candlesticks; they even wounded some of the soldiers, but the arms were too unequal; eighteen monks were killed or mortally wounded, and their blood, says the contemporary chronicle, poured down the steps of the altar. Another historian says, that he could recite many facts similar to this, but that he prefers to pass them over in silence, as equally painful to write and to read.

In the year 1083 died Matilda, wife of king William. An old narrative says that the counsels of this lady more than once softened the soul of the conqueror; that she often disposed him to clemency towards the English, but that after her death. William abandoned himself without reserve to his tyrannical humour. Facts are wanting to substantiate this aggravation of oppression and misery for the conquered people, and the imagination can scarcely supply the deficiency, for it is difficult to add a single shade to the dark picture of the unhappiness of the preceding years. The only difference observable between the epoch of the conquest which followed the death of

Matilda, and those which have been already narrated is, that William, having nothing further to gain in power over the natives, began to create for himself a personal domination over his companions in victory.

Necessity had probably as large a share in this enterprise as ambition; nothing remaining to take from the English, the king found himself obliged to levy contributions on the Normans themselves for the maintenance of the common property. In the year 1083 he exacted sixpence in silver for every hide of land throughout the kingdom, without distinction of possessor. The Norman warrior, worn out by twenty years of combats, found himself obliged to pay, out of the revenues of the domain he had conquered in the days of his youth and strength, the hire of a new army.

From this epoch dates a spirit of mutual distrust and secret hostility between the king and his old friends; they accused each other of avarice and selfishness. William reproached the Norman chiefs with caring more for their private interest than for the common safety; with thinking more of building farms, raising flocks, or forming studs, than of holding themselves in readiness against the native or foreign enemy. In their turn, the chiefs reproached the king with being beyond all measure greedy of gain, and with desiring to appropriate to himself, under false pretexts of general utility, the wealth acquired by the labour of all. In order to rest his demand of contributions, or money services, on a fixed basis, William ordered a general territorial inquest to be made, and a register prepared of all the mutations of property brought about in England by the conquest; he desired to know into what hands throughout the country the Saxon domains had passed, and how many of these still retained their possessions in virtue of special agreements with himself or his barons, how many acres of land there were in each domain, how many were sufficient for the maintenance of a man-at-arms, and how many men-at-arms there were in each province or county of England; what was the gross amount derived in various ways from the cities, towns, boroughs and hamlets, what was the exact property of each earl, baron, knight, or sergeant-at-arms; what land, how many men holding fiefs on that land, how many Saxons, how much cattle, and how many ploughs each possessed.

This undertaking, in which modern historians have thought they discerned the stamp of administrative genius, was simply the result of the peculiar position of the Norman king, as chief of a conquering army, and of the necesity of establishing some kind of order in the chaos of the conquest. This is so entirely the case, that in other conquests, the details of which have been transmitted to us, for example, in that of Greece by the Latin crusaders in the thirteenth century, we find the same kind of inquest instituted by the chiefs of the invasion, on a wholly similar plan.

In virtue of the orders of king William, Henry de Ferrieres, Walter Giffard, Adam, brother of Eudes the seneschal, and Remi, bishop of Lincoln, with other personages selected from among the officers of justice and of the Exchequer, made a progress through the counties of England, establishing a court of inquiry in each place of any importance. They summoned before them the Norman viscount of each province, or of each Saxon shire, a personage whom the Saxons, in their language, still called by the ancient title of shire-reve or sheriff. They then summoned, or caused the viscount to summon, all the Norman barons of the neighbourhood, and called upon them to state the precise limits of their possessions and of their territorial jurisdictions; then some of the inspectors, or commissioners delegated by them, proceeded to each large domain and to each district, or hundred, as the Saxons called it. There they made the French men-at-arms of each seigneur, and every English inhabitant of the hundred, declare upon oath how many free-holders or lease-holders there were on the domain, what portion each occupied in full and modified property, the names of the actual holders, the names of those who had possessed them before the conquest, and the various mutations of property that had taken place since. So that they required, say the narratives of the time, three declarations concerning each estate; what it had been in the time of king Edward; what it was when William gave it, and what it was at the time being. Under each particular return was inscribed this form: "This is what has been sworn by all the Frenchmen and all the Englishmen of the hundred."

In each town they inquired what taxes the inhabitants had paid to the ancient kings, and what the town produced to the officers of the Conqueror; how many houses the war of the conquest or the construction of fortresses had done away with; how many houses the conquerors had taken; how many Saxon families, reduced to utter poverty, were not in a condition to pay anything. In cities, they took the oath from the high Norman authorities, who convoked the Saxon citizens in their old Guildhall, now become the property of the king or of some foreign baron; lastly, in places of less importance, they took the oath of the royal provost, of the priest, and of six Saxons or villeins, as the Normans called them, of each town. This survey occupied six years, during which the commissioners of king William went over all England, with the exception of the mountainous districts, north and west of Yorkshire, that is to say, the five modern counties of Durham, Northumberland, Cumberland, Westmoreland, and Lancashire. Perhaps the lands in this district, cruelly devastated on two separate occasions, were not deemed valuable enough or fixedly appropriated enough to make their survey useful or even practicable; perhaps, too, the Norman commissioners feared, lest, if they extended their inquiries into the towns of Northumbria, the Saxon words which had been the signal for the massacre of bishop Vaulcher and his hundred men, might sound in their ears also.

However this may be, the register, or, to use the old term, the terrier of the Norman conquest, makes no mention of the domains conquered beyond the province of York. The compilation of this roll for each county mentioned in it, was formed on an uniform plan. The king's name was placed at the head, with the list of his lands and revenues in the county; then followed the names of the chiefs and lesser proprietors, in the order of their military rank and territorial wealth. The Saxons who had been spared by special grace in the great spoliation, figured only in the last ranks; for the few men of that race who remained free proprietors, or tenants, en chef du roi, as the conquerors expressed it, possessed only very small estates. They were inserted at the end of each chapter under the name of thanes of the king, or with various qualifications derived from offices in the royal household. The other names of Anglo-Saxon aspect which occur here and there in the roll, belonged to men who farmed portions, of greater or less extent, of the domains of the Norman earls, barons, knights, sergeants-at-arms or cross-bow-men.

Such is the form of the authentic and still existing book, whence have been derived most of the facts as to expropriations given in the present work. This precious volume, in which the conquest was registered in its entirety, so that its memory might never be effaced, was called by the Normans, le grand rôle, le rôle royale, or le rôle de Winchester, because it was preserved in the treasury of the cathedral of that city. The Saxons called it by a more solemn name, Dom-boc, or

Doomsday Book, because it contained their sentence of irrevocable expropriation. But if this book was a sentence of dispossession for the English nation, it was so equally for some of the foreign usurpers. Their chief skilfully availed himself of it to effect numerous changes of property in his own favour, and to legitimate his personal pretensions to many lands usurped and occupied by others. He asserted himself proprietor, by inheritance, of all that Edward, the last king but one of the Anglo-Saxons, Harold, the last king, and the whole family of Harold had possessed; by the same title, he claimed all public property and the lordship of all cities, except where he had expressly divested himself of it, either wholly or in part, by a formal deed, par lettre et saisine, as the old jurisconsults call it.

In the moment of victory, no one had thought of the formalities of lettre or saisine, and each of those to whom William, before the battle of Hastings, said: "What I take, you shall take," had carved out his own portion: but after the conquest, the soldiers felt transferred to their own shoulders some of the weight of that power which they had brought upon the shoulders of the English. It was thus that the right of William de Warenne to the estates of two free Englishmen in Norfolk was contested, because these lands had once formed part of one of Edward's royal manors. It was the same with the domain of one Eustache, in Huntingdonshire, and with fifteen acres of land held by one Miles, in Berkshire. An estate that Engelry occupied in Essex was, in the language of the great roll, seized into the hands of the king, because Engelry sent no one to justify his titles. The king, in like manner, seized all estates over which he had any pretension, and of which the occupier, although a Norman, could not or would not render an account.

Another claim on his part was, that every domain which had paid any rent or service to king Edward, should pay the same rent or service to him, although held by a Norman. This claim, founded on a regular succession to the rights of the English king, which could not be admitted by those who had forcibly dispossessed the English race, was at first ill received by the conquerors. Exemption from taxes or any money service beyond a voluntary contribution now and then, appeared to them the inviolable prerogative of their victory, and they regarded the condition of customary tax-payers as peculiar to the subjugated nation. Many resisted the demands of the king, scorning to have personal servitude imposed upon them for the land which they had conquered. But others submitted; and their compliance, whether voluntary or purchased by William, weakened the opposition of the rest. Raoul de Courbespine long refused to pay any rent for the houses he had taken in the city of Canterbury; and Hugh de Montfort for the lands he occupied in Essex. These two chiefs might act thus cavalierly with impunity; but the haughtiness of less powerful and less considerable men was sometimes severely punished. One Osbern le Pecheur (Fisher), having refused to pay the dues which his land formerly paid to king Edward, as depending on his domain, was appropriated by the royal agents, and his land offered to any one who would pay the dues demanded. Raoul Taille-Bois paid, says the great roll, and took possession of the domain forfeited by Osbern le Pecheur.

The king thus endeavoured to levy from his own countrymen, in the cities and lands of his demesne, the tax established by the Saxon law. As to the English in these cities and demesne lands, besides the tax rigorously exacted, as being the custom of the place, and which was often doubled or tripled, they were further subject to a casual, arbitrary, variable impost, capriciously and harshly levied, which the Normans called taille or taillage (tallagium). The great roll enumerates the tallagable burgesses of the king, in cities, towns, and hamlets. "The following are the burgesses of the king at Colchester: Keolman, who holds a house and five acres of land; Leofwin, who holds two houses and twentyfive acres; Ulfrik, Edwin, Wulfstan, Manwn, &c." The Norman soldiers and chiefs also levied tallage on the Saxons who had fallen to their lot in town or country. This is what, in the language of the conquerors, was called having a free burgess or Saxon; and in this way the free men were reckoned by the head, were sold, given, exchanged, lent, or even divided among the Normans. The great roll mentions that a certain viscount had in the town of Ipswich two Saxon burghers, the one on loan, the other in pledge; and that king William, by authentic deed, had lent the Saxon Edwig to Raoul Taille-Bois, to keep him so long as he should live.

Many intestine disputes among the conquerors for the spoil of the conquered, many invasions of Normans upon Normans, as the roll expresses it, were also recorded in every part of England; for example, William de Warenne, in Bedfordshire, had disseised Walter Espec of a half-hide or half-acre of land, and had taken from him two horses. Elsewhere, Hugh de Corbon had usurped from Roger Bigot the half of a free Englishman—that is to say, five acres of land. In Hampshire, William de la Chesnaye claimed from Picot a certain portion of land, under pretext that it belonged to the Saxon whose property he had taken. The last fact, and many others of the same kind, prove that the Normans regarded as their legitimate property all that the ancient proprietor could have legally claimed, and that the foreign invader, considering himself a natural successor, made the same claims, prosecuted the same civil suits, that the natural heir of the Saxon would have done. He summoned the English inhabitants of the district as witnesses to establish the extent of the rights which his substitution in place of the man he had killed or expelled had communicated to him. Frequently, the memory of the inhabitants, disturbed by the suffering and confusion of the conquest, was not equal to these appeals; frequently, also, the Norman who sought to dispute the right of his countrymen, refused to abide by the deposition of the vile populace of the conquered. In this case, the only means of terminating the dispute was by judicial combat between the parties, or a trial in the king's court.

The Norman terrier speaks in many places of unjust invasions, disseizins, and wrongful pretensions. It seems curious to find the word justice in the register of the expropriation of an entire people; a book which cannot be properly understood, unless we bear in mind throughout every page that the word inheritance means the spoliation of an Englishman; that every Englishman despoiled by a Norman takes thenceforth the name of predecessor of the Norman; that the being just, with a Norman, meant the abstaining from invasion of lands or houses of an Englishman killed or expelled by another Norman, and that the contrary is called injustice, as is proved by the following passage: "In the county of Bedford, Raoul Taille-Bois has unjustly disseized Nigel of five hides of land, notoriously forming part of the inheritance of his predecessor, and part of which is still occupied by the concubine of the said Nigel."

Some of the dispossessed Saxons ventured to present themselves before the commissioners of inquiry to set forth their claims; many of these are registered, couched in terms of humble supplication that no Norman employed. These men declared themselves poor and miserable; they appealed to the clemency and compassion of the king. Those who, by the most abject servility, succeeded in preserving some slight portion of their paternal inheritance, were obliged to pay for this favour with degrading or fantastic services, or received it under the no less humiliating title of alms. Sons are inscribed in the roll as holding the property of their fathers by alms. Free women retain their field as alms. One woman preserves her husband's land on condition of feeding the king's dogs. A mother and her son receive their own property in gift, on condition of each day saying prayers for the soul of Richard, the king's son.

This Richard, son of William the Conqueror, died in 1081, crushed by his horse against a tree in the New Forest. This was a space of thirty miles, newly planted with trees, between Salisbury and the sea. This district, before being converted into wood land, contained more than sixty parishes, which the conqueror broke up, and whose inhabitants he expelled. It is not known whether the reason for this singular proceeding was purely politic, and whether William's special object was to provide a secure place of debarkation for his succours from Normandy, a place where they would encounter no Saxon enemy; or whether, as most of the ancient historians say, he merely designed to satisfy his passion and that of his sons for the chase. It is to this inordinate passion that are also attributed the strange and cruel regulations he made respecting the carrying arms in the forests of England; but there is reason to suppose that these regulations had a graver motive, and that they were directed against the English, who, under the pretext of hunting, might meet in arms for political purposes. "He ordered," says a contemporary chronicle, "that whoever should kill a stag or a hind should have his eyes picked out; the protection given to stags extended also to wild boars; and he even made statutes to secure hares from all danger. This king loved wild beasts as though he had been their father." These laws, rigorously enforced against the Saxons, greatly increased their misery; for many of them had no means of subsistence but the chase. "The poor murmured," adds the chronicle just cited, "but he made no account of their ill will, and they were fain to obey under pain of death."

William comprised within his royal demesne all the great forests of England, formidable places to the conquerors, the asylum of their last adversaries. These laws, which the Saxon historians ridicule as laws to protect the life of hares, were a powerful protection to the life of the Normans; and, in order that their execution might be the better assured, hunting in the royal forests became a privilege, the concession of which appertained to the king alone, who could at will grant and interdict it. Many high personages of Norman race, more alive to their own convenience than to the interests of the conquest, were indignant at this exclusive law. But so long as the spirit of nationality remained among the conquered, this objection of the Normans did not prevail against the will of their kings. Sustained by the instinct of political necessity, the sons of William preserved, as exclusively as he had done, the privilege of the chase; and it was only when this privilege ceased to be necessary, that their successors found themselves constrained, however unwillingly, to surrender it.

Then, that is to say, in the thirteenth century, the parks of the Norman proprietors were no longer included within the royal forests, and the lord of each domain obtained the free enjoyment of his woods; his dogs were no longer subjected to mutilation of limbs, and the royal foresters, verderers, or viewers, no longer prowled incessantly round his house to surprise him in some offence against the forest laws, and to make him pay a heavy fine. On the contrary, the royal law for the preservation of game, great and small, was extended in favour of the descendants of the rich Normans, enabling them to have game-keepers of their own to kill with impunity the poor Englishman who might be detected laying wait for deer or hares. At a later period, the poor man himself, the descendant of the Saxons, having ceased to be formidable to the rich heirs of the other race, was only punished, when he dared to hunt, with a year's imprisonment, and the providing responsible bail to answer for his not committing any such crime for the future, "in parks, or forests, or warrens, or fish-ponds, or anywhere, against the peace of our lord the king."

The last peculiarity that we shall cite, as exhibited by the great register of the Norman conquest, is that we find there the proof that king William established as a general law, that every title to property anterior to his invasion, and every act of transfer or transmission of property made by a man of English race posterior to the invasion, was null and void, unless he himself had formally ratified it. In the first terror caused by the conquest, some Englishmen had made over part of their lands to churches, either in actual gift, for the good of their souls and bodies, or in feigned gift, to secure that portion to their sons, should the domains of the saints of England be respected by the Normans. This precaution was futile, and when the churches could not produce written proof that the king had confirmed the gift, or, in other words, that he himself had made it, the land was seized to his account. Such was the case with the domain of Ailrik, who, before departing for the war against the Saxons, had assigned his manor to the convent of St. Peter, in Essex; and it was so with the estate of one Edrik, made over before the conquest to the monastery of Abingdon.

This law was more than once put in force, and all title to property whatsoever utterly effaced and annihilated for the sons of the Anglo-Saxons. This fact is attested by the Norman Richard Lenoir, bishop of Ely about the middle of the twelfth century. He relates that the English, daily dispossessed by their lords, addressed great complaints to the king, saying that the ill treatment they had to undergo from the other race, and the hatred exhibited towards them by it, left them no resource but to abandon the country. After long deliberation, the kings and their council decided that in future all that a man of English race obtained from the lords, as payment for personal services, or as the result of a legal agreement, should be irrevocably secured to him, but on condition that he should renounce all right founded upon anterior possession. "This decision," adds the bishop of Ely, "was sage and beneficial; and it obliged the sons of the conquered to seek the good graces of their lords by submission, obedience, and devotion. So that now no Englishman possessing lands or houses or other property, is proprietor thereof by title of inheritance or paternal succession, but only in virtue of a donation made to him in recompence for his loyal services."

It was in the year 1086 that the compilation of the Great Roll of the Normans—the Book of Judgment of the Saxons—was finished; and in the same year there was a great convocation of all the conquering chiefs, laymen and priests. In this council were discussed the various claims registered in the roll of inquest, and the discussion did not terminate without quarrels between the king and his barons; there were grave conferences between them, says a contemporary chronicle, upon the important distinction as to what ought to be definitively regarded as legitimate in the occupations under the conquest. Most of the individual invasions were ratified; but as some exceptions were made, there was a discontented minority among the conquerors. Several barons and knights renounced their homage, quitted William and England, and, crossing the Tweed, went to offer to Malcolm, king of Scotland, the service of their horses and their arms. Malcolm received them favourably, as, before them, he had received the emigrant Saxons; and distributed among them portions of land, for which they became his liege-men, his soldiers towards and against all. Thus Scotland received an accession of population entirely different from those which had hitherto mingled together there. The Normans, united by a common exile and a common hospitality with the English who had but lately fled before them, became, under a new banner, their companions and brothers-in-arms. Equality reigned beyond the Tweed between two races of men who, on the other side of the same river, were of so different a condition; a fusion rapidly took place of manners and even of language, and the recollection of diversity of origin did not sever their sons, because there was mingled with it no recollection of foreign insult or oppression.

While the conquerors were thus occupied in regulating their internal affairs, they were suddenly disturbed by an alarm from without. The report spread that a thousand Danish vessels, sixty Norwegian vessels, and an hundred vessels from Flanders, furnished by Robert de Frison, the new duke of that country and an enemy of the Normans, were assembling in the gulf of Lymfiord, for the purpose of making a descent upon England and delivering the Anglo-Saxon people. The kings of Denmark, who, for twenty years past, had successively encouraged and betrayed the hopes of this people, could not, it would seem, resolve entirely to abandon them. The insurrection which, in 1080, caused the death of the bishop of Durham, appears to have been encouraged by the expectation of a descent of the northmen; for we find these words in the official despatches addressed, at the time, to that bishop: "The Danes are coming: carefully provide your castles with provisions and arms." The Danes did not come, and perhaps the extraordinary precautions recommended to bishop Vaulcher on their account occasioned the failure of the outbreak in which he perished.

But this false alarm was nothing compared with that which spread through England in the year 1085. The great body of the Norman forces was at once marched into the eastern provinces; poets were established on the coasts; cruisers put to sea; the recently erected fortresses were surrounded with additional works, and the walls of the old cities, dismantled by the conquerors, were rebuilt. King William published through Gaul the ban he had proclaimed twenty years before, when first about to cross the Channel. He promised pay and reward to every horse or foot soldier, who would enrol in his service. An immense number arrived from all parts. Every country that had furnished invaders to effect the conquest, furnished garrisons to defend it. Fresh soldiers were quartered in the towns and villages; and the Norman earls, viscounts, bishops, and abbots were ordered to lodge and support them in proportion to the extent of their respective jurisdictions or domains. To meet the expense of this great armament, the king revived the old impost called Dane-gheld, which, prior to its being levied by the Scandinavian conquerors, had been raised for the defence of the country against their invasions. It was re-established at the rate of twelve pence in silver for each acre of land. The Normans upon whom this tax immediately fell, reimbursed themselves out of the pockets of their Anglo-Saxon farmers or serfs, who thus paid to repel the Danes coming to their aid, that which their ancestors had paid to repel them as enemies.

Bodies of troops overran the north-eastern counties of England, in all directions, to devastate them and render them uninhabitable either by the Danes, if they landed, or by the English, whom they suspected of favouring their landing. There remained on the sea coast, within reach of the vessels, neither man, nor beast, nor fruit tree. The Saxon population was necessarily driven inland, and, by way of additional precaution against any communication between that population and the Danes, a royal ban, published by sound of trumpet in all places lying near the sea, ordered the English to assume Norman attire, Norman weapons, and to shave their beards in the

Norman fashion. This singular order was designed to deprive the Danes of the means of distinguishing the friends whom they came to succour, from the enemies whom they came to fight.

The fear which inspired these precautions was not without foundation; there was really a numerous fleet, destined for England, at anchor on the coast of Denmark.

Olaf Kyr, king of Norway, son and successor of that Harold who, seeking to conquer England, had obtained but seven feet of land there, now came to aid the nation which had vanquished and killed his father, without, perhaps, heeding the change in the destiny of that people, and thinking that he was going to avenge Harold. As to the king of Denmark, Knut the son of Swen, promoter of the war and chief commander of the armament, he understood the revolution effected in England by the Norman conquest, and it was with a full knowledge of the subject that he went to succour the conquered against the conquerors. "He had yielded," say the Danish historians, "to the supplications of the exiled English, to the messages received from England, and to the pity inspired in his bosom by the miseries of a race of men allied to his own, a race whose chiefs, whose rich men, whose notable personages had been killed or banished, and which found itself reduced to servitude under the foreign race of French, who are also called Romans."

These were, in fact, the only two names by which the Norman nation was known in the north of Europe, since the last remains of the Danish language had perished at Rouen and at Bayeux. Though the seigneurs of Normandy might still readily prove their Scandinavian descent, in forgetting the idiom which was the visible sign of that descent, they had lost their title to the family compact which, despite frequent hostilities, the result of transient passions, united the Teutonic populations one with another. But the Anglo-Saxons were still entitled to the benefit of this fraternity of origin; and this, say the chroniclers of his nation, the king of Denmark acknowledged; so that if his enterprise was not wholly free from infusion of views of personal ambition, it was at least ennobled by the sentiment of a duty of humanity and relationship. His fleet was detained in port longer than he had expected, and, meanwhile, emissaries from the Norman king, able and cunning as their master, corrupted with English gold many of the counsellors and captains of the Danes.

The delay, at first involuntary, was protracted by these intrigues. The men secretly sold to William, and especially the Danish bishops, most of whom allowed themselves to be gained over, repeatedly succeeded in preventing king Knut from putting to sea, by creating all sorts of embarrassments and obstacles. Meantime, the soldiers, tired of a futile encampment, complained and murmured in their tents. They demanded not to be thus mocked, and that they should be either sent upon their expedition, or be allowed to return to their homes, their labours, and their commerce. They held meetings, and signified to the king by deputies their resolution to disband, if the order for departure was not given forthwith. King Knut attempted to use rigour in order to re-establish discipline. He imprisoned the leaders of the revolt, and sentenced the whole army to pay a fine of so much each man. The general exasperation far from being calmed by these measures, increased to such a degree, that in July, 1086, there was a general mutiny, in which the king was killed by the soldiers: this was the signal for a civil war, which spread over all Denmark; and from that time the Danish people, occupied with its own quarrels, forgot the Anglo-Saxons, their servitude, and their wrongs.

This was the last occasion on which the sympathy of the Northern Teutons was exercised in favour of the Teutonic race which inhabited England. By degrees, the English, despairing of their own cause, ceased to recommend themselves and their cause to the remembrance and support of the northern nations. The exiles of the conquest died in foreign lands, and left there children, who, forgetting the country of their ancestors, knew no other than the land which had given them birth. Finally, the Danish ambassadors and travellers who visited England, hearing in the houses of the great and wealthy none but the Romane tongue of Normandy, and paying little heed to the language spoken by the traders in their shops, or the neatherds in their yards, imagined that the whole population of the country was Norman, or that the language had changed since the invasion of the Normans. Seeing French trouveres in every castle and city constituting the pastime of the higher classes in England, who, in fact, could have supposed that, sixty years before, the scalds of the north had been held in the same favour there? England accordingly, from the twelfth century, was regarded by the Scandinavian nations as a country of an absolutely foreign tongue. This opinion became so decided, that, in the Danish and Norwegian law of escheat, the English were classed in the rank of the least favoured nations. In the code bearing the name of king Magnus, under the article of successions, we find the following words: "If men of English race, or others even still greater strangers to us—If Englishmen or other men speaking an idiom bearing no resemblance to our own. . . ." This want of resemblance could not mean mere diversity of dialects; for, even in the present day, the brogue of the northern provinces of England is to a certain extent intelligible to a Dane or Norwegian.

About the close of the year 1086, there was a general meeting of all the conquerors and sons of the conquerors, at Salisbury, or, according to some writers, at Winchester. Each person of dignity, layman or priest, came at the head of his men-at-arms and the feudatories of his domains. There were present sixty thousand men, all possessors of at least a portion of land sufficient to maintain a horse, or provide a complete suit of armour. They renewed in succession their oath of faith and homage to king William, touching his hands and pronouncing this form: "I become your man from this day forth for life, for limb, and for worldly honour, and unto you shall be true and faithful, and bear you forth for the land that I hold of you, so help me God."

The armed colony then separated, and it was probably then that the royal herald published, in his name, the following ordinances:

"We will and order that the earls, barons, knights, sergeants, and all the free men of this kingdom, be and hold themselves fitly provided with horses and arms, that they may be ready at all times to do us the lawful service they owe us for their domains and holdings.

"We will that all the free men of this kingdom be leagued and united as sworn brothers-in-arms, to defend, maintain, and guard it to the best of their power.

"We will that all the cities, towns, castles, and hundreds of this kingdom be guarded every night, and that the inhabitants in turn keep watch and ward against all enemies and evil doers.

"We will that all the men brought by us from beyond sea, or who have followed us, shall be, throughout the kingdom, under our peace and special protection; that if one of them be killed, his lord, within the space of five days, shall seize the murderer; if he fail in so doing, he shall pay us a fine, conjointly with the English of the hundred in which the murder has been committed.

"We will that the free men of this kingdom hold their lands and possessions well and in peace, free from all unjust exaction and all tallage, so that nothing be taken or demanded from them for the free service they owe us and are bound to do us in all perpetuity.

"We will that all shall observe and maintain the law of king Edward with those which we have established, for the benefit of the English and the common weal of the kingdom."

This vain word, the law of king Edward, was all that remained for the future to the Anglo-Saxon nation of its ancient existence; for the condition of each individual had been wholly changed by the conquest. From the greatest to the smallest, each conquered man had been brought lower than his former position: the chief had lost his power, the rich man his wealth, the free man his independence; and he, whom the hard custom of the period had made to be born a slave in the house of another, became the serf of a stranger, no longer enjoying the greater or less consideration which the habit of living together and the community of language had procured for him on the part of his former master.

The English towns and villages were unceremoniously farmed out by the Norman earls and viscounts, to men who then worked them for their own profit, and as though they were their own property. "He let out to the highest bidder," say the chronicles, "his towns and his manors; if there came a bidder who offered more, he let the farm to him; if a third arrived, who offered a still higher price, it was to the third that he adjudged it. He gave it to the highest bidder, quite regardless of the enormous crimes which the farmers committed in levying taxes upon the poor people. He and his barons were avaricious to excess, and capable of doing anything by which they could gain money."

William, for his share of the conquest, had nearly fifteen hundred manors: he was king of England, supreme and irremovable chief of the conquerors of the country; and yet he was not happy. In the sumptuous courts he held thrice a year, the crown on his head, at London, Winchester, or Gloucester, when his companions in victory, and the prelates whom he had instituted, were ranged around him, his countenance was sad and stern; he appeared uneasy and full of care, and the possibility of a change of fortune haunted his mind. He doubted the fidelity of his Normans, and the submission of the English. He tormented himself as to his future career, and the fate of his children; and consulted, respecting his forebodings, certain men renowned as sages, in this period when divination was a part of wisdom. An Anglo-Norman poet of the twelfth century represents him seated in the midst of his bishops of England and Normandy, and soliciting them, with childish earnestness, to throw some light upon the fate of his posterity.

After having subjected the variable and turbulent results of the conquest to something like regular if not legitimate order, William quitted England for the third time, and crossed the Channel, loaded, say the old historians, with innumerable maledictions. He crossed it, never again to return: for death, as we shall soon see, kept him on the opposite shore. Among the laws and ordinances that he left behind him, two only are worthy of being mentioned as relating specially to the preservation of the rule established by the conquest. The first of these two laws, which is merely the accomplishment of a proclamation already cited (if the proclamation itself be not another version of it), had for its object to repress the assassinations committed on the members of the victorious nation; it was couched in these terms: "When a Frenchman is killed, or found dead in any hundred, the men of the hundred shall apprehend the murderer and bring him to justice within eight days; or, in default of this, shall pay a fine of forty-seven silver marks as murdrum."

An Anglo-Norman writer of the twelfth century explains the grounds of this law in the following terms: "In the first years of the new order of things, those of the English who were allowed to live, spread a thousand snares for the Normans, assassinating all those whom they met alone in desert or bye places. To suppress these assassinations, king William and his barons for some years employed punishment and exquisite tortures against the subjected people; but these chastisements producing little effect, it was decreed that every district or hundred, as the English call it, in which a Norman should be found dead, without any one there being suspected of the assassination, should nevertheless pay a large sum of money to the royal treasury. The salutary fear of this punishment, inflicted on all the inhabitants in a body, would, it was thought, procure safety for travellers, by inducing the men of each district to denounce and deliver up the culprit, whose single fault would otherwise cause an enormous loss to the whole place."

To avoid this loss, the men of an hundred in which a Frenchman—that is to say, a Norman by birth, or an auxiliary of the Norman army—was found dead, hastened carefully to destroy every external indication capable of proving that the body was that of a Frenchman, for then the hundred was not responsible, and the judge did not pursue an inquiry. But these judges soon detected the trick, and frustrated it by a regulation equally singular. Every man found assassinated was deemed a Frenchman unless the hundred could judicially prove that he was a Saxon by birth, which had to be proved before the royal judge by the oaths of two men, near relations of the deceased on the father's side, and two women on the mother's. Without these four witnesses, the quality of Englishman, Englisherie, as the Normans called it, was not sufficiently proved, and the hundred had to pay the fine. Nearly three centuries after the invasion, if we may believe the antiquaries, this inquest was still held in England on the body of every assassinated man; and, in the legal language of the time, it was called presentment of Englisherie.

The other law of the Conqueror to which we have referred was designed to increase in an exorbitant manner the authority of the bishops of England. These bishops were all Normans: it was deemed just and necessary that their power should be wholly exercised for the advantage of the conquest; and as the warriors who had effected this conquest maintained it with sword and lance, so the churchmen were called upon to maintain it by political address and religious influence. With these motives of public utility was combined another, more personal with regard to king William; it was, that the bishops of England, although installed by the common counsel of all the Norman barons and knights, had been selected from among the chaplains, the creatures, or the intimate friends of the king. No intrigue, during the life of William, ever disturbed this arrangement; never did he create a bishop who had any other will than his. The position of things changed, it is true, under the kings his successors; but the Conqueror could not foresee the future, and the experience of his whole reign justified him when he made the following law:—

"William, by the grace of God, king of England, to the earls, viscounts, and all the men of England, French and English, greeting. Know, you and all my other faithful subjects, that by the common counsel of the archbishops, bishops, abbots, and lords of my kingdom, I have thought fit to reform the episcopal laws, which unfitly and contrary to all the canons have been, up to the time of my conquest, in force in this country. I order that, for henceforth, no bishop or archdeacon shall attend the courts of justice, to hold pleads of episcopal causes, or shall submit to the judgment of secular men causes which relate to the government of the soul. I will that whosoever is summoned for any cause whatever to appear before the episcopal justice seat, shall go to the house of the bishop, or to some place which the bishop shall himself have chosen and named; let him there plead his cause, and do right before God and the bishop; not according to the law of the country, but according to the canons and episcopal decrees. If any one, through excess of pride, refuse to appear before the tribunal of the bishop, he shall be summoned once, twice, thrice; and if, after these three consecutive summonings, he does not appear, he shall be excommunicated, and, if necessary, the power and justice of the king and the viscount shall be employed against him."

It was in virtue of this law that was effected in England the separation of the civil and ecclesiastical tribunals, which established for the latter an absolute independence of all political power, an independence which they had never possessed in the time of Anglo-Saxon nationality. At that period, the bishops were obliged to attend the court of justice, which was held twice a year in each province and three times a year in each district; they added their accusations to those of the ordinary magistrates, and judged conjointly with them and the free men of the district the cases in which the custom of the age permitted them to interfere, those of widows, orphans, and churchmen, of divorce and marriage. For these cases, as for all others, there was but one law, one justice, and one tribunal. The only difference was that, when they were tried, the bishop seated himself beside the sheriff and the alderman, or elder of the province; and then, according to usage, sworn witnesses testified as to the facts, and the judges determined the law. The change in these national customs dates only from the Norman conquest. It was the Conqueror who, bursting through the ancient rules of civil equality, gave power to the high clergy of England to hold courts in their own palaces, and to employ the public power in enforcing the attendance of the contumacious; he thus subjected the royal power to the obligation of executing the decrees rendered by the ecclesiastical power, in virtue of a legislation which was not that of the country. William imposed this obligation on his successors, knowingly and purposely, from policy and not from devotion or from fear of his bishops, who were all devoted to him. Nor had the fear of pope Gregory VII. any influence upon this determination. For, notwithstanding the services which the court of Rome had formerly rendered him, the king was ever prepared with a stern denial when the pontiff's demands were not agreeable to him. The tone of one of his letters to Gregory shows with what freedom of thought he considered the pontifical pretensions and his own engagements towards the Roman church. The pope had to complain of some delay in the payment of the Peter's pence stipulated in the treaty of alliance concluded at Rome in the year 1066; he wrote to remind William of this stipulation, and the money was immediately sent. But this was not all; in raising the banner of the holy see against the English, the Conqueror seemed to have acknowledged himself vassal of the church, and Gregory, availing himself of this circumstance, did not hesitate to summon him to do homage for his conquest, and to swear the oath of fealty and vassalage between the hands of a cardinal. William answered in these terms: "Thy legate has required me, on thy part, to send money to the Roman church, and to swear fealty to thee and thy successors; I have admitted the first of these demands; as to the second, I neither have nor will admit it. I will not swear fealty to thee, because I have not promised it, and because none of my predecessors have sworn fealty to thine."

In concluding the narrative of the events just related, the chroniclers of English race give way to touching regrets as to the miseries of their nation. "There is no doubt," exclaim some of them, "that God will no longer permit us to be a nation, or to possess honour and security." Others complain that the name of Englishman has become an opprobrium; and it is not only from the pens of contemporaries that such complaints proceed; the remembrance of a great misfortune and of a great national shame is reproduced, century after century, in the writings of the sons of the Saxons, although more faintly as time advances. In the fifteenth century, the distinction of ranks in England was still attached to the conquest; and a monastic historian, not to be suspected of revolutionary theories, wrote these remarkable words: "If there be amongst us such a distance between the various conditions, one must not be astonished at it; it is because there is diversity of race; and if there be so little mutual confidence and affection among us, it is because we are not of the same blood." Lastly, an author who lived in the beginning of the seventeenth century, recals the Norman Conquest in these words: the "memorie of sorrowe," and uses touching expressions in speaking of the families then disinherited, and since fallen into the class of the poor, of labourers and peasants; it is the last glance of regret thrown back on the past, upon the event which had brought into England kings, nobles, and chieftains of foreign race.

If, retracing in his own mind the facts he has read, the reader would form to himself a just idea of what was the England conquered by William of Normandy, he must represent to himself, not a mere change of government, nor the triumph of one competitor over another, but the intrusion of a whole people into the bosom of another people, broken up by the former, and the scattered fragments of which were only admitted into the new social order as personal property, as clothing of the earth, to speak the language of the ancient acts. We must not place on one side, William, king and despot, and on the other, subjects high or low, rich or poor, all inhabitants of England, and consequently all English; we must imagine two nations, the English by origin and the English by invasion, divided on the surface of the same country; or rather imagine two countries in a far different condition: the land of the Normans, rich and free from taxes, that of the Saxons, poor, dependent, and oppressed with burdens; the first adorned with vast mansions, with walled and embattled castles; the second, sprinkled with thatched cabins or half ruined huts; that peopled with happy, idle people, warriors and courtiers, nobles and knights; this inhabited by men of toil and sorrow, farm labourers and mechanics; on the one side, luxury and insolence; upon the other, misery and envy, not the envy of the poor at sight of the riches of others, but the envy of the despoiled in the presence of their spoilers.

Lastly, to complete the picture, these two countries in a manner are entwined one in the other; they touch each other at every point, and yet they are more distinct than if the sea rolled between them. Each has its separate idiom, an idiom foreign to the other; the French is the language of the court, of the castles, of the rich abbeys, of all the places where power and luxury reign: the ancient language of the land is confined to the hearth of the poor, of the serf. Long, from generation to generation, did these two idioms continue to subsist without mixing with each other, remaining the one the token of nobility, the other the token of base estate. This is expressed with a sort of bitterness, in some verses of an old poet, who complains that England in his time offers the strange spectacle of a country abnegating its own language.

* Thus come lo! Engelond into Normannes honde.

* And the Normannes ne couthe speke tho bote her owe speche

* And speke French as dude atom, and her chyldren dude also teche;

* So that beymen of this lond that of her blod come

* Holdeth alle thulke speche that hii of hem nome,

* Ac lowe men holdeth to englyss and to her kunde speche gut.

BOOK VII. FROM THE DEATH OF WILLIAM THE CONQUEROR, TO THE LAST GENERAL CONSPIRACY OF THE ENGLISH AGAINST THE NORMANS.

1087—1137.

Quarrel between king William and Philip I., king of France—King William burns the town of Mantes—Last moments of king William—His death—His funeral—Election of William Rufus—The goldsmith Otho. banker of the invasion—Verses in praise of the Conqueror—Civil war among the Normans—Termination of the civil war—Treaty between William Rufus, king of England, and his brother Robert, duke of Normandy—Revolt of the English monks of the convent of St. Augustin—Conspiracy of the monks of this convent against their Norman abbot—Alliance between the monks and the citizens of Canterbury—Tyranny of the Norman bishops and counts—Fresh vexations inflicted upon the monks of Croyland—New quarrels among the Normans—Moderation of Eudes Fitz-Hubert—Heavy burdens imposed upon the English—Terror of the English on the approach of the king—Severity of the forest laws—Last chase of William Rufus—His death—Henry elected king of England—He addresses himself to the English—Utter insincerity of his promises—He wishes to marry an Englishwoman—Opposition of the Norman nobles to the contemplated match—Marriage of the king to Editha, Edgar's niece—More civil war—Revolt of earl Robert de Belesme—His banishment—State of the English population—Renewed quarrel between the king and his brother Robert—Levy of money in England—Duke Robert becomes his brother's prisoner—The son of duke Robert takes refuge in France—Foreign abbots installed into English monaster's—Sufferings and complaints of the English monks—Popular superstitions—Embarkation of the children of king Henry—Their shipwreck—Indifference of the English to the calamity thus endured by the king and the Norman families—Invectives of the English historians on this occasion—Mabile, daughter of Robert Fitz-Aymon—Norman anecdote—English anecdote—Trial and sentence of the Saxon Brihtstan—Anglo-Norman tribunals—Oath taken to Matilda, surnamed the Empress—Marriage of Matilda with the earl of Aujou—Festivities at Rouen on the occasion—Election of Stephen of Blois—His popularity with the Norman barons—His rupture with them—Conspiracy of the

English—Flight of the conspirators—Subsequent insurrections—Difficulties experienced by the historian.

During his stay in Normandy, in the first months of the year 1087, king William occupied himself in terminating an old dispute with Philip I., king of France. Favoured by the troubles which followed the death of duke Robert, the county of Vexin, situated between the Epte and the Oise, had been dismembered from Normandy, and re-united to France. William flattered himself that he should be able to recover this portion of his inheritance without a war; and, pending the result of the negotiations, he reposed from his fatigues at Rouen; he even kept his bed, by the advice of his physicians, who were seeking to reduce his excessive corpulence by a rigorous diet. Thinking he had little to fear from a man absorbed in such cares, Philip gave evasive replies to the demands of the Norman; and, on his part, the latter seemed to take the delay patiently. But the king of France having one day said jestingly to his friends: "By my faith, the king of England is very long about his lying-in; there will be great rejoicing at his churching," this sarcasm, reported to William, offended him to such a degree that he forgot everything but vengeance. He swore by his greatest oath, by the splendour and birth of God, that he would be churched at Nôtre Dame-de-Paris, with ten thousand lances for his candles.

Suddenly resuming his activity, he assembled his troops, and in the month of July entered France through the territory of which he claimed possession. The wheat was still in the fields, and the trees laden with fruit. He ordered everything to be laid waste on his way; the harvests were trodden under foot by the cavalry, the vines torn up, and the fruit trees cut down. The first town he came to was Mantes-sur-Seine; it was fired by his order, and he himself, in a sort of destructive phrenzy, rode in the midst of the flames, to enjoy the spectacle and encourage his soldiers.

As he was galloping over the ruins, his horse placed his feet upon some burning embers, started, fell, and wounded his rider in the stomach. The agitation into which he had thrown himself by riding about and shouting, the heat of the fire and of the weather, rendered his wound dangerous; he was conveyed very ill to Rouen, and thence, unable to support the noise of the streets, to a monastery outside the city. He languished for six weeks, surrounded by physicians and priests, and his illness growing worse and worse, he sent money to Mantes, to rebuild the churches he had burnt; he also sent sums to the convents and poor of England, to obtain, says an old English poet, pardon for the robberies he had committed there. He ordered the Saxons and Normans whom he had imprisoned to be set at liberty. Among the former were Morkar, Siward Beorn, and Ulfnoth, brother of king Harold, (one of the two hostages for whose deliverance Harold made his fatal journey.) The Normans were Roger, formerly earl of Hereford, and Eudes bishop of Bayeux, William's half-brother by the mother's side.

William, surnamed Rufus, and Henry, the king's two youngest sons, did not quit his bedside, waiting with impatience for him to dictate his last will. Robert, the eldest of the three, had been absent since his last quarrel with his father. It was to him that William, with the consent of the barons of Normandy, had formerly left his title of duke; and, notwithstanding the malediction he had since pronounced upon Robert, he did not seek to divest him of this title, which the wishes of the Normans had destined for him. "As to the kingdom of England," he said, "I leave it to no one, because I did not inherit it, but acquired it by force, and at the price of blood; I replace it in the hands of God, contenting myself with expressing the wish that my son William, who has ever been submissive to me in all things, may obtain it, if it please God, and prosper in it." "And what will you give me then, my father?" energetically demanded Henry, the youngest son. "I give thee," said the king, "five thousand pounds in silver, from my treasury." "But what can I do with this money, if I have neither land nor house?" "Content ye, my son, and have confidence in God; allow thy elder brothers to precede thee; thy time will come after theirs." Henry immediately withdrew to receive the five thousand pounds; he had them carefully weighed, and deposited in a coffer, strongly banded with iron and supplied with good locks. William Rufus departed at the same time for England, in order to get crowned.

On the 10th of September, at sunrise, king William was awakened by the sound of bells, and asked what it meant; he was answered that they were ringing prime at the church of Saint Mary. He raised his hands, saying: "I commend my soul to Mary, the holy mother of God," and almost immediately expired. His physicians and the other attendants who had passed the night with him, seeing him dead, hastily mounted their horses, and went to look after their property. The servants and vassals of lower rank, after the flight of their superiors, carried off the arms, plate, clothes, linen, and everything portable, and also fled, leaving the body almost naked upon the floor. It remained, thus abandoned, several hours; for throughout Rouen the people had become as it were intoxicated, not with grief, but with fear for the future; they were, says an old historian, as much troubled as though they had seen an hostile army before the gates of their city. The men ran wildly to and fro, asking advice from their wives, their friends, from the first person they met; they removed and concealed their goods, or endeavoured to sell them at a loss.

At last the churchmen, priests, and monks, having recovered their senses and their strength, arranged a procession. Dressed in the habits of their order, with the cross, candles, and censors, they came to the corpse, and prayed for the soul of the deceased. The archbishop of Rouen, William, ordered that the body of the king should be transported to Caen, and buried in the cathedral of Saint Stephen the proto-martyr, which the king had built. But his sons, his brothers, all his relations had deserted him; none of his officers was present; not one appeared to take charge of his obsequies; and it was a private country gentleman, named Herluin, who, out of good nature and for the love of God, say the historians of the time, undertook the trouble and the expense of the ceremonial. He hired men and a hearse at his own expense, removed the body to the banks of the Seine, and thence upon a boat, by river and by sea, to Caen. Gilbert, abbot of Saint Stephens, came, with all his monks, to meet the body; many priests and laymen joined them; but a fire which suddenly broke out dissolved the procession, and priests and laymen all hastened to extinguish it. The monks of Saint Stephen alone remained, and carried the body of the king to their house.

The inhumation of the great chief, the famous baron, as the historians of the period style him, was not completed without fresh incidents. All the bishops and abbots of Normandy were assembled for the ceremony; they had prepared the grave in the church, between the choir and the altar; the mass was finished; they were about to lower the body, when a man, advancing from the crowd, said aloud: "Priests and bishops, this land is mine; it was the site of my father's house; the man for whom you are now praying took it from me by force, to build his church upon it. I have not sold my land; I have not pawned it; I have not forfeited it; I have not given it: it is mine by right, and I demand it. In the name of God, I forbid the body of the spoiler to be placed here, or to be covered with my glebe." The man who thus spoke was Asselin Fitz-Arthur, and all present confirmed the truth of what he had said. The bishops made him approach, and agreed to pay him sixty pence for the immediate place of sepulture, and to give him equitable recompence for the rest of the land. The king's body was without a coffin, clothed in its royal habit; when they proceeded to place it in the grave, which had been constructed in masonry, the aperture was found to be too narrow; in forcing the body in, it burst. They burnt abundance of incense and perfumes, but in vain; the people dispersed in disgust, and the priests themselves, hastening the ceremony, soon quitted the church.

William Rufus, on his way to England, learned the death of his father at the port of Wissant, near Calais. He hastened to Winchester, the city where the royal treasure was deposited, and gaining over William de Pont-de-l'Arche, the keeper of the treasure, obtained the keys. He had an inventory taken of it, and weighed it carefully; he found it to consist of 60,000 pounds of fine silver, with much gold, and a quantity of jewels. He next assembled all the high Norman barons then in England, announced the death of the Conqueror, was chosen king by them, and crowned by archbishop Lanfranc in the cathedral of Winchester, while the lords who had remained in Normandy were holding a council as to the succession. Many of the latter were desirous that the two countries should have but one and the same government; they wished to give the crown to duke Robert, who had returned from exile; but the activity of William anticipated them.

His first act of royal authority was again to imprison the Saxons Ulfnoth, Morkar, and Siward Beorn, whom his father had restored to liberty; he then drew from the treasury a great quantity of gold and silver, which he gave to the goldsmith Otho to be converted into ornaments for the tomb of him whom he had abandoned on his death bed. The name of the goldsmith Otho merits a place in this history, because the territorial register of the conquest mentions him as one of the great proprietors newly created. Perhaps he had been the banker of the invasion, and had advanced part of the funds upon mortgage of English lands; we may easily believe this, for the goldsmiths of the middle ages were also bankers; perhaps, also, he had merely made commercial speculations in the domains acquired by the lance and the sword, giving to the adventurers, those men-at-arms errant, a class of men so common at that period, gold in exchange for their lands.

A sort of literary competition was now entered into between the Latin versifiers of England and of Normandy, for the epitaph which was to be cut on the tomb of the deceased king; it was Thomas, archbishop of York, who carried off the honours. Several pieces of verse and prose in praise of the Conqueror have been preserved to our days, and amongst the eulogies bestowed on him by the priests and literary men of the period, there are some very singular: "English nation!" exclaims one of them, "why hast thou troubled the repose of this prince, so much the friend of virtue?" "O! England," cries another, "thou wouldst have cherished him, thou wouldst have esteemed him in the highest degree, had it not been for thy folly and thy wickedness." "His reign was pacific and fruitful," says a third; "and his soul was benevolent." None of the epitaphs remain which the conquered nation pronounced upon him, unless we regard as an instance of the popular exclamations occasioned by his death, these verses of an English poet of the thirteenth century: "The days of king William were days of vexation and sorrow, so that much people of England thought his life too long."

Meantime, the Anglo-Norman barons who had not concurred in the election of William Rufus returned to England, furious at his having become king without their consent; they resolved to depose him, and to substitute for him his eldest brother, Robert, duke of Normandy. At the head of this party was Eudes de Bayeux, brother to the Conqueror, who had just come out of prison, and many rich Normans or English-Frenchmen, as the Saxon chronicle calls them. The Red king (for so the historians of the time designate him), seeing that his countrymen conspired against him, called to his aid the men of English race, conciliating their support by the hope of some mitigation of their sufferings. He summoned around him several of those whom the recollection of their past power still caused to be regarded by the English nation as their natural chiefs; he promised them the best laws they should themselves require, the best which had ever been in the country; he restored to them the right to carry arms, and the right of the chase; he stayed the levy of imposts and of all odious tributes; but this did not last long, say the contemporary annals.

For these concessions of a few days, and perhaps also from a secret desire to come to blows with the Normans, the Saxon chiefs consented to defend the king's cause, and published in his name and their own this ancient proclamation of war, that which once aroused every Englishman capable of bearing arms: "Let each man that is not a nothing, whether in the town or country, leave his house and come." Thirty thousand Saxons assembled at the appointed place, received arms, and were enrolled under the king's banner. They were nearly all foot-soldiers; William led them by a rapid march, with his cavalry, composed of Normans, to the city of Rochester, where bishop Eudes and the other recusant chiefs had fortified themselves, awaiting the arrival of duke Robert, to march upon Canterbury and London.

It appears that the Saxons of the royal army displayed great ardour at the siege of Rochester. The besieged closely pressed, soon demanded to capitulate, on condition of acknowledging William for their king, and of retaining under him their lands and honours. William at first refused; but the Normans of his army, not having the same zeal as the Saxons in this war, which was for them a civil war, and not desiring to reduce their countrymen and relations to extremity, considered the king too inveterate against the defenders of Rochester.

They sought to appease him: "We who have aided thee in danger," said they, "pray thee to spare our countrymen, our relatives, who are also thine, and who aided thy father to conquer England." The king gave way, and at last granted the besieged liberty to quit the city with their arms and horses. Bishop Eudes endeavoured further to obtain that the king's military music should not play in token of victory at the departure of the garrison, but William angrily refused, and said, that he would not make this concession for a thousand gold marks; the Normans of Robert's party quitted the city which they had not been able to defend, with colours lowered, to the sound of the royal trumpets. At this moment loud clamours arose from the English in the royal army: "Bring us cords," they cried; "we will hang this traitor bishop, with all his accomplices. O king! why dost thou let him go free? He is not worthy to live, the traitor, the perjured murderer of so many thousand men."

It was amidst these imprecations that the prelate who had blessed the Norman army at the battle of Hastings quitted England, never more to return. The war amongst the Normans lasted some time longer; but this family quarrel gradually subsided, and terminated in a treaty between the two parties and the two brothers. The domains that the friends of Robert had lost in England, for having embraced his cause, were restored to them, and Robert himself resigned his pretensions to the crown in consideration of large territorial possessions. It was agreed between the two parties, that the king, if he survived the duke, should have the duchy of Normandy, and that in the contrary case, the duke should have the kingdom of England; twelve men on the part of the king, and twelve on the part of the duke, confirmed this treaty by oath. Thus ended both the Norman civil war and the alliance which this war had occasioned between the English and the king. The popular concessions that the latter had made, were all revoked, his promises belied, and the Saxons returned to their position of oppressed subjects.

Near the city of Canterbury was an ancient monastery, founded in honour of the missionary Augustin, who converted the Saxons and Angles. Here were preserved, in a higher degree than in the religious houses of less importance, the national spirit, and the remembrance of ancient liberty. The Normans perceived this, and early endeavoured to destroy this spirit by reiterated humiliations. The primate Lanfranc commenced by abolishing the ancient privilege of the monks of Saint Augustin, of being exempt from all ecclesiastical discipline but that of their own abbot. Although the abbot, at this time, was a Norman, and as such little liable to any suspicion of indulgence towards the men of another race, Lanfranc deprived him of the charge of his monks, which he himself assumed; he then forbad the bells of the monastery to be rung before the office had rung from the cathedral, paying no respect, says the historian, to this maxim of the Holy Scriptures: Where the spirit of the Lord is, there is liberty. The Saxon monks murmured at being subjected to this restriction, and, to manifest their discontent, they celebrated the offices late, negligently, and with all sorts of irregularities, such as reversing the crosses, and walking in procession barefooted against the course of the sun. "They do violence to us," said they, "in contempt of the canons of the church; well, we will violate the canons in the service of the church." They requested the Norman, their abbot, to transmit a protest from them to the pope; but the only reply of the abbot was to punish them as rebels, and to shut up the building, so that they could not go out. This man, who sacrificed his personal independence out of hatred to the Saxons, died in the year 1088, and then archbishop Lanfranc himself proceeded to the monastery, taking with him a Norman monk, called Guy, a man much beloved by the king. He called upon the monks of St. Augustin, in the name of the royal authority, to receive and instal the new abbot forthwith; but all emphatically answered that they would do nothing of the sort. Lanfranc, furious at this resistance, ordered that those who refused to obey should immediately quit the monastery. They almost all departed, and the Norman was installed in their absence with the usual ceremonies. The prior of the monastery, named Elfwin, and several other monks, all of Saxon birth, were then seized and imprisoned. Those who had departed at the command of the archbishop went and seated themselves on the ground under the walls of the castle of Canterbury. They were informed that a certain number of hours was granted them within which to return to the monastery, but that after that time they would be regarded and treated as vagabonds; they remained for awhile undecided, but the hour for refection came; they suffered from hunger, and many, repenting, sent to archbishop Lanfranc and promised obedience. He made them swear on the relics of St. Augustin to remain faithful to this promise. They who refused to take the oath were imprisoned, until weariness of captivity should render them more docile. One of them, named Alfred, who fled and was afterwards found wandering by the road-side, was put in irons in the archiepiscopal palace at Canterbury. The spirit of resistance was appeased for some months, and then again became still more violent than before; a conspiracy was formed against the life of the new abbot of foreign race. One of the conspirators, named

Colomban, was taken, brought before the archbishop, and questioned as to his design of killing the Norman. "I had that intention," answered the monk boldly, "and assuredly would have executed it." Lanfranc ordered him to be tied naked to the doors of the monastery, and to be publicly whipped.

In the year 1089, the primate Lanfranc died; and the monks, delivered from the terror with which he had inspired them, commenced a third revolt, of a more serious character than the two others. They called to their aid the Saxon inhabitants of Canterbury, who, embracing this quarrel as a national quarrel, came armed to the house of the abbot of Saint Augustin, and attacked it. The abbot's people resisted, and on both sides there were several men wounded and killed. Guy, with great difficulty, escaped from his adversaries, and hastened to shut himself up in the cathedral. On hearing of the affair, the Normans, Gaucelme, bishop of Winchester, and Gondulph, bishop of Rochester, hastened to Canterbury, whither numerous detachments of troops were sent by the king's order. The monastery of Saint Augustin was occupied militarily; the trial of the monks was commenced, and they were condemned in a body to receive corporal punishment, which two foreign monks, Guy and Le Normand, inflicted on them at the discretion of the bishops; they were then distributed in various parts of England, and in their place twenty-four monks and a prior came from the continent. All those inhabitants of Canterbury who were taken by the Norman troops in arms were condemned to lose their eyes.

These struggles, fruits of the hatred and despair of the conquered, were reproduced at the same time in many churches of England; and generally, wherever Saxons, united in a body, and not reduced to the last degree of slavery, encountered the chiefs or governors of foreign race. These chiefs, whether priests or laymen, differed only in their dress; under the coat of mail, or under the cope, it was the same insolent, cruel, avaricious conqueror, treating the conquered as beings of an inferior race to his own. Jean de la Villette, bishop of Wells, formerly a physician at Tours, pulled down the houses of the canons of his church to build himself a palace with their materials. Renouf Flambard, bishop of Lincoln, formerly a valet to the duke of Normandy, committed such depredations in his diocese, that the inhabitants wished to die, said an ancient historian, rather than live under his authority. The Norman bishops went to the altar, as the earls to their military reviews, between two rows of lances; they passed the day in playing at dice, hunting, hawking, and drinking. One of them, in a fit of gaiety, had prepared for his Saxon monks, in the great hall of the monastery, a repast at which he made them eat meats forbidden by their order, and served up by women with dishevelled hair and half naked. Those of the monks who at this sight desired to withdraw, or who even turned away their eyes, were maltreated and called hypocrites by the Norman prelate and his friends.

Against such adversaries the remnant of the Anglo-Saxon clergy could not maintain any very protracted combat; every day, age and persecution removed some of the old monks or priests; the resistance, at first energetic, was gradually extinguished. The fact of being peopled by a majority of men of English race was with any monastery ground for the hatred and oppression of the great. This was experienced under William Rufus, by the monastery of Croyland, already so ill treated at the time of the conquest. After a conflagration which had consumed part of their houses, the Norman count of the district in which it stood, presuming that the charters of the abbey had perished in the flames, summoned the monks to appear in his court at Spalding, to produce their title. On the appointed day they sent one of their number, Trig, who took with him their ancient charters in the Saxon language, confirmed by the Conqueror, whose seal was appended. The monk displayed his parchments before the count and his officers, who laughed at and insulted him, saying that these barbarian and unintelligible scrawls were of no authority. The sight of the royal seal, however, produced some effect; the Norman viscount, who dared not break it or publicly seize the charters to which it was attached, allowed the monk to depart; but he sent servants after him, armed with sticks, to seize him on the road, and take the charters from him. Trig only avoided them by following a bye road.

The peace which reigned among the conquerors of England was once more disturbed in the year 1094, by the revolt of several chiefs against the king. One of the causes of this revolt was the exclusive right to hunt in the forests of England, established by William the Bastard and vigorously maintained by his son. At the head of the malcontents was Robert, son of Roger de Molbray, earl of Northumberland, who possessed two hundred and eighty manors in England. Robert did not appear at the court of the king on one of the days fixed for the political conferences of the barons and Anglo-Norman knights. His absence excited suspicion, and the king issued a proclamation that every great landholder who did not appear at his court at the approaching feast of Whitsuntide, should be excluded the public peace. Robert de Molbray did not attend, from fear of being seized and imprisoned; whereupon William despatched the royal troops to Northumberland. He besieged and took several castles; he blockaded that of Bamborough, to which earl Robert had withdrawn, but he could not make himself master of it. After many useless efforts, the king constructed opposite Bamborough a wooden fortress, which he called, in his Norman language Malveisin, or bad neighbour, left a garrison in it, and returned southwards. The garrison of the new fortress surprised Robert in a sortie, wounded and made him prisoner. He was condemned to perpetual imprisonment, and his accomplices were exiled from England.

The estates of these banished men, in town and country, remained for some time without a master and without cultivation. It appears that the king's favourites allowed them to remain untilled, after having taken from them everything of any value, indifferent as to property, the origin of which and the uncertainty of political events, rendered it too precarious. On their part, the royal officers, in order that the exchequer might lose none of its revenues, continued to levy from the town or hundred to which the vacant property appertained the entire amount of the territorial tax, a charge that fell upon the men of English race. The people of Colchester, according to an old narrative, returned great thanks to Eudes Fitzhubert, viscount or governor of the town, for assuming in his own name the lands of the disinherited Normans, and consenting to pay the taxes demanded in respect of them. If we may credit the same account, this Eudes gained the love of the people of Colchester by his equitable and mild administration. He is the only chief imposed upon the English by the foreign power to whom history bears such a testimony.

This exception to the law of the conquest did not extend beyond one single town; everywhere else things followed their course, and the royal officers, say the chronicles, were worse than robbers; they pillaged without mercy the cornloft of the peasant, and the shop of the trader. Oxford was governed by Robert d'Ouilly, who spared neither poor nor rich; in the north, Odineau d'Omfreville seized the goods of the English in his vicinity, in order to compel them to hew and carry stones for the construction of his castle. Around London, the king also levied by force troops of men to construct a new wall for the Conqueror's tower, a bridge over the Thames, and in Westminster a palace or hall of audience, for the assemblies of his barons.

"The counties to whose share these works fell," says the Saxon chronicle, "were cruelly afflicted; every year that passed was heavy and full of sorrow, on account of the vexations without number and the multiplied taxes."

Historians less laconic have transmitted to us some details of the sorrows and torments that the conquered nation suffered. Wherever the king passed in his journeys through England, the country was ravaged by his people. When they could not themselves use all the provisions or goods that they found in the houses of the English, they made the owner himself carry them to the neighbouring market, and sell them for their profit; at other times they burned them for amusement, or if it were wine or other beverage, washed the feet of their horses with it. "The ill treatment to which they subjected the heads of families, their outrages upon the women and girls," adds the contemporary historian, "one would blush to relate; accordingly, at the first rumour of the king's approach, all fled from their abodes, and retired, with whatever they could carry, to the depths of the forest or other desert places."

Fifty Saxons who, by some happy chance or perhaps by a little political cowardice, had managed to retain a remnant of their property, were accused, falsely or justly, of having hunted in the royal forests, and of having killed, taken, and eaten deer; such were the terms of the criminal charge brought against them. They denied the charge, and the Norman judges inflicted on them the ordeal by fire, which the ancient English laws only sanctioned when demanded by the accused. "On the appointed day," says an eye-witness, "all underwent the sentence, without any mercy; it was piteous to behold; but God, in preserving their hands from burning, showed clearly their innocence, and the wickedness of their persecutors." When it was reported to king William that after three days the hands of the accused were unscathed: "What of that," said he; "God is no judge of these things; these matters concern me, and it is I who ought to judge them." The historian does not relate what the new sentence was, or what the fate of the unhappy English, whom now no pious fraud could save.

The Saxons, persecuted by William Rufus for transgressing the laws of the chase, far more rigorously than they had been even by his father, had no other way of revenging themselves than by calling him, in derision, keeper of the forests, and wild beast-herd, and spreading sinister rumours as to these forests, into which no man of English race could enter armed without risking his life. They said that the devil, under terrible forms, appeared there to the Normans, and told them of the terrible fate that he reserved for the king and his counsellors. This popular superstition obtained authority by the singular chance which rendered hunting in the forest of England, and especially in the New Forest, fatal to the race of the Conqueror. In the year 1081, Richard, eldest son of William the Bastard, had mortally wounded himself there; in the month of May of the year 1100, Richard, son of duke Robert, and nephew of William Rufus, was killed there by an arrow carelessly shot; and, singular circumstance, this king himself also met with the same death there in the July of the same year.

On the morning of his last day, he held a grand breakfast with his friends in Winchester castle, and then prepared for the proposed chase. While he was fastening his shoes, jesting with his guests, a workman presented to him six new arrows. He examined them, praised the workmanship, took four to himself, and gave the two others to Walter Tirel, saying: "Sharp arrows for the best shot." Walter Tirel was a Frenchman who had great possessions in Poix and Ponthieu; he was the king's most cherished intimate, and constant companion. At the moment of departure there came in a monk of St. Peter's abbey at Gloucester, bearing despatches from his superior. The latter, a Norman by birth and named Serlon, sent word, expressing the utmost uneasiness at the circumstance, that one of his monks (probably of English race) had had a vision of ill-omen in his sleep; that he had seen Jesus Christ seated upon a throne, and at his feet a woman, who supplicated him saying: "Saviour of the world, look down with pity upon thy people, who suffer under the yoke of William." On hearing this message, the king burst into loud laughter. "Do they take me for an Englishman, with their dreams?" said he; "do they think I am one of the idiots that turn back because an old woman dreams or sneezes? Come, Walter de Poix, to horse!"

Henry, the king's brother, William de Breteuil, and several other lords, accompanied him to the forest: the hunters dispersed, but Walter Tirel remained with the king, and their dogs hunted together. Both were at their post opposite each other, the arrow in the cross-bow and the finger on the trigger, when a large stag, turned up by the huntsmen, advanced between the king and his friend. William pulled the trigger, but the cord of his crossbow breaking, the arrow did not fly, and the stag, astonished at the sharp sound, stopped and looked around. The king signed to his companion to shoot, but the latter did not obey the signal, either because he did not see it or because he did not understand it. Thereupon William impatiently exclaimed: "Shoot, Walter, shoot, in the devil's name!" And on the instant an arrow, either that of Walter of from another hand, pierced his chest; he fell without uttering a word and expired. Walter Tirel ran to him; but finding him without life, he remounted his horse, galloped to the coast, passed over to Normandy, and thence into France.

At the first rumour of the king's death, all participating in the chase hastily quitted the forest to see to their affairs. His brother Henry galloped to Winchester to the royal treasury; and the body of William Rufus remained on the ground, abandoned as that of the Conqueror had been. Some charcoal burners, who found him pierced with the arrow, placed him in their cart, wrapped in rags through which the blood trickled along the road. In this manner were the remains of the second Norman king conveyed to Winchester castle. Henry, already arrived there, imperiously demanded the keys of the royal treasury. As the keepers were hesitating, William de Breteuil himself, arriving from the New Forest, entered all out of breath, and opposed this demand: "Thou and I," he said to Henry, "ought loyally to remember the fealty we swore to the duke Robert thy brother: he has received our oath of homage, and, absent or present, he is entitled to it." A violent quarrel ensued; Henry drew his sword, and, with the aid of his attendants, who flocked in, took possession of the treasure and of the royal ornaments.

It was certainly true that, in the terms of the treaty of peace concluded between William and duke Robert, and sworn to by all the Anglo-Norman barons, the crown was due to the duke; but he was then far from England and from Normandy. The exhortations of pope Urban II. to all Christians to recover the Holy Land, had produced a powerful effect upon his adventurous spirit, and he was among the first who had departed with the great levy en masse made to the cry of Dieu le Veut, in the year 1096, and which, three years after, attained the object of its pilgrimage in the capture of Jerusalem. When the death of his brother William happened, Robert was on his return to Normandy; but, little suspecting what the delay would cost him, he stayed some time to prosecute a love affair at the court of one of the Norman lords settled in Italy. Thus taken by surprise, and without a leader, his partisans could not withstand those of Henry. The latter, master of the royal treasure, came to London, where the principal Normans assembled; and, three days after the death of his brother, he was elected king by them and solemnly crowned. The prelates favoured him, because he was greatly attached to them and to the literature of the period, a circumstance which procured for him the surname of Clerc, or Beauclerc. It is even said that the Saxons preferred him to his competitor, because he had been born and brought up in England. He promised at his coronation to observe the good laws of king Edward; but declared that he would, like his father, retain the exclusive enjoyment of the forests.

King Henry, the first of the name, had neither the faults nor the good qualities of his eldest brother Robert. The latter was volatile and fanciful, but generous and of good faith; the other was an able administrator, greatly given to dissimulation. Notwithstanding the facility with which he had ascended the throne, he thought it prudent not to rely too entirely on the faith of those who had elected him. He suspected the fidelity of the Normans, and resolved to create for himself in England a power independent of them, and to arouse, for his own purposes, the patriotism of the Saxons. He extended his hand to the poor conquered natives, who were ever flattered in the hour of danger and crushed when that hour had passed away. He convoked their leading men, and, by an interpreter, addressed them in the following terms:—

"My friends and liegemen, natives of this country, in which I was myself born. You know that my brother would have my crown. He is a haughty man, who cannot live in repose; he openly despises you, holding you as cowards and gluttons, and would trample you under his feet. But I, a mild and pacific king, propose to maintain you in all your ancient liberties, and to govern you by your own counsels, with moderation and prudence. I will give you, if you require it, a writing to this effect, signed with my own hand, and will confirm it by oath. Stand firm, then, by me; for, supported by English valour, I fear not the mad menaces of the Normans."

The writing promised by the king to the English, or, to use the language of the period, his royal charter, was drawn up; as many copies of it made as there were Norman counties in England, and, to invest it with the more solemnity, a new seal, made for the purpose, was affixed to it. The copies were deposited in the principal church of each county, but they did not remain there long; all were removed when the king retracted his promises, and, in the phrase of an ancient historian, impudently falsified his word. Three copies only remained which escaped by chance; one at Canterbury, one at York, and the other at Saint Albans.

The same policy that induced Henry I. to take this step with the English, led him to adopt another still more decisive; this was to take a wife of Anglo-Saxon race. There was then in England an orphan daughter of Malcolm, king of Scotland, and of Margaret, sister of king Edgar. She was named Edith, and had been brought up in the abbey of Rumsey, in Hampshire, under the care of another of Edgar's sisters, Christina, who, after taking refuge in Scotland with her brother, had assumed the veil in the year 1086. As a king's daughter, many of the high Norman barons had sought Edgar's niece in marriage; she was demanded of William Rufus by Alain de Breton, lord of Richmond, in Yorkshire; but Alain died before the king had given her to him. William de

Garenne (Warenne), earl of Surrey, then sought her; but for some reason or other the marriage did not take place. It was this lady whom king Henry's ablest counsellors proposed to him as a wife, with a view thus to gain the support of the whole Anglo-Saxon race against Robert and his partisans.

On their part, many of the English conceived the futile hope of witnessing the return of the old Saxon times, when the granddaughter of the Saxon kings should wear the crown. Those who had any relations with the family of Edith went to her, and intreated her not to refuse this union. She showed much repugnance, it is not precisely known for what reason; but they who urged her were not discouraged, and so beset her, says an ancient author, that she at last said yea, out of sheer weariness of saying nay. "Noble and gracious lady," they urged, "it is in thy power to retrieve the ancient honour of England; thou wilt be a sign of alliance, a pledge of reconciliation, but if thou persist in thy refusal, eternal hatred will remain between the two races, and blood will not cease to flow."

As soon as Edgar's niece had given her assent, they changed her name, and instead of Edith, she was called Matilda, which sounded more agreeably in Norman ears. This was not the only precaution that became necessary; for a strong party was formed against the marriage, principally composed of those who openly or secretly favoured duke Robert, whose numbers were augmented by many who, from national pride, thought it unworthy of the conquerors of England to have a Saxon woman for their queen. Their ill will raised up all sorts of unforeseen obstacles; they alleged that Matilda, brought up from her infancy in a convent, had been consecrated to God by her parents; it was reported that she had been seen publicly wearing the veil, and this report suspended the celebration of the marriage, to the great joy of those who were opposed to it.

There was at this time, in the archiepiscopal throne of Canterbury, a monk of Bec, named Anselm, a man of learning and virtue, to whom the historians of the period render this honorable testimony, that the native English loved him as though he had been one of themselves. Anselm had come by chance to England, in the reign of the first William, at the time when Lanfranc, seeking to destroy the reputation of the saints of English race, was fiercely attacking the sanctity of archbishop Elfeg, murdered by the Danes. Entirely absorbed with his project, the primate conversed with the Norman monk on the history of the Saxon Elfeg, and what he called his pretended martyrdom. "For my part," answered Anselm, "I think this man a martyr and truly a martyr; for he preferred to die rather than injure his country. He died for justice, as Saint John for truth, and both for Christ, who is truth and justice."

Become primate in his turn, under William Rufus, Anselm persevered in the spirit of equity which had inspired this answer, and in his good will towards the English. He was one of the most zealous partisans of the marriage sought by the latter, but when he learned the reports respecting Edgar's niece, he declared that nothing should induce him to take from God one who was his spouse, to unite her to a carnal husband. Wishing, however, to assure himself of the truth, he questioned Matilda, who denied that she had been consecrated to God; she even denied that she had ever worn the veil of her own accord, and offered to prove this before all the prelates of England. "I must confess," she said, "that I have sometimes appeared veiled; but only for this reason: in my youth, when I was under the care of my aunt Christina, she, to protect me, as she said, from the libertinism of the Normans, who assailed the honour of every woman they met, used to place a piece of black stuff on my head, and when I refused to wear it, she treated me harshly. In her presence, I wore this cloth, but as soon as she left me, I threw it on the ground, and trampled on it in childish anger."

Anselm, unwilling to act in this great difficulty upon his own judgment, convoked an assembly of bishops, abbots, monks, and lay-lords, in Rochester. Several witnesses cited before this council confirmed the truth of the girl's statement. Two Norman archdeacons, William and Humbault, were sent to the convent in which Matilda had been educated, and on their return, deposed that the public voice, as well as the testimony of the sisters, agreed with her declaration. At the moment when the assembly was about to deliberate, archbishop Anselm withdrew, that he might not be suspected of using any influence upon it; and when he returned, he who spoke for all the rest announced, in these terms, the common decision: "We think that the girl is free, and may dispose of her person, relying herein upon the authority of a judgment pronounced in a similar case, by the venerable Lanfranc, at a time when the Saxon women, who had sought shelter in the nunneries, through fear of the great William's soldiers, demanded their liberty."

Archbishop Anselm replied that he fully concurred in this decision, and, a few days after, celebrated the marriage of the Norman king and the niece of the last king of English race; but before pronouncing the nuptial benediction, desirous of dissipating all suspicion, and disarming malignity, he ascended a platform raised for the purpose in front of the church door, and related to the people the inquiry that had been made and the decision that had been given in accordance with it. These facts are stated by an eye-witness, Edmer, a Saxon by birth and monk of Canterbury.

All these precautions could not overcome what the historian Edmer calls the heart-malice of certain men, that is to say, the repugnance of many of the Normans to what they deemed the misalliance of their king. They amused themselves at the expense of the newly-married pair, calling them Godrik and Godiva, employing these Saxon names by way of derision. "Henry knew it and heard it," says an ancient chronicler, "but he affected to laugh at it heartily, adroitly concealing his anger." When duke Robert had landed in Normandy, the irritation of the malcontents assumed a more serious character; many Anglo-Norman lords crossed the Channel to support the rights of the dispossessed brother, or sent him encouraging messages, inviting him to hasten to England, and assuring him of their fidelity, pursuant to the compact formerly concluded with William Rufus. And accordingly, on Robert's landing in England, his army was rapidly augmented by a great number of barons and knights; but the bishops, the common soldiers, and the men of English race, remained on the king's side. The latter more especially, with their old instinct of national hatred, ardently desired that the two factions should fight. There was no battle on the duke's disembarkation, because Robert landed on the coast of Hampshire, while Henry awaited him on that of Sussex. Some days elapsed before the armies could meet, and the least inveterate among the Normans of both parties, availing themselves of the interval, interposed, and appeased this quarrel between brothers and countrymen. It was arranged that Robert should once more renounce his pretensions to the kingdom of England, for an annual pension of two thousand pounds of silver, and that the confiscations made by the king upon the duke's friends, and by the duke upon the king's, should be restored.

This treaty deprived the English of an occasion of satisfying with impunity their national aversion to the conquerors, and of killing the Normans under the covert of a Norman banner. But, ere long, this occasion again presented itself, and was eagerly seized. Robert de Belesme, one of the most powerful earls of Normandy and England, was cited before the general assembly to answer to forty-five charges. Robert appeared, and demanded, as was the custom, permission freely to seek his friends and take counsel with them as to his defence; but once out of the council-hall, he mounted his horse, and hastened to one of his strongholds. The king and lords, who had vainly awaited his answer, declared him a public enemy unless he presented himself at the next assembly. But Robert de Belesme, preparing for war, supplied with ammunition and arms his castles of Arundel and Tickhill, and the citadel of Shrewsbury, which was in his keeping. He also fortified Bridgenorth, near the Welsh frontier; and it was towards this point, that the royal army marched to assail him.

King Henry had been besieging Bridgenorth three weeks, when the Norman earls and barons interposed to terminate the war, and to reconcile Robert de Belesme with the king. "For they thought," says an old historian, "that the victory of the king over earl Robert would give him the means to bend them all to his will." They came in a great body to Henry, and demanded a conference, or, as it was termed in the French tongue, a parlement, to treat of peace. The assembly was held in a plain near the royal camp. On the side of the neighbouring hill was a body of three thousand English, who, knowing the object of the conference of the Norman chiefs, were greatly excited, and cried: "O king Henry, believe them not; they seek to lay a snare for thee; we are here, we will aid thee, and make the attack for thee; agree to no peace with the traitor until thou holdst him fast, dead or alive." For this once, the Normans did not succeed in their attempt at conciliation; the siege of Bridgenorth was vigorously prosecuted, and the fortress taken; the capture of that of Shrewsbury soon followed, and Robert de Belesme, compelled to capitulate, was dispossessed and banished.

The vanity of the English enrolled under the royal banner might be flattered by their military successes against the insurgent Normans, but the nation at large derived no relief from it; and, if it was avenged on some of its enemies, it was for the profit of another enemy. Though the king had married a Saxon wife and had received a Saxon nickname from the Norman chiefs, he was a Norman at heart. His favourite minister, the count de Meulan, was conspicuous among all the other foreign dignitaries for his hatred to the natives. It is true that the popular voice surnamed Matilda the good queen; she counselled the king, it is said, to love the people; but facts reveal no trace of her counsels or of her influence. The following is the manner in which the Saxon chronicle of the monastery of Peterborough prefaces its account of the events that followed the so eagerly-desired marriage of Henry with Edgar's niece: "It is not easy to recount all the miseries with which the country was afflicted this year, by the unjust and constantly-renewed taxes. Wherever the king travelled, the people in his train vexed the poor people, and committed in various places murders, and set fire to places." Each succeeding year in the chronological series is marked by a repetition of the same complaints, set forth nearly in the same terms, and this very monotony gives an additionally gloomy colouring to the recital. "The year 1105 was most miserable, owing to the loss of the harvest, and the taxes, the levy of which never ceased. The year 1110 was full of misery, owing to the bad season, and the taxes which the king raised for the portion of his daughter." This daughter, named Matilda, after her mother, and who was at this time five years old, was married to Henry, fifth of the name, emperor of Germany. "All this," says the Saxon chronicle, "cost the English nation dear."

That which cost it still dearer, was an expedition which king Henry undertook against his brother, the duke of Normandy. Personally, Henry had no motive to be the first to break the peace that existed between himself and Robert, since the latter had renounced all pretensions to the kingdom of England. But a short time previous, the duke had paid a visit to his brother, as to a dear friend; and had even, in return for the hospitality he received, given to his sister-in-law Matilda the pension which, in the terms of their treaty, the king was to pay him. This act of courtesy was not the only good office that Henry had experienced on the part of his eldest brother, the most generous and least politic of this family. Formerly, when Henry was without lands, and discontented with his condition, he had endeavoured to seize Mont Saint-Michel in Normandy. Robert and William Rufus besieged him there, and closely pressing him, reduced him to a want of water. The besieged sent to entreat his brothers not to deny him the free enjoyment of that which belongs to all men, and Robert, touched by this appeal, ordered his soldiers to allow those of Henry to supply themselves with water. Hereupon, William Rufus was enraged with Robert: "You show great skill in warfare," said he, "you who supply your enemy with drink; you have now only to furnish him with meat too."—"How!" answered the duke, "should I leave a brother to die of thirst? what other brother have we, were we to lose him?"

The recollection of this service and of this fraternal affection vanished from Henry's mind as soon as he became king. He essayed by every means to injure Robert, and even to avail himself of his heedless character, facile even to imprudence, and which rendered the duke of Normandy quite unfit to manage his affairs. Many abuses and disorders were introduced into his duchy, and, as a consequence, there were many malcontents, whom Robert's volatility prevented him from heeding and his easy nature from punishing. King Henry artfully availed himself of these circumstances to interfere in the quarrels between the Normans and their duke; at first in the character of an intercessor, and then, removing the mask when discord recommenced, as the protector of Normandy against the ill government of his brother. He called upon Robert to cede the duchy to him in exchange for a sum of money. "Thou hast the title of lord," he said to him in his message, "but thou art no longer a lord in reality; for they who should obey thee, scorn thee." The duke indignantly refused to accede to this proposition, and Henry at once proceeded to compass his brother's downfall by force of arms.

Preparing to depart for Normandy, he ordered a great subsidy of money to be raised in England, to defray the expenses of this expedition; and his collectors exercised the most cruel violence towards the Saxon citizens and peasants. They drove from their poor cabins those who had nothing to give; they took out their doors and windows, and carried off even the least article of furniture. Against those who appeared to possess anything, frivolous charges were instituted: they dared not appear before the courts of justice, and their property was then confiscated. "Many persons," says a contemporary, "saw nothing new in these grievances, knowing that they existed during the whole reign of William, brother of the present king, not to speak of what passed in the time of their father. But, in our days, there was a reason why these vexations were more hard and insupportable than ever: it was that they were employed against a people despoiled of all, utterly ruined, and against whom their masters were furious because they had nothing." Another writer of the period relates that troops of labouring men used to come to the king's palace or meet him on his rides, and throw before him their ploughshares in token of distress, and as if to declare that they renounced the cultivation of their native land in despair.

The king departed for Normandy, conquered duke Robert, and made him prisoner, with his most trusty friends, in a battle fought near the castle of Tinchebray, three leagues from Mortain. A remarkable incident in this victory was, that the Saxon king, Edgar, was among the prisoners. Having renounced all hopes for his country and for himself, he had settled in Normandy with duke Robert, whom he soon loved as a brother, and whom he even accompanied to the Holy Land. He was brought to England, and the king, who had married his niece, granted him a small pension, upon which he lived for the remainder of his days, in the country, solitary and obscure. Duke Robert experienced, on the part of his brother, more rigorous treatment; he was sent, under a strong guard, to Cardiff castle in South Wales, opposite Gloucester, in a district recently taken from the Welsh. Robert, separated from England by the Severn, at first enjoyed a degree of liberty; he could walk about the adjacent country; but one day he attempted to escape, and seized a horse; he was pursued, and brought back to his prison, which he never again quitted. Some historians, but of the following century, relate that his eyes were put out by order of his brother.

At the time of his defeat, Robert had a son still under age, named William, whom king Henry endeavoured to get possession of, but who was taken to France by one of his father's friends. Louis, king of the French, adopted him, and had him brought up in his palace; he gave him horses and armour, according to the custom of the period, and feigning to take an interest in his misfortunes, converted him into a means of disquieting the duke-king his neighbour, whose power gave him umbrage. In the name of this son of Robert, the king of France formed a league which was joined by the Flemings and the Angevins. King Henry was attacked on every part of his Norman frontier; he lost towns and castles one after another; and, at the same time, the friends of duke Robert conspired against his life. For several years he never slept without having a sword and buckler at his bed's-head. But however formidable the confederation of his external and internal enemies, it did not prevail against the power which he derived from combined Normandy and England.

Robert's young son continued to live on the wages of the king of France, as his vassal, and to follow this king in his wars. They went together to Flanders, after a sedition in which had perished the duke of Flanders, Karle or Charles, son of Knut, king of the Danes, who had himself also been killed in a revolt. The king of France entered Flanders, with the sanction of the most powerful men of the country, to punish the murderers of the late duke: but, without such sanction and solely by virtue of feudal suzerainty (a right greatly questioned), he placed young William on the throne of the late duke, in furtherance of his object to render him powerful and then to oppose him to king Henry. There was little resistance to this unpopular king, so long as the king of France and his troops remained in Flanders; but, after their departure, a general revolt broke out against the new lord imposed upon the country by foreigners. The war proceeded with various success between the barons of Flanders and the son of Robert. The insurgents placed at their head the count of Alsace, Thiedrik, of the same race with themselves, and a descendant of one of their ancient dukes. This popular candidate attacked the protegé of the king of France, who, wounded at the siege of a town, died shortly afterwards. Thiedrik of Alsace succeeded him, and king Louis found himself obliged, despite his lofty pretensions, to acknowledge as legitimate duke of the Flemings, the man whom they had themselves chosen.

Prior to his departure for the Continent to sustain the protracted war which his nephew and the king of France had excited against him, Henry had, with the consent of his bishops and barons, introduced an extensive creation of abbots and prelates. According to the Saxon chronicle, there had never been so many abbots made at once, as in the forty-first year of the reign of the French in England. At this period, while the daily intercourse with the church held so great a place in men's lives, such an event, although of little moment in our eyes, was far from uninfluential upon the destiny of the English population, in as well as out of the cloister. "Of these new shepherds," says the contemporary Edmer, "most were rather wolves than shepherds. We must suppose that such was not the king's intention; and yet this were more probable, had he selected at least a few of the natives of the country. But if you were English, no degree of virtue or merit could procure you the lowest employment, whilst a foreigner by birth was, as such, judged worthy of any position. We live in evil days."

Among the new abbots instituted by king Henry, in the year 1107, was conspicuous a certain Henry de Poitou, who had come to England because it was a country in which priests made their fortune more speedily than elsewhere, and lived under less restraint. This Poitevin obtained from the king the abbey of Peterborough, and "he demeaned himself there," says the contemporary chronicle, "as a hornet in a hive, seizing upon all he could find to take in the convent and out of the convent, and transmitting all he got to his own country." He was a monk of Cluny, and had promised the superior of that order, by oath on a relic of the true cross, to procure for him the entire property of the abbey of Peterborough, with all its possessions in land and goods. At the time the Saxon chronicler wrote, the abbot had made his request to the king, and the royal decision was pending; "May God," says the Saxon author, "have mercy on the monks of Peterborough, and this unfortunate house! truly it is now that they need the aid of Christ, and of every Christian nation."

These sufferings, to which we cannot refuse our compassion, since they were undergone by men, and that the foreign government rendered them common to both priests and laymen, by daily depressing more and more the hearts and minds of the English, appear to have increased in them the superstitious tendencies of their nation and their time; they seem to have derived some consolation from imagining that God from time to time revealed his anger against their oppressors by terrible signs. The Saxon chronicle affirms that, when abbot Henry the Poitevin entered Peterborough, there appeared at night, in the forests between the monastery and the town of Stamford, black huntsmen, tall and of fearful forms, who, leading black dogs with glaring eyes, and mounted on black horses, chased black hinds: "People worthy of belief have seen them," says the narrator, "and for forty nights consecutively the sound of their horns was heard." At Lincoln, on the tomb of a Norman bishop, Robert Bluet, a man infamous for his debaucheries, other phantoms were visible for several nights. Accounts were circulated of terrible visions, which, said the story, had appeared to king Henry in his sleep, and so terrified him that three times in the same night he had sprung from his bed and seized his sword. It was about this time that the pretended miracles at the tomb of Waltheof were renewed; those of king Edward, whose beatification was not contested by the Normans, on account of his relationship to William the Conqueror, also occupied the imagination of the English. But these vain fireside stories, these superstitious regrets for the men and days that were past, gave the people neither relief for the present, nor hope for the future.

The son of king Henry and Matilda inherited none of his mother's good will towards the English. He was heard publicly to say, that if ever he reigned over those miserable Saxons he would make them draw the plough, like oxen. When this son, named William, formally received his knightly arms, all the Norman barons accepted him as successor to the king, and swore fealty to him. Shortly after this, he married the daughter of Foulques, earl of Anjou. This union detached the Angevins from the confederation formed by the king of France, who himself ere long abandoned the war, on condition that William, son of Henry, should acknowledge himself his vassal for Normandy and do him homage for it. Peace being thus completely re-established, in the year 1120, in the beginning of winter, king Henry, his legitimate son William, several of his natural children, and the Norman lords of England, prepared to return home.

The fleet was assembled in the month of December, in the port of Barfleur. At the moment of departure, one Thomas Fitzstephen came to the king, and offering him a gold mark, said: "Stephen, son of Erard, my father, served thy father all his life upon the sea, and it was he who commanded the vessel which bore thy father to the conquest; lord-king, I entreat thee to grant me in fief the same office: I have a vessel called La Blanche Nef, fitly provided." The king answered that he had already chosen a vessel for himself, but that to meet the request of Fitzstephen, he would confide to his charge his two sons, his daughter, and their suite. The vessel which bore the king sailed first, with a south wind, at sunset, and next morning reached England in safety. Somewhat later in the evening, La Blanche Nef set sail; the sailors who manned it had asked for wine previous to their departure, which the young and joyous passengers had distributed in profusion. The vessel was worked by fifty rowers: Thomas Fitzstephen held the helm, and the ship went rapidly on, in the moonlight, along the coast near Barfleur. The sailors, excited by the wine, made every effort to overtake the king's ship. Too intent upon this object, they heedlessly involved themselves among the breakers at a place then called the Ras de Catte, now known as the Ras de Catteville. The Blanche Nef, going at her utmost speed, struck on a rock, which drove in her left side: the crew sent forth a cry of distress, which was heard by the king's vessels, already on the open sea; but no one suspected its cause. The water poured in, and the vessel sank with all in it, to the number of three hundred persons, among whom were eighteen women. Two men alone clung to the main-mast, as it floated on the water: a butcher of Rouen, named Berauld, and a young man of higher birth, named Godefroi, son of Gilbert de Laigle.

Thomas, the master of La Blanche Nef, after having sunk once, returned to the surface; perceiving the heads of the two men who held on to the mast, "And the king's son," said he, "what has become of him?"—"He has not appeared, neither he, nor his sister, nor any of their company." "Woe is me!" exclaimed Fitzstephen; and he plunged beneath the waves. This December night was extremely cold, and the most delicate of the two survivors, losing his strength, relinquished his hold on the most that supported him, and sank, commending his companion to the mercy of God. Berauld, the poorest of all, still supported himself afloat, in his jacket of sheep-skin, and he alone again saw the day; some fishermen picked him up in their boat, and it is from him that the details of the event were learned.

Most of the English chroniclers, in relating this catastrophe, so grievous to their masters, express but little compassion for the misfortune of the Norman families. They call it a Divine vengeance, a judgment of God, and discern something supernatural in this shipwreck in fine weather and a calm sea. They recal the contemptuous and malignant language of young William with reference to the Saxons. "The proud man said, I shall reign," exclaims a contemporary; "but God said, It shall not be, impious one, it shall not be; and the brow of the wicked, instead of wearing a diadem of gold, has been dashed against the rocks." They accused the young man, and those who perished with him, of infamous vices, unknown, they said, to England, before the arrival of the Normans. The invectives and accusations of these writers, indeed, often exceed all bounds; as in other cases do their flatteries and their obsequiousness, manifesting them men who at once hate and fear. "Thou hast seen," says one of them, in a letter which was intended to remain secret, "thou hast seen Robert de Belesme, that man who made murder his most agreeable recreation; thou hast seen Henry, earl of Warwick, and his son Roger, the ignoble soul; thou hast seen king Henry, the murderer of so many men, the violator of his oaths, the gaoler of his brother. . . . . Perhaps thou wilt ask me, why in my history I so highly praised this Henry: I have said that he was remarkable among kings for his wisdom, his courage, and his wealth; but these kings, to whom we all take the oath, before whom the very stars of heaven seem to bow, and whom the women, the children, and the idlers among men, gaze at on their way, rarely throughout their kingdom is there one man to be found so guilty as they; and this has given rise to the expression, royalty is crime."

According to the old historians, king Henry was never seen to smile after the shipwreck of his children. Matilda, his wife, was dead, and reposed at Winchester, within a tomb, the epitaph on which was partly in English, a circumstance that for many years did not recur on the monuments of the rich and great of England. Henry married a second wife, not of Anglo-Saxon race, which had now again fallen into contempt because the son of the Conqueror no longer needed it. This new marriage of the king was sterile, and all his tenderness was now concentrated upon a natural son, named Robert, the only son who remained to him. At about the time this son became old enough to marry, it happened that one Robert Fitz-Aymon, a rich Norman, possessor of great domains in Gloucestershire, died, leaving as heiress of his property an only daughter, called Aimable, and familiarly Mable or Mabile. King Henry negotiated with the relations of this girl a marriage between her and his son Robert; the relations consented, but Aimable refused, and persisted in her refusal for a long time, without explaining the motives of her repugnance, until at last, driven to extremity, she declared that she would never be the wife of a man who had not two names.

The two names, or the double name, composed of a Christian name and a surname, either purely genealogical, or indicating the possession of an estate or the exercise of some office, was one of the signs by which the Norman race in England was distinguished from the other race. In bearing only his own name, in the centuries which followed the conquest, a man incurred the risk of passing for a Saxon; and the provident vanity of the heiress of Robert Fitz-Aymon was alarmed at the idea that her future husband might be confounded with the mass of the natives. She fairly confessed this scruple in a conversation she had with the king, and which is related in the following manner, by a chronicle in verse:—

"Sire," said the young Norman, "I know that your eyes are fixed on me, much less for myself than for my inheritance; but having so great an inheritance, were it not great shame to take a husband who has not a double name? In his lifetime my father was called Sir Robert Fitz-Aymon. I will not belong to a man whose name does not also show whence he comes." "Well said, damsel," answered king Henry; "Sir Robert Fitz-Aymon was the name of thy father; Sir Robert Fitz-Roi shall be the name of thy husband." "A fair name, I grant, and honourable for him all his life; but how shall be called his sons, and his son's sons?" The king understood this question, and immediately answered: "Damsel, thy husband shall bear a name without reproach for himself and his heirs; he shall be called Robert of Gloucester, for I will create him earl of Gloucester, him and all who shall descend from him."

By the side of this anecdotal illustration of the life and manners of the conquerors of England, may be placed some others, less amusing, of the fate of the natives. In the year 1124, Raoul Basset, chief justiciary, and several other Anglo-Norman barons, held a great assembly in Leicestershire; here they summoned before them a number of Saxons, charged with highway robbery; that is to say, with partisan warfare, which had succeeded to more regular defensive operations against the foreign power. Forty-four of these, accused of robbing with arms in their hands, were condemned, by judge Basset and his assessors, to death, and six others to lose their eyes. "Persons worthy of credit," says the contemporary chronicle, "attest that most of them died an unjust death; but God, who sees all, knows that his unhappy people are oppressed beyond all justice; first, they are despoiled of their goods, and then they are deprived of life. This year was hard to bear; he who possessed anything, however little, was robbed of it, by the taxes and the decrees of the powerful; he who had nothing, died of hunger."

A circumstance which occurred some time before this may throw some light upon these decrees, which despoiled the unhappy Saxons of all. In the sixteenth year of the reign of Henry I., a man named Brithtstan, living in Huntingdonshire, wished to devote himself, with all he possessed, to the monastery of St. Ethelride. Robert Malartais, the Norman provost of the hundred, conceived that the Englishman only desired to become a monk, in order to escape the punishment of some secret offence against the foreign power, and he hereupon accused him, as it would appear, altogether at random, of having found a treasure and appropriated it to his own use, which was an infringement upon the king's rights; for the Norman kings claimed to be born-possessors of all money found underground. Malartais, in the king's name, forbad the monks of Saint Ethelride to receive Brithtstan into their monastery; he then seized the Saxon and his wife, and sent them before the justiciary Raoul Basset, at Huntingdon. The accused denied the crime imputed to him; but the Normans called him liar, insulted him for his short stature and his excessive corpulence, and pronounced a sentence which adjudged him and all that he possessed to the king. Immediately after sentence, they demanded from the Englishman a declaration of his property, real and personal, with the names of his debtors. Brithtstan gave it; but the judges, not satisfied with the statement, told him several times that he was an impudent liar. The Saxon answered in his language: "My lords, God knows that I speak the truth;" he repeated these words patiently several times, says the historian, "without anything further." His wife was obliged to give up fifteen pence and two rings that she had about her, and to swear that she retained nothing. The condemned man was then taken, bound hand and and foot, to London, thrown into prison, and loaded with iron chains, the weight of which exceeded his strength.

The sentence of the Saxon Brithtstan was pronounced, according to the testimony of the ancient historian, in the assembly of justice; or, as the Normans called it, la cour du comté, the county court of Huntingdon. These courts, in which all causes were tried, except those concerning the high barons, which were reserved for the King's Bench, were presided over by the viscount of the county, whom the English called sheriff, or by a circuit judge, a justicier errant, as it was called in the Norman tongue. In the county-court sat, as judges, the possessors of free tenements, whom the Normans called Franc tenants, and the natives franklings, adding a Saxon termination to the French adjective. The county-court, like that of the king, had periodical sessions, and those who failed to attend them paid a certain fine for having, as the legal acts of the time express it, left justice without judgment. None had a right to sit there, unless he wore the sword and baldric, the insignia of Norman liberty, and unless, moreover, he spoke French. The judges attended girt with their swords, and thus kept away the Saxons, or, in the language of the old acts, the villeins, the country people, and all men of ignoble and low race. The French language was, so to speak, the criterion of a capacity to act as a judge; and there were even cases in which the testimony of a man, ignorant of the language of the conquerors, and thus betraying his English descent, was not considered valid. This is proved by a fact posterior, by more than sixty years, to the period at which we are now arrived. In 1191, in a dispute affecting the abbot of Croyland, four persons gave evidence against him; these were Godfrey de Thurleby, Gaultier Leroux de Hamneby, William Fitz-Alfred, and Gilbert de Bennington. "The false testimony given by them was registered," says the old historian, "and not the truth spoken by the abbot; but all present thought that the judgment would be favourable to him, because the four witnesses had no knightly fief, were not girt with the sword, and one of them even could not speak French."

Of king Henry's two legitimate children, Matilda still lived, the wife of Henry V., emperor of Germany. She became a widow in the year 1126, and returned to her father; notwithstanding her widowhood, the Normans continued in courtesy to style her empress. At Christmas, Henry held his court, in great pomp, at Windsor castle, and all the Norman lords of both countries, assembled by his invitation, promised fealty to Matilda, both for the duchy of Normandy and for the kingdom of England, swearing, after her father's death, to obey her as they had obeyed him. The first who took this oath was Stephen, son of the earl of Blois and of Adele, daughter of William the Conqueror, one of the king's most intimate friends, and almost the favourite. In the same year, Foulqnes, earl of Anjou, seized with the new enthusiasm of the century, became what was called a soldier of Christ, assumed the cross, and departed for Jerusalem. Uncertain as to his return, he gave the earldom to his son Geoffroy, surnamed Plante Genest, from his habit of wearing a sprig of flowering broom in his hat, instead of a feather.

King Henry conceived a great liking for his young neighbour, earl Geoffroy d'Anjou, for his personal attractions, the elegance of his manners, and his valour; he became his knightly godfather, and defrayed, at his own cost, the ceremony, at Rouen, of his admission to chivalry. After the bath, into which, according to custom, the young knight was immersed, Henry gave him, as his knightly godson, a Spanish charger, a suit of mail, lance and sword proof, gold spurs, a shield emblazoned in gold with the three lions, a helmet set with jewels, an ash lance with a head of Poitiers steel, and a sword, of temper so fine that it passed for the work of Waland, the fabulous smith of northern traditions. The king of England's friendship was not confined to these proofs, and he resolved to marry the earl to his daughter Matilda, the empress, and the union was celebrated, but without the previous consent of the lords of Normandy and England; a circumstance attended with most serious consequences to the fortunes of the married pair. Their nuptials were celebrated in the Whitsuntide of the year 1127, and the rejoicings continued for three weeks. On the first day, heralds in their state costume went through all the squares and streets of Rouen, making this singular proclamation: "By order of king Henry, let no man here present, native or foreigner, rich or poor, noble or villein, be so bold as to absent himself from the royal rejoicings; whoever takes not his share in the entertainments and sports, shall be held guilty of offence towards his lord the king."

Of this marriage was born, in the year 1133, a son who was called Henry, after his grandfather, and whom the Normans surnamed Fitz-empress, son of the empress, to distinguish him from the elder Henry, whom they called Fitz-Guilliaume-Conquéreur. On the birth of his grandson, the Norman king once more convoked his barons of Normandy and England, and required them to acknowledge as his successors, the children of his daughter after him and after her; they outwardly consented, and swore fealty. The king died two years after, in Normandy, thinking that he left an undisputed crown to his daughter and his grandson; but it happened far otherwise; on the first intelligence of his death, Stephen of Blois, his nephew, sailed for England, where he was elected king by the prelates, earls, and barons, who had sworn to give the kingdom to Matilda. The bishop of Salisbury declared that this oath was void, because the king had married his daughter without the consent of the lords: others said that it would be shameful for so many noble knights to be under the orders of a woman. Stephen's election was sanctioned by the benediction of the primate of Canterbury, and, what was highly important at this period, approved by a bull of pope Innocent II.

"We have learned," said the pontiff to the new king, "that thou hast been elected by the common voice and unanimous consent of the lords and people, and that thou hast been crowned by the prelates of the kingdom. Considering that the suffrages of so great a number of men cannot have been combined in thy favour without a special co-operation of the Divine grace; that besides thou art a near relation of the late king, and that thou didst promise obedience and reverence to Saint Peter on the day of thy coronation, we admit all that has been done for thee, and adopt thee specially, with paternal affection, for the son of the blessed apostle Peter, and of the holy Roman church."

Stephen of Blois was very popular with the Anglo-Normans, because of his tried valour, and his affable and generous disposition. He promised, on receiving the crown, to give to each of his barons the free enjoyment of the forests which had been appropriated by king Henry, after the example of the two Williams, and to secure by proper instruments the liberties of the church and of the nation. The first portion of the new reign was peaceful and happy, at least for the Norman race. The king was lavish and magnificent in his tastes, and most generous to those around him. He drew largely upon the treasure that the Conqueror had amassed and his two successors augmented; he alienated or distributed in fiefs the lands that William had reserved as his share of the conquest, and which was called the royal demesne; he gave independent earls and viscounts to districts and towns hitherto administered for the sole benefit of the king by royal governors. Geoffroy of Anjou, Matilda's husband, agreed to remain at peace with him, for a pension of five thousand marks, and Robert of Gloucester, natural son of the late king, who at first manifested an intention of vindicating the rights of his sister, took the oath of allegiance and homage to Stephen.

But this calm did not last long; towards the year 1137 many young barons and knights who had fruitlessly demanded of the new king a portion of his demesne lands and castles, proceeded to take possession of them by force. Hugh Bigot seized Norwich castle; one Robert that of

Badington; the king recovered both, but the spirit of opposition went on gaining strength from the moment that it had first manifested itself. The bastard son of king Henry suddenly broke the peace he had sworn to Stephen, and sent from Normandy a message defying him, and renouncing his homage. "That which induced Robert to take this step," says a contemporary, "was the answers given him by many religious men whom he consulted, and especially an apostolical sentence, as it was called, of the pope, which enjoined him to obey the oath he had taken to Matilda his sister, in presence of their father." Thus was annulled the brief of the same pope in favour of king Stephen; and war could now alone decide between the two competitors. The malcontents, encouraged by the defection of the late king's son, were in movement throughout England, preparing for the contest. "They have made me king," said Stephen, "and now they abandon me; but, by the birth of God, they shall never call me a deposed king." To secure an army on which he could depend, he collected mercenaries from all parts of Gaul. "As he promised good pay, the soldiers hastened to enrol themselves; horsemen and light infantry, especially Flemish and Bretons."

The conquering population of England was thus again divided into two hostile factions. The state of things became the same as under the two preceding reigns, when the sons of the conquered took part in the quarrels of their masters, and turned the scale on one side, in the vain hope of improving their condition. But now that a similar juncture presented itself, taught by past experience, the English stood apart. In the quarrel between Stephen and the partisans of Matilda, they were neither for the established king, who pretended that his cause was that of order and of the public peace, nor for the daughter of the Norman prince and the Saxon princess: they resolved to be for themselves; and there was formed that which had not been seen since the dispersion of the camp of Ely, a national conspiracy for the freedom of the country. "On an appointed day," says a contemporary author, "all the Normans in England were to be massacred."

The historian does not detail how this plot had been arranged, who were its chiefs, what classes of men joined it, or in what places and at what signal it was to break out. He only relates that the conspirators of 1137 had renewed the former alliance of the patriot Saxons with the men of Wales and Scotland, and that they had even the intention of placing a Scotsman at the head of their emancipated kingdom, perhaps David, the reigning king of Scotland, son of Margaret, Edgar's sister. The enterprise failed, because a disclosure, or perhaps mere hints of it, reached the Norman Richard Lenoir, bishop of Ely, under the seal of confession. At this period, even the strongest minds never exposed themselves to the probable danger of death without having set their consciences in order; and when the attendance of penitents was more than usually numerous, it was an almost certain sign of some political movement. In watching in this way the proceedings of the Saxons, the clergy of Norman race fulfilled the principal object of their admission to office: for by means of insidious questions put to penitents overflowing with devotion, it was easy to discover the hidden thought of revolt; and rarely could the man whom the priest thus interrogated defeat the craft of him whom he deemed to have the power to bind and loose upon earth and in heaven. The bishop of Ely communicated his discovery to the other bishops, and superior agents of authority: but notwithstanding the promptitude of their measures, "many, and these the most important of the conspirators," says the contemporary author, "had time to fly." They withdrew to Wales, and sought to excite her population to make war upon the Normans. The numbers who were taken, perished on the gibbet or by other means.

This event took place sixty-six years after the last defeat of the insurgents of Ely, and seventy-two after the battle of Hastings. Whether the chroniclers have not told us all, or whether after this time the tie which bound Saxon to Saxon and made of them one people, could not be renewed, it would certainly appear that no further projects of deliverance, formed by common accord among all classes of the Anglo-Saxon population, occurred in the succeeding centuries. The old English cry, Down with the Normans! no longer resounds in history; the later insurrections have for their rallying cry terms indicating not national but civil war: thus, in the fourteenth century, the English peasants, in insurrection, shouted No gentlemen! and in the seventeenth, the people in town and country cried, No more proud lords and rotten hearted bishops! We shall still, however, to a certain extent, discover in the facts we are about to relate, traces of the old hostility of the two races.

It has now become very uncertain how long the terms noble and rich were, in the popular feelings of the English, synonymous with those of usurper and foreigner; the exact value of the language of the old historians is too often a problem for the modern historian. The former addressed themselves to people who knew, respecting their own social position, many secrets which have not come down to posterity; they could safely, therefore, be vague and cautiously unexplicit, for they were understood at half a word. But for us, how is it possible to understand the old chroniclers, if we are not first acquainted with the aspect and physiognomy of the times in which they wrote? And where can we study these times but in the chronicles themselves? This is the vicious circle in which all the moderns who seek to portray with fidelity the historic scenes of the old world, and the happy or miserable fate of the generations that are gone, are constantly and necessarily turning. Their work, full of difficulties, can never produce a perfect fruit; thanked, then, let them be, for even the small portion of truth which their toils so painfully resuscitate.

APPENDIX.

No. I. ARYMES PRYDYN VAWR. THE GREAT ARMED CONFEDERACY OF BRITAIN.

*

o Dysgogan awen: dygobryssyn!

o Marannedd a meuedd, a hêdd genhyn,

o A phennaeth ehelaeth, a fraeth unbyn;

o A, gwedy dyhedd, anhedd ymhob mehyn.

o Gwyr gwychyr yn trydar casnar dengyn:

o Escaud yn gnovud ryhyd dyvin:

o Gwaethyl gwyr hyt Gaer Wair gwascarawdd allmyn.

o Gwnahawnt gorvoledd gwedy gwehyn,

o A chymod Cymry, a gwyr Dulyn,

o Gwyddyl Iwerddon, Mon, a Phrydyn,

o Cernyw a Cludwys, eu cynnwys genhyn.

o Atporion vydd Brython pan dyorphyn.

o Pell dysgoganer amser dybyddyn

o Teyrnedd, a bonedd eu go rescyn:

o Gwyr gogledd, ynghyntedd yn eu cylchyn,

o Ymhervedd eu rhagwedd y ddisgynnyn.

o Dysgogan Merddin. Cyvervydd hyn.

o *

o Yn Anber Peryddon, meirion mechdeyrn

o (A chyn ni bai unrhaith) llaith a Gwynyn.

o O un ewyllys bryd, ydd ymvrthvynnyn.

o Meirion eu trethau, dychynnullyn

o Yngnedoedd Cymry nadd oedd a delyn:

o Y sydd wr dyledawg a levair hyn—

o "Ni ddyfai a dalai yngheithiwed."

o *

o Mab Mair, mawr ei air! Pryd na thardded

o Rhag pennaeth Saeson, ac eu hofed!

o Pell bwynt cychmyn i Wrtheyrn Gwynedd!

o Ev gyrhaut Allmyn i alltudedd.

o Nis arhaeddwy neb, nis dioes daear;

o Ni wyddynt py dreiglynt ymhob aber.

*

o Pan brynasant Danet, drwy fled calledd

o Gan Hors a Hengys oedd yn eu rhyssedd,

o Eu cynnydd bu y wrthym yn anvonhedd:

o Gwedi rhin dilein, ceith ym ynver.

o Dychymmydd medddawd mawr wirawd o vedd!

*

o Dychymmyn angau angen Hawer!

o Dychymmydd anaelau, dagrau gwragedd,

o Dychyfroy edgyllaeth peunaeth lledfer!

o Dychymmydd tristyd byd a ryher,

o Pan vydd cechmyn Danet an teyrnedd!

*

o Gwrthotted trindawd dyrnawd a bwyller—

o Y ddilein gwlad Vrython, a Saeson yn anned!

o Poet cynt eu rheges yn alltudedd,

o Na myned Cymry yn ddivröedd!

*

o Mab mair mawr ei air! pryd nas terddyn

o Cymry, rhag goeir breyr ag unbyn!

o Cyneircheid, cyneilweid, unrhaith cwynyn!

o Un gôr, un gyngor, un eisor ynt.

o Nid oedd er mawred nas lleverynt;

o Namyn er hepcor goeir nas cymmodynt.

o I Dduw a Dewi ydd ymorchmynnynt:

o Taled gwrthotted fled i Allmyn!

o Gwnawnt hwy aneireu eisiau trevddyn

o Cymry a Saeson cyvervyddyn,

o I amlan ymdreulaw ag ymwrthryn.

o O ddirvawr vyddinawr pan ymbrovyn,

o Ag amallt lavnawr a gawr a gryn,

o Ag am Gwy gair cyvergeir, y am Peurllyn,

o A lluman a ddaw a garw ddisgyn;

o A, mal balaon, Saeson syrthyn.

*

o Cymry cynyrcheid cyfun Ddullyn.

o Blaen wrth vôn, granwynion, cyvyng oeddyn

o Meirion, yngwerth eu gau, yn eu creinhyn.

o Eu byddyn yngwaedlin, yn eu cylchyn,

o Eraill, ar eu traed, trwy goed Cilhyn,

o Trwy Vwrch y Ddinas foras föyn.

o Rhyvel heb ddychwel i dir Prydyn,

o Attor, trwy law gyngor, mal morlithryn.

o Meirion Caer Geri ddivri cwynant

o Rhai i ddyfryn a bryn nis dirdwadant;

o I Aber Peryddon ni mad ddoethant:

o Anaelau drethau dychynullant:

o Naw ugain canhwr a ddisgynnant;

o Mawr watwar, namyn pedwar, nid atcorant.

o Dyhedd i eu gwragedd a ddywedant;

o Eu crysseu yn llawn creu aroclhant.

*

o Cymry cyneirchaie, enaid dichwant—

o Gwyr Dehau eu trethau a amygant.

o Llym lliveid llavnawr, llwyr y lladdant:

o Ni bydd i veddyg mwyn o'r a wnaant.

o Byddinoedd Cadwaladyr cadyr i deuant.

o Ryddyrchavwynt Cymry. Cad a wnaant—

o Llaith, anolaith ryddysgyrchasant.

o Yn gorphen eu trethau angau a wawdant.

o Eraill ar osgail ryphlanhasant:

o Oes oeseu, eu tretheu nid esgorant.

*

o Ynghoed, ym maes, ym mryn,

o Canhwyll, yn nhywyll, a gerdd genhyn—

o Cynan yn rhagwan ymhob disgyn.

o Saeson rhag Brython gwae a gênyn.

o Cadwaladir yn baladir gan ei unbyn,

o Trwy synwyr, yn llwyr yn eu dychlyn,

o Pan syrthwynt en clas dros eu herchwyn

o Ynghustudd, a chreu rhudd ar rudd allmyn.

o Yn ghorphen pob angrheith, anrheith dengyn.

o Seis ar hynt, hyd Gaer Wynt, cynt pwy cynt techyn.

*

o Gwyn eu byd hwy Cymry, pan adroddynt

o Rymgwarawd y Drindawd o'r travallawd gynt

o Na chryned Dyved na Glywyssyg

o Nis gwnaho molawd meirion mechdeyrn;

o Na chynhorion Saeson cefyn ebryn,

o "Nis gwnaw, meddut, meddawt genhyn,

o Heb daled o dynged." Maint a gefyn

o O ymddiveid veibion, ac eraill ryn.

o Trwy eiriawl Dewi a seint Prydyn,

o Hyd frwd Argelo fohawr allan.

*

o Dysgogan awen. Dyddaw y dydd

o Pan ddyfo i wys, i un gyssul,

o Un gôr, un gynghor; a Lloeyr llosgyd,

o Yr gobaith Arreiraw ar yn phrydaw lluydd;

o A cherdd arallvro, a fo beunydd.

o Mi wyr cwdd ym dda cwdda cwdd vydd.

o Dy chyrchwynt gywarth mal arth o vynydd,

o I dalu gwynieith, gwaed eu hennydd,

o Atoi peleidral dyval dillydd,

o Nid arbetwy car corph eu gilydd:

o Atoi pen gaflaw heb emennydd:

o Atoi gwragedd gweddw, a meirch gweilydd;

o Atoi' r brein uthr rhag uthur cedwyr,

o A lliaws llaw amhar, cyn gwascar lluydd.

*

o Cennadau angau dychyvervydd,

o Pan favwynt galanedd wrth eu henydd.

o Ev dialawr ar werth ei dreth beunydd,

o A'r mynych genhadau a'r gau luydd.

*

o Dygorvu Cymry trwy gyvergyr,

o Yn gywair, gydair, gydson, gydfydd:

o Dygorvi Cymry i beri cad,

o A llwyth lliaws gwlad a gynhullant,

o A lluman glan Dewi a ddyrchavant,

o J dywysaw Gwyddyl drwy Lieingant:

o A gynheu Dulyn genhyn a savant,

o Pan ddyfont l'r gâd nid ymwadant.

TRANSLATION.

*

o The muse foretels the speedy coming to the people of the enjoyment of wealth and peace.

o An ample domimon, and eloquent princes:

o But, after tranquillity, there will be commotion in every tribe,

o The mighty men contending with barbarous wrath:

o The Scots resolving to make an assault;

o The Germans scattered the disturbers as far as Caer Wair.

o After the expulsion they make a triumph,

o And reconciled the Cymry, the men of Dublin,

o The Gwyddyl of Ireland, Anglesey, and Scotland.

o Cornwall, and the men of Alclwyd, to their reception amongst us.

o In the end the Britons will recover their sovereignty.

o Long since has it been predicted that they shall become

o Princes, and the felicity of their enterprise,

o Is when the men of the north, who dwell upon their borders,

o Shall make a descent into the bowels of their land.

o 'Tis Merddin that foretels. This will come to pass.

*

o In Aber Peryddon, the deputies of a Saxon king,

o (Even before there was a public stipulation) stirred up slaughter.

o By an unanimous arbitrary act, the deputies, with violence,

o Demanded, and proceeded to collect, a tribute.

o The Cymry resolved, they were under no obligation to pay:

o But it was a man of authority that made this declaration—

o "He that pays shall not go into captivity!"

*

o O, Son of Mary, whose word is sacred! woe's the time that we sprung not forth

o To resist the dominion of the Saxons—that we cherished them!

o Far be the cowards of Vortigern of Gwynedd!

o The Germans might have been banished by them from hence.

o No one would have seized, no one would have stripped the land;

o But they knew not those that lingered in every harbour.

*

o When the Germans purchased Thanet by imposing craftiness,

o In which Horse and Hengist chiefly excelled,

o Their aggrandizement was to us a degradation:

o After concerting the plot of death, the slaves return.

o Reflect on the intoxication at the great banquet of mead!

o Reflect on the violent deaths of many guests!

o Reflect on the incurable wounds—the tears of nations,

o When woeful mourning was roused by the cruel pagan!

o Reflect on the calamitous lot that will befal us,

o When the lurkers of Thanet become our princes!

*

o May the Trinity avert the stroke I have mentioned—

o That the Saxons should dwell in the land of the annihilated Britons!

o May utter banishment be their portion, rather

o Than the Cymry should be deprived of their country!

*

o O, Son of Mary, whose word is sacred! woe's the time

o When the Cymry withstood not the base decrees of nobles and princes!

o Let them be summoned—let them be called together—let them rise unanimous!

o They have one heart, one opinion, one common cause.

o They remained silent (not abashed by the presence of the great)

o But to withhold their consent from a base decree which they disapproved,

o Let them now commit their cause to God and to Dewi,

o Who shall render or refuse to the Germans the reward of treachery,

o Let our foes be discordant for want of a regulating chief,

o But let the Cymry and the Saxons meet in the field,

o For the decision of the confused conflict, and the strife of valour

o When the foe tries the fortune of the mighty leader;

o When the grove trembles with the warrior's shout:

o When the battle is joined for the Wye and the land of lakes,

o The standard shall advance, and the terrible assault;

o And the Saxons shall drop like the buds of the forest.

*

o The Cymry were strengthened by the social forces of Dublin.

o The van of the deputies was confused with the rear; with pallid cheek, in utter perplexity,

o They wallowed on the field, as the reward of perfidy;

o While their army lay around them in a lake of gore:

o And the remnant, on foot, through the wood of Killin,

o And through Bwrch y Ddinas fled, in disorder.

o This war which will return no more to the land of Prydyn,

o Rolls away, at the signal, like a billow on the deep.

o The deputies of Caer Geri dolefully complain

o Of those that will not resign their claim to their vallies and hills.

o To Aber Peryddon they came in an evil hour,

o And fatal were the tributes they collected:

o The descent was made by eighteen thousand men;

o With great disgrace four hundred only returned.

o They told a tale of peace to their wives,

o Who smelled their garments full of gore.

*

o Let the Cymry be collected, regardless of life—

o The men of the south will defend themselves from paying tribute.

o Keen let the swords be ground: they will utterly destroy;

o The surgeon shall reap no advantage from what they do.

o The mighty hosts of Cadwallader shall advance.

o Let the Cymry exalt themselves. They shall make a slaughter,—

o The destruction, the demolition of the foe, which they have freely de-

o manded.

o In putting an end to their vassalage, they will mock at death.

o Strangers have they repeatedly planted with their shafts;

o But never, no never will they deliver a tribute.

*

o In the forest, in the field, in the mountain—

o A lamp in darkness shall attend them—

o Conan, their leader in every inroad.

o The Saxons, before the Britons, shall sing the song of woe,

o Cadwallader, a pillar amongst his princes,

o By his wise conduct shall utterly dismember the Germans,

o When they drop over the limits of their sanctuary

o In misery, and the ruddy gore stains their brow.

o Thus will be put an end to their violence and plunder inhuman,

o And the Saxons in their way to Caerwint shall fly in the utmost disorder.

*

o Thrice happy the Cymry when they shall relate

o How the Trinity delivered them from past calamity,

o Let not Dyved nor Gliwyssig be alarmed,

o The deputies of the king shall acquire no glory;

o Nor the leaders of the Saxons obtain forage.

o "We shall acquire," say they, "no possession among them

o Without paying the debt of fate." Multitudes may they have

o Of fatherless sons—of others, a small number.

o Through the intercession of Dewi and the Saints of Prydyn.

o They shall fly out of the land as far as the stream of Argelo.

*

o The prophetic song declares the day shall arrive

o When men shall assemble, unanimous in council,

o With one heart, one design; and Lloegyr shall be wasted with fire.

o Arreiraw shall rely upon our torrent-hosts.

o The alien shall remove—the pagan shall be put to flight.

o And well I know success awaits us, whatever chance befals.

o Let the Cymry rush to conflict, like a bear from the mountain,

o To revenge the treacherous murder of their ancestors:

o And in condensing the quick piercing spears

o Let not friends protect the bodies of each other,

o Let them multiply the brainless skulls of German worthies,

o Let them multiply their widow'd matrons, and steeds without riders,

o Let them multiply the greedy ravens before the valiant warriors,

o And let there be many a maimed hand before our host separates.

*

o The messenger of death shall meet the Saxon chief,

o When the carcases of his men are heaped about him;

o We shall be revenged on the pagan for his oppressive tribute, o His frequent messages, and his treacherous sway.

*

o The Cymry have been victorious in the conflict,

o True to their cause, of one voice, one language, one faith

o The Cymry will again be victorious, demanding the fight:

o Their tribes, the multitude of their land will they collect,

o And the sacred banner of Dewi will they display

o To conduct the Gwyddil through Lieingant:

o And the leaders of Dublin will stand firm in our behalf,

o When they come into the battle they will not desert the cause.

No. II. Decree of the Emperors Theodosius and Valentinian, relative to the Subjection of the Bishops of Gaul to the Pope of Rome. (A.D. 445.)

Impp. Theodosius et Valentinianus AA. Aetio v. inl. comiti et magistro utriusque militiæ et patricio.

Certum est, et nobis et imperio nostro unicum esse præsidium in supernæ divinitatis favore, ad quem promerendum præcipue christiana fides, et veneranda nobis religio suffragatur. Cum igitur sedis apostolicæ primatum sancti Petri meritum, qui princeps est episcopalis coronæ, et romanæ dignitas Civitatis, sacræ etiam synodi firmarit auctoritas, ne quid præter auctoritatem sedis istius inlicitum præsumptio adtentare nitatur. Tunc enim demum ecclesiarum pax ubique servabitur, si rectorem suum agnoscat universitas. Hæc cum hactenus inviolabiliter fuerint custodita, Hilarius Arelatensis, sicut venerabilis viri Leonis romani papæ fideli relatione comperimus, contumaci ausu inlicita quædam præsumenda tentavit; et ideo transalpinas ecclesias abominabilis tumultus invasit; quod recens maxime testatur exemplum. Hilarius enim, qui episcopus Arelatensis vocatur, ecclesiæ romanæ Urbis inconsulto pontifice, indebitas sibi ordinationes episcoporum sola temeritate usurpans invasit. Nam alios incompetenter removit, indecenter alios, invitis et repugnantibus civibus, ordinavit. Qui quidem, quoniam non facile ab his qui non elegerant recipiebantur, manum sibi contrahebat armatam, et claustra murorum, in hostilem morem, vel obsidione cingebat, vel aggressione reserabat, et ad sedem quietis pacem prædicaturus per bella ducebat. His talibus et contra imperii majestatem, et contra reverentiam apostolicæ sedis admissis, per ordinem religiosi viri Urbis papæ cognitione discussis, certa in eum ex his, quæ male ordinaverat, lata sententia est. Et erat quidem ipsa sententia per Gallias etiam sine imperiali sanctione valitura. Quid enim tanti pontificis auctoritati in ecclesias non liceret? Sed nostram quoque præceptionem hæc ratio provocavit, ne ulterius vel Hilario, quem adhuc episcopum nuncupari sola mansueti præsulis permittit humanitas, nec cuiquam alteri ecclesiasticis rebus arma miscere, aut præceptis romani antistitis liceat obviare. Ausibus etiam talibus fides et reverentia nostri violatur imperii. Nec hoc solum, quod est maximi criminis, submovemus: verum, ne levis saltem inter ecclesias turba nascatur, vel in aliquo minui religionis disciplina videatur, hoc perenni sanctione decernimus, ne quid tam episcopis gallicanis, quam aliarum provinciarum, contra consuetudinem veterem liceat, sine viri venerabilis papæ Urbis æternæ auctoritate, tentare; sed illis omnibusque pro lege sit, quidquid sanxit vel sanxerit apostolicæ sedis auctoritas. Ita ut quisquis episcoporum ad judicium romani antistitis evocatus venire neglexerit, per moderatorem ejusdem provinciæ adesse cogatur, per omnia servatis, quæ divi parentes nostri romanæ ecclesiæ detulerunt, Aeti P. K. A. Unde inlustris et præclara magnificentia tua, præsentis edictalis legis auctoritate, faciet quæ sunt superius statuta servari, decem librarum auri multa protinus exigenda ab unoquoque judice, qui passus fuerit præcepta nostra violari. Et manu divina Divinitas te servet per multos annos, parens carissime. Datum VIII. Idus junias Romæ, Valentiniano Augusto VI. Consule.—(Script. ier. Gallic. et Francic., i. 768.)

No. III. Conference of the Catholic and Arian Bishops for the Conversion of the King of the Burgundians.

Collatio episcoporum, præsertim Aviti Viennensis coram Gundebaldo Burgundionum rege, adversus Arianos.

Providente Domino ecclesiæ suæ, et inspirante pro salute totius gentis cor domni Remigii, qui ubique altaria destruebat idolorum, et veram fidem potenter cum multitudine signorum amplificabat, factum est ut episcopi plures non contradicente rege congregarentur, si fieri posset, ut Ariani, qui religionem christianam scindebant, ad unitatem possent reverti. Quod ut melius fieret videreturque id non consilio accidisse sed occasione, domnus Stephanus scripsit ad episcopos multos, et invitavit illos ad festivitatem sancti Justi quæ instabat, in qua ob frequentiam miraculorum fiebat concursus plurimus populorum. Venerunt itaque de Vienna Avitus, de Arelate Æonius, de Valentia...de Massilia...jus, et plures alii, omnes catholicæ professionis et laudabilis vitæ in Domino. Qui omnes ad salutationem regis cum domno Stephano ad Sarbiniacum, ubi tunc erat, profecti sunt. Erant quidam inibi de potentioribus arianis cum eo, qui si potuissent, prohibuissent nostrorum accessum ad regem, sed, Domino cooperante, nihil profecerunt.

Post salutationem factam, domnus Avitus, cui, licet non esset senior nec dignitate nec ætate, tamen plurimum deferebatur, dixit ad regem: "Si Excellentia vestra vellet procurare pacem ecclesiæ, parati sumus fidem nostram tam clare demonstrare esse secundum Evangelium et apostolos quod nulli dubium erit, quam retinetis non esse secundum Deum et ecclesiam. Habetis hie de vestris qui sunt instructi in omnibus scientiis, jubeatis ut nobiscum alloquantur, et videant si possint respondere rationibus nostris, ut parati sumus respondere rationibus eorum. Ad quæ rex respondit: Si vestra fides est vera, quare episcopi vestri non impediunt regem Francorum, qui mihi bellum indixit, et se cum inimicis meis sociavit, ut me destruerent? Nam non est fides ubi est appetentia alieni, sitis sanguinis populorum; ostendat fidem per opera sua."

Tune humiliter respondit domnus Avitus, faciem habens angelicam ut et sermonem: "Ignoramus, o rex, quo consilio, et qua de causa rex Francorum facit quod dicitis; sed Scriptura nos docet quod propter derelictionem legis Dei sæpe subvertuntur regna, et suscitantur inimici omni ex parte illis, qui se inimicos adversus Deum constituunt. Sed redite cum populo vestro ad legem Dei, et ipse dabit pacem in finibus vestris. Nam si habetis pacem cum illo, habebitis et cum ceteris, et non prævalebunt inimici vestri." Cur rex: "Nonne legem Dei profiteor? Sed quia nolo tres Deos, dicitis quia non profiteor legem Dei; in scriptura sancta non legi plures esse Deos, sed unum." Ad quæ domnus Avitus...et cum videret regem pacifice audientem, protelavit sermonem, et dixit: "O si vellet sagacitas vestra cognoscere quam bene fundata sit nostra fides, quantum boni vobis et populo vestio inde proveniret! Nam et cœlestis gloria vobis non deesset, et pax et abundantia in turribus vestris. Sed vestri cum sint inimici Christi, super regnum vestrum et super populum iram desuper accendunt, quod, ut speramus, non esset, si velletis audire monita nostra, et jubere ut vestri sacerdotes de his nobiscum colloquantur coram sublimitate vestra et populo vestro; ut sciatis quia Dominus Jesus est æterni Patris æternus Filius, et utrique coæternus Spiritus Sanctus, unus Deus benedictus in sæcula, simulque ante tempora, et absque ullo initio."

Cum hæc dixisset, procidit ad pedes regis, et amplectens eos, flebat amare; procubuerunt et omnes episcopi cum eo. Unde rex valde commotus est, et inchnans se usque ad eos, erexit domnum Avitum cum ceteris, quibus amicabiliter dicit se responsum daturum illis super petitionibus illorum. Quod est crastina die factum. Nam rex per Sagonam rediens ad urbem, misit ad domnos Stephanum et Avitum, ut venirent apud illum. Qui cum venissent, rex dixit ad illos: "Habetis quod postulatis, nam sacerdotes mei parati sunt vobis ostendere, quod nullus potest esse coæternus et consubstantialis Deo. Sed nolo ut id fiat coram omni populo, ne turbæ excitentur, sed tantum coram senatoribus meis, et aliis quos eligam, sicut vos eligetis ex vestris quos volueritis, sed non in magno numero, et id fiet die crastina in hoc loco." Quo dicto episcopi salutato rege discesserunt, et reversi sunt ut omnia intimarent aliis episcopis. Erat autem vigilia sollemnitatis sancti Justi: et licet optavissent quod hoc fieret die sollemnitatem sequenti, noluerunt tamen propter tantum bonum amphus procrastinare. Sed unanimiter decreverunt apud S. Justi sepulcrum pernoctare, ut illo intercedente obtinerent a Domino petitiones cordis sui. Evenit autem ut ea nocte cum lector secundum morem inciperet lectionem a Moyse, inciderit in illa verba Domini: Sed ego indurabo cor ejus, et multiplicabo signa et ostenta mea in terra Ægypti, et non audiet vos. Deinde cum post psalmos decantatos recitaret ex prophetis, occurrerunt verba Domini ad Esaiam dicentis: Vade et dices populo huic: Audite audientes, et nolite intelligere, et videte visionem, et nolite cognoscere. Excæca cor populi ejus, et aures ejus aggrava, et oculos ejus claude, ne forte videat oculis suis, et auribus audiat, et intelligat suo corde, et convertatur, et sanem eum. Cumque adhuc psalmi fuissent decantati, et legeret ex evangelio, incidit in verba quibus Salvator exprobrat Judæis incredulitatem: Væ tibi Corrazaim, væ tibi Betzaida, quia, si in Tyro et in Sidone virtutes factæ fuissent quæ sunt factæ in vobis, jam dudum in cilicio et cinere pœnitentiam egissent. Denique cum lectio fieret ex apestolo, pronuntiata sunt verba illa: An divitias bonitatis ejus et patientiæ et longanimitatis contemnis? Ignoras quoniam sustinentia Dei ad pœnitentiam te adducit? Secundum autem duritiam tuam et impœnitens cor thesaurizas tibi iram in tempore iræ. Quod cum ab omnibus episcopis observatum fuisset, cognoverunt lectiones illas sic occurrisse volente Domino, ut scirent induratum esse cor regis, Deumque illum in sua impœnitentia relinquere, ad ostendendum divitias justitiæ suæ; unde valde tristes effecti, noctem in lacrymis transegerunt. Non destiterunt tamen veritatem nostræ religionis contra arianos asserere.

Igitur tempore que rex jusserat conveniunt omnes episcopi, et simul ad regiam vadunt cum multis sacerdotibus et diaconibus, et quibusdam de catholicis, inter quos erant Placidus et Lucanus, qui erant de præcipuis militiæ regis. Venerunt etiam ariani cum suis. Cum ergo sedissent coram rege, domnus Avitus pro catholicis, Bonifacius pro arianis, sermonem habuerunt. Sed postquam domnus Avitus proposuit fidem nostram cum testimoniis sacræ Scripturæ, ut erat alter Tullius, et Dominus inspirabat gratiam omnibus quæ dicebat; tanta consternatio cecidit super arianos, et qui satis amicabiliter audientiam præbuerat Bonifacius, nihil omnino respondere posset ad rationes domni Aviti, sed tantum quæstiones difficiles proponeret, quibus videbatur velle regem fugitare. Sed cum ab Avito urgeretur ut responderet ad antedicta, promittens se etiam responsurum ad ea quæ proposuerat, non potuit respondere ad unam de rationibus quæ fuerant a domno Avito propositæ, neque ullam pro defensione suæ partis allegare; sed tantum os suum in conviciis aperiebat, et dicebat catholicos esse præstigiatores, et colere multitudinem deorum. Quod solum cum diceret, videretque rex confusionem suæ sectæ, surrexit de sua sede, dicens quod in crastinum responderet Bonifacius. Discesserunt ergo omnes episcopi: et quia adhuc dies non erat inclinata, iverunt simul cum ceteris catholicis ad basilicam domni Justi, confitentes Dominum quoniam bonus, et laudantes eum, qui dederat illis talem victoriam de inimicis suis.

Sequenti vero die iterum ad regiam profecti cum his qui in præcedenti aderant. Cumque ingrederentur, invenerunt Aredium, qui eis persuadere volebat ut regrederentur: dicebat enim quod tales rixæ exasperabant animos multitudinis, et quod non poterat aliquid boni ex eis provenire. Sed domnus Stephanus, qui sciebat illum favere arianis, ut gratiam regis consequeretur, licet fidem nostram profiteretur, respondit ei quod non timendum erat ne rixæ procederent ex inquisitione veritatis, et amore salutis fratrum suorum; imo nihil esse utilius ad jungendos animos in sancta amicitia, quam cognoscere apud quos esset veritas, quia ubicumque est amabilis est, et professores ejus reddit amabiles. Addidit insuper omnes huc venisse secundum jussionem regis: contra quod responsum non est ausus Aredius amplius resilire. Ingressi sunt ergo; et cum rex eos vidisset, surrexit in occursum eorum, mediusque inter domnum Stephanum et domnum Avitum, adhuc multa locutus est contra Francorum regem, quem dicebat sollicitare fratrem suum contra se. Sed cum responderent præfati episcopi quod non esset melior via ineundi pacem, quam concordare in fide, et operam suam, si gratam haberet, pollicerentur pro tam sancto fœdere conciliando, nihil amplius locutus est: sed unusquisque locum, quem præcedenti die tenuerat, occupavit.

Cum itaque sedissent, domnus Avitus tam lucide probavit quod catholici non plures deos adorabant, ut sapientiam ejus tam catholici quam adversarii cum stupore mirarentur. Id autem fecit, ut responderet conviciis quæ Bonifacius in nostram fidem jecerat. Postquam ergo conticuit, ut locum daret responsionibus Bonifacii, nihil aliud potuit ille dicere, quam quod præcedenti die fecerat: et conviciis addens convicia, tanto impetu clamabat, ut præ raucitate non posset amplius loqui, et quasi suffocaretur. Quod cum rex vidisset, et satis diu exspectasset, tandem surrexit vultu indignationem prætendens contra Bonifacium. Tunc domnus Avitus dixit ad regem: "Si sublimitas vestra vellet jubere, ut hi responderent propositionibus nostris, ut posset judicare quænam fides esset retinenda." Sed nihil respondit, neque ceteri ariani qui erant cum illo. adeo stupefacti erant de doctrina et sapientia domni Aviti. Qui cum videret eorum silentium, subjunxit: "Si vestri non possunt responderre rationibus nostris, quid obstat cur non omnes simul conveniamus in eadem fide?" Tunc murmurantibus illis, de sua fide securus in Domino, addidit: "Si rationes nostræ non possunt illos convincere, non dubito quin Deus fidem nostram miraculo confirmet. Jubeat sublimitas vestra ut tam illiquam nos eamus ad sepulcrum hominis Dei Justi, et interrogemus illum de nostra fide, similiter et Bonifacius de sua: et Dominus pronuntiabit per os servi sui in quibus complaceat." Rex attonitus annuere videbatur: sed inclamare cœperunt ariani, et dicere se pro fide sua manifestanda facere nolle, ut fecerat Saul, et ideo maledictus fuerat; aut recurrere ad incantationes et illicita, sufficere sibi et habere Scripturam, quæ sit fortior omnibus præstigiis; et hæc semper repetentes et boantes potius quam vociferantes. Rex qui jam surrexerat, accipiens per manus domnum Stephanum et domnum Avitum, duxit eos usque ad cubiculum suum; et cum intraret, amplexus est eos, dicens ut orarent pro eo. Cognoverunt quidem illis perplexitatem et angustias cordis ejus; sed quia Pater eum non traxerat, non potuit venire ad Filium, ut veritas impleretur: Non est volentis, neque festinantis, sed miserentis Dei.—(Script. rer. Gallic. et Francic. iv. 99-101.)

No. IV. Speech of a Northumbrain Chief.

Anglo-Saxon Text.

Thyslic me is gesewen Cyning this andwarde lif manna on eorthan to withmetenysse thære tide the us uncuth is. swa gelic swa thu [Editor: illegible word] swæsendum sitte mid thinum ealdormannum and thegnum on winter tide. And sy fyr onæled and thin heall gewyrmed. and hit rine and sniwe and styrme ute. Cume thonne an spearwa and hrædlice the lius thurli fieo. thur othre duru in. thurh othre ut gewite: · hwet he on tha tid the he inne bith. ne bith ryned mid thy storme thæs wintres. ac that bith an eagan brihtm and the læste fœc. ac he sona of wintra in winter eft cymeth. Swa thonne this monna lif to medmyclum fæce ætyweth. Hwæt ther foregange. oththe hwæt thœr afterfylige we ne cunnon: · Forthon gif theos niwe lare owiht cuthlicre and gerisenlicre bringe. heo thæs wirthe is that we thære fyligean: ·—(Saxon translation of Bede's Ecclesiastical History, by king Alfred, lib. ii. cap. xii.)

No. V. National Song of the Anglo-Saxons, on the Victory of Brunanburgh.

Athelstan king of earls the lord, rewarder of heroes, and his brother eke, Edmund Atheling elder of ancient race, slew with the edge of their swords the foe at Brumby. The sons of Edward their board-walls clove, and liewed their banners with the wrecks of their hammers So were they taught by kindred zeal, that they at camp oft, 'gainst any robber their land should defend, their hoards and homes. Pursuing fell the Scottish clans; the men of the fleet in numbers fell; 'midst the din of the field, the warrior swate. Since the sun was up in morning tide, gigantic light! glad over grounds, God's candle bright, eternal Lord! 'till the noble creature sat in the western main: there lay many of the Northern heroes under a shower of arrows, shot over shields; and Scotland's boast, a Scythian race, the mighty seed of Mars! with chosen troops, throughout the day the West Saxons fierce pressed on the loathed bands; hew'd down the fugitives, and scattered the rear, with strong mill-sharpen'd blades. The Mercians too the hard hand-play spared not to any of those that with Anlaf over the briny deep in the ship's bosom sought this land for the hardy fight. Five kings lay in the field of battle, in bloom of youth pierced with swords.

So seven eke of the earls of Anlaf; and of the ship's crew unnumber'd crowds. There was dispersed the little band of hardy Scots, the dread of Northern hordes; urged to the noisy deep, by unrelenting fate! The king of the fleet with his slender craft escaped with his life on the felon flood; and so too Constantine the valiant chief returned to the north in hasty flight. The hoary Hildrine cared not to boast among his kindred. Here was his remnant of relations and friends slain with the sword in the crowded fight. His son too he left in the field of battle mangled with wounds, young at the fight. The fair-hair'd youth had no reason to boast of the slaught'ring strife. Nor old Inwood and Anlaf the more with the wrecks of their army could laugh and say that they on the field of stern command, better workmen were in the conflict of banners, the clash of spears, the meeting of heroes, and the rustling of weapons, which they on the field of slaughter played with the sons of Edward. The Northmen sail'd in their nailed ships, a dreary remnant on the roaring sea; over deep water Dublin they sought, and Ireland's shores in great disgrace. Such then the brothers both together, king and Atheling sought their country, West-Saxon land in fight triumphant. They left behind them raw to devour the sallow kite the swarthy raven with horny nib and the hoarse vulture with the eagle swift to consume his prey; the greedy gos-hawk, and that grey beast the wolf of the weald. No slaughter yet was greater made e'er in this island, of people slain before this same with the edge of the sword as the books inform us of the old historians since hither came from the eastern shores the Angles and Saxons over the broad sea, fierce battle-smiths, o'ercame the Welsh, most valiant earls, and gain'd the land.

(Saxon Chronicle, by Ingram, London, 1823.)

No. VI. 'Song composed in Brittany on the Departure of a Young' Breton follower of the Normans, and on his Shipwreck.

*

o Etré parrez Pouldrégat ha parrez Plouaré,

o Ez-euz tudjentil iaouank o sével eunn armé

o Evit monet d'ar brezel dindan mab ann Dukés

o Deuz dastumet kalz a dud euz a beb korn a Vreiz;

*

o Evit monet d'ar brezel dreist ar mor, da Vro-zoz.

o Me meuz ma mab Silvestik ez-int ous hé c'hortoz.

o Me meuz ma mab Silvestik ha ne meuz né met-hen,

o A ia da heul ar strollad, ha gand ar varc'héien.

*

o Eunn noz é oann em' gwélé, ne oann ket kousket mad,

o Me glévé merc'hed Kerlaz a gané son ma mab;

o Ha mé sevel ém' c'hoanzé raktal war ma gwelé:

o —Otrou doué! Silvestik, pelec'h oud-de bremé?

*

o Martézé émoud ouspenn trich'ant léo dious va zi

o Pé tolet barz ar mor braz d'ar pesked da zibri;

o Mar kérez béa chommet gant da vam ha da dad,

o Te vize bet dimézet bréman dimézet mâd;

*

o Té vizé bet dimézet hag eureujed timad

o D'ar braoa plac'h dious ar vro, Mannaik Pouldrégat,

o Da Manna da dousik-koant, ha vizez gen-omp-ni

o Ha gand da vugaligou trouz gant-hé kreiz ann ti.

*

o Me em euz eur goulmik glas tostik dious ma dor,

o Ma hi é doull ar garrek war benn ar roz o gor;

o Me stago dious hi gouk me stago eul lizer

o Gant séiennen va eured, ra zeui ma mab d'ar ger.

*

o —Sav a-lé-sé, va c'houlmik, sav war da ziou-askel

o Da c'hout mar te a nichfé, mar té a nichfé pell;

o Da c'hout mar té a nichfé gwall bell dreist ar mor braz,

o Ha wifez mai d-é ma mab, ma maber buhé c'hoaz?

*

o Da c'hout mar te a nichfe tré-beteg ann armé

o Ha gasfez euz va mab paour timad kélou dimé?

o —Setu koulmik glaz va mamm a gané kreiz ar c'hoat,

o Mé hi gwell érru d'ann gwern me hi gwel oc'h rézat.

*

o —Eurvad d'hoc'h hu, Silvestik, eurvad d'hoc'h, ha klévet:

o Ama emeuz eul lizer zo gan-in d'hoc'h kaset.

o —Benn tri bloaz hag eunn devez me erruo da vad

o Benn tri bloaz hagg eunn devez gant ma mamm ha ma zad.—

*

o Achuet oa ann daou vloaz, achuet oa ann tri:

o —Kénavo did, Silvestik, né az gwelinn két mui;

o Mar gaffenn da eskern paour tolet gand ar maré

o Ha mé ho dastuméfé hag ho briatefé.—

*

o Ne oa két he c'homz gant-hi, hé c'homz peur-lavaret

o Pa skoaz eul lestr a Vreiz war ann ot, hen kollet,

o Pa skoaz eul lestr a vro penn-da-benn hen frezet,

o Kollet gant-hen hé raonnou hag hé gwernou bréet.

*

o Leun a oa a dud varo, den na ouffé lavar,

o Na gout pe géit so amzer n'hé deuz gwelet ann douar.

o Ha Silvestik oa eno, hogen na mamm na tad,

o Na minon, né doa siouaz, sarret hé zaou lagad!

TRANSLATION.

Between the parish of Pouldregat and the parish of Plouare, young gentlemen levy an army to go to war, under the orders of the son of the duchess, who has collected many people from all parts of Brittany.

To go to war, beyond the sea, in the land of the Saxons. I have a son Silvestik, whom they expect; I have a son, an only son, my Silvestik, who departs with the army, in the train of the knights.

One night that I lay sleepless in my bed, I heard the girls of Kerlaz singing the song of my son; forthwith I sat up, and said—Lord! Lord! Silvestik, where art thou now?

Peradventure thou art more than three hundred leagues hence, or perhaps beneath the waters of the great sea, the food of fishes. Hadst thou consented to remain with thy father and mother, thou wouldst by this time be espoused, well espoused.

Thou wouldst be espoused to the prettiest girl of these parts, to Mannack of Pouldregat—Manna, thy sweet fair one, and thou wouldst be with us, and have little ones playing and making a noise around thee.

I have there, outside my door, a little white dove that makes its nest in the hollow of the rock on the hill: I will fasten a letter to its neck, with my wedding riband, and my son will return.

Ascend, my little dove, ascend on thy light wings: fly, fly far hence, beyond the great sea, to learn whether my son is still alive.

Fly to the army, and bring me tidings of my poor boy.

Ah! here cometh my mother's white dove, that used to coo in the woods around our dwelling; it passes through the masts of the fleet, it skims the waves.

Blessings on thee, Silvestik—blessings on thee! Hear me: I have here a letter for thee.

—In three years and a day I will return: in three years and a day, I will be once more with my father and my mother.

Two years passed away: three years passed away.

—Adieu, Silvestik, I shall never again see thee! Oh, could I but find some of thy bones on the shore, oh, I would gather them up, I would kiss them, and press them to my bosom.

She had scarce uttered the words, when a ship from Britain was cast upon the shore, a ship of the country, without oars, the masts broken, and filling with water. It was cast upon the rocks.

It was full of dead men; no one could say how long it had been straggling on the fierce waters. Silvestik was among these dead men: neither father, nor mother, nor friend had closed his eyes!

No. VII. POETICAL NARRATIVE OF THE BATTLE OF HASTINGS. NARRATIVE OF GEOFFROI GAIMAR.

V jors après sont arivez

François ot IX mile niefs

A Hastinges desur la mier

Ilœc firent chastel fermer.

Li reis Harald, quant ceo oit,

L'évesque Tared idonc saisit

Del grant avoir et del hernois

K'il out conquis sur les Norreis,

Merleswein idonc lessa,

Pur ost mander el suth ala,

V jors i mist al assembler;

Mès ne pout gères auner

Pur la grant gent ki ert oscise

Quant des Noreis fist Dieu justise.

Tresqu'en Suthsexe Harald ala

Tieus come pout od li mena.

Ses II frères gent assemblèrent,

A la bataille od lui alèrent,

Li uns fut Gérard, l'autre Leswine,

Contre la gent de ultre marine.

Quant les escheles furent rengées

Et de ferir apparaillées,

Mult i out genz d'ambes douz parz

De hardement semblent leoparz.

Un des François done se hasta,

Devant les autres chevaucha.

Talifer ert cil appellez,

Juglère hardi esteit assez,

Armes avoit et bon cheval,

Si ert hardiz et noble vassal.

Devant les autres cil se mist,

Devant Englois merveilles fist.

Sa lance prist par le tuet

Si com ceo fust un bastonet,

Encontre mont halt l'engetta

Et par le fer receue l'a.

III fois issi getta sa lance,

La quarte foiz puis s'avance,

Entre les Englois la launça,

Parmi le cors un en navera,

Puist trest s'espée, arère vint

Et getta l'espée, qu'il tint,

Encontre mont haut le receit.

L'un dit à l'autre, qi ceo veit,

Que ceo estoit enchantement.

Cil se fiert devant la gent

Quant III foiz out getté l'espée.

Le cheval ad la goule baée,

Vers les Englois vint eslessé,

Auquanz quident estre mangé

Pur le cheval q'issi baout.

Li jugléour enprès venout,

De l'espée fiert un Engleis,

Le poign li fet voler maneis;

Un autre férit tant cum il pout,

Mau guerdon le jour en out;

Car li Englois de totes parz

Li launcent gavelocs et darz,

Si l'occistrent et son destrer:

Mar demanda le coup primer.

Après iço Franceis requèrent,

E li Englois encontre fièrent.

Assez i out levé grant cri.

D'ici q'au vespre ne failli

Ne le ferir ne le launcer.

Mult i out mort meint chevalier.

Ne's sai nomer, ne ruis mentir.

Li Englois alèrent bien férir.

Li quiens Alain de Bretaigne

Bien i férit od sa compaigne.

Cil i férit come baron.

Mult bien le firent Breton.

Od le roi vint en ceste terre

Pur lui aider de sa guerre.

Son cosin ert, de son lignage,

Gentilhome de grant parage,

Le roi servit et ama,

Et il bien le guerdona

Richement li donna el north

Bon chastel et bel et fort.

En plusurs lius en Engleterre

Li rois li donna de sa terre.

Lunges la tint et puis finit,

A Saint-Edmon l'om l'enfouit.

Ore ai dit de cel baron,

Repairer voil à ma raison.

Lui et li autre tant en firent

Que la bataille bien venquirent.

Et ceo sachez qu'au chef de tour

Englois furent li péjour,

Et tournent à fuie el pré.

Meint cors fut de l'alme voidé.

Harald remist et ses II freres.

Par eus sont morz et fiz et pères,

Et multz autres des lignages,

Dont mult estoit granz damages.

Leswine et Gérard furent occis.

Li quiens William out le pais.

Narrative of Benoit de Sainte-Maure.

Pas sis jorz, furent amassées

Les fières gens des granz contrées,

Dunc chevaucha vers les Herberges.

La nuit que li ceus fu teniègres,

Soprendre quidout l'ost normant

En la pointe de l'ajornant,

Si qu'el champ out ses genz armées

Et ses batailles diséés;

Enz la mer out fait genz entrer

Por ceus prendre, por ceus garder

Qui de la bataille fuireient

Et qui as nefs revertireient.

Treis cenz en i orent e plus.

Dès ore ne quident que li dux

Lor puisse eschaper ne seit pris

Ou en la grant bataille occis.

A ce vout mult li dux entendre

Que l'om n'eì peust sopprendre.

Le seir en l'anuitant oscur

Que tuit en fussent plus seur,

Lor out lor cors faiz toz armer

Ci que le jor parut tot cler.

Samadis ert, ce sui lisantz.

Dunc prist treis légions mult granz,

En treis ordres les devisa

Et s'autre gent r'apareilla,

Archers, serjanz e ceus à pié.

Quant tuit furent apareillié,

Si fu l'enseigne despleiée,

Que l'apostoile out enveié [e]

De la sainte iglise de Rome.

Assous, confès, c'en est la sume,

Chevauchèrent, lor escuz pris,

Contre lor mortex enemis.

Cume sage, proz e discrez,

Les out li dux amonestez;

Remembre lor lor grant honor,

Que puisqu'il l'orent à seignor

Ne furent en nul leu vencuz.

Or est li termes avenuz

Que lor valors estuet dobler,

Creistre e pareistre e afiner.

Ci n'a mestier hobeléiz,

Mais od les branz d'acer forbiz

Deffendre les cors et les vies,

Kar od tant seront acomplies

Les granz paines e les travailles,

Ici finiront les batailles,

Ci receveront les granz loiers

Qu'aveir deivent bons chevaliers

Les terres, les fieus, les honors,

Plus c'unc n'orent lor anceisors.

Par lor valor, par lor proeces,

Auront dès or les granz richesces,

Les granz tenures e les fieus;

Mais trop est perillos li gieus.

Si la victoire n'en est lor

Et se il ne sunt venqueor,

Mort sunt, en ce n'a recovrer;

Kar fuie n'i aureit mestier,

Recet ne chastel ne boschage;

Mais qui or sera proz e sage

S'il mostre e face apareissant,

E il sera par tot aidant

Chadel et escuz et deffense;

E si chascun d'eus se porpense,

Si trovera c'unc Engleterre

Ne vout gaires nus hom conquerre,

Qu'Engleis la peussent deffendre;

E si deivent à ce entendre,

Que mult poent estre seur

Dunt Heraut est vers lui parjur.

Faus, enchaaiz, vient al estor

Od tote sa grant déshonor;

Morz est, vencuz e trespassez,

E il vivront mais honorez

Del grand conquest qu'iloc feront,

Qu'ensemble od lui départiront.

Or n'i a plus mais del férir

E de vassaument contenir

Que la bataille aient veneue

Ainz que la nuit seit avenge

Tant out Heraut ses genz menées

Par poi qu'as lor ne sunt jostées,

Tant out conreiz faiz et sevrez

Qui ne vos serreint devisez,

Si bel armez, si richement,

Que des armes d'or et d'argent

Resplent la terre d'environ:

Tant riche enseigne e tant penor.

I despleient à l'avenir.

Alez se sunt entre-férir

Si durement et od tel ire,

Jà n'orrez mais si fier martire.

Assemblez sunt d'anbes deuz parz,

Volent saettes, volent darz

A teu fuison senz plus tenir,

Riens n'i ose l'oil descovrir.

Li sun des cors, li hu, li cri,

Sunt entendu loing e oi,

Od ire assembla cel ovraigne,

Por tel ensangla[n]ta la plaigne.

Sempres assez en petit d'ore

Se corrent si morteument sore,

Od les haches danesches lées

E od les lances acérées

S'entre-fierent si durement

E si très airéement,

Que des costez e des eschines,

Des chés, des braz et des peitrines

S'en ist li sans à fais vermeilz.

Tant i a d'eus pasmez e freiz

Que ce n'est si merveille non.

Comencée est la contençon

Od les fiers glaives esmoluz

Si pesme, dunt dis mile escuz

Sunt despeciez e estroez

Et les forz haubers effundrez,

E li boel et li panceil

Eissi que de cler sanc vermeil,

Qui des cors lor chet et devale,

En i a jà deu mile pâle.

Ne fu si l'ovre non à gas

De ci que oiz fu li fiers glas

Sor les heaumes des branz d'acier;

Mas là sorst dol e encombrer

A ceus qui trébuchent des seles

Et qui l'om espant les cerveles

E qui l'om trauche les viaires.

Eissi dura tant li afaires

Que li coart e li preisié,

Cil à cheval et cil à pié

D'ambesdeus parz furent à un.

Dunc fu le chaple si comun

Ci qu'a hore de midi

Que nus de tant espie forbi,

Ne de tant glaive reluisant,

Ne de tant espée trenchant

Ne de tante hache esmolue,

Ne de tante sajette ague,

Ne quide eschaper ne eissir.

Tuit s'abandonent à morir.

A ce veient l'ovre atorner,

Kar, ke en cors que en sanc cler,

Sunt en maiz jusqu'as genoilz.

Unc tante dolerose voiz,

Ne tanz morteus orribles criz

Ne furent en un jor oiz.

En ceste ovraigne amère e fière

Orent Engleis en teu manière

Avantage, cum je vos dirai:

Dunt li nostre orent grant esmai,

Qu'encombros ert li leus e haut

Ou estaient les genz Heraut.

Ce les fist tant le jor tenir

Qu'à eus faiseit mal avenir.

Se il fussent à plain trovez,

Mult fust ainceis li chans finez:

Mais mult greja les noz le jor

E qu'en igal n'esteit l'estor.

A grant meschef les requereient

Là ù forment se defendeient,

Si que je truis escrit senz faille

Qu'à senestre de la bataille,

Où li nostre èrent au contenz,

Vint un morteus esmaiemenz;

Kar ne sai par quel aventure

Qui trop dut estre pesme et dure

Distrent e quidèrent plusor

Que li dux fust mort en l'estor:

C'en fist à mil les dos virer

Por fuir tot dreit à la mer.

A ce comença teu merveile

Qu'autretel mais ne sa pareille

Ne fu oie en itant d'ore,

Qu'Engleis corent à Normanz sore;

Fièrent, dérompent les à faiz.

Ici sorst dolor e esmais.

N'i eut rien deu retenir,

Ne deu champ jà plus maintenir,

Si deu nen feist marvaument;

Mais quant li dux veit e entent

Que sa gent est si dérompue

E morte, e guenchie, e vencue,

Si d'eus hastif conrei ne prent,

Dol à sis quers e dolor sent;

Par un sol poi n'esrage vifs,

Set qu'il creient qu'il seit ocis,

E por lui qu'il quident mort

Lor est venu cest desconfort.

Son chef desarme en la bataille

E del heaume e de la ventaille;

En si périllos leu mortal

Où fenissent tant bon vassal,

Mostrer se vout apertement

Que bien sachent certainement

Qu'il est toz seins e toz seurs,

Qu'à lui tornera li bons eurs;

A ceus qui jà erent fuiant

Lor vait, l'espée el poing, d'avant,

Si très durement les manace

Dunt guerpi unt e champ e place

Que riens n'en saureit reconter.

Qui dunc l'oist en haut crier

"Qu'avez oi, genz senz valor?

Ne veez-vos vostre seignor

Délivre e bien aidanz e sains

E de victorie tot certains?

Tornez arière au féréiz,

Kar jà les verreiz desconfiz."

Dunc vint poignant quens Eustace

Qui le duc effreie e manace

E dit: "Morz est, por veir, sens faille,

S'il ne se part de la bataille;

Nul recovrer n'a mais ès suens."

Ci pout grant honte aveir li quens,

Qu'à trop mauvaise e à trop fole

Fu puis tenue la parole;

E li dux ses gens tant sermone

Que quers e hardement lor done;

E quant ce est que sain le veient,

De nule rien plus ne s'effreient,

R'adrècent les chès des chevans;

E li bons dux, li bons vassaus

Lor mostre la veie premiers.

Iloc par fu teus chevaliers

E tel esforz i fist le jor

Od le tranchant brant de color,

Que chevaliers fendi armez

De ci qu'ès nuz des baudrez;

Hurte et abat, détrenche e tue,

E sa grant gent se resvertue,

Trovent Engleis desconréez

Qui jà s'erent abandonez

A enchaucier e à occire.

Donc i out d'eus fait teu martire

Si trés doleros e si granz

Que milliers, si cum sui lisanz,

I chairent que tuit finèrent,

Idunc quant Normant recovrèrent,

En sanc èrent vers les jenoiz.

Ainz que partist icil tooilz,

Fu reis Heraut morz abatuz,

Parmi les deus costez féruz

De treis granz lances acérées

Et par le chef de dous espées

Qui entrèrent jusqu'as oreilles

Que les plantes en out vermeilles.

Ne fu pas tost aperceu:

Por ce se sunt mult puis tenu

Cil devers lui estrangement.

A cel estor, à cel content,

Dunt ci vos di e dunt je vos cont,

Robert, fiz Roger de Baumunt,

Vos di qui fu teus chevaliers

Si proz, si hardiz e si fiers

E si aidanz que ceste istoire

Me fait de lui mult grant mémoire,

Mult redélivrent forz les places

Il e ses gens quens Eustaces.

Si n'a durée acer ni fer

Vers Guillaume le fiz Osber,

Qu'Engleis ateigne si garniz

De la mort ne puisse estre fiz.

Chevaliers i est forz e durs

E sage, e sofranz, e seurs:

E li bons visquens de Toarz

N'i est ne mauvais ne coarz,

Qui est apelé Eimeris;

Mult i reçut le jor grant pris.

Gauter Gifart, savum de veir,

Qui out le jor grant estoveir,

Qu'abatuz fu de son destrier

Eissi que cinc cenz chevalier

Des lor l'aveient jà outré,

Toz ert li secors oublié,

Quant li bons dux de Normendie,

Od l'espée d'acer forbie,

L'ala secorre e délivrer

E faire sempres remonter,

En si fait lieu n'iert mais retrait

Que tel esforz cum ceu seit fait

Par un prince qui au munt vive.

Nus ne content ne nus n'estrive

Que le pris n'en fust suens le jor

De la bataille et de l'estor;

Poi out de mort crieme e regart

A rescorre Gauter Gifart.

N'en i r'out gaires de plus buens

Qui fu le jor Hues li quens,

E Guillaume cil de Warenne

R'ida à conquerre le règne

Cum buens chevalers et hardiz.

Uns Taillefer, ce dit l'escriz,

I aveit mult grant pris conquis;

Mais il i fu morz e occis.

Tant esteit grant sis hardemenz

Qu'en mi les presses de lor genz

Se colout autresi seur

Cume s'il i fust clos de mur;

Et puis qu'il out plaies mortex,

Puis i fu-il si proz e teus

Que chevalier de nul parage

N'i fist le jor d'eus teu damage,

Ne's non pas toz, ne cil ne fist

Que l'estoire primes escrit,

Qui riche furent et vassal

El dur estor pesme e mortal.

Si vousisse lor faiz escrire,

Trop lunge chose fust à dire;

En treis quaers de parchemin

N'en venissé je pas à fin:

Par ce covient l'ovre à finer,

Que tost s'ennuient d'escouter,

Eschis e pensis e destreiz,

Auquant plusor soventes feiz

Qui à neient volent entendre

Mieuz qu'as buenz faiz oir n'aprendre.

[S]i dès prime, quant fu jostée,

De ci qu'à haute relevée

Dura la bataille plénière,

Que nus ne s'en fu traiz arère;

Mais quant la chose fu seue

E entre Engleis aperceue

Que Heraut ert mort à devise

E le plus de sa gent occise

E sis frère e baron plusors

N'en i atendent nul secors;

Lus sunt e vain, e feible, e pâle

Del sanc qui des cors lor déval[e];

Veient sei rompre e départir

E de totes parz envaïr,

Veient lor genz ocis e morte

E vient la nuit qui's desconforte,

Veient Normanz resvigorer

E lor force creistre e dobler,

Veient n'i a deffension,

Qui ne garra par esperon

Ou par mucer ou par foir

Certains e fis est de morir;

Virent les dos, n'i a retor;

Le deffendre laissent li lor.

Teus fu lor perte e lors esmais

Que derompu sunt à un fais.

Adonc i out glaive e martire

Si grant n'el vos saureiet riens dire,

Cele occise, cele dolor.

Tint tant cum point I out deu jor,

Ne la nuit ne failli la paine

Ci que parut le diemaine,

Ce que la terre ert encombrose

E fossée e espinose,

C'ocist Engleis plus e destruist,

Qué nus à peine s'i esduist.

La trébuchoent e chaeient,

E cil a pié les occieient,

Ne quid ne l'sai ne je ne l'lis

Ne en nule istoire ne l'truis

C'unc si granz genz fust mais jostée,

Si péri n'eissi alée

N'eissi à neient revertue.

Si fu la bataille vencue

Le premier jor d'oitovre dreit:

E si quide-l'om bien e creit

Qu'à cinc milliers furent esmé

Cil des lor qui furent trové

Sol eu grant champ del féreiz

Quant qu'il fussent desconfiz

Estre l'occise et le martire

Qui fu tute la nuit à tire.

Au retorner parmi les morz

Veissiez esjoir les noz;

Mais li dux est pleins de pitié

De lermes a le vis moillié

Quant il esgarde les ocis.

S'il tuit li furent enemis

Morteus vers lui e vers les suens,

Dunt mult li unt ocis de buens,

S'il tot deit aveir joie grant

D'aver si vencu un tirant

Vers lui parjur, faus, desleié

Totevies a-il pietie

Que li plus bel e li meillor

E Deu règne tote la flor

Seient eissi peri e mort

Par sa grant coupe et par son tort.

Cerchez fu sis cors e trovez,

En plus de tresze leus nafrez;

Kar devers lui, si cum je qui,

N'out meillor chevaler de lui;

Mais Deu ne crienst ne serement

E por ce l'emprist malement.

Lez lui furent trové ocis

Andui si frère, ce m'est vis;

Ne se voudrent de lui partir:

Toz treis les i covint morir.

Eissi l'en prent qui sieu désert:

Qui tot coveite le tot pert.

Cest glaive e ceste grant dolor

Que li Normant unt fait des lor

Aveient piaçà déservie

Quant par lor très grant felonie.

Occistrent auvré e tanz

De ses bons compaignons Normanz,

C'unc puis ne fu ne s'haissent

E qu'a ce ne s'atendissent,

Qu'or en unt fait à ceste feiz

Cumparé unt lor grant desleiz.

Tant aveit lor mautez durée

Qu'or es fenie e trespassée.

Alée est tote lor vertu

Si qu'à neient sunt revertu.

Deu règne ert mais la seignorie

As eirs estraiz de Normendie;

Cunquise l'unt cum chevalier

Au fer trenchant e al acier.

Au bie[n] matin, emprès mangier,

A fait li dux les morz cercher.

Mult i out piez e mains e buille;

Mais les armes e la despuille

Firent coillir et amasser;

Dunc fist toz les suens enterrer.

Li reis Heraut fu seveliz;

E si me retrait li escriz

Que sa mère por lui aveir

Vout au duc donner grant aveir;

Mais n'en vout unques dener prendre

Ne por riens nule le cors rendre;

Mais à un Guillaume Malet,

Qui n'ert tosel pas ne vaslet,

Mais chevaliers durs et vaillanz.

Icist l'en fu tant depreianz

Qu'il li donna à enfoir

Là où li vendreit à plaisir.

Narrative of Robert Wace.

Li dus e li soens plus n'i firent,

A lor herberges revertirent,

Tuit asseur e tuit certain

D'aveir la bataille à demain.

Dunc veissiez hanstes drecier,

Haubers e helmes afaitier,

Estrieus e seles atorner,

Couires emplir, ars encorder,

Eissi tot appareillier

Ke à cumbattre aveit mestier.

Quant la bataille dut joster,

La nuit avant, ço oi conter,

Furent Engleiz forment haitiez,

Mult riant e mult enveisiez;

Tote nuit mangièrent e burent,

Unkes la nuit el lit ne jurent.

Mult les veissiez démener,

Treper e saillir e chanter;

Bublie, crient, e weissel

E laticome e drincheheil,

Drinc Hindrewart e Drintome

Drinc Helf e drinc Tome.

Eissi se contindrent Engleiz,

E li Normanz e li Franceiz

Tote nuit firent oreisons,

E furent en aflicions.

De lor péchiez confez se firent,

As proveires les regehirent,

Et qui n'en out proveires prez,

A son veizin se fist confez.

Por ço ke samedi esteit,

Ke la bataille estre debveit,

Unt Normanz pramis e voé,

Si com li cler l'orent loé,

Ke à cet jor mez s'il veskeient,

Char ne saunc ne maingereient.

Giffrei, éveske de Coustances,

A plusors joint lor pénitances;

Cil reçut li confessions,

E dona li béneiçons.

Cil de Baieues ensement,

Ki se contint mult noblement;

Eveske fu de Baessin,

Odes aveit nom, filz Herluin,

Frère li dus de par lor mère;

Granz esforz mena od son frère

De chevaliers e d'altre gent;

Manant fu mult d'or e d'argent.

D'oitovre al quatorzième di

Fut la bataille ke jo vos di.

Li proveires par lor chapeles,

Ki esteient par l'ost noveles,

Unt cele noit tote veillié,

Dex réclamé e Dex préié.

Junes font et aflicions

E lor privées oroisons;

Salmes dient e misereles,

Létanies e kerieles;

Dex requièrent e merci crient.

Patenostres e messes dient;

Li uns: Spiritus Domini,

Li altres: Salus populi,

Plusors: Salve, sancte parens,

Ki aparteneit à cel tens,

Kar samedi cel jor esteit

A cel jor bien aparteneit.

Quant li messes furent chantées,

Ki bien matin furent finées,

Tuit li baron s'entr'asemlèrent,

E l'duc vindrent, si porpalèrent

Ke treis cunreis d'armes fereient

Et en treis lieus les assaldreient.

En un tertre s'estut li dus,

De sa gent pout veir li plus;

Li baron l'unt avironé,

Hautement a à els parlé:

"Mult vos deis, dist-il, toz amer,

E mult me pois en vos fier,

Mult vos dei e voil mercier

Ke por mei avez passé mer,

Estes venu en cele terre,

Ne vos en puiz, ço peize mei,

Tel graces rendre comme jo dei,

Maiz quant jo porrai, les rendrai,

E ço aureiz ke jo aurai:

Se jo cunquier, vos cunquerrez,

Se jo prens terre, vos l'anrez.

Maiz jo di bien veraiement:

Jo ne vins mie solement

Por prendre ço ke je demant,

Maiz por vengier li félunies,

Li traisuns, li feiz menties,

Ke li homes de cest pais

Unt fet à notre gent toz dis.

Mult unt fet mal à mes parenz;

Mult en unt fet à altres gens;

Par traisun font kank' il font,

Jà altrement mal ne feront.

La nuit de feste saint Briçan

Firent orrible traisun,

Des Daneiz firent grant dolor,

Toz les ocistrent en un jor.

Ne kuid mie ke pechie seit

D'ocire gent ki miex ne creit:

Ensemle od els mangié aveient,

E en dormant les ocieient;

D'Alwered avez bien oi

Come Guigne mult le trai:

Salua li, poiz cil beisa,

Ensemle od li but è menga,

Poiz le trai, prist e lia,

E à felun rei le livra,

Ki en lisle d'Eli le mist,

Les oils li creva, puiy l'ocist.

A Gedefort fist toz mener

Cels de Normendie e diesmer:

Et quant la diesme fu partie,

Oez com faite felonie,

Por ço ke trop grant li sembla,

La diesme de rechief diesma,

Teles félunies e plusors

K'il unt fete à nos ancessors

Et à nos amis ensement,

Ki se contindrent noblement,

Se Dex plaist nos les vengeron,

Et kant nos veineu les aron,

Ke nos feron légièrement,

Lor or aron e lor argent,

E lor aveir donc plenté ont,

E li maneirs ki riches sont.

En tot li mond n'a altretant

De si fort gent ne si vaillant

Come vos estes asemblez;

Vos estes toz vassals provez."

—E cil comencent à crier:

"Jà n'en verrez un coarder,

Nus n'en a de morir poor,

Se mestier est por vostre amor."

—Il lor répont: "Les vos merciz,

Por Dex, ne seiez esbahiz,

Ferez les bien al comencier;

N'entendez mie à gaaingner;

Li gaain nos iert tot comun;

A plenté en ara chescun;

Vos ne porreiz mie garir

Por estre en paiz ne por fuir,

Jà Engleiz Normanz n'ameront

Ne jà Normanz n'esparneront;

Félons furent e felons sont,

Faus furent et faus seront.

Ne fetes mie malvaistié,

Kar jà n'aront de vos pitié.

Ne li coart por bien fuir,

Ne li hardi por bien ferir,

N'en iert des Engleiz plus preisiez.

Ne n'en sera plus esparniez.

Fuir poez jusk'à la mer.

Vos ne poes avant aler;

N'i troverez ne nef ne pont,

Et esturmans vos faldront;

Et Engleiz là vos ateindront,

Ki à honte vos ociront.

Plus vos morreiz en fuiant

Ke ne fereiz en combatant;

Quant vos par fuie ne garreiz,

Cumbatez vos e si veincrez.

Jo ne dot pas de la victoire,

Venuz somes por aveir gloire;

La victoire est en notre main,

Tuit en poez estre certain."

—A ço ke Willame diseit

Et encor plus dire voleit,

Vint Willame li filz Osber,

Son cheval tot covert de fer.

—"Sire, dist-il, trop demoron;

Armons nos tuit, alon, alon!"

—Issi sunt as tentes alé,

Al miex k'il poent se sunt armé.

Li dus fu mult en grant trepeil,

Tuit perneient à li cunseil

Mult enorout toz li vassals,

Mult donout armes a chevals.

Quant il s'apareilla d'armer,

Sun boen haubert fist demander,

Sor sez bras l'a uns hoem levé,

Devant li dus l'a aporte.

Maiz al lever l'a trestourné

Sainz k'il ne fist ço de sun gré:

Sun chief a li duz enz boté,

Preuf l'aveit jà tot endosse,

Cels derriers a devant torné,

Arrière l'a mult tost jeté;

Cil en furent espoenté;

Ki li haubert unt esgardé.

—"Maint home, dist-il, ai veu:

Se issi li fust avenu,

Jà hui maiz armes ne portast

Ne en hui maiz en champ n'entrast,

Mais unkes en sort ne crei

Ne ne creirai; en Dex me fi,

Kar il fet d'el tot son pleisir,

E ço k'il velt fet avenir.

Unkes n'amai sortiseors,

Ne ne crei devineors:

A Dam le Deu tut me comant,

Ch'à mon haubert n'alez dotant;

Li haubert ki fu tresturné,

Et puiz me r'est à dreit doné

Senefie la tresturnée,

De la chose ki rert muée.

Li nom ki ert de duché

Verreiz de duc en rei torné;

Reis serai ki duc ai esté,

N'en aiez mie altre pensé."

—Dunc se signa, li haubert prist,

Beissa sun chief, dedens le mist,

Laça sun helme et ceint s'espée,

Ke un varlet out aportée.

Sun boen cheval fist demander,

Ne poeit l'en meillor trover;

D'Espaingne li out enveié

Un reis par mult grant amitié;

Armes ne presse ne dotast

Se sis sires l'esperonast.

Galtier Giffart l'out amené,

Ki à Saint-Jame aveit esté;

Tendi sa main, li règnes prist,

Pié en estrieu, desuz s'asist;

Li cheval poinst e porsailli,

Torna e point e s'esverti.

Li visquens de Toarz guarda

Coment li dus armes porta;

A sa gent a entor sei dit:

—"Home mez si bel armé ne vit,

Ki si gentement chevalchast,

Ne ki si bel arme portast

N'a ki haubert si avenist,

Ne ki lance si bien brandist,

Ni en cheval si bien seist,

Ki si tornast ne si tenist.

Soz ciel tel chevalier n'en a

Beau quiens et beau rei sera;

Cumbate sei et si veincra;

Tot seit honi ki li faldra."

—Li dus fist chevals demander,

Plusors en fist très li mener,

Chescun out à l'arcon devant

Une espée bone pendant;

Et cil ki li chevals menèrent,

Lances acérées portèrent.

Dunc furent armé li baron,

Li chevalier e li gueldon,

En treis compaignes se partirent,

Et treiz compaignes d'armez firent.

A chescune des treiz compaignes

Out mult seignors à chevetaignes,

K'il ne feissent coardie

Por perdre membre ne por vie.

Li Dus apela un servant,

Son gonfanon fist traire avant

Ke li pape li enveia,

E cil le traist, cit le despleia;

Li duz le prist, suz le dreça,

Raol de Conches apela;

Portez, dist-il, mon gonfanon

Ne vos voil feire se dreit non;

Par dreit e par anceissorie

Deivent estre de Normandie

Vostre parent gonfanonnier,

Mult furent tuit boen chevalier.

Grant merci, dist Raol, aiez,

Ke nostre dreit reconoissiez;

Maiz li gonfanon, par ma fei,

Ne sera hui porte par mei.

Hui vos claim quite cest servise;

Si vos servirai d'altre guise,

D'altre chose vos servirai:

En la bataille od vos irai,

Et as Engleiz me combatrai

Tant ke jo vis estre porrai;

Saciez ke ma main plus valdia

Ke tels vint homes i aura.

E li Dus guarda d'altre part,

Si apela Galtier Giffart;

Pel gonfanon, dist-il, pernez,

En la bataille le portez.

Galtier Giffart li respondi:

Sire, dist-il, per Dex merci,

Veiez mon chief blanc e chanu,

Empeirie sui de ma vertu,

Ma vertu m'est afebliée.

E m'aleine mult empeiriée.

L'ensuigne estuet à tel tenir,

Ki lonc travail poisse soffrir,

E jo serai en la bataille;

N'aveiz home ki mielx i vaille,

Tant i kuid ferir od m'espée,

Ke tot en iert ensanglantee.

Dunc dist li dus, par grant fierté:

Seignors, par la resplendor Dé,

Vos me volez, ço crei, trair,

E à cel grand busuing faillir.

Sire, dist Giffart, non feron;

Jamez ne feron traison,

Nel' refus' mie par félonie,

Maiz jo ai grant chevalerie

De soldéiers e de mon fieu;

Unkes mez jo n'out si bon lieu

De vos servir com jo ore ai.

Or se Dex plaist vos servirai;

Se mestier ert, por vos morreie,

Por vostre cor, li mien metreie.

En meie fei, ço dist li dus.

Jo vos amoe, or vos aim' plus;

Se jo en puiz escarper vis,

Mielx vos en sera mez toz dis.

Dunc apela un chevalier

Ke mult aveit or preisier,

Tosteins filz Rou-le-Blanc out non

Al Bec en Caux aveit meison;

Li gonfanon li a livré

E cil l'en a seu bon gré,

Parfondement l'en a cliné:

Volentiers l'a e bien porté

Encor en tienent quitement

Lor éritage lor parent.

Quitement en deivent aveir

Lor éritages tuit ses eir.

Willame sist sor son destrier;

Venir a fet avant Rogier

Ke l'en dist de Montgomeri:

Forment, dist-il, en vos me fi:

De cele part de là ireiz,

De cele part les assaldreiz,

E Guillaume, un seneschal,

Li filz Osber un boen vassal,

Ensemble od vos chevalchera

Et ovec vos les assaldra.

Li Boilogneiz e li Pohiers.

Aureiz e toz mes soldeiers.

De l'altre palt Alain Fergant

Et Aimeri li cumbatant,

Poitevinz meront e Bretons

E del Maine toz li barons

E jo, od totes mes granz genz

Et od amiz et od parenz,

Me cumbatrai par la grant presse

U la bataille iert plus engresse.

Armé furent tuit li baron

E li chevalier e li gueldon.

La gent à pié fu bien armée,

Chescun porta arc et espée;

Sor lor testes orent chapels,

A lor piez liez lor panels;

Alquanz unt bones coiriés,

K'il unt à lor ventre liés;

Plusors orent vestu gambais,

Couires orent ceiz et archais.

Chevaliers ont haubers e branz,

Chauces de fer, helmes luizanz,

Escuz as cols, as mains lor lances;

E tuit orent fet cognoissances,

Ke Normant altre coneust,

Et k'entreposture n'eust;

Ke Normant altre ne férist,

Ne Franceiz altre n'oceist.

Cil à pié aloient avant

Serréement, lor ars portant;

Chevaliers emprez chevalchoent,

Ki les archiers emprez gardoent.

Cil à cheval et cil à pié,

Si com il orent comencié

Tindrent lor eire e lor compas,

Serréement lor petit pas

Ke l'un l'altre ne trespassout,

Ne n'aprismout ne n'esloignout;

Tuit aloent serréement,

E tuit aloent fièrement.

D'ambedui parz archiers esteient,

Ki à travers traire debveient.

Heraut out sez homes mandez,

Cels des chastels e des citez,

Des ports, des viles e des bors,

Contes, barons et vavassors.

Li vilain des viles aplouent,

Tels armes portent com ils trovent,

Machues portent e granz pels,

Forches ferrées e tinels.

Engleiz orent un champ porpris:

Là fu Heraut od ses amis

Et od li baronz del pais,

Ke il out semons e requis.

Venuz furent delivrement

Cil de Lundres e cil de Kent,

Cil de Herfort e cil d'Essesse,

Cil de Surée e de Sussesse,

De Saint Edmund e de Sufoc,

E de Norwis e de Norfoc,

De Cantorbiere e de Stanfort,

E cil vindrent de Bedefort,

E cil ki sunt de Hundetone;

Venu sunt cil de Northantone,

D'Eurowic e de Bokinkeham,

De Bed et de Notinkeham:

De Lindesie et de Nichole

Vindrent qui sorent la parole.

Dechà deverz soleil levant

Veissiez venir gent mult grant

De Salebiere e de Dorsete

E de Bat e de Sumersete;

Mult en i vint deverz Glocestre,

E mult en vint de Wirecestre,

De Wincestre e de Hontesire

Et del conté de Brichesire.

Mult en vint d'altres cuntrées

Ke nos n'avon mie nomées;

Ne poon mie tot nomer,

Ne ne volon tot aconter.

Tuit cil ki armes porter porent

Ki la novele del duc sorent,

Alerent le terre desfendre

D'icels ki la voloent prendre.

D'ultre li humbre n'i vint gaires,

Quer cil orent altres affaires;

Daneiz les orent damagiez

E Tosti les out empiriez.

Heraut sont ke Normanz viendreient,

E ke par main les assaldreient;

Un champ out par matin porpris

U il a toz ses Engleiz mis;

Par matin les fist toz armer

Et la bataille conréer,

Et il out armes et ator,

Ki conveneit à tel seignor.

Li dus, ço dist, le deit requerre,

Ki conquerre velt Engleterre,

Et il, ço dist, le deit attendre,

Ki la terre li deit défendre.

A sa gent dist e comanda

Et à ses baronz cunscilla

Ke tuit ensemble se tenissent

Et ensemble se défendissent,

Quer se diloc se desparteient,

A grant peine se rescovreient.

Normanz, dist-il, sunt boen vassal,

Vaillant à pié et à cheval;

A cheval sunt boen chevalier

Et de cumbatre costumier;

Se dedenz noz poent entrer,

Nient iert puiz del recovrer.

Lungues lances unt et espées,

Ke de lor terres unt aportées,

E vos avez lances aigues

Et granz gisarmes esmolues.

Cuntre vos armes ki bien taillent

Ne kuid les lor gaires ne vaillent;

Trenchiez quant ke trenchier porreiz

Et jà mar rien espanereiz.

Heraut out grant pople e estult,

De totes parz en i vint mult;

Mais multitude petit vaut

Se la virtu du ciel i faut.

Plusor et plusor unt poiz di

Ke Heraut aveit gent petit,

Por ço ke à li meschai;

Maiz plusors dient e jel di,

Ke cuntre un home altre enveia

La gent al duc poi foisonna,

Maiz li dus aveit veirement

Plusors baronz e meillor gent:

Plenté out de boens chevaliers

E grant plenté de boens archiers.

Geldons Engleiz haches portoent,

E gisarmes ki bien trenchoent;

Fet orent devant els escuz

De fenestres e d'altres fuz,

Devant els les orent levez

Come cleies joinz e serrez;

N'i lessièrent nule jointure,

Fet en orent devant closture.

Par ù Normanz entr'elz venist,

Ke descunfire les volsist.

D'escuz e d'aiz s'avironèrent,

Issi desfendre se kuidèrent;

Et s'il se fussent bien tenu,

Jà ne fussent li jor veincu.

Jà Normant ne si embastist,

Ke l'alme à hunte ne perdist,

Fust par hache, fust par gisarme,

U par macliue u par altre arme.

Corz haubers orent e petit

E helmes de soi lor vestis.

Li Reis Heraut dist e fist dire

E fist banir com lor sire

Ke chescun tienge à tort son vis

Tot dreit contre lor anemis;

Nus ne tort de là ù il est,

E ki viendra là les truis prest:

Ke ke Normant el altre face,

Chescun defende bien sa place.

Dunc rova cels de Kent aler

Là ù Normanz durent joster,

Kar ço dient ke cil de Kent

Deivent férir primièrement;

U ke li reis auge en estor,

Li primier colp deit estre lor.

Cil de Lundres, par dreite fei,

Deivent garder li cors li Rei,

Tut entur li deivent ester,

E l'estandart deivent garder;

Cil furent miz à l'estandart,

Ke chescun le défent e gart.

Quant Heraut out tot apresté,

E ço k'il volt out comande,

Emmi les Engleiz est venu,

Lez l'estendart est descendu;

Lewine e Guert furent od lui;

Frère Heraut furent andur;

Asez out entur li baronz.

Heraut fu lez si gonfanonz;

Li gonfanon fu mult vaillanz,

D'or e de pierres reluisanz;

Willame pois ceste victoire

Le fist porter à l'Apostoile,

Por mostrer e metre en mémoire

Sun grant cunquest e sa grant gloire.

Engleiz se sunt tenu serré,

Tuit de cumbatre atalenté;

Un fossé unt d'une part fait,

Ki parmi la champaigne vait.

Entretant Normanz aparurent,

D'un pendant surstrent ù il furent,

D'une valée e d'un pendant

Sort un cunrei ki vint avant.

Li reis Heraut de luing les vit,

Guert apela, si li a dit:

Frère, dist-il, ù gardes-tu?

As-tu li dus qui vient veu?

De cele gent ke jo vei là,

La nostre geut nul mal n'ara;

Il a poi gent à nos cunquerre,

Mult ai grant gent en cele terre,

Encore ai jo tuz cumbatanz

Ke chevaliers ke paisanz

Par quatre foiz chent mil armez.

Par fei, dist Guert, grant gent avez,

Mais mult petit poise en bataille

Assemblee de vilanaille.

Grant gent avez en sorquetot,

Mult creim Normanz e mult les dot;

Tuit cil ki vienent d'outremer

Sunt mult à craindre e à doter,

Bien sunt arme, à cheval vunt,

Nos maisnies défolerunt.

Mult unt lances, mult unt escuz,

Mult unt haubers, helmes aguz,

Mult unt glaives, mult unt espées,

Ars e saetes barbelées

Les saetes sunt mult isneles,

Mult plus tost vunt ke arondeles.

Guert, dist Heraut, ne t'esmaier,

Dex nos pot bien, s'il volt aidier:

Jà par la gent ke jo là vei

Ne nos estuet estre en esfrei.

Endementrez ke il parloent

De celz Normanz k'il esgardoent

Sort un altre cunrei plus grant,

Emprez l'altre serréement;

A une part del champ tornerent,

E si k'as altres s'asemblèrent.

Heraut les vit, si les garda,

Guert apela, si li mostra:

Guert, dit-il, nos anemiz creissent,

Chevaliers vienent et espeissent,

Mult part en vient, grant poor ai:

Unkes maiz tant ne m'esmaai,

De la bataille ai grant freor,

Mi cors en est en grant poor.

—Heraut, dist-il, mal espleitas

Quant de bataille jor nomas;

Ço peise mei ke chà venis

E k'à Lundres ne remainsis,

U à Lundres u à Wincestre.

Mais ore est tart, ne pot maiz estre.

Sire frère, Heraut a dit,

Cunseil arière velt petit;

Desfendon nos, se nos poon.

Ne sai mez altre garison.

Se tu, dist Guert, à Lundres fusses

De vile en vile aler peusses,

E jà li dus ne te quérist,

Engleiz dotast e tei cremist

Arière alast u paix feist,

Et tes règnes te remainsist.

Unkes creire ne me volsis,

Ne me preisa ço ke jo dis;

De la bataille jor meis

Et à cel jor terme asseis,

Et de ton gre si le quesis.

Guert, dist Heraut, por bien le fis;

Jor li assis à samedi,

Por ço ke samedi naski

Ma mère dire me soleit

Ke à cel jor bien m'aviendreit.

Fol est, dist Guert, ki en sort creit,

Jà nul prudhoem creire n'i deit,

Nul prudhoem ne deit creire en sort.

A son jor a chescun sa mort;

Tu dis ke samedis naskis,

A cel jor pos estre occis.

Atant est sorse une cumpaigne

Ki covri tute la champaigne;

Là fu li gonfanon levez,

Ki de Rome fu aportez;

Joste l'ensuigne ala li dus:

Là fu li mielx, là fu li plus,

Là furent li boen chevalier,

Li boen vassal, li boen guerrier;

Là furent li gentil baron,

Li boen archier, li boen geldon,

Ki debveient li dus garder,

Et entur li debveient aler.

Li garchon e l'altre frapaille;

Ki mestier n'orent en bataille,

Ki le menu herneiz gardèrent,

De verz un teltre s'en tornèrent.

Li proveire e li ordoné

En som un tertre sunt monté

Por Dex preier et por orer,

E por la bataille esgarder.

Heraut vit Willame venir,

E li chams vit d'armes covrir,

E vit Normanz en treiz partir,

Ki de treiz parz voldrent férir:

Ne sai kels deie plus doter,

A paine pout itant parler:

Nos somes, dist-il, mal bailli,

Mult criem ke nos seions honi.

Li quens de Flandres m'a trai;

Mult fis ke fol ke jel' créi,

Kar par son brief m'aveit mandé,

E par messaige esseuré

Ke Willame ne porreit mie

Aveir si grant chevalerie;

Por ço, dist-il, me suiz targiez,

Ke me suis tant poi porchaciez;

Ço peise me ke ai si fait,

Sun frère Guert à sei a trait,

Miz se sunt juste l'estandart;

Chescun prie ke Dex le gart.

Envirun els lor parenz furent

E li Baron ke il conurent;

Toz jes unt preié de bien faire.

Nus ne s'en pot d'iloc retraire;

Chescun out son haubert vestu,

Espée ceinte, el col l'escu;

Granz haches tindrent en lor cols.

Dunc il kuident ferir granz cols.

A pié furent serréement,

Mult se contindrent fièrement;

Maiz s'il seussent deviner

Mult deussent plaindre e plorer

Por la dolorose advanture,

Ki lor avint mult male e dure.

Olicrosse sovent crioent

E Godemite reclamoent;

Olicrosse est en engleiz

Ke Sainte Croix est en franceiz,

E Godemite altretant

Com en frenceiz Dex tot poissant.

Normanz orent treiz cumpaignies

Por assaillir en treiz parties;

En treiz cumpaignes se partirent,

E treiz cumpaignes d'armes firent.

Li primiers e li secund vint,

E poiz li tiers ki plus grant tint:

Ço fu li dus ovec sa gent,

Tuit alèrent hardiement,

Dez ke li dous ost s'entrevirent,

Grant noise e grant temulte firent;

Mult oïssiez graisles soner

E boisines e cors corner:

Mult veissiez gent porfichier,

Escuz lever, lances drecier,

Tendre lor ars, saetes prendre,

Prez d'aissaillir, prez de desfendre.

Engleiz à estal se teneient

E li Normanz toz tems veneient.

Quant il virent Normanz venir

Mult veissiez Engleiz fremir,

Genz esmover, ost estormir;

Li uns rouii, li altres palir;

Armes seisir, escuz lever;

Hardiz saillir, coarz trembler.

Taillefer, ki mult bien cantout,

Sor un cheval ki tost alout,

Devant li dus alout cantant

De Karlemaine e de Rollant,

E d'Oliver e des vassals

Ki morurent en Renchevals.

Quant ils orent chevalchié tant

K'as Engleis vindrent aprismant:

Sires, dist Taillefer, merci,

Jo vos ai lungement servi,

Tut mon servise me debvez;

Hui si vos plaist me le rendez.

Por tut guerredun vos requier,

E si vos voil forment preier;

Otreiez mei, ke jo n'i faille,

Li primier colp de la bataille.

E li dus respont: Je l'otrei.

E Taillefer point à desrei,

Devant toz li altres se mist;

Un Engleiz feri, si l'ocist;

De soz le pis, parmie la pance

Li fist passer ultre la lance

A terre estendu l'abati.

Poiz trait l'espée, al're féri,

Poiz a crié: Venez, venez.

Ke fetes vos? Férez, férez.

Dunc l'unt Engleiz avironé;

Al secund colp k'il out doné,

Eis vos noise levé e cri,

D'ambedui pars pople estormi.

Normanz à assaillir entendent,

E li Engleiz bien se défendent;

Li uns fierent, li altres botent,

Tant sunt hardi ne s'entre dotent.

Eis vos la bataille assemblée,

Dunc encore est grant renomée

Mult oissiez grant corneiz

E de lances grant froisseiz,

De machues grant fereiz,

E d'espées grant chapleiz.

A la feie Engleiz rusèrent,

Et à la feie retornèrent,

E cil d'ultre mer assailleient,

E bien sovent se retraeient.

Normanz escrient: Dex are;

La gent englesche: Ut s'escrie.

Lors véissiez entre serjanz,

Gelde d'Engleiz e de Normanz,

Granz barates e granz medlees,

Buz de lances e colps d'espées.

Quant Engleiz cheient, Normanz crient,

De paroles se cuntralient,

E mult sovent s'entre défient,

Maiz ne sevent ke s'entre dient;

Hardiz fierent, cuarz s'esmaient;

Normanz dient k' Engleiz abaient,

Por la parole k'il n'entendent.

Cil empierent e cil amendent.

Hardiz fierent, cuarz grandissent

Come hoems font ki escremissent.

A l'assaillir Normanz entendent,

E li Engleiz bien se défendent,

Hauberz percent et escuz fendent,

Granz colps receivent, granz colps rendent,

Cil vunt avant, cil se retraient:

De mainte guise s'entre assaient.

En la champaigne out un fossé;

Normanz l'aveient adossé:

En belliant l'orent passé,

Ne l'aveient mie esgardé.

Engleiz unt tant Normanz hasté,

E tant empeint e tant boté;

El fossé les unt fet ruser.

Chevals et homes jambeter:

Mult veissiez homes tumber

Li uns sor li altres verser,

E tresbuchier et adenter;

Ne s'en poeient relever.

Des Engleiz i moreit asez,

Ke Normanz unt od els tirez.

En tut li jor n'out mie tant

En la bataille occiz Normant,

Com el fossé dedenz perirent,

Ço distrent ki li morz virent.

Vasletz ki as herneiz esteient,

E li herneiz garder debveient.

Voldrent guerpir tut li herneiz,

Por li damage des Franceiz,

K'el fossé virent tresbuchier,

Ki ne poeient redrecier;

Forment furent espoenté,

Por poi k'il ne s'en sunt torné;

Li herneiz voleient guerpir

Ne saveient kel part garir.

Quand Odes li boen corunez,

Ki de Bareues ert sacrez,

Poinst, si lor dist: Estez, estez;

Seiez en paiz, ne vos movez;

N'aiez poor de nule rien,

Kar se Dex plaist nos viencron bien

Issi furent asséuré,

Ne se sunt mie remué,

Odes revint puignant arière

U la bataille esteit plus fière.

Forment i a li jor valu,

Un haubergeon aveit vestu,

Desor une chemise blançhe,

Lé fut li cors, juste la manche;

Sor un cheval tot blanc seeit,

Tote la gent le congnoisseit

Un baston teneit en son poing.

Là ù veeit li grant besoing,

Faseit li chevaliers torner,

E là les faseit arrester:

Sovent les faseit assaillir,

E sovent les faseit ferir.

Dez ke tierce del jor entra,

Ke la bataille comença,

De si ke none trespassa

Fust si de si, fust si de là.

Ke nus ne sout lequel veincreit,

Ne ki la terre conquerreit.

De tutes parz si se teneient,

E si sovent se cumbateient,

Ke nus ne saveit deviner

Ki debveit l'altre sormonter.

Normanz archiers ki ars teneint,

As Engleiz mult espez traeient

Maiz de lor escuz se covreient,

Ke en char férir ne s' poeient;

Ne por viser, ne por bien traire,

Ne lor poeient nul mal faire.

Cunseil pristrent ke halt traireient;

Quat li saetes descendreient,

De sor lor testes dreit charreient,

Et as viaires les ferreient.

Cel cunseil ont li archier fait,

Sor li Engleiz unt en halt trait;

Quant li saetes reveneient,

De sor les testes lor chaeient,

Chiés e viaires lor perçoent,

Et à plusors les oilz crevoent;

Ne n'osoent les oilz ovrir,

Ne lor viaires descovrir.

Saetes plus espessement

Voloent ke pluie par vent

Mult espès voloent saetes

Ke Engleiz clamoent wibetes.

Issi avint k'une saete,

Ki deverz li ciel ert chaete

Féri Heraut desus l'oil dreit,

Ke l'un des oilz li a toleit;

Et Heraut l'a par air traite,

Getée a les mains, si l'a fraite.

Por li chief ki li a dolu

S'est apuié sor son escu.

Por ço soleient dire Engleiz,

E dient encore as Franceiz

Ke la saete fu bien traite

Ki à Heraut fu en halt traite,

E mult les mist en grant orgoil,

Ki al rei Herant creva l'oil.

Normanz aperchurent è virent

Ke Engleiz si se desfendirent,

Et si sunt fort por els desfendre,

Peti poeient sor els prendre.

Privéement unt cunseillié,

Et entr'els unt aparaillié

Ke des Engleiz s'esluignereient,

E de fuir semblant fereient,

Tant que Engleiz les porsivront

E par les chams s'espartiront.

Si les poeient despartir,

Mielx les porreient assaillir,

E lor force sereit mult piere,

Si porreient mielx descunfiere.

E com ils l'orent dit, si firent,

E li Engleiz les parswirent;

Poi e poi vunt Normanz fuiant,

E li Engleiz les vunt suiant.

Tant cum Normanz plus s'esluignièrent

E li Engleiz plus s'aprochièrent.

Par l'esluignement des Franceiz

Kuidèrent è distrent Engleiz,

Ke cil de France s'enfueient,

Ne jà mez ne retornereient.

La feinte fuie les dechut,

Par la fuie grant mal lor crut;

Kar se il se fussent tenu,

Ke il ne se fussent meu,

Mult se fussent bien desfendu,

A grant paine fussent veincu;

Maiz come fol se despartirent,

Et come fol les parswirent.

Mult veissiez par grant veisdie

Retraire cels de Normendie;

Lentement se vunt retraiant

Por fere Engleiz venir avant.

Normanz fuient et Engleiz chacent,

Lances aloignent, haches haucent.

Quant il furent bien esbaudi,

E par la champaigne esparti,

Engleiz les aloent gabant

E de paroles leidissant.

Cuarz, font-il, mar i venistes

Ki nos terres aveir volsistes

Nostre terre aveir kuidastes,

Folz fustes quant vos i entrastes;

Normendie vos iert trop luing.

N'i vendrez mie à cel besuing;

Nient iert mez d'arrière aler;

S'à un saut n'i poez voler.

Filz e filles perduz avez

Se la mer tot ne bevez.

Cil escotoent e soffreietn

Ne saveient ke il diseient,

Ço lor ert vis k'il glatisserent,

Kar lor langage n'entendeient.

Al arester et al torner

Ke Normant voldrent recovrer,

Oissiez baronz rapeler,

E Dex aie en halt crier.

Lor erre unt Normanz repris

Torné lor sunt emmi le vis;

Donc veissiez Normanz torner,

E ès Eugleiz entremesler;

Li uns li altres encuntrer,

E cels ferir e cels boter;

Cil fiert, cil faut, cil fuit, cil chace,

E eil assome, e cil manace;

Normanz encuntre Engleiz s'arestent,

E de ferir Normanz s'aprestent.

Mult veissiez par plusurs places

Beles fuies e beles chaces;

Grant fu la gent, la place lée,

Estur espez, dure meslée;

De tutes parz bien se cumbatent,

Granz sunt li colps, bien s'entrebatent,

Bien le faseient li Normant,

Quant un Engleiz vint acorant;

En sa cumpaigne out chent armez,

De plusors armes atornez,

Hache noresche out mult bele,

Plus de plain pié out l'alemele,

Bien fu armé à sa manière,

Grant ert e fier, o bele chiere.

En la bataille el primer front,

La ù Normanz plus espez sont,

En vint saillant plus tost ke cers;

Maint Normant mit li jor envers

Od sa cumpaigne k'il aveit,

A un Normant s'en vint tot dreit,

Ki armé fu sor un destrier;

Od la hache ki fu d'acier

El helme férir le kuida,

Maiz li colp ultre escolorja;

Par devant l'arcon glaceia

La hache ki mult bien trencha

Li col del cheval en travers

Colpa k'a terre vint li fers,

E li cheval chai avant

Od tot son mestre à terre jus.

Ne sai se cil le féri plus,

Maiz li Normanz ki li colp virent,

A grant merveille s'esbahirent.

L'assalt aveient tot guerpi,

Quant Rogier de Montgomeri

Vint poignant, la lance beissié;

Onc ne leissa por la coignié

K'il aveit sus el col levée,

Ki mult esteit lonc enhanstée,

Ke il Engleiz si ne férist,

K'à la terre platir le fist;

Dunc s'écria: ferez, Franceiz;

Nostre est li champ sor les Engleiz

Dunc veissiez dure medlée,

Maint colp de lance e maint d'espée.

E veissiez Engleiz desfendre,

Chevals tuer et escuz fendre.

Un soldeier i out de France

Ki fu de noble cuntenance,

Sor un cheval sist merveillos;

Dous Engleiz vit mult orguillos,

Ki s'esteient acumpaignié

Por ço ke bien erent preisié.

Ensemble debveient aler,

Li uns debveit l'altre garder,

En lor cols aveient levées

Dui gisarmes lunges e lées;

As Normanz feseient granz mals,

Homes tuoent e chevals.

Li soldeier les esgarda,

Vi li gisarmes, si dota;

Son boen cheval perdre creineit,

Kar ço ert li mielx k'il aveit;

Volentiers altre part tornast,

Se cuerdise ne semblast,

Maiz tost fu en altre pensé,

Sun cheval a esperuné;

Poinst li cheval, li frein lascha

E li cheval tost le porta.

Por la crieme des dons gisarmes

L'escuz leva par les énarmes:

Un des Engleiz féri tot dreit,

Od la lance ke il teneit,

Sos li menton en la petrine;

Li fer passa parmi l'eschine.

Endementrez ke il versa,

Se lance chai e froissa,

Et il a le gibet seisi

Ki a sun destre bras pendi;

L'altre Engleiz a féru amont

Ke tot li chief li casse e font.

Rogier li viel, cil de Belmont,

Assalt Engleiz el primier front,

A merveilles pris en i ont:

Ço pert as eirs ki riches sont;

Bien poet l'en saveir as plusors,

Ke il orent boens ancessors,

E furent bien de lor seignors

Ki lor donérent tels enors.

De cel Rogier en descendant

Vint li lignage de Mellant.

Guillame ke l'en dit Mallet,

Hardiement entr'els se met;

Od l'espée ki resflambie,

As Engleiz rent dure escremie;

Maiz son escu si estroèrent,

E son cheval soz li toèrent,

Et il meisme eussent mort,

Quant vint li sire de Montfort

Et dam Willame de Vez-Pont;

Od granz maisnies ke il ont

Le rescotrent hardiement.

Mult i perdirent de lor gent;

Mallet firent monter maneiz

Sor un destrier tot freiz.

Bien firent cel de Beessin,

E li baronz de Costentin,

E Neel de Saint-Salveor

Mult s'entremet d'aveir l'amor

E li boen gré de son seignor;

Assalt Engleiz o grant vigor,

Od la petrine du destrier

En fist maint li jor tresbuchier,

Et od l'espee al redrecier

Veissiez bien baron aidier.

Grant pris en out cil de Felgières,

Ki de Bretaigne ont gent mult fières,

Henri li sire de Ferrières,

E cil ki dunc gardout Tillières;

Od cels baronz grant gent s'asemble,

Sor Engliez fierent tuit ensemble;

Morz est u pris ki ne s'en emble;

Tote la terre crole et tremble.

De l'altre part out un Engleiz

Ki leidisseit mult li Franceiz;

Od une hache mult trenchant,

Les alout mult envaissant.

Un helme aveit tot fait de fust,

Ke kolp el chief ne receust;

A ses draz l'aveit atachié,

Et envirun son col lacié,

Un chevalier de Normendie

Vit li forfeit à l'estoltie

K'il alout des Normanz faisant;

Sor un cheval sist mult vaillant;

Eve ne feu nel' retenist,

Se li sire bien le poinsist;

Li chevalier l'esperuna

E li cheval tost le porta.

Sor li helme l'Engleiz feri,

De suz les oils li abati,

Sor li viaire li pendi

E li Engleiz sa main tendi

Li helme voleit suz lever,

E son viaire délivrer;

E cil li a un colp doné,

Li puing destre li a colpé,

E sa hache à terre chai.

Et un Normand avant sailli;

Od ses dous mains l'a relevée,

Ke il aveit mult golosée;

M'aiz mult li out corte dure,

K'il l'out sempres cumperée.

Al beissier ke il faseit

A la hache ke il perneit,

Un Engleiz od une coignié,

Ke il aveit lungue emmanchié,

L'a si féru parmi li dos

Ke toz li fet croissir les os:

Tote poet l'en veir l'entraille.

E li pomon e la coraille.

Li chevalier al boen cheval

S'en retorna ke il n'out mal;

Maiz un Engleiz ad encuntre,

Od li cheval l'as si hurté,

Ke mult tost l'a acraventé,

Et od li piez tot défolé.

Li boen citean de Roem

Et la jovente de Caem,

Et de Faleise, e d'Argentoen,

E d'Anisie, e de Matoen;

Cil ki ert sire d'Aubemare,

E dam Willame de Romare,

E li sire de Litehare,

E cil de Touke e de la Mare,

E li sire de Néauhou,

Et un chevalier de Pirou,

Robet li sire de Belfou,

E cil ki ert sire d'Alnou,

Li chamberlenc de Tancharvile,

E li sire d'Estotevile,

Et Wiestace d'Abevile,

Et li sire de Magnevile,

Willame ke l'en dist Crespin,

E li sire de Saint-Martin,

E dam Willame des Moslins,

E cil ki ert sire des Pins;

Tuit cil furent en la bataille;

N'i a cil d'els ki mult n'i vaille.

Un vassal de Grentemesnil

Fu muli li jor en grant peril;

Kar sun cheval li tresporta,

Por poi ke il ne tresbucha

A un boissun k'il tressailli:

Par li regnes le frein rompi,

E li cheval sailli avant,

Vers les Engleiz ala corant;

E li Engleiz ki s'aperchurent,

Haches levées li corurent;

Maiz li cheval s'espoenta

Arière vint, dunc il torna.

De Meaine li vieil Gifrei,

E de Bohon li vieil Onfrei,

De Cartrai Onfrei e Maugier,

Ki esteit novel chevalier;

De Garenes i vint Willeme,

Mult li sist bien el chief li helme;

Et li vieil Hue de Gornai,

Ensemle o li sa gent de Brai.

Ot la grant gent ke cil menèrent

Mult en ocistrent e tuèrent.

Et Engerran de Laigle i vint,

L'escu el col, la lance tint,

Sor Engleiz fiert de grant air,

Mult se peine del duc servir;

Por terre qu'il li out pramise

S'entremist mult de son servise.

E li visquens cil de Toarz

Ne fu mie li jor coarz.

D'Avrencin i fu Richarz,

Ensemble od li cil de Biarz,

E li sire de Solignie.

E li boteillier d'Aubignie,

Cil de Vitrie e de Lacie,

De val de Saire e de Tracie,

E cil furent en un conrei,

Sor Engleiz fierent demanei;

Ne dotoent pel ne fossé,

Maint hoem unt cel jor enversé:

Maint boen cheval i unt tué,

E d'els maint hoem i out nafré.

Hue li sire de Montfort,

Cil d'Espiné e cil de Port,

Cil de Corcie e cil de Jort,

I unt cel jor maint Englès mort.

Cil ki fu sire de Reviers,

Grant plenté out de chevaliers;

Cil i férirent as primiers,

Engleiz folent od li destriers.

Li viel Willame de Moion

Out avec li maint cumpaigner

De Cingueleiz Raol Teisson

E li viel Rogier Marmion

S'i contindrent come baron,

Poiz on orent grant guerredon.

Joste la cumpaigne Néel

Chevalcha Raol de Gael;

Bret esteit e Bretonz menout,

Por terre serveit ke il out,

Maiz il la tint asez petit,

Kar il la forfist, ço fu dit.

Des Biarz i fu avenals,

Des Mortiers-Hubert Paienals,

Robert Bertram ki esteit torz,

Mult i out homes par li morz.

Li archier du Val de Roil,

Ensemle od els cels de Bretoil,

A maint Engleiz crevèrent l'oil

Od li saetes acérées

K'il aveient od els aportées.

Cels de Sole e cels d'Oireval,

De Saint Johan e de Brehal,

Cels de Brius e celz de Homez

Veissiez férir mult de prez;

Li escuz sor lor chiés meteient,

Li colps de haches receveient;

Mielx voleient iloc morir,

Ke à lor dreit seignor faillir

Cil de Saint Sever e de Caillie,

E li sire de Semillie;

De Basquevile i fu Martels,

De joste li cil de Praels,

Cil de Goviz e de Sainteals,

Del viez Moléi e de Monceals,

Cil ki ert sire de Pacie,

E li seneschals de Corcie,

Et un chevalier de Lacie,

Ensemle o els cils de Gascie,

E cil d'Oillie e de Sacie,

E li sire de Vaacie,

Del Tornéor e de Praeres,

E Willame de Columbieres,

E Gilbert li viel d'Asnieres,

De Chaaignes e de Tornières,

Li viel Luce de Bolebec

E Dam Richart ki trent Orbec.

E li sire de Bonnesboz,

E cil de Sap e cil de Gloz,

E cil ki dunc teneit Tregoz;

Dous Engleiz fist tenir por soz;

L'un od sa lance acraventa,

L'altre od s'espée escervela,

Poinst li cheval, si retorna,

Si ke Engleiz ne le tocha;

E li sire de Monfichet,

Ki de boz garder s'entremet;

L'ancestre hue li Bigot,

Ki aveit terre a Maletot

Et as Loges et à Chanon;

Li dus soleit en sa maison

Servir d'une séneschaucie;

Mult out od li grant cumpaignie;

E fieu esteit son séneschals,

E mult esteit noble vassals.

Cil de corsage esteit petiz,

Maiz mult esteit proz e hardiz,

E por ço as Engleiz hurta

Od la grant gent ke il mena.

La oissiez noises c criz

E de lances grant froisseiz;

Encuntre Engleiz furent as lices,

De lor lances firent esclices.

Od gisarmes et od coignies

Lor unt lor lances pesciés;

Et cil unt lor espées traites,

Li lices unt totes fraites,

E li Engleis par grant déhait

Se sunt à l'estandart retrait.

Là esteient tuit assemblé

Li meshaignié e li nafré;

Dunc point li sire de La Haie,

Nus n'espargne ne ne manaie,

Ne nus ne fiert k'à mort ne traiei

Ne poet garir k'il fet plaie.

Cil de Vitrie e d'Urinie,

Cil de Monbrai e de Saie

E li sire de la Ferté

Maint Engleiz unt acraventé;

Grant mal i firent li plusor,

E mult i perdirent des lor;

Botevilain e Trossebot,

Cil ne dotent ne colp ne bot,

Mult si firent cel jor d'air

As colps recheivre et al férir.

Willame Patric de la Lande

Li reis Heraut forment demende;

Co diseit, se il le veeit,

De perjure l'appellereit.

A la Lande fu l'aveit veu,

E Heraut out iloc geu

E bar la Lande fu passez.

Quant il fu al duc amenez,

Ki à Avrenches dunc esteit,

Et en Bretaigne aler debveit.

Lá le fist li dus chevalier,

Armes e dras li fist bailler

A li et à sez cumpaingnons,

Poiz l'enveia sor li Bretons.

Patric fu lez li dus armez,

E mult esteit de li privez,

Mult i out chevaliers de Chauz,

Ki jostes firent et assauz.

Engleiz ne saveient joster,

Ne à cheval armes porter;

Haches et gisarmes teneient,

Avec tals armes se cumbateient.

Hoem qui od hache volt férir,

Od sez dous mainz l'estuet tenir,

Ne pot entendre à sei covrir,

S'il velt ferir de grant air;

Bien ferir et covrir ensemble

Ne pot l'en faire, ço me semble.

Deverz un tertre unt pris estal,

Normanz unt miz deverz li val.

Normanz à pié e à cheval,

Les assaillirent comme vassal.

Dunct puinst Hue de Mortemer

Od li sire d'Auviler;

Cil d'Onebac e de Saint-Cler

Engleiz firent mult enverser.

Robert ki fu filz Erneis,

La lance aluigne, l'escu pris,

A l'estandart en vint puignant;

De son glaive ki fu tranchant

Fiert un Engleiz ki ert devant,

Mort l'abati de maintenant,

Poiz trait l'espée demaneiz,

Maint colp feri sor les Engleiz.

A l'estandart en alout dreit,

Por ço k'abatre le voleit,

Maiz li Engleiz l'avironèrent,

Od lor gisarmes le tuèrent:

La fu trové quant il fu quis,

Lez l'estandart mort et occis.

Li quens Robert de Moretoing

Ne se tint mie del duc loing;

Frère ert li dus de par sa mère,

Grant aie fist à son frère.

Li sire poinst de Herecort,

Sor un cheval ki mult tost cort

De kant k'il pot li dus secort.

De Crievecoer e de Driencort

E li sire de Briencort

Sueient li dus kel part k'il tort.

Cil de Combrai e cil d'Alnei,

E li sire de Fontenei,

De Robercil e del Molei

Vunt demandant Heraut li rei.

As Engleiz dient: çà estez,

U est li reis ke vos servez,

Ki à Guillame est parjurez?

Morz est s'il pot estre trovez,

Altres barons i out assez,

Ke jo n'ai mie encor nomez;

Maiz jo ne poiz à toz entendre,

Ne de toz ne poiz raisun rendre

Ne poiz de toz li colps retraire

No jo ne voil lunge ovre faire;

Ne sai nomer toz li barons

Ne de toz dire li sornons

De Normendie e de Bretaigne,

Ke li dus out en sa cumpaigne.

Mult out Mansels et Angevins

E Tuarceiz e Poitevins

E de Pontif e de Boloigne.

Grant ert la gent, grant la busoigne;

De mainte terre out soldeiers,

Cels por terre, cels por deniers.

Li dus Willame se cumbat,

En la greignur presse s'embat,

Mult en abat, n'est ki rescoe;

Bien pert ke la busoigne ert soe.

E cil ki tient son gonfanon

(Tostein filz Rou li Blanc out non;

Del Bec joste Fescam fu nez,

Chevalier proz e renomez;

Et quant li dus tournout, tournout,

Et quant arestout, arestout)

Par li granz presses s'embateit,

Là ù il plus Engleiz veeit,

E li Normanz les ocieient

E tueient et abateient.

Out li dus mult grant cumpaignie;

De vavassors de Normendie,

Ki por lor seignor garantir

Se lesseient as cor férir.

Alain Fergant, quens de Bretaigne,

De Bretons mene grant cumpaigne;

C'st une gent fière e grifaigne,

Ki volentiers prent e gaaingne.

Cil en ocist mult e méhaigne,

Ne fiert Engleis ki sus remaigne.

Bien se cumbat Alainz Ferganz,

Chevalier fu proz e vaillanz;

Li Bretonz vaid od sei menant,

Des Engleiz fait damage grant.

Li sire de Saint Galeri,

E li Quens d'Ou bien i feri,

E Rogier de Mongomeri

E de Toarz Dam ameri

Se cuntindrent come hardi;

Ki li fierent, mal son bailli.

Li dus Willame mult s'engoisse,

Sor li Engleiz sa lance froisse;

D'aler à l'estendart se peine

Od li grant pople ke il meine;

Mult s'entremet de Heraut querre,

Ke par li est tute la guerre.

Normanz vunt lor seignor quérant,

E mult le vunt avironant;

As Engleiz vunt granz colps donant,

E cil se vunt mult desfendant;

Forment, s'esforcent e desfendent,

Lor anemiz à colps atendent.

Un i en out de grant vigor,

Ke l'en teneit por luiteor;

Od une hache k'il teneit,

As Normanz grant mal faiseit;

Trestuit li pople le cremeit,

Kar les Normanz mult destrureit

Li dus poinst, si l'ala férir;

Maiz cil guenchi, cil fist faillir,

En travers sailli un grant saut,

El col leva la hache en haut;

A retor ke li dus faiseit

Por la hache ke il cremeit

S'acorsa; cil de grant vertu

Sus a li dus el chief féru,

Li helme li a mult pléié,

Maiz ne l'a pas granment blecié.

Por poi k'il ne l' fist tresbuchier,

Maiz as estrieus s'est porfichiez,

Delivrement s'est redreciez;

E kant il se kuida vengier

Et occire li pautonier,

Li pautonier s'est trait arière;

Crieme a del duc k'il ne l' fière.

Entre les Engleiz vint saillant,

Maiz n'i pout mie avoir garant,

Kar Normanz ki l'orent veu

L'ont parsui e conseu,

As fers des lances l'ont cosu,

A terre l'unt mort abatu,

Là ù la presse ert plus espesse;

Là cil de Kent e cil d'Essesse

A merveille se cumbateient.

E li Normanz ruser faiseient,

En sus les faiseient retraire,

Ne lor poeient grant mal faire.

Li dus vit sa gent resortir

E les Engleiz trop esbaudir;

Par les enarmes prinst l'escu,

Porfichie s est de grant vertu,

Une lance a prise e drecié,

Ke un vaslet li a baillié,

Joste li prist sun gonfanon.

Plus de mil armez environ,

Ki del duc grant garde perneient

E là ù il puigneit puigneient,

Serréement si com il durent,

Verz les Engleiz férir s'esmurent;

Od la force des boens destriers

Et od li colps des chevaliers

La presse unt tote desrompue

Et la turbe avant els fendue.

Li boen dus avant les conduit,

Maint enchaça e maint s'emfuit.

Mult veissiez Engleiz tumber,

Gésir à terre e jambeter,

Et as chevals cels defoler

Ki ne se poent relever;

Mult veissiez voler cerveles

Et à terre gésir boeles.

Mult en chai à cel enchaus

Des plus riches et dus plus haus.

Engleiz par places se astreignent,

Cels ocient ke il ateignent,

E plus k'il poent s'esvertuent,

Homes abatent, chevals tuent.

Un Engleiz a li dus veu,

A li ociere a entendu;

Od une lance k'il portout

Férir le volt, mais il ne pout,

Kar li dus l'a enceiz féru

E à terre jus abatu.

Grant fu la noise e grant l'occise;

Maint alme i out forz de cors mise;

Li vifz de suz li morz trespassent,

D'ambes parz de férir se lassent.

Ki déroter pot, si dérote,

E ki ne pot férir, si bote;

Li forz cuntre li forz estrivent,

Li uns morent, li altres vivent;

Li cuarz se vont retraiant

Et li hardez passent avant.

Mal est bailli ki entrels chiet,

Grant poor a ainz k'il reliet,

E maint en chiet, ki ne relieve,

Par la grant presse maint encrieve.

Tant unt Normant avant empeint,

K'il unt à l'estandart ateint.

Heraut à l'estandart esteit,

A son poer se desfendeit,

Maiz mult esteit de l'oil grevez,

Por ço k'il li esteit crevez.

A la dolor ke il senteit

Del colp del oil ki li doleit,

Vint un armez par la bataille;

Heraut feri sor la ventaille,

A terre le fit tresbuchier;

E quant k'il se volt redrecier,

Un chevalier le rabati,

Ki en la cuisse le féri,

En la cuisse parmi le gros,

La plaie fu de si en l'os.

Guert vit Engleiz amenuisier,

Vit k'il n'i out nul recovier,

Vit son lignage déchaeir;

De sei garir n'out nul espeir,

Fuir s'en volt, mais ne poeit,

Ke la presse toz tems cresseit.

A tant puinst li dus, si l'ateint,

Par grant air avant l'empeint,

Ne sai se de cel colp morut,

Maiz ço fut dit ke pose jut.

L'estandart unt à terre mis,

E li reis Heraut unt occis

E li meillor de ses amis;

Li gonfanon à or unt pris.

Tel presse out à Heraut occire,

Ke jo ne sai ki l'occist dire.

Mult unt Engleiz grant dol eu

Del rei Heraut k'il unt perdu,

E del duc ki l'aveit vencu

E l'estandart out abatu.

Mult lungement se cumbatirent

E lungement se desfendirent,

De si ke vint â la parfin

Ke li jor torna el déclin.

E dunc unt bien aperceu,

E li alkanz recogneu

Ke l'estandart esteit cheu,

E la novele vint e crut

Ke mort esteit Heraut por veir.

Ne kuident maiz secors aveir;

De la bataille se partirent,

Cil ki porent fuir fuirent.

Ne sai dire ne jo nel di,

Ne jo n'i fu, ne jo ne l' vi,

Ni à mestre dire n'oi

Ki li reis Heraut abati,

Ne de kel arme il fu nafrez,

Maiz od li morz fu morz trovez,

Mort fu trovez entre li morz,

Ne l' pout garir ses granz esforz.

Engleiz ki del champ eschapèrent,

De si à Lundres ne finerent:

Co diseient e so creimeient

Ke li Normanz prez les sueient.

Grant presse out à passer li pont,

E l'ewe fu desoz parfont;

Por la presse li pont froissa,

E maint en l'ewe tresbucha.

Willame bien se cumbati,

En mainte presse s'embati,

Maint colp dona, maint colp reçut,

E par sa main maint en morut.

Douz chevals out soz li occis,

E li tiers a par busuing pris,

Si k'il à terre ne chai,

Ne de sanc gute n'i perdi.

Coment que chescun le feist,

Ki ke morust ne ki vesquist,

Veir est ke Willame veinqui.

Des Engleiz mult del cham fui

E maint en morut par li places:

A Dex Willeme en rent graces.

Li dus Willame par fierté,

Là ù l'estendart out esté

Rova son goufanon porter,

E là le fist en haut lever;

Ço fu li signe qu'il out veincu

E l'estandart out abatu.

Entre li morz fist son tref tendre,

E là rova son hostel prendre;

Là fist son mangier aporter

Et aparaillier son souper.

Eis vus Galtier Giffart puignant:

Sire, fet-il, k'alez faisant?

Vos n'estes mie avenament

Remez od ceste morte gent.

Maint Engleiz gist ensanglenté

Entre li morz sain u nafré,

Ki de lor sanc se sunt soillié,

Et od li morz de gré couchié,

Ki par noit kuident relever,

E par noit kuident escaper;

Mais mult se kuident ainz vengier,

E mult se kuident vendre chier.

Ne chaut chescun de sa vie,

Ne li chaut poix ki l'ocie,

Mais ke il ait un Normant mort.

Nos lor faison, ço dient, tort.

Aillors deussiez herbergier,

E faire vos eschargaitier

A mil u à douz mil armez

De cels ù plus vos fiez

Seit ennuit faite l'eschargaite;

Nos ne savons ki nos agaite;

Fière jornée avon hui faite,

Maiz la fin bien me plaist e haite.

Giffart, dist li dus, Dex merci,

Bien l'avome fet trésqu'ici,

Et se Dex le velt cunsentir,

E ke à li viengi à pleisir,

Bien le feron d'ore en avant;

De tot traion Dex à garant.

Issi s'en est Giffart tornez

Et Willame s'est désarmez,

A la guige del col oster,

Et à l'helme del chief sevrer

Et à l'hauber del dos verser

Vinrent baronz e chevaliers

E dameisels et esquiers;

Li colps virent granz en l'escu

E li helme ont quasse veu.

A grant merveille unt lot tenu

E dient tuient: tel ber ne fu

Ki si poinsist e si férist,

Ne ki d'armes tels faiz si fist;

Poiz Rollant ne poiz Olivier

N'out en terre tel chevalier.

Mult le preisent, mult le loent,

De ço k'il unt veu s'esjoent,

Maiz dolens sunt de lor amis,

Ki sunt en la bataille occis.

Li dus fu entr'els en estant

De bele groisse e de bel grant;

Graces rendi al rei de gloire

Par ki il out eu victoire,

Li chevaliers a merciez,

Et li morz sovent regretez.

A la champaigne la nuit jut,

Entre li morz mainga e but.

Diemaine fu el demain;

Cil ki orent ju à cel plain

E ki orent veillié as chans

E sofert orent mainz ahans,

Par matin furent el jor levez;

Par la champaigne sunt alé,

Lor amis unt fait enterrer,

Cels k'il porent morz trover.

Li nobles dames de la terre

Sunt alees lor maris querre;

Li unes vunt quérant lor pères,

U lor espos, u fils, u frères;

A lor villes les emportèrent,

Et as mostiers les enterrèrent.

Clers e proveires del pais

Par requeste de lor amis

Unt cels ke il trovèrent pris;

Charniers unt fait, cil unt enz mis.

Li reis Heraut fut emportez,

Et à Varham fu enterrez,

Maiz jo ne sais ki l'emporta,

Ne jo ne sais ki l'enterra.

Maint en remest el champ gisant,

Maint s'en ala par nuit fuiant.

No. VIII. Letter from M. Augustin Thierry to M. de la Fontenelle de Vaudore, Corresponding Member of the Institute.

"Sir,

"You request my opinion of Mr. Bolton Corney's Researches and Conjectures on the Bayeux Tapestry; I will give it you as succinctly as I can. Mr. Bolton Corney's theory comprises two principal propositions:, that the Bayeux tapestry was not a gift to the chapter of Bayeux from queen Matilda, nor, indeed, from any other person, but was manufactured for the cathedral by the order and at the expense of the chapter;, that this venerable monument is not contemporary with the conquest of England by the Normans, but dates from the period when Normandy was reunited to France. The first proposition appears to be quite supported by evidence; the second I consider inadmissible.

The tradition which assigned to queen Matilda the execution of the piece of tapestry preserved at Bayeux, a tradition in itself quite recent and thoroughly refuted by M. de la Rue, is now no longer admitted by any one. As to the second question, whether this tapestry was or was not a present made to the church of Bayeux, Mr. Corney resolves it in the negative, and this in what appears to be a very decisive manner. The inference from the entire silence on the subject of the ancient inventories of the church, he corroborates by proofs derived from the monument itself, demonstrating that its details are very decidedly impressed with the stamp of locality; that the conquest of England by the Normans is considered there almost entirely as it were with reference to the city and church of Bayeux. One bishop alone figures on the tapestry, and this the bishop of Bayeux, who repeatedly makes his appearance, and is sometimes designated merely by his title, Episcopus. Again, of all the lay personages represented around duke William, there is no one who bears an historical appellation. The names constantly recurring are Turold, Wadard, Vital, all of them probably popular men at Bayeux; indeed, the two latter, Wadard and Vital, are registered in Domesday Book, among the feudatories of the church of Bayeux, in Kent, Oxfordshire, and Lincolnshire. If we combine with this reason those which Mr. Corney deduces from the peculiar form and application of the monument, we cannot but concur in his opinion that the tapestry was ordered by the chapter of Bayeux, and executed according to its commission.

I proceed to the second proposition, that the Bayeux tapestry was worked after the reannexation of Normandy to France. This hypothesis needs no very diffuse refutation, for its author bases it upon one sole circumstance, the use of the term Franci in designating the Norman army. "William of Poitiers," he writes, "calls those who formed part of the army Normanni; the tapestry always terms them Franci, French. I regard this as a mistake, indicative of the period at which the monument was executed." Now, in point of fact, there is no mistake in the matter, no grounds whatever for the presumption that the Bayeux tapestry is otherwise than contemporary with the conquest of England by the Normans. The Anglo-Saxons themselves used to designate by the term French (Frencan, Frencisee men) all the inhabitants of Gaul, without distinction of province or of race. The Saxon Chronicle, in the thousand places where it mentions the chiefs and soldiers of the Norman army, invariably calls them French. In England this name served to distinguish the conquerors from the indigenous population, not merely in ordinary language, but also in legal acts. We read in the laws of William the Conqueror, under the article Murdrum, these words, Ki Franceis occist, and in the Latin version of these laws, Si Francigena interfectus fuerit. The employment of the word Franci instead of Normanni is not, then, any proof at all that the Bayeux tapestry is of a date posterior to the conquest. If it proved anything, it would be that the tapestry was executed not in Normandy but in England, and that it was to workmen and workwomen of the latter country that the chapter of Bayeux gave its commission.

This theory, indeed, which I submit to the opinion of archaiologists, appears further confirmed by the orthography of certain words and the employment of certain letters in the legends we read on the monument. We find even in the name of duke William, and in that of the city of Bayeux, traces of Anglo-Saxon pronunciation: Hic Wido adduxit Haroldum ad Wilgelmum Normannorum ducem; Willem venit Bagias; Wilgelm for Wilielm, Bagias for Baycux. The diphthong ea, one of the peculiarities of Anglo-Saxon orthography, is exhibited in the legends which contain the name of king Edward; Hic portatur corpus Eadwardi. Another legend presents this name of a place, given with exact accuracy in its Saxon form; At foderetur castellum ad Hestenca castra. Lastly, the name of Gurth, (pronounced Gheurth) brother of king Harold, as spelt with three Saxon letters; g having the sound of ghè; y, having that of eu, and the d having that of the modern English th.

Thus, then, I think with the majority of the Saxons who have written on the Bayeux tapestry, that this tapestry is contemporaneous with the great event it represents; I think with Mr. Bolton Corney that it was executed at the order and cost of the chapter of Bayeux, and I add, as a conjecture of my own, that it was manufactured in England and by English workers, according to a design transmitted from Bayeux

Receive, Sir, the assurances, &c.

No. IX. The valiant Courage and Policy of the Kentishmen which overcame William the Conqueror, who sought to take from them their Ancient Laws and Customs, which they retain to this day.

*

o When as the duke of Normandy

o With glistering spear and shield,

o Had entered into fair England,

o And foil'd his foes in field:

*

o On Christmas-day in solemn sort

o Then was he crowned here,

o By Albert archbishop of York,

o With many a noble peer.

*

o Which being done, he changed quite

o The customs of this land,

o And punisht such as daily sought

o His statutes to withstand:

*

o And many cities he subdu'd,

o Fair London with the rest;

o But Kent did still withstand his force,

o And did his laws detest.

*

o To Dover then he took his way,

o The castle down to fling,

o Which Arviragus builded there,

o The noble British king.

*

o Which when the brave archbishop bold

o Of Canterbury knew,

o The abbot of saint Augustine's eke,

o With all their gallant crew:

*

o They set themselves in armour bright,

o These mischiefs to prevent;

o With all the yeomen brave and bold

o That were in fruitful Kent.

*

o At Canterbury did they meet,

o Upon a certain day,

o With sword and spear, with bill and bow,

o And stopt the conqueror's way.

*

o "Let us not yield, like bond-men poor,

o To Frenchmen in their pride,

o But keep our ancient liberty,

o What chance so e'er betide:

*

o "And rather die in bloody field,

o With manly courage prest,

o Than to endure the servile voke,

o Which we so much detest."

*

o Thus did the Kentish commons cry

o Unto their leaders still.

o And so march'd forth in warlike sort,

o And stand at Swanscomb-hill:

*

o There in the woods they hid themselves

o Under the shadow green,

o Thereby to get them vantage good,

o Of all their foes unseen.

*

o And for the conqueror's coming there

o They privily laid wait,

o And thereby suddenly appal'd

o His lofty high conceit;

*

o For when they spied his approach,

o In place as they did stand,

o Then marched they to him with speed,

o Each one a bough in hand.

*

o So that unto the conqueron's sight,

o Amazed as be stood;

o They seem'd to be a walking grove,

o Or else a moving wood.

*

o The shape of men he could not see,

o The boughs did hide them so:

o And now his heart with fear did quake,

o To see a forest go.

*

o Before, behind, and on each side,

o As he did cast his eye,

o He spi'd the wood with sober pace

o Approach to him full nigh:

*

o But when the Kentishmen had thus

o Enclos'd the conqueror round;

o Most suddenly they drew their swords,

o And threw their boughs to ground;

o

o Their banners they display in sight,

o Their trumpets sound a charge,

o Their ratling drums strike up alarms,

o Their troops stretch out at large.

o

o The conqueror, with all his train,

o Were hereat sore aghast,

o And most in peril, when they thought

o All peril had been past.

o

o Unto the Kentishmen he sent,

o The cause to understand;

o For what intent, and for what cause

o They took this war in hand;

o

o To whom they made this short reply:

o "For liberty we fight,

o And to enjoy king Edward's laws,

o The which we hold our right."

*

o Then said the dreadful conqueror:

o "You shall have what you will,

o Your ancient customs and your laws,

o So that you will be still;

*

o "And each thing else that you will crave

o With reason at my hand;

o So you will but acknowledge me

o Chief king of fair England."

*

o The Kentishmen agreed thereon,

o And laid their arms aside;

o And by this means king Edward's laws

o In Kent doth still abide:

*

o And in no place in England else

o These customs do remain:

o Which they by manly policy

o Did of duke William gain.

No. X. Details of the Surrender of London, extracted from a contemporary Poem, attributed to Guy, Bishop of Amiens.

* Intus erat quidam contractus debilitate

* Renum, sicque pedum segnis ab officio;

* Vulnera pro patria quoniam numerosa recepit,

* Lectica vehitur, mobilitate carens.

* Omnibus ille tamen primatibus imperat urbis,

* Ejus et auxilio publica res agitur.

* Huic, per legatum, clam rex potiora revelat

* Secreti, poscens quatenus his faveat.

* "Solum rex vocitetur, ait, sic eommoda regni,

* Ut jubet Ansgardus, subdita cuncta regat."

* Ille quidem cautus caute legata recepit,

* Cordis et occulto condidit in thalamo.

* Natu majores, omni levitate repulsa,

* Aggregat, et verbis talibus alloquitur:

* "Egregii fratres, tum vi, tum sæpius arte

* (Est ubi nec sensus vester, et actus ubi?)

* Cernitis oppressos valido certamine muros,

* Et circumseptos cladibus innumeris;

* Molis et erectæ transcendit machina turres,

* Ictibus et validis mœnia scissa ruunt,

* Casibus a multis, ex omni parte ruina

* Eminet, et nostra corda timore labant;

* Atque manus populi, nimio percussa pavore,

* Urbis ad auxihum segniter arma movet.

* Nosque foris vastat gladius, pavor angit et intus:

* Et nullum nobis præsidium superest.

* Ergo, precor, vobis si spes est ulla salutis,

* Quatenus addatis viribus ingenium;

* Est quum præcipuum, si vis succumbat in actum,

* Quod virtute nequit, fiat ut ingenio.

* Est igitur nobis super hoc prudenter agendum,

* Et pariter sanum quærere consilium.

* Censeo quapropter, si vobis constat honestum,

* Hostes dum lateant omnia quæ patimur,

* Actutum docilis noster legatus ut hosti

* Mittatur, verbis fallere qui satagat;

* Servitium simulet nec non et fœdera pacis

* Et dextras dextræ subdere si jubeat"

* Omnibus hoc placuit; dicto velocius implent;

* Mittitur ad regem vir ratione capax,

* Ordine qui retulit decorans sermone faceto

* Utile fraternum, non secus ac proprium.

* Sed quamvis patula teneatur compede vulpes.

* Fallitur a rege fallere quem voluit.

* Namque palam laudat rex, atque latenter ineptat

* Quidquid ab Ansgardo nuntius attulerat.

* Obcæcat donis stolidum verbisque fefellit,

* Præmia promittens innumerosa sibi.

* Ille retro rutilo gradiens oneratus ab auro,

* A quibus est missus talia dicta refert:

* "Rex vobis pacem dicit, profertque salutem,

* Vestris mandatis paret et absque dolis.

* Sed, Dominum testor, cui rerum servit imago,

* Post dictum regem nescit habere parem;

* Pulchrior est sole, sapientior est Salomone,

* Promptior est Magno largior et Carolo.

* Contulit Etguardus quod rex donum sibi regni

* Monstrat et affirmat, vosque probasse refert.

* Hoc igitur superest, ultra si vivere vultis,

* Debita cum manibus reddere jura sibi."

* Annuit hoc vulgus, justum probat esse senatus,

* Et puerum regem cœtus uterque negat.

* Vultibus in terra deflexis, regis ad aulam

* Cum puero pergunt, agmine composito,

* Reddere per claves urbem, sedare furorem

* Oblato quærunt munere cum manibus.

* Novit ut adventum factus rex obvius illis,

* Cum puero reliquis oscula grata dedit,

* Culpas indulsit, gratanter dona recepit.

* Et sic susceptos tractat honorifice,

* Per fider speciem proprium commendat honorem,

* Et juramentis perfida corda ligat.

No. XI. Names of the Provinces and Principal Towns of England as given in the Saxon Chronicles.

Cant (Kent); Cantwaraburh (Canterbury).

Suthseaxe (Sussex); Cissanceaster (Chichester).

Sudrige (Surrey).

Middelseaxe (Middlesex); Lundene (London).

Eastseax (Essex); Colneceaster (Colchester)

Heortfordscyre (Hertfordshire).

Buccinggahamscyre (Buckinghamshire).

Oxnafordscyre (Oxfordshire).

Bearwukscyre (Berkshire).

Hamtunscyre (Hampshire); Wintanceaster (Winchester).

Wiltunscyre (Wiltshire); Searbyrig (Salisbury)

Dornsetas (Dorset).

Sumurset (Somerset).

Defnascyre (Devonshire); Exanceaster (Exeter)

Cornweallas (Cornwall).

Gleawanceasterscyre (Gloucestershire).

Wigreceasterscyre (Worcestershire).

Weringwicscyre (Warwickshire).

Nordhamtunscyre (Northamptonshire).

Huntandunescyre (Huntingdonshire).

Bedanfordscyre (Bedfordshire).

Grantanbrycgscyre (Cambridgeshire).

Suthfolc (Suffolk); Gipeswic (Ipswich).

Northfolc (Norfolk); Northwic (Norwich).

Lygraceaster (Leicester).

Steffordscyre (Staffordshire).

Scrobscyre (Shropshire); Scrobbesbyrig (Shrewsbury).

Ceasterscyre (Cheshire).

Deorabyscyre (Derbyshire).

Snotingahamscyre (Nottinghamshire).

Lincolnescyre (Lincolnshire).

Eoforwicscyre (Yorkshire).

Westmoringaland (Westmoreland).

Cumbraland (Cumberland).

Northanhumbraland (Northumberland).

No. XII. Ancient List of the Conquerors of England.

List published by André Duchesne, from a Charter in Battle Abbey.

* Aumerle.

* Audeley.

* Angilliam.

* Argentoun.

* Arundell.

* Avenant.

* Abel.

* Awgers.

* Angenoun.

* Archer.

* Aspervile.

* Amonerdvile.

* Arey.

* Akeny.

* Albeny.

* Asperemound.

* Bertram.

* Buttecourt.

* Brœchus.

* Byseg.

* Bardolf.

* Basset.

* Bohun.

* Baylife

* Bondeville.

* Barbason.

* Beer.

* Bures.

* Bonylayne.

* Barbayon.

* Berners.

* Braybuf.

* Brand.

* Bonvile.

* Burgh.

* Busshy.

* Blundell.

* Breton.

* Belasyse.

* Bowser.

* Bayons.

* Bulmere.

* Brone.

* Beke.

* Bowlers.

* Banestre.

* Belomy.

* Belknape.

* Beauchamp.

* Bandy.

* Broyleby.

* Burnel.

* Belot.

* Beufort.

* Baudewine.

* Burdon.

* Berteviley.

* Barte.

* Bussevile.

* Blunt.

* Beawper.

* Bret.

* Barret.

* Barnevale.

* Barry.

* Bodyt

* Bertevile.

* Bertine.

* Belew.

* Buschell.

* Beleners.

* Buffard.

* Boteler.

* Botvile.

* Brasard.

* Belhelme.

* Braunche

* Bolesur.

* Blundel.

* Burdet.

* Bigot.

* Beaupount.

* Bools.

* Belefroun.

* Barchampe.

* Camos.

* Chanville.

* Chawent.

* Chancy.

* Couderay.

* Colvile.

* Chamberlaine.

* Chambernoune.

* Cribet.

* Corbine.

* Corbet.

* Coniers.

* Chaundos.

* Coucy.

* Chaworthe.

* Claremaus.

* Clarell.

* Camnine.

* Chaunduyt.

* Clarways.

* Chantilowe.

* Colet.

* Cressy.

* Courtenay.

* Constable.

* Chancer.

* Cholmelay.

* Corlevile.

* Champeney.

* Carew.

* Chawnos.

* Clarvaile.

* Champaine.

* Carbonell.

* Charles.

* Chareberge.

* Chawnes.

* Chawmont

* Cheyne.

* Cursen.

* Conell.

* Chayters.

* Cheynes.

* Cateray.

* Cherecourt.

* Chaunvile.

* Clereney.

* Curly.

* Clyfford.

* Deauvile.

* Dercy.

* Dine.

* Dispencer.

* Daniel.

* Denyse.

* Druell.

* Devaus.

* Davers.

* Doningsels.

* Darell.

* Delabere.

* De la Pole.

* De la Lind.

* De la Hill.

* De la Wate.

* De la Watche.

* Dakeny.

* Dauntre.

* Desuye.

* Dabernoune.

* Damry.

* Daveros.

* De la Vere.

* De Liele.

* De la Warde.

* De la Planch.

* Danway.

* De Hewse.

* Disard.

* Durant.

* Divry.

* Estrange.

* Estutaville.

* Eseriols.

* Engayne.

* Evers.

* Esturney.

* Folvile.

* Fitz Water.

* Fitz Marmaduk.

* Fibert.

* Fitz Roger.

* Fitz Robert.

* Fanecourt.

* Fitz Philip.

* Fitz William.

* Fitz Paine.

* Fitz Alyne.

* Fitz Raulfe.

* Fitz Browne.

* Foke.

* Frevile.

* Faconbridge.

* Frissel.

* Filioll.

* Fitz Thomas.

* Fitz Morice.

* Fitz Hughe.

* Fitz Warren.

* Faunvile.

* Formay.

* Formiband.

* Frison.

* Finer.

* Fitz Urcy.

* Furnivall.

* Fitz Herbert.

* Fitz John.

* Gargrave.

* Graunson.

* Gracy.

* Glaunvile.

* Gover.

* Gascoyne.

* Gray.

* Golofer.

* Grauns.

* Gurly.

* Perot.

* Picard.

* Pudsey.

* Pimeray.

* Pounsey.

* Punchardon.

* Pynchard.

* Placy.

* Patine.

* Pampilion.

* Poterell.

* Pekeney.

* Pervinke.

* Penicord.

* Quincy.

* Quintine.

* Rose.

* Ridle.

* Rynel.

* Rous.

* Russel.

* Rond.

* Richmond.

* Rocheford.

* Reymond.

* Seuche.

* Seint-Quintine.

* Seint-Omer.

* Seint-Amand.

* Seint-Léger.

* Gurdon.

* Gamages.

* Gaunt.

* Hansard.

* Hastings.

* Haulay.

* Husie.

* Herne.

* Hamelyn.

* Harewell.

* Hardel.

* Hecket.

* Hamound.

* Harecord.

* Jarden.

* Jay.

* Janvile.

* Jasparvile.

* Karre.

* Karron.

* Kyriell.

* Lestrange.

* Levony.

* Latomere.

* Loveday.

* Logenton.

* Level.

* Lescrope.

* Lemare.

* Litterile.

* Lucy.

* Lisley or Liele.

* Longspes.

* Lonschampe.

* Lastels.

* Lindsey.

* Loterel.

* Longvaile.

* Lewawse.

* Loy.

* Lave.

* Le Despenser.

* Marmilon.

* Moribray.

* Morvile.

* Manley.

* Malebranche.

* Malemaine.

* Muschampe.

* Musgrave.

* Mesni-le-Villers.

* Sovervile.

* Sanford.

* Somery.

* Seint-George.

* Seint-Lés.

* Savine.

* Seint-Clo.

* Seint-Albine.

* Seinte-Barbe.

* Sandevile.

* Seint-More.

* Seint-Scudemor

* Tows.

* Toget.

* Talybois.

* Tuchet.

* Truslot.

* Trusbut.

* Traynel.

* Taket.

* Talbot.

* Tanny.

* Tibtote.

* Trussell.

* Turbevile.

* Turvile.

* Torel.

* Tavers.

* Torel.

* Mortmaine.

* Muse.

* Marteine.

* Mountbocher.

* Malevile.

* Mountney.

* Maleherbe

* Musgros.

* Musard.

* Mautravers.

* Merke.

* Murres.

* Montagu.

* Montalent.

* Mandute.

* Manle.

* Malory.

* Merny.

* Muffet.

* Menpincoy.

* Mainard.

* Morell.

* Morley.

* Mountmartin Yners.

* Mauley.

* Mainwaring.

* Mantell.

* Mayel.

* Morton.

* Nevile.

* Neumarche.

* Norton.

* Norbet.

* Norece.

* Newborough.

* Neele.

* Normanvile.

* Otenel.

* Olibef.

* Olifaunt.

* Oysell.

* Oliford.

* Oryoll.

* Pigot.

* Pecy.

* Perecount.

* Pershale.

* Power.

* Paynel.

* Peche.

* Peverell.

* Tirell.

* Totels.

* Taverner.

* Valence.

* Vancord.

* Vavasour.

* Vender.

* Verder.

* Verdon.

* Aubrie de Vere.

* Vernoune.

* Verland.

* Verlay.

* Vernois.

* Verny.

* Vilan.

* Umframvile.

* Unket.

* Urnall.

* Wake.

* Waledger.

* Warde.

* Wardebus.

* Waren.

* Wate.

* Wateline.

* Watevile.

* Woly.

* Wywell.

List from Bromton's Chronicle.

Vous qe desyrez assaver

Les nons de grauntz delà la mer,

Qe vindrent od le conquerour

William Bastard de graunt vigoure,

Lours surnons issi vous devys

Com je les trova en escris.

Car des propres nons force n'y a

Purce q'ill i ssont chaungés sà et là,

Come de Edmonde en Edwarde,

De Baldwyn en Bernard,

De Godwyne en Godard.

De Elys en Edwyn,

Et issint des touz autrez nons

Come ils sont levez du fons;

Purce lour surnons que sont usez,

Et ne sont pas sovent chaungez,

Vous ay escript; ore escotez

Si vous oier les voylleth.

Maundevyle et Daundevyle,

Ounfravyle et Downfrevyle,

Bolvyle et Baskarvyle,

Evyle et Clevyle,

Morevyle et Colevyle,

Warbevyle et Carvyle,

Botevyle et Stotevyle,

Deverous et Cavervyle,

Mooun et Boun,

Vipoun et Vinoun,

Baylon et Bayloun,

Maris et Marmyoun,

Agulis et Aguloun,

Chaumburleyn et Chaumbursoun,

Vere et Vernoun,

Verdyers et Verdoun,

Cryel et Caroun,

Dummer et Dommoun,

Hastyng et Cammois,

Bardelfe Bote et Boys,

Warenne et Wardeboys,

Rodes et Deverois,

Auris et Argenten,

Botetour et Boteveleyn,

Malebouch et Malemeyn,

Hautevyle et Hauteyn,

Danvey et Dyveyn,

Malure et Malvesyn,

Morten et Mortimer,

Braunz et Columber,

Seynt-Denis et Seynt-Cler,

Seynt-Aubyn et Seynt-Omer,

Seynt-Fylbert Fyens et Gomer,

Turbevyle et Turbemer,

Gorges et Spenser,

Brus et Boteler,

Crevequel et Seynt-Quinteyn,

Deverouge et Seynt-Martin,

Seynt-Mor et Seynt-Leger,

Seynt-Yigor et Seynt-Per,

Avynel et Paynell,

Peyvere et Peverell,

Rivers et Rivel,

Beauchamp et Beaupel,

Lou et Lovell,

Ros et Druell,

Mountabours et Mountsorell,

Trussebot et Trussell,

Bergos et Burnell,

Bra et Boterell,

Riset et Basset,

Malevyle et Malet,

Bonevyle et Bonet,

Nervyle et Narbet,

Coynale et Corbet,

Mountayn et Mounfychet,

Geynevyle et Gyffard,

Say et Seward,

Chary et Chaward,

Pyryton et Pypard,

Harecourt et Haunsard,

Musegrave et Musard,

Mare et Mantravers,

Fernz et Ferers,

Bernevyle et Berners,

Cheyne et Chalers,

Daundon et Daungers,

Vessi Gray et Graungers,

Bertram et Bygod,

Traillyz et Tragod,

Penbri et Pypotte,

Freyn et Folyot,

Dapisoun et Talbote,

Sanzaver et Saunford,

Vadu et Vatorte,

Montagu et Mounford,

Forneus et Fornyvaus,

Valens Yle et Vaus,

Clarel et Claraus,

Aubevyle et Seynt-Amauns,

Agantez et Dragans,

Malerbe et Maudut,

Brewes et Chaudut,

Fizowres et Fiz de lou,

Cantemor et Cantelou,

Braybuffe et Huldbynse,

Bolebeke et Molyns,

Moleton et Besyle,

Richford et Desevyle,

Watervyle et Dayvyle,

Nebors et Nevyle,

Hynoys Burs Burgenon,

Ylebon et Hyldebrond Holyon,

Loges et Seint-Lou,

Maubank et Seint-Malou,

Wake et Wakevyle,

Coudree et Knevyle,

Scales et Clermount,

Beauvys et Beaumount,

Mouns et Mountchampe,

Nowers et Nowchaumpe,

Percy Crus et Lacy,

Quincy et Tracy,

Stokes et Somery,

Seynt-Johan et Seynt-Jay,

Greyle et Seynt-Walry,

Pynkeney et Panely,

Mohant et Mountchensy,

Loveyn et Lucy,

Artoys et Arcy,

Grevyle et Courcy,

Arras et Cressy,

Merle et Moubray,

Gornay et Courtnay,

Haunstlayng et Tornay,

Husee et Husay,

Pounchardon et Pomeray,

Longevyle et Longespay,

Peyns et Pountlarge,

Straunge et Sauvage.

List published by Leland.

Un role de ceux queux veignont in Angleterre ovesque roy William le Conquereur.

Faet asavoir que en l'an du grace nostre seigneur Jesu Christe mil sisaunt ses, per jour de samadi en la feste S. Calixte, vint William Bastarde duc de Normandie, cosin à noble roy seint Edwarde le fiz de Emme de Angleter, et tua le roy Haraude, et lui tali le terre par l'eide des Normannez et aultres gents de divers terres. Entre quils vint ovesque lui monseir William de Moion le Veil, le plus noble de tout l'oste. Cist William de Moion avoit de sa retenaunde en l'ost tous les grauntz sieignors après nomez, si come il est escript en le liver des conquerors, s'est à savoir: Raol Taisson de Cinqueleis; Roger Marmion le Veil; Monsieur Nel de Sein Saviour; Raol de Gail qui fust Briton; Avenel de Giars; Hubert Paignel; Robert Berthram; Raol le archer de Val et le seir de Bricoil; li sires de Sole et le sires de Sureval; li sires de S. Jehan, et li sires de Breal; li sires de Breus et due sens des homez; li sires de S. Seu et li sires de Cuallie; li sires de Cennllie, et li sire de Basqueville; li sires de Praels, et li sires de Souiz; li sires de Samtels et li sires de vientz Moley; li sires de Mouceals et li sires de Pacie; li séneschals de Corcye et li sires de Lacye; li sires de Gacre et li sires Soillie; li sires de Sacre; li sires de Vaacre; li sires de Torneor et li sires de Praerers; William de Columbiers et Gilbert Dasmeres le Veil; li sires de Chaaiones; li sires de

Coismieres le Veil; Hugh de Bullebek; Richard Orberk; li sires de Bouesboz, et lí sires de Sap; li sires de Gloz et li sires de Tregoz; li sires de Monfichet et Hugh Bigot; li sires de Vitrie, et li sires Durmie; li sires de Moubray et li sires de Saie, li sires de la Fert et li sire Botenilam; li sire Troselet et William Patrick de la Lande; Monseir Hugh de Mortimer et li sires Damyler; li sires de Dunebek et li sires de S. Clere et Robert Fitz Herveis, le quel fust occis en la bataille; Tous ycels seigners desus nomé estoient à la retenaunce Monseir de Moion, si cum desus est diste.

Another List from Leland.

Et fait asavoir que toutes cestes gentez dount lor sor nouns y sont escritz vindrent ove William le Conquerour a de primes.

Aumarill et Deyncourt.

Bertrem et Buttencourt.

Biard et Biford.

Bardolf et Basset.

Deyville et Darcy.

Pygot et Percy,

Gurnay et Greilly.

Tregos et Treylly.

Camoys et Cameville.

Hautein et Hauville.

Warenne et Wauncy.

Chauent et Chauncy.

Loveyne et Lascy.

Graunson et Tracy.

Mohaud et Mooun.

Bigot et Boown.

Marny et Maundeville.

Vipount et Umfreville.

Morley et Moundeville.

Baillof et Boundeville.

Estraunge et Estoteville.

Moubray et Morvile.

Veer et Vinoun.

Audel et Aungeloun.

Vuasteneys et Waville.

Soucheville Coudrey et Colleville.

Fererers et Foleville.

Briaunsoun et Baskeville.

Neners et Nereville.

Chaumberlayn et Chaumberoun.

Fiz Walter et Werdoun.

Argenteyn et Avenele.

Ros et Ridel.

Hasting et Haulley.

Meneville et Mauley.

Burnel et Buttevillain.

Malebuche et Malemayn.

Morteyne et Mortimer.

Comyn et Columber.

S. Cloyis et S. Clere.

Otinel et S. Thomer.

Gorgeise et Gower.

Bruys et Dispenser.

Lymesey et Latymer.

Boys et Boteler.

Fenes et Felebert.

Fitz Roger et Fiz Robert.

Muse et Martine.

Quyncy et S. Quintine.

Lungvilers et S. Ligiere.

Griketot et Grevequer.

Power et Panel, alias Paignel.

Tuchet et Trusselle.

Peche et Peverelle.

Daubenay et Deverelle.

Sainct Amande et Adryelle.

Ryvers et Ryvel.

Loveday et Lovel.

Denyas et Druel.

Mountburgh et Mounsorel.

Maleville et Malet.

Newmarch et Newbet.

Corby et Gorbet.

Mounfey et Mountfichet.

Gaunt et Garre.

Maleberge et Marre.

Geneville et Gifard.

Someray et Howarde.

Perot et Pykarde.

Chaundoys et Chaward.

Delahay et Haunsard.

Mussegros et Musard.

Maingun et Mountravers.

Fovecourt et Feniers.

Vescy et Verders.

Brabasoun et Bevers.

Challouns et Chaleys.

Merkingfel et Mourreis.

Fitz Philip et Fliot.

Takel et Talbot.

Lenias et Levecote.

Tourbeville et Tipitot.

Saunzauer et Saunford.

Montagu et Mountfort.

Forneux et Fournivaus,

Valence et Vaus.

Clerevalx et Clarel.

Dodingle et Darel.

Mautalent et Maudict.

Chapes et Chaudut.

Cauntelow et Coubray.

Sainct Tese et Sauvay.

Braund et Baybof.

Fitz Alayne et Gilebof.

Maunys et Meulos.

Souley et Soules.

Bruys et Burgh.

Neville et Newburgh.

Fitz William et Watervile.

De Lalaund et de l'Isle.

Sorel et Somery.

S. John et S. Jory.

Wavile et Warley

De la Pole et Pinkeney.

Mortivaus et Mounthensy.

Crescy et Courteny.

S. Leo et Luscy.

Bavent et Bussy.

Lascels et Lovein

Thays et Tony.

Hurel et Husee.

Longvil et Longespe

De Wake et De la War.

De la Marche et De la Marc.

Constable et Tally

Poynce et Paveley

Tuk et Tany.

Mallop et Marny.

Paifrer et Plukenet.

Bretonn et Blundet.

Maihermer et Muschet.

Baius et Bluet.

Beke et Biroune.

Saunz pour et Fitz Simoun.

Gaugy et Gobaude.

Rugetius et Fitz Rohaut.

Peverel et Fitz Payne.

Fitz Robert et Fitz Aleyne.

Dakeny et Dautre.

Menyle et Maufe.

Maucovenaunt et Mounpinson.

Pikard et Pinkadoun.

Gray et Graunsoun.

Diseney et Dabernoun.

Maoun et Mainard.

Banestre et Bekard.

Bealum et Beauchaump.

Loverak et Longchaump.

Baudyn et Bray.

Saluayn et Say.

Ry et Rokel.

Fitz Rafe et Rosel.

Fitz Brian et Bracy.

Playce et Placy.

Damary et Deveroys.

Vavasor et Warroys.

Perpounte et Fitz Peris.

Sesee et Solers.

Nairmere et Fitz Nele.

Waloys et Levele.

Chaumpeneys et Chaunceus.

Malebys et Mounceus.

Thorny et Thornille.

Wace et Wyvile.

Verboys et Waceley.

Pugoys et Paiteny.

Galofer et Gubioun.

Burdet et Boroun.

Daverenge et Duylly.

Sovereng et Suylly.

Myriet et Morley.

Tyriet et Turley.

Fryville et Fresell.

De la River et Rivel.

Destraunges et Delatoun.

Perrers et Pavillioun.

Vallonis et Vernoun.

Grymward et Geroun.

Hercy et Heroun.

Vendour et Veroun.

Glauncourt et Chamount.

Bawdewyn et Beaumont.

Graundyn et Gerdoun.

Blundet et Burdoun.

Fitz-Rauf et Fihol.

Fitz-Thomas et Tibol.

Onatule et Cheyni.

Mauliverer et Mouncy.

Querru et Coingers.

Mauclerk et Maners.

Warde et Werlay.

Musteys et Merlay.

Barray et Bretevil.

Tolimer et Treville.

Blounte et Boseville.

Liffard et Osevile.

Benny et Boyvile.

Coursoun et Courtevile.

Fitz-Morice et S. More.

Broth et Barbedor.

Fitz-Hugh et Fitz-Henry.

Fitz-Arviz et Esturmy.

Walangay et Fitzwarin.

Fitz-Raynald et Roscelin.

Baret et Bourte.

Heryce et Harecourt.

Venables et Venour.

Hayward et Henour.

Dulee et De la laund.

De la Valet et Veylaund.

De la Plaunche et Puterel.

Loring et Loterel.

Fitz-Marmaduk et Mountrivel.

Kymarays et Kyriel.

Lisours et Longvale.

Byngard et Bernevale.

La Muile et Lownay.

Damot et Damay.

Bonet et Barry.

Avenel et S. Amary.

Jardyn et Jay.

Tourys et Tay.

Aimeris et Aveneris.

Vilain et Valeris.

Fitz Eustace et Eustacy.

Mauches et Mascy.

Brian et Bidin.

Movet et S. Martine.

Surdevale et Sengryn.

Buscel et Bevery

Duraunt et Doreny.

Disart et Doynell.

Male Kake et Mauncel.

Bernevile et Bretevile.

Hameline et Hareville.

De la Huse et Howel.

Tingez et Gruyele.

Tinel et Travile.

Chartres et Chenil.

Belew et Bertine.

Mangysir et Mauveysin.

Angers et Aungewyne.

Tolet et Tisoun.

Fermband et Frisoun.

S. Barbe et Sageville.

Vernoun et Watervile.

Wemerlay et Wamervile.

Broy et Bromevile.

Bleyn et Breicourt.

Tarteray et Chercourt.

Oysel et Olifard.

Maulovel et Maureward.

Kanceis et Kevelers.

Liof et Lymers.

Rysers et Reynevil.

Busard et Belevile.

Rivers et Ripers.

Percehay et Pereris.

Fichent et Trivet.

NOTE FROM THE ABBE DE LA RUE'S WORK,

Recherches sur la Tapisserie de Bayeux. Caen, 1824.

"Wace est loin d'avoir transcrit les noms de tous les sergneurs qui aidèrent le duc Guillaume dans son expédition. Aussi, d'après nos recherches, nous sommes certains qu'il existe encore dans notre province beaucoup de familles qui ont eu des branches établies dans la Grande-Bretagne, lors et depuis la conquête, et qui ont conservé les mêmes noms et souvent les mêmes armes. Mais comme ces noms ne sont pas tous inscrits dans le catalogue de Wace, nous transcrivons ici avec plaisir ceux que nos recherches nous ont fait connaître:

* Achard,

* D'Angerville,

* D'Annervile,

* D'Argouges,

* D'Auray,

* De Bailleul,

* De Briqueville,

* De Canouville,

* De Carbonel,

* De Clinchamp,

* De Courcy,

* De Couvert,

* De Cussy,

* De Fribois,

* De Harcourt,

* D'Héricy,

* De Houdetot,

* Mallet de Granville,

* De Mathon,

* Du Merle,

* De Montfiquet,

* D'Orglande,

* De Percy,

* De Pierre Pont,

* De St-Germain,

* De Ste-Marie d'Aigneaux.

* De Touchet,

* De Tournebu,

* De Tilli,

* De Vassi,

* De Vernois,

* De Verdun,

* Le Viconte."

No. XIII. Enumeration of the Lands of Brihtrik, possessed by Queen Matilda.

Infra scriptas terras tenuit Brictric, et post regina Mathildas.

Rex tenet Levia. Tempore regis Edwardi geldebat pro i hida et una virgata terræ. Terra est et uno ferling xii carucatæ. In dominio iiii carucatæ et vii servi et xx villani et vii bordarii cum x carucatis. Ibi xxx acræ prati et x acræ silvæ. Pasturæ viii quarentenæ longitudinis et iiii quarentenæ latitudinis. Reddit ix libras ad numerum.

Halgewelle geldebat T. R. E. pro una virgata terræ. Terra est v carucatæ. In dominio sunt ii carucatæ et vi servi et x villani et i bordarius cum v carucatis. Ibi xl acræ prati et ii acræ silvæ. Pastura i leuca longitudinis et ii quarentenæ latitudinis. Reddit lxx solidos ad numerum.

Clovelie T. R. E. geldebat pro iii hidis. Terra est xii carucatæ. In dominio sunt v carucatæ et x servi et xvi villani et xi bordarii cum vii carucatis. Ibi xxx acræ prati et xl acræ silvæ. Pastura i leuca longitudinis et dimidia leuca latitudinis. Reddit xii libras ad numerum. Olim reddebat vi libras.

Bedeford T. R. E. geldebat pro iii hidis. Terra est xxvi carucatæ. In dominio sunt iiii carucatæ et xiiii servi et xxx villani et viii bordarii cum xx carucatis. Ibi x acræ prati xx acræ pasturæ et cl acræ silvæ. Reddit xvi libras. Huic manerio adjacebat una piscaria. T. R. E. reddit xxv solidos.

Liteham T. R. E. geldebat pro una hida. Terra est viii carucatæ. In dominio sunt: una est carucata et vii servi et xii villani et iii bordarii cum iiii carucatis. Ibi x acræ prati et xx acræ pasturæ et lx acræ silvæ. Reddit iii libras.

Langetrev T. R. E. geldebat pro ii hidis dimidia virgata minus. Terra est xx carucatæ. In dominio sunt ii carucatæ et viii servi et xxiiii villani et ii bordarii cum xvi carucatis. Ibi xv acræ prati. Silva i leuca longitudinis et tantumdem latitudinis. Reddit vii libras et v solidos.

Edeslege T. R. E. geldebat pro iii hidis. Terra est xxii carucatæ. In dominio sunt iiii carucatæ et xv servi et xxiiii villani cum xvi carucatis. Ibi xv acræ prati; silva ii leucæ longitudinis et una leuca latitudinis. Reddit xiiii libras. De hac terra tenet Walterus de rege unam virgatam terræ. Terra est iii carucatæ. Aluuare tenuit de Brictric T. R. E. nec poterat ab eo separari. Huic manerio pertinent ii virgatæ erræ et dimidia.

In Tavetone Hundert.

Wincheleie T. R. E. geldebat pro v hidis et dimidia. Terra est xl carucatæ. Valet xx solidos. In dominio sunt viii carucatæ et xvi servi et lx villani cum xl carucatis et x porcariis. Ibi quatuor xx acræ prati et quingentæ acræ silvæ. Pastura i leuca longitudinis et alia latitudinis et parcus bestiarum. Reddit xxx libras ad numerum. De ipsa terra tenet Norman unam virgatam terræ et dimidiam. Valet xii solidos et vi denarios.

Aisse T. R. E. geldebat pro ii hidis dimidia virgata minus. Terra est xv carucatæ. In dominio sunt ii carucatæ, et x servi et xiiii villani et vi bordarii cum x carucatis. Et ii porcarii reddunt x porcos. Ibi xx acræ prati et cc acræ silvæ. Pastura dimidia leuca longitudinis et tantumdem latitudinis. Reddit vii libras ad numerum.

Slapeford T. R. E. geldebat pro ii hidis et dimidia. Terra est xi carucatæ. In dominio sunt iii carucatæ, et vi servi et vii porcarii et xviii villani et xii bordarii cum viii carucatis. Ibi xx acræ prati et x acræ pasturæ et cxxx acræ silvæ. Valet xii libras et xii solidos. Huic manerio adjacet Ervescome et ibi est dimidia virgata terræ.

Bichentone T. R. E. geldebat pro i hida et ii virgatis terræ et dimidia. Terra est xvi carucatæ. In dominio sunt ii carucatæ et iii servi et xiiii villani et ii bordarii cum vii carucatis. Ibi viii acræ prati et c acræ pasturæ et c acræ silvæ. Reddit xii libras. Huic manerio addita est Bichenelie quæ pertinebat in Tavestoch T. R. E. reddit in Bichentone iiii libras.

Morchet T. R. E. geldebat pro dimidia hida. Terra est viii carucatæ. In dominio sunt ii carucatæ et ii servi et viii villani cum iii carucatis. Ibi ii acræ prati et xi acræ silvæ. Reddit iiii libras ad numerum.

Holecumbe T. R. E. geldebat pro i hida. Terra est vii carucatæ. In dominio sunt ii carucatæ et iiii servi et x villani et viii bordarii cum v carucatis. Ibi cx acræ silvæ. Reddit viii libras et xv solidos.

Halsbretone T. R. E. geldebat pro v hidis. Terra est xxviii carucatæ. In dominio sunt iiii carucatæ et viii servi et xliii villani et x bordarii cum xxii carucatis. Ibi ii molini reddunt x solidos et xxxvi acræ prati. Pastura v quarentenæ longitudinis et xiii quarentenæ latitudinis. Silva xvi quarentenæ longitudinis et xiii quarentenæ latitudinis. Reddit xxvii libras. De hac terra hujus manerii tenit Goscelmus unam virgatam terræ et ibi habet i carucatam cum i servo et i bordario. Reddit x solidos in Alsbretone.

Aisbertone T. R. E. geldebat pro iii hidis. Terra est x carucatæ. In dominio sunt ii carucatæ et iiii servi et vii villani et viii bordarii cum iii carucatis. Ibi ii piscariæ et una salina et iii acræ prati et xl acræ pasturæ. Silva i leuca longitudinis et dimidia leuca latitudinis. Reddit iiii libras. Juhel tenebat de regina.

Rex tenet Ulwardesdone. Boia tenuit T. R. E. et geldebat pro una virgata terræ et dimidia. Terra est ii carucatæ quæ ibi sunt cum iii villanis et ii servis. Ibi iii acræ prati et ii quarentenæ pasturæ. Silva ii quarentenæ longitudinis et una quarentena latitudinis. Reddit x solidos. Adolfus tenet de rege.

No. XIV. Narrative of the Imprisonment of the Saxon Brihtrik.

* ...Malde de Flandres fu née,

* Meis de Escoce fu appelée

* Pur sa mère ke fu espusé

* Al roi de Escoce ki l'out rové,

* Laquele jadis, quant fu pucele,

* Ama un conte d'Engleterre.

* Bric'trich Mau le oi nomer,

* Après le rois ki fu riche ber.

* A lui la pucele envela messager

* Pur sa amur à lui procurer;

* Meis Brictrich Maude refusa:

* Dunt ele mult se coruça.

* Hastivement mer passa

* E à Willam Bastard se maria.

* Quant Willam fu coruné

* E Malde sa femme a reine levé,

* Icele Malde se purpensa

* Coment vengier se purra

* De Brictriche Mau k'ele ama,

* Ki à femme prendre la refusa.

* Tant enchanta son seignor,

* Le rei Willam le Conquéror,

* Ke de Brictrich Mau l'ad granté

* De faire de lui sa volente.

* La reine partot le fist guerreier,

* K'ele li volt déshériter.

* Pris fu à Haneleye à son maner,

* Le jor que saint Wlstan li ber

* Sa chapele avait dédié;

* A Wincestre fu amené,

* Ilokes morut en prison

* Brictrich Mau par treison.

* Quant il fu mort senz heir de sei,

* Son héritage seisit le rei

* E cum escheit tint en sa main,

* Dekes il feoffa Robert fiz Haim

* Ki oveke lui do Normondie

* Vint od mult grant chevalerie.

* La terre ke Brictrich li leissa,

* Franchement à Robert dona.

No. XV. Extract from Domesday-Book relative to the State of the Towns immediately after the Conquest.

DOVERE (Dover).

Dovere tempore regis Edwardi reddebat xviii libras, de quibus denariis habebat rex E. duas partes et comes Godwinus tertiam: contra hoc habebant canonici de Sancto Martino medietate maliam. Burgenses dederunt xx naves regi una vice in anno ad xv dies; et in unaquaque navi erant homines xx et unus. Hoc faciebant pro eo quod eis perdonaverat sacam et socam. Quando Missatici regis veniebant ibi, dabant pro caballo transducendo iii denarios in hieme et ii in æstate. Burgenses vero inveniebant stiremannum et unum alium adjutorem: et sí plus opus esset, de pecunia ejus conducebatur.

A festivitate S. Michaelis usque ad festum sancti Andreæ, Treuva (i. e. pax) regis erat in villa. Si quis eam infregisset, inde præpositus regis accipiebat communem emendationem.

Quicumque manens in villa assiduus reddebat regi consuetudinem, quietus erat de thelonio per totam Angliam. Omnes hæ consuetudines erant ibi, quando Wilhelmus rex in Angliam venit. In ipso primo adventu in Angliam, fuit ipsa villa combusta; et ideo pretium ejus non potuit computari quantùm valebat, quando episcopus Baiocensis eam recepit. Modo appretiatur xl lib.

et tamen præpositus inde reddit liv lib., Regi quidem xxiiii lib. de denariis qui sunt xx in Ora, comiti vero xxx lib. ad numerum.

In Dovere sunt xxix mansuræ, de quibus rex perdidit consuetudinem. De his habet Robertus de Romenel duas. Radulfus de Curbespine iii. Wilhelmus filius Tedaldi i. Wilhelmus filius Ogeri i. Wilhelmus filius Tedoldi et Robertus Niger vi. Wilhelmus Gaufredi iii.; in quibus erat Gihalla burgensium. Hugo de Montforts i domum. Durandus i. Ranulphus de Columbel i. Wadardus vi. Filius Modberti unam. Et hi omnes de his domibus revocant episcopum Baiocensem ad protectorem et liberatorem (vel datorem.)

De illa mansura quam tenet Ranulfus de Columbels, quæ fuit cujusdam exulis (vel utlagi), concordant quod dimidia terra est regis, et Ranulphus ipse habet utrunque. Hunfridus (Loripes) tenet i mansuram, de qua erat forisfactura dimidia regis. Rogerus de Ostreham fecit quamdam domum super aquam regis, et tenuit huc usque consuetudinem regis. Nec domus fuit ibi T. R. E.

CANTUARIA (Canterbury.)

In civitate Cantuaria habuit rex Edwardus l et i Burgenses, reddentes gablum, et alios cc et xii super quos habebat sacam et socam, et iii molendina de xl sol. Modo Burgenses gablum reddentes sunt xix. De xxxii aliis, qui fuerunt, sunt vastati xi in fossato civitatis: et archiepiscopus habet ex eis vii, et abb. S. Augustini alios xiv pro excambio castelli; et adhuc sunt cc et xii burgenses, super quos habet rex sacam et socam et molend. iii reddunt c et viii sol. et theloneum redd lxviii sol. Ibi viii acræ prati, quæ solebant esse legatorum regis, modo reddunt de censu xv sol. et mille acræ silvæ infructuosæ de qua exeunt xxiv solidi. Intra totum T. R. E. valuit li lib. et tantumdem quando vicecomes (Hamo) recepit; et modo l lib. appreciatur. Tamen qui tenet nunc reddit xxx lib. arsas et pensatas et xxiv lib. ad numerum. Super hæc omnia habet vicecomes c et x sol.

Burgenses habuerunt xlv mansuras extra civitatem, de quibus ipsi habebant gablum et consuetudinem; rex autem habebat sacam et socam. Ipsi quoque burgenses habebant de rege xxxiii acras terræ in gildam suam. Has domus et hanc terram tenet Ranulfus de Columbels; habet etiam quatuor xxi acras terræ super hæc, quas tenebant burgenses in alodia de rege. Tenet quoque v acras terræ, quæ juste pertinent uni ecclesiæ. De his omnibus revocat isdem Ranulfus ad protectorem epis. Baiocensem.

Radulfus de Curbespine habet iv mansuras in civitate, quas tenuit quædam concubina Heraldi, de quibus est saca et soca regis, sed usque nunc non habeit.

Isdem Radulfus tenet alias xi mansuras de Epispoco (Baiocens) in ipsa civitate quæ fuerunt Sbern Biga, et reddunt xi sol. et ii denarios et i obolum. Per totam civitatem Cantuariæ habet rex sacam et socam, excepta terra Ecclesiæ S. Trinitatis et S. Augustini, et Eddewe reginæ, et Alnold cild, et Eiber Biga, et Siret de Cilleham.

ROVECESTER (Rochester.)

Civitas Rovecester T. R. E. valeb. c sol. Quando episcopus recepit, similiter. Modo val. xx lib. tamen ille qui tenet reddit xl lib.

CASTRUM HARUNDEL (Arundel.)

Robertus filius Tetbaldi habet (in castro Harundel) ii hagas de xii sol. et de hominibus extraneis habet suum theloneum. Morinus habet consuetudinem de ii burgensibus de xii denar. Ernaldus unum burgensem de xii denariis. S. Martinus i burgensem de xii denariis. Radulfus unam hagam de xii denariis. Will. v hagas de v sol. Nigellus v hagas quæ faciunt servitium.

BURGUM DE LEWES (Lewes.)

Burgum de Lewes T. R. E. reddebat vi libras et iv sol. et iii obolos de gablo et de theloneo. Ibi rex E. habebat cxxvii burgenses in dominio. Eorum consuetudo erat, si rex ad mare custodiendum sine se mitterre suos voluisset, de omnibus hominibus, cujuscunque terra fuisset, colligebant xx sol. et hos habebant qui in navibus arma custodiebant. Qui in burgo vendit, dat præposito nummum; et qui emit, alium. De bove obolum. De homine iv denarios, quocumque loco emat infra rapum.

Sanguinem fundens emendat per vii sol. et iv denarios. Adulterium vel raptum faciens, viii sol. et iv denarios emendat homo, et femina tantundem. Rex habet hominem adulterum, archiepiscopus feminam. De fugitivo si recuperatus fuerit viii sol. et iv denarios. Cum moneta revocatur, dat xx sol. unusquisque monetarius. De his omnibus erant ii partes regis et tertia comitis. Modo per omnia reddunt Burgens. sicut tunc, et xxxviii sol. de super plus. De rapo de Pevenesel. xxxix mansuræ hospitatæ et xx inhospitatæ, ex quibus rex habet xxvi sol. et vi denarios et de his habet Will. do Warene medietatem. T. R. E. valebant xxvi lib. Rex medietatem et comes aliam habet. Modo val. xxxiv lib. et de nova moneta c sol. et xviii.

De his omnibus habet Will. medietatem et rex alteram.

GILDEFORD (Guildford.)

In Gildeford habet rex Willelmus lxxv hagas, in quibus manent clxxv homines. T. R. E. reddebant xxiii lib. et iii denarios. Modo appreciantur xxx lib. et tamen reddunt xxii lib. De supra dictis hagis habet Ranulfus clericus iii hagas, ubi manent vi homines; et inde habet isdem Ranulfus sacam et socam, nisi commune geldum in villa venerit, unde nullus evadat. Si homo ejus in villa delinquit, et divadiatus evadat, nil inde habet præpositus regis. Si vero calumniatus ibi fuerit et divadiatus, tunc habet rex emendam. Sic tenuit eas Stigandus (arch.)

Ranulfus (vicecomes) tenet i hagam, quam huc usque tenuit de episcopo Baiocensi: homines vero testificantur quia non adjacet alicui manerio, sed qui tenebat eam T. R. E. concessit eam Tovi præposito villæ pro emendatione unius suæ forisfacturæ.

Altera domus est quam tenet præpositus episcopi Baiocensis de Manerio Bronlei. De hoc dicunt homines de comitatu, quod non habet ibi aliam rectidudinem, nisi quod quandam viduam, cujus erat domus, accepit præpositus villæ, et ideo misit episcopus domum illam in suo manerio et huc usque perdidit rex consuetudines, episcopus autem habet.

Dicunt etiam homines qui juraverunt de alia domo quæ jacet in Brunlei, propter hoc tantum quod præpositus Ple ipsa villa fuit amicus hominis illius qui hanc domum habebat, et eo mortuo convertit eam ad M. de Bronlei.

Walterannus quoque desaisivit quendam hominem de una domo, unde rex E. habebat consuetudinem. Modo tenet eam Otbertus cum consuetudine, sicut dicit, per regem W. Robertus de Watevile tenet i domum quæ reddebat omnem consuetudinem T. R. E. Modo nichil reddit.

WALINGFORD (Wallingford.)

In Burgo de Walingeford habuit rex Edwardus viii. virgatas terræ: et in his erant ccvxxvi hagæ, reddentes xi lib. de gablo, et qui ibi manebant faciebant servitium regis cum equis vel per aquam usque ad Blidberiam, Reddinges, Sudtone, Besentone, et hoc facientibus dabat præpositus mercedem (vel conredium) non de censu regis, sed de suo.

Modo sunt in ipso Burgo consuetudines omnes ut ante fuerunt. Sed de hagis sunt xiii minus pro castello, sunt viii destructæ, et monetarius habet unam quietam, quamdiu facit monetam. Saulf de Oxenford habet unam; filius Alsi de Ferendone unam, quam rex ei dedit, ut dicit Hunfridus; Wisdelew habet unam, de qua reclamat regem ad Warant. Nigellus unam de Henrico per hæreditatem Soarding, sed burgenses testificantur se nunquam habuisse. De istis xiii non habet rex consuetudinem et adhuc Will. de Ware habet unam hagam, de qua rex non habet consuetudines, etc.

DORECESTRE (Dorchester.)

In Dorecestre, tempore regis Edwardi, erant clxxii domus. Hæ pro omni servitio regis se defendebant et geldebant pro x hid. scilicet ad opus huscarlium unam markam argenti, exceptis consuetudinibus quæ pertinent ad firmam noctis. Ibi erant ii monetarii, quisque eorum reddebat regi unam markam argenti et xx sol. quando moneta vertebatur.

Modo sunt ibi quatuor xx et viii domus, et c penitus destructæ a tempore Hugonis vicecomitis usque nunc.

BRIDEPORT (Bridport.)

In Brideport, tempore regis Edw. erant cxx domus et ad omnes servitium regis defendebant se et geldebant pro v hidis; scilicet ad opus huscarlium regis dimid. markam argenti, exceptis consuetudinibus quæ pertinent ad firmam unius noctis: ibi erat unus monetarius, reddebat regi i mark. argenti et xx sol. quando moneta vertebatur.

Modo sunt ibi c domus et xx sunt ita destructæ, quod qui in eis manent geld. solvere non valent.

WARHAM (Wareham.)

In Warham tempore regis Edwar. erant cxliii domus in domin. regis. Hæc villa ad omne servitium regis se defendebat et geldebat pro x hid. scilicet i markam argenti huscarlis regis, exceptis consuetudinibus quæ pertinent ad firmam unius noetis; ibi erant ii monetarii, quisque reddebat i markam argenti regi, et xx sol. quando moneta vertebatur.

Modo sunt ibi lxx domus et lxiii sunt penitus destructæ à tempore Hugonis vicecomitis, etc.

SCEPTESBERIE (Shaftesbury.)

In burgo Sceptesberie T. R. E. erant c et iv domus in dominio regis. Hæc villa ad omne servitium regis se defendebat, et geldebat pro xx hid. scilicet ii mark. argenti huscarlis regis; ibi erant iii monetarii, quisque reddebat i mark. argenti et xx sol. quando moneta vertebatur, etc.

EXONIA (Exeter.)

In civitate Exonia habet rex ccc domus xv minus, reddentes consuetudinem: hæc reddit xviii lib. per annum. De his habet B. Vicecomes vi lib. ad pensum et arsuram, et Columus xii lib. ad numerum, in ministeriis Eddid reginæ.

In hac civitate sunt vastatæ xlviii domus, postquam rex venit in Angliam.

Hæc civitas, T. R. E., non geldebat nisi quando Londonia, et Eboracum, et Wibtonia geldebant, et hoc erat dimid. markam argenti, ad opus militare. Quando expeditio ibat per terram aut per mare, serviebat hæc civitas quantum v hidæ terræ. Barnestapla vero et Lidesord et Totenais serviebat quantum ipsa civitas.

Burgenses Exoniæ urbis habent extra civitatem terram xii carucarum, quæ nullam consuetudinem reddunt nisi ad ipsam civitatem.

BURGUM HERTFORD (Hertford.)

Burgum Hertforde pro x hidis se defendebat T. R. E. et modo non facit. Ibi erant cxlvi Burgenses in soca regis Edwardi, nullam consuetudinem reddiderunt nisi geldum regis quando colligebatur.

OXENEFORD (Oxford.)

Tempore regis Edwardi reddebat Oxeneford pro theloneo et gablo et omnibus aliis consuetudinibus per annum, regi quidem xx lib. et vi sextaria mellis, comiti vero Algaro x lib. adjuncto molino quem infra civitatem habebat. Quando rex ibat in expeditionem, burgenses xx ibant cum eo pro omnibus aliis, vel xx lib. dabant regi, ut omnes essent liberi.

Modo reddit Oxeneford lx lib. ad numerum de xx in Ora.

In ipsa villa, tam intra murum quam extra, sunt ccxliii domus reddentes geld. et exceptis his sunt ibi quingentæ domus, xxii minus, ita vastatæ et destructæ quod geldum non possent reddere.

Rex habet xx mansiones murales quæ fuerunt Algari (comitis) T. R. E. reddentes tunc et modo xiv sol. ii denar. minus, etc.

Propterea vocantur murales mansiones quia si opus fuerit, et rex præcepit, murum reficient viz. unam ex his habuit antecessor Walterii dono regis E. ex viii virg. quæ consuetudinariæ erant T. R. E., etc.

Hi omnes præscripti tenent has prædictas mansiones liberas propter reparationem muri.

Omnes mansiones quæ vocantur murales T. R. E. liberæ erant ab omni consuetudine, excepta expeditione et muri reparatione.

Alwimus i (tenet) domum liberam pro muro reficiendo; de hac habet xxxii den. per annum. Et si murus, dum opus est, per eum qui debet non restauratur, aut xl sol. regi emendabit, aut domum suam perdit.

Omnes burgenses Oxeneford habent communiter extra murum pasturam reddentem vi sol. et viii denarios.

GLOWECESTRE (Gloucester.)

Tempore regis Edwardi reddebat civitas de Glowecestre xxxvi lib. numeratas et xii sectaria mellis ad mensuram burgi, et xxxvi dicras ferri et c virgas ferreas ductiles ad clavos navium regis, et quasdam alias minutas consuetudines in aula et in camera regis.

Modo reddit ipsa civitas regi lx lib. de xx in Ora; et de moneta habet rex xx lib., etc., cum alia consuetudine, quæ dat gablum sed aliam consuetudinem retinet.

Omnes istæ mansiones reddebant regalem consuetudinem T. R. E. Modo rex W. nichil inde habet, etc., sed etiam domus erant ubi sedet castellum, etc.

WIRECESTRE (Worcester.)

In civitate Wirecestre, habebat rex Edw. hanc consuetudinem. Quando moneta vertebatur, quisque monetarius dabat xx sol. ad Lundoniam pro cuneis monetæ accipiendis. Quando comitatus geldebat, pro xv hid. se civitas adquietabat. De eadem civitate habebat ipse rex x lib. et comes Edvinus viii lib. Nullam aliam consuetudinem ibi rex capiebat, præter censum domorum, sicut unicuique pertinebat. Modo habet rex W. in dominio et partem regis et partem comitis. Inde reddit vicecomes xxiii lib. et v sol. ad pensum, de civitate et de dominicis maneriis regis reddebat cxxiii lib. et iv sol. ad pensum. De comitatu vero reddebat xvii lib. ad pensum. Et adhuc reddit x lib. denariorum de xx in Ora, aut accipitrem (norresc) et adhuc c sol. reginæ ad numerum, et xx sol. de xx in Ora pro summario. Hæ xvii libræ ad pensum et xvi lib. ad numerum sunt de placetis comitatus et hundretis, et si inde non accipit, de suo proprio reddit.

HEREFORD (Hereford.)

In Hereford civitate tempore regis Edwardi erant c et iii homines commanentes intus et extra murum, habebant has subterscriptas consuetudines.

Si quis eorum voluisset recedere de civitate, poterat concessu præpositi domum suam vendere alteri homini, servitium debitum inde facere volenti, et habebat præpositus tertium denarium hujus venditionis. Quod si quis paupertate sua non potuisset servitium facere, relinquebat sine precio domum suam præposito, qui providebat ne domus vacua remaneret et ne rex careret servitio.

Intra murum civitatis unaquaque integra masura reddebat vii denarios et obolum, et iv denarios ad locandos caballos, et iii diebus in Augusto secabat ad Maurdine, et una die ad fenum congregandum erat, ubi vicecomes volebat. Qui equum habebat ter in anno pergebat cum vicecomite ad placita et ad hundret ad Urmelavia. Quando rex venatui instabat, de unaquaque domo per consuetudinem ibat unus homo ad stabilitionem in silva. Alii homines non habentes integras masuras, inveniebant inewardos ad aulam, quando rex erat in civitate.

Burgensis cum caballo serviens, cum moriebatur, habebat rex equum et arma ejus. De eo qui equum non habebat, si moreretur, habebat rex aut x sol. aut terram ejus cum domibus.

Si quis morte præventus non divisisset quæ sua erant, rex habebat omnem ejus pecuniam. Has consuetudines habebant in civitate habitantes et alii similiter extra murum manentes, nisi tantum quod integra masura foris murum non dabat nisi iii denar. et obolum. Aliæ consuetudines erant communes.

Cujuscunque uxor brazabat intus et extra civitatem, dabat x denarios per consuetudinem.

Sex fabri erant in civitate: quisque eorum de sua forgia reddebat unum denarium, et quisque eorum faciebat cxx ferra de ferro regis, et unicuique eorum dabantur iii denarii inde per consuetudinem, et isti fabri ab omni alio servitio erant quieti.

Septem monetarii erant ibi. Unus ex his erat monetarius episcopi. Quando moneta renovabatur, dabat quisque eorum xviii sol. pro cuneis recipiendis; et ex eo die quo redibant usque ad unum mensem, dabat quisque eorum regi xx sol. et similiter habebat epis. de suo monetario xx sol.

Quando veniebat rex in civitatem quantum volebat denar. faciebant ei monetarii, de argento scilicet regis, et hi vii habebant sacam et socham suam.

Moriente aliquo regis monetario, habebat rex xx sol. de relevamento. Quod si moreretur non diviso censu suo, rex habebat omnem censum.

Si vicecomes iret in Wales cum exercitu, ibant hi homines cum eo. Quod si quis ire jussus non iret, emendabat regi xl sol.

In ipsa civitate habebat Heraldus (comes) xxvii burgenses, easdem consuetudines habentes quas et alii burgenses.

De hac civitate reddebat præpositus xii lib. regi (E.) et vi lib. comiti (Heraldo) et habebat in suo censu supradictas omnes consuetudines.

Rex vero habebat in suo dominio tres forisfacturas, hoc est pacem suam infractam, et heinfaram, et forestellum.

Quicunque horum unum fecisset, emendabat c sol. regi cujuscumque homo fuisset.

Modo habet rex civitatem Hereford in dominio, et anglici burgenses ibi manentes habent suas priores consuetudines: Francigenæ vero burgenses habent quietas per xii denarios omnes forisfacturas, præter tres supradictas.

Hæc civitas reddit regi lx lib. ad numerum, de candidis denariis, intra civitatem et xviii maneria quæ in Hereford reddunt firmas suas, computantur cccxxxv lib. et xviii sol. exceptis placitis de hund. de comitatu.

GRENTEBRIGE (Cambridge.)

Burgum de Grentebrige pro uno hundret se defend T. R. E. In hoc Burgo fuerunt et sunt decem custodiæ. In prima custodia liv masuræ, ex his ii sunt vaste. In hac prima custodia habet Alanus comes v burgenses nichil reddentes, etc. Hæc eadem una custodia pro duabus computabatur T. R. E.; sed pro castro sunt destructæ xxviii domus.

In secunda custodia fuerunt xlviii masuræ T. R. E., etc.

In tercia custodia T. R. E. fuerunt xli masuræ, etc.

In quarta custodia T. R. E. fuerunt xlv masuræ.

De consuetudinibus hujus villæ vii lib. per annum, et de Landgable vii lib. et ii Oræ et duo denar.

Burgenses T. R. E. accommodabant vicecomiti carrucas suas ter in anno. Modo novem vicibus exiguntur.

Nec averas nec currus T. T. E. inveniebant, quæ modo faciunt per consuetudinem impositam. Reclamant autem super Picotum vicecomitem, communem pasturam sibi per eum (et ab eo) ablatam.

De Harieta Lagemannorum habuit isdem Picot. vii lib. et unum palfridum, et unius militis arma.

HUNTEDUN (Huntingdon.)

Huntedun burg defendebat se ad geld. regis pro quarta parte de hyrstingestan hund. pro l hid.; sed modo non geldat ita in illo hund. postquam rex W. geldum monetæ posuit in burgo. De toto hoc burgo exibant T. R. E. de Landgable x lib. inde comes tertiam partem habebat, rex duas. De hoc censu remanent nunc supra xx mansuræ, ubi castrum est xvi sol. et viii denar. inter comitem et regem. Præter hæc habebat rex xx lib. et comes x lib. de firma burgi, aut plus aut minus, sicut poterat collocare partem suam, etc.

Hanc terram colunt burgenses, et locant per ministros regis et comitis. Infra prædictum censum sunt iii piscatores iii sol. reddentes.

In hoc burgo fuerunt iii monetarii reddentes xl sol. inter regem et comitem; sed modo non sunt. T. R. E. reddebant xxx lib., modo similiter.

BEDEFORD (Bedford.)

Bedeford T. R. E. pro dimidio hund, se defendebat, et modo facit, in expeditione et in navibus. Terra de hac villa nunquam fuit hidata, nec modo est, præter unam hidam, quæ jacuit in ecclesia S. Pauli in elemosina, etc.

LEDECESTRE (Leicester.)

Civitas de Ledecestre tempore regis Edwardi reddebat per annum regi xxx lib. ad numerum de xx in Ora et xv sextaria mellis.

Quando rex ibat in exercitu per terram, de ipso burgo xii burgenses [Editor: illegible word] cum eo. Si vero per mare in hostem ibat, mittebant ei iv equos de eodem burgo usque Londoniam, ad comportandum arma, vel alia quæ opus esset.

Modo habet rex W. pro omnibus redditibus civitatis ejusdem et comitatus xlii lib. et x sol. ad pondus; pro uno accipitre x lib. ad numerum: pro summario xx sol. De monetariis xx lib. per annum de xx in Ora. De his xx lib. habet Hugo de Grentemaisnil tertium denarium.

WARWIC (Warwick.)

In burgo de Warwic, habet rex in dominio suo cxiii domus, et barones regis habent cxii de quibus omnibus rex habet geldum suum, etc. Episcopus de Wirecestre habet lx masuras, et sic de cæteris; præter has supradictas masuras sunt in ipso burgo xix burgenses qui habent xix masuras cum saca et soca et omnibus consuetudinibus et ita habebant T. R. E.

SCIROPESBERIE (Shrewsbury.)

Hæc civitas T. R. E. geldabat pro c hidis. De his habebat S. Almundus ii hid. et sic de ceteris.

Dicunt Angligenæ burgenses de Sciropesberie multùm grave sibi esse, quod ipsi reddunt totum geldum, sicuti reddebant T. R. E. quamvis castellum comitis occupaverit li masuras et aliæ l masuræ sint vastatæ, et xliii Francigenæ burgenses teneant masuras geldantes T. R. E. et abbatiæ quam facit ibi comes dederit ipse xxxix burgenses, olim similiter cum aliis geldantes.

Intra totum sunt cc masuræ, vii minus, quæ non geldant.

EBORACUM (York.)

In Eboraco civitate tempore regis Edwardi præter scyram archiepiscopi fuerunt vi scyræ; una ex his est vastata in castellis.

In quinque scyris fuerunt mille et quadringentæ et xviii mansiones hospitatæ. De una harum scyrarum habet archiepiscopus adhuc tertiam partem. In his nemo alius habebat consuetudinem nisi ut burgensis, præter Merlesvainan una domo quæ est infra castellum, et præter canonicos ubi[Editor: illegible letter]unque mansissent, et præter iv judices, quibus rex dabat hoc donum per [Editor: illegible letter]num brevem, et quamdiu vivebant.

Archiepiscopus autem de sua scyra habebat plenam consuetudinem.

De supra dictis omnibus mansionibus sunt modo hospitatæ in manu regis reddentes consuetudinem quadringentæ, ix minus, inter magnas et parvas; et cccc mansiones non hospitatæ, quæ reddunt melior i denarium. et aliæ minus; et quingentæ et xl mansiones ita vacuæ, quod nil omnino reddunt, et cxlv mansiones tenent Francigenæ.

LINCOLIA (Lincoln.)

In civitate Lincolia erant, tempore regis Edwardi, novies centum et lxx mansiones hospitatæ. Hic numerus Anglice computatur i centum pro cxx.

In ipsa civitate erant xii Lagemanni, id est habentes sacam et socam, Hardecnut, Suartin, F. Grimboldi, Ulf filius Suertebrand, qui habuit Thol et Them, Walraven, Alwold, Brictric, Guret, Ulbert, Godric, F. Eddeve, Siward (presbyter), Leuwine (presbyter), Aldeve (presbyter).

Modo sunt ibi totidem habentes similiter sacam et socam. Suardinc (i) loco Hardecnut patris sui, Suartinc (ii), Sortebrand (iii) loco Ulf patris sui, Agemund (iv) loco Walraven patris sui, Aluwold (v), Goduinus (vi) filius Brictric, Normanus (vii), Crassus loco Guret, Ulbert (viii), frater Ulf adhuc vivit, Pethrus (ix) de Valonges loco Godric filii Eddeve, Ulnoldus (x) presbyter loco Siward, presb. Buruolt (xi) loco patris sui Leuwine, qui modo est monachus, Ledewinus (xii) filius Ravene loco Aldene presbyteri.

Tochi filius Outi habuit in civitate xxx mansiones præter suam hallam, et ii ecclesias et dimidiam; et suam hallam habuit quietam ab omni consuetudine et super alias xxx mansiones habuit locationem, et præter hoc de unaquaque unum denarium, id est Langdable. Super has xxx mansiones habebat rex theloneum et forisfacturam, ut burgenses juraverunt. Sed his jurantibus contradicit Ulviet presbyter, et offert se portaturum judicium quod non ita est sicuti dicunt, etc.

Radulfus Pagenel habet i mansionem, etc., et sic de ceteris.

Aluredus nepos Turoldi habet iii. Toftes de terra sybi, quantum rex sibi dedit, in quibus habet omnes consuetudines, præter geldum de Monedagio.

Consuetudines regis et comitis in Sudlincolia reddunt xxiii lib.

In Nortreding consuetudines regis et comitis reddunt xxiv lib.

In Westreding consuetudines regis et comitis reddunt xii lib.

In Sudtreding consuetudines regis et comitis reddunt xv lib.

Pax manu regis vel sigillo ejus data, si fuerit infracta, emendatur per xviii hundret. Unum quoque hund. solvit viii lib. duodecim. hund. emendant regi et vi comiti.

NORWIC (Norwich.)

Hoc de Norwic. In Norwic erant tempore regis Edwardi mcccxx burgenses. Quorum unas ita dominicus regis, ut non posset recedere nec homagium facere sine licentia ipsius cui erat nomen Edstan, etc.

Tota hæc villa reddebat T. R. E. xx lib. regi et comiti x lib. et præter hoc xxi sol. et iv denar. præbendarios, et vi sextarios mellis, et i ursum et [Editor: illegible word] canes ad ursum; et modo lxx lib. pensum regis et c sol. ad numerum de gersuma reginæ, et i asturconem et xx lib. blancas comiti et xx sol. gersuma ad numerum G., etc.

Franci de Norwic in novo burgo xxxvi burgenses et vi Anglici et ex annua consuetudine reddebat unusquisque v denar. præter forisfacturas. De hoc toto habebat rex rex ii partes et comes tertiam. Modo xli burgenses franci in dominio regis et comitis et Rogerius Bigot habet l et sic de aliis.

Tota hæc terra burgensium erat in dominio comitis Rad. et concessit eam regi in commune ad faciendum burgum inter se et regem, ut testatur vicecomes. Et omnes terræ istæ, tam militum quam burgensium, reddunt regi suam consuetudinem.

CESTRE (Chester.)

Civitas de Cestre, tempore regis Edwardi, geldabat pro l hidis. Tres et dimidium, quæ sunt extra civitatem (hoc est, una hida et dimidium ultra pontem, et duæ hidæ in Neutone, et Redolive et in burgo episcopi); hæ geldabant cum civitate.

Tempore regis Edwardi erant in ipsa civitate cccc et xxxi domus geldantes; et præter has habebat episcopus lvi domus geldantes. Tunc reddebat hæc civitas x marcas argenti et dimidiam: duæ partes erant regis et tertia comitis...

Tempore regis Edwardi erant in civitate hac septem monetarii, qui dabant septem libras regi et comiti extra firmam, quando moneta vertebatur.

Tunc erant xii judices civitatis; et hi erant de hominibus regis et episcopi et comitis; horum si quis de hundret remanebat die quo sedebant, sine excusatione manifesta, x solidis emendabat inter regem et comitem.

Ad murum civitatis et pontem reædificandum de unaquaque hida comitatus unum hominem venire præpositus edicebat; cujus homo non veniebat, dominus ejus xl solidos emendabat regi et comiti; hæc forisfactura extra-firmam erat.

Hæc civitas tunc reddebat de firma xlv libras, et tres timbres pellium martrinium; tertia pars erat comitis et duæ regis.

Quando Hugo comes recepit, non valebat nisi xxx libras. Valde enim erat vastata: ducentæ et quinque domus minus ibi erant quam tempore regis Edwardi fuerunt: modo totidem sunt ibi quot invenit.

Hanc civitatem Mundret tenuit de comite pro lxx libris et una marka auri.

Ipse habuit ad firmam, pro l libris et una marka auri, omnia placita comitis in comitatu et hundretis præter Inglefeld.

Terra in qua est templum sancti Petri, quam Robertus de Rodelend clamabat ad Teiland (sicut diratiocinavit comitatus), nunquam pertinuit ad manerium extra civitatem, sed ad burgum pertinet, et semper fuit in consuetudine regis et comitis, sicut aliorum burgensium.

No. XVI. Narrative of the Exploits and Death of Hereward.

* Un an après l'évesque Elwine

* Et Siward Bern en la marine

* Meurent d'Escoce od noef esnecces,

* Tresq'en Humbre siglent ès brecces.

* Li quiens Morgar encontre vint,

* Ès niefs entra, od eus se tint;

* A Welle encontrèrent les Englois,

* Fuiz sont à Willam li rois.

* Tant ont parlé de compaignie,

* Chescuns vont faire à autre aie.

* Un gentil home lur sire estoit.

* Des utlaghes mult i avoit.

* Par la terre sont alez

* Et vont degastant le régné.

* Li rois Willam, quant il ceo sout,

* Mult fu irez, si l'en pesout;

* S'ost somonst, manda guerroiers,

* François, Anglois et chevaliers;

* Devers la mier mist marinaus,

* Bucecarles, valez as peaus

* E autres genz, dont tant i out.

* Nul des assis aler n'i pout;

* E derichef par les boscages

* Furent gardez tuz les passages,

* E li marchis tut environ

* Fut bien gardé par contençon.

* Après ceo comanda li rois

* Faire ponz outre les marois

* Et dist que tuz les destruieroit;

* Jà nuls n'en eschaperoit.

* Quant il ceo seurent en Ely,

* Si se sont mis en sa merci;

* Tuz alèrent merci crier

* Fors Ereward, qui mult fu bier.

* Il eschapa od poi de gent,

* Geri od lui, un son parent

* Od eus eurent v compaignons.

* Uns homs qui amenoit peissons

* As gardeins long le mareis,

* Fist qe prodom et qe surpreis

* En un batel les recuillit,

* De ros, de glais tuz les coverit,

* Vers les gardeins prist à nager.

* Si come un soir deit anuiter,

* Vint près des loges od sa nief.

* François estoient en un tref,

* Wid le viesconte en ert seignour,

* Bien conuissoit le pescheour,

* Et bien seurent q'il venoit,

* De lui nule garde n'avoit;

* Le pescheour virent nager,

* Nuit ert et sistrent au manger.

* Fors de la nief ist Ereward,

* De hardement sembloit leopard,

* Si compaignon apres issirent,

* Desouz un bois le tref choisirent.

* A eus ala le pescheour,

* Ereward ert seins son seignour.

* Q'en dirroie? Li chevaler

* Furent suspris à lur manger.

* Cil entrent, haches en lur mains;

* De bien ferir ne sont vilains,

* Normanz occistrent et desconfirent,

* Cil qui poeient s'enfuirent.

* Grant fut l'effrei par les osteaus,

* De la fuite sont communaus,

* Chevaus lessent enseelez.

* Les outlaghes i sont montez

* Tut à leisir et seinement,

* Onques n'eurent desturbement;

* A eise erent de fere mal.

* Chescuns choisit très bon cheval.

* Li bois sont près, enz sont entré,

* Il n'alèrent pas esgarré,

* Bien seurent tut cel païs,

* Mult i avoit de lur amis.

* A une ville où sont turnez

* Trovèrent x de lur privez.

* Od Ereward cil se sont pris,

* Einz furent vi ore sont plus de dis.

* Dis e huit sont li compaignon;

* Einz qu'il passèrent Huntedon,

* Eurent cent homes bien armez,

* De Ereward liges privez.

* Si home erent et si fideil.

* Einz qu'au demain levast soleil,

* vii cenz sont à lui venuz,

* En Bruneswald l'ont aconseuz

* Ore fut grant la compaignie

* Une cité ont assaillie,

* Burgh assaillirent cil forfet:

* Bien tost en fut le meur tut fret

* Entrent dedenz, assez ont pris

* Or et argent et veir et gris.

* Autre hernois i ont assez,

* La chose as moignes ont tensez.

* D'ilœc s'en vont à Estamford,

* De ceo que pernent ne font tort;

* Car li burgois eurent bracé

* Que Ereward en fut déchacé,

* Meslé l'eurent envers le roi

* A mult grant tort et à deslei.

* S'il se vengoit, ne fut nul tort,

* De ceux de Burgh et de Stanford.

* Qu'en dirroie? Par plusurs anz

* Tint Ereward contre Normanz,

* Il et Winter son compaignon

* E dan Geri un gentil hom,

* Alveriz, Grugan, Saiswold, Azecier.

* Icil et li altre guerreier

* Guerreièrent issi Franceis;

* Si un d'els encontrout treis

* Ne s'en alasent sanz asalt.

* Ço pert uncore en Bruneswald,

* Là ù Gier se combati,

* Ki mult fu fort e fier e hardi.

* Lui setme asailli Hereward,

* Sul par son cors, n'i out reguard,

* Les quatre oscist, les treis fuirent:

* Naffrez, sanglant, cil s'en partirent

* En plusurs lius ceo avint.

* En contre vii très bien se tint,

* De vii homes avoit vertu,

* Onques plus liardi ne fut veu.

* Par plusurs anz tant guerroia

* Si qe une dame le manda,

* Que de li out oi parler;

* Par meinte foiz l'ad fet mander

* Q'à lui vensist, si li plesoit;

* L'onor son pière li dorroit;

* Et, s'il la pernoit à muiller,

* Bien porroit François guerreier.

* Ceo fut Alfued qe ço manda

* A Ereward, qe mult ama;

* Par plusurs foiz tant le manda

* Qe Ereward s'apresta.

* Vers lui ala ad mult de gent,

* Triwes avoit tut veirement,

* Au roi se devoit acorder;

* Dedenz cel mois passer la mer

* Devoit pur guerroier Mansaus,

* Qui ont au roi tolet chasteaus.

* Il i avoit ainceis esté,

* Walter del Bois avoit maté,

* Et dan Geffrei cil de Meine

* Tint en prison une simeine.

* Ereward, qui doit aler en pees,

* D'or et d'argent avoit meint fès.

* Quant li Normant ceo entendirent.

* Fruissent la pès, si l'assaillirent,

* A son manger l'ont assailli.

* Si Ereward en fust garni,

* Le plus hardi semblast couard.

* Malement le gaita Aaelward,

* Son chapelein: le deust gaiter,

* Si s'endormit sus un rocher.

* Qu'en dirroie? Suspris i fu;

* Mès gentement s'est contenu,

* Si se contint come leon,

* Il et Winter son compaignon.

* Quant nul haubert n'i pout aveir

* Ne ses armes pur soi armer,

* Ne sur destrer ne pout saillir,

* Un escu prist q'il vist gisir

* Et une lance et une espée.

* L'espée ceinst, si l'ad nuée,

* Devant trestuz ses compaignuns

* S'est acemez come uns leons,

* Mult fièrement dist as François:

* "Triwes m'avoit doné li rois;

* Mès vus venez ireement,

* Le mien pernez, tuez ma gent,

* Suspris m'avez à mon manger;

* Fel traitres, vendrai moi cher."

* iii gavelocs un sergant tint,

* Sis homs estoit, devant li vint,

* L'un en bailla à son seignour.

* Un chevalier aloit entour,

* Par tout le champ aloit quérant

* E Ereward mult demandant.

* De ses homes aveit oscis

* E morz getez dès-ci k'à dis.

* Si come il l'alout demandant,

* Li bier li est venu devant,

* Le gaveloc i fet aler,

* Parmi l'escu le fet voler.

* L'auberc rumpit, pas ne se tint,

* Le queor trencha, issi avint;

* E cil chait, ne pout el estre,

* A son morir n'ont point de prestre.

* Donc l'assaillirent li Normant,

* Traient à lui et vont lançant,

* De totes parz l'avironèrent,

* En plusurs lius son cors nafrèrent;

* Et il fiert eus come sengler

* Tant com la lance pout durer;

* Et quant la lance li faillit,

* Del brant d'ascer grant coup férit.

* Tiel le quida mult vil trover,

* De son cors l'estuet achater;

* Et quant le trœvent si amer,

* Asquanz n'i osent arester;

* Car il férit vigerousemens,

* Si's requist menu e sovent,

* Od s'espée iiii en occist,

* Dès qu'il fiert le bois retentist;

* Mès donc brusa le brant d'ascer

* Desus l'elme d'un chevalier,

* Et il l'escu en ses mains prist,

* Si en fiert qe ii Franceis occist;

* Mès iiii vindrent à son dos

* Qui l'ont féru par mi le cors,

* Od iiii lances l'ont féru;

* N'est merveille s'il est cheu,

* A genuillons s'agenuilla,

* Par tiel air l'escu getta

* Que uns de ceus qi l'ont féru

* Fiert en volant si del escu

* Qu'en ii moitiez li freint le col.

* Cil out à non Raol de Dol,

* De Tuttesbire estoit venuz.

* Ore sont amdui mort abatuz

* E Ereward e li Breton,

* Raol de Dol avoit à non;

* Mès Alselin le paroccist.

* Cil de Ereward le chef prist.

* Si jura Dieu et sa vertu,

* Et li autre qui l'ont veu

* Par meinte foiz l'ont fort juré,

* Que oncques si hardi ne fut trové,

* Et s'il eust eu od lui trois,

* Mar i entrassent li François;

* E s'il ne fust issi occis,

* Touz les chaçast fors del païs.

End of Volume 1

"THE CHARTER OF KING STEPHEN CONCERNING THE LIBERTIES OF THE CHURCH AND KINGDOM OF ENGLAND.

"I, Stephen, by the grace of God, and by consent of the clergy and people, king of England, and consecrated by William, archbishop of Canterbury, and legate of the holy Roman church; and afterwards confirmed by Innocent, pontiff of the holy Roman see;—do hereby grant, in respect and love of God, that the holy church shall be free; and I confirm all reverence due to it. I promise to act nothing in the church, nor in ecclesiastical affairs, simoniacally, nor will I permit it to be done. I defend and confirm that the power, justice, and dignities, of ecclesiastical persons and all clerks, and the distribution of their goods, shall be in the hands of the bishops. I grant and establish, that the dignities of churches confirmed by their privileges and the customs held by ancient tenure, shall remain inviolable. All the possessions and tenures of churches, which they held on that day when king William my grandfather was alive and dead, I grant to be free and absolute to them, without any false reclamation: but if the church shall hereafter claim any of those things which were possessed or enjoyed before the death of the king, and which it now may want, I reserve that to my indulgence and dispensation, to be either discussed or restored. But whatsoever hath been bestowed upon it since the king's death, either by the liberality of the king, or the gift of great persons, or the oblation, purchase, or any exchange, of faithful men, I confirm, and shall be conferred upon them. I promise to preserve peace and justice in all things to the utmost of my power. The forests which William, my grandfather, and William, my uncle, have made and held, I reserve to myself: but all the rest, which king Henry had superadded, I restore, and grant, quit, and discharged to the churches and the kingdom. If any bishop, or abbot, or other ecclesiastical person, shall reasonably distribute his goods before his death, or appoint them to be so distributed, I grant that it shall remain firm: but if he be prevented by death, distribution of them shall be made by consent of his church for the good of his soul. Whilst episcopal sees shall remain vacant of pastors, both they and all their possessions shall be committed to the power and keeping of clerks, or other honest men of the same church, until a pastor shall be canonically substituted. All exactions, injustice, and miskennings, wickedly introduced either by sheriffs, or by any others, I totally abolish. The good and ancient laws and just customs in murders, pleas, and other causes, I will observe, and do hereby establish and command to be observed. But all this I grant, saving my royalty and just dignity. Witnesses: William, archbishop of Canterbury, Hugh, bishop of Rouen, Henry (de Blois), bishop of Winchester, Roger, bishop of Salisbury, Alexander, bishop of Lincoln, Nigel, bishop of Ely, Everard, bishop of Norwich, Simon, bishop of Worcester, Bernard, bishop of St. David's, Audoen, bishop of Evreux, Richard, bishop of Avranches, Robert (de Bethun), bishop of Hereford, Æthelwulf, bishop of Carlisle, and Roger, the chancellor, and Henry, the king's nephew, and Robert (consul), earl of Gloucester, William, earl of Warren, Ranulph, (Randle de Gernons,) earl of Chester, Robert, (Roger de Newburgh,) earl of Warwick, Robert de Vere, and Milo de Gloucester, Bryan Fitz-Earl, Robert D'Oyly, the constable, William Martell, Hugh Bigod, Humphrey de Bohun, Simon de Beauchamp the Sewer, William de Albini, Eudonius Martell the Butler, Robert de Ferrers, William Penr', of Nottingham, Simon de Sainthz, William de Albain, Payne Fitz-John, Hamon de St. Clare, and Ilbert de Lacy. At Oxford, in the year from the Incarnation of our Lord. 1136, namely the first of my reign."

The other Charter of Liberties granted by this sovereign, was a short general one for the whole realm; it was also written in Latin, without date, and is preserved in an ancient entry in the

Cottonian manuscript, Claudius D. II., Art. 25, fol. 75, or 68 b, whence the following translation has been made: "Stephen, by the grace of God, king of England, to the justiciaries, sheriffs, barons, and all his officers and faithful subjects, French and English, greeting. Know ye that I have granted, and by this present charter have confirmed to all my barons and people of England, all the liberties and good laws and customs, which Henry, my uncle, gave and granted to them, which were had in the time of king Edward. Wherefore I will, and strictly command, that they have and hold all those good laws and liberties of me and of my heirs, for them and for their heirs, freely, fully, and securely, and prohibit any one to cause any molestation or impediment upon them,—upon my forfeiture. Witnessed by William Martel, at London."—Thomson, Essay on Magna Charta,.

"Dover, in the time of king Edward, rendered xviii pounds, of which sum Edward had ii portions and earl Godwin a third. Besides this, the canons of St. Martins had another portion. The burgesses provided xx ships for the monarch, once each year, for xv days, and in each ship were xxi men. They rendered this service because the king had liberated them from Sac and Soc. When the messengers of the monarch came to this port, they paid iii pence in winter and ii pence in summer for the transportation of a horse; but the burgesses found a pilot and one assistant; if more were required, they were furnished at the king's expense.

"From the festival of St. Michael to St. Andrew, the royal peace was maintained in the town. Whoever violated it, paid to the king's officer the customary forfeit.

"Every inhabitant of this town that paid the royal customs, was quit of toll throughout the realm of England. All these customs existed when king William came to this country. At his first arrival, this vill was destroyed by fire, and therefore its value could not be estimated when the bishop of Bayeux received it. At the present period, it is valued at xl pounds, yet the mayor pays liv pounds, xxiv to the king in money, of xx pence in the ore, and xxx to the earl, in tale.

"In Dover there are xxix houses, of which the king has lost the customary payments. Of these, Robert de Romenil (Romney) has ii, Radulf de Curbespine (Crookthorne) iii, William Fitz-Tydald i, William Fitz-Oger i, William Fitz-Tedold and Robert le Noir vi, William Fitz-Geoffroi iii, one of which was the Guild-hall of the burgesses; Hugh de Montfort i, Durand i, Ranulf de Columbel (Colville) i, Wadard vi, Fitz-Modbert i. And all these depend on the bishop of Bayeux as their protector and donor.

"Of the house which Ralph Colville occupies, heretofore the property of an exile or outlaw, it is agreed that one half of it belongs to the king, and the other to Ranulf. Hunfrid has i house, one half of it belongs to the king. Roger of Easterham erected a certain house upon the king's water, and has hitherto observed the king's customs. There was no house there in the time of king Edward.

CANTUARIA (Canterbury).

"In the city of Canterbury king Edward had li burgesses paying rent, ccxii others rendering suit and service to his court, and iii mills of xl shillings. At the present time there are xix burgesses paying rent. Of the xxxii other houses, xi were destroyed to make way for the city ditch. The archbishop has vii, and the abbot of St. Augustin's xiv, in exchange for the castle; there are still ccxii burgesses rendering Sac and Soc to the king; the iii mills produce cviii shillings, and the toll yields lxviii shillings. There are viii acres of meadow which formerly belonged to the lieutenants of the king; they now yield a rent of xv shillings; and there are m acres of unproductive wood, rented at xxiv shillings. The total value under king Edward was li pounds, and it was the same when viscount Hamo received it; now it is valued at l pounds: yet the mayor now pays xxx pounds of pure silver coin, and xxiv pounds in tale. Besides all this, the viscount receives cx shillings.

"The burgesses had xlv houses beyond the precincts of the city, from which they received rent and customary payments; but the king had Sac and Soc therefore. The burgesses also had xxxiii acres of land from the king for their guild. These houses and this land Ralph Colville holds; besides these, he has lxxx acres of allotted land, which the ourgesses held from the monarch. He has v other acres, which rightly belong to a church. For all these, Ranulf appeals to the bishop of Bayeux for protection," &c. &c.

BOOK VIII. FROM THE BATTLE OF THE STANDARD TO THE INSURRECTION OF THE POITEVINS AND BRETONS AGAINST HENRY II.

A.D. 1137—1189.

Vassalage of the kings of Scotland—Political state of Scotland—Populations of Scotland—Social equality and language of the Scots—Highland and island clans—Hostility of the Scots to the Anglo-Normans—Entry of the Scots into England—Assembling of the Anglo-Norman army—Battle of the Standard—Invasion of the Welsh—Conquests of the Normans in Wales—Bernard de Neuf Marché—Richard d'Eu, called Strongbow—Norman monks and priests in Wales—Norman bishops driven out by the Welsh—Manners and character of the Welsh—Civil war among the Anglo-Normans—Vexations and ravages committed by the Normans—King Stephen besieges Bristol—Attack on the Isle of Ely—Stephen made prisoner—Matilda elected queen of England—Her arrogance—Matilda driven from London by the citizens—Revival of the party of Stephen—Landing of Henry, son of Matilda—Termination of the civil war—Eleanor, duchess of Aquitaine—Marriage of Eleanor with the son of Matilda—State of southern Gaul—Its population—Its social state—Henry II. of England—Expulsion of the Flemings—Mixture of races—Saxon genealogy of Henry II.—War of Henry II. against his brother—War against the Bretons—Submission of Brittany—National insurrection of the Bretons—Their defeat—Insurrection of the Poitevins—Peace between the kings of France and England—Termination of Breton independence—Message of a Welsh chieftain to the king of France—War against the Toulousans—Character of the southern Gauls.

The friendship which, at the period of William's conquest, had been suddenly formed between the Anglo-Saxon people and that of Scotland, although cooled since by several circumstances, had never been entirely broken. On the day, indeed, when Malcolm Kenmore, king Edgar's brother-in-law, was constrained to confess himself the vassal of the Conqueror, a kind of moral barrier was raised between the Scottish kings and the English by race; but Malcolm himself and his successors ill endured this condition of vassalage that force had imposed on them. More than once, seeking to throw it off, they became aggressors of the Anglo-Normans by way of reprisal, and marched south of the Tweed; more than once, also, the Normans passed that river, and the oath of feudal subjection was, by turns, broken and renewed, according to the chances of war. Besides, the kings of Scotland never reckoned among the duties they had contracted in accepting the title of liegemen, the obligation to close their country against the Anglo-Saxon emigrants.

The multitude of men of all ranks and conditions who, after a futile struggle against the invaders, expatriated themselves to Scotland, considerably augmented there the previous mass of Germanic population established between the Tweed and the Forth. The kings who succeeded Malcolm were not less generous than he to these refugees; they gave them lands and offices, and admitted them into their state-council, where gradually the true Scottish language, the Gaelic or Erse, was supplanted by the Anglo-Danish dialect, spoken in the lowlands of Scotland. By the same revolution, the Scottish kings discarded the patronymic surnames which recalled to mind their Celtic origin, and only retained simple proper names, Saxon or foreign, as Edgar, Alexander, David, &c.

The hospitality which the chiefs of Scotland accorded to the men of Saxon race flying from the Normans, was, as we have already seen, offered by them also to men of Norman race, discontented with the share which had fallen to them in the division of the conquest, or banished from England by the sentence of their own chiefs. These sons of the conquerors came, in great numbers, to seek fortune where the conquered had found refuge. Most of them were tried soldiers; the Scottish kings took them into their service, delighted to have Norman knights to oppose to the Normans beyond the Tweed. They received them into their intimacy, confided high commands to them, and even, to render their court more agreeable to these new guests, studied to introduce into the Teutonic language spoken there, many French words and idioms. Fashion and custom gradually naturalized these exotic terms throughout the country south of the Forth, and in a short time the national language became there a singular medley of Teutonic and French, in about equal proportions.

This language, which is still the popular dialect of the inhabitants of southern Scotland, retained but very few Celtic words, Erse or Breton, most of them expressing features peculiar to the country, such as the various accidents of an extremely various soil. But, notwithstanding the little figure made by the remains of the ancient idiom of the Scottish plains in the new language, it was easy to see, in the spirit and manners of the population of these districts, that it was a Celtic race, in which other races had mingled without entirely renewing it. Vivacity of imagination, the taste for music and poetry, the custom of strengthening the social bond by ties of relationship, marked out and recognised in the most distant degree, are original features which distinguished then, and still distinguish, the inhabitants of the left bank of the Tweed from their southern neighbours.

Further westward in the plains of Scotland, these features of Celtic physiognomy appeared more strongly impressed, because the people there were more removed from the influence of the royal cities of Scone and Edinburgh, whither the multitude of foreign emigrants flocked. In the county of Galloway, for instance, the administrative authority was, up to the twelfth century, only regarded as a fiction of paternal authority; and no man sent by the king to govern this country could exercise his command in peace, unless he was accepted as head of the family, or chief of the clan, by the people whom he was to rule. If the inhabitants did not think fit to assign this title to the king's officer, or if the old hereditary chief of the tribe did not voluntarily yield him this privilege, the tribe would not recognise him, for all his royal commission, and he himself was soon fain to resign or sell this commission to the chief preferred by the people.

In the places where the emigrants from England, Saxons or Normans, obtained territorial domains on condition of fealty and service, they built a church, a mill, a brewery, and some houses, for their people, which the Saxons called the hirède, and the Normans la menie. The collection of all these edifices, surrounded by a palisade or a wall, was called l'enclos or the tun, in the language of the lowlands of Scotland. The inhabitants of this inclosure, masters and servants, proprietors and farmers, composed a sort of little city, united like a Celtic clan, but by other ties than relationship, by those of service and pay, obedience and command. The chief, in his square tower, built in the midst of the more humble dwellings of his vassals or labourers, resembled in general appearance the Norman of England, whose fortress dominated the huts of his serfs. But there was a great difference between the real condition of the one and of the other. In Scotland, the subordination of the poor to the rich was not servitude; true, the name of lord, laird, in the Teutonic language, and of sire in the French, was given to the latter, but as he was neither a conqueror, nor the son of a conqueror, he was not hated, and none trembled before him. A sort of familiarity brought more or less nearly together the inhabitant of the tower and the dweller in the cottage; they knew that their ancestors had not bequeathed to them mortal injuries to revenge upon each other.

When war assembled them in arms, they did not form two separate peoples, the one horse, the other foot; the one clothed in complete steel, the other denied spurs under penalty of ignominious punishment. Every man, armed according to his means, in a coat of mail or a quilted doublet, rode his own horse, well or ill-caparisoned. In Scotland, the condition of labourer on the domain of another man, was not humiliating as in England, where the Norman term villain has become, in the vernacular tongue, the most odious of epithets. A Scotch farmer was commonly called the gude-man; his lord could only demand from him the rents and services mutually settled between them; he was not taxed haut et bas, as in a conquered country; and accordingly no insurrection of peasants was ever seen in Scotland; the poor and rich sympathized, because poverty and riches were not derived from victory and expropriation. The races of men, like the different idioms, were mingled in every rank, and the same language was spoken in the castle, the town, and the hut.

This language, which, from its resemblance to that of the Anglo-Saxons, was called Anglisc or English, had a very different fate in Scotland and in England; in the latter country, it was the idiom of the serfs, the artizans, the shepherds; the poets, who wrote for the upper classes, composed only in pure Norman; but, north of the Tweed, English was the favourite tongue of the minstrels attached to the court; it was polished, refined, elaborate, graceful, and even distinguished, whilst, on the other side of the same river, it was becoming rude and inelegant, like the unfortunate people who spoke it. The few popular poets who, instead of rhyming in French for the sons of the Normans, continued to rhyme in English for the Saxons, felt this difference, and complained of their inability to employ, under penalty of not being understood, the fine language, the bold flights, and the complex versification of the southern Scots. "I have put," says one of them, "into my simple English, out of love for simple folk, what others have written and said more elegantly; for it is not to the proud and noble I address myself, but to those who could not understand a more refined English." In this polished English of the lowlands of Scotland were clothed old British traditions, which remained in the memory of the inhabitants of the banks of the Clyde, long after the British language had perished in those districts. In the lowlands of the south-west, Arthur and the other heroes of the Cambrian nation were more popular than the heroes of the ancient Scots, than Gaul-Mac-Morn, and Fin-Mac-Gaul, or Fingal, father of Oshinn, or Ossian, sung in the Gaelic language in the highlands and islands.

The population which spake this language, almost entirely similar to that of the natives of Ireland, was still, in the twelfth century the most numerous in Scotland, but the least powerful, politically, since its own kings had deserted its alliance for that of the inhabitants of the south-east. It knew this, and remembering that the plains occupied by these new comers had been of old the property of its ancestors, it hated them as usurpers, and denied them the name of Scots, under which foreigners confounded them with it, and gave them instead that of Sassenachs, that is to say Saxons, because whatever their origin, all of them spoke the English language. The children of the Gaels long regarded as mere acts of reprisal the incursions of war and pillage made upon the lowlands of Scotland. "We are the heirs of the plains," said they; "it is just we should resume our own."

This national hostility, the effects of which the inhabitants of the plain greatly dreaded, rendered them ever ready to encourage in the kings of Scotland all sorts of arbitrary and tyrannical measures, tending to destroy the independence of the highlanders. But it would seem as though there were in the manners, as in the language of the Celtic populations, a principle of eternity which mocks the efforts of time and of man. The clans of the Gael perpetuated themselves under their patriarch chieftains, whom the members of the clan, all bearing the same name, obeyed as sons obey their father. Every tribe not having a patriarch and not living as one family, was considered base; few incurred this dishonour, and to avoid it, the poets and historians, adepts in genealogies, were always careful to make each new chief descend from the primitive chief, from the common ancestor of the whole tribe. In token of this descent, which was never to be interrupted, the reigning chief added to his own name a patronymic surname, which all his predecessors had borne before him, and which his successors were to take after him; and, according to Celtic etiquette, this surname served them in lieu of a title. The feudal style of the public acts of Scotland was never current in the highlands or islands, and the same man, who at the court of the kings entitled himself duke or earl of Argyle, on his return to Argyleshire, in the bosom of his tribe, again became Mac-Callam-More, that is, the son of Callam the great.

All the tribes spread over the western coast of Scotland from the Mull of Cantyre to the North Cape, and in the Hebrides, which were also called Innis Gail or the islands of the Gael, lived in separate societies under this patriarchal authority; but above all their peculiar chiefs, there was in the twelfth century a supreme chief, who, in the language of the lowlanders, was called the lord or king of the Isles. This king of the whole Gaelic population of Scotland had his residence at Dunstaffnage, upon a rock on the western coast, the ancient abode of the Scottish kings, prior to their emigration to the east; sometimes, also, he inhabited the fortress of Artornish in Mull, or the island of Ilay, the most fertile if not the largest of the Hebrides. Here was held a high court of justice, the members of which sat in a circle, on seats cut out of the rock. Here also was a stone, seven feet square, upon which the king of the Isles stood on the day of his coronation. Erect on this pedestal, he swore to preserve to every one his rights, and to do justice at all times; then, the sword of his predecessor was put into his hands, and the bishop of Argyle and seven priests crowned him in the presence of all the tribes of the Isles and of the mainland.

The authority of the king of the Hebridean isles extended sometimes over Man, situated more southward, between England and Ireland, and sometimes this island had a king of its own, issue of Irish race, or of the old Scandinavian chiefs who had rested here after their sea excursions. The kings of the western isles acknowledged as their suzerains, sometimes the kings of Scotland and sometimes those of Norway, as self-interest or compulsion dictated. The natural aversion of the Gael to the lowland Scots aided to maintain the independence of this purely Gaelic kingdom, which still existed in all its plenitude at the time which this history has now attained, and the king of the Isles treated, on terms of equality, with him of Scotland, his rival in ordinary times, but his natural ally against a common enemy, for example, against the kings of England; for the instinct of national hatred, which had so often impelled the ancient Scots towards southern Britain, had not yet disappeared from among the Scottish highlanders.

In the lowlands of Scotland, a war against the Anglo-Normans could not fail to be extremely popular; for while the Saxons by origin, who inhabited that country, burned with a desire to revenge their own misfortunes and those of their ancestors, by a singular concurrence of circumstances, the Norman refugees in Scotland themselves yearned to cross swords with their countrymen who had banished them from England. The desire to regain the domains they had formerly usurped, not less ardent in them than in the hearts of the Anglo-Saxons was the wish to recover their country and their hereditary property, occasioned, in the council of the kings of Scotland, where the new citizens sat in great numbers, an almost universal vote for war with the conquerors of England. Gael, Saxons, Normans, Highlanders, Lowlanders, though from different motives, all agreed on this point; and it was probably this unanimity, well known by the native English, which encouraged the latter to count on the support of Scotland, in the great conspiracy framed and discovered in the year 1137.

For some time past, emissaries from the English people had come in crowds to the court of the Scottish kings, nephews of the last Anglo-Saxon king, conjuring them, by the memory of their uncle Edgar, to march to the assistance of the oppressed nation to which they were related. But the sons of Malcolm Kenmore were kings, and, as such, little disposed to commit themselves in a national revolt, without powerful motives of personal interest. They remained deaf to the complaints of the English and the suggestions of their own courtiers during the life of Henry I., with whom they had some ties of relationship through his wife, Matilda, daughter of Malcolm. When Henry made the Norman barons swear to give the kingdom, after his death, to his daughter by Matilda, David, then king of Scotland, was present and took the oath as vassal of Henry I.; but when the lords of England, violating their word, instead of Matilda, chose Stephen of Blois, the king of Scotland began to think the cause of the Saxons the best. He promised to assist them in their project of exterminating all the Normans, and perhaps, in return for this vague promise, he stipulated, as was rumoured at the time, that he should be made king of England, did the enterprise succeed.

The enfranchisement of the English did not take place, as we have seen above, owing to the vigilance of a bishop. The king of Scotland, however, who had only joined that people because he had, on his side, warlike projects against the Normans, assembled an army and marched towards the south. It was not in the name of the oppressed Saxon race that he entered England, but in the name of Matilda, his cousin, dispossessed, he said, by Stephen of Blois, usurper of the kingdom.

The English people cared little more for the wife of Geoffroy of Anjou than for Stephen of Blois, and yet the populations nearest the frontiers of Scotland, the men of Cumberland, Westmoreland, and all the valleys whose rivers run to swell the waters of the Tweed, impelled by the simple instinct which leads us to seize with avidity every means of escape, received the Scots as friends and joined them. These valleys, of difficult access and scarce subjected by the Normans, were in great measure peopled with Saxons whose fathers had been banished at the time of the Conquest. They came to the camp of the Scots in great numbers and without any order, upon little mountain horses, their only property.

In general, with the exception of the cavalry of Norman or French origin, whom the king of Scotland brought with him, and who were clad in complete and uniform mail, the great body of the troops presented a most disorderly variety of arms and attire. The inhabitants of the eastern lowlands, men of Danish or Saxon descent, formed the heavy infantry, armed with cuirasses and strong pikes; the inhabitants of the west, and especially those of Galloway, who still retained a marked impress of their British descent, were, like the ancient Britons, without defensive arms, and carried long javelins, the points of which were sharp, and the wood slender and fragile; lastly, the genuine Scots, highlanders and islanders, wore caps ornamented with the feathers of wild fowl, and large mantles of striped wool, fastened round the waist with a leathern belt, whence hung a long broad-sword; they carried a round shield of light wood, covered with a thick leather, on the left arm; and some of the island tribes used two-handed axes, like the Scandinavians; the equipment of the chiefs was the same as that of the men of the clan; they were distinguished only by their longer feathers, lighter, and floating more gracefully.

The numerous, and for the most part irregular, troops of the king of Scotland, occupied without resistance all the country between the Tweed and the northern limits of the province of York. The Norman kings had not as yet erected in this district the imposing fortresses which they afterwards raised there, and thus no obstacle stayed the progress of the Scottish ants, as an old author calls them. It appears that this army committed many cruelties in the places through which it passed; the historians talk of women and priests massacred, of children thrown into the air and caught on the points of lances; but, as they talk with little precision, it is not known whether these excesses fell only upon men of Norman descent, and were the reprisals of the English by race, or whether the native aversion of the Gaelic population for the inhabitants of England was exercised indifferently on the serf and on the master, on the Saxon and on the Norman. The northern lords, and especially the archbishop of York, Toustain, profited by the report of these atrocities, spread vaguely, and, perhaps, in an exaggerated form, to counteract, in the minds of the Saxon inhabitants of the banks of the Humber, the interest they would naturally feel in the cause of the enemies of the Norman king.

To induce their subjects to march with them against the king of Scotland, the Norman barons skilfully flattered old local superstitions; they invoked the names of the saints of English race, whom they themselves had once treated with such contempt; they adopted them, as it were, as generalissimos of their army, and archbishop Toustain raised the banners of St. Cuthbert of Durham, of St. John of Beverly, and of St. Wilfred of Ripon.

These popular standards, which, since the Conquest, had scarce seen the day, were taken from the dust of the churches, and conveyed to Cuton Moor, near Elfer-tun, now North Allerton, thirty-two miles north of York, the place where the Norman chiefs resolved to await the enemy. William Piperel and Walter Espec, of Nottinghamshire, and Guilbert de Lacy and his brother Walter, of Yorkshire, assumed the command. The archbishop, who could not attend, on account of illness, sent in his place Raoul, bishop of Durham, probably driven from his diocese by the invasion of the Scots. Around the Saxon banners, raised by lords of foreign race in the camp of Allerton, a half religious, half patriotic instinct drew together a number of the English inhabitants of the surrounding towns and plains. These no longer bore the great battle-axe, the favourite weapon of their ancestors, but were armed with large bows and arrows a cloth yard long. The Conquest had worked this change in two different ways: first, those of the natives, who had stooped to serve the Norman king in battle, for food and pay, had necessarily applied themselves to Norman tactics; and next, those who, more independent, had adopted the life of partisans on the roads and of free-hunters in the forests, had also found it desirable to lay aside the weapons adapted for close combat, for others better fitted to reach, from a distance, the knights of Normandy and the king's stags. The sons of both these classes having been from their infancy exercised in drawing the bow, England had become, in less than a century, the land of good archers, as Scotland was the land of good lances.

While the Scottish army was passing the Tees, the Norman barons actively prepared to meet its attack. They raised upon four wheels, a mast, having at its summit a small silver box, containing a consecrated host, and around the box floated the banners which were to excite the English to fight well. This standard, of a kind common enough in the middle ages, was in the centre of the army. The Anglo-Norman knights took up their post around it, after having sworn together by faith and oath, to remain united for the defence of the country, in life and death. The Saxon archers flanked the battle array, and formed the vanguard. On the news of the approach of the Scots, who were rapidly advancing, the Norman Raoul, bishop of Durham, ascended an eminence in the midst of the army, and delivered in French the following harangue:

"Noble lords of Norman race, you who make France tremble, and have conquered England; the Scots, after having done you homage, seek to drive you from your lands. But if our fathers in so few numbers subjected a great part of Gaul, shall we not conquer these half-naked people, who oppose to our swords nothing but the skin of their bodies, or a leathern buckler? Their pikes are long, it is true, but the wood is fragile, and the iron of poor temper. These people of Galloway have been heard to say, in their vain boasting, that the sweetest drink to them were the blood of a Norman. Do ye so that not one of them shall return to his family to boast of having killed a Norman."

The Scottish army, having for its standard a simple lance with a guidon, marched in several bodies. The young Henry, son of the king of Scotland, commanded the lowlanders and the English volunteers of Cumberland and Northumberland; the king himself was at the head of all the clans of the highlands and islands; and the knights of Norman origin, armed at all points, formed his guard. One of them, named Robert de Brus, a man of great age, who sided with the king of Scotland, by reason of his fief of Annandale, and had no personal enmity against his countrymen of England, approached the king, as he was about to give the signal of attack, and addressing him in a mournful tone, said: "O king, dost thou reflect against whom thou art about to fight? It is against the Normans and the English, who have ever served thee so well and promptly in council and in the field, and have subjected to thee thy people of Gaelic race. Thou thinkest thyself, then, sure of the submission of these tribes? Thou hopest, then, to hold them to their duty, with the sole aid of thy Scottish men at arms? remember that it was we who first placed them in thy hands, and that hence sprung the hatred which they bear our countrymen." This speech seemed to make a great impression on the king; but William, his nephew, exclaimed, impatiently: "these are the words of a traitor." The old Norman replied to this insult, by abjuring, in the formula of the period, his oath of faith and homage, and then galloped to the enemy's camp.

The highlanders who surrounded the king of Scotland raised their voices, and shouted the ancient name of their country, "Albyn! Albyn!" This was the signal for combat. The men of Cumberland, of Liddesdale, and of Teviotdale, made a firm and rapid charge upon the centre of the Norman army, and, to adopt the expression of an ancient historian, broke it like a spider's web; but ill supported by the other bodies of Scots, they did not reach the standard of the Anglo-Normans. The latter recovered their ranks, and repulsed the assailants with great loss. At a second charge, the long javelins of the south-western Scots broke against the hauberks and shields of the Normans. The highlanders then drew their long swords to fight hand to hand; but the Saxon archers, deploying on the sides, assailed them with a shower of arrows, while the Norman horse charged them in front, in close ranks, and with lances low. "It was a noble sight," says a contemporary, "to see the stinging flies issue humming from the quivers of the southern men, and fall upon the foe thick as hail."

The Gael, brave and hardy men, but ill adapted for regular military evolutions, dispersed the moment they found they could not break the enemy's ranks. The whole Scottish army, compelled to retreat, fell back upon the Tyne. The conquerors did not pursue it beyond this river, and the district which had risen in insurrection upon the approach of the Scots, remained, notwithstanding their defeat, emancipated from Norman domination. For a long period after this battle, Westmoreland, Cumberland, and Northumberland formed part of the kingdom of Scotland; and the new position of these three provinces prevented the Anglo-Saxon spirit and character from degenerating there so much as in the more southern portions of England. The national traditions and popular ballads survived and perpetuated themselves north of the Tyne, and it was thence that English poetry, annihilated in the districts inhabited by the Normans, returned once more at a later period, to the southern provinces.

While these things were passing in the north of England, the Welsh, who had promised to aid the Saxons in their great plan of deliverance, executing this promise, notwithstanding the failure of the enterprise elsewhere, commenced upon the whole line of their frontiers an attack upon the strongholds erected by the Normans. The Cambrians, an impetuous and vehement race of men, rushed to this sudden aggression with a sort of national fanaticism; there was no quarter for any man who spoke the French tongue; the barons, knights, and soldiers, who had usurped estates in Wales, the priests and monks who had intruded upon the churches and churchlands, all these were slaughtered, or driven from the properties they occupied. The Cambrians exhibited much cruelty in these acts of reprisal, but then they themselves had undergone unprecedented sufferings at the hands of the Anglo-Normans. Hugh-le-Loup, and Robert de Maupas, had almost exterminated the native population of Flintshire; Robert de Ruddhlan had seized the Welsh in his district and made serfs of them; Robert de Belesme, earl of Shrewsbury, say the historians of the period, tore the Welsh with claws of iron.

The conquerors of England, not content with possessing the fertile lands of that country, had early begun, with equal avidity, to invade the rocks and marshes of Cambria. The chiefs of the bands established in the western provinces, almost all solicited from king William or his sons, as a sort of supplementary pay, licence to conquer from the Welsh: such is the language of the old acts. Many obtained this permission; others dispensed with it, and, equally with the first, attacked the Welsh, who resisted bravely, and defended their country inch by inch. The Normans, having made themselves masters of the eastern extremities of Wales, erected there, according to their custom, a line of strongholds.

These fortresses had gradually become so numerous and so near to each other, that when, in 1138, the Welsh undertook to break through the chain, nearly the whole of South Wales, the valleys of Glamorganshire and Brecknockshire, and the great promontory of Pembrokeshire, were already severed from ancient Cambria. Various circumstances had contributed to facilitate these conquests. First, in the reign of William Rufus, a civil war among the southern Welsh (an event but too common with them) introduced into Glamorganshire, as hired auxiliaries of one of the contending parties, a band of Norman adventurers, commanded by Robert Fitz-Aymon. This Robert (the same whose daughter refused to accept a husband without two names), after fighting for a Welsh chieftain, and receiving his wages, on his return to his domain in Gloucestershire reflected upon the terrible effect that his steel-clad men and horses had produced upon the Cambrians, and the reflection suggested to him the project of visiting as a conqueror the chieftain he had served as a mercenary. He collected a more numerous band than before, entered the valley of Glamorganshire, and took possession of the districts nearest to the Norman frontier. The invaders divided out the country among themselves, according to their ranks. Robert Fitz-Aymon had for his share three towns, and became earl of the conquered territory. Among his principal companions, history mentions Robert de St. Quentin, Pierre-le-Sourd, Jean-le-Flamand, and Richard de Granville, or Grainville, as the Normans pronounced it. They had each of them whole villages or vast domains, and from poor hirelings became, in the eye of posterity, the stock of a new race of nobles and powerful barons.

At about the same time, Hamlin, son of Dreux de Balaon, built a castle at Abergavenny, and one William, who constructed a fortress at Monmouth, assumed the name of William de Monemue, according to the Norman euphony: this William, for the salvation of his soul, made a donation of a Welsh church to the monks of St. Florent at Saumur; in the same neighbourhood, Robert de Candos or Chandos founded and endowed a priory for a body of monks from Normandy. During the wars which a numerous party of Normans carried on against William Rufus and Henry I., in favour of duke Robert, these kings summoned to their aid all the soldiers of fortune they could collect. These, for the most part, like the soldiers of the Conqueror, required in compensation for their services, the promise of territorial possessions, for which they did homage beforehand to the kings. In payment of these debts, there were first appropriated the lands confiscated from the Normans of the opposite party, and when this resource was exhausted, the adventurers had letters of marque upon the Welsh.

Several captains of free companies who received their wages in this coin, distributed out among themselves, before they had conquered them, the counties around Glamorganshire, and added the name of each portion so self-allotted, to their own name; then upon the expiration of their time of service in England, they took their way westward, to assume possessession, as they phrased it, of their inheritances. Thus, in the reign of William Rufus, Bernard de Neuf-Marché seized upon Brecknockshire, and dying, left it, say the acts, in lawful property to his daughter Sybil. In the time of king Henry, one Richard, a Norman by birth, count of Eu, conquered the Welsh province of Divet or Pembroke, with a small army of Brabançons, Normans, and even of English, whom the miseries of their own subjection had reduced to the condition of adventurer-invaders of other men's lands. Richard d'Eu in this campaign received from his Flemings and his English the Teutonic surname of Strongboghe or Strongbow, and by a singular chance, this soubriquet, unintelligible to the Normans, remained hereditary in the family of the Norman earl.

Strongbow and his companions in arms proceeded by sea to the westernmost point of the land of Divet, and landing there, drove back eastward the Cambrian population of the coast, massacring all who resisted them. The Brabançons were at this period the best infantry in Europe, and the land invaded, generally level in its character, enabled them to make full advantage of their heavy armour. Effecting a rapid conquest, they divided out the towns, houses, and lands, and built castles to secure themselves from the incursions of the vanquished. The Flemings and Normans, who occupied the first rank in the conquering army, were the most favoured in the division of the spoil, and their posterity constituted the new proprietors and new nobles of the land. Several centuries afterwards, these nobles and proprietors were still distinguishable by the French turn of their names, preceded by the particle de, or the word fils or fitz, according to the old orthography. The descendants of the English who took part in the expedition, composed the middle class of small landowners and free farmers; their language became the common tongue of the vanquished district, whence it expelled the Welsh idiom, a circumstance which gave to Pembrokeshire the cognomen of Little England beyond Wales. A remarkable monument of this conquest long subsisted in the country: a road along the crest of the mountains, and which, constructed by the conquerors for the purpose of facilitating their marches and securing more rapid intercommunication, retained for several centuries the name of the Fleming way.

Encouraged by the example of Richard Strongbow, earl of Pembroke, other adventurers landed in Cardigan bay; and one Martin de Tours or des Tours, invaded the land of Keymes or Kemys, in company with Guy de Brionne and Guerin de Mont Cenis, or, as it was called in Norman, Mont Chensey. Martin de Tours assumed the title of lord of Keymes, as sovereign administrator of the country in which his men at arms established themselves. He opened an asylum there for all the French, Flemish, and even English by birth, who chose to come and augment his colony, swear fealty and homage to him against the Welsh, and receive lands on condition of service, with the title of free guests of Keymes. The town which these adventurers founded was called Le Bourg neuf (Newtown), and the spot where the war-chief who had become lord of the country erected his principal dwelling, was long called Château-Martin (Castle Martin), pursuant to the genius of the old French tongue. To sanctify his invasion, Martin built a church and a priory, which he peopled with priests, brought, at a great expense, from the abbey of St. Martin de Tours, and whom he selected, either because the town of Tours was his native place, or because its name was the same with his own. On his death, he was buried in a marble tomb, in the nave of the new church, and the Touravese priests of the lordship of Keymes recommended to the benedictions of every Christian, the memory of their patron, who, said they, had by his pious zeal revived in that land the tottering faith of the Welsh.

The imputation thus thrown out, which the Norman prelates had made so much use of to authorize their intrusion and the dispossession of all the clergy of English race, was renewed against the Cambrians, by those to whom the conquerors of Wales gave churches or abbeys. To colour by some sort of pretext the violent expulsion of the former bishops and priests of this country, they declared them en masse heretics and false Christians. Yet the bishops of Cambria had long since been reconciled with the Romish church, had re-entered, as it was then termed, the Catholic unity, and one of them, the bishop of St. David's, had even received the pallium. They complained bitterly to the pope of the usurpation of their churches by men of foreign race and impious lives. But he paid no heed to them, considering those who had re-established the tax of Peter's pence as excellent judges of what was good for men's souls. After this useless appeal, the Welsh, driven to extremity, vindicated justice for themselves, and in many places expelled, in their turn, by force of arms, the foreign priests who had expelled their priests and disposed of the property of the church as of private patrimony.

These acts of national vengeance were more frequent in the maritime districts, further removed from the centre of Anglo-Norman power. On the coast facing the isle of Anglesea, conquered simultaneously with that island by the soldiers of the earl of Chester, there was an episcopal city called Bangor, where king Henry I. had established a Norman prelate, named Hervé. To fulfil to the king's satisfaction his pastoral functions, amidst a country scarce subjected, Hervé, says an ancient author, drew his double-edged sword, launching forth daily anathemas on the Cambrians, while he made war upon them at the head of a troop of soldiers. The Welsh did not allow themselves to be excommunicated and massacred without resistance; they defeated the bishop's army, killed one of his brothers, and many of his men, and compelled him to make a hasty retreat. Hervé returned to king Henry, who congratulated him on having suffered for the faith, and promised him a recompence. The reigning pope, Pascal, wrote with his own hand to the king, recommending to him this victim of what he called the persecution and ferocity of the barbarians.

Yet at this period, the Welsh nation was, perhaps, of all Europe, that which least merited the epithet of barbarian; despite the evil which the Anglo-Normans inflicted upon them every day, those who visited them unarmed, as simple travellers, were received with cordial hospitality; they were at once admitted into the bosom of the best families, and shared the highest pleasures of the country, music and song.

"They who arrive in the morning," says an author of the twelfth century, "are entertained until evening with the conversation of the young women, and the sounds of the harp." There was a harp in every house, however poor it might be, and the company, seated in a circle round the musician, sang, alternately, stanzas, sometimes extemporised; challenges passed for improvisation and song, from man to man, and sometimes from village to village.

The vivacity natural to the Celtic race, was further manifested in the Cambrians by an excessive taste for conversation, and their promptitude in repartee. "All the Welsh, without exception, even in the lowest ranks," says the ancient author already quoted, "have been gifted by nature with a great volubility of tongue, and extreme confidence in answering before princes and nobles; the Italians and French seem to possess the same faculty; but it is not found among the English of race nor among the Saxons of Germany nor among the Allemans. The present servitude of the English will, doubtless, be alleged as the cause of this want of assurance in the English; but such is not the true reason of this difference, for the Saxons of the continent are free, and yet the same defect is to be remarked in them."

The Welsh, who never, like the Germanic tribes, undertook invasive expeditions out of their own country, and who, in one of their national proverbs, wished that "every ray of the sun were a poniard to pierce the friend of war," never, on the other hand, made peace with the foreigner, so long as he occupied their territory, how long soever he remained there, how firmly fixed soever in castles, villages, and towns. The day on which one of these castles was demolished, was a day of universal rejoicing, in which, to use the words of a Welsh writer, the father deprived of an only son forgot his calamity. In the great insurrection of 1138, the Normans, attacked along the whole line of their marches, from the mouth of the Dee to the Severn, lost numerous fortified posts, and for some time, were obliged, in their turn, to assume a defensive attitude. But the advantage obtained by the Cambrians was of no great importance, because they did not prosecute the war beyond the limits of their mountains and their valleys. Their attack, however vigorous, gave, therefore, less alarm to the conquerors of England, than the invasion of the king of Scotland, and was of still less utility to the Saxon people, who had placed their hopes in it.

King Stephen deemed it unnecessary to quit his southern residence to march against either the Scots or the Welsh. But, shortly afterwards, the Norman partisans of Matilda, daughter of Henry I., gave him deeper uneasiness. Invited to England by her friends, Matilda landed on the 22nd September of the year 1139, threw herself into Arundel Castle on the coast of Sussex, and thence gained that of Bristol, which was held by her brother, Robert earl of Gloucester. On the news of the pretender's arrival, many secret discontents and intrigues revealed themselves. Most of the northern and western chiefs solemnly renounced their homage and obedience to Stephen of Blois, and renewed the oath they had taken to the daughter of king Henry. The whole Norman race of England seemed divided into two factions, which observed each other for awhile with wary distrust, ere they came to blows. "Neighbour," say the historians of the time, "suspected neighbour; friend, friend; brother, brother."

Fresh bands of Brabançon soldiers, hired by one or other of the two rival parties, came with arms and baggage by different ports and various roads, to the rendezvous respectively assigned by the king and by Matilda, each side promising them the lands of the opposite faction as pay. To meet the expenses of this civil war, the Anglo-Normans sold their domains, their villages and their towns in England, with the inhabitants, body and goods. Many made incursions upon the domains of their adversaries, and carried off horses, oxen, sheep, and the men of English race, who were seized even in towns, and taken away, bound back to back.

"Every rich man," says the Saxon chronicle, "built castles, and defended them against all, and they filled the land full of castles. They greatly oppressed the wretched people, by making them work at these castles, and when the castles were finished, they filled them with devils and evil men. Then they took those whom they suspected to have any goods, by night and by day, seizing both men and women, and they put them in prison for their gold and silver, and tortured them with pains unspeakable, for never were any martyrs tormented as these were. They hung some up by their feet, and smoked them with foul smoke; some by their thumbs, or by the head, and they hung burning things on their feet. They put a knotted string about their heads, and writhed it till it went into the brain. They put them into dungeons wherein were adders, and snakes, and toads, and thus wore them out. Some they put into a crucet-house, that is, into a chest that was short and narrow, and not deep; and they put sharp stones in it, and crushed the man therein, so that they broke all his limbs. There were hateful and grim things, called sachenteges, in many of the castles, and which two or three men had enough to do to carry. The sachentege was made thus: it was fastened to a beam, having a sharp iron to go round a man's throat and neck, so that he might no ways sit, nor lie, nor sleep, but that he must bear all the iron. Many thousands they exhausted with hunger. I cannot and I may not tell of all the wounds and all the tortures that they inflicted upon the wretched men of this land; and this state of things lasted the nineteen years that Stephen was king, and ever grew worse and worse. They were continually levying an exaction from the towns, which they called tensery, and when the miserable inhabitants had no more to give, then plundered they and burned all the towns; so that well mightest thou walk a whole day's journey, nor even shouldest thou find a single soul in a town or its lands tilled.

"Then was corn dear, and flesh, and cheese, and butter, for there was none in the land. Wretched men starved with hunger; some lived on alms, who had been erewhile rich; some fled the country; never was there more misery, and never acted heathens worse than these. At length they spared neither church nor churchyard, but they took all that was valuable therein, and then burned the church and all together. Neither did they spare the lands of bishops or of abbots or of priests, but they robbed the monks and the clergy, and every man plundered his neighbour, as much as he might. If two or three men came riding to a town, all the township fled before them, and thought that they were robbers. The bishops and clergy were ever cursing them, but this to them was nothing, for they were all accursed, and forsworn, and reprobate. The earth bare no corn; you might as well have tilled the sea, for the land was all ruined by such deeds, and it was said openly that Christ and his saints slept. These things, and more than we can say, did we suffer during nineteen years, because of our sins."

The greatest terror prevailed in the environs of Bristol, where the empress Matilda and her Angevins had established their head-quarters. All day long men were brought into the city, bound and gagged with a piece of wood or an iron bit. Troops of disguised soldiers were constantly leaving the castle, who, concealing their arms and language, and attired in the English habit, spread through the town and neighbourhood, mingling with the crowd in the markets and streets, and there, suddenly seizing those whose appearance denoted easy circumstances, carried them off to their quarters and put them to ransom. It was against Bristol that king Stephen first directed his army. This strong and well-defended city resisted, and the royal troops revenged themselves by devastating and burning the environs. The king next attacked, one by one and with better success, the Norman castles along the Welsh frontier, the seigneurs of which had nearly to a man declared against him.

While he was engaged in this protracted and troublesome war, insurrection broke out in the eastern districts of the country; the marshy lands of Ely, which had served as a refuge to the last of the free Saxons, became a camp for the Normans of the Angevin faction. Baldwin de Reviers or Redvers, earl of Devonshire, and Lenoir, bishop of Ely, raised against king Stephen intrenchments of stone and mortar in the very place where Hereward had erected a fortress of wood. This district, always considered formidable by the Norman authority, on account of the facilities it presented for hostile assemblage and defence, had been placed by Henry I. under the authority of a bishop, whose superintendence was to be combined with that of the earl or viscount of the province. The first bishop of the new diocese of Ely was the same Hervé whom the Welsh had expelled from Bangor; the second was Lenoir, who discovered and denounced the great conspiracy of the English in the year 1137. It was not out of personal zeal for king Stephen, but from patriotism as a Norman, that the latter served the king against the Saxons; and as soon as the Normans had declared against Stephen, Lenoir joined them, and undertook to make the islands of his diocese a rendezvous for the friends of Matilda.

Stephen attacked his adversaries in this camp as William the Conqueror had formerly attacked the Saxon refugees there. He constructed bridges of boats, over which his cavalry passed, and completely routed the troops of Baldwin de Reviers and bishop Lenoir. The bishop fled to Gloucester, where the daughter of Henry I. then was with her principal partisans. Her friends in the west, encouraged by the king's absence, repaired the breaches in their castle-walls, or, transforming into fortresses the towers of the great churches, furnished them with war-machines, and dug moats round them, even in the churchyards, so that the bodies were laid bare and their bones scattered. The Norman prelates did not scruple to participate in these military operations, and were not the least active in torturing the English to make them give ransom. They were seen, as in the first years of the Conquest, mounted upon war-horses, clad in armour, and a lance or bâton in their hands, directing the works and the attacks, or casting lots for the spoil.

The bishop of Chester and the bishop of Lincoln were remarkable among the most warlike. The latter rallied the troops beaten at the camp of Ely, and re-formed, upon the eastern coast, an army which king Stephen came to attack, but with less success than before; his troops, victorious at Ely, dispersed near Lincoln: abandoned by those who surrounded him, the king defended himself alone for some time; but at last, obliged to yield, he was taken to Gloucester, to the quarters of the countess of Anjou, who, by the advice of her council of war, imprisoned him in the donjon of Bristol. This defeat ruined the royal cause. The Normans of Stephen's party, seeing him conquered and captive, passed over in crowds to Matilda. His own brother, Henry, bishop of Winchester, declared himself for the victorious faction; and the Saxon peasants, who equally detested both parties, profited by the misfortune of the conquered to despoil them and maltreat them in their flight.

The grand-daughter of William the Conqueror made her triumphal entry into the city of Winchester; bishop Henry received her at the gates, at the head of the clergy of all the churches. She took possession of the royal ornaments, and of Stephen's treasure, and convoked a great council of prelates, earls, barons, and knights. The assembly decided that Matilda should assume the title of queen, and the bishop who presided pronounced the following form:—"Having first invoked, as was befitting, the assistance of Almighty God, we elect, for lady of England and Normandy, the daughter of the glorious, rich, good, and pacific king Henry, and promise her faith and support." But the good fortune of queen Matilda soon made her disdainful and arrogant; she ceased to solicit the counsel of her old friends, and treated with little favour those of her adversaries who sought to make peace with her. The authors of her elevation, when they requested aught of her, often underwent a refusal; and when they bowed before her, says an old historian, she did not rise to acknowledge the homage. This conduct cooled the zeal of her most devoted partisans, and the majority of them, quitting her, without, however, declaring for the dethroned king, awaited the result in repose.

From Winchester, the new queen went to London. She was the daughter of a Saxon, and the Saxon citizens, from a kind of national sympathy, were better pleased to see her in their city, than they were to see there the king of pure foreign race; but the enthusiasm of these serfs of the Conquest made little impression on the proud heart of the wife of the count of Anjou, and the first words she addressed to the citizens of London, were a demand for an enormous subsidy. The citizens, whom the devastations of war and the exactions of Stephen had reduced to such distress that they were in fear of a speedy famine, intreated the queen to pity them, and to wait until they had recovered from their present misery, ere she imposed new tributes on them. "The king has left us nothing," said the deputies from the citizens, submissively. "I understand," said the daughter of Henry I., disdainfully; "you have given all to my adversary; you have conspired with him against me; and you would have me spare you." Obliged to pay the tax, the citizens of London seized the occasion to present an humble petition to the queen: "Noble lady," said they, "let it be permitted us to follow the good laws of king Edward, thy great uncle, instead of those of thy father the king Henry, which are harsh and ill to bear." But, as if she blushed for her maternal ancestors and abnegated her Anglo-Saxon descent, Matilda became furious at this petition, treated those who dared to address it to her as the most insolent of serfs, and threatened them fiercely. Deeply aggrieved, but dissimulating their anger, the citizens returned to the Guildhall, where the Normans, become less suspicious, allowed them to assemble to arrange among themselves the payment of the taxes; for the government had adopted the custom of imposing these upon the towns in the mass, without troubling themselves as to the manner in which the impost should be raised by individual contributions.

Queen Matilda waited in full security, either in the Tower or in the new palace of William Rufus at Westminster, for the citizens to come and present to her on their knees the gold she had demanded, when suddenly the bells of the town rang the alarm: an immense crowd filled the streets and squares. From every house issued a man, armed with the first weapon that had come to hand. An ancient author likens the multitude who thus tumultuously assembled to bees quitting a hive. The queen and her Norman and Angevin barons, thus surprised, and not daring to risk, in the narrow and tortuous streets, an encounter in which the superiority of arms and of military skill could be of no avail, speedily mounted their horses and fled. They had hardly passed the last houses of the suburbs, when a troops of English hastened to the lodgings they had occupied, broke open the doors, and not finding the men, seized upon all they had left behind. The queen hastened along the Oxford road with her barons and knights; from time to time some of these quitted her to retreat in greater safety alone by cross roads and bye paths; she entered Oxford with her brother the earl of Gloucester, and the few who had followed the road she pursued as the safest, or who forgot their own danger in hers.

This danger, however, was not great; the people of London, satisfied with having driven the new queen of England from their walls, did not pursue her. Their insurrection, the result of an ebullition of fury, without any previous project and without connexion with any other movement, did not constitute the first act of a national insurrection. The expulsion of Matilda and her adherents, however, while it did not profit the English, served the partisans of king Stephen, who entering London, occupied the city and garrisoned it with their troops, under colour of alliance with the citizens. The wife of the imprisoned king repaired hither also, and took up her quarters in the Tower; all that the citizens obtained was permission to enrol a thousand of their number, with helmet and hauberk, among the troops who assembled in the name of Stephen, to serve, as auxiliaries of the Normans, under William and Roger de la Chesnaye.

The bishop of Winchester, seeing his brother's party regaining some strength, deserted the opposite faction, and declared once more for the prisoner of Bristol; he unfurled the king's flag on Winchester castle and on his own episcopal palace, which he had fortified and embattled like a castle. Robert of Gloucester and the partisans of Matilda came to besiege it. The garrison of the castle, constructed in the centre of the city, set fire to the surrounding houses, in order to harass the besiegers; and in the mean time, the London army attacking the latter unexpectedly, compelled them to retire to the churches, which were set on fire as a mode of driving them out.

Robert of Gloucester was taken prisoner, and his followers dispersed. Barons and knights threw aside their arms, and travelling on foot to avoid recognition, traversed, under assumed names, the towns and villages. But, besides the king's partisans, who followed them closely, they encountered on their way other enemies, the Saxon peasants, furious against them in their defeat, as they had been just before against the opposite party, under similar circumstances; they stopped the proud Normans, whom, despite their efforts to disguise themselves, they recognised by their language, and compelled them to run before them, by blows of their whips. The archbishop of Canterbury, other bishops, and a number of seigneurs, were maltreated in this way and despoiled of their horses and clothes. Thus, this war was for the native English at once a source of misery and of joy—of that frantic joy we feel amidst suffering, in returning evil for evil. The grandson of a man who had died at Hastings, now found himself master of the life of a Norman baron or prelate, and the English women, who turned the spinning-wheel in the service of noble Norman dames, laughed as they heard related the sufferings of queen Matilda on her departure from Oxford; how she had fled with three knights, on foot, and by night, through the snow; and how she had fearfully passed the enemy's posts, trembling at the least sound of men and horses, or at the voice of the sentinels.

Soon after the brother of Matilda, Robert earl of Gloucester, had been taken prisoner, the two parties concluded an agreement, by which the king and the earl were exchanged, one for the other, so that the dispute resumed its first position. Stephen quitted Bristol castle and resumed the exercise of royalty, his government extending over the portion of the country where his partisans predominated; that is to say, over the central and eastern provinces of England. As to Normandy, none of his orders reached it; for during his captivity, the whole of that country had yielded to earl Geoffroy, the husband of Matilda, who, shortly afterwards, with the consent of the Normans, transferred the title of duke of Normandy to his eldest son Henry. The party of Stephen thus lost the hope of recruiting itself beyond seas; but as he was master of the coast, he was in a position to prevent any succour thence to his adversaries at home, who were shut up in the west. Their only resource was to hire bodies of Welsh, who, though ill armed, by their bravery and singular tactics, arrested, for awhile, the march of the king's partisans.

While the struggle was thus languidly prolonged on both sides, Henry, son of Matilda, left Normandy with a small army, and succeeded in landing in England. On the first rumour of his arrival, many nobles began to abandon the cause of Stephen; but, as soon as they learned that Henry had but a few followers and very little money, most of these returned to the king, and the desertion ceased. The war went on in the same way as before; castles were taken and retaken, towns pillaged and burnt. The English, flying from their houses, through force or fear, raised huts under the walls of the churches; but they were soon driven from them by one or the other party, who converted the church into a fortress, embattling its towers, and furnishing them with war machines.

Stephen's only son, Eustache, who had more than once signalized himself by his valour, died, after having pillaged a domain consecrated to Saint Edmund, king and martyr; his death was, according to the English, the consequence of the outrage he had dared to commit on this saint of English race. Stephen having now no son to whom he could desire to transmit the kingdom, proposed to his rival, Henry of Anjou, to terminate the war by an accommodation; he required that the Normans of England, and of the continent, should allow him to reign in peace during his life, on condition that the son of Matilda should be king after him. The Normans consented to this, and peace was re-established. The tenour of the treaty, sworn by the bishops, earls, barons, and knights of both parties, is presented to us under two very different aspects by the historians of the time, according to the faction they favour. Some say that king Stephen adopted Henry as his son, and that in virtue of this preliminary act, the lords swore to give in heritage to the adopted son, his father's kingdom; others, on the contrary, assert that the king positively acknowledged the hereditary right of the son of Matilda to the kingdom, and that in return the latter benevolently granted him permission to reign for the remainder of his life. Thus contemporaries, equally worthy of belief, deduce from two principles, entirely opposite, the legitimacy which they accord to the grandson of Henry I. Which are we to believe on this point? neither the one nor the other; the truth is, that the same barons who had elected Stephen despite the oath sworn to Matilda, and who afterwards elected Matilda despite the oath sworn to Stephen, by a new act of will, designed, as successor to Stephen, the son of Matilda and not the mother: from this all-potent will was derived the royal legitimacy.

Shortly before his expedition to England, Henry had married the divorced wife of the king of France, Eleanor, or Alienor, or, more familiarly, Aanor, daughter of William, earl of Poitou and duke of Aquitaine, that is to say, sovereign of all the western coast of Gaul, from the mouth of the Loire to the foot of the Pyrenees. According to the custom of this country, Eleanor enjoyed there all the power that her father had exercised; and, moreover, her husband, though a foreigner, could share the sovereignty with her. King Louis VII. had enjoyed the privilege so long as he remained united to the daughter of earl William, and he maintained officers and garrisons in the towns of Aquitaine; but, as soon as he had repudiated her, he found himself under the necessity of recalling his seneschals and troops. It was in Palestine, whither Eleanor had followed her husband to the crusades, that their misunderstanding broke out. Persuaded, right or wrong, that the queen played him false with a young Saracen, Louis solicited and obtained the divorce refused by the church to common people, but frequently granted to princes.

A council was held at Beaugency-sur-Loire, before which the queen of France was summoned. The bishop who acted as accuser, announced that the king demanded a divorce, "because he had no confidence in his wife, and should never feel assured as to the lineage issuing from her."

The council, passing this scandalous proposition over in silence, declared the marriage null, under pretext of consanguinity, perceiving, somewhat late after a union of sixteen years, that Eleanor was her husband's cousin, within one of the prohibited degrees. The divorced wife, on her return to her own country, stopped for awhile at Blois. During her stay in this town, Thibaut, earl of Blois, endeavoured to conciliate her and to obtain her hand. Indignant at the refusal he received, the earl resolved to retain the duchess of Aquitaine in prison in his castle, and even to marry her by force. She suspected this design, and departing by night, descended the Loire to Tours, a town which then formed part of the earldom of Anjou. On hearing of her arrival, Geoffroy, the second son of the earl of Anjou and the empress Matilda, seized with the same desire as Thibaut de Blois, placed himself in ambush at Port de Piles, on the frontiers of Poitou and Touraine, to stop the progress of the duchess, seize her and marry her; but Eleanor, says the historian, was warned by her good angel, and suddenly took another road to Poitiers.

It was hither that Henry, the eldest son of Matilda and of the earl of Anjou, more courteous than his brother, repaired to solicit the love of the daughter of the duke of Aquitaine. He was accepted, and conducting his new wife to Normandy, he sent bailiffs, justiciaries, and Norman soldiers to the cities of southern Gaul. To the title of duke of Normandy he thenceforward added those of duke of Aquitaine and earl of Poitou; and his father already possessing Anjou and Touraine, their combined sovereignty extended over the whole western portion of Gaul, between the Somme and the Pyrenees, with the exception of Brittany. The territories of the king of France, bounded by the Loire, the Saone, and the Meuse, were far from having so great an extent. This king grew alarmed at seeing the aggrandizement of the Norman power, the rival of his own ever since its birth, and still more so since the conquest of England. He had made great efforts to prevent the union of young Henry with Eleanor of Aquitaine, and had required him, as his vassal for the duchy of Normandy, not to contract marriage without the consent of his suzerain lord. But the obligations of the liegeman to the suzerain, even when the two parties had expressly acknowledged and consented to them, were of small value between men of equal power. Henry took no heed to this prohibition to marry; and Louis VII. was fain to content himself with the new oaths of homage which the future king of England made to him for the earldom of Poitou and the duchy of Aquitaine.

Oaths of this kind, vague in their tenour, taken unwillingly, and in some sort a mere form, had long been the only tie existing between the successors of the ancient Frank kings and the sovereign chiefs of the country comprised between the Loire and the two seas; for the Frank domination had not taken root in these districts so deeply as in those nearer Germany. In the seventh century, the nations of Europe who had relations with Gaul, already designated it all by the name of France; but in the Gaulish territory itself this name was far from possessing such universality. The course of the Loire formed the southern limit of Frankish Gaul, or of the French country; beyond this was the Roman territory, differing from the other in language and manners, and especially in civilization.

In the south, the inhabitants, high or low, rich or poor, were nearly all of pure Gaulish race, or at least their German descent was not accompanied there by the same superiority of social condition which was attached to it in the north. The men of Frankish race who had come into southern Gaul, either as conquerors or as agents and commissioners of the conquerors, settled north of the Loire, did not succeed in propagating themselves as a distinct nation amidst a numerous population collected in great towns; and accordingly, the inhabitants of France and Burgundy usually employed the term Romans to designate those of the south.

Many of the successors of Clodowig added to their title of king of the Franks, that of prince of the Roman people; in the decline of that first dynasty, the population of Aquitaine and Provence chose native dukes and counts, or, what is more remarkable, obliged the descendants of their governors of Teutonic race to revolt with them. But this enfranchisement of southern Gaul was scarcely accomplished, when the accession of a second race of kings restored to the Frank nation its pristine energy, and again directed it to the conquest of the south.

Once more masters of these beautiful lands, the Gallo-Franks placed there governors and judges, who, under the form of tribute, carried off all the money in the country; but, on the first favourable occasion, the southerns refused to pay, rose, and drove out the foreigners. Hereupon the Franks descended from the north to reassert their right of conquest; they came to the banks of the Loire at Orleans, Tours, or Nevers, to hold their Champ-de-Mai in arms. The war commenced between them and the inhabitants of the Limousin or Auvergne, then the outpost of the Gallo-Roman population. If the Romans (to speak in the language of the period) found themselves too weak to contend, they proposed to the chief of the Frenchmen to pay him the impost every year, preserving their political independence. The Frank prince submitted this proposition to his leudes, in their assembly, held in the open air; if the assembly voted against peace, the army continued its march, cutting down the vines and fruit trees, and carrying off men, cattle and horses. When the cause of the south had been completely defeated, the judges, the Frank grafs and skepen, re-installed themselves in the towns, and, for a more or less extended period, this form figured at the head of the public acts: "In the reign of the glorious king Pepin; in the reign of the illustrious emperor Karle."

Karle, or Charlemagne, with the consent of all the Frank lords, established as king of Aquitaine his son Lodewig, whom the Gauls called Louis. This Louis became, in his turn, emperor or keisar of the Franks, and under this title, ruled at once Germany, Italy, and Gaul. In his own lifetime, he desired his sons to enjoy this immense authority, and the unequal division he made excited discord among them. The southern Gauls took part in these quarrels, in order to envenom them and thus contribute to weaken their masters. While awaiting the moment to revolt under chiefs of their own race and language, they gave the crown of their country to members of the imperial family, indeed, but these such as neither the emperor nor the supreme assembly of the Franks desired to reign; hence resulted protracted wars and fresh devastations in the towns of Aquitaine. The great struggle for royalty which arose towards the close of the ninth century, and continued for a century, gave some relief to the Aquitans. Indifferent to the two rival parties, having no common interest either with the family of Charlemagne or with the kings of new race, they kept aloof, and made use of the dispute as a pretext for resisting alike the power of both. When the Gallo-Franks, renouncing the Austrasian Karle, called Le Gros, chose for their king the Neustrian Eudes, count of Paris, a national king, named Ranulf, then arose in Aquitaine, who, shortly after, under the modest titles of duke of the Aquitans and count of the Poitevins, reigned in full sovereignty, from the Loire to the Pyrenees. King Eudes quitted France to subject Aquitaine; but he did not succeed in this object. With their material resistance, the inhabitants of the south combined a sort of moral opposition; they set themselves up as defenders of the rights of the old dispossessed family, for the sole reason that the French would no longer acknowledge these rights.

Hereupon nearly all the independent chiefs of Aquitaine, Poitou, and Provence, proceeded to assert themselves descendants of Charlemagne on the female side, and applied this hypothetical descent as authority for denouncing as usurpers the kings of the third dynasty. After Charles le Simple, the legitimate heir of Charlemagne, had been imprisoned in Peronne, his name was placed at the head of the public acts in Aquitaine, as though he still reigned; when his son had recovered the power, the Aquitans would not allow him to exercise the slightest authority over them, directly or indirectly.

The victory of the French over the second and third Germanic dynasties was permanently decided by the election of Hugh, surnamed Capet or Shapet in the Romane language of Outre-Loire. The people of the south took no part in this election, and did not acknowledge king Hugh;

the latter, at the head of his people between the Meuse and the Loire, made war upon Aquitaine; but, after repeated efforts, he only succeeded in establishing his suzerainty over the provinces nearest the Loire, Berry, Touraine, and Anjou. As the reward of his adhesion, the count of the latter province obtained the hereditary title of seneschal of the kingdom of France; and, at solemn banquets, had the charge of serving the meats at the king's table on horseback. But the attraction of such honours did not seduce the counts or dukes of the more southern districts; they maintained the combat, and the great mass of population who spoke the language of oc, did not acknowledge, in reality or in semblance, the authority of the kings of the country in which they said oui. The south of Gaul, distributed into various principalities, according to the natural divisions of the land or the ancient circumscription of the Roman provinces, thus appeared, towards the eleventh century, freed from every remnant of the subjection which the Franks had imposed on it, and the people of Aquitaine had thenceforth for their sovereigns men of their own race and language.

It is true, that north of the Loire, from the end of the tenth century, one same language was also common to kings, lords, and commons; but in this country, where the conquest had never been controverted, the seigneurs loved not the people; they felt in their hearts, perhaps without noting it, that their rank and their power were derived from a foreign source. Although severed for ever from their old Teutonic stock, they had not renounced the manners of the conquest they alone in the kingdom enjoyed territorial property and personal freedom. On the contrary, in the petty southern sovereignties, though there were ranks among men, though there were higher and lower classes, castles and cottages, insolence in wealth and tyranny in power, the soil belonged to the body of the people, and none contested with them its free possession, the franc-aleu, as it was termed in the middle ages. It was the popular mass which, by a series of efforts, had recovered this soil from the invaders of Outre-Loire. The duchies, the countships, the viscountships, all the lordships, were, more or less, national: most of them had originated in periods of revolt against the foreign power, and had been legitimised by the consent of the people.

But, inferior to the southern provinces in social organization, in civil liberty, and in traditions of government, the kingdom of France was powerful from its extent, and formidable abroad; none of the states which shared with it the ancient territory of Gaul, equalled it in power; and its chiefs often made the dukes and counts of the south tremble in their large cities, enriched by arts and by commerce. Often, to secure the continuance of peace with France, they offered their daughters in marriage to French princes, who, by this false policy, were admitted among them as relations and allies. It was thus that the union of the daughter of duke William with king Louis VII. opened, as we have seen, the towns of Aquitaine and Poitou to foreign garrisons. When, after the divorce of Eleanor, the French had withdrawn, her second marriage introduced Angevins and Normans, who, like the French, said oui and nenny, instead of oc and no. Perhaps there was more sympathy between the Angevins and the inhabitants of the south, than between the latter and the French, because civilization increased in Gaul the further south it lay. But the difference of language, and more especially of accent, necessarily reminded the Aquitains that Henry Fitz-Empress, their new lord, was a foreigner.

Shortly after the marriage, which made him duke of Aquitaine, Henry became earl of Anjou, by the death of his father, but upon the express condition of transferring that province to his younger brother on the day he himself should become king. He swore this oath with every demonstration of solemnity, on the corpse of the departed, but the oath was broken, and Henry retained the earldom of Anjou, when the Norman barons, more faithful than he to their word, called him to England, to succeed king Stephen. As soon as he had taken possession of the crown, he denounced Stephen as an usurper, and proceeded to abolish all that he had done. He drove from England the Brabançons who had settled there after aiding the royal cause against Matilda. He confiscated the lands which these men had received as their pay, and demolished their strongholds, in common with those of all the other partisans of the late king; desiring, he said, to reduce the number to what it had been under king Henry, his grandfather. The bands of foreign auxiliaries who had come to England during the civil war, had committed infinite pillage on the Normans of the party opposed to that which they served; their chiefs had seized upon domains and mansions, and had then fortified them against the dispossessed Norman lords, imitating the fathers of the latter, who had in like manner fortified the habitations taken from the English. The expulsion of the Flemings was for the whole Anglo-Norman race a subject of rejoicing, as great as their own expulsion would have been for the Saxons. "We saw them all," says a contemporary author—"we saw them all cross the sea to return from the camp to the plough, and again become serfs, after having been masters."

Every man who in the year 1140 had, on the invitation of king Stephen, unharnessed his oxen to cross the Channel to the battle of Lincoln, was thus treated as an usurper by those whose ancestors had, in 1066, unharnessed theirs to follow William the Bastard. The conquerors of England already looked upon themselves as the legitimate possessors; they had effaced from their memory all recollection of their forcible usurpation and of their former condition, fancying that their noble families had never exercised any other function than that of governing men. But the Saxons had a longer memory: and in the complaints drawn from them by the cruelty of their lords, they said of many an earl or prelate of Norman race: "He drives us and goads us, as his father goaded his plough-oxen on the other side of the Channel."

Despite this consciousness of their own position and of the origin of their government, the Saxon race, worn out by suffering, gave way to an apathetic resignation. The little English blood which the empress Matilda had transmitted to Henry II., was, they said, a guarantee for his goodwill towards the people; and they forgot how this same Matilda, though more Saxon than her son, had treated the citizens of London. Writers, either from sheer simplicity of good faith, or hired to extol the new reign, proclaimed that England at length possessed a king, English by nation; that she had bishops, abbots, barons, and knights, the issue of both races, and that thus national hatred had, for the future, no basis. No doubt, the Saxon women, seized upon and married by force after the battle of Hastings, or after the defeats of York and Ely, had, amid their despair, borne sons to their masters; but these sons of foreign fathers, did they deem themselves brothers of the citizens and serfs of the land? Would not the desire to efface the stain of their birth in the eyes of the Normans of pure race, render them still more overbearing, even than the latter, towards their maternal countrymen? It is also true, that, in the first years of the invasion, William the Conqueror had offered women of his nation and even of his own family to Saxon chiefs, still free; but these unions were few in number; and as soon as the conquest seemed complete, no Englishman was held noble enough for a Norman woman to honour him with her hand. Besides, even supposing that many English in birth, by denying the cause of their country, by unlearning their own language, by playing the part of flatterers and parasites, had raised themselves to the privileges of the men of foreign race, this individual fortune did not weaken, in reference to the mass of the conquered, the mournful effects of the Conquest.

Perhaps, indeed, the mixture of races was in England, at this time, more favourable to the oppressors than to the oppressed; for, as the former lost their foreign character, if we may so express it, the inclination to resist diminished in the hearts of the latter. A violent reaction, the only efficacious resource against the iniquities of the conquest, became less possible. To the fetters of usurped domination were superadded moral bonds, the respect for men for their own blood, and those kindly affections which render us so patient under domestic despotism. Accordingly, Henry II. was pleased to see the Saxon monks, in the dedications of their books, set forth his English genealogy, and without mentioning either his grandfather, Henry I., or his great grandfather, the Conqueror, place him as the descendant of king Alfred. "Thou art the son," they said, "of the very glorious empress Matilda, whose mother was Matilda, daughter of Margaret, queen of Scotland, whose father was Edward, son of king Edmund Ironsides, the great grandson of the noble king Alfred."

Whether by chance or design, predictions were circulated at the same time, announcing the reign of Henry of Anjou as an epoch of relief, and, in some measure, of resuscitation, for the English. One of these prophecies was attributed to king Edward on his death bed; and it was said that he delivered it, in order to reassure those who then feared for England the ambitious projects of the duke of Normandy. "When the green tree," he said to them, "after having been cut down and moved from its root to a distance of three acres, shall itself approach its root once more, shall flourish and bear fruit, then a better time will come." This allegory, invented for the purpose, was readily interpreted. The felled tree was the family of Edward, which had lost the crown on the election of Harold; after Harold had come William the Conqueror, and his son William Rufus; these completed the number of three kings foreign to the ancient family; for it is to be observed that the interpreters omitted Edgar, because he still had relations in England or Scotland, to whom, in a question of descent from the noble king Alfred, the Angevin Henry would have had very inferior pretensions. The tree again approached its root when Matilda married Henry I.; it flourished in the birth of the empress Matilda, and, lastly, it bore fruit in that of Henry II. These miserable tales only merit a place in history on account of the moral effect they produced on the men of former times. Their object was to divert from the person of the king the hatred which the Saxons nourished against all Normans; but nothing could prevent Henry II. from being regarded as the representative of the conquest: it was in vain that his friends mystically surnamed him the corner stone of junction for the two walls, that is to say, the two races: no union was possible amidst such utter inequality of rights, properties, and power.

Difficult as it was for an Anglo-Saxon of the twelfth century to recognise as natural successor of the kings of English race, a man who could not even say king in English, the pertinacious reconcilers of the Saxons with the Normans put forward assertions still more extraordinary; they undertook to prove the Conqueror himself the legitimate heir of king Alfred. A very ancient chronicle, cited by an ancient author, relates that William the Bastard was the own grandson of king Edmund Ironsides. "Edmund," says this chronicle, "had two sons, Edwin and Edward, and also a daughter, whose name history does not mention, on account of her ill life, for she had illicit intercourse with the king's tanner." The king, greatly enraged, banished his skinner from England, with his daughter, who was then pregnant. Both passed into Normandy, where, living on public charity, they had successively three daughters. One day, as they were begging at Falaise, at the door of duke Robert, the duke, struck with the beauty of the wife and her three children, asked her who she was. "I am," she answered, "an Englishwoman, and of royal blood." At this answer, the duke treated her honourably, took the tanner into his service, and received into his palace one of their daughters, who afterwards became his mistress and the mother of William, surnamed the Bastard, who, for the greater probability, always remained the grandson of a tanner of Falaise; although by his mother he was a Saxon and a descendant of Saxon kings.

The violation of the oath which Henry II. had, as we have seen, sworn to his brother Geoffroy, involved him, soon after his arrival in England, in a war on the continent. With the assistance of the partisans of his right to the earldom of Anjou, Geoffroy obtained possession of several strongholds. Henry sent an army of Englishmen against him. The English, animated by the antipathy they had borne, ever since the conquest, to the populations of Gaul, vigorously prosecuted the war, and in a short time secured a triumph to the ambitious and unjust brother. The conquered Geoffroy was obliged to accept, in exchange for his lands and his title of earl, a pension of a thousand pounds English and two thousand livres of Anjou. He had become once more a simple Angevin baron, when, by a fortunate chance for him, the people of Nantes made him count of their town and territory. By this election, they detached themselves from the government of Bretagne, with which it had been formerly incorporated by conquest, but which they had preferred to the domination of the Frank kings, without, however, any very vehement attachment, owing to the difference of language.

Aggrandized by fortunate wars, in the interval between the ninth to the eleventh century, Brittany was in the twelfth century torn by internal divisions, the result of its very prosperity. Its frontiers, which extended beyond the Loire, comprehended two populations of different race, one of which spoke the Celtic idiom, the other the Romane tongue of France and Normandy; and as the earls or dukes of the whole country enjoyed the favour of the one of these two races of men, they were disliked by the other. The Nantese who elected Geoffroy of Anjou as their earl, naturally belonged to the former of these two parties, and they only called on the Angevin prince to govern them in order to release themselves from the authority of a seigneur of pure Celtic race. Geoffroy of Anjou did not long enjoy his new dignity, and on his death, the town passed, if not freely, at least without repugnance, under the sovereignty of Conan, hereditary earl of Brittany, and possessor in England of Richmond castle, built in the time of the conquest, by the Breton, Alain Fergant. Hereupon, king Henry II., on a pretension entirely novel, claimed the town of Nantes, as a portion of the inheritance of his brother; he treated the earl of Brittany as an usurper, confiscated the estate of Richmond, and then crossing the sea, came with a large army to compel the citizens of Nantes to acknowledge him as lord, and to reject earl Conan. Incapable of resisting the forces of the king of England, the citizens obeyed against their will; the king placed a garrison within their walls, and occupied all the country between the Loire and the Vilaine.

Having thus gained a footing on the Breton territory, Henry II. extended his ambition still further, and concluded with the same Conan, from whom he had just taken the town of Nantes, a treaty which threatened the independence of all Brittany. He affianced his youngest son, Geoffroy, eight years of age, to Constance, daughter of Conan, and then five years old. In the terms of this treaty, the Breton earl engaged to make the future husband of his daughter heir to his dominions, and the king, in return, guaranteed to Conan possession for life of the earldom of

Brittany, promising him aid, succour, and support, towards and against all. This treaty, the inevitable result of which would be the extension, at some future day, of the domination of the Anglo-Normans over the whole of Western Gaul, greatly alarmed the king of France; he negotiated with the pope, Alexander III., to engage him to prohibit the union of Geoffroy and Constance, on account of consanguinity; Conan being the grandson of a bastard daughter of Henry the second's grandfather; but the pope would not recognise this relationship, and the precocious nuptials of the young couple were celebrated in the year 1166.

Shortly after, a national insurrection broke out in Brittany, against the chief who trafficked with a foreign king in the independence of his country. Conan summoned Henry II. to his assistance, and in the terms of their treaty of alliance, the king's troops entered Brittany by the Norman frontier, under pretext of defending the legitimate earl of the Bretons against the insurgents. Henry gained possession of Dol, and of several smaller towns, in which he placed garrisons. Soon after, half voluntarily, half compulsorily, earl Conan resigned his power into the hands of his protector, allowing him to exercise the administrative authority and to levy tributes throughout Brittany. The timid and feeble waited on the Angevin king in his camp, and, according to the ceremonial of the time, did him homage for their lands; the clergy hastened to compliment, in the Latin tongue, the man who came in the name of God to visit and console Brittany. But the divine right of this foreign usurpation was not universally recognised, and the friends of old Brittany, assembling from all its districts, formed against king Henry a sworn confederation for life and death.

The bond of nationality was already too weak in Brittany for this country to derive from itself sufficient resources for its rebellion. The insurgents accordingly opened a correspondence abroad; they came to an understanding with their neighbours the people of Maine, who, since the reign of William the Bastard, had given a most unwilling obedience to the Norman princes. Numbers of Manseaux entered the league sworn in Brittany against the king of England, and all the members of this league adopted as their patron the king of France, the political rival of Henry II., and the most powerful of his competitors. Louis VII. promised assistance to the insurgent Bretons, not from love of their independence, which his predecessors had assailed so fiercely during so many centuries, but through hatred to the king of England, and the desire to acquire for himself in Brittany that supremacy which his enemy might lose there. To attain this object at small cost, he contented himself with mere promises to the confederates, leaving upon them all the burden of an enterprise of which he was to share the profits. Speedily attacked by the entire forces of king Henry, the Breton insurgents were defeated, and lost the towns of Vannes, Léon, Auray, and Fougères, their castles, domains, soldiers, wives and daughters, whom the king took for hostages, and whom he amused himself with dishonouring, by seduction or by violence: one of them, the daughter of Eudes, viscount de Porrhoët, was his cousin in the second degree.

About the same time, a distaste for the domination of the king of England became strongly felt by the inhabitants of Aquitaine, more especially by those of Poitou and the Marche de France, who, being the children of a mountainous country, were of a fierce temperament, and were in a better position to carry on a patriotic war. Though husband of the daughter of the earl of Poitou, Henry II. was a foreigner to the Poitevins, who ill endured to see officers of foreign race violating or destroying the customs of their country by ordinances drawn up in the Angevin or Norman language. Many of these new magistrates were driven forth, and one of them, a native of

Perche, and earl of Salisbury, was killed at Poitiers by the people. An extensive conspiracy was formed under the direction of the principal lords and rich men of north Aquitaine, the count De la Marche, the duke d'Angoulême, the viscount De Thouars, the abbot of Charroux, Aymery de Lezinan or Luzignan, Hugh and Robert de Silly. The Poitevin conspirators placed themselves, as the Bretons had done, under the patronage of the king of France, who demanded hostages from them, and engaged, in return, not to make peace with king Henry without including them in it; but they were crushed, as the Bretons had been, Louis VII. remaining a mere spectator of their war with the Angevin king.

The leading men among them capitulated with the conqueror; the others fled to the territory of the king of France, who, unfortunately for them, began to grow weary of war with king Henry, and to desire a truce. These two princes, after having long laboured to injure each other, at length came to a formal reconciliation in the little town of Montmirail in Perche. It was agreed that the king of France should secure to the other king possession of Brittany, and should give up to him the refugees of that country and of Poitou; that, in return, the king of England should expressly acknowledge himself the vassal and liegeman of the king of France, and that Brittany should be comprehended in the new oath of homage. The two rivals shook hands and embraced cordially; then, in virtue of the new sovereignty which the king of France acknowledged in him over the Bretons, and pursuant to the treaty, Henry II. instituted as duke of Brittany, Anjou, and Maine, his eldest son, who in this quality took the oath of vassalage between the hands and on the lips of the king of France. In this interview the Angevin king gave utterance to sentiments of tenderness, most absurd in their exaggeration, towards a man who, the day before, was his mortal enemy. "I place," said he, "at your disposal myself, my children, my lands, my forces, my treasures, to use and to abuse, to keep or to give, at your pleasure and good will." It would seem as though his reason was somewhat deranged by the joy of having the Poitevin and Breton emigrants in his power. King Louis gave them up to him, upon the derisive condition that he should receive them into favour, and restore to them their property. Henry promised this, and even gave them publicly the kiss of peace, as a guarantee of this promise, but most of them ended their days in prison or on the scaffold.

The two kings having separated under this appearance of perfect harmony, which, however, was not of long continuance, Henry, the eldest son of the king of England, transferred to his young brother, Geoffroy, the dignity of duke of Brittany, only retaining for himself the earldom of Anjou. Geoffroy did homage to his brother, as the latter had done to the king of France; he then proceeded to Rennes to hold his court, and receive the submission of the lords and knights of the country. Thus did the two hereditary enemies of the liberty of the Bretons deprive them, by mutual accord, of the sovereignty of their native land, the Angevin prince making himself immediate lord, the French prince, suzerain lord, and this great revolution took place without apparent violence. Conan, the last earl of pure Breton race, was not deposed, but his name did not again appear in the public acts: thenceforth there was, properly speaking, no longer any nation in Brittany; there was a French party and an Angevin or Norman party, labouring in opposite directions for one or the other power.

The ancient national language, abandoned by all who desired to please either of the two kings, became gradually corrupted in the mouths of the poor and the peasants, who, however, still remained faithful to it, and preserved it, in great measure, for centuries, with the tenacity of memory and of will which characterizes the Celtic race. Despite the desertion of their national chiefs to foreigners, Normans or French, and the public and private servitude which was the result, the populace of Lower Brittany have never ceased to recognise in the nobles of their country the children of the soil. They have never hated them with that violent hatred which was elsewhere borne to the lords, issue of a foreign race; and under the feudal titles of baron and knight, the Breton peasant still saw the tierns and the mactierns of the time of his independence; he obeyed them with zeal in good and in evil, engaged in their intrigues and their political quarrels, often without understanding them, but through habit and that instinct of devotion which the Welsh tribes and the highlanders of Scotland had for their chieftains.

It was not alone the populations contiguous to France, such as the Bretons and Poitevins, which, in their quarrels with the king of England, sought to make common cause with his political rival. After the rupture of the peace of Montmirail, Louis VII. received from a country with which he had before had no relations, and of whose existence he was almost ignorant, a despatch conceived in the following terms:—

"To the most excellent king of the French, Owen, prince of Wales, his liegeman and faithful friend: greeting, obedience, and devotion.

"The war which the king of England had long meditated against me, broke out last summer, without any provocation on my part; but, thanks to God and to you, who occupied his forces elsewhere, he lost more men than I on the fields of battle. In his rage, he has wickedly mutilated the hostages held from me; and retiring, without concluding any peace or truce, he has ordered his men to be ready by next Easter, to march once more against us. I therefore intreat your Clemency to inform me, by the bearer of these presents, if you propose to make war upon him at that period, so that on my part I may serve you, by harassing him as you may desire. Let me know what you would counsel me to do, and also what succours you will give me, for without aid and counsel from you, I fear I shall not be strong enough against our common enemy."

This letter was brought by a Welsh priest, who presented it to the king of France in his plenary court. But the king, having scarce in his whole life heard of Wales, suspected the messenger to be an impostor, and would not recognise either him or Owen's despatch. The latter was accordingly obliged to write a second missive to authenticate the contents of the first: "You did not believe," said he, "that my letter was really from me; but it was, I affirm, and call God to attest it." The Cambrian chief again styled himself, "faithful servant and vassal of the king of France." This circumstance is worthy of mention, because it teaches us, not to take literally or without a strict examination, the forms and phrases of the middle ages. The words vassal and lord often, indeed, expressed a real relationship of subordination and dependence, but they were also often a mere form of politeness, especially when the weak sought the alliance of the strong.

The duchy of Aquitaine or of Guienne, as it came to be called, did not extend beyond the eastern limits of the second of the ancient Aquitanian provinces, and thus the towns of Limoges, Cahors, and Toulouse were not comprised in it. This last city, the ancient residence of the Visigoth kings and of the Gallo-Roman chiefs, who after them governed the two Aquitaines combined to resist the Franks, had become the capital of a small separate state, which was called the county of Toulouse. There had been great rivalries in ambition between the counts of Toulouse and the dukes of Guienne, and, on both sides, various attempts to subject to one sole authority all the country between the Rhone, the Ocean, and the Pyrenees. Hence had arisen many disputes, treaties, and alliances, by turns made and unmade, in accordance with the instability natural to the people of the south. Henry II., become duke of Aquitaine, examined the records of these former conventions, and finding among them a sort of pretext for annulling the independence of the county of Toulouse, he advanced troops, and laid siege to the town. Raymond de Saint Gilles, count of Toulouse, raised his banner against him, and the commune of Toulouse, a corporation of free citizens, also raised theirs.

The common council of the city and suburbs (such was the title borne by the municipal government of the Toulousans,) opened, through their chief, negotiations with the king of France to obtain assistance from him. This king marched to Toulouse by Berri, which, for the most part, belonged to him, and through the Limousin, which gave him free passage; he compelled the king of England to raise the siege of the town, and was received in it with great joy by the count and the citizens. The latter, collected in a solemn assembly, voted him a letter of acknowledgments, in which they thanked him for having succoured them as a patron and as a father, an expression of affectionate gratitude which implied no acknowledgment of civil or feudal subjection on their part.

But this habit of imploring the patronage of one king against another became a cause of dependence, and the period when the king of England, as duke of Aquitaine and earl of Poitou, obtained influence over the affairs of the south of Gaul, was, for its inhabitants, the commencement of a new epoch of decay and misfortune. Placed thenceforth between two rival and equally ambitious powers, they attached themselves sometimes to one, sometimes to the other, according to circumstances, by turns supported, abandoned, betrayed, sold by both. From the twelfth century, the Southerns were never well off, except when the kings of France and England were at war: "When will this truce end between the Sterlings and the Tournois?" they cried, in their political songs; and their eyes were ever turned towards the north, asking: "What are the two kings about?"

They detested all foreigners, yet a restless turbulence, a wild passion for novelty and movement, impelled them to seek their alliance, whilst within they were torn by domestic quarrels and petty rivalries between man and man, town and town, province and province. They were vehemently fond of war, not from the ignoble thirst for gain, nor even from the elevated impulse of patriotic devotion, but for that which war presents of the picturesque and poetical; for the excitement, the noise, the display of the battle field; to see the lances glitter in the sun, and to hear the horses neigh in the wind. One word from a woman sufficed to send them to a crusade under the banner of the pope, for whom they had small liking, and risk their lives against the Arabs, of all the nations in the world that with which they had most sympathy and moral affinity.

With this volatility of character, they combined the graces of imagination, a taste for the arts and for refined enjoyments; they were industrious and rich; nature had given them all, all except political prudence and union, as descendants of the same race, as children of one country: their enemies combined to destroy them, but they would not combine to love each other, to defend each other, to make one common cause. They paid a severe penalty for this, in losing their independence, their wealth, and even their learning. Their language, the second Roman language, almost as polished as the first, has, in their own mouths, given place to a foreign tongue, the accentuation of which is repugnant to them, while their natural idiom, that of their liberty and of their glory, that of the noblest poetry of the middle ages, has become the patois of the peasant. But regret for these changes is futile: there are ruins made by time which time will never repair.

BOOK IX. FROM THE ORIGIN OF THE QUARREL BETWEEN KING HENRY II. AND ARCHBISHOP THOMAS BEKET, TO THE MURDER OF THE ARCHBISHOP.

A.D. 1160—1171.

Adventures of Gilbert Beket—Birth and education of Thomas Beket—Thomas, archdeacon and chancellor of England—Political conduct of Thomas Beket—Disputes between the king and the Anglo-Norman clergy—Beket archbishop of Canterbury—Coolness between the king and him—First quarrel between them—Excommunication of an Anglo-Norman baron—Hatred of the Anglo-Norman barons to the archbishop—Council of Clarendon—New laws of Henry II.—Importance of the quarrel between the king and the archbishop—Policy of the pope in the affair of Beket—The archbishop seeks to withdraw from England—A new assembly at Northampton—Archbishop Thomas accused and condemned—Second citation of the archbishop—His firmness—Appeal of the king and the bishops to the pope—Counter appeal of Beket—Flight of Beket—Letter of Henry II. to the king of France—Beket cordially received by the king of France—Conduct of pope Alexander III.—Thomas retires to the abbey of Pontigny—Excommunications pronounced by Beket—Intrigues of the court of Rome—Interview between the king and the two legates—Beket driven from Pontigny—Congress of Montmirail—Thomas abandoned by the king of France—Negotiations of Henry II.—Persecution of the Welsh priests—Affection of the Welsh people for Beket—Reconciliation of the king of France with Beket—Two new legates arrive in Normandy—Conference between these legates and Henry II.—Complaints of Beket against the court of Rome—The pope is compelled to declare his real views—Negotiations between the king and the archbishop—Interview and reconciliation of the king and the archbishop—Departure of archbishop Thomas for England—Attempts of the Normans against him—Two bishops denounce him to the king—Conspiracy of four Norman knights—Murder of the archbishop—Insurrection of the inhabitants of Canterbury—Beket regarded by the native English as a saint—Girauld de Barri elected bishop of St. David's—His banishment—His return and reinstallation—Persecution exercised upon him—He repairs to the court of Rome—He is condemned by the pope—Gratitude of the Welsh towards him—Petition of eight Welsh chieftains to Alexander III.—National motives for appeals to the pope in the middle ages.

In the reign of Henry I., there lived at London a young citizen, of Saxon origin, but sufficiently rich to associate with the Normans of that city, whom the historians call Beket. It is probable that his real name was Bek, and that the Normans among whom he lived, added to this a diminutive familiar to them, and made it Beket, as the English of race and language called it Bekie. About the year 1115, Gilbert Bekie or Beket, assumed the cross, either to accomplish a vow of penance, or to seek fortune in the Christian kingdom of Jerusalem. But he was less fortunate in Palestine than the squires and sergeants of Normandy had been in England, and instead of becoming like them, powerful and opulent by conquest, he was taken prisoner and reduced to slavery.

Degraded and despised as he was, the English slave inspired the daughter of a Saracen chief with love. He escaped by her assistance, and returned to his own country; and his deliverer, unable to live without him, soon abandoned the paternal roof and went in quest of him. She knew but two words intelligible to the people of the west: London and Gilbert. By aid of the former, she reached England in a ship laden with merchants and pilgrims; and by means of the latter, going from street to street, and repeating Gilbert! Gilbert! to the crowd who surrounded her, she found the man she loved. Gilbert Beket, after obtaining the opinion of several bishops on this wondrous incident, had his mistress baptised, changed her Saracen name into that of Matilda, and married her. This marriage made a great sensation by its singularity, and became the subject of several popular romances, two of which, preserved to our own times, exhibit the most touching details. In the year 1119, Gilbert and Matilda had a son, who was called Thomas Beket, according to the mode of double names introduced into England by the Normans.

Such, according to the narrative of some ancient chroniclers, was the romantic origin of a man destined to trouble in so violent and unexpected a manner the great grandson of William the Conqueror in the enjoyment of his power. This man, born to torment the Anglo-Norman race, received an education peculiarly calculated to give him access to the nobles and great men, and to gain their favour. At an early age he was sent to France, to study the laws, sciences, and language of the continent, and to lose the English accent, which was then considered in England altogether vulgar. Thomas Beket, on his return from his travels, was in a position to converse and associate with the most refined people of the dominant nation, without shocking their ears or their taste by a word or gesture recalling to mind his Saxon origin. He soon put this talent to use, and, still very young, insinuated himself into the familiar friendship of one of the rich barons resident near London. He became his daily guest, and the companion of his pleasures. He rode the horses of his patron, and sported with his birds and his dogs, passing the day in these amusements, forbidden to every Englishman who was not either the servant or associate of a man of foreign origin.

Thomas, full of gaiety and supple address, ingratiating, refined, obsequious, soon acquired a great reputation in high Norman society. The archbishop of Canterbury, Thibaut, who, from the primacy instituted by the Conqueror, was the first person next after the king, hearing the young Englishman spoken of, sent for him, and, liking him, attached him to his person. Having induced him to take orders, he appointed him archdeacon of his metropolitan church, and employed him in several delicate negotiations with the court of Rome. Under Stephen, archdeacon Thomas conducted with pope Eugenius an intrigue of the bishops of England, partisans of Matilda, the object of which was to obtain from the pope a formal prohibition to crown the king's son. When, a few years after, the son of Matilda had obtained the crown, Thomas Beket was presented to him as a zealous servant of his cause during the usurpation; for so was the reign of Stephen now designated by most of those who had before elected, crowned, and defended him against the pretensions of Matilda. The archdeacon of Canterbury made himself so agreeable to the new king, that a few years saw him raised by the royal favour to the high office of chancellor of England, that is to say, Keeper of the seal of three lions, the legal emblem of the power founded by the Conquest. Henry II. further confided to the archdeacon the education of his eldest son, and attached to these two offices large revenues, which, by a singular chance, were derived from places of fatal memory to the English: from the prebend of Hastings, the custody of the castle of Berkhamsted, and the governorship of the Tower of London.

Thomas was the assiduous companion and the intimate friend of king Henry, sharing his most frivolous and most worldly amusements. Raised in dignity above all the Normans of England, he affected to surpass them in luxury and seigneural pomp. He maintained in his pay seven hundred knights completely armed. The trappings of his horses were covered with gold and silver; his plate was magnificent, and he kept open table for persons of high rank. His purveyors procured, from the most remote places and at great expense, the rarest delicacies. The earls and barons esteemed it an honour to visit him: and no person coming to his house left it without a present of sporting dogs or birds or of horses or rich vestments. The great lords sent their sons to serve in his house and to be brought up there; he kept them for a considerable time, then armed them knights, and, in dismissing them, furnished each with a complete military equipment.

In his political conduct, Thomas demeaned himself as a true and loyal chancellor of England, in the sense which already attached to these words; that is to say, he laboured with all his might to maintain and even to augment the personal power of the king towards and against all men, without distinction of race or state, Normans or Saxons, priests or laymen. Although a member of the ecclesiastical order, he more than once engaged in a struggle with that order on behalf of the fisc or of the royal exchequer. When Henry undertook the war against the count of Toulouse, there was levied in England, to defray the expenses of the campaign, the tax which the Normans called escuage, the tax of shields, because it was payable by every possessor of an estate large enough to maintain a man-at-arms, who, within the time prescribed by the summons, did not appear at the muster, armed, and with his shield on his arm. The rich prelates and the rich abbots of Norman race, whose warlike spirit had mitigated since there had been no occasion for pillaging the Saxons, and no civil war among the Normans, excused themselves from obeying the military summons, because, they said, holy church forbad their shedding blood; they refused, further, for the same reason, to disburse the fine for non-appearance; but the chancellor insisted upon their paying it. The high clergy hereupon launched out in invectives against the audacity of Thomas: Gilbert Foliot, bishop of London, publicly accused him of plunging a sword into the bosom of his mother the church, and archbishop Thibaut, his former patron, threatened to excommunicate him. Thomas was in no way moved by these ecclesiastical censures; and shortly afterwards he again exposed himself to them, by fighting with his own hands in the war of Toulouse, and, deacon as he was, being the first to mount to the assault of the fortresses. One day, in an assembly of the clergy, several bishops asserted exaggerated maxims of independence as regarded the royal power: the chancellor, who was present, gainsaid them openly, and reminded the prelates, in a severe tone, that they were bound to the king in the same oath as the men of the sword were, by the oath to aid in preserving his life, his limbs, his dignity, and his honour.

The harmony which had subsisted in the first years of the Conquest, between the Norman barons and prelates, or, to speak in the language of the period, entre l'empire et le sacerdoce, had not been of long duration. Scarcely installed in the churches that William and his knights opened for them with their spears, they became ungrateful to those who had thus given them their titles and their possession. Concurrently with the disputes between the kings and the barons, differences arose between the barons and the clergy, between this order and royalty: these three powers became disunited, when the power, hostile to all three, the Anglo-Saxon race, ceased to be feared. The first William was wholly wrong in his calculation of an enduring union, when he gave to the ecclesiastical power established by the Conquest, a power before unknown in England. He thought to obtain by this means an augmentation of personal power; perhaps he was right, as far as regarded himself, but he did a great injury to his successors.

The reader is already acquainted with the royal decree by which, destroying the former responsibility of the priests to the civil judges, and giving to the members of the high clergy the privilege of being judges, William had instituted episcopal courts, taking cognizance of certain lay cases and of all proceedings instituted against priests. The Norman priests, priests of fortune, if we may use the expression, soon exhibited in England the most disorderly habits; they committed murders, rapes, and robbery, and as they were only responsible to their own order, these crimes were seldom punished, a circumstance which multiplied them to a fearful extent. Not long after the accession of Henry II., men reckoned up one hundred murders committed by priests who still remained alive and at liberty. The only means of checking and punishing these disorders was to abolish the ecclesiastical privilege established by the Conqueror, the temporary necessity for which had ceased, since the rebellions of the English were no longer feared. It was a reasonable reform, and, moreover, from a motive less pure, for the extension of their own territorial jurisdictions, the men of the sword desired it, and loudly censured the law decreed by their ancestors in the great council of king William the First.

For the sake of the temporal power of which he was the sovereign depositary, and actuated also, we may fairly believe, by motives of justice and reason, Henry II. determined to execute this reform; but that he might effect it easily and without disturbance, it was necessary that the primacy of Canterbury, that species of ecclesiastical royalty, should be in the hands of a man devoted to the person of the king, to the interests of the royal power, and the cause of the barons against the churchmen. It was also necessary that this man should be insensible to the greater or less degree of suffering of the native English; for the absurd law of clerical independence, formerly directed especially against the conquered population, after having greatly injured it while it still resisted, had become favourable to it. Every Saxon serf, who managed to be ordained priest, was thenceforth for ever exempt from servitude, because no action brought against him as a fugitive slave, either by the royal bailiff or by the officers of the seigneurs, could oblige him to appear before secular justice; as to the other justice, it would not consent to allow those who had become the anointed of Christ to return to the plough. The evils of national subjugation had multiplied in England the number of these priests from necessity, who had no church, who lived upon alms, but who, at least, differing from their fathers and their countrymen, were neither attached to the glebe, nor penned up within the walls of the royal towns. The faint hope of this resource against foreign oppression was, at this time, next to the miserable success of servility and adulation, the most brilliant prospect for a man of English race. The lower classes were accordingly as zealous for the clerical privileges as their ancestors had been against the resistance of the clergy to the common law of the country.

The chancellor, having passed his youth amongst men of high birth, seemed likely to have lost all national interest in the oppressed people of England. On the other hand, all his friendships were with laymen; he appeared to know no other rights in the world than those of royal power;

he was the favourite of the king, and the functionary best versed and most able in state affairs: the partisans of ecclesiastical reform, accordingly, thought him a peculiarly fit person to become the principal instrument in it; and long before the death of archbishop Thibaut, it was commonly rumoured at court that Thomas Beket would obtain the primacy. In the year 1161, Thibaut died, and the king immediately recommended his chancellor to the choice of the bishops, who rarely hesitated to elect a candidate thus introduced to them. On this occasion, however, they opposed an unwonted resistance. They declared that it would be against their conscience to raise to the see of the blessed Lanfranc a hunter and a war rior by profession, a man of the world and its turmoil.

On their part, the Norman lords who lived apart from the court, and more especially those across the Channel, violently opposed the nomination of Thomas. The king's mother used every effort to dissuade him from making the chancellor archbishop. Perhaps, too, many who had not seen Beket often enough or closely enough to place full assurance in him, felt a kind of presentiment of the danger of intrusting such great power to a man of English origin; but the king's confidence was unbounded. He persisted against all remonstrances, and swore by God that his friend should be primate of England. Henry II. was at this time holding his court in Normandy, and Thomas was with him. In one of their daily conferences on affairs of state, the king told him he must prepare to cross the sea on an important mission. "I will obey," answered the chancellor, "as soon as I shall have received my instructions." "What!" said the king, in an expressive tone, "dost thou not then guess what I mean, and that I am firmly resolved that thou shalt be archbishop?" Thomas smiled, and raising the lappet of his rich dress—"Look," said he, "at the edifying man, the holy man whom you would charge with such sacred functions. Besides, you have views as to ecclesiastical matters to which I could never lend myself; and I fear that if I were to become an archbishop, we should soon cease to be friends." The king received this answer as mere badinage, and immediately one of his justices, sir Richard de Lucy, conveyed to the bishops of England, who for thirteen months had delayed the election, the formal order to nominate the court candidate without delay. The bishops yielding to what they then called the royal hand, obeyed with apparent readiness.

Thomas Beket, the fifth primate since the Conquest, and the first of English race, was ordained priest, the Easter Saturday, June, of the year 1162, and the day after was consecrated archbishop by the prelate of Winchester, in the presence of the fourteen suffragans of the see of Canterbury. A few days after his consecration, those who saw him did not recognise him. He had laid aside his rich vestments, disfurnished his sumptuous house, broken with his noble guests, and made friends with the poor, with beggars, and Saxons. Like them he wore a coarse dress, lived on vegetables and water, and presented an humble and mournful air; it was for them only that his banquet-hall was thrown open and his money expended. Never was change of life more sudden, exciting so much anger on one side, so much enthusiasm on the other. The king, the earls, the barons, all those whom Beket had formerly served, and who had contributed to his elevation, deemed themselves betrayed and insulted. The Norman bishops and clergy, his old antagonists, remained in suspense, closely watching him; but he became the idol of the lower classes: the monks, the inferior clergy, and the natives of every rank saw in him a brother and a protector.

The astonishment and anger of the king passed all bounds when he received, in Normandy, a message from the primate, returning to him the royal seal, with a short message, "that he desired him to provide himself with another chancellor, for he could hardly suffice to the duties of one office, much less of two." Henry regarded as hostile an abdication by which the archbishop seemed desirous of releasing himself from every tie of dependence on him; and he was all the more irritated at this that he had in no degree expected it. His friendship was converted into bitter aversion, and on his return to England, he received his former favourite disdainfully, affecting to despise, in a monk's dress, him whom he had so often entertained in the habit of a Norman courtier, with a poniard at his side, a plumed cap on his head, and shoes with long points turned up like ram's horns.

The king at once commenced against the archbishop a regular system of attack and personal vexations. He took from him the archdeaconry of Canterbury, which he had continued to hold with the episcopal see; he next set up in opposition to him one Clerambault, a monk from Normandy, a man of daring character and ill life, who had cast aside his clerical habit in his own country, and whom the king now made abbot of the monastery of Saint Augustin at Canterbury. Clerambault, backed by the court, refused to take the oath of canonical obedience to the primate, in contravention of the order decreed by Lanfranc for the purpose of destroying the independence of the monks of Saint Augustin, when the Saxon monks still resisted the Normans. The new abbot grounded his refusal upon the plea that formerly, that is to say, before the Conquest, his monastery had enjoyed full and entire liberty. Beket asserted the prerogative which the first Norman kings had attached to his see. The dispute grew warm on both sides; and Clerambault, by the advice of the king and the courtiers, referred his cause to the judgment of the pope.

There were at this time two popes, the cardinals and Roman nobles not having been able to agree in their choice. Victor was acknowledged legitimate by the emperor of Germany, Frederick, but disowned by the kings of France and England, who recognised his competitor, Alexander, the third of that name, who, driven from Rome by his adversaries, was now in France. It was to the latter that the new abbot of Saint Augustin addressed a protest against the primate of England, in the name of the ancient liberties of his convent; and, singular circumstance, these same liberties, formerly annihilated by the authority of pope Gregory VII. in the interest of the Norman Conquest, were declared inviolable by pope Alexander III., at the request of a Norman abbot against an archbishop of English race.

Thomas, irritated at this defeat, returned the courtiers attack for attack, and as they had availed themselves against him, of rights anterior to the Conquest, he, too, proceeded to claim all that his church had lost since the invasion of the Normans. He summoned Gilbert de Clare to restore to the see of Canterbury the domain of Tunbridge, which his ancestor had received in fief; and he advanced pretensions of the same kind against several other barons, and against the officers of the royal demesne. These demands tended, indirectly, to shake to its foundation the right of property of all the Anglo-Norman families, and thus occasioned general alarm. Prescription was invoked, and Beket roundly replied that he knew of no prescription for injustice, and that whatever had been taken without a good title ought to be restored. The sons of the companions of William the Bastard thought the soul of Harold had descended into the body of him whom they themselves had made primate.

The archbishop did not give them time to recover from this first agitation; and in defiance of one of the customs most respected since the Conquest, he placed a priest of his own choice, one

Lawrence, in the vacant living of Eynesford, in Kent, in the domain of the Norman knight, William d'Eynesford, a tenant-in-chief of the king. This William, in common with all the Normans, claimed to dispose and had hitherto in fact disposed, of all the churches on his fief, just as much as of the farms. He named priests at his pleasure, as he did farmers, administrating, by men of his choice, religious aid and instruction to his Saxons, freemen and serfs; a privilege called the right of patronage. In virtue of this right, William d'Eynesford expelled the priest sent by the archbishop; but Beket excommunicated William for having done violence to a priest. The king interposed against the primate; he complained that, without previous reference to him, one of his tenants-in-chief had been excommunicated, a man liable to be called to his council and his court, and entitled to present himself before him at all times and in all places; a circumstance that had exposed his royal person to the danger of coming unwittingly in contact with an excommunicated man. "Since I was not informed of it," said Henry II., "and since my dignity has been injured in this essential point, the excommunication of my vassal is null; I require the archbishop, therefore, to withdraw it." The archbishop gave an unwilling assent, and the king's hatred grew more bitter than ever. "From this day forth," he said, publicly, "all is at an end between this man and me."

In the year 1164, the royal justiciaries, practically revoking the ancient law of the Conqueror, cited before them a priest, accused of rape and murder; but the archbishop of Canterbury, as supreme ecclesiastic of all England, declared the citation void, in virtue of the privileges of the clergy, as ancient in the country as those of the Norman royalty. He ordered his own officers to arrest the culprit, who was brought before an ecclesiastical tribunal, deprived of his prebend, whipped publicly with rods, and suspended from any office for several years. This affair, in which justice was respected to a certain point, but in which the royal judges were completely set aside, created a great sensation. The men of Norman descent were divided into two parties, one of which approved, and the other greatly blamed the primate. The bishops were for him; the men of the sword, the court and the king, against him. The king, naturally self-willed, suddenly converted the private dispute into a legislative question; and convoking, in a solemn assembly at Westminster, all the lords and prelates of England, he set forth to them the numerous crimes committed daily by priests. He added, that he had discovered a means of suppressing these crimes, in the ancient customs of his predecessors, and especially in those of his grandfather Henry I. He demanded, according to custom, of all the members of the assembly, whether they did not think it were well to revive the customs and laws of his ancestors. The laymen replied in the affirmative; but all the priests, with Thomas at their head, answered: "Saving the honour of God and of holy church." "There is poison in these words," answered the king furiously, and immediately departed, without saluting the bishops, and the affair remained undecided.

A few days after, Henry II. summoned separately to him, Roger, archbishop of York, Robert de Melun, bishop of Hereford, and several other prelates of England, whose purely French names sufficiently indicate their origin. By means of promises, long explanations, and perhaps insinuations, as to the presumed designs of the English Beket against all the nobles of England, and by various other reasonings, which the historians do not detail, the Anglo-Norman bishops were nearly all gained over to the king's party. They promised to favour the re-establishment of the alleged customs of Henry I., who, in truth, had never practised others than those of William the Conqueror, the founder of ecclesiastical privilege. Moreover, for the second time since his differences with the primate, the king addressed himself to pope Alexander; and the pope, complaisant to excess, without investigating the affair, declared him perfectly in the right. He even sent a special messenger with apostolical letters, enjoining all the prelates, and especially him of Canterbury, to accept and observe the laws of the king of England, whatever they might be. Left alone in his opposition, and deprived of all hope of support, Beket was fain to yield. He went to the king at his residence at Woodstock, and, in common with the other bishops, promised to observe faithfully, and without any restriction, all the laws that should be made. In order that this promise might be renewed authentically amidst a solemn assembly, king Henry convoked in the village of Clarendon in Wiltshire, not far from Winchester, the great council of the Anglo-Norman archbishops, bishops, abbots, priors, earls, barons, and knights.

The council of Clarendon was held in the month of March, 1164, under the presidency of John, bishop of Oxford. The king's officers set forth the reforms and new ordinances which he chose to entitle the ancient customs and liberties of his grandfather, Henry I. The bishops solemnly gave their adhesion to all they had heard; but Beket refused his, and accused himself of insane weakness in having promised to observe, without reserve, the laws of the king, whatever they might be. The whole Norman council was in a state of excitement. The bishops implored Thomas, and the barons threatened him. Two knights of the Temple begged of him, with tears in their eyes, not to dishonour the king; and as this scene was taking place in the great hall, there were discerned through the open doors, men in the adjoining apartment, buckling on their armour and their swords. The archbishop grew alarmed, and gave his word to observe the customs of the king's grandfather without restriction, only asking leave to examine them more at leisure and to verify them. The assembly appointed three commissioners to draw up these articles, and adjourned till the next day.

Towards evening, the archbishop departed for Winchester, where he was sojourning. He was on horseback, with a numerous train of priests, who, on the way, talked of the events of the past day. The conversation, at first tranquil, grew animated by degrees, and at length became a dispute, in which every one took the side accordant with his views. Some praised the conduct of the primate, or excused him for having yielded to the force of circumstances: others blamed him warmly, saying, that ecclesiastical liberty was about to perish in England through the fault of one man. The most excited of all was a Saxon, named Edward Grim, who carried the archbishop's cross; inflamed by the discussion, he spoke loud, and with great gesticulation: "I see plainly," said he, "that now-a-days those only are esteemed who exhibit towards princes boundless compliance; but what will become of justice? who will fight for her when the general has allowed himself to be conquered? or what virtues shall we henceforth find in him who has lost courage?" The latter words were heard by Thomas, whose attention had been attracted by the agitation and vehemence of the speaker's voice. "With whom are you angry, my son?" he said to the cross-bearer. "With yourself," answered the latter, full of a sort of enthusiasm; "with you, who have renounced your conscience in raising your hand to promise the observance of these detestable customs." This violent reproach, in which national feeling had, perhaps, as great a share as religious conviction, did not anger the archbishop, who, after a moment's reflection, addressing his countryman in gentle tones, said: "My son, you are right; I have committed a great fault, and I repent me of it."

Next day, the pretended customs or constitutions of Henry I. were produced in writing, divided into sixteen articles, containing an entire system of regulations, contrary to the ordinances of

William the Conqueror. Among them were several special regulations, one of which prohibited the ordaining as priests, without the consent of their lord, those who, in the Norman language, were called natifs or naifs, that is to say, serfs, all of whom were of native race. The bishops were required to affix their seals in wax at the foot of the parchment which contained the sixteen articles: they all did this, with the exception of Thomas, who, without openly retracting his first adhesion, demanded further delay. But the assembly completed the signatures, and this refusal of the archbishop did not prevent the new laws from being forthwith promulgated. Letters were sent from the royal chancery addressed to all the Norman judges or justiciaries of England and the continent. These letters ordered them, in the name of Henry, by the grace of God, king of England, duke of Normandy, duke of Aquitaine, and earl of Anjou, to have executed and observed by the archbishops, bishops, abbots, priests, earls, barons, burgesses, and peasants, the ordinances decreed in the great council of Clarendon.

A letter from the bishop of Poitiers, who received one of these despatches, brought to his diocese by Simon de Tournebu and Richard de Lucy, justiciaries, gives us in detail the instructions they contained. It is curious to compare these instructions with the laws published eighty years before, in the name of William I. and his barons; for, on the two sides, we find the same threats and the same penalties sanctioning contrary orders.

"They have forbidden me," says the bishop of Poitiers, "to summons before me any of my diocesans, on the demand of any widow, orphan, or priest, unless the officers of the king or of the lord of the fief, in which the cause in question arose, have made denial of justice; they have declared that if any one obey my summons, all his goods shall be forthwith confiscated and himself imprisoned; lastly, they have signified to me that if I excommunicate those who refuse to appear before my episcopal justice, such excommunicated persons may, without displeasing the king, attack my person or that of my priests, and my own property or that of my church."

From the moment when these laws, made by Normans in a village of England, were decreed as obligatory upon the inhabitants of nearly all the west of Gaul, upon the Angevins, Manseaux, Bretons, Poitevins and Aquitans, and all these various populations took sides in the quarrel between Henry and archbishop Thomas Beket, the court of Rome observed with more attention an affair which in so short a time had assumed such importance. This profoundly political court now meditated how to derive the greatest possible advantage, whether from war or from peace. Rotrou, archbishop of Rouen, a man less immediately interested than the Normans of England in the conflict between royalty and the English primacy, came on a mission from the pope to observe things more closely, and to propose, on speculation, an accommodation, under pontifical mediation; but the king, elevated with his triumph, replied that he would not accept this mediation, unless the pope would previously confirm the articles of Clarendon by an apostolic bull; the pope, who had more to gain than to lose by delay, refused to give his sanction until he was better informed on the subject.

Hereupon, Henry II. soliciting, for the third time, the aid of the pontifical court against his antagonist Beket, sent a solemn embassy to Alexander III., soliciting for Roger, archbishop of York, the title of apostolical legate in England, with the power of making and unmaking, appointing and deposing. Alexander did not grant this request, but he conferred on the king himself, by a formal commission, the title and powers of legate, with supreme authority to act as he thought fit in all points but one, the deprivation of the primate. The king, seeing that the pope's intention was to avoid coming to a conclusion, received this novel commission with displeasure, and at once sent it back. "We will employ our own power," said he, "and we think it will suffice to make those return to their duty who assail our honour." The primate, abandoned by the Anglo-Norman bishops and barons, and having only on his side poor monks, burgesses, and serfs, felt he should be too weak against his antagonist, if he remained in England, and he accordingly resolved to seek aid and an asylum elsewhere. He proceeded to the port of Romney, and twice went on board a vessel about to sail; but twice the wind was adverse, or the captain of the ship, fearing the king's anger, refused to sail.

Some months after the council of Clarendon, Henry II. convoked another at Northampton; and Thomas, in common with the other bishops, received his writ of summons. He arrived on the day appointed, and hired lodgings in the town; but he had scarce taken them, when the king filled them with his men and horses. Enraged at this insult, the archbishop sent word that he would not attend the parliament until his house was vacated by the king's horses and people. It was restored to him, indeed, but the uncertainty of the result of this unequal struggle made him fearful of engaging further in it, and however humiliating it was for him to be a suppliant to a man who had just insulted him, he repaired to the king's apartments, and demanded an audience. He waited vainly the whole day, while Henry was amusing himself with his falcons and his dogs. Next day, he returned and placed himself in the king's chapel during mass, and when the latter came out he left it, and approaching him with a respectful air, asked his permission to proceed to France. "Ay," answered the king; "but first you must give an account of several matters, and, especially, repair the injury you have done to John, my marshal, in your court."

This John, surnamed le Maréchal from his office, had some time previously appeared before the episcopal court of justice at Canterbury to demand an estate in the diocese, which he said he was entitled to hold in hereditary fief. The judges had rejected his claim as unfounded; whereupon the plaintiff had faussé the court, that is to say, protested on oath that it denied him justice. "I admit," said Thomas to the king, "that John le Maréchal appeared before my court; but far from receiving any wrong there from me, it is I who received wrong and insult from him; for he produced a psalter, and swore upon it that my court was false and denied him justice; whereas, according to the law of the land, whoever desires to impugn the court of any man, must swear upon the Holy Gospels." The king affected to regard this explanation as altogether frivolous. The accusation of denial of justice brought against the archbishop, was prosecuted before the great Norman council, who condemned him, and by their sentence, placed him at the king's mercy, that is to say, adjudged to the king all that he might be pleased to take of the property of the condemned man. Beket was at first inclined to protest against this sentence, and fausser jugement, as it was then termed, but the sense of his weakness determined him on making terms with his judges, and he compounded for a fine of 500 pounds of silver.

Beket returned to his house; his heart saddened with the annoyances he had experienced, grief threw him into an illness. As soon as the king heard this, he hastened to send him an order to appear next day before the council of Northampton, to account for the public moneys and revenues of which he had had the management when chancellor. "I am weak and suffering," he replied to the royal officers; "and besides, the king knows as well as I, that the day on which I was consecrated archbishop, the barons of his exchequer and Richard de Lucy, grand justiciary of England, declared me free and discharged from all bonds, all accounts, and all demands whatever." The legal citation remained in force; but Thomas did not appear to it, alleging his illness. Officers of justice, who came on several occasions to ascertain whether he was really incapable of walking, brought him a schedule of the king's demands, amounting to forty-four thousand marks. The archbishop offered to pay two thousand marks to relieve himself from this process, so disagreeable in itself, and so full of bad faith, but Henry refused any kind of accommodation, for it was not the money that influenced him in the affair. "Either I will be no longer king," said he, "or this man shall no longer be archbishop."

The delays allowed by law had expired: it was necessary for Beket to present himself, and, on the other hand, he had been warned that if he appeared at court, it would not be without danger for his liberty or his life. In this extremity, collecting all his strength of soul, he resolved to go forth, and to be firm. On the morning of the decisive day, he celebrated the mass of Saint Stephen, the proto-martyr, whose service commences by the words: "The princes sat and spoke against me." After the mass, he put on his pontifical robes, and taking his silver cross from the hands of him who usually bore it, he set forth, holding it in his right hand and the reins of his horse in the left. Alone, and still bearing his cross, he entered the great hall of council, traversed the crowd, and seated himself. Henry II. was then in a more retired apartment with his private friends, occupied in discussing, in this privy council, the means of getting rid of the archbishop with the least possible disturbance. The news of the unexpected array in which he had appeared confounded the king and his counsellors. One of them, Gilbert Foliot, bishop of London, hastily left the private apartment, and advancing to the place where Thomas was seated: "Why dost thou come thus," said he, "armed with thy cross?" and he laid hands upon the cross, in order to take possession of it, but the primate held it forcibly. The archbishop of York then joined the bishop of London, and said to Beket: "It is defying the king, our lord, to come thus in arms to his court, but the king has a sword whose edge is sharper than that of a pastoral staff." The other bishops, manifesting less violence, contented themselves with counselling Thomas, for his own sake, to place his dignity of archbishop at the king's mercy, but he did not heed them.

While this scene was passing in the great hall, Henry was greatly angered to find his adversary sheltered under his pontifical attire; the bishops, who, at first, had perhaps consented to projects of violence against their colleague, were now silent, taking care not to encourage the courtiers to lay hands on the stole or cross. The king's counsellors were at a loss what to do, when one of them said: "Why not suspend him from all his rights and privileges by an appeal to the holy father? This were a way to disarm him." This advice, hailed as a sudden inspiration, singularly pleased the king, and, by his order, the bishop of Chichester, advancing to Thomas Beket, at the head of his colleagues, addressed him thus:

"Some time thou wert our archbishop, and we were bound to obey thee; but because thou hast sworn fealty to our sovereign lord the king, that is, to preserve to the utmost of thy power, his life, limbs, and royal dignity, and to keep his laws, which he requires to be maintained, and, nevertheless, dost now endeavour to destroy them, particularly those which in a special manner concern his dignity and honour; we therefore declare thee guilty of perjury, and owe for the future no obedience to a perjured archbishop. Wherefore, putting ourselves and all that belongs to us under the protection of our lord the pope, we cite thee to his presence, there to answer to these accusations."

To this declaration, made with all the solemnity of legal forms, and all the emphasis of assured confidence, Beket merely replied: "I hear what you say!" The great assembly of lords was then opened, and Gilbert Foliot charged before it the late archbishop with having celebrated, in contempt of the king, a sacrilegious mass, under the invocation of the evil spirit; then came the demand of accounts of the revenues of the office of chancellor, and the claim of forty-four thousand marks. Beket refused to plead, alleging the solemn declaration which had theretofore released him from all ulterior responsibility. Hereupon the king rising, said to the barons and prelates: "By the faith ye owe me, do me prompt justice on this my liegeman, who, duly summoned, refuses to answer in my court." The Norman barons having put the matter to the vote, pronounced a sentence of imprisonment against Thomas Beket. When Robert, earl of Leicester, charged to read the sentence, pronounced in the French language, the first words of the accustomed form: "Hear the judgment pronounced against you," the archbishop interrupted him: "Son earl," said he, "hear you first. You are not ignorant how serviceable and how faithful, according to the state of this world, I have been to the king. In respect whereof it has pleased him to promote me to the archbishopric of Canterbury, God knows, against my own will. For I was not unconscious of my weakness; and rather for the love of him than of God, I acquiesced therein: which is this day sufficiently apparent; since God withdraws both himself and the king from me. But in the time of my promotion, when the election was made, prince Henry, the king's son, to whom that charge was committed, being present, it was demanded in what manner they would give me to the church of Canterbury? And the answer was, 'free and discharged from all the bonds of the court.' Being therefore free and discharged, I am not bound to answer, nor will I, concerning those things, from which I am so disengaged." Hereupon the earl said: "This is very different from what the bishop of London reported to the king." To which the archbishop replied, "Attend, my son, to what I say. By how much the soul is of more worth than the body, so much are you bound to obey God and me rather than an earthly king: nor does law or reason allow that children should judge or condemn their father: wherefore I disclaim the judgment of the king, of you, and of all the other peers of the realm, being only to be judged, under God, by our lord the pope: to whom, before you all, I here appeal, committing the church of Canterbury, my order, and dignity, with all thereunto appertaining, to God's protection and to his. In like manner do I cite you, my brethren and fellow-bishops, because you obey man rather than God, to the audience and judgment of the sovereign pontiff; and so relying on the authority of the catholic church, and the apostolical see, I depart hence."

After this sort of counter appeal to the power which his adversaries had first invoked, Beket rose and slowly traversed the crowd. A murmur arose on every side; the Normans cried: "The false traitor, the perjurer, whither goes he? Why let him to depart in peace? Remain here, traitor, and hear thy sentence." At the moment of quitting the hall, the archbishop turned round, and, looking coldly around him: "If my sacred order," said he, "did not forbid, I could answer in arms those who call me traitor and perjurer." He mounted his horse, went to the house where he lodged, had the tables laid for a great repast, and gave orders to assemble all the poor people in the town. Numbers came, whom he fed. He supped with them, and that same night, while the king and his Norman chiefs were prolonging their evening repast, he quitted Northampton, accompanied by two brothers of the Cistercian order, one of English race, named Skaiman, and the other of French origin, called Robert de Caune. After three days journeying, he reached the marshes of Lincolnshire, and concealed himself in the hut of a hermit. Thence, under a complete disguise and the assumed name of Dereman, the Saxon turn of which insured obscurity, he reached

Estrey, near Canterbury, where he stayed eight days; he then proceeded to the coast near Sandwich. It was now the 10th of November, a period at which to cross the Channel becomes dangerous. The archbishop went on board a small vessel, in order to avoid suspicion, and after a perilous transit, landed near Gravelines, and thence, on foot, and in a wretched plight, reached the monastery of Saint Bertin, in the town of Saint Omer.

On the news of his flight, a royal edict was published in all the provinces of the king of England, upon both shores of the ocean. In the terms of this edict, all the relations of Thomas Beket, in ascending and descending line, even the old men, pregnant women, and young children, were condemned to banishment. All the possessions of the archbishop and of his adherents, or of those who were asserted to be such, were sequestrated into the hands of the king, who made presents of them to those whose zeal he had experienced in this affair. John, bishop of Poitiers, who was suspected of friendship towards the primate and of favour to his cause, received poison from an unknown hand, and only escaped death by chance. Royal missives, in which Henry II. called Thomas his enemy, and forbad any counsel or aid being given to him or his friends, were sent to all the dioceses of England. Other letters, addressed to the earl of Flanders and all the high barons of that country, requested them to seize Thomas, late archbishop, a traitor to the king of England, and a fugitive with evil designs. Lastly, the bishop of London, Gilbert Foliot, and William, earl of Arundel, waited on the king of France, Louis VII., at his palace of Compiegne, and gave him a despatch, sealed with the great seal of England, and conceived in the following terms:—

"To his lord and friend, Louis, king of the French, Henry, king of England, duke of Normandy, duke of Aquitaine, and earl of Anjou—

"Know that Thomas, late archbishop of Canterbury, after a public sentence, rendered in my court by the high court of the barons of my kingdom, has been convicted of fraud, of perjury, and treason towards me, and has since traitorously fled my kingdom, with evil designs; I earnestly intreat you, therefore, not to allow this man, laden with crimes, or any of his adherents, to dwell on your lands, or any of your subjects to lend to my greatest enemy help, aid or counsel; for I protest that your enemies, or those of your kingdom, should receive none from me, or from any of my people. I expect from you that you will assist me in the vindication of my honour and the punishment of my enemy, as you would have me to do for you, did you need it."

From his asylum at Saint Bertin, Thomas awaited the effect of Henry's letters to the king of France and the earl of Flanders, in order to know in what direction he might proceed without peril. "The dangers are many, the king's hands are long" (wrote one of his friends, whom he had desired to feel the ground with Louis VII. and at the papal court, then established at Sens). "I have not yet applied to the Roman church," continues the same correspondent, "not knowing what to seek there as yet; they will do much against you, and little for you. Powerful and rich men will come to them, scattering money with both hands, which has ever greatly influenced Rome; whereas, poor and unaided as we are, what will the Romans care for us? You tell me to offer them two hundred marks; but the opposite party will propose four hundred, and I warrant you that—through love for the king and respect for his ambassadors—they will rather take the greater sum than wait for the less." The king of France gave a favourable reception to Thomas Beket's messenger, and after having taken counsel with his barons, granted to the archbishop and his companions in exile peace and security in his kingdom, adding graciously, that it was one of the ancient flowers of the crown of France to give protection to exile against their persecutors.

As to the pope, who had then no interest in counteracting the king of England, he hesitated two days ere he received those who came to Sens on the part of the archbishop; and when they asked him to send Thomas a letter of invitation to his court, he positively refused. But, with the aid of the free asylum granted him by the king of France, Beket came to the papal court without invitation. He was received coldly by the cardinals, most of whom at first treated him as a firebrand, and said he must check his enterprising temperament. He set forth to them the origin and whole history of his quarrel with Henry II. "I do not boast of great wisdom," said he, "but I should not be so mad as to oppose a king for trifles; for know, that had I consented to do his will in all things, there would now not be in his kingdom a power equal to mine." Without taking any decisive part in the dispute, the pope gave the fugitive permission to receive assistance in money and provisions from the king of France. He allowed him also to excommunicate all who had seized and detained the property of his church, excepting only the king, who had distributed it. At length, he asked from him a statement in detail of the articles of Clarendon, which pope Alexander himself, at the solicitation of king Henry, had approved, as it would seem, without having very carefully read them, if at all. Alexander, however, now deemed the sixteen articles utterly opposed to the honour of God and of holy church. He denounced them as tyrannical usurpations, and harshly reproached Beket with the passing adhesion he had given to them on the formal injunction of a pontifical legate. The pope excepted from this reprobation six articles only, and among them that which deprived the serfs of enfranchisement on becoming priests; and he solemnly pronounced anathema against the partisans of the other ten.

The archbishop then enlarged upon the ancient liberties of the church of Canterbury, to whose cause he said he had devoted himself; and then accusing himself of having been intrusively forced into his see, in contempt of those liberties, by the royal power, he resigned his ecclesiastical dignity into the hands of the pope. The pope reinvested him with it, saying, "that he, who had hitherto lived in affluence and delights, should now be taught, by the instructions of poverty, the mother of religion, to be the comforter of the poor when he returned to his see: wherefore he committed him over to one of the poor of Christ, from whom he was to receive, not a sumptuous, but simple entertainment, such as became a banished man and a champion of Christ." Beket was recommended to the superior of the abbey of Pontigny, on the confines of Burgundy and Champagne, where he was, for the present, to live as a simple monk. He submitted, assumed the habit of the Cistercian monks, and followed in all its rigour the discipline of monastic life.

In his retreat at Pontigny, Thomas wrote and received many letters, and among them several from the bishops of England and the whole body of Anglo-Norman clergy, full of bitter irony. "Fame has brought us the news that, renouncing for the future all plots against your lord and king, you humbly submit to the poverty to which you are reduced, and are expiating your past life by study and abstinence. We congratulate you hereupon, and counsel you to persevere in this good path." The same letter reproached him, in humiliating terms, with the lowness of his birth and his ingratitude towards the king, who, from the rank of a Saxon and a nothing, had raised him high as himself. Such were the views of the bishops and lords of England with reference to Beket. They were indignant at what they called the insolence of the parvenu; but among the lower classes, whether of clergy or laity, he was beloved and pitied, and ardent, though silent prayers were offered up that he might succeed in all he should undertake. In general, he had as adherents all those who were hostile to the Anglo-Norman government, whether as subjects by conquest or as political opponents. One of those who most courageously exposed themselves to persecution to follow him, was a Welchman named Culin. Another, a Saxon by birth, was thrown into prison, and remained there a long time, on his account; and the poison given to the bishop of Poitiers seems to prove that there was fear entertained of his partisans in southern Gaul, whose population unwillingly obeyed a king of foreign race; he had also zealous friends in Lower Brittany; but it does not appear that he had any warm partisans in Normandy, where obedience to king Henry was regarded as a national duty. The king of France favoured the antagonist of Henry II. from motives of a less elevated character, wholly exempt from any real affection, and simply for the purpose of embarrassing his political rival.

In the year 1166, Henry II. went to Normandy, and on the news of his landing, Thomas quitted the abbey of Pontigny and proceeded to Vezelay, near Auxerre. Here, in presence of the people assembled in the principal church on Ascension-day, he mounted the pulpit, and with the greatest solemnity, amid the ringing of bells and the light of the tapers, pronounced a sentence of excommunication against the defenders of the constitutions of Clarendon, against the detainers of the sequestered property of the church of Canterbury, and against those who kept priests or laymen imprisoned on his account. Beket also pronounced, by name, the same sentence against the Normans Richard de Lucy, Jocelin Bailleul, Alain de Neuilly, Renouf de Broc, Hugh de Saint Clair, and Thomas Fitz-Bernard, courtiers and favourites of the king. Henry was then at Chinon, a town in his earldom of Touraine, and on the new sign of life given by his adversary, a fit of violent fury seized upon him; carried beyond all self-possession, he cried that the traitor sought to kill him body and soul; that he was most unhappy in having none around him but traitors, not one of whom thought of freeing him from the annoyances he endured at the hands of one single man. He took off his cap, and threw it on the ground, unbuckled his belt, divested himself of his clothes, and snatching the silk coverlid from his bed, rolled in it before all his nobles, biting the mattress and tearing the wool and hair with his teeth.

Coming a little to himself, he dictated a letter to the pope, reproaching him with protecting traitors, and he sent to the clergy of Kent an order to write in their own name to the sovereign pontiff, saying that they repudiated the sentences of excommunication pronounced by the archbishop. The pope replied to the king—begging him not to communicate his letters to any living soul—that he was ready to give him full satisfaction, and that he had deputed two extraordinary legates to him with power to absolve all excommunicated persons. And, in point of fact, he sent to Normandy, under this title and with this power, William and Otho, cardinal-priests, the first openly sold to the king, and the second ill-disposed to the archbishop. While these two ambassadors were traversing France, announcing on their way that they were about to content the king of England and confound his enemy, the pope, on his return to Italy, sent word to Thomas to place all confidence in them, and begged him, in consideration of the care which he had shown in choosing men favourable to his cause, to employ himself with the earl of Flanders in obtaining alms for the Roman church.

But the archbishop was warned of the little confidence these assurances merited, and bitterly complained, in a letter addressed to the pope himself, of the duplicity employed against him.

"There are some," said he, "who say that you have purposely prolonged my exile, and that of my companions in misfortune for a year, in order to make, at our expense, a more advantageous bargain with the king. I hesitate to believe this; but to give me as judges such men as your two legates, is it not truly giving me the chalice of passion and of death?" In his indignation, Thomas sent to the papal court despatches in which he did not spare the king, calling him a tyrant full of malice; these letters were given, and perhaps sold, to Henry II. by the Roman chancery. Before entering, according to their instructions, upon a conference with the king, the legates invited the archbishop to a private interview; he went to it full of a distrust, and a contempt ill concealed. The Romans conversed with him solely on the grandeur and power of king Henry, of the low estate from which the king had raised him, and of the danger he ran in braving a man so powerful and so beloved by holy church.

Arrived in Normandy, the pontifical envoys found Henry II. surrounded by Anglo-Norman lords and prelates. The discussion opened with the causes of the quarrel with the primate; Gilbert Foliot, bishop of London, stated the case; he said that the dispute arose from a sum of forty-four thousand marks, of which the archbishop obstinately refused to give an account, pretending that his ecclesiastical consecration had exempted him from all debt, as his baptism had freed him from all sin. Foliot added to these witticisms other jests about the excommunications pronounced by Beket, saying that they did not receive them in England from pure economy of horses and men, seeing that they were so numerous that forty couriers would not suffice to distribute them all. At the moment of separating, Henry humbly intreated the cardinals to intercede for him with the pope, that he would deliver him from the torment caused him by one single man. In pronouncing these words, the tears came into his eyes; cardinal William, who was sold to him, wept as from sympathy; cardinal Otho could scarce refrain from laughter.

When pope Alexander, reconciled with all the Romans by the death of his competitor Victor, had returned to Italy, he sent from Rome letters to Henry II., wherein he announced that Thomas should assuredly be suspended from all authority as archbishop, until he should regain the king's favour. Nearly at the same time, a diplomatic congress was held at Ferté-Bernard in Vendomois, between the kings of England and France. The former publicly exhibited the pope's letters, saying with a joyous air: "Thank Heaven, our Hercules is without his club. He can do nothing for the future against me or against my bishops, and his terrible threats are now merely ridiculous, for I hold in my purse the pope and all his cardinals." This confidence in the success of his intrigues gave the king of England a new ardour of persecution against his antagonist; and shortly after, the general chapter of Citeaux, of which the abbey of Pontigny was a dependent, received a despatch, wherein Henry II. signified to the priors of the order that if they valued their possessions in England, Normandy, Anjou, and Aquitaine, they must cease to harbour his enemy.

The reception of this letter caused great alarm in the chapter of Citeaux. The superior immediately set out for Pontigny, with a bishop and several abbots of the order. He came to Beket, and, in the name of the order, said to him mildly, but significatively: "God forbid the chapter should, on such injunctions, expel you; but it is a notification we give you, that you may in your prudence decide what is to be done." Thomas replied, without hesitation, that he would prepare for his departure. He quitted the monastery of Pontigny in the month of November 1168, after two years residence there, and then wrote to the king of France to request another asylum. On receiving his letter, the king exclaimed: "Oh, religion! religion! what has become of thee?

They who call themselves dead to the world banish, for the world's sake, an exile in the cause of God!" He received the archbishop on his territory, but it was evidently as a matter of policy that he showed himself, on this occasion, more humane than the monks of Citeaux.

About a year after, a reconciliation took place between the kings of France and of England; a meeting was appointed at Montmirail in Perche, to settle the terms of the truce; for, since the Normans had reigned in England, there had been but brief intervals of peace between the two countries. Meantime frequent assemblies were held in or near the towns on the frontiers of Normandy, Maine, and Anjou; and the contending interests were discussed with the greater facility, that the kings and lords of France and of England spoke exactly the same language. The former brought Thomas Beket with them to the congress of Montmirail. Availing themselves of the influence which his state of dependence on them gave them over him, they had induced him to consent to make, under their auspices, his submission to the king of England, and to become reconciled with him, the archbishop yielding to their interested solicitations, from weariness of his wandering life, and of the humiliation he felt in eating the bread of strangers.

When the two antagonists met, Thomas, quelling his pride, placed one knee on the ground, and said to the king: "My lord, the whole quarrel existing between us, I submit entirely to your judgment, as sovereign arbiter, in every point, saving the honour of God." But the moment this fatal reservation passed the lips of the archbishop, the king, setting at nought his conciliatory proceeding and his humble posture, overwhelmed him with a torrent of abuse, calling him proud, ungrateful, and heartless; then, turning to the king of France: "Know you," said he, "what would befal me, were I to admit this reservation? He would pretend that all that pleases me, and does not please him, is contrary to the honour of God; and by means of these two words, he would render me a nullity. But I will make him a concession. Certes, there have been before me in England kings less powerful than I, and, doubtless, also, there have been in the see of Canterbury, archbishops more holy than he; let him only act towards me as the greatest and most holy of his predecessors has acted towards the least of mine, and I shall be content."

To this evidently ironical proposition, comprehending fully as much mental reservation on the part of the king as Thomas had comprised in the clause, saving the honour of God, the whole assembly, French and English, cried out that it was quite enough, that the king humbled himself sufficiently; and, the archbishop remaining silent, the king of France, in his turn, said to him: "Well, why do you hesitate? here is peace offered you." The archbishop calmly replied that he could not in conscience accept peace, yield himself up and his liberty of action, unless saving the honour of God. At these words, the whole assembly, of both nations, vied with each other in charging him with measureless pride, of outrecuidance, as it was then called. One of the French barons loudly exclaimed, that he who resisted the counsel and unanimous will of the lords of two kingdoms was no longer worthy of an asylum. The kings remounted their horses, without saluting the archbishop, who withdrew, deeply dejected. No one in the name of the king of France offered him food or lodging, and on his return he was compelled to live on the alms of priests and of the populace.

That his vengeance might be complete, Henry II. only needed somewhat more decision on the part of pope Alexander. To obtain the deprivation, the object of all his efforts, he exhausted the resources which the diplomacy of the time placed at his disposal, resources far more extensive that we at all imagine at the present time. The Lombard towns, the national cause of which was then combined with that of the pope against the emperor Frederic I., almost all received messages from the king of England. He offered the Milanese three thousand marks of silver, and to defray the expenses of repairing their walls, which the emperor had destroyed; to the Cremonese, he offered three thousand marks; a thousand to the Parmesans, and as many to the Bolognese, if they would solicit from Alexander III., their ally, the degradation of Beket, or at least his translation to an inferior see. Henry also applied to the Norman lords of Apulia to employ their credit in favour of a king, issue of the same race with themselves. He promised to the pope himself as much money as he should require to extinguish at Rome the last remnant of schism, and, further, ten thousand marks for himself, with power absolutely to dispose of the nomination to the bishoprics and archbishoprics vacant in England. The last offer proves that, in his hostility against archbishop Thomas, Henry II., at this time, by no means aimed at the diminution of the papal authority. New edicts forbad, under extremely severe penalties, the admission into England of the friends or relations of the exile, or of letters from him or his friends, or of letters from the pope, favourable to his cause, letters which might well be apprehended in the very probable event of some diplomatic manœuvring on the part of the pontifical court.

To maintain a correspondence with England, despite this prohibition, the archbishop and his friends employed the disguise of Saxon names, which, on account of the low condition of those who bore them, awakened little disquietude in the Norman authorities. John of Salisbury, one of the ablest authors of the age, and who had lost his property from his attachment to the primate, wrote under the name of Godrik, and styled himself a knight in the pay of the commune of Milan. As the Milanese were then at war with the emperor Frederic, he put down, in his letters, to the account of the latter, all the reproaches he intended to apply to the king of England. The number of those whom the Norman authority persecuted on account of this affair was considerably augmented by a royal decree, couched in these terms: "Let every Welshman, priest or layman, who shall enter England without letters of licence from the king, be seized and thrown into prison, and let all Welsh persons be expelled the schools in England." To understand the reason of this ordinance and the point which most sensibly wounded the interests of the king and the Anglo-Norman barons in the resistance of Thomas Beket, the reader must turn his attention for a moment to the territories recently acquired or conquered from the Cambrian nation.

Wales, overrun, as we have seen, by invasions in every direction, exhibited the same scenes of oppression and of national struggle which England had presented in the first fifty years of the Conquest. There were daily insurrections against the conquerors, especially against the priests who had come in the train of the soldiers, and who, soldiers themselves, under a peaceful habit, devoured with their relations, settled with them, what war had spared. Forcing themselves on the natives as spiritual pastors, they seized, in virtue of the patent of a foreign king, the sees of the former prelates, elected by the clergy and people of the country. To receive the sacraments of the church from the hands of a foreigner and an enemy was, for the Welsh, an insupportable affliction, perhaps the most cruel tyranny of the conquest. Accordingly, from the moment when archbishop Beket raised his front against the king of England, the national opinion in Cambria strongly declared itself for the archbishop, first for the popular reason that every enemy of an enemy is a friend, and next, because a prelate of Saxon race, struggling with the grandson of the conqueror of the Saxons, seemed in some measure the representative of the religious rights of all the men forcibly united under the Norman domination. Although Thomas Beket was entirely a stranger to the Cambrian nation in affection as in birth, although he had never manifested the slightest indication of interest for it, this nation loved him, and in the same way, would have loved also any stranger who, however distant, however indirectly, however uninfluenced by friendly views to it, had awakened in it the hope of obtaining once more priests born in its bosom and speaking its language.

This patriotic sentiment, deeply rooted in the people of Wales, was manifested with invincible determination in the ecclesiastical chapters, where foreigners and natives were mingled together. It was searcely ever possible to induce the latter to give their votes to any but a Welshman of pure race without any admixture of foreign blood; and, as the choice of such candidates was never confirmed by the royal power of England, and as, on the other hand, nothing could overcome the inveteracy of the voters, there was a sort of perpetual schism in most of the churches of Cambria, a schism more reasonable than many that have made more noise in the world. It was thus that with the cause of archbishop Thomas, whatever his personal motives, whether ambition, love of opposition and self-will, or the conscientious conviction of a great duty, was combined, in every direction, a national cause, that of the races of men reduced to servitude by the ancestors of the king whose adversary he had declared himself.

The archbishop, deserted by the king of France, his former protector, and reduced to subsist upon alms, lived at Sens, in a poor inn. One day, while seated in the common room, conversing with his companions in exile, a messenger from king Louis presented himself, and said to them: "The king my lord, invites you to proceed to his court." "Alas!" cried one of the spectators, "it is doubtless to banish us, and so we shall be excluded from both kingdoms, and have no hope of assistance but from those thieves of Romans, who occupy themselves solely in seizing the spoils of the unfortunate and the innocent." They followed the messenger, sad and thoughtful, as men anticipating a great calamity. But to their great surprise, the king received them with extraordinary marks of affection and even of tenderness. He wept on seeing them, and casting himself at Thomas's feet, said to him: "It is you, my father, it is you alone who saw justly; all the rest of us were blind, in counselling you against God. I repent, my father, I repent, and promise, for the future, no more to desert you and yours." The true cause of this sudden change was a new project of war on the part of the king of France against Henry II.

The pretext of this war was the vengeance exercised by the king of England upon the Breton and Poitevin refugees, whom the other king had given up to him on condition of his receiving them into his grace. It is probable that, in signing the treaty of Montmirail, king Louis had in no degree supposed that the clause in their favour, inserted out of very shame, would be executed; but shortly after, when Henry II. had put the richest of the Poitevins to death, the king of France, having reasons of self-interest for renewing the war, availed himself of the bad faith of the Angevin towards the refugees, and his first act of hostility was to restore to Thomas Beket his protection and support. Henry II. complained, by a special message, of this flagrant violation of the treaty of Montmirail. "Go," said the king of France to the messenger, "go and tell your king, that if he adheres to the customs of his ancestor, I may surely adhere to my hereditary right to aid the exiled."

Ere long, the archbishop, resuming the offensive, hurled new sentences of excommunication against the courtiers, servants, and chaplains of the king of England, and especially against the retainers of the property of the see of Canterbury. He excommunicated so great a number, that, in the doubt whether the sentence had not been secretly ratified by the pope, there was not, in the king's chapel, a single priest who at the service of the mass dared give him the kiss of peace. Thomas further sent to the bishop of Winchester, Henry, Stephen's brother, and consequently a secret enemy of Henry II., a mandate interdicting in England all religious ceremonies, except the baptism of infants and the confession of the dying, unless the king, within a certain time, gave satisfaction to the church of Canterbury. One English priest, upon this mandate, refused to celebrate mass; but his archdeacon reprimanded him, saying: "If you were ordered by the archbishop not to eat again, would you abstain from eating?" The sentence of interdict not having obtained the sanction of any bishop in England, was not executed; and the bishop of London departed for Rome, with messages and presents from the king. He brought back, purchased at heavy cost, a formal declaration, affirming that the pope had not ratified and would not ratify, the sentences of excommunication pronounced by the archbishop. The pope himself wrote to Beket, ordering him to recal these sentences with the shortest delay.

But the court of Rome, always careful to procure personal sureties on every occasion, required that each excommunicated person, on receiving absolution, should take an oath never to separate from the church. All of them, and especially the king's chaplains, would readily have consented to this, but the king would not permit it, preferring to leave them under the sword of Saint Peter (gladius beati Petri, spiculum beati Petri, as the phrase ran) than to deprive himself of a means of disquieting the Romish church. To terminate this new dispute, two legates, Vivian and Gratian, went to Henry, at Domfront. He was hunting at the time of their arrival, and returned from the forest to visit them at their lodgings. During his interview with them, the whole band of hunters, with young Henry, the king's eldest son, at their head, came to the inn where the legates were, shouting and sounding their horns to announce the taking of a stag. The king abruptly interrupting his conversation with the envoys from Rome, went to the hunters, complimented them, said that he made them a present of the animal, and then returned to the legates, who exhibited no anger, either at the strange incident, or at the cavalier manner in which the king treated them and the object of their mission.

A second conference took place in the park of Bayeux; the king proceeded thither on horseback, with several bishops of England and Normandy. After some unimportant conversation, he asked the legates if they had clearly decided not to absolve his courtiers and chaplains without conditions. The legates said this was impossible. "Then, by the eyes of God," exclaimed the king, "I never again in my life will hear speak of the pope," and he hastened to his horse. The legates, after some show of resistance, granted all he asked. "Then," said Henry II., "you will proceed to England, in order that the excommunication may be raised as solemnly as possible." The legates hesitated to answer. "Well," said the king, impatiently, "do as you please; but know that I take no account either of you or of your excommunications, and care no more for them than for an egg." He hastily mounted his horse, but the Norman archbishops and bishops ran after him, calling to him to dismount and renew the conversation. "I know, I know as well as you what they can do," said the king, still continuing his way; "they will place my lands under interdict; but I, who can take a walled town every day, can punish a priest who shall come and place my kingdom under interdict."

At last, the excitement on both sides being appeased, a new discussion was entered upon respecting the king's quarrel with Thomas Beket. The legates said that the pope desired to see an end of this scandalous affair; that he would do much to obtain peace, and that he would undertake to make the archbishop more docile and tractable. "The pope is my spiritual lord and father," said the king, greatly softened; "and I consent, for my part, to do much at his request; I will even restore, if necessary, to him of whom we speak, his archbishopric and my peace, for him and all those who, on his account, are banished from my lands." The interview at which the terms of peace were to be agreed upon was fixed for the next day; but at this conference, king Henry practised the expedient of reservations for which he so reproached the archbishop, and sought to insert the condition, "saving the honour and dignity of his kingdom." The legates refused to accede to this unexpected clause; but their modified refusal, though suspending the final decision of the affair, did not destroy the good understanding between them and the king. They gave full power to Rotrou, archbishop of Rouen, to go and by the pope's authority relieve Gilbert Foliot, bishop of London, from his sentence of excommunication. They sent at the same time, letters to Beket, recommending him, in the name of the obedience he owed to the church, humility, gentleness, and circumspection towards the king.

It will be remembered with what assiduity William the Bastard and his councillor, Lanfranc, laboured to establish, for the better maintenance of the conquest, the absolute supremacy of the see of Canterbury. It will also be remembered that one of the privileges attached to this supremacy, was the exclusive right of crowning the kings of England, least the metropolitan of York might one day be led, by the rebellion of his diocesans, to oppose a Saxon king, anointed and crowned by him, to kings of the conquering race. This danger no longer existing, after a century of possession, the politicians of the court of Henry II., to weaken the power of Thomas Beket, resolved to create a king of England, anointed and crowned without his participation.

For this purpose, king Henry presented his eldest son to the Anglo-Norman barons, and set forth, that, for the welfare of his vast provinces, a colleague in the royalty had become necessary to him, and that he desired to see Henry his son decorated with the same title as himself. The barons offered no obstacle to the views of their king, and the young man received the royal unction from the hands of the archbishop of York, assisted by the suffragan bishops of the province of Canterbury, in Westminster Abbey, immediately dependent on the latter see. All these circumstances constituted, according to the ecclesiastical code, a complete violation of the privileges of the English primacy. At the banquet which followed the coronation, the king waited on his son at table, saying, in the effusion of his paternal joy, that from that day the royalty no longer belonged to him. He little expected, that in a few years, this phrase, so heedlessly uttered, would be raised up against him, and that his own son would call upon him no longer to bear the title of king, since he had solemnly abdicated it.

The violation of the ancient rights of the primacy took place with the consent of the pope; for previous to undertaking it, Henry II. had provided himself with an apostolic letter, authorising him to crown his eldest son how he pleased and by whom he pleased. But, as this letter was to remain secret, the Roman chancery did not scruple to send Thomas Beket another letter, equally private, in which the pope protested that the coronation of the young king by the archbishop of York had been performed against his will, and that equally against his will had the bishop of London been relieved from his excommunication. At these manifest falsehoods, Beket lost all patience; and he addressed to a Roman cardinal, named Albert, in his own name and that of his companions in exile, a letter full of reproaches, the bitterness of which passed all bounds:

"I know not how it is that at the court of Rome it is ever the cause of God that is sacrificed; so that Barabbas is saved and Christ is put to death. This is the seventh year in which, by the authority of that court, I remain proscribed, and the church in suffering. The unfortunate, the banished, the innocent, are condemned before you, for the sole reason that they are weak, because they are the poor of Jesus Christ, and that they demand justice. I know that the envoys of the king distribute or promise my spoils to the cardinals and courtiers; let the cardinals rise against me, if they will; let them arm for my destruction, not only the king of England, but the whole world: I will never swerve from the fidelity due to the church, in life or in death, placing my cause in the hands of God, and ready to endure proscription and exile. It is my firm resolve never again to solicit the pontifical court. Let those repair to it who avail themselves of iniquity, and who return full of pride at having trampled on justice and made innocence a prisoner."

This energetic attack had not the effect of making ultramontane policy retrograde one single step; but positive menaces on the part of the king of France, then at open rupture with the other king, lent efficacious aid to the remonstrances of the exile. "I demand," wrote Louis VII. to the pope; "I demand that you at length renounce your deceitful and dilatory proceedings." Pope Alexander, who found himself, as he expressed it, in the position of an anvil between two hammers, seeing that the hammer of the king of France was raised to strike, became all at once of opinion that the cause of the archbishop was really the cause of Heaven. He sent to Thomas a brief, suspending the archbishop of York and all the prelates who had assisted at the coronation of the young king; and even went so far as to menace Henry II. with ecclesiastical censure, unless he forthwith vindicated the primate against the courtiers who held his property and the bishops who had usurped his privileges. Henry II., alarmed at the good understanding between the pope and the king of France, yielded for the first time; but it was from motives of interest, and not from fear of a banished man, whom all his protectors abandoned and betrayed in turns.

The king of England accordingly announced that he was prepared to open definitive negotiations for peace. The archbishop of York and the bishops of London and Salisbury sought to dissuade him from this. Labouring with their utmost efforts to prevent any reconciliation, they told the king that peace would be of no advantage to him, unless the donations made out of the property of the see of Canterbury were permanently ratified. "And it is known," they added, "that the annulling of these royal gifts will be the principal feature of the archbishop's demands." Grave reasons of external policy determined Henry II. not to adopt these counsels, though they perfectly agreed with his personal aversion to Thomas Beket. Negotiations commenced; there was an exchange of letters between the king and the archbishop, indirectly and by third hands, as between two contracting powers. One of Thomas's letters, drawn up in the form of a diplomatic note, is worth giving as a curious specimen of the diplomacy of the middle ages.

"The archbishop," said Beket, speaking of himself, "insists that the king, if the reconciliation take place, shall give him the kiss of peace publicly; for this formality is a solemn custom with all nations and all religions, and nowhere, without it, has any peace been concluded between persons previously enemies. The kiss of any other than the king, of his son, for example, would not answer the end, for it might be inferred that the archbishop had re-entered into grace with the son rather than with the father; and if once this idea were spread abroad, what resources would it not furnish to the malevolent? The king, on his part, might pretend that his refusal to give the kiss meant that he did not engage himself willingly, and might, therefore, afterwards break his word, without subjecting himself to the brand of infamy. Besides, the archbishop remembers what happened to Robert de Silly and the other Poitevins who made their peace at Montmirail; they were received into the grace of the king of England with the kiss of peace, and yet, neither this token of sincerity publicly given nor the consideration due to the king of France, mediator in the affair, secured to them peace or life. It is not, therefore, too much to demand this guarantee, in itself, even if given, so insecure."

On the 22nd July, 1170, in a vast meadow between Freteval and Laferté-Bernard, a solemn congress was held for the double pacification of the king of France with the king of England and of the latter with Thomas Beket. The archbishop proceeded thither, and when, after the discussion of political affairs, the assembly approached his own, he had a conference apart, in the centre of the field, with his adversary. The archbishop demanded of the king, first, that he should be allowed to punish the injury done to the dignity of his church by the archbishop of York and his own suffragans. "The coronation of your son by another than myself," said he, "has enormously wounded the ancient rights of my see." "But who then," asked the king, warmly, "who then crowned my great grandfather William, the conqueror of England? Was it not the archbishop of York?" Beket replied, that at the period of the conquest the church of Canterbury was without a legitimate pastor; that it was, so to speak, captive under one Stigand, an archbishop repudiated by the pope, and, in this emergency, it was necessary that the prelate of York, whose title was better founded, should crown the Conqueror. After this historical reference, the worth of which the reader can appreciate, and some other arguments, the king promised to remedy all Beket's complaints; but as to the demand for the kiss of peace, he politely evaded it, saying to the archbishop: "We shall soon meet in England, and will embrace there."

On leaving the king, Beket saluted him, bending his knee; and with a reciprocal courtesy, which astonished all present, Henry II., as he mounted his horse, arranged his robes, and held the stirrup for him. Next day some return of their old familiarity was remarked between them. Royal messengers conveyed to the young Henry, the colleague and lieutenant of his father, a letter couched in these terms: "Know that Thomas of Canterbury has made his peace with me, to my entire satisfaction. I command you then to give him and his all their possessions freely and peaceably." The archbishop returned to Sens to make ready for the journey; his friends, poor and dispersed in various places, prepared their slight luggage, and then assembled to wait upon the king of France, who, in their own words, had not rejected them when the world abandoned them. "You are then about to depart?" said Louis VII. to the archbishop: "I would not for my weight in gold have given you this counsel; and, if you will believe me, do not trust your king until you have received the kiss of peace."

Several months had already elapsed since the reconciliation interview; yet, notwithstanding the ostensible order despatched by the king to England, no instance was known wherein the usurpers of property of the church of Canterbury had been made to restore it; on the contrary, they publicly ridiculed the credulity and simplicity of the primate, in thinking himself restored to favour. The Norman, Renouf de Broc, went so far as to say that, if the archbishop came to

England, he would not have time given him wherein to eat a whole loaf. Beket further received from Rome letters warning him that the king's peace was only a peace in words, and recommending him, for his own safety, to be humble, patient, and circumspect. He solicited a second interview, for the purpose of having an explanation upon these fresh points of complaint, and the meeting took place at Chaumont, near Amboise, under the auspices of the earl of Blois. On this occasion Henry's manner was frigid, and his people affected not to notice the archbishop. The mass celebrated in the royal chapel was a mass for the dead, selected expressly, because, in this service, those present do not mutually give the kiss of peace at the gospel. The archbishop and the king, before they separated, rode some way together, loading each other with bitter reproaches. At the moment of leavetaking, Thomas fixed his eyes upon Henry, in an expressive manner, and said to him solemnly: "I believe I shall never see you again." "Do you then take me for a traitor?" warmly exclaimed the king, who understood the meaning of these words. The archbishop bowed and departed.

Several times on the day of reconciliation, Henry II. had promised that he would come to Rouen to meet the prelate, pay all the debts he had contracted in exile, and thence accompany him to England, or, at least, direct the archbishop of Rouen to accompany him. But on his arrival at Rouen, Beket found neither the king, nor the promised money, nor that any order to accompany him had been transmitted to the archbishop. He borrowed three hundred livres, and by means of this sum proceeded to the coast near Boulogne. It was now the month of November, the season of storms; the primate and his companions were obliged to wait some days at the port of Wissant, near Calais. One day that they were walking upon the beach, they saw a man running towards them, whom they at first took to be the master of their vessel, coming to summon them on board; but the man told them that he was a priest, and dean of the church of Boulogne, and that the count, his lord, had sent him to warn them not to embark, for that troops of armed men were waiting on the coast of England, to seize or kill the archbishop. "My son," answered Thomas, "were I sure of being dismembered and cut to pieces on the other shore, I would not stay my steps. Seven years absence is enough both for the pastor and for his flock." The travellers embarked; but willing to derive some advantage from the warning they had received, they avoided a frequented port, and landed in Sandwich bay, at the spot nearest to Canterbury.

Notwithstanding their precautions, the report spread that the archbishop had landed near Sandwich. Hereupon the Norman Gervais, viscount of Kent, marched to that town, with all his men-at-arms, accompanied by Renouf de Broc and Renauld de Garenne, two powerful lords and Beket's mortal enemies. At the same report, the burgesses of Dover, men of English race, took up arms, on their part, to defend the archbishop, and the people of Sandwich armed for the same purpose, when they saw the Norman horse approach. "If he has the audacity to land," said the viscount Gervais, "I will cut his head off with my own hand." The ardour of the Normans was somewhat modified by the attitude of the people; they advanced, however, with drawn swords, when John, dean of Oxford, who accompanied the prelate, rushed to meet them, exclaiming: "What are you doing? Sheathe your swords; would you have the king pass for a traitor?" The populace collecting, the Normans returned their swords to their scabbards, contented themselves with searching the coffers of the archbishop for any papal briefs they might contain, and returned to their castles.

Upon the whole road from Sandwich to Canterbury, the peasants, artisans, and tradesmen came to meet the archbishop, saluting him, shouting, and collecting in great numbers; but scarcely any man of wealth, or rank, or simply of Norman race, welcomed the exile on his return; on the contrary, they avoided the places through which he passed, shutting themselves up in their houses, and spreading from castle to castle the report that Thomas Beket was letting loose the serfs in town and country, who were following him, drunk with frenzied joy. From his metropolitan city, the primate repaired to London, to salute the son of Henry II. All the citizens of the great city were collected in the streets to receive him; but he had scarcely entered it when a royal messenger stayed his progress in the name of the young king, and communicated to him the formal order to return to Canterbury and to remain there. At this moment, a London citizen, enriched by commerce despite the exactions of the Normans, advanced to Beket, and offered him his hand. "And you, too!" cried the messenger, "you, too, speak with the king's enemy?—return at once whence you came!"

The archbishop received with disdain the young king's order, and said that, if he retraced his steps, it was only because he was recalled to his church by a great approaching solemnity—that of Christmas. Beket returned to Canterbury, surrounded by poor men, who, at their own peril, arming themselves with shields and rusty lances, formed an escort for him. They were several times insulted by men who appeared seeking to excite a quarrel, in order to furnish the royal soldiers with a pretext for interfering and killing the archbishop, without scandal, amidst the tumult. But the English bore all these provocations with imperturbable calmness. The order intimated to the primate to remain within the walls of the dependences of his church was published by sound of trumpet in every town, as an edict of the public authority; other edicts denounced as enemies to the king and kingdom all who should manifest any favour to him or his; and a great number of the citizens of London were cited before the Norman judges to answer a charge of high treason for their reception of the archbishop, "the king's enemy," in their city. All these proceedings of the men in power warned Beket that his end was nigh; and he wrote to the pope, asking him to have the prayers for the dying offered up in his name. He ascended the pulpit, and in presence of the people assembled in the cathedral of Canterbury, preached a sermon on this text: "I am come to die amongst you."

The court of Rome, pursuing its constant policy of never allowing disputes in which it could interfere completely to subside, after having sent to the archbishop an order to absolve the prelates who had crowned the son of the king, had given him a fresh permission to excommunicate the prelate of York, and to suspend the other bishops. This time, it was Henry II. who was deceived by the pope; for he was entirely ignorant that Beket had gone to England provided with such letters. The latter had at first intended to employ them merely as a minatory means of making his enemies capitulate. But the fear lest these papers should be seized on his landing, made him afterwards determine upon sending them on before him, and thus the pope's letter and the new sentences of excommunication became prematurely public; the resentment of the bishops, thus unexpectedly attacked, exceeded all measure. The archbishop of York and several others, hastened across the Channel to Henry, who was still in Normandy, and presenting themselves before him: "We intreat you," they said, "to protect the crown, the priesthood; your bishops of England are excommunicated because, according to your orders, they crowned the young king, your son." "Ha!" cried the king, in a tone which showed his utter surprise; "then, if all who consented to the coronation of my son are excommunicated, by the eyes of God, I am so too!" "Sire, this is not all," continued the bishops; "the man who has done you this injury is setting the whole kingdom in a flame; he marches about with armed bodies of horse and foot, prowling round the fortresses, and seeking to take them."

On hearing this grossly exaggerated statement, the king was seized with one of those fits of passion to which he was subject; he changed colour, and beating his hands together: "What!" he exclaimed, "shall a man who has eaten my bread, who came to my court upon a lame horse, lift his foot to strike me? shall he insult the king, the royal family, and all the kingdom, and not one of the lazy servants whom I nourish at my table do me right for such an affront?" These words went not forth in vain from the king's lips; four knights of the palace, Richard le Breton, Hugh de Morville, William de Traci, and Renault Fitz-Ours, who heard him, making a vow together for life and death, suddenly departed for England, on Christmas day. Their absence was not perceived, or still less, its cause suspected; and even while they were galloping to the coast, the council of Norman barons, assembled by the king, named three commissioners to arrest and imprison Thomas Beket, on a charge of high treason; the conspirators, however, who were in advance of the royal commissioners, left them nothing to do.

Five days after Christmas-day, the four Norman knights arrived at Canterbury. This city was all excitement on account of new excommunications which the archbishop had just pronounced against persons who had insulted him, and, in particular, against Renouf de Broc, who had amused himself with cutting off the tail of one of his horses. The four knights entered Canterbury with a troop of armed men whom they had collected from the castles on their way. They first required the provost of the city to order the citizens to march in arms, on the king's service, to the archbishop's palace; the provost refusing, the Normans ordered him, at least to take measures that, throughout the day, no citizen should stir, whatever might happen. The four conspirators, with twelve of their friends, then proceeded to the palace and to the apartment of the primate.

Beket had just finished dinner, and his followers were still at table; he saluted the Normans on their entrance, and demanded the object of their visit. They made no intelligible answer, but sitting down, looked fixedly at him for some minutes. Renault Fitz-Ours at length spoke: "We come from the king," said he, "to demand that the excommunicated be absolved, that the suspended bishops be re-established, and that you yourself do penance for your offences towards the king." "It was not I who excommunicated the archbishop of York," replied Beket, "but the sovereign pontiff; it is he, consequently, who alone has the power to absolve him. As to the others, I will re-establish them if they will make their submision to me." "But of whom, then," asked Renault, "do you hold your archbishopric? from the king, or from the pope?"—"I hold the spiritual rights from God and from the pope, and the temporal rights from the king." "What! it is not, then, the king who gave you all?"—"By no means," replied Beket. The Normans murmured at this answer, denounced the distinction as a quibble, and became impatient, moving about on their chairs and twisting their gloves. "You threaten me, it would appear," said the primate; "but 'tis in vain; were all the swords in England drawn against me, you would get nothing from me." "We will do more than threaten," answered Fitz-Ours, suddenly rising, and the others followed him to the door, crying: "To arms!"

The door of the apartment was immediately closed behind them; Renault armed himself in the outer court, and taking an axe from the hands of a carpenter who was at work there, struck the door to force it open. The archbishop's people, hearing the blows, intreated the primate to seek refuge in the church, which communicated with his apartment by a cloister or gallery; he refused, and they were impelling him thither, when one of the attendants remarked that the vesper bell had rung. "Since it is the hour for my duty, I will go to the church," said the archbishop; and having his cross borne before him, he slowly traversed the cloister, and advanced towards the high altar, separated from the nave by an iron grating, the door of which was open. He had scarcely set foot on the steps of the altar, when Renault Fitz-Ours appeared at the other end of the church, in his coat of mail, his long, two-edged sword in his hand, crying: "A moi, à moi, vassaux du roi!" The other conspirators were immediately behind him, armed like himself from head to foot, and brandishing their swords. The persons who were with the primate proposed to shut the grating; he forbad this, and left the altar to prevent it; they earnestly intreated him to take refuge in the subterranean church, or to ascend the stairs, which, by many windings, led to the roof of the edifice. This advice was equally rejected. Meantime, the knights advanced; a voice exclaimed: "Where is the traitor?" No one answered. "Where is the archbishop?" "Behold him," replied Beket, "but there is no traitor here; what came you to do in the house of God, in such attire? what is your object?" "Your death." "I am prepared to die; you will not see me avoid your swords; but in the name of Almighty God, I forbid you to touch any of my companions, priest or layman, great or small." At this moment he received a blow from the flat of a sword on his shoulders, and he who struck him said: "Fly, or thou diest." He did not stir; the knights endeavoured to drag him out of the church, feeling scrupulous of killing him in it. He struggled with them, and declared firmly that he would not withdraw but would compel them to execute their intentions or their orders in the sacred place.

During this struggle, the priests in attendance upon the primate all fled and abandoned him, with one sole exception, the cross-bearer, Edward Grim, the same who had so fearlessly expressed his opinions after the council at Clarendon. The conspirators, seeing that he was totally unarmed, took little notice of him, and one of them, William de Tracy, raised his sword to strike the archbishop on the head; but the faithful and courageous Saxon immediately extended his right arm to parry the blow: the arm was cut off, and Thomas received but a slight wound. "Strike, strike, all of you!" cried the Norman to his companions; and a second blow on the head prostrated the archbishop with his face to the earth; a third blow split his skull, the stroke being so violent that the sword broke on the pavement. A man-at-arms, named William Maltret, contemptuously kicked the motionless body, saying: "Thus die the traitor who troubled the kingdom and excited the English to revolt."

And, indeed, an historian relates that the inhabitants of Canterbury arose and collected tumultuously in the streets. Among them was seen not one rich man or noble; all these remained within their houses, and semeed intimidated by the popular excitement. Men and women, by their dress readily recognisable as Saxons, hastened to the cathedral church and rushed in at every door. At sight of the body, still extended near the steps of the altar, they wept, and exclaimed that they had lost their father; some kissed the feet and hands, and others dipped their garments in the blood which covered the pavement. On their side, the Norman authorities did not remain inactive; and an edict, proclaimed by sound of trumpet, forbad any one to say publicly that Thomas of Canterbury was a martyr. The archbishop of York ascended the pulpit to announce his death as an effect of the divine vengeance, saying that he had perished like Pharaoh, in his crime and in his pride. Other bishops preached that the body of the traitor ought not to repose in holy ground, but should be cast on a dunghill or left to rot on a gibbet. An attempt was even made by the soldiers to get possession of the body of the Norman king's enemy; but the priests were warned in time, and hastily buried it in the vaults of their church.

These efforts of the powerful to persecute even beyond the tomb the man who had dared to withstand them, rendered his memory still more dear to the oppressed population; they made a saint of him, in defiance of the Norman authority and without the sanction of the Roman church. As Waltheof before him, Thomas Beket worked, upon the spot where he had died, miracles visible to Saxon imaginations, and the report of which, hailed with enthusiasm, spread over England. Two years elapsed ere the new saint was acknowledged and canonized at Rome; and all that time it was with no slight danger that those who believed in him named him in their masses, and that the poor and sick visited his tomb. The cause he had maintained with such inflexible determination, was that of mind against power, of the weak against the strong; and, above all, that of the conquered of the Norman conquest against the conquerors. Under whatever aspect we view his story, this national attribute is discernible; it may be deemed subordinate to others, but its existence cannot be denied. It is certain that the popular voice associated in the same regret the memory of St. Thomas of Canterbury and the recollection of the conquest. It was said, incorrectly perhaps, but with a poetry, the meaning of which is unequivocal, that the death of the saint had been sworn in the same castle and in the same chamber, in which was sworn the oath of Harold, and the oath of the chiefs of the army to the Bastard, previous to the expedition against England.

A circumstance worthy of remark is, that the only primate of Norman race who, prior to the English Beket, had opposed lay authority, was a friend to the Saxons, and, perhaps, the only friend they had found among the race of their conquerors. This was Anselm, he who pleaded against Lanfranc the cause of the saints of old England. Anselm, become archbishop, endeavoured to revive the ancient custom of ecclesiastical elections in lieu of the absolute right of royal nomination, introduced by William the Conqueror. He had to combat at once William Rufus, all the bishops of England, and pope Urban, who supported the king and the bishops. Persecuted in England and condemned at Rome, he was compelled to retire to France, and in exile wrote as Thomas Beket wrote after him: "Rome loves money more than justice; there is no help in her for him who has not wherewithal to purchase it." After Anselm came other archbishops, more docile to the traditions of the conquest; Raoul, William de Corbeil, and Thibaut, Beket's predecessor. None of them attempted to enter into opposition with the royal power, and union reigned between royalty and the priesthood, as in the time of the invasion, until the fatal moment when an Englishman by birth obtained the primacy.

A fact no less remarkable is, that a few years after the death of Thomas Beket, a priest arose in Wales, who, following his example, but from motives more unequivocally national, and with a less tragic result, struggled against Henry II. and against John, his son and second successor. In the year 1176, the clergy of the ancient metropolitan church of Saint David, in Pembrokeshire, chose for a bishop, subject to the ultimate approbation of the king of England, Girauld de Barri, archdeacon, the son of a Norman, and the grandson of a Norman and a Welshwoman. The priests of St. David selected this candidate of mixed origin, because they knew perfectly well, says Girauld de Barri himself, that the king would never allow a Cambrian of pure race to become the chief of the principal church of Wales. This moderation was vain, and the choice of a man born in the country, and Welsh by his grandmother, was regarded as an act of hostility to the royal power. The property of the church of Saint David was sequestrated, and the principal priests of that church were cited to appear before king Henry in person, at his castle of Winchester.

Henry asked them menacingly how they had dared, of themselves and without his order, not merely to choose a bishop, but to elect him; then, in his own bed-chamber, he ordered them to elect forthwith a Norman monk named Peter, whom they did not know, who was not introduced to them, and whose name only was told to them. They accepted him tremblingly, and returned to their country, where shortly after bishop Peter arrived, escorted by a number of servants, and accompanied by relations, male and female, among whom he distributed the territorial possessions of the church of Saint David. He imposed a tax on the priests of that church, took the tithe of their cattle, and exacted from all his diocesans extraordinary aids and presents at the four great festivals of the year. He so cruelly afflicted the people of the country that, despite the danger they incurred in resisting a bishop imposed by the Anglo-Normans, they drove him from his church, after having endured him for eight years.

Whilst the elected of king Henry II. was pillaging the church of St. David, the elected of the clergy of that church was living proscribed and an exile in France, without aid or encouragement, for the king considered, that by protecting an obscure bishop of the petty country of Wales, he could not do the king of England any material injury or annoyance. Girauld, destitute of all resources abroad, found himself obliged to return home, notwithstanding the danger he might incur there; and on the eve of quitting Paris he went to pray in the chapel which the archbishop of Reims, brother of king Louis VII. had consecrated to the memory of Thomas Beket, in the church of Saint Germain l'Auxerrois. Arrived in England, his powerless position secured him exemption from maltreatment; nay, by a private arrangement with the Norman prelate whom the Welsh had driven from Saint David's, he was charged ad interim and simply as bishop's substitute with the episcopal functions. But he soon renounced his office in disgust at the vexations to which he was subjected by his principal, who every day sent him orders to excommunicate one or more of his own partisans and most devoted friends. The Normans of England had just undertaken the conquest of Ireland. They offered Girauld, whom they did not wish to be a bishop in his native land, three bishoprics and an Ireland; but, though the grandson of one of the conquerors of Cambria, Girauld would not consent to become an instrument of oppression to a foreign nation. "I refused," he says, in his narrative of his own life, "because the Irish, like the Welsh, will never accept or receive as bishop, unless upon compulsion, a man not born amongst them."

In the year 1198, in the reign of John, son of Henry II., the Norman bishop of Saint David's died in England; and hereupon the Welsh chapter, by an unanimous act of will and of courage, without awaiting the order of the king of England, again proceeded to an election, and, for the second time, nominated Girauld de Barri. On receiving this intelligence, king John flew into a violent passion. He had the election declared null by the archbishop of Canterbury, in virtue of the pretended right of religious supremacy over all Britain, which six hundred years before the Cambrians had so energetically refused to acknowledge. The elect of Saint David's denied this supremacy, declaring that his church had been, from all antiquity, metropolitan and free, without subjection to any other, and that consequently no primate had power to revoke its elections. Such had, in fact, been the right of the church of Saint David's, previous to the conquest of

Pembrokeshire in the reign of Henry I. One of the first operations of Norman authority had been to abolish this prerogative, and to extend over the Cambrians the ecclesiastical unity established in England as a curb for the Anglo-Saxons. "Never in my life," said Henry I., "will I permit the Welsh to have an archbishop."

Thus the dispute as to ecclesiastical privilege between Girauld and the see of Canterbury, was nothing more or less than one of the phases of the great question of the subjection of Wales. A strong army could alone settle the dispute, and Girauld had no army. He went to Rome to the pope, the common resource of men who had no other, and found at the pontifical court an envoy from the king of England, who had anticipated him, laden with magnificent presents for the sovereign pontiff and the cardinals. The elected of Saint David's brought with him nothing but old, worm-eaten title-deeds, and the supplications of a nation which had never been rich.

In anticipation of the decree to be procured from the Sacred College by king John's ambassador, Regnault Foliot, (who, by a curious chance, bore the same name with one of Beket's mortal foes,) that at no time had there been an archbishop of Saint David's, all the possessions of that church and the private property of Girauld de Barri were confiscated. Proclamations denounced as traitor to the king the self-styled elect of the Cambrians, the audacious man who sought to raise against the king his subjects of Wales. Raoul de Bienville, bailiff of Pembroke, a gentle ruler, merciful to the conquered, was deprived of his office, and one Nicolas Avenel, notorious for his ferocious character, came from England to replace him. This Avenel published an address to the Welsh in these terms: "Know all that Girauld the archdeacon is the king's enemy, and aggressor against the crown; if any of you dare to hold correspondence with him, such man's house, his land, and his goods shall be given to the first comer." In the intervals of three journeys that Girauld made to Rome, and between which he had to remain in concealment to avoid violence, menacing injunctions were conveyed to his former residence. One of them ran thus: "We order and counsel thee, as thou lovest thy body and thy limbs, not to hold any chapters or synods in any place within the king's territory; and consider thyself warned that thy body and all that belongs to thee, wherever thou mayst be found, will be placed at the mercy of the lord king in good custody."

After a period of five years, during which the court of Rome, following its usual policy, prefaced its final sentence by vague decisions alternately favourable and unfavourable to both parties, Girauld was formally condemned, upon the testimony of some Welshmen, induced by poverty and fear to sell themselves to the Normans, and whom Regnault Foliot took to Rome with great ceremony to bear witness against their own country. Terror and bribes at length brought even the members of the chapter of Saint David to desert the bishop of their choice, and to acknowledge the supremacy of a foreign metropolis. When Girauld de Barri, after his deprivation, returned to his country, none dared open their doors to him; and the persecuted of the conquerors was shunned as a leper. The Normans, however, had no desire to make him undergo the fate of Thomas Beket, and he was only cited before a synod of bishops in England, to be censured and to receive his sentence of canonical degradation. The Norman prelates amused themselves with rallying him on his vast labours and their small success. "You must be mad," said the bishop of Ely, "to take so much trouble to do people a good which they do not desire, and to make them free in spite of themselves; for you see that they now disown you." "You say the truth there," answered Girauld, "and I was far from expecting such a result. I did not think that the priests of St. David, who so recently were members of a free nation, were capable of bowing beneath the yoke like you English, so long since serfs and slaves, and with whom slavery has become a second nature."

Girauld de Barri renounced all public affairs, and, devoting himself entirely to literature, under the title of Giraldus Cambrensis, Girauld the Cambrian, he obtained greater celebrity in the world as an elegant writer, than he had done as the antagonist of power. In fact, few people in Europe, in the twelfth century, took any interest in the question whether or no the last remnant of the ancient population of the Celts should lose its religious and civil independence among foreigners. There was small sympathy abroad in such a calamity; but in the heart of Wales, in that portion of the country whither the terror of the Norman lances had not yet penetrated, the exertions of Girauld for Wales were an universal subject of conversation and of praise. "Our country," said the chief of Powis, in a political assembly, "has sustained great struggles with the men of England; but none of us ever did so much against them as the elected of Saint David's; for he has stood as a rock against their king, their primate, their priests, against all of them, for the honour of Wales." At the court of Llewellyn, the chief of North Wales, at a solemn banquet, a bard arose, and took his harp to celebrate the devotion of Girauld to the cause of Saint David and of the Welsh nation. "So long as our land shall endure," said the poet, in extempore verse, "let his noble daring be commemorated by the pens of those who write and the mouths of those who sing."

We of the present day may well smile at these squabbles between kings and bishops, which made so much noise in centuries less enlightened than our own; but we must acknowledge that among these disputes there were some, at least, of a very grave nature. To the Roman chancery, the centre of the diplomacy of the middle ages, there often came appeals founded upon justice and upon truly national interests; and such, we must confess, were seldom deemed worthy of being the objects of a pontifical bull. Neither bull nor brief of pope Alexander III. menaced Henry II. when eight Welsh chiefs appealed to that pope against the foreign bandits whom the kings of England quartered upon them under the titles of priests and bishops. "These bishops, come from another land," said the chiefs in their petition, "detest us, us and our country; they are our mortal enemies; how can they take an interest in the welfare of our souls? They have been placed among us, as in ambush, to shoot at us from behind, like Parthians, and excommunicate us at the first order they receive. Whenever an expedition is making ready in England against us, suddenly the primate of Canterbury places an interdict upon the territory they purpose to invade; and our bishops, who are his creatures, hurl anathema upon the whole people in a body, and, by name, upon the chiefs who arm to fight at their head. Thus all among us who perish in the defence of our country die excommunicate."

If the reader will picture to himself the horror of such a situation, at a time when catholicism reigned dominant from one end of Europe to the other, he will at once comprehend how fearful an engine of subjection the Christian conquerors possessed, who had a reserve of churchmen in the train of their steel-clad battalions. He will readily conceive how men of courage and natural good sense addressed themselves to the pope, supplicated him, and put their trust in him; he will conceive that men, who were neither prebendaries nor monks, rejoiced, in the middle ages, to see those who crushed the people under the feet of their chargers, themselves called upon to render an account to a power too often their accomplice in oppression and in contempt of man. He will feel less pity for the grandees of the age when the dart of excommunication chances to fall on their mailed cuirass; for they often applied it to strike unarmed populations. Having once planted in another man's field their bandroled lance, they denounced for every defender of the paternal inheritance, death in this life, and, by the mouth of the priests, everlasting damnation in the next; over the body of the dying they held out their hand to the sovereign pontiff, and dividing with him the spoil of the vanquished people, nourished by voluntary tributes those ecclesiastical thunders which sometimes glanced upon themselves, but which, when hurled in their service, struck a sure and mortal blow.

BOOK X. FROM THE INVASION OF IRELAND BY THE NORMANS ESTABLISHED IN ENGLAND TO THE DEATH OF HENRY II.

A.D. 1171—1189.

Character of the Irish—Attempts of the popes upon Ireland—Their indifferent success—Ecclesiastical revolution in Ireland—Unpopularity there of the papal power—Enterprise of Henry II. and the pope against Ireland—Bull of Adrian IV.—Norman settlers in Wales—Alliance between them and an Irish king—First establishment of the Anglo-Normans in Ireland—Their election of a leader—Their conquests—Jealousy of them on the part of Henry II.—He proceeds to Ireland—Submission of several Irish chieftains—Cowardice of the Irish bishops—Disquietudes of Henry II.—Conduct of the clergy of Normandy—Fictitious narrative of the death of Thomas Beket—Letter of Henry II. to the pope—Departure of the king for Normandy—His reconciliation with the court of Rome, and rehabilitation of Beket—Scenes of hypocrisy—Bull of Alexander III.—Domestic troubles of Henry II.—Discovery of a conspiracy—Prince Henry acknowledged king in France—His manifesto—Progress of the quarrel—General abandonment of Henry II.—His return to England, and penance at the tomb of Beket—Motives and results of this proceeding—Bertrand de Born—The Troubadours—Reconciliation of the royal family—Hostilities between Richard and Henry—Interview between king Henry and prince Geoffroy at Limoges—Death of Henry the younger—Interview between king Henry and Bertrand de Born—Re-establishment of peace—Fresh revolt of Richard—The kings of France and England assume the cross—The crusades—Resumption of hostilities—Death and burial of Henry II.

The reader must now quit Britain and Gaul, to which this history has hitherto confined him, and, for some moments, transport himself to the Western Isle, called by its inhabitants Erin, and by the English Ireland. The people of this island, brothers of the Scottish highlanders, and forming with them the last remains of a great population, which, in ancient times, had covered Britain, Gaul, and part of the Spanish peninsula, had several of the physical and moral characteristics which distinguish the original races of the south. The major portion of the Irish were men with dark hair and impetuous passions, loving and hating with vehemence, prompt to anger, yet of a sociable disposition. Enthusiasts in many things, and especially in religion, they mixed up Christianity with their poetry and their literature, the most cultivated, perhaps, of all western Europe. Their island counted a host of saints and learned men, venerated in England and in Gaul, for no country had furnished more Christian missionaries, uninfluenced by other motives than pure zeal to communicate to foreign nations the opinions and faith of their own land. The Irish were great travellers, and always ingratiated themselves with the people they visited, by the extreme facility with which they conformed to their customs and modes of life.

This facility of manner was combined in them with an intense love of their national independence. Invaded at various periods by different nations of the north and of the south, they had never admitted a prescription of conquest or made voluntary peace with the sons of the stranger; their old annals contain narratives of terrible acts of vengeance exercised, often after the lapse of a century, by the natives on their conquerors. The remnant of the ancient conquering races, or the small bands of adventurers who from time to time had sought lands in Ireland, avoided the effects of this patriotic intolerance, by incorporating themselves with the Irish tribes, by submitting to the ancient social order established among the natives, and by learning their language. This was the case with the Danish and Norwegian pirates, who, in the course of the eighth and ninth centuries, founded on the eastern coast several colonies, where, renouncing their former life of robbery, they built towns and practised commerce.

When the Roman church had established its dominion in Britain by the conversion of the Anglo-Saxons, she laboured incessantly to extend over Erin the empire she claimed to exercise over all the worshippers of Jesus Christ. As in Ireland there were no pagan conquerors to convert, the popes were fain to content themselves with seeking, by letters and messages, to induce the Irish to establish in their island an ecclesiastical hierarchy similar to that of the continent, and, like it, calculated to serve as a step to the pontifical throne. The men of Erin, like the Britons of Cambria and of Gaul, having spontaneously organized Christianity in their country, without in any way conforming to the official organization decreed by the Roman emperors, had no fixed and determinate episcopal sees. Their bishops were simple priests, to whom had been confided, by election, the purely honorary charge of superintending or visiting the churches. They did not constitute a body superior to the rest of the clergy; there were no different degrees of hierarchy among them; in a word, the church of Ireland had no archbishop, and not one of its members needed to visit Rome to solicit or buy the pontifical pallium. Thus enjoying full independence of foreign churches, and administered, like any other free society, by elective and revocable chiefs, this church was at an early period stigmatized as schismatic by the consistory of Saint John Latran; a continuous system of attack was directed against it, with that perseverance inherent in the successors of the old senate, who, by dint of one unvarying will applied to one unvarying purpose, had subjugated the universe.

The new Rome had not, like the old, legions issuing from her gates to conquer nations; all her power was in address and in her skill to make alliance with the strong; an unequal alliance for the latter, which, under the names of friends and sons, rendered them subjects and vassals. The victories of the conquerors, and especially those of the still pagan barbarians, presented, as may have been observed more than once in this history, the most ordinary occasions for the political aggrandizement of the pontifical court. It carefully watched the rise of the first thought of ambition in the invading kings, as the moment at which to enter into association with them; and, in default of foreign conquests, it loved and encouraged internal despotism. Hereditary monarchy was the system it best liked, because under hereditary monarchy it only needed to gain possession of the mind of one family to acquire absolute authority over a whole nation.

Had such a system prevailed in Ireland, it is probable that the religious independence of this country would have been early destroyed by mutual agreement between the popes and the kings. But, although the Irish had chiefs to whom the Latin title of reges might be applied, and was, in fact, applied in public acts, the greater number of these kings, and their perpetual dependence on the various Irish tribes, whose simple name served them as a title, gave slight hold to Roman policy. There was, indeed, in Erin, a chief superior to all the rest, who was called the great king or the king of the country, and who was chosen by a general assembly of the chiefs of the different provinces; but this elective president of the national confederation swore to the whole nation the same oath which the chiefs of the tribes swore to their respective tribes, that of inviolably observing the ancient laws and hereditary customs. Moreover, the share in power of the great king was rather the execution than the decision of general affairs, all of which were regulated in councils held in the open air, upon a hill, surrounded by a deep ditch; here, the laws of the land were made, and here the disputes between province and province, town and town, and occasionally between man and man, were contested, sometimes in a very tumultuous manner.

It may be easily understood that such a social order, whose basis was the people themselves, and where the impulsion always emanated from the variable and passion-led mass, was little favourable to the projects of the court of Rome. Accordingly, despite all their efforts with the kings of Ireland, during the four centuries and a half which elapsed between the conversion of the Anglo-Saxons and the descent of the Normans into England, the popes effected not the slightest change in the religious practices and organization of the clergy of Erin, or the smallest tribute from the inhabitants of the island. After the conquest of England, the intrigues of the primate Lanfranc, a man devoted to the simultaneous aggrandisement of the papal power and of the Norman domination, energetically directed upon Ireland, began to make some slight impression on the national mind of the priests of this island; Lanfranc combining with his credit as a man of learning and eloquence, other efficacious means of persuading and seducing, for he had accumulated great wealth, the result of his share of the pillage of the Anglo-Saxons, and, if ancient testimonies are to be believed, of selling to the bishops of Norman race the pardon of their violence and excesses.

In the year 1074, an Irishman, named Patrick, after having been elected bishop by the clergy and people, and confirmed by the king of his province and by the king of all Ireland, went to be consecrated at Canterbury, instead of contenting himself, as was the ancient custom, with the benediction of his colleagues; this was the first act of obedience to the laws of the Roman church, which required that every bishop should be consecrated by an archbishop who had received the pallium, and it was not long ere these new seeds of religious servitude bore their fruit. From that time, several Irish bishops accepted in succession the title of pontifical legate in Hibernia; and about the period at which this history has arrived, Christian, bishop of Lismore and papal vicar, conjointly with Papirius, a Roman cardinal, undertook to reorganize the church of Ireland, according to the views and interests of the court of Rome. After four years' efforts he succeeded, and in a synod attended by the bishops, abbots, kings, chiefs, and other magistrates of Hibernia, with the consent of all present, say the old acts, and by apostolical authority, four archbishops were instituted, to whom were assigned, as fixed sees, the cities of Armagh, Dublin, Cashel, and Tuam. But notwithstanding the appearance of national consent given to these measures, the ancient spirit of independence still prevailed: the clergy of Ireland exhibited little docility in their submission to the new hierarchal order, and the people had infinite repugnance towards the foreign practices, and especially to the money-tributes which it was sought, under various names, to levy for the benefit of the ultramontane church. Still dissatisfied with the Irish, despite their concessions, the court of Rome continued to call them bad Christians, lukewarm Christians, rebels to apostolical discipline; it watched as closely as ever an occasion to obtain better hold upon them, by associating its ambition with some temporal ambition, and this occasion soon offered itself.

When Henry, son of Geoffroy Plantegenest, became king of England, it occurred to him to signalize his accession as first king of Angevin race, by a conquest almost as important as that of his paternal ancestor, the Norman William. He resolved to take possession of Ireland, and, following the example of the Conqueror of England, his first care was to send to the pope a proposition to concur in this new enterprise, as his predecessor, Alexander II., had taken part in the first. The reigning pope was Adrian IV., a man of English birth, whose family name was Breakspear, and who, by expatriating himself at a very early age, had escaped the miseries of his condition. Too proud to work in the fields or to beg in England, says an ancient historian, he adopted a bold resolution, inspired by necessity; he went to France, then to Provence, then to Italy, entered a rich abbey as secretary, became abbot, then bishop, and finally pope; for the Roman church was thus far liberal, that she made the fortune of all who devoted themselves to her service, without distinction of origin. On the pontifical throne, Adrian seemed to have forgotten all the resentment of an Englishman against the oppressors of his nation; far from showing anything of that spirit which, a few years afterwards, animated the opposition of Thomas Beket, he exhibited the greatest complaisance towards king Henry II. He received very graciously his message relative to the project of subjugating Ireland, and with the sanction of the sacred college, replied to it in a bull, from which we will make some extracts:—

"Adrian, bishop, servant of the servants of God, to his dearly beloved son in Jesus Christ, the illustrious king of England, salutation and apostolic benediction.

"Thou hast let us to know, dearly beloved son in Jesus Christ, that thou desirest to enter the island of Hibernia, to subject the people there to the yoke of the laws, to extirpate the seeds of vice, and also to enforce the payment to the blessed apostle Peter, of the annual pension of a penny for each house. According to this laudable and pious desire, the favour it merits, and a gracious reply to thy request, we consent that, to extend the limits of holy church, to arrest the course of vice, to reform men's manners, implant virtue, and propagate the Christian religion, thou enter into that island, and execute there, according to thy prudence, whatever thou shalt judge fitting for the honour of God and the salvation of souls. We command that the people of that country receive thee and honour thee as their lord and master, saving the right of the churches, which must remain intact, and also the annual pension of a penny from every house to the blessed Peter and to the most holy Roman church.

"If, then, thou thinkest fit to put into execution what thou hast conceived in thought, employ all thy care in forming that people to good manners, so that, by thy efforts and by those of men of known sufficiency in faith, word, and life, the church may in that country be adorned with a new lustre; that the religion of Christ may be planted there and grow; that, in a word, everything concerning the honour of God and the salvation of souls may, by thy prudence, be ordered in such a manner that thou mayest become worthy to obtain in heaven eternal recompence, and upon earth a glorious name in all ages."

This flow of mystic eloquence served, we may see, as a sort of decent envelop for a political compact exactly similar to that of William the Bastard with pope Alexander II. Henry II. would probably have hastened to accomplish, like William, his singular religious mission, if another conquest, that of Anjou from his own brother Geoffroy, had not at the precise moment diverted his attention. He next fought against the Bretons and Poitevins, who, unluckily for their safety, preferred their national independence to the yoke of a friend of the church. Lastly, the rivalry of the king of France, ever at work openly or secretly, and, above all, the long and serious quarrel with the primate of Canterbury, prevented his going to conquer in Ireland temporal royalty for himself, and for the pope spiritual royalty and the rent of a penny for each house. When Adrian IV. died, his bull still slept, awaiting employment, in the treasure-chest of the royal charters of England, and it would perhaps have ripened there during the whole of the king's life, had not unexpected events created an occasion for bringing it out to daylight.

We have seen above how Norman and Flemish adventurers had conquered Pembrokeshire and part of the western coast of Wales. In establishing themselves in the domains usurped by them, these men had not quitted their old manners for habits of order and repose; they consumed in gaming and debauchery all the revenues of their lands, which they drained instead of bettering, calculating upon new expeditions, rather than upon economy, for the repair of their fortunes. Briefly, in the condition of great landed proprietors, of rich seigneurs terriens, to use the language of the epoch, they had retained the character of soldiers of fortune, ever disposed to run the chances of a foreign war, either on their own account or in the pay of others. It was under this aspect they were remarked by the people of Erin, who, in the prosecution of their commerce, often visited the coasts of Wales. For the first time, they saw, in the vicinity of Ireland, a colony of men trained to wear those complete suits of steel which the language of the period called armure Française; the sight of the coats of mail and great Flemish war-horses of the companions of Richard Strongbow, a new thing for the Irish, who were only acquainted with light arms, caused them great surprise. The travellers and merchants on their return spread marvellous accounts of the strength and warlike skill of the new inhabitants of the west of Britain. Just at this time, the chief of one of the eastern provinces of Ireland was at war with a neighbouring chief; struck with the accounts he heard of the conquerors of Pembrokeshire, he bethought himself of asking some of them to enlist in his service for high pay, and to aid him in destroying his enemy, whose downfal he prosecuted with that passionate fury which the Irish ever exhibited in their civil wars.

The Normans and Flemings of Wales, although decorated since their conquest with the titles of honour designating the rich and powerful, in the French language of the middle ages, saw nothing strange in the proposition of the Irishman Dermot Mac Morrogh, chief or king of the province of Lagheniagh, or Leinster. Having made an agreement with him as to the pay and the duration of the service, they embarked, four hundred knights, squires and archers, under the command of Robert Fitz-Stephen, Maurice Fitz-Gerauld, Hervè de Mont-Maurice and David de Barry. They sailed in a straight line from the westernmost point of Wales to the easternmost point of Ireland, and landed near Wexford, a town founded by the Danes in one of their expeditions of mixed piracy and commerce. This town, which formed part of the territory of

Dermot Mac Morrogh, had been taken from him by a stratagem of his adversary and the defection of the inhabitants. Its present garrison came out to meet the hostile army and its auxiliaries; but, when they saw the horses barbed with iron and the steel-clad warriors of Wales, in all their panoply, wholly new to them, a sort of panic terror seized upon them; though far more numerous, they dared not venture an engagement in the open fields, and burning in their retreat all the surrounding villages and all the provisions they could not carry with them, they shut themselves up within the walls of Wexford.

Dermot and the Normans besieged it, and made upon it three consecutive assaults, with little success, because the great horses, the lances twelve feet long, the cross-bows, and cuirasses of mail of the assailants, were mainly of advantage in the open field. But the intrigues of the bishop of Wexford, who had influence enough to reconcile the inhabitants with their king, opened the gates to the ally of the foreigners, who, entering the town without striking a blow, immediately marched in a north-westerly direction to pursue his adversaries and deliver his kingdom. In this expedition, the military skill and complete armour of his allies were a vast assistance to him. The most formidable weapons of the people of Erin were a small steel axe, long javelins, and short, but very sharp arrows. The Normans, secured by their armour from injuries by such weapons as these, rode in upon the natives, and while the shock of their great chargers overthrew the small horses of Ireland, attacked with their strong lances or large swords, the rider, whose only defensive armour was a shield of light wood and long tresses of hair, plaited on each side of the head. The whole province of Leinster was reconquered by Mac Morrogh, who, delighted with the prodigious aid given him by the Normans, after having faithfully paid them their hire, invited them to dwell with him, and offered them, as an inducement, more lands than they possessed elsewhere. In the effusion of his gratitude, he gave to Robert Fitz-Stephen and to Maurice Fitz-Gerauld the government and revenue of the town of Wexford and its precincts; to Hervé de Mont-Maurice two districts on the coast, between Wexford and Waterford; and to the rest, lands proportionate to their rank and military talent.

This intervention of strangers in the internal quarrels of the country, and above all, the establishment of these foreigners in permanent colonies in the towns and on the territory of the king of Leinster, alarmed all the surrounding provinces, and private enmity to Dermot was converted into national hostility. He was placed, as a public enemy, under the ban of the Irish confederation, and, instead of one king, well-nigh all the kings of the country declared war against him. The new colonists, seeing their cause closely bound up with his, resolved to exert every effort to support him while defending themselves, and at the first murmur of the gathering storm they sent some of their followers to England to collect fresh vagabond-adventurers, Normans, French, and even English. They were promised pay and lands; numbers came, whom king Dermot received as he had done the first, raising the fortune of each on his landing far above its previous condition, the depression of which was self-declared by the surnames of some of them, such as Raymond le Pauvre, who, without changing the appellation, became a high and puissant baron on the eastern coast of Ireland.

The foreign colony, gradually augmented under the auspices of the chief of Leinster, who now saw in it his only protection, had, despite its engagements, a tendency to separate its cause from that of the Irish king, and to form of itself an independent society. Ere long, the adventurers disdained to march to battle under the leadership of the man whose pay they were receiving, a man ignorant of skilled warfare—of, as the phrase then ran, les faits d'armes de la chevalerie. They desired to have a captain of great military reputation, and invited over to command them, Richard, son of Gilbert Strongbow, and grandson of the first earl of Pembroke. This man, noted among the descendants of the conquerors of Wales as possessor of the most extensive domains, was at this time so impoverished by his excessive expenditure, and so harassed by his creditors, that, to avoid their pursuit and to repair his fortunes, he did not hesitate to comply with the summons of the Normans in Ireland.

His reputation and his rank procured for him many followers. He landed, with several vessels filled with soldiers and munitions of war, at the same spot where the allies of Dermot had landed two years before, and was received with great honours by his countrymen and by the king of Leinster, fain to welcome this new friend, who might yet one day become formidable to himself. Richard, joining with his army the Norman colony, assumed the command of the united forces, and attacked Waterford, a city of the kingdom of Mumham or Munster, nearest to the territory occupied by the Normans. This city, founded by the northern corsairs, as is evidenced by its Teutonic name, was taken by assault.

The Normans left a garrison in it, and, advancing northwards, attacked Dyvlin or Dublin, another city founded by the Danes, and the largest and richest on the eastern coast. Supported by all the troops of king Dermot, they took Dublin, whence they made incursions in different directions upon the open country, seizing upon some districts, obtaining others by capitulation, and laying the foundations of many fortresses, edifices still rarer in Ireland than they had been in England before the conquest.

The Irish, vividly struck with the rapid progress of the foreigners, attributed it to the Divine anger, and, mingling a sentiment of humanity with their superstitious fears, thought to allay the scourge come upon them from England, by emancipating all the men of English race who, captured by pirates or purchased, had become slaves in Ireland. This generous resolution, decreed in a great council of the chiefs and bishops of the country, did not sheathe the sword of Richard Fitz-Gilbert. Master of the kingdom of Leinster, in the name of the Irishman Dermot, whose daughter he married, and who became the protégé and vassal of his late mercenaries, the Norman threatened to conquer all the country with the help of new supplies of adventurers whom he summoned from England.

But the rumour of the prodigious aggrandisement of this new power reaching king Henry II. aroused his jealousy. So far he had beheld without uneasiness, and even with satisfaction, the establishment of the warriors of Pembroke on the coasts of Ireland, and their connexion with one of the kings of the country, who was thus engaged against his countrymen in an hostility favourable to the designs of the king of England, should he ever realise his plan of conquest. But the possession of a great portion of the island by a man of Norman race, who every day augmented his forces by opening an asylum to adventurers, and who could already, if he chose, pay to the pope the rent of a penny for each house, greatly alarmed the king's ambition. He issued a threatening proclamation, ordering all his liegemen then in Ireland to return to England before the approaching festival of Easter, under penalty of forfeiture of all their property, and perpetual banishment. He also forbad any vessel from his territories in England or the continent to proceed to Ireland under any pretext. This prohibition arrested the progress of Richard Strongbow, who suddenly found himself cut off from all supplies of men, provisions, or arms.

From want of personal daring, or of the means of maintaining himself by his own strength, Richard endeavoured to negotiate an accommodation with the king, and sent one of his lieutenants, Raymond le Gros, to wait upon him in Aquitaine. The envoy was ill received by the king, who would not reply to any of his propositions, or rather replied to them in a very expressive manner by confiscating all Richard's domains in England and Wales. At the same time, the Norman colony in Leinster underwent a fierce attack from the men of Danish race established on the north-eastern coast of Ireland, in conjunction with the native Irish. The confederates were supported by Godred, king of the Isle of Man, a Scandinavian by name and origin, and chief of a mixed people of Gauls and Teutons. They attempted to recover Dublin; the Normans resisted, but fearing the effects of this new league formed against them at a moment when they were deprived of all external aid in consequence of the royal ordinances, they thought they could not do better than to reconcile themselves with the king, at whatever cost. Henry II. required very hard conditions, but the earl of Pembroke and his companions submitted to them. They gave to the king the city of Dublin and the best of the other towns they had conquered. In return, the king gave back to Richard Fitz-Gilbert his confiscated domains, and confirmed to the Normans in Ireland their territorial possessions there, to hold in fief of him on condition of fealty and homage. From supreme chief that he then was, Richard Strongbow became seneschal in Ireland of the king of England; and the king himself immediately set forth to visit the new possessions he had thus easily acquired.

The rendezvous assigned to the royal army was on the western coast of Pembrokeshire. Before going on board his vessel, Henry II. paid his devotions in the church of Saint David, and recommended to Heaven the expedition he was about to undertake, as he said, for the advancement of holy church. He landed at Waterford, where the Norman chiefs of the kingdom of Leinster, and Dermot Mac Morrogh, still king in name, but whose titular royalty necessarily expired on the landing of the foreign king, received him as, in that century, vassals received a sovereign lord. Their troops formed a junction with his army, and marching westward, the combined forces reached the city of Cashel without opposition. The inhabitants of the surrounding districts, hopeless of successfully resisting so powerful an army, emigrated in crowds to the mountainous country beyond the Shannon. The kings of the southern provinces, left by this panic terror at the mercy of the foreigner, were obliged to obey his summons, to swear fealty to him, and to declare themselves tributaries. The Normans divided out among themselves the lands of the fugitive Irish; and when the latter returned, driven back by distress, the conquerors received them in the quality of serfs on their own fields. Norman garrisons were placed in the towns, Norman officers superseded the old national chiefs and a whole kingdom, that of Cork, was given by king Henry to Robert Fitz-Stephen, one of the captains of adventurers who had opened for him so facile a road into Ireland.

After having thus shared out and organized the provinces of the south, the king proceeded northwards to the great city of Dublin. Immediately upon his arrival, in the name of his right of lordship, founded, as he said, upon donation by the church, he summoned all the Irish kings to appear at his court to take the oath of faith and homage. The kings of the south attended, but the sovereign of the great western province of Connaught, to whom belonged at this time the supremacy over all the rest, and the national title of king of the country, replied that he would attend no man's court, he himself being the only chief of all Ireland. The altitude and ruggedness of the mountains, and the extent of the marshes of his province, permitted him with impunity to set this example of patriotic haughtiness. It was alike in vain that the summons of the king of England reached the north of the island; not a chief of the province of Thuall or Ulster came to do homage at the Norman court of Dublin; and the nominal sovereignty of Henry II. remained bounded by a line from north-east to south west, from the mouth of the Boyne to that of the Shannon.

A palace of wood, polished and painted in the Irish fashion, was constructed at Dublin, and it was here that the chiefs who had consented to place their hands as vassals in those of the foreign king, passed Christmas. Here was displayed for several days all the pomp of Norman royalty; and the Irish, a docile and sociable race, fond of novelty and susceptible of vivid impressions, took pleasure, if we may believe the ancient authors, in viewing the splendour which surrounded their masters, their horses, their arms, and the gold adorning their dresses. The members of the clergy, and especially the archbishops, installed a few years before by the pontifical legates, played a great part in this submission to the law of the strongest. The prelates of the western and northern provinces, indeed, did not, any more than the political chiefs of these provinces, attend at Dublin; but those of the south and east swore fidelity to king Henry, towards and against all men. They addressed the bearer of the bull of Adrian IV. in this verse, so often applied by the clergy to conquerors: "Blessed is he who cometh in the name of the Lord." But Henry II. was not content with these uncertain proofs of obedience and resignation; he required others of a more solid nature, demanding that every Irish bishop should give him letters, signed and sealed, in the shape of a formal charter, by which all declared that of their own free will and motion they had constituted "king and lord of Ireland, the glorious Henry Fitz-Empress, and his heirs for ever."

King Henry resolved to send these letters to the reigning pope, Alexander III., to obtain from him a formal confirmation of the bull of pope Adrian. To prove in a striking manner his intention to execute the clauses stipulated in that bull for the advantage of the Romish church, he assembled in the city of Cashel a synod of Irish bishops and Norman priests, chaplains, abbots, or simple monks, to arrange the definitive establishment of the papal dominion in Hibernia. This synod prescribed the strict observance of the canons prohibiting marriage within the sixth degree of consanguinity, a law quite new to Ireland, where, in the utmost innocence, were contracted a host of unions reprobated by the church in the other Christian countries. The council of Cashel also passed other resolutions, having for their object the general enforcement of canonical discipline, and it was decreed that the services of the churches of Ireland should for the future be modelled upon those of the churches of England. "Hibernia," said the acts of this council, "being now, by the grace of divine providence, subjected to the king of England, it is just that she should receive from that country the order and the rules best adapted for reforming her, and for introducing into her a better manner of life."

These events took place nearly two years after the murder of Thomas Beket, at a period when king Henry found himself compelled by political necessity to display infinite humility towards the pope; all his former haughtiness in reference to cardinals and legates, and his resolution to maintain against the episcopal power what he then called the rights and dignity of his crown, had now vanished. The need to obtain the sanction and support of the sovereign pontiff for the securing his authority in Ireland, was not the only cause of this change; the death of the primate of Canterbury had also contributed to it. However great the king's desire had been to be relieved of his antagonist; however emphatically he might have expressed this desire in his passion, the circumstances of the assassination, committed in broad daylight, at the foot of the altar, displeased and disquieted him. "He was vexed," says a contemporary, "at the manner in which the martyrdom took place, and feared to be called a traitor, for having, in sight of all men, given his full peace to the holy man, and then immediately sent him to perish in England."

The political enemies of Henry II. had eagerly availed themselves of this accusation of treason and perjury; they disseminated it zealously, and gave the name of the field of traitors to the meadow in which the reconciliation of the primate and the king of England had taken place. The king of France exhausted himself in invectives and messages to excite in every quarter hatred towards his rival, and more especially to renew the insurrection of the provinces of Aquitaine and Brittany. Following the example of the Anglo-Saxon population, but from wholly different motives, king Louis did not await a decree of the Roman church to exalt as a saint and martyr him whom he had by turns assisted, abandoned, and again assisted, at the dictate of his own interest. The impression of horror which the murder of the archbishop had produced on the continent furnished him with a pretext for breaking the truce with king Henry, and he flattered himself that he should have the sovereign pontiff as an auxiliary in the war he proposed to recommence. "Let the sword of Saint Peter," he wrote, "be drawn from the scabbard to avenge the martyr of Canterbury. For his blood cries aloud in the name of the universal church, and demands satisfaction from the church." Thibaut, earl of Blois, vassal of the king of France, who desired to extend, at the expense of the other king, his territories around Touraine, was still more violent in the despatches he sent to the pope. "The blood of the just," he said, "has been spilled; the dogs of the court, the familiars, the servants of the king of England, became the ministers of his crime. Most holy father, the blood of the just cries to you; may the Father Almighty inspire you with the will, and give you the power to avenge it."

Lastly, the archbishop of Sens, who styled himself primate of the Gauls, pronounced a sentence of interdict upon all the continental provinces of the king of England. This was a potent means of arousing popular discontent in these provinces, for the execution of a sentence of interdict was accompanied by lugubrious forms, which made a deep impression on the mind. The altars were stripped, the crucifixes placed on the ground, the bones of the saints were taken from their shrines and strewed over the pavement of the churches, the doors were taken away and replaced by heaps of bushes and thorns, and no religious ceremony took place, except the baptism of infants and the confession of the dying.

The Norman prelates, who bore no political hatred to Henry II., did not execute this sentence; and the archbishop of Rouen, who assumed the authority of primate of the continental provinces subject to the king of England, forbad, by pastoral letters, the bishops of Anjou, Brittany, and Aquitaine, to obey the interdict until it had been ratified by the pope. Three bishops and several Norman priests departed on an embassy to Rome to exonerate Henry II. from the accusation of murder and perjury. No member of the Aquitan clergy took part in this mission, the king distrusting them, from their having manifested a disposition unfavourable to his cause. We can judge of the spirit which animated them by the following letter, addressed to the king himself, by William de Trahinac, prior of the abbey of Grandmont, near Limoges, an abbey to which Henry was greatly attached, and the church of which he was at this time rebuilding. "Ah! lord king, what is this I hear of you? I would not have you ignorant that, since the day I learned you had fallen into a mortal sin, I sent away the workmen who, in your pay, were building the church of our house of Grandmont, in order that there might no longer be anything in common between you and us."

While the king of France and the other enemies of Henry II. were directly charging him with the murder of the archbishop of Canterbury, and endeavouring to represent the crime of the four Norman knights as the result of an express mission, the friends of the king were labouring to spread an entirely different version of the affair. They represented the violent death of Thomas Beket as a mere accident, in which the king's animosity had no share. A fictitious narrative of the facts, drawn up and signed by a bishop, was sent to pope Alexander III., in the name of all the clergy of Normandy. The Norman prelates related, that being one day with the king to discuss the affairs of the church and of the state, they had suddenly learned from some persons just returned from England, that certain enemies of the archbishop, driven to extremities by his provocations, had thrown themselves upon him and killed him; that this melancholy news had been for some time concealed from the king, but that at last it had necessarily reached his ears, it being impossible to allow him longer to remain ignorant of a crime, the punishment of which appertained to him by the right of power and the sword; that at the first words of this sad recital, he had burst into lamentations, and given way to a grief which revealed the soul of the friend rather than that of the prince, now appearing stupified, now uttering cries and sobs; that he had passed three whole days shut up in his chamber, refusing all nourishment and all consolation, and seeming to have the project of putting an end to his life. "So much so," added the narrators, "that we, who at first lamented the fate of the primate, began to despair of the king, and to believe that the death of the one would calamitously involve that of the other. At length his intimate friends ventured to ask him what afflicted him to this degree, and prevented his returning to himself: 'It is,' he answered, 'that I fear the authors and accomplices of this abominable crime have promised themselves impunity, relying upon my former displeasure towards the archbishop, and that my reputation may suffer from the malevolence of my enemies, who will not fail to attribute all to me; but, by Almighty God, I have in no way concurred therein, either by will or by acquiescence, unless it be construed into a crime on my part that heretofore I misliked the archbishop.' "

This story, in which the exaggeration of the sentiments, the dramatic display, the attempt to exhibit the king as the tender friend of the primate, are manifest proofs of falsity, obtained little credit at the court of Rome or elsewhere. It did not prevent the malevolent from propagating the equally false report, that Thomas Beket had been killed by the express order of Henry II. To weaken this impression, the king resolved himself to address to the pope an account of the murder and of his own deep regret, more conformable with the truth than that of the prelates of Normandy, but still inexact. The king took care not to admit that the four assassins had left his court after having heard him utter an exclamation of fury which might pass for an order, and he exaggerated his kindness towards the primate, alike with the offences of the latter. "I had," he said, "restored to him my friendship and the full possession of his property; I had allowed him to return to England at my expense; but, on his return there, instead of the joys of peace, he brought with him sword and flame. He questioned my royal dignity, and excommunicated my most zealous followers without reason. Then, those whom he had excommunicated, and others, no longer able to support the insolence of this man, threw themselves upon him and killed him, which I cannot relate without great grief."

The court of Rome at first made a great noise about the sacrilegious outrage committed upon the Lord's anointed; and when the Norman clergy sent thither, presented their credentials, and pronounced the name of Henry, by the grace of God, king of England, all the cardinals arose, exclaiming: "Hold! hold!" But when, on quitting the hall of audience, each had privately seen the glitter of the king's gold, they became much more tractable, and consented not to consider him a direct accomplice in the murder. Thus, despite the public clamour and the efforts of his enemies, the king of England was not excommunicated; and two legates proceeded from Rome to receive his justification and to absolve him. Things had arrived at this point, when Henry II. departed for Ireland, and by its easy conquest gave a diversion to his disquietude. But this very success placed him in a new relation of dependence on the papal power. In the midst of his military and political labours in the country he had just conquered, he had his eyes unceasingly fixed upon the opposite coast, anxiously awaiting the coming of the Roman ambassadors. When, at length, in the Lent which closed the year 1172, he learned that the cardinals Albert and Theodin had arrived in Normandy, he laid aside everything else to visit them, and departed, leaving his conquests in Ireland to the care of Hugh de Lacy.

King Henry had already obtained from the court of Rome the erasure of his name from the list of persons excommunicated for the murder of Thomas Beket; but this court, then sovereign in such cases, still allowed the accusation of indirect complicity to weigh upon him. An absolute and definitive pardon was not to be pronounced until after fresh negotiations and fresh pecuniary sacrifices. In case the king should not submit to the conditions of the treaty, the legates were charged to lay England and the continental possessions of England under interdict, which would open to the king of France admission to Brittany and Poitou. But, on the other hand, if Henry II. yielded to all their demands, the legates were to oblige the king of France, by the threat of a similar sentence, immediately to conclude peace with the other king.

The first interview of the king of England with the two cardinals took place in a convent near Avranches. The demands of the Romans, thoroughly alive to the difficult position in which the king was placed, were so exorbitant, that the latter, notwithstanding his resolution to go a great way to please the church, refused to submit to their proposals. He said, on leaving them: "I return to Ireland, where I have much to do; as to you, go in peace throughout my territories, wherever you please, and accomplish your mission." But Henry II. reflected that the weight of his affairs in Ireland would soon be too heavy for him, unsupported by pontifical favour; and on their side, the cardinals became less exacting. They again met, and after mutual concessions, peace was concluded between the court of Rome and the king, who, according to the official report of the legates, manifested great humility, fear of God, and obedience to the church. The conditions imposed upon Henry II. were, a money tribute towards the expenses of the war against the Saracens, the obligation to repair in person to that war, or to take the cross, as it was then called, and lastly, the abolition of the statutes of Clarendon, and of all other laws, ancient or modern, which should be condemned by the pope.

In pursuance of previous arrangement, the king went in state to the cathedral of Avranches and, laying his hand on the Gospel, swore before all the people, that he had neither ordered nor desired the death of the archbishop of Canterbury, and that, on learning it, he had felt more grief than joy. The legates repeated to him the articles of peace and the promises he had made, and he swore to execute them all in good faith and without fraudulent reservation. Henry, his eldest son and colleague in royalty, swore this at the same time with him; and, as a guarantee of this double promise, the conditions were drawn up in a charter, at the foot of which was affixed the royal seal. This king, so lately full of haughty assumption in reference to the pontifical power, called upon the cardinals not to spare him. "Lord legates," he said, "here is my body; it is in your hands; and know, for a certainty, that whatever you order, I am ready to obey it." The legates contented themselves with making him kneel before them as they gave him absolution for his indirect complicity, exempting him from the obligation to receive upon his bare back the stripes ordinarily administered to penitents. The same day he forwarded to England letters sealed with his great seal, announcing to all the bishops that they were thenceforth dispensed from keeping their promise to observe the statutes of Clarendon, and to the nation, that peace was re-established, to the honour of God and of the church, of the king and of the kingdom. A pontifical decree, declaring the archbishop saint and martyr, with which the legates had come provided as a diplomatic document necessary to their purpose, was also sent to England, with orders to promulgate it in the churches, public squares, and in all the places where previously those who had dared to call the assassination of the king's enemy a crime, had been flogged and pilloried.

On the arrival of this news and of the brief of canonization, there was great commotion among the high personages of England, laymen and clergy, thus suddenly called upon to change their language and opinion, and to adopt as an object of public worship the man whom they had persecuted with such fierce inveteracy. The earls, viscounts, and barons who had awaited Thomas Beket on the sea-shore, to kill him, the bishops who had insulted him in his exile, who had envenomed the king's hatred against him, and brought to Normandy the denunciation which occasioned his death, assembled in the great hall of Westminster, to hear the reading of the papal brief, which was couched in these terms:—

"We give you all to wit, whoever you be, and enjoin you by our apostolic authority, solemnly to celebrate the memory of Thomas, the glorious martyr of Canterbury, every year on the day of his passion, so that by addressing your prayers and vows to him, you may obtain the pardon of your offences, and that he, who living underwent exile, and dying suffered martyrdom for the cause of Christ, being invoked by the faithful, may intercede for us with God."

Scarcely was the reading of this letter concluded, when all the Normans, priests and laymen together, raised their voices and exclaimed: "Te Deum laudamus." While some of the bishops continued to chant the verses of the hymn of thanks-giving, the others burst into tears, saying, with passionate sobs: "Alas! miserable creatures that we are! we had not for our father all the respect we owed him, neither in his exile, nor when he returned from exile, nor even after his return. Instead of assisting him in his troubles, we obstinately persecuted him. We confess our error and our iniquity." And as though these individual exclamations were not enough to prove to king Henry II. that his faithful bishops of England could turn whichever way the wind of his royal will blew, they arranged among themselves that one of them should, in public, in the name of the others, pronounce their solemn confession. Gilbert Foliot, bishop of London, once the most eager persecutor of the primate, the man most deeply compromised with the pontifical court for the part he had taken in the persecution of the new saint, and in the catastrophe which had crowned them, swore publicly that he had not participated in the death of the archbishop, either by deed, word, or writing. He was one of those who, by their complaints and their false statements, had so violently excited the king's anger against the primate; but an oath wiped out all; the Romish church was satisfied, and Foliot retained his see.

The political advantages which were to result from this great change were speedily obtained by the king of England. First, by the mediation of the legates, he had an interview with the king of France on the frontiers of Normandy, and concluded peace upon conditions as favourable as he could hope for. Next, as the price of the relinquishment he had just made of his former projects of ecclesiastical reform, he received from pope Alexander III. the following bull relative to the affairs of Ireland: "Alexander, bishop, servant of the servants of God, to his dearly beloved and illustrious son Henry, king of England, salutation, grace, and apostolic benediction.

"Seeing that the gifts granted for good and valid cause by our predecessors, ought to be ratified and confirmed by us, having maturely weighed and considered the grant and privilege of possession of the land of Hibernia, belonging to us, delivered by our predecessor Adrian, we ratify, confirm, and grant, in like manner, the said grant and privilege, reserving the annual pension of a penny from each house, due to Saint Peter and the Roman church, as well in Hibernia as in England, and providing also that the people of Hibernia be reformed in their lives and in their abominable manners, that they become Christian in fact as in name, and that the church of that country, as rude and disorderly as the nation itself, be brought under better laws." In support of this donation of an entire people, body, and goods, a sentence of excommunication handed over to Satan all who should dare to deny the rights of king Henry and his heirs over Ireland.

Everything now appeared settled in the most satisfactory manner, for the great grandson of the conqueror of England. The man who had troubled him for nine years was no more; and the pope who had made use of the obstinate determination of that man to alarm the ambition of the king, now amicably aided the king in his projects of conquest. That nothing might disturb his repose, he dispensed him, by absolution, from all the remorse which might trouble his conscience, after a murder committed, if not by his order, at least to please him. He even exempted him, by implication, from the obligation of punishing those who had committed that murder, in excess o zeal for his interest; and the four Normans, Traci, Morville, Fitz-Ours, and Le Breton, dwelt safely and at peace in a royal castle in the north of England. No justice prosecuted them but that of public opinion, which spread a thousand sinister reports respecting them; for example, that even animals were horrified at their presence, and that the dogs refused to touch the bones from their table. In gaining the sanction of the pope against Ireland, Henry II. was, by this augmentation of external power, amply recompensed for the diminution of his influence over ecclesiastical affairs; and there is nothing to show that he did not readily assent to the latter sacrifice. A pure taste for good was not the motive which had actuated him in his legislative reforms; and it will be remembered that he had already more than once proposed to the pope to abandon to him the statutes of Clarendon, and still more, if on his side he would consent to sacrifice Thomas Beket. Thus, after protracted turmoil and agitation, Henry II. enjoyed in repose the delight of satisfied ambition: but this calm was of brief duration; new vexations, with which, by a singular fatality, was again mixed up the memory of the archbishop, soon afflicted the king.

The reader bears in mind that, during the life of the primate, Henry, being unsuccessful in persuading the pope to deprive him of his title, had resolved to abolish the primacy itself, and with this view had caused his eldest son to be crowned by the archbishop of York.

This step, apparently of no other importance than that it attacked in its foundation the hierarchy established by the conquest, had consequences which none had foreseen. As there were two kings of England, the courtiers and flatterers having, as it were, double employment, divided themselves between the father and the son. The younger and more active in intrigue sided with the latter, whose reign offered a longer perspective of favour. A peculiar circumstance more especially procured him the affection of the Aquitans and Poitevins, able, insinuating, persuasive men, eager after novelty, and prompt to avail themselves of any opportunity of weakening the Anglo-Norman power, which they obeyed with reluctance. The good understanding between Eleanor of Guienne and her husband had long ceased to exist. The latter, once in possession of the honours and titles which the daughter of earl William had brought to him as her portion, and for which, as the old historians say, he had alone loved and married her, kept mistresses of every rank and nation. The duchess of Aquitaine, passionate and vindictive as a woman of the south, endeavoured to inspire her sons with aversion towards their father, and by treating them with the utmost tenderness and indulgence, to raise up in them a support against him. Ever since the eldest had shared the royal dignity, she had given him friends, councillors, and confidants, who, during the father's numerous absences, excited as much as possible the ambition and pride of the young man. They had little difficulty in persuading him that his father, in crowning him king, had fully abdicated in his favour; that he alone was king of England, and that no other person ought to assume the title or exercise the sovereign authority.

The old king, as Henry II. was now designated, soon perceived the evil designs which the confidants of his son sought to inculcate upon him; he several times obliged him to change his friends, and to dismiss those whom he most loved. But these measures, which the continual occupations of Henry II. upon the continent and in Ireland prevented him from following up, angered the young man without correcting him, and gave him a sort of right to call himself persecuted, and to complain of his father. Things were in this position when peace was re-established, by the mediation of the pope, between the kings of France and of England. One of the causes of their last quarrel was that king Henry, when crowning his son by the hands of the archbishop of York, had not, at the same time, crowned his son's wife, Marguerite, the daughter of the king of France. This grievance was now remedied; and Marguerite, crowned queen, requested to visit her father at Paris. Henry II., having no reasons to oppose to this demand, allowed the young king to accompany his wife to the court of France; and, on their return, found his son more discontented than ever: he complained of being a king without land or treasure, and of not having a house of his own in which to live with his wife; he went so far as to ask his father to resign to him, in full sovereignty, the kingdom of England, the duchy of Normandy, or the earldom of Anjou. The old king counselled him to remain quiet, and to have patience until the time when the succession to all his territories would fall to him naturally. This answer raised the anger of the young man to the highest point; and from that day forth, say the contemporary historians, he did not address a single word of peace to his father.

Henry II. entertaining fears as to his conduct, and desiring closely to observe him, made him travel with him in the province of Aquitaine. They held their court at Limoges, where Raymond, count of Toulouse, quitting his alliance with the king of France, came to do homage to the king of England, pursuant to the vacillating policy of the southerns, ever balancing and passing alternately from one to the other of the kings their enemies. Count Raymond made a fictitious transfer to his ally of the territory he governed, which was then by a similar legal fiction returned to him to hold in fief, he taking in respect of it the oath taken by a vassal to whom a lord really conceded an estate. He swore to observe to Henry fealty and honour, to give him aid and counsel towards and against all, never to betray his secrets, and to reveal to him, on occasion, the secrets of his enemies. When the count of Toulouse came to this last portion of the oath of homage:—"I have to warn you," he said to the king, "to secure your castles of Poitou and Guienne, and to distrust your wife and son." Henry took no public notice of this information, indicating a plot which the count of Toulouse had been solicited to join; but he availed himself of several large hunting-parties, as they seemed, composed of his most devoted adherents, to visit the fortresses of the country, place them in a state of defence, and assure himself of the men who commanded them.

On their return from this progress in Aquitaine, the king and his son stopped to sleep at Chinon, and in the night, the son, without notice to his father, quitted him, and proceeded to Alençon. The father pursued, but failed to overtake him; the young man went to Argentan, and thence during the night into the territory of France. As soon as the old king heard this, he mounted his horse, and with the utmost possible rapidity visited the whole frontier of Normandy, inspecting the fortresses, and placing them in a state of defence against surprise. He then sent despatches to all his castellans of Anjou, Brittany, Aquitaine, and England, ordering them to repair and guard with redoubled care their fortresses and towns. Messengers also repaired to the king of France, to learn what were his intentions, and to claim the fugitive in the name of paternal authority. King Louis received these ambassadors in full court, having at his right hand young Henry, attired in royal robes. When the messengers had presented their despatches, according to the ceremonial of the time: "From whom bring you this message?" asked the king of France. "From Henry, king of England, duke of Normandy, duke of Aquitaine, earl of the Angevins and of the Manceaux." "That is false," answered the king, "for here at my side is Henry king of England, who has nothing to say to me through you. But if it be the father of this king, the late king of England, to whom you give these titles, know that he is dead since the day on which his son assumed the crown; and if he still pretends to be king, after having, in the sight of the world resigned the kingdom to his son, it is a matter we shall soon remedy."

And, in effect, young Henry was acknowledged sole king of England, in a general assembly of all the barons and bishops of the kingdom of France. King Louis VII. and, after him, all the lords, swore, their hands on the Gospel, to assist the son with all their power to conquer the territories of his father. The king of France had a great seal made with the arms of England, that Henry the Younger might affix this token of legality to his charters and despatches. As a first act of sovereignty, the latter made donations of lands and honours in England and upon the continent to the principal lords of France, and to other enemies of his father. He confirmed to the king of Scotland the conquests which his predecessor had made in Northumberland; and gave to the earl of Flanders the whole county of Kent, with the castles of Dover and Rochester. He gave to the count of Boulogne a vast domain near Lincoln, with the county of Mortain in Normandy; and to the earl of Blois, Amboise, Chateau Reynault, and five hundred pounds of silver from the revenues of Anjou. Other donations were made to several barons of England and Normandy, who had promised to declare against the old king; and Henry the Younger sent despatches, sealed with his new royal seal, to his own friends, his mother's friends, and even to the pope, whom he endeavoured to gain over by the offer of greater advantages than the court of Rome then derived from its friendship with Henry II. This last letter was, in some measure, the manifesto of insurrection; for it was to the sovereign pontiff that were then made the appeals which, in our times, are addressed to public opinion.

A singular peculiarity of this manifesto is, that Henry the Younger assumes therein all the titles of his father, except that of duke of Aquitaine, doubtless the better to conciliate the favour of the people of that country, unwilling to acknowledge any right over them but that of the daughter of their last national chief. A still more remarkable circumstance is the origin which the young king attributes to his quarrel with his father, and the manner in which he justifies himself for having violated the commandment of God, which prescribes honour to father and to mother. "I pass over in silence," says the letter, "my own personal injuries, to come to that which has most powerfully influenced me. The reprobate villains who, even in the very temple, massacred my foster father, the glorious martyr of Christ, Saint Thomas of Canterbury, remain safe and unharmed; they have still deep root in the land; no act of royal justice has pursued them after so frightful a crime. I could not endure this negligence, and this was the first and principal cause of the present discord. The blood of the martyr cried out to me; I could not comply with his demand, I could not give him the vengeance and the honours due to him; but I at least evinced my respect for him by visiting his sepulchre, in the sight and to the astonishment of the whole realm. My father was greatly incensed against me for so doing; but I, certes, heed not the offending a father, when the alternative is offending Christ, for whom we ought to abandon both father and mother. This is the origin of our dissensions; hear me then, most holy father, and judge my cause; for it will be truly just, if it be justified by thy apostolic authority."

To appreciate these assertions at their just value, it will be sufficient to recal to mind the proclamations issued by the young king himself, when Thomas Beket came to London. Then, it was by his express command that access to the capital and to all the towns in England, except Canterbury, was forbidden to the archbishop, and that every man who had presented his hand to him, in token of welcome, was declared a public enemy. The remembrance of these notorious facts was still fresh in the memory of the people, and hence, doubtless, the general surprise occasioned by the visit of the persecutor to the tomb of the persecuted, if the visit, indeed, be not altogether fabulous. To this statement, set forth with all the forms of deference that could flatter the pride of the Roman pontiff, the young king added a sort of scheme of the new administration which he proposed to institute throughout his father's states. Should God grant him permission to conquer them, he intended, he wrote, to reinstate ecclesiastical elections in all their liberty, without the intervention in any way or degree of the royal power; he proposed that the revenues of vacant churches should be reserved for the future incumbent, and no longer be levied for the revenue, not being able to endure that the "property of the cross acquired by the blood of the Crucified, should administer to that luxury and splendour, without which kings cannot live." That the bishops should have full power to excommunicate and to interdict, to bind and to loose, throughout the kingdom, and that no member of the clergy should ever be cited before lay judges, as Christ before Pilate. Henry the Younger offered further to add to these regulations any which the pope might be pleased to suggest, and lastly, intreated him to write officially to all the clergy of England, "that by the inspiration of God, and the intercession of the new martyr, her king had conferred liberties upon them which would excite their joy and gratitude." Such a declaration would indeed have been of great assistance to the young man, who, looking upon his father as already dead, styled himself Henry the Third. But the court of Rome, too prudent lightly to abandon the certain for the uncertain, was in no haste to answer this despatch, and until fortune should declare herself in a more decisive manner, preferred the alliance of the father to that of the son.

Besides this son, who was commonly called the young king, in the Norman language, li reys Josnes, and lo reis Joves in the dialect of the southern provinces, the king of England had three others: Richard, whom, notwithstanding his youth, his father had created earl of Poitiers, and who was called Richard of Poitiers; Geoffroy, earl of Brittany, and lastly, John, surnamed Sans-terre (Lackland), because he alone, of them all, had neither government nor province. The latter was too young to take a part in the quarrel between his father and his eldest brother; but the two others embraced the cause of the latter under the influence of their mother, and secretly urged on by their vassals of Poitou and Brittany.

It was with the vast portion of Gaul now united under the authority of Henry II., as it had been with the whole of Gaul, in the time of the Frank emperor, Lodewig, commonly called Louis-le-pieux, or le Debonnaire. The populations who dwelt south of the Loire would no more be associated with those who resided north of that river, or with the people of England, than the Gauls and Italians of the empire of Charlemagne with the Germans under the sceptre of a German king. The rebellion of the sons of Henry II. concurring with these national distastes, and associating with them, as formerly that of the children of Louis-le-Debonnaire, could not fail to reproduce, although in a more limited arena, the dark scenes which signalized the discords of the family of the Frank Cæsars. The sword once drawn between father and son, neither would be permitted to return it at his pleasure to the scabbard; for connected with the two rival parties in this domestic war there were nations, there were popular interests, which would not turn with the vacillations of paternal indulgence or of filial repentance.

Richard of Poitiers and Geoffroy of Brittany quitted Aquitaine, where they resided with their mother Eleanor, to join their eldest brother at the court of France. Both arrived there in safety; but their mother, on her way to the same court, was arrested, disguised as a man, and thrown into prison by order of the king of England. On the arrival of the two young brothers, the king of France made them swear solemnly as their elder brother had done, never to conclude a peace or truce with their father, but through the barons of France. The war then commenced on the frontiers of Normandy. As soon as the news of these events spread over England, the whole country was in a state of excitement. Many men of Norman race, and especially the younger men, declared for the son's party; the Saxon population, as a body, remained indifferent to the dispute; individually, the serfs and vassals took the side which their lord adopted. The citizens were enrolled, whether they would or no, in the cause of the earls or viscounts who governed the towns, and armed, either for father or son.

Henry II. was now in Normandy, and well nigh each day witnessed the departure from his palace of one or more of his most trusted courtiers, men who had eaten at his table, and to whom he had, with his own hands, given the belt of knighthood. "It was for him," says a contemporary, "the extreme of grief and despair to see, leaving him for the enemy, one after the other, the guards of his chamber, those to whom he had confided his person and his life; for almost every night some one departed, whose absence was discovered at the morning call." In this deserted condition, and amidst the dangers it presented, the king displayed much apparent tranquillity. He followed the chase more earnestly than ever; he was gay and affable to the companions who remained with him, and replied with gentleness to the demands of those who, profiting by his critical position, required exorbitant remuneration for their fidelity. His greatest hope was in the assistance of foreigners. He sent to great distances, soliciting the aid of kings who had sons. He wrote to Rome, soliciting from the pope the excommunication of his enemies; and in order to obtain in this court an influence superior to that of his adversaries, he made to the apostolic see that admission of vassalage, which William the Conqueror had so haughtily refused. His letter to pope Alexander III. contained the following passages: "You, whom God has raised to the sublimity of the pastoral functions, to give to his people the knowledge of salvation, though absent in body, present in mind, I throw myself at your feet. To your jurisdiction appertains the kingdom of England, and I am bound and held to you by all the obligations which the law imposes on feudatories. Let England then experience what the Roman pontiff can effect, and as you do not employ material weapons, defend the patrimony of the blessed Peter with the spiritual sword."

The pope met this demand by ratifying the sentences of excommunication which the bishops who remained faithful to the king had hurled against the partisans of his sons. He sent, moveover, a special legate, charged to re-establish domestic peace, and to take care that this peace, whatever its conditions in other respects, should be productive of some new advantage to the princes of the Roman church.

Meantime, on one side the king of France and Henry the Younger, and on the other, the earls of Flanders and Brittany, passed in arms the frontier of Normandy. Richard, the second son of the king of England, had repaired to Poitou, and most of the barons of that country rose in his cause, rather from hatred to the father than from love for the sons. Those who, in Brittany, some years before, had formed a national league, revived their confederation, and armed apparently for count Geoffroy, but in reality for their own independence. Thus attacked at once on several points, the king of England had no troops on whom he could fully rely, but twenty thousand of the mercenaries, then called Brabançons, Cotereaux, or Routiers, bandits in time of peace, soldiers in time of war, serving indifferently every cause; as brave as any other troops of the period, and better disciplined. With a portion of this army, Henry II. arrested the progress of the king of France; the other portion he sent against the revolted Bretons, who were defeated in a pitched battle by the military experience of the Brabançons, and compelled to retreat to their castles and to the town of Dol, which the king of England besieged and took in a few days.

The defeat of the Bretons diminished the ardour, not of the sons of king Henry and their Norman, Angevin, or Aquitan partisans, but of the king of France, who, above all things, desired to carry on the war at the least possible expense. Fearing to be involved in a too great expenditure of men and money, or desirous of essaying other political combinations, he one day said to the rebellious sons, that they would do well to effect a reconciliation with their father. The young princes, constrained by the will of their ally to a sudden return of filial affection, followed him to the place appointed for the conference of peace. Not far from Gisors, in a vast plain, there stood a gigantic elm, whose branches had been artificially bent down to the earth, forming a covered circle, under which, from time immemorial, the interviews of the dukes of Normandy and the kings of France had taken place. Thither came the two kings, accompanied by their archbishops, bishops, earls, and barons. The sons of Henry II. made their demands, and the father seemed disposed to make them considerable concessions. He offered to the eldest, one half of the royal revenues of England and four good fortresses in that country, if he chose to reside there, or, if he preferred it, three castles in Normandy, one in Maine, one in Anjou, and one in Touraine, with all the revenues of his ancestors the earls of Anjou, and half the revenues of Normandy. He offered, in like manner, lands and revenues to Richard and Geoffroy. But this facility on his part, and his earnest desire to remove permanently every source of dissension between his sons and himself, alarmed the king of France, who, no longer desiring peace, allowed the partisans of Henry's sons, who greatly feared it, to create obstacles and intrigues tending to break off the negotiations thus favourably commenced. One of these men, Robert de Beaumont, earl of Leicester, went so far as to insult the king of England to his face, and to lay his hand on his sword. He was withheld from actual violence by the surrounding nobles; but the tumult which ensued stayed all accommodation, and hostilities soon recommenced between the father and the sons. Henry the Younger and Geoffroy remained with the king of France; Richard returned to Poitou; and Robert de Beaumont, who had personally menaced the king, went to England to join Hugh Bigot, one of the richest barons of the land, and a zealous partisan of the rebellion.

Ere earl Robert could reach his town of Leicester, it was attacked by Richard de Lucy, the king's grand justiciary. The earl's men-at-arms made a vigorous defence, and compelled the Saxon burgesses to fight for them; but part of the rampart giving way, the Norman soldiers retreated into the castle, leaving the town to its fate. The burgesses continued their resistance, unwilling to yield at discretion to men who deemed it a venial sin to kill an insurgent Englishman. Obliged at length to capitulate, they purchased, for three hundred pounds of silver, permission to withdraw from the town, and to proceed wherever they thought fit. They sought a refuge upon the lands of the church: some went to Saint Alban's, and many to Bury Saint Edmund's, named after a martyr of English race, who, according to the popular notion, was ever ready to protect his countrymen against the tyranny of the foreigners. On their departure, the town was dismantled by the royal troops, who broke down the gates and levelled the walls. While the English of Leicester were thus punished because their Norman governor had taken part in the revolt, one of the lieutenants of that governor, Anquetil Malory, having collected a body of earl Robert's vassals and partisans, attacked Northampton, held by its viscount for the king. The viscount obliged the burgesses to take up arms for his party in the same way that those of Leicester had been compulsorily armed on the other side. A great number were killed and wounded, and two hundred taken prisoners. Such was the calamitous part played by the population of English race in the civil war of the sons of their conquerors.

The natural sons of king Henry had remained faithful to their father, and one of them, Geoffroy, bishop of Lincoln, vigorously urged on the war, besieging the castles and fortresses of the barons on the other side. Meantime, Richard had been fortifying the towns and castles of Poitou and Angoumois, and it was against him that the king now marched with his faithful Brabançons, leaving Normandy, where he had most friends, to combat the king of France. He laid siege to Saintes, then defended by two castles, one of which bore the name of the Capitol, a reminiscence of old Rome preserved in several cities of southern Gaul. After taking the fortresses of Saintes, Henry attacked with his war machines the two towers of the episcopal church, wherein the partisans of Richard had fortified themselves. He took it, with the fort of Taillebourg and several other castles, and, on his return to Anjou, devastated all the frontier of Poitou, burning the houses, and uprooting the vines and fruit trees. He had scarcely arrived in Normandy, when he learned that his eldest son and the earl of Flanders, having assembled a large naval force, were preparing to make a descent upon England. This news decided him upon immediately returning to that country; he took with him, as prisoners, his wife Eleanor, and his daughter-in-law Marguerite, the daughter of the king of France.

From Southampton, where he landed, the king proceeded to Canterbury, and, as soon as he beheld its cathedral church, at three miles distance, he dismounted from his horse, quitted his silken robes, took off his shoes, and continued his journey barefoot upon the stony and, at that moment, muddy road. Arrived at the church which contained the tomb of Thomas Beket, he prostrated himself with his face to the earth, weeping and sobbing, in sight of all the people of the town, attracted thither by the ringing of the bells. The bishop of London, the same Gilbert Foliot who had been the greatest enemy of Beket in his lifetime, and who, after his death, had proposed to throw his body upon a dunghill, mounted the pulpit, and, addressing the congregation: "All you here present," he said, "know that Henry, king of England, invoking, for the salvation of his soul, God and the holy martyr, protests before you that he neither ordered, wished, nor wilfully caused, nor desired in his heart the death of the martyr. But, as it is possible, that the murderers availed themselves of some words imprudently escaping him, he declares that he seeks penitential chastisement of the bishops here assembled, and consents to submit his bare back to the discipline of the rod."

And in effect, the king, accompanied by a great number of Norman bishops and abbots, and by all the Norman and Saxon priests of the chapter of Canterbury, proceeded to the subterranean church, where two years before the body of the archbishop had been placed as in a fortress to remove it from the insults of the royal officers. Here, kneeling upon the tomb-stone, and stripping off his clothes, he placed himself, with bare back in the posture in which his justiciaries had placed the English who were publicly whipped for having received Thomas on his return from exile, or for having honoured him as a saint. Each of the bishops, the parts being previously arranged, took one of those whips with several lashes, used in the monasteries to inflict ecclesiastical correction, and which, for that reason, were called disciplines. Each struck two or three gentle blows on the king's shoulders, saying: "As thy Redeemer was scourged for the sins of men, so be thou scourged for thy own sin." From the hands of the bishops, the whips passed into those of the priests, who were in great numbers, and for the most part of English race. These sons of the serfs of the conquest impressed the marks of the whip upon the flesh of the grandson of the Conqueror, with a secret satisfaction, revealed by some bitter jests in the contemporary narratives of the affair.

But neither this joy nor this triumph of a moment, produced any fruit for the English population; on the contrary, that population was duped in this scene of hypocrisy acted before it by the king of Angevin race. Henry II. seeing the greater number of his continental subjects turning against him, recognised the necessity of rendering himself popular with the Saxons in order to gain their support. He thought lightly of a few strokes of a whip, could he at such a price obtain the loyal services which the English populace had rendered to his ancestor, Henry I. In fact, since the murder of Thomas Beket, the love of this new martyr had become the passion, or more accurately, the madness of the English nation. The religious worship with which the memory of the archbishop was surrounded, had weakened, had superseded, well nigh every patriotic reminiscence. No tradition of national independence was more powerful than the deep impression produced by those nine years, during which a primate of Saxon race had been the object of the hopes, the prayers, the conversation of every Saxon. A marked proof of sympathy with this popular sentiment was, then, the most effective attraction by which the king could draw the native English to him, and render them, in the words of an old historian, "manageable in bit and harness." This was the true cause of the pilgrimage of Henry II. to the tomb of him whom he had, at first, loved as the companion of his pleasures, and afterwards mortally hated as his political opponent.

"After having been thus whipped, of his own free will," says the contemporary narration, "he persevered in his prayers to the holy martyr, all day and all night, taking no nourishment, leaving the church for no need; as he had come, so he remained, allowing no carpet or similar thing to be placed under his knees. After matins, he made the circuit of the upper church, prayed before all the altars and all the relics, and then returned to the tomb of the saint. On Saturday, when the sun had risen, he heard mass; then, having drunk water blessed by the martyr, and filled a flask with it, he joyously departed from Canterbury."

This ostentatious display of contrition had entire success; it was with perfect enthusiasm that the burgesses of the towns, and the serfs of the country, heard it preached in the churches that the king had reconciled himself with the blessed martyr, by penitence and tears. It happened, by chance, that at the same time, William, king of Scotland, who had made an hostile incursion upon the English territory, was defeated and made prisoner near Alnwick in Northumberland. The Saxon population, passionately intent upon the honour of Saint Thomas, viewed in this victory a manifest token of the benevolence and protection of the martyr, and from that day forth sided with the old king, whom the saint thus evidently favoured. Acting upon this superstitious impulse, the native English enrolled themselves in crowds under the royal banner, and fought with ardour against the accomplices of revolt. Poor and despised as they were, they formed the great mass of the population, and nothing can resist such a power when it is organized. The enemy were defeated in every county, their castles taken by assault, and numbers of earls and barons made prisoners. "So many were taken," says a contemporary, "that they could hardly procure cords enough wherewith to bind them, or prisons enough wherein to confine them." This rapid series of victories arrested the project of descent upon England formed by Henry the Younger and the earl of Flanders.

But on the continent, where the populations subject to the king of England had no national affection for the English Beket, the affairs of Henry II. prospered no better after his visit and his flagellation at the martyr's tomb than before. On the contrary, the Poitevins and Bretons recovered from their first defeat, and renewed more firmly their patriotic associations. Eudes de Porrhoet, whose daughter the king of England had formerly dishonoured, and whom the same king had subsequently banished, returned from exile, and again rallied in Brittany all who were weary of the Norman domination. The malcontents made some daring excursions that gave to Breton temerity celebrity all over the continent. In Aquitaine, Richard's party also resumed courage, and fresh troops of insurgents assembled in the mountainous parts of Poitou and Perigord, under the same chiefs who, a few years before, had risen in arms at the instigation of the king of France. Hatred of the foreign power collected around the lords of the castles the inhabitants of the towns and villages, men free in body and goods; for servitude did not exist south of the Loire, as it did north of that river. Barons, castellans, and portionless sons of castellans, also adopted the same side, from a motive less pure, the hope of making a fortune by the war. They opened the campaign by attacking the rich abbots and bishops of the country, most of whom, according to the spirit of their order, supported the cause of established power. They pillaged their domains, or, arresting them on the highways, shut them up in their castles till they paid ransom. Among these prisoners was the archbishop of Bordeaux, who, according to the papal instructions, had excommunicated the enemies of the elder Henry in Aquitaine, as the archbishop of Rouen excommunicated them in Normandy, Anjou, and Brittany.

At the head of the insurgents of Guienne figured, less from his fortune and rank, than from his indefatigable ardour, Bertrand de Born, seigneur of Haute-Fort, near Perigueux, a man who combined in the highest degree all the qualities necessary to the fulfilment of a distinguished part in the middle ages. He was a warrior and a poet, a man ever under the impulsive influence of an excessive need of action, of emotion; of an activity and an ability which he employed wholly in political affairs. But this agitation, vain and turbulent in appearance, was not without a real object, without a close reference to the welfare of his native land. This extraordinary man appears to have had the profound conviction, that his country, adjoining the states of the kings of France and of England, had no other escape from the dangers which ever threatened it, on one side or the other, but in war between its two enemies. Such seems to have been the idea which, during Bertrand's life, guided his actions and his conduct. "At all times," says his Provençal biographer, "he desired that war should be between the king of France and the king of England, and if the kings made peace or truce, he worked and toiled to undo that peace or that truce." With this view, Bertrand employed all his address to develop and envenom the quarrel between the king of England and his sons; he was one of those who, gaining an ascendancy over the mind of young Henry, aroused his ambition and excited him to revolt. He gained equal influence over the other sons, and even over their father, ever to their detriment and to the profit of Aquitaine. This is the testimony rendered of him by his ancient biographer, with all the pride of a man of the south, setting forth the moral superiority of one of his countrymen over the kings and princes of the north: "He was master whenever he pleased of king Henry of England and his sons, and always did he desire that they should all of them, the father, the sons and the brothers, be at war with each other."

His efforts, crowned with complete success, obtained for him an ill reputation with those who saw in him only a counsellor of domestic discord, a man seeking maliciously, to speak the mystic language of the period, to raise blood against flesh, to divide the head from the members. It is for this reason that Dante makes him, in his Inferno, suffer a punishment analogous with the figurative expression by which his offence was designated. "I saw, and still seem to see, a body without a head advancing towards us, carrying its severed head in its hand by the hair, like a lantern. Know that I am Bertrand de Born, he who gave ill counsel to the young king."

But Bertrand did something more: he was not content with giving to young Henry that counsel against his father which the poet terms ill counsel; he gave to him similar counsel against his brother Richard, and when the young king was dead, to Richard against the old king; and lastly, when the latter was dead, to Richard against the king of France, and to the king of France against

Richard. He never allowed them to remain for an instant upon a good understanding, but constantly animated them one against the other, by the sirventès or satirical songs so greatly in vogue at that time.

Poetry then played a great part in the politics of the countries south of the Loire. No peace, no war, no revolt, no diplomatic transaction, took place that was not announced, proclaimed, praised or blamed in verse. These verses, often composed by the very men who had taken an active part in the events that formed their subject, were of an energy almost inconceivable to him who regards the ancient idiom of southern Gaul, in the effeminate aspect it has assumed since the French dialect has replaced it as a literary language. The songs of the trobadores, or Provençal, Toulousan, Dauphinese, Aquitainan, Poitevin, and Limousin poets, rapidly circulated from castle to castle, from town to town, doing in the twelfth century the office of newspapers, in the country comprised between the Vienne, the Isere, the mountains of Auvergne and the two seas. There was not as yet in this country any religious inquisition; men there freely and openly criticised that which the people of the other portions of Gaul scarcely dared to examine. The influence of public opinion and of popular passions, was everywhere felt, in the cloisters of the monks as in the castles of the barons; and, coming to the subject of this history, the dispute between Henry II. and his sons so vividly excited the men of Aquitaine, that we find the impress of these emotions even in the writings, generally characterized by very little animation, of the Latin chroniclers. One of these, an anonymous dweller in an obscure monastery, cannot refrain from interrupting his narrative with a poetical prose version of the war song of the partisans of Richard.

"Rejoice, land of Aquitaine, rejoice, land of Poitou; the sceptre of the northern king recedes. Thanks to the pride of that king, the truce is at length broken between the realms of France and of England; England is desolate, and Normandy mourns. We shall see the king of the south coming to us with his great army, with his bows and his arrows. Woe to the king of the north, who dared raise his lance against the king of the south, his lord; his downfall approaches, and the stranger will devour his land."

After this outburst of joy and of patriotic hate, the author addresses Eleanor, alone of the family of Henry II. dear to the Aquitans, because she was born among them.

"Thou wert taken from thy native land and carried among strangers. Reared in abundance and delicacy, thou didst enjoy a regal liberty, thou didst live in the bo om of riches, thou wert amused by the sports of thy women, by their songs, sung to the sound of the guitar and of the drum; and now, thou lamentest, thou weepest, thou art consumed with grief; return to thy cities, poor prisoner.

"Where is thy court? where are thy young companions? where thy counsellors? Some, dragged far from their country, have suffered an ignominious death; others have been deprived of their sight; others, banished men, wander over the face of the earth. Thou criest, and none listen to thee, for the northern king keeps thee inclosed like a besieged city: cry out then, cease not to cry out; raise thy voice as a trumpet, that thy sons may hear thee, for the day approaches in which they will deliver thee, and thou shalt again behold thy native land."

To these expressions of love for the daughter of the ancient national chiefs, succeeds a malediction upon the cities, which, of choice or necessity, still stood out for the king of foreign race, and warlike exhortations to those of the other side, menaced with an attack of the royal troops.

"Woe to the traitors of Aquitaine! for the day of chastisement is at hand. Rochelle dreads that day; she doubles her walls and her moats; she surrounds herself on every side with the sea, and the sound of this great work is heard beyond the mountains. Flee before Richard, duke of Aquitaine, ye who inhabit that shore; for he will overthrow the proud, he will destroy the chariots and those who guide them; he will annihilate all, from the highest to the lowest, who refuse him admittance to Saintonge. Woe to those who seek aid from the king of the north! Woe to you, rich men of Rochelle, who confide in your riches! the day will come when there will be no escape for you, when flight will not save you; when the bramble, instead of gold, will fill your mansions; and when the nettle will grow on your walls.

"And thou, maritime citadel, whose bastions are high and strong, the sons of the stranger will come to thee; but soon they will all flee to their own country, in disorder and covered with shame. Fear not their threats, raise thy front boldly against the north; stand upon thy guard, place thy foot on thy entrenchments; call thy neighbours, that they may come in strength to thy aid; range in a circle around thee all who inhabit thy bosom and cultivate thy land, from the southern frontier to the gulf wherein the ocean foams."

The success of the royal cause in England soon allowed Henry II. to cross the Channel with his faithful Brabançons and a body of Welsh mercenaries, less disciplined than the Brabançons, but more impetuous, and disposed, from the very hatred they bore the king, to wage furious war upon his sons. These men, skilled in the art of military ambuscade and of partisan warfare among woods and marshes, were employed in Normandy to intercept the convoys and provisions of the French army, then besieging Rouen. They succeeded so well in this by dint of activity and address, that this great army, apprehending famine, suddenly raised the siege and withdrew. Its retreat gave king Henry the opportunity of assuming the offensive. He regained, inch by inch, all the territory that his enemies had occupied during his absence; and the French, once more weary of the enormous expenses they had so fruitlessly undergone, again informed Henry the Younger and his brother Geoffroy that they could no longer assist them, and that if they could not alone maintain the war against their father, they must be reconciled with him. The two princes, whose power was limited without foreign aid, were fain to obey. They allowed themselves to be conducted to an interview between the two kings, at which they made, perforce, diplomatic protestations of repentance and filial tenderness.

A truce was agreed upon, which would give the king of England time to go to Poitou, and force his son Richard to submit like the two others. The king of France swore that he would give Richard no more aid, and imposed the same oath on the two brothers, Henry and Geoffroy. Richard was indignant on learning that his brothers and his ally had concluded a truce from which he was excluded. But, incapable of resisting alone the forces of the king of England, he returned to him, implored his pardon, restored the towns he had fortified, and quitting Poitou, followed his father to the frontiers of Anjou and France, where a general congress or parliament was held to settle the peace. Here, under the form of a political treaty, was drawn up the act of reconciliation between the king of England and his three sons. Placing their hands in those of their father, they swore to him the oath of liege homage, the ordinary form of every compact of alliance between two men of unequal power, and so solemn in this age as to establish between the contracting parties ties reputed more inviolable than those of blood. The historians of the epoch are careful to observe that, if the sons of king Henry II. now declared themselves his men, and swore allegiance to him, it was to remove from his mind every suspicion as to the sincerity of their return.

This reconciliation of the Angevin princes was a calamitous event for the various populations which had taken part in their quarrels. The three sons, in whose name they had revolted, kept their oath of homage by delivering up these populations to the vengeance of their father, and themselves undertaking to execute it. Richard, especially, more imperious and of a more rugged temperament than his brothers, inflicted all the injury he could on his former allies of Poitou; these, reduced to despair, maintained against him the national league at the head of which they had before placed him, and pressed him so closely that the king was obliged to send him powerful succours, and to go in person to his assistance. The excitement of the people of Aquitaine increased with the danger. From one end of that vast country to the other, a war broke out, more truly patriotic than the former, because it was against the whole family of the foreign princes; but for this very reason, the success was necessarily more doubtful, and the difficulties greater. During nearly two years the Angevin princes and the barons of Aquitaine fought battle after battle, from Limoges to the foot of the Pyrenees, at Taillebourg, at Angouleme, at Agen, at Dax, and at Bayonne. All the towns which had adopted the party of the king's sons, were militarily occupied by Richard's troops, and overwhelmed with taxes, in punishment of their revolt.

Whether from policy or good feeling, Henry the Younger took no part in this odious and dishonourable war; he even maintained relations of friendship with many of the men who had supported him and his brothers. Thus he lost none of his popularity in the southern provinces, and this circumstance was, for the family of Henry II., a fresh source of discord, which the able and indefatigable Bertrand de Born laboured with all his energies to develop. He attached himself more than ever to the young king, over whom he resumed all the ascendancy of a man of strong mind and resolute determination. Out of this connexion arose a second league, formed against Richard by the viscounts of Ventadour, Limoges, and Turenne, the count of Perigord, the seigneurs de Montfort and de Gordon, and the burgesses of the country, under the auspices of Henry the Younger and the king of France. Consistently with his usual policy, this king entered into only vague engagements with the confederates, but Henry the Younger made them positive promises; and Bertrand de Born, the soul of the confederation, proclaimed it in a poem designed, says his biographer, to confirm his friends in their common resolution.

Thus war recommenced in Poitou between Henry and earl Richard. But, at the very outset, Henry the Younger breaking his word, listened to propositions of accommodation with his brother, and, for a sum of money and an annual pension, consented to quit the country and desert the insurgents. Without thinking any more of them or their fate, he visited foreign courts, those of France, Provence, and Lombardy, spending the price of his treachery, and acquiring wherever he went high renown for magnificence and chivalry; conspicuous in warlike jousts, which were just coming into fashion, tourneying, resting, sleeping, solacing himself, as an ancient historian relates.

In this way he passed more than two years, during which the barons of Poitou, Angoumois, and Perigord, who had confederated under his auspices, had to sustain a fierce war at the hands of the earl of Poitiers. Their towns and their castles were besieged, and their lands laid waste by fire. Among the towns attacked, Taillebourg was the last to surrender, and when all the barons had submitted to Richard, Bertrand de Born alone still resisted in his castle of Haute-Fort. Amidst the fatigues and anxieties attending this desperate struggle, he retained sufficient freedom of thought to compose verses on his own position, and satires on the cowardice of the prince who passed in amusements the days which his old friends were passing in war and in suffering.

"Since the lord Henry has no land, and seeks not to have any, let him be named the king of cowards.

"For cowardly is he who lives on the wages and wears the livery of another. The crowned king who takes the pay of another, resembles not the gallant knight of former days; since he has deceived the Poitevins, and lied to them, let him no longer hope to be loved by them."

Henry the Younger felt these reproaches when, satiated with the pleasure of being cited as a spendthrift and chevalereux, he again turned his attention to the more solid advantages of power and territorial wealth. He then returned to his father, and pleaded with him the cause of the people of Poitou, whom Richard was overwhelming, he said, with unjust vexations and tyrannical domination. He went so far as to censure the king for not protecting them as he ought, he who was their natural defender. He accompanied these complaints with personal demands, again asking for Normandy or some other territory, where he might live in a manner worthy of his rank, with his wife, and out of whose revenues he could pay the wages of his knights and sergeants. Henry II. at first firmly objected to this demand, and even constrained the young man to swear that for the future he would claim no more than one hundred Angevin livres a day for his expenses, and ten livres of the same money for his wife. But things did not long remain in this position; Henry the Younger renewed his complaints, and the king, now yielding, ordered his two other sons to swear to their eldest brother the oath of homage for the provinces of Poitou and Brittany. Geoffroy consented; but Richard refused point-blank, and, in indication of his firm intention to resist the order, placed all his towns and castles in a state of defence.

Henry the Younger and Geoffroy, his vassal, then marched against him, with their father's consent; and, on their entering Aquitaine, the country once more rose against Richard. The confederacy of the towns and barons was renewed, and the king of France declared himself the ally of the young king and of the Aquitans. Henry II., alarmed at the serious turn which this family quarrel thus suddenly assumed, recalled his two sons, but they disobeyed the order, and persisted in warring upon the third. Obliged to take a decisive part, unless he chose to witness the triumph of the independence of Poitou and of the ambitious aims of the king of France, he joined his forces to those of Richard, and went in person to besiege Limoges, which had opened its gates to young Henry and Geoffroy. Thus the domestic war recommenced under a new aspect. It was no longer the three sons leagued together against the father, but the eldest and the youngest fighting against the other son and the father.

The historians of the south, eye-witnesses of these events, seem to have comprehended the active part taken in them by the populations, whose country was their theatre, and the national interests involved in these rivalries which appeared wholly personal. The historians of the north, on the contrary, only view in them the unnatural war of the father against the sons, and of the brothers among themselves, under the influence of an evil destiny hanging over the race of Plantagenet, in expiation of some great crime. Several sinister tales as to the origin of this family passed from mouth to mouth. It was said that Eleanor of Aquitaine had, at the court of France, a love affair with Geoffroy of Anjou, her husband's father; and that this same Geoffroy had married the daughter of Henry I. during the life of the emperor her husband; a circumstance which, in the opinion of the period, amounted to a kind of sacrilege. Lastly, it was rumoured of a former countess of Anjou, grandmother of the father of Henry II., that her husband having remarked with terror that she went rarely to church, and always left it before the mass, resolved to retain her forcibly, by four squires, during that celebration; but at the moment of the consecration, the countess, throwing off the mantle by which they held her, flew out at a window and was never after seen Richard of Poitiers, according to a contemporary, used to relate this adventure, and to observe: "Is it to be wondered at, that, coming from such a source, we live ill one with the other? What comes from the devil, must return to the devil!"

A month after the renewal of hostilities, Henry the Younger, whether from apprehension of the results of the unequal struggle in which he had engaged against his father and the most powerful of his brothers, or from a revival of filial tenderness, once more abandoned the Poitevins. He went to the camp of Henry II., revealed to him all the secrets of the confederation formed against Richard, and intreated him to interpose as mediator between his brother and himself. His hand on the Gospel, he swore solemnly that never again would he separate from Henry, king of England, but would be faithful to him, as to his father and his lord. This sudden change of conduct was not imitated by Geoffroy, who, more pertinacious and more loyal towards the revolted Aquitans, remained with them and continued the war. Messengers then came to him from the old king, urging him to terminate a quarrel, which was advantageous only to the common enemies of his family. Among other envoys was a Norman priest, who, holding a cross in his hand, intreated earl Geoffroy to spare the blood of the Christians, and not to imitate the crime of Absalom. "What! thou wouldst have me relinquish my birthright?" said the young man. "God forbid, monseigneur," answered the priest; "I seek nothing to your detriment." "Thou dost not understand my words," rejoined the earl of Brittany; "it is the destiny of our family not to love each other. That is our heritage, and none of us will ever renounce it."

Notwithstanding his reiterated treachery to the barons of Aquitaine, the young Henry, a man of wavering mind, and incapable of a firm decision, still maintained personal relations with several of the conspirators, and especially with Bertrand de Born. He undertook to play the part of mediator between them and his brother Richard, flattering himself with the chimerical hope of arranging the national quarrel at the same time with the family quarrel. To this end he made several advances to the chiefs of the league of Poitou, but he received from them nothing but haughty and hostile replies. As a last attempt, he proposed to them a conference at Limoges, offering to repair thither himself, with his father, and but a small train, to remove all distrust. The town of Limoges was at this time under siege by the king of England; it is not known whether the confederates formally consented to allow their enemy to enter, or whether the young man, eager to make himself of importance, promised more in their name than he was warranted in doing. However this may have been, when Henry II. arrived before the gates of the town, he found them closed, and he received from the ramparts a flight of arrows, one of which penetrated his doublet, and another wounded one of his knights who rode beside him. This affair passed as a mistake, and, after a fresh explanation with the insurgent chiefs, it was agreed that the king should freely enter Limoges, to confer with his son Geoffroy. They met in the great market-place; but during the interview, the Aquitans who formed the garrison of the castle, and who could not calmly witness the commencement of negotiations which would ruin all their projects of independence, shot at the old king, whom they recognised by his dress and the banner carried beside him; the bolt of a crossbow aimed at him from the ramparts of the citadel, pierced his horse's ear. The tears came into his eyes; he had the arrow picked up, and presenting it to Geoffroy: "Say, my son," he exclaimed, "what has thy unhappy father done to thee to deserve that thou should render him a mark for thy archers?"

Whatever the faults of Geoffroy towards his father, he was not to blame in this matter; for the archers who had aimed at the king of England were not soldiers in his pay, but his independent allies. The northern writers reproach him for not having sought out and punished them; but he had no such authority over them, and since he had bound up his cause with their national hostility, he had, whether he would or no, to undergo all the consequences. Henry the Younger, piqued at finding his efforts defeated by the obstinacy of the Aquitans, declared them all incurable rebels, and that he would never make peace or truce with them, but would be faithful to his father at all times and in all places. In token of this submission, he gave his horse and arms into the king's keeping, and remained several days with him, under every appearance of the warmest friendship.

But by a sort of fatality in the life of king Henry's eldest son, it was ever at the moment when he was making to one party the strongest protestations of devotion, that he was most immediately about to separate from it, and to engage with the opposite party. After having, in the words of an historian of the time, eaten at the same table with his father, and placed his hand in the same dish, he suddenly quitted him, leagued again with his adversaries, and proceeded to Le Dorat, a town on the frontiers of Poitou, which the insurgents had made their head-quarters. He ate with them at the same table, as he had done with the king, swore loyalty to them towards and against all, and a few days after abandoned them to return to the other camp. Fresh scenes of tenderness took place between the father and the son, and the latter thought he acquitted his conscience in intreating the king to be merciful to the rebels. He rashly promised, in their name, the surrender of the castle of Limoges, and announced that it would suffice to send messengers to the garrison to receive its oaths and hostages. But it was not so, and those who went on this mission from the king of England were nearly all put to death by the Aquitans. Others, who were sent at the same time to Geoffroy to negotiate with him, were attacked in his presence; two were killed, a third seriously wounded, and the fourth thrown into the river from the bridge. It was thus that the national spirit, severely, cruelly inflexible, mocked the hopes of the princes and their projects of reconciliation.

Shortly after these events, Henry II. received a message announcing to him that his eldest son, having fallen dangerously ill at Chateau-Martel, near Limoges, asked to see him. The king, whose mind was full of that which had just happened to his people, and of what had happened to himself in the two conferences at Limoges, suspected some snare on the part of the insurgents:

he feared, says a contemporary author, the wickedness of these conspirators, and notwithstanding the assurances of the messenger, he did not go to Chateau-Martel. A second messenger soon came to inform him that his son Henry had died on the 11th of June, in his twenty-seventh year. The young man, in his last moments, had manifested great signs of contrition and repentance: he had insisted on being drawn from his bed by a cord, and placed on a heap of ashes. This unexpected loss occasioned the king great affliction, and augmented his anger against the Aquitans, to whose perfidy he attributed the feeling of timidity that had kept him away from his dying son. Geoffroy himself, touched with his father's grief, returned to him, and abandoned his allies, who then found themselves alone in presence of the family whose dissensions had constituted their strength. The day after the funeral of Henry the Younger, the king of England vigorously attacked the town and fortress of Limoges by assault, and took them, with the castles of several of the confederates, which he completely demolished. He pursued Bertrand de Born with even greater inveteracy than all the others; "for he believed," says an ancient narrative, "that Bertrand had been the cause of all the wars that the young king, his son, had made against him; and for this he came to Haute-Fort to take and destroy it."

The castle of Haute-Fort did not long hold out against all the king's forces, united with those of his two sons, Richard and Geoffroy of Brittany. Forced to surrender at discretion, Bertrand de Born was led to his enemy's tent, who, before pronouncing the sentence of a conqueror on the conquered, desired to enjoy, for a space, the pleasure of revenge, in treating with derision the man who had inspired him with fear, and who had boasted that he felt no fear on his own part. "Bertrand," said he, "you who once said that you never needed more than half your sense, know that this is an occasion upon which the whole would do you no harm." "My lord," answered the man of the south, with that habitual assurance which the feeling of his intellectual superiority gave him, "it is true I said so, and I said the truth." "And I," rejoined the king, "think that you have lost your sense." "Yes, sire," answered Bertrand, gravely, "I lost it on the day when the valiant young king, your son, died; on that day I lost both my sense and my reason." At the name of his son, which he did not expect to hear pronounced, the king of England burst into tears, and fainted. When he came to himself, he was changed; his projects of revenge had disappeared, and he now saw in the man before him only the former friend of the son whom he lamented. Instead of the bitter reproaches and the sentence of death which Bertrand might have expected: "Sire Bertrand, sire Bertrand," he said to him, "well may you have lost your senses for my son; for he loved you more than he loved any man in the world; and I, for the love of him, restore to you your life, your possessions, and your castle. I give you my friendship and my favour, and I grant you five hundred silver marks for the damage you have sustained."

The misfortune which had struck the family of Henry II. reconciled not only the sons and the father, but also the father and the mother, a far more difficult thing, from the nature of the enmity existing between them. Common tradition accuses Eleanor of having poisoned one of her husband's mistresses, the daughter of an Anglo-Norman baron, named Rosamonde or Rosemonde. A good understanding, however, was now effected between them, and the queen of England, after an imprisonment of ten years, was restored to liberty. In her presence the family peace was solemnly sworn and confirmed by writing and by oath, as an historian of the time expresses it, between king Henry and his sons, Richard, Geoffroy, and John, the latter of whom hitherto had been too young to take a part in his brothers' intrigues. The continual affliction which the revolts of the others had occasioned the king, had led him to place the greatest affection upon John; and this preference itself had contributed to embitter the minds of the elder brothers, and to make the period of concord very brief. After a few months of union, the peace was again disturbed by the ambition of Geoffroy. He demanded the earldom of Anjou, in addition to his duchy of Brittany, and on the rejection of his application, passed into France, where, awaiting an occasion to recommence the war, he occupied himself with the amusements of the court. Thrown from his horse in a tournament, he was trodden under foot by the horses, and died of his wounds. After his death, it was earl Richard's turn to unite in friendship with the king of France against the will of his father.

The crown of France had just fallen to Philip, second of that name, a young man, who affected towards Richard still more friendship than his father, Louis VII., had manifested to Henry the Younger. "Every day," says a contemporary historian, "they ate at the same table and from the same dish, and at night they slept in the same bed." This vast friendship gave umbrage to the king of England, and much uneasiness as to the future. He sent repeated messages to France, summoning his son home; Richard regularly replied that he was coming, but he did not come. At length he departed, as if for his father's court; but passing by Chinon, where a portion of the royal treasure was deposited, he carried off the greatest part of it, despite the resistance of the keepers. With this money he proceeded to Poitou, and fortified, garrisoned, and provisioned several castles. Recent events had substituted for the former effervescence of the Aquitans an entire apathy, and the hatred which Richard had excited by his want of faith and his cruelties was still too vivid to allow men, however discontented with the Angevin government, to repose confidence in him. He remained therefore alone, and, unable to commence operations without the concurrence of the barons of the country, he made up his mind to return to his father, and implore his pardon, rather from necessity than from goodwill. The old king, who had gone through every solemn form of reconciliation between himself and his sons, essayed, on this occasion, to bind Richard by an oath on the Gospel, which he made him take in presence of a great assemblage of clergy and laymen.

The late attempt of the earl of Poitiers remaining without effect, produced no rupture of peace between the kings of France and England. The two kings had long since agreed to hold a conference, at which permanently to regulate those points of contending interests which might, if not settled, produce renewed misunderstanding. They met, in January 1187, between Trie and Gisors, at the Great Elm already referred to. The Christian conquerors of Syria and Palestine were at this time undergoing great reverses; Jerusalem and the wood of the true cross had just fallen once more into the power of the Mohammedans, under the command of Salah-Eddin, popularly called Saladin. The loss of this precious relic renewed that public enthusiasm for the crusades which had somewhat cooled in the past half century. The pope overwhelmed the princes of Christendom with messages, urging them to make peace among themselves and combined war upon the infidels. The cardinals promised to renounce riches and pleasures, to receive no present, and not to mount a horse until the Holy Land should be reconquered; they promised, further, to be the first to take the cross, and to march at the head of the new pilgrims, begging alms. Preachers and missionaries repaired to all the courts, to all the assemblies of the great and the rich; several came to the interview of the kings of France and England; and, among others, William, archbishop of Tyre, one of the most celebrated men of the time for learning and eloquence.

This prelate had the ability to induce the two kings, who could not agree about their own affairs, to concur in making war on the Saracens, setting aside the while their own personal differences. They confederated together as brothers-in-arms, in what was termed the cause of God, and, in token of their engagement, received from the hands of the archbishops a cross of cloth, which they attached to their attire; that of the king of France was red, that of the king of England white. In receiving them, they signed themselves on the forehead, the mouth, and the breast, and swore not to lay aside the cross of the Lord on land or sea, in country or in town, until they returned from the great passage. Many lords of both kingdoms took the same oath, influenced by the example of the kings, by the desire to obtain the remission of all their sins, by the constant inculcation of the subject from every pulpit, and even by the popular songs which in every street glorified all who should fight in the Holy Land against the Paynim foe. One of these, composed by a priest of Orleans, reached as far as England, and there excited, says a contemporary writer, many men to take up the cross; although written in a learned language, this poem bears a sufficient impress of the ideas and style of the epoch to merit translation:—

"The wood of the cross is the standard that the army will follow, it has never given way; it has gone onward by the power of the Holy Spirit.

"Let us go to Tyre, 'tis the meeting-place of the brave: 'tis there should go they who, in European courts, so arduously labour, without good fruit, to acquire the renown of chivalry.

"The wood of the cross is the standard that the army will follow.

"But, for this war, there needs robust combatants, and not effeminate men; they who are too assiduous as to their persons gain not God by prayers.

"The wood of the cross, etc.

"He who has no money, if he be faithful, sincere faith will suffice for him: the body of the Lord is provision enough on the way for him who defends the cross.

"The wood of the cross, etc.

"Christ, in giving his body to the executioner, lent to the sinner; sinner, if thou wilt not die for Him who died for thee, thou returnest not that which God has lent thee.

"The wood of the cross, etc.

"Listen, then, to my counsel; take up the cross, and say, in making thy vow, I recommend myself to Him who died for me, who gave for me His body and His life.

"The wood of the cross is the standard that the army will follow."

The king of England, wearing the white cross on his shoulder, proceeded to Mans, where he assembled his council to discuss the means of defraying the expenses of the holy war in which he had just engaged. It was decided that, in all the countries subject to the Angevin sway, every man should be made to pay the tenth part of his yearly revenue and of his personal property; but, from this universal decimation, were excepted, the arms, horses, and vestments of the knights, the horses, books, vestments, and ornaments of the priests, and jewels and precious stones, both of laymen and of priests. It was also ordered that the priests, knights, and sergeants-at-arms, who should take up the cross, should pay nothing; but that the burgesses and peasants who should join the army, without the express consent of their lords, should not the less pay their tithe.

The subsidy, decreed at Mans for the new crusade, was levied without much violence in Anjou, Normandy, and Aquitaine. The only minatory measure employed in these various countries, where the authority of Henry II. was modified by traditions of national administration, was a sentence of excommunication, pronounced by the archbishops and bishops, against all who should not faithfully pay their quota to the persons charged with collecting the tax. The collection was made in each parish by a commission formed of the officiating priest, a templar, a hospitaller, a royal officer, a clerk of the king's chapel, and an officer and chaplain of the seigneur of the place. The composition of this council, in which men of the locality had a place, offered to the inhabitants some guarantee of impartiality and justice. Moreover, if a dispute arose as to the proportion of the sum demanded, four or six notables of the parish were to be assembled to declare, upon oath, the value of the personalty of the appellant, whom their testimony condemned or absolved. These precautions, employed, even in the middle ages, in countries where the public administration was not properly a government of conquest, were probably practised also in England with reference to the earls, barons, knights, bishops, in a word, to all the men of Norman race; but they were wholly omitted with regard to the Saxon burgesses, and replaced by a more expeditious and entirely different process, which deserves mention.

King Henry crossed the Channel, and while his officers, lay and clerical, were collecting, in the terms of his ordinances, the tax from the landholders, he had a list drawn up of the richest citizens in all the towns, whom he summoned to personally appear before him at a fixed day and place. The honour of being admitted into the presence of the descendant of the Conqueror was in this way granted to two hundred citizens of London, to an hundred of York, and to a proportionate number of the inhabitants of other cities and towns. The letters of summons admitted no excuse or delay. The citizens did not all meet on the same day; for king Henry liked great assemblies of the English no better than his ancestors liked them. They were received in parties, on different days and in different places. On their introduction to the royal presence, the sum required from them was signified to them by an interpreter, "and thus," says a contemporary, "the king took from them the tenth of all their property, according to the estimate of the notables who were acquainted with their means. The refractory he imprisoned until they had paid the last farthing. In like manner he acted towards the Jews of England; which procured him incalculable sums." This assimilation of the men of English race with the Jews affords the exact estimate of their political state at the commencement of the second century after the conquest. It should be observed also that the convocation of the inhabitants of the towns by the king, far from being a sign of civil liberty, was, on the contrary, in this and in many similar cases, a mark of servitude and a means of vexation applied especially to men of inferior condition.

Notwithstanding the treaty and the oath of the two kings, it was to anything but the recovery of Jerusalem that the money raised from the Saxons and Jews of England, and the contributions of the nobles of that country and of the continental provinces, were applied. The enemy of old did not sleep, say the historians of the time, and his malice soon rekindled the flame of war between those who had just sworn not to bear arms against Christians until their return from the Holy Land. The occasion of this rupture was a difference of interests between Richard of Poitiers and the count of Toulouse, Raymond de Saint Gilles. The Aquitans and the Poitevins, who had regained strength and energy since their last defeat, availed themselves of the confusion occasioned by this quarrel to form new plots and new leagues against the Anglo-Norman power. On his side, the king of France, pursuant to the policy of his ancestors, could not abstain from siding with the party opposed to the Normans, and from attacking in Berri the fortresses belonging to the king of England. The war soon extended along the whole frontier of the countries governed by the two kings. On both sides many towns were taken and retaken, farms burned, vineyards devastated; at length, the rival powers, weary of fruitlessly damaging each other, resolved to treat for peace. The kings Henry and Philip met under the Great Elm, but they separated without having come to an accommodation upon any point. The youngest of them, irritated at the failure of the conference, vented his anger upon the tree under which it had been held, and had it cut down, swearing by the saints of France, his favourite oath, that no parliament should ever again be held on that spot.

During this war, Richard, against whom, ostensibly at least, king Philip had commenced it, manifested a tendency to go over to this monarch, a circumstance that greatly alarmed his father. He went so far as a proposal to refer to the judgment of the barons of France, the quarrel between him and count Raymond de Saint Gilles. Henry II. would not consent to this, and distrusting his son, refused to treat for peace, except in a personal interview with Philip. At this conference, which took place near Bonmoulins, in Normandy, the king of France made propositions in which Richard's interests were so closely bound up with his own, that they seemed the result of some secret compact previously concluded between them.

At one of the truces formerly sworn between Henry II. and Louis, the father of Philip, it had been agreed that Richard should marry Alix or Aliz, daughter of the king of France, and receive with her, as a marriage portion, the county of Vexin, hitherto a constant subject of contest between the two crowns. As a guarantee for the faithful execution of this treaty, Aliz, still a child, was placed in the hands of the king of England, that he might have the custody of her, until she was old enough to marry. But war having soon afterwards again broken out, and the sons of the king of England having leagued with the king of France, the marriage was deferred, Henry still retaining the young girl who had been confided to him. He affected only to keep her as an hostage; but it was generally believed that political reasons did not influence him in detaining her a captive in an English castle, but that he had conceived a violent passion for her, which he even satisfied, say several historians, after the death of his mistress, Rosamond. Some writers assure us that during the wars against his sons he had resolved to take Aliz for his wife, repudiating Eleanor, so as to obtain for himself the aid which the king of France gave to his adversaries. But it was in vain that he solicited a divorce of the court of Rome, and, to obtain it, loaded the pontifical legates with presents.

In the conferences he had previously held with the king of England, Philip had repeatedly demanded the solemnization of the marriage of his sister Aliz with the earl of Poitiers, and this was the first condition that he put forward at the congress of Bonmoulins. He further demanded that his future brother-in-law should be forthwith declared heir to all the states of king Henry, and in this character receive the oath of homage of the barons of England and of the continent. But Henry II. would not consent to this, apprehending a recurrence of the vexations that had formerly resulted from the premature elevation of his eldest son. On this refusal, Richard, furious with passion, again did that which he had already so often done: in the very presence of his father, turning to the king of France, and placing his joined hands in those of that monarch, he declared himself his vassal, and did homage to him for the duchies of Normandy, Brittany, and Aquitaine, and for the earldoms of Poitou, Anjou, and Maine. In return for this oath of fealty and homage, Philip gave him in fief the towns of Chateauroux and Issoudun.

This usurpation of all Henry's rights on the continent was the hardest blow that Richard had yet struck at his father; it was the commencement of a new domestic quarrel, as violent as that first dispute which, as we have seen, arose out of the attempts at usurpation made by Henry the Younger. The discontented populations appreciated the importance for them of the occasion, and were at once agitated with a movement of revolt. The barons, who for more than two years had remained quiet, the men of Poitou, late the sworn enemies of Richard, declared for him the moment they thought him at mortal enmity with the king. Henry II. came to Saumur to make his preparations for war; meanwhile his barons and knights quitted him in crowds to follow his son, whose party, supported by the king of France and by all the southern provinces, seemed likely to be the most powerful. The king of England had with him the majority of the Normans, of the Angevins, and of those who feared the sentences of excommunication, the aid of which the pope's legate lent him. But while the priests of Anjou were pronouncing these ecclesiastical sentences in their churches, the Bretons, entering in arms, devastated the country, and attacked the king's fortresses and castles. Overwhelmed by the ill fortune which had so long pursued him, almost without cessation, Henry fell ill with grief, and taking no military measures, left his defence wholly to the legates and archbishops. They multiplied their decrees of excommunication and interdict, and sent message after message to Richard and to the king of France, in turns conciliatory and menacing. These had little influence on the mind of Richard, but more on that of Philip, ever as disposed for peace as for war, provided he could gain as much by the one as by the other.

The king of France consented to hold a conference with the other king, which Richard was fain to attend, and whither came the cardinal John of Anagni, the pope's legate, and the archbishops of Reims, Bourges, Rouen, and Canterbury. Philip proposed to the king of England much the same conditions as at the interview of Bonmoulins—namely, the marriage of Aliz with Richard, and the nomination of the latter as heir to all his father's territories, under the guarantee of the oath of homage of all the barons of England and the continent. But Henry II., who had now, even more than at the former conference, reason to distrust Richard, again rejected these demands, and proposed to marry Aliz to John, his other son, who hitherto had always shown himself obedient and affectionate towards him. He said that if this marriage were adopted, he should have no objection to declare John heir to all his continental provinces. This proposition involved Richard's ruin; and either from a scruple of honour, or from a want of confidence in Henry's youngest son, the king of France refused to sanction it and to abandon his ally. Cardinal John then interposed, and declared that, pursuant to his express mission, he should lay France under interdict. "Lord legate," said Philip, "pronounce thy decree, if thou so please; I fear it not. The Roman church has no right to proceed against France, either by interdict or otherwise, when her king thinks fit to arm against rebellious vassals in vindication of his own injuries and the honour of his crown; I see thou hast touched the king of England's sterlings." Richard, whose interests were far more deeply involved, did not content himself with rallying the pontifical envoy; he drew his sword, and would have proceeded to some act of violence, had not those present restrained him.

The old king, compelled to fight, assembled his army; but his best soldiers had abandoned him to join his son. In a few months he lost the towns of Mans and Tours, with all their territory; and while the king of France was attacking him in Anjou by the northern frontiers, the Bretons advanced by the west, and the Poitevins by the south. Without any means of defence, and without authority, enfeebled in body and in mind, he resolved to seek peace in assenting to all the other party's demands. The conference between the two kings (for Richard did not attend, awaiting elsewhere the result of the negotiations) was held in a plain between Tours and Azay-sur-Cher. Philip's demands were, that the king of England should expressly acknowledge himself his liegeman, and place himself at his mercy and discretion; that Aliz should be confided to the care of five persons, chosen by Richard, until the return of the latter from the crusades, for which he was to depart with the king of France at mid-Lent; that the king of England should renounce all right of suzerainty over the towns of Berri, formerly dependent on the dukes of Aquitaine, and that he should pay to the king of France twenty thousand silver marks, as ransom for that monarch's conquests; that all those who had attached themselves to the party of the son against the father should remain vassals of the son, and not of the father, unless of their own motion they returned to the latter; lastly, that the king should receive his son into his grace by the kiss of peace, and should sincerely and in good faith abjure all rancour and all animosity against him.

The old king had no means or hope of obtaining gentler conditions; he armed himself, therefore, with patience, as well as he could, and conversed with king Philip, listening to him with a docile air, as one man receiving the law from another. Both were on horseback in the middle of the plain, and whilst they conversed together, says a contemporary, it suddenly thundered, though the sky was cloudless, and a fierce flash of lightning fell between them, without doing them any harm. They immediately separated, both greatly terrified, and, after a short interval, rejoined each other; but a second clap of thunder, louder and more terrible than the first, burst forth almost at the same moment. The king of England, whom the distressed position to which he was reduced, mental grief and physical malady, rendered more susceptible of excited emotions, perhaps connecting this natural incident with his own destiny, was so agitated, that he abandoned the reins of his horse, fell forward on his saddle, and would have fallen to the ground, had not his attendants supported him. The conference was suspended, and as Henry II. was too ill to attend a second interview, the articles of peace, drawn up in writing, were taken to his chamber for his formal consent.

The messengers of the French king found him in bed. They read to him the treaty of peace, article by article. When they came to that which related to the persons, secretly or openly, of Richard's party, the king asked their names, that he might know how many men there were whose fealty he had to renounce. The first person named to him was John, his youngest son. On hearing this name pronounced, the king, with an almost convulsive movement, rose on his seat, and, casting fearful glances around with his haggard eyes, exclaimed: "Is it true, indeed, that John, my heart, my favourite son, he whom I cherished more than all the rest; he, my love for whom has brought upon me all my misfortunes, is it indeed true that he has abandoned me?" He was answered that it was so. "Well, then," he murmured, falling back on his bed, and turning his face to the wall, "let all things go as they will; I care no longer for myself or for the world." A few moments after, Richard approached the bed, and demanded the kiss of peace from his father, in execution of the treaty. The king gave it him with apparent calmness; but, as Richard withdrew, he heard his father mutter to himself: "If God would only spare my life till I were revenged on thee!" On his arrival at the French camp, the earl of Poitiers repeated this to king Philip and his courtiers, who all shouted with laughter, and jested upon the fine peace thus concluded between father and son.

The king of England, feeling his malady increase, had himself removed to Chinon, where, in a few days, he was reduced to the point of death. In his last moments he was heard to utter these broken sentences, in reference to his misfortunes and to the conduct of his sons: "Shame!" he exclaimed; "shame to a conquered king! Cursed be the day on which I was born, and cursed of God be the sons whom I leave behind me." The bishops and clergy around him sought by every effort to induce him to recal this malediction on his children, but he persisted in it to his last breath. After his death, his body was treated by his servants as that of William the Conqueror had been; all abandoned him, after having stripped him of his clothes and seized upon every valuable in the room and in the house. King Henry had desired to be buried at Fontevrault, a celebrated nunnery, a few leagues south of Chinon; scarcely could men be found to envelop the body in a shroud, or horses to convey it. The corpse was already deposited in the great church of the abbey, awaiting the day of sepulture, when earl Richard learned, from public report, his father's death. He came to the church, and found the king lying in a coffin, his face uncovered, and still exhibiting, by the contraction of his features, the signs of an agonized death. This sight occasioned the earl of Poitiers an involuntary shudder. He knelt and prayed before the altar; but he rose in a few moments, after the interval of a paternoster, say the historians of the period, and quitted the church, never to return to it. The same contemporary writers assure us that, from the moment Richard entered the church until he left it, the blood incessantly flowed in abundance from the nostrils of the deceased. Next day the funeral took place. The officiating priests wished to decorate the corpse with some insignia of royalty; but the keepers of the treasury of Chinon would supply none, and after infinite intreaties only sent an old sceptre and a ring of no value. In default of a crown, the head was encircled with a sort of diadem, made with some gold fringe from a woman's dress; and thus singularly attired did Henry, son of Geoffroy Plantagenest, king of England, duke of Normandy, Aquitaine, and Brittany, earl of Anjou and Maine, lord of Tours and Amboise, descend to his last abode.

A contemporary author views in the misfortunes of Henry II. a sign of Divine vengeance upon the Normans, the tyrants of invaded England. He connects this miserable death with those of William Rufus, of the sons of Henry I., of the brothers of Henry II., and of his two eldest sons, who all died a violent death in the flower of their age: "Such," said he, "was the punishment of their unlawful reign." Without adopting this superstitious view, it is certain that the calamities of king Henry were a result of the events which placed the southern provinces of Gaul under his domination. He had rejoiced infinitely in this augmentation of power; he had given his sons the territories of others in appanage, glorying to see his family reign over many nations of different race and of different manners, and to reunite, under the same sceptre, that which nature had divided. But nature did not lose her rights; and at the first movement made by the peoples to regain their independence, division entered the family of the foreign king, who saw his own children serve his own subjects as instruments against him, and who, whirled to and fro, up to his last hour, by domestic feuds, experienced on his death-bed the bitterest feeling a man can carry with him to the tomb, that of dying by a parricide.

[Back to Table of Contents]

BOOK XI.

FROM THE ACCESSION OF KING RICHARD I. TO THE EXECUTION OF THE SAXON, WILLIAM LONGBEARD.

1190—1196.

State of Ireland under the Anglo-Normans—Three populations in Ireland—Insurrection of the Irish—Political conduct of a papal legate—Conquest of the kingdom of Ulster—Invasion of that of Connaught—Prince John, son of Henry II., sent into Ireland—Insult offered to the Irish chieftains—Fresh insurrection—Inveterate hostility of the two races—Petition of the Irish to the pope—Cruelties of the Anglo-Irish—Unyielding patriotism of the native Irish—Tenacity of the Cambrian race—Popular belief respecting king Arthur—Pretended discovery of the tomb of Arthur—Prediction of a Welshman to Henry II.—Accession of Richard I.—His first administrative measures—He departs for the Crusades—His quarrel with the people of Messina—Misunderstanding between him and the king of France—Their reconciliation—Ordinance of the two kings—Taking of Acre—Return of the king of France—State of affairs in England—Quarrel between the chancellor William de Longchamp and earl John, king Richard's brother—Impeachment of the chancellor—Convocation of the citizens of London—Dismissal of the chancellor—His flight—His arrest—Accusations brought by the king of France against king Richard—Feigned apprehensions of assassination—Institution of the gardes-du-corps—Fresh complaints of Philip against Richard—Departure of king Richard—He lands on the coast of Istria—His arrest and imprisonment—Intrigues of the king of France and of earl John—King Richard acknowledges himself vassal of the emperor—Alliance between earl John and the king of France—Richard ransomed—His release and return to England—Siege of Nottingham—Visit of the king to Sherwood Forest—Robert, or Robin Hood, king of the outlaws—Popularity of the outlaws—Character of Robin Hood—Popular ballad on Robin Hood—His long celebrity—Tradition respecting his death—Outlaws of Cumberland—Adam Bell, Clym of the Clough, and William of Cloudesly—Freebooting loses its patriotic colouring—King Richard resumes his crown—Ambition of the king of France—War between the two kings—Treachery of earl John—Restoration of peace—Policy of the northern populations—Interview of the two kings—State of Auvergne—The king of France attacks that country—Sirventes of king Richard and of the earl of Auvergne—State of England—Saxon families—Assemblies of the London citizens—Character of William Longbeard—Conspiracy of the Londoners—Longbeard tried and executed—He popularly passes for a martyr—Observations.

The impossibility of combining every fact in one narrative, now compels the historian to return to the epoch at which Henry II. received from pope Alexander III. the bull investing him with the lordship of all Ireland. The king hereupon immediately despatched the Normans, William Fitz-Elme, and Nicholas, dean of Wallingford, who, on their arrival in Ireland, convoked a synod of all the high clergy of the newly conquered provinces. The diploma of Alexander III. and the bull of Adrian IV. were solemnly read in this assembly, and ratified by the Irish bishops, involved by their first submission in fresh acts of weakness. Several, however, soon repented, and took part in the conspiracies which were secretly carried on in the places occupied by the Norman garrisons, or even in the open resistance of the still free provinces on the Shannon and the Boyne. Lawrence, archbishop of Dublin, one of the first who had sworn fealty to the conqueror, engaged in several patriotic insurrections, and from the friend of the foreigners, became the object of their hatred and persecution. They replaced him by a Norman, John Comine, who, to accomplish his new mission, conducted himself in such sort towards the natives, that his countrymen gave him, in jest, the surname of Ecorche-villain.

In a few years, the conquest extended as far as the eastern and southern frontiers of the kingdoms of Connaught and Ulster. A line of fortresses and palisadoed redoubts, stretching along the frontier of the invaded territory, procured it the Norman appellation of Pal or the Pale. Every foreign baron, knight, or squire, quartered within the Pale, had taken care to fortify his domain; each had a castle, great or small, according to his rank and wealth. The lowest class of the conquering army, and in particular the English soldiers, labourers, or merchants, dwelt together in entrenched camps, formed round the castles of their leaders, or in the towns which the natives had partly abandoned. The English language was spoken in the streets and market-places of these towns, and the French in the fortresses newly erected by the lords of the conquest. All the names of these chiefs that history has preserved, are French, as Raymond de Caen, Guillaume Ferrand, Guillaume Maquerel, Robert Digarre, Henri Bluet, Jean de Courcy, Hughes le Petit, and the numerous family of the Fitz-Geraulds, who were also called Gerauldines. Thus the English who had come to Ireland in the train of the Anglo-Normans, were in a middle state between the latter and the natives, and their language, the most despised in their own country, held in the island of Erin an intermediate rank between that of the new government and the Gallic idiom of the conquered. All that remained of Irish population within the inclosure of the Pale, or the Anglo-Norman territory, was soon confounded in one common servitude, no distinction remaining between the friend of the foreigners and the man who had resisted them; all became equal in the eyes of the conquerors, as soon as they no longer needed assistance. In the kingdom of Leinster, as elsewhere, they only left to the inhabitants of their land and property that which was not worth the taking from them. They who had called in the Normans and fought with them, repented and revolted; but wanting organization, they could not carry on their revolt, and the foreigners accused them of fickleness and perfidy. These interested reproaches passed into contemporary history, which at every page lavishes them upon all of Irish race.

Towards the year 1177, the men of Connaught and Ulster, not content with defending the approaches to their own country, resolved to attempt the enfranchisement of the invaded territory. They advanced as far as Dublin; but, unskilled in the art of besieging, they did not succeed in gaining possession of this city, which had been recently fortified, and were thus arrested in their progress. The Normans, to compel them to retreat by a powerful diversion, entered Ulster, under the command of John de Courcy. This manœuvre obliged the king of Connaught to quit the south-eastern country, and to return northwards; many of the ancient chiefs, and even of the Irish bishops of the Anglo-Norman territory, joined his army.

At this time a cardinal, named Vivian, who had been sent by the pope to Scotland to collect money, having succeeded in his mission, landed in the north of Ireland, in the district whither the war had just been transferred. Notwithstanding all the evil that the Roman church had inflicted upon Ireland, the legate was received with great honour by the chiefs of the Irish army; they intreated him, with deference, to counsel them, and to tell them whether it was not lawful for them to oppose with all their power the usurpation of the king of England. From fear or calculation, the pontifical legate gave them the reply they desired, and even exhorted them to fight to the death in defence of their country. This encouragement excited an universal joy and a warm friendship towards the cardinal, who, without losing any time, announced that he would make a collection for the church of Rome. In the fulness of their content, the chiefs of the army and the people gave as much as they could, and the legate, continuing his journey, entered the Anglo-Norman territory.

Arrived at Dublin, he was ill received by the king's barons and justiciaries, who reproached him with having encouraged the Irish to resistance, and ordered him to depart forthwith, unless he chose publicly to retract what he had said. The cardinal, without hesitation, proclaimed king Henry II. sovereign and lawful master of Ireland, and, in the name of the church, fulminated a decree of excommunication against every native who did not acknowledge him. The Normans were as delighted at this sentence as their adversaries had been at the approbation bestowed on their patriotic devotion, and the legate filled his coffers at leisure throughout the conquered part of the island. He then went to visit the Norman army, which had just invaded Ulster. This army suffered greatly from a scarcity of provisions, because, at their approach, the inhabitants hid or burned their provisions, or stored them in the churches, to stay the pillage of the foreigners by the fear of sacrilege. If such scruples did not wholly check the soldiers, they, at least, produced in them a certain degree of moral restraint, which, added to their physical privations, delayed the progress of the campaign. The chief of the expedition, John de Courcy, asked the cardinal if they who fought for the rights of king Henry, could not, without sin, force open the doors of the churches and take the provisions from them? "In this case," answered the accommodating Roman, "the Irish alone would be guilty of sacrilege, who, to sustain their rebellion, dare to transform the church of God into a granary and a storehouse."

The invasion of Ulster was successful, though incomplete: the maritime towns and low country fell into the hands of the foreigners; but the mountainous districts remained free, and the natives collected there, and carried on a guerilla warfare. While John de Courcy was fortifying himself in his new conquest, the Norman Mile or Milon, who styled himself Mile de Cogham, because he possessed an estate of that name in England, crossed the river Shannon with six hundred horse, and entered the province of Connaught. He was followed thither by Hugh de Lacy, who was accompanied by greater forces. On their approach, the inhabitants withdrew to the forests, driving their cattle before them, taking away all they could, and burning the rest, together with their houses. This system of defence would probably have succeeded, had not the king of Connaught, who hitherto had shown himself the bravest man in Ireland, requested to capitulate, and consented to acknowledge himself liegeman of the king of England. His defection weakened the spirit of his people; but the nature of their country, the most mountainous in the island, and intersected by lakes and marshes, prevented the Anglo-Normans from completely effecting its conquest. They obtained few lands there, and settled in but a limited number; the only bond of subjection by which they retained their authority over this part of Ireland being the oath of vassalage sworn by the chief who had become their friend.

Hugh de Lacy married one of the daughters of this chief, and his companions in victory, dispersed among the native population, married, like himself, women of the country. Whether from the tendency to imitation, natural to man, or from a politic desire to ingratiate themselves with the natives, they gradually quitted the manners and customs of the Normans for those of the Irish, having at their banquets a harper, and preferring music and poetry to tournaments and warlike jousts. This change greatly displeased the barons settled in the southern and eastern provinces, where the natives, reduced to servitude and held in contempt by their lords, inspired the latter with no desire to imitate them. They treated those who adopted the usages or married the women of the country, as degenerate and misallied, and the children born of these marriages were regarded as very inferior in nobility to those of pure Norman race. Moreover, they distrusted them, fearing least the tie of relationship should some day attach them to the cause of the conquered people; which, however, did not take place until many centuries after.

On the other hand, the king of England distrusted the lords settled in Ireland, alarmed at the idea that, sooner or later, one of them might undertake to found a new empire in that island. To avert this danger, Henry II. resolved to send one of his sons to represent him, under the title of king of Ireland; and, as he could not trust any of the three eldest, who were alone capable of properly fulfilling the mission, he selected John, the youngest of all, scarcely as yet fifteen. The day on which this prince received knighthood at Westminster, his father made all the conquerors of the isle of Erin swear to him the oath of vassalage. Hugh de Lacy and Mile de Cogham did homage to him for Connaught, and John de Courcy for Ulster. The south-western part of the island was not yet subjected: it was offered in fief to two brothers, Herbert and Josselin de la Pommeraye, upon the sole condition that they should conquer it; they refused the gift, which seemed to them too onerous. But Philip de Brause accepted it, and did homage for it to the new king of Ireland, declaring that he held of him, for the service of sixty men, a district into which no Norman had yet penetrated.

The fourth son of Henry II. embarked in April 1185, and landed at Waterford, accompanied by Robert le Pauvre, his marshal, and a great number of young men, brought up at the court of England, who had never seen Ireland, and who, alike strangers to the conquerors of the country and to the natives, followed the new king, in the hope of making a rapid fortune at the expense of both. Upon landing, John proceeded to Dublin, where he was received with great ceremony by the archbishops and all the Anglo-Normans of the district. Many of the Irish chiefs who had sworn fealty to king Henry and to the foreign barons, came to salute the young prince, according to the form of their country.

This ceremonial was much less refined than that of the Norman court; it left each man free to give to the person invested with sovereign power, the token of affection he thought fit, and in the way he thought fit. The Irish had no idea but that they were to follow the ancient customs, and, accordingly, one simply bowed before the son of king Henry, another shook hands with him, a third wished to embrace him; but the Normans regarded this familiarity as impertinent, and treated the native chiefs as rude, unmannerly, untaught churls. Amusing themselves with insulting them, they pulled their long beards, or their hair, which hung down on each side of the head, or touched their dress with a contemptuous air, or pushed them towards the door. These insults did not remain unavenged, and the same day all the Irish chiefs left Dublin in a body. Many people of the surrounding districts, taking with them their children and their goods, followed them, and sought refuge, some in the south with the king of Limerick, who still struggled against the conquest; others with the king of Connaught, who soon placed himself at the head of a new patriotic insurrection.

In the almost general war which then arose between the Irish and their conquerors, a circumstance favourable to the former was the jealousy of the young king's courtiers towards the barons and knights of the conquest. Having nothing to lose in this war, they looked upon it as an occasion presented to them of supplanting the first settlers in their commands and their position. They accused and calumniated them to the son of Henry II., who, frivolous, careless, and devoted to the companions of his pleasures, despoiled in their favour the founders and supporters of the Norman power in Hibernia. He spent in debauchery all the money received from England for the payment of the troops; his army, ill commanded and discontented, obtained little success against the insurgents, and the cause of the conquerors began to be in danger. As soon as this peril was felt, the young king and his courtiers fled and quitted the island, taking with them all the money they could collect, and leaving the two populations really interested in the war, to fight it out between them.

The struggle of these two races of men continued for a long period, under every form, in open country and in towns, by strength and by stratagem, by open attack and by assassination. The same spirit of hatred to the foreign power which, in England, had strewed with Norman corses the forests of Yorkshire and Northumberland, now filled with them the lakes and marshes of Erin. A feature giving a peculiar character to the conquest of the latter country is, that the conquerors of Ireland, ranking as oppressors in reference to the natives, were reduced to that of oppressed, in reference to their countrymen who had remained in England. The evil that the sons of the conquerors inflicted upon the subjugated nation, was in part retaliated upon them by the kings of whom they held, who, doubting their fidelity, regarded them almost as a foreign race. There was, however, infinite difference between the tyrannies which the English, established in Ireland, underwent from the government of England, and those which they themselves inflicted on the natives for a long series of ages. A document of the fourteenth century may answer the purpose of much detail, and complete, for the reader, the idea of a conquest in the middle ages.

"To pope John, Donald O'Neyl, king of Ulster, and the inferior kings of that territory, and all the population of Irish race.

"Most holy father, we transmit to you some exact and true information of the state of our nation and the injustice we suffer, and which our ancestors have suffered, from the kings of England, and their agents, and the English barons born in Ireland. After having driven us by violence from our spacious habitations, from our fields and our paternal inheritances; after having forced us, in order to save our lives, to fly to the mountains, the marshes, the woods, and the hollows of the rocks, they continually harass us in these miserable asylums to expel us thence, and appropriate the whole of our country to themselves. From this there results between them and us an implacable enmity; and it was a former pope who placed us in this deplorable situation. They had promised this pope to form the people of Hibernia to good manners, and to give them good laws:

but far from so doing, they have destroyed all the written laws which heretofore governed us. They have left us without laws, the better to accomplish our ruin; or have established perfectly detestable laws, of which the following are examples.

"It is a rule in the courts of justice of the king of England in Ireland, that any man, not of Irish race, may bring any sort of action against an Irishman, while this power is prohibited to all Irishmen, lay or clerical. When, as too often happens, an Englishman assassinates an Irishman, priest or layman, the assassin is not corporally punished, or even made to pay a fine: on the contrary, the more considerable among us the assassinated man, the more is the murderer excused, honoured, and recompensed by his countrymen, even by the ecclesiastics and bishops. No Irishman may dispose of his property on his death-bed, but the English appropriate it all. All the religious orders established in Ireland upon the English territory are forbidden to receive any Irishman into their houses.

"The English, who have dwelt among us for many long years, and who are called men of mixed race, are not less cruel towards us than are the others. Sometimes they invite to their table the greatest men of our land, and treacherously kill them at board, or while they sleep. It is thus that Thomas de Clare, having invited to his house Brien the Red, of Thomond, his brother-in-law, put him to death by surprise, after having partaken with him of the same consecrated host, divided into two parts. These crimes they deem honourable and praiseworthy; it is the belief of all their laity, and many of their churchmen, that there is no more sin in killing an Irishman than in killing a dog. Their monks boldly assert that, for having killed a man of our nation (which too often happens), they would not abstain one single day from saying mass. As a proof of this, the monks of the order of Citeaux, established at Granard, in the diocese of Armagh, and those of the same order at Ynes, in Ulster, daily attack in arms, wound and kill the Irish, and yet regularly say mass. Brother Simon, of the order of Minorites, a relation of the bishop of Coventry, has publicly declared from the pulpit that there is not the slightest sin in killing or robbing an Irishman. In a word, all maintain that they are at full liberty to take from us, if they can, our lands and our goods, and their conscience does not reproach them for this, even at the hour of death.

"These grievances, added to the difference of language and of manners which exists between them and us, destroy every hope of our ever enjoying peace or truce in this world, so great on their side is the desire to rule, so great on ours the legitimate and natural desire to throw off an insupportable servitude, and to recover the inheritance of our ancestors. We preserve in our heart's core an inveterate hatred, the result of long memories of injustice, of the murder of our fathers, our brothers, our cousins, which will never be forgotten, either by us or by our sons. Thus, then, without regret or remorse, so long as we shall live, we shall fight them in defence of our rights, ceasing only to combat and injure them when they themselves, through want of power, shall cease to do us evil, and when the Supreme Judge shall take vengeance on their crimes, which we firmly hope will happen sooner or later. Until then, we will, for the recovery of that independence which is our natural right, make war upon them to the death, constrained as we are thereto by necessity, and preferring to confront the peril as brave men than to languish amidst insult and outrage."

This promise of war to the death, made more than four hundred years ago, is not yet forgotten; and, melancholy circumstance, but well worthy to be remarked, blood has been shed in our own times, in Ireland, in the old quarrel of the conquest. The hour when this quarrel will be terminated, belongs to a future that we cannot as yet discern; for, notwithstanding the mixture of races, the intercommunion of every kind brought about by the course of centuries, hatred to the English government still subsists, as a native passion, in the mass of the Irish nation. Ever since the hour of invasion, this race of men has invariably desired that which their conquerors did not desire, detested that which they liked, and liked that which they detested. She whose misfortunes were in a degree caused by the ambition of the popes, attached herself to the doctrines of popery with a sort of fury, the instant that England emancipated herself from them. This indomitable pertinacy, this faculty of preserving through centuries of misery the remembrance of their lost liberty, and of never despairing of a cause always defeated, always fatal to those who have dared to defend it, is perhaps the strangest and the noblest example ever given by any nation.

Something of the tenacity of memory and of the national spirit which characterize the Irish race has been exhibited, at the same epochs, by the native Welsh. Weak as they were at the close of the twelfth century, they still hoped not only to recover the conquered portion of their own immediate country, but a return of the time when they possessed the island of Britain. Their immoveable confidence in this chimerical hope, made such an impression upon those who observed it, that in England, and even in France, the Welsh were considered to possess the gift of prophecy. The verses in which the ancient Cambrian poets had expressed, with effusion of soul, their patriotic wishes and expectations, were looked upon as mystic predictions, the exposition of which it was sought to discover in the great events of the day. Hence the singular celebrity which Myrdhin, a bard of the seventh century, enjoyed five hundred years after his death, under the name of Merlin the Enchanter. Hence also, the extraordinary renown of king Arthur, the hero of a petty nation, whose existence was scarcely known upon the continent. But the books of this petty nation were so full of poetry, they had so powerful an impress of enthusiasm and conviction, that once translated into other languages, they became most attractive reading for foreigners, and the theme upon which the romance writers of the middle ages most frequently constructed their fictions. It was thus that the old war-chief of the Cambrians appeared, in the fabulous histories of the Norman and French trouvères, the ideal of a perfect knight, and the greatest king that ever wore crown.

Not content to adorn this personage with every knightly perfection, many foreigners believed in his return, well nigh as firmly as did the Welsh themselves; this opinion gained ground even among the conquerors of Wales, whom it terrified despite all their efforts to conquer the impression; various reports, each more fantastic than the rest, nourished this belief. Now it was said that pilgrims, returning from the Holy Land, had met Arthur in Sicily, at the foot of Mount Etna; now, that he had appeared in a wood in Lower Brittany, or that the foresters of the king of England, in making their rounds by moonlight, often heard a great noise of horns, and met troops of hunters, who said they formed part of the train of king Arthur. Lastly, the tomb of king Arthur was nowhere to be found; it had often been sought but never discovered, and this circumstance seemed a confirmation of all the reports in circulation.

The contemporary historians of the reign of king Henry II. admit that all these things formed for the Welsh a groundwork for national enthusiasm, and great encouragement in their resistance to foreign rule. The stronger minded among the Anglo-Normans ridiculed what they called the Breton Hope; but this hope, so vivid, so real, that it communicated itself by contagion even to the enemies of the Cambrians, gave umbrage to the statesmen of the court of England. To give it a mortal blow, they resolved to discover the tomb of Arthur, and this they did in the following manner. About the year 1189, a nephew of the king, named Henry de Sully, ruled the abbey of Glastonbury, raised on the site of the building whither popular tradition related that the great Cambrian chief had retired, to await the cure of his wounds. This abbot all at once announced, that a bard of Pembrokeshire had had a revelation as to the sepulchre of king Arthur; and hereupon extensive excavations were commenced within the walls of the monastery, care being taken the while to keep apart all persons who were likely to raise doubts on the subject. The desired discovery was of course made, and there was found, say the contemporaries, a Latin inscription engraved on a metal plate, and bones of an extraordinary size. These precious remains were raised with great marks of respect, and Henry II. had them placed in a magnificent coffin, of which he did not grudge the expense, thinking himself amply repaid by the injury done to the Welsh, in depriving them of their long cherished hope, of the superstition which animated their courage, and shook that of their conquerors.

The patriotic determination of the Cambrians, however, survived the hope of king Arthur's return, and they were still far from resigning themselves to foreign rule. This disposition of mind gave them confidence in themselves, so undoubting that it almost seemed to partake of insanity. In an expedition which king Henry II. made in person to the south of Wales, a Cambrian chief, under the influence of one of those family feuds which were the capital vice of the nation, came to his camp and joined him, The king received him as a valuable auxiliary, and questioning him on the probable chances of the war: "Dost thou think," he said, "that the rebels can withstand my army?" At this question, patriotic pride awakened in the heart of the Welshman. Looking at the king with an air at once calm and assured, he answered: "King, your power may, to a certain extent, weaken and injure this nation, but utterly to destroy it requires the anger of God. In the day of judgment no other race, no other tongue than that of the Kymrys will answer for that corner of the earth to the Sovereign Judge."

The historians do not say in what terms Henry II. replied to these words, so impressed with imperturbable conviction; but the idea of the prophetic skill of the Welsh was not without power over him; at least, so his flatterers thought, for his name is found, by interpolation, in many of the old poems attributed to the bard Myrdhin.

One day, as the same king, returning from Ireland, passed through Pembrokeshire, a countryman accosted him, to communicate an entirely religious prediction, remarkable only for the circumstances which accompanied it. The Welshman, thinking that a king of England must needs understand English, addressed Henry II. in that language, thus: "God holde ye, king." This salutation was followed by an harangue of which the king understood but a few words; wishing to answer, and unable to do so, he said in French to his squire: "Ask this peasant if he is telling us his dreams." The squire, whose less elevated position enabled him to converse with Saxons, served as an interpreter between his master and the Cambrian. Thus, to the fifth king of England since the Conquest, the English language was almost a foreign tongue. The son and successor of Henry II., Richard, upon whose reign our history now enters, could just as little converse in English; but then he spoke and wrote equally well the two Romane languages of Gaul, that of the north and that of the south, the tongue of oui and the tongue of oc.

The first administrative act of Richard I., when his father (as we have seen) was buried in the church of Fontevrault, was to arrest Stephen de Tours, seneschal of Anjou and treasurer of Henry II. He shut him up, chained hand and foot, in a dungeon, which he did not quit until he had given up to the new king all the deceased king's money, and his own too. Richard then crossed the Channel, accompanied by his brother John, and, on his arrival in England, took the same precautions as on the continent; he hastened to the various royal treasuries in different cities, and had their contents collected, weighed and enumerated. The love of gold was the first passion manifested by the new monarch; and as soon as he had been consecrated and crowned, according to ancient custom, he began to sell everything he possessed, lands, castles, towns, his whole demesne, and in some places the domains of others, if we are to credit an historian of the time.

Many rich Normans, priests and laymen, profited by the opportunity, and bought, at a cheap rate, portions of the large share of the conquest which William the Bastard had reserved for himself and his successors. The Saxon burgesses of many towns belonging to the king, clubbed together to purchase their houses, and to become, for an annual rent, proprietors of the place they inhabited. By the operation of such a compact or treaty, the town making it became a corporation, regulated by officers responsible to the king for the payment of the municipal debt, and to the citizens for the employment of the money raised by personal contributions. The reigns of the successors of Richard I. exhibit many of these conventions by which the cities of England gradually emerged from the condition to which the Norman Conquest had reduced them, and it is wholly probable that he himself used this mode of filling his coffers, at a time when he seemed to neglect no means of so doing. "I would sell London," he said to his courtiers, "if I could find a purchaser."

The money thus accumulated by the king of England in the first months of his reign, seemed destined to the expenses of the expedition to the Holy Land, which he had sworn to accomplish in common with Philip of France. Yet Richard displayed little haste to set out; his companion in pilgrimage was obliged to send ambassadors to England to remind him of his plighted word, and to inform him that the time of departure was definitively fixed for the festival of Easter. Richard, seeing no excuse for further delay, convoked at London a general assembly of his earls and barons, at which all those who with him had made a vow to take up the cross, swore to be at the place of meeting without fail. The ambassadors took this oath upon the soul of the king of France, and the barons of England upon the soul of their own king. Vessels were collected at Dover, and Richard crossed the sea.

Upon the point of departure for the new crusade, the kings of England and France made a compact of alliance and brotherhood-in-arms, swearing that each would maintain the life and honour of the other; that neither would fail the other in the hour of danger; that the king of France would defend the rights of the king of England, as he would his own city of Paris, and the king of England those of the other king, as he would those of his own city of Rouen. Richard sailed from one of the ports of southern Gaul, which, from the frontiers of Spain to the coast of Italy, between Nice and Venitimille, were all free, depending nominally on the crown of Arragon. King Philip, who had no maritime town on the Mediterranean, went to Genoa, and embarked in vessels furnished him by this rich and powerful city. The fleet of the king of England joined him by the Straits of Gibraltar; and the two kings, having coasted along Italy, took up their winter quarters in Sicily.

This island, conquered a century before by the Norman lords of Apulia and Calabria, formed, with the opposite territory, a kingdom acknowledging the suzerainty of the holy see. In the year 1139, Roger, first king of Sicily and Naples, had received from pope Innocent II. investiture by the standard. After the reign of his son and that of his grandson, the crown fell to one of his natural sons, named Tancred, who had acceded shortly previous to the arrival of the two kings at Messina. Both were received with great marks of respect and friendship; Philip had lodgings provided for himself and his barons within the town; and Richard established himself outside the walls, in a house surrounded by a vineyard.

One day that he was walking in the environs of Messina, accompanied by a single knight, he heard the cry of a falcon in the house of a peasant. Falcons, like all other birds of chase, were at this time in England, and even in Normandy, noble property, prohibited to villeins and burghers, and reserved for the amusement of barons and knights. Richard, forgetting that in Sicily things were not exactly as they were in his own kingdom, entered the house, seized the bird, and was about to carry it away; but the Sicilian peasant, though the subject of a king of Norman race, was not accustomed to suffer what the English endured; he resisted, and, calling his neighbours to his aid, he drew his knife upon the king. Richard endeavoured to use his sword against the peasants who collected around him, but the weapon breaking in his hands, he was fain to flee, pursued with sticks and stones. Shortly after this adventure, the habit of going any length in England with the villeins and burghers, involved the king in a more serious affair. There was, near Messina, on the coast of the Straits, a monastery of Greek monks, which its position rendered very strong: Richard, thinking the building commodious for holding his stores, expelled the monks and placed a garrison in it. But the inhabitants of Messina, resolved to show the foreign prince how greatly this act of contemptuous arrogance towards them displeased them, closed their gates, and refused the king of England's people admission to the city. On hearing this, Richard, furious with anger, hastened to the palace of Tancred, and required him to chastise, without delay, the citizens who had dared to oppose a king. Tancred commanded the Messinese to abstain from hostilities, and peace seemed re-established; but Sicilian vindictiveness did not subside at the dictate of political considerations. Some days after, a troop of the most indignant and bravest of the citizens of Messina assembled on the heights around the quarters of the king of England, for the purpose of assailing him unexpectedly when he should pass with a limited train. Weary of waiting, they attacked the house of a Norman officer, Hugh le Brun; there ensued a combat and a great tumult, which coming to the ears of Richard, who was then in conference with king Philip upon the affairs of the holy war, he hastened to arm himself and his people. With superior forces, he pursued the citizens to the gates of the town: the latter entered, but admission was refused to the Normans, upon whom there rained from the walls above, a shower of arrows and stones. Five knights and twenty sergeants of the king of England were killed; at length, his whole army coming up, broke down one of the gates, and, taking possession of the city, planted the banner of Normandy on all the towers.

During this combat, the king of France had remained a tranquil spectator, without, say the historians, offering any aid to his brother-in-pilgrimage; but when he saw the standard of the king of England floating on the ramparts of Messina, he demanded that this flag should be removed and replaced by his own. This was the commencement of a quarrel between the brothers-in-arms, which time only embittered. Richard would not yield to the pretensions of the king of France; but, lowering his banner, committed the city to the custody of the knights of the

Temple until he obtained satisfaction from king Tancred for the conduct of the Messinese. The king of Sicily granted everything that was asked, and, more timid than a handful of his subjects had shown themselves, he made his great officers swear, by his soul and their own, that he and his people, by land and by sea, would at all times maintain faith and peace with the king of England and all his people.

In proof of his fidelity to this oath, Tancred gave Richard a letter, which he assured him had been sent to him by king Philip, and in which that monarch said that the king of England was a traitor, who had not observed the conditions of the last peace made with him, and that if Tancred and his people would fall upon him, by day or by night, the army of France would aid them. Richard kept this communication for some time secret; but in one of the frequent disputes resulting from their prolonged stay in the same place, he suddenly presented the letter to the king of France, and asked him if he recognised it? Without replying to this question, Philip assailed the king of England: "I see what it is," said he; "you seek a quarrel with me, as a pretext for not marrying my sister Aliz, whom you have sworn to wed; but be sure that if you abandon her, and take another wife, I will be a life-long enemy of you and yours." "I cannot marry your sister," calmly answered Richard; "for it is certain that she had a child by my father; as I can prove by good testimony, if you so require." This was not a discovery that Richard had only just made respecting his affianced bride; he had known of the affair at the time when, to injure his father, he showed as we have seen, so great a desire to conclude this marriage. But that which he had promised, ambitious to reign, he did not, as crowned king, deem himself bound to accomplish; and he made Philip undergo the proof, by evidence, of his sister's shame. The facts, as it would seem, were incontestable; and the king of France, unable to persist in his demand, released Richard from his promise of marriage, in consideration of ten thousand marks of silver, payable in four years. On this condition, says the contemporary narrator, he gave him leave to marry whomsoever he pleased.

Once more friends, the two kings set sail for the Holy Land, after having again sworn upon the relics and upon the Gospel, faithfully to sustain each other, going and returning. On the eve of departure, the following ordinance was published in the two camps:—

"Know that it is forbidden to every one in the army, except the knights and priests, to play for money at any game whatever, during the transit; the priests and knights may play so long as they lose no more than twenty sous in one day and night, and the kings may play for as much as they will.

"In the company of the kings, or in their ship, and with their permission, the royal sergeants-at-arms may play up to twenty sous; and so in the company of the archbishops, bishops, earls, counts, and barons, and with their permission, their sergeants may play to the same amount.

"But if, of their own authority, sergeants-at-arms, labourers or sailors, presume to play, the former shall be flogged once a day for three days; and the latter shall be plunged three times into the sea, from the top-mast."

God, say the historians of the time, blessed the holy pilgrimage of these pious and sage kings. Philip arrived first off the city of Ptolemais or Saint Jean-d'Acre, then besieged by the Christians whom Salah-Edin had driven from Jerusalem and Palestine; Richard joined him here after a long delay, during which he had conquered the island of Cyprus from a prince of the race of Comnena. As soon as the two kings had united their forces, the siege of Acre advanced rapidly; their heavy guns, their pierriers, their mangonneaux, and their trebuchets did such execution upon the walls, that a breach was opened in a few days, and the garrison obliged to capitulate. This victory, which produced the most vivid enthusiasm among the Christians of the east, did not, however, assure concord between the crusader princes. Despite the oath taken by the two kings upon the Gospel, they and their soldiers hated and abused and calumniated each other inveterately.

Most of the chiefs of the army, whatever their rank or their country, were divided by rivalries, ambition, avarice, or pride. On the day of the taking of Acre, the king of England, finding the banner of the duke of Austria planted on the walls beside his own, had it taken down, torn, and thrown into a sewer. Shortly after, the marquis of Montferrat, who disputed with Guy de Lusignan the vain title of king of Jerusalem, was assassinated at Tyre by two fanatic Arabs, and the king of England was charged with having hired them to do the deed. Lastly, a few months afterwards, the king of France falling ill, thought, or feigned to think, that he had been poisoned by some secret agent of the king of England. Under this pretext he abandoned the enterprise he had vowed to achieve, and left his companions in pilgrimage to fight alone against the Saracens. Richard, more obstinate than he, continued with every effort the difficult task of reconquering the holy city and the wood of the true cross.

While performing, with little result, exploits that rendered his name an object of terror throughout the east, his kingdom of England was the theatre of great troubles caused by his absence. The native English had not, indeed, essayed a revolt against their lords of Norman race; but misunderstandings had arisen among the latter. On his departure for the crusade, king Richard had confided no authority to his brother John, who then bore no other title than that of earl of Mortain. Faithful to that old instinct of discord which he himself ascribed to all the members of his family, Richard distrusted and disliked his brother. A stranger to the family, a stranger even to Anjou and to Normandy, William de Longchamp, bishop of Ely, a native of Beauvais, had been charged by the king with the supreme direction of affairs, under the title of chancellor and grand justiciary of England. Lastly, king Richard had made his natural brother Geoffroy swear that he would not set foot in England until three years after his departure, his expectation being that he should return within that time.

The chancellor, William de Longchamp, master of the entire royal power, used it to enrich himself and his family; he placed his relations and friends of foreign birth in all the posts of profit and honour; confided to them the custody of the castles and towns, which he took, under various pretences, from men of pure Norman race, whom, equally with the English he made to feel the weight of insupportable exactions. The authors of the time say that, thanks to his rapine, no knight could keep his silver-plated baldric, no noble his gold ring, no woman her necklace, no Jew his merchandize. He affected the manners of a sovereign, and sealed the public acts with his own seal, instead of with the seal of England; a numerous guard was posted round his palace; wherever he went, a thousand horse and more accompanied him, and if he lodged in any man's house, three years' income did not suffice to repair the expense he and his train had occasioned in one single day. He procured at great expense from France, trouveres and jongleurs to sing in the public squares, verses wherein it was affirmed that the chancellor had not his equal in the world.

John, earl of Mortain, the king's brother, a man no less ambitious and no less vain than the chancellor, beheld with envy this power and pomp, which he would fain himself have displayed. All whom the exactions of William de Longchamp angered, or who desired a political change wherein to make their fortune, formed a party around the earl, and an open struggle was soon established between the two rivals. Their enmity broke forth in reference to one Gerard de Camville, a man of Norman race, whom the chancellor sought to deprive of the governorship, or, as it was then called, the viscounty of Lincoln, which the king had sold to him. The chancellor, who wished to give this office to one of his friends, ordered Gerard to surrender the keys of the royal castle of Lincoln; but the viscount resisted the order, declaring that he was liegeman of the earl John, and that he would not give up his fief, until he had been judged and condemned to forfeiture in the court of his lord. On this refusal, the chancellor came with an army to besiege the castle of Lincoln, took it, and expelled Gerard de Camville, who demanded reparation for this violence from John, as his suzerain and protector. As a sort of reprisal for the injury done to his vassal, earl John seized upon the royal castles of Nottingham and Tickhil, placed his knights there, and unfurled his banner, protesting, says an ancient historian, that if the chancellor did not promptly do justice to Gerard, his liegeman, he would visit him with a rod of iron. The chancellor was alarmed, and negotiated an accommodation, by which the earl remained in possession of the two fortresses he had seized upon; this first step of prince John towards the authority his brother had feared to confide in him, was soon followed by more important attempts.

Geoffroy, the natural son of Henry II., who had been elected archbishop of York during his father's life, but had long remained without confirmation by the pope, at length obtained from Rome permission to receive consecration from the prelate of Tours, the metropolitan of Anjou. Immediately after his consecration he departed for England, notwithstanding the oath which the king his brother had obliged him to take. The chancellor received information of this; and as the archbishop was about to sail from the port of Wissant, messengers came to him, and forbad him, in the king's name, to cross the sea. Geoffroy took no heed to this prohibition, and armed men were posted to seize him on landing. Having evaded them by disguising himself, he reached a monastery at Canterbury, the monks of which received him, and concealed him in their house. But the rumour of his presence there soon spread; the monastery was invested by soldiers, and the archbishop, seized in the church as he was saying mass, was imprisoned in the castle of the city, under the charge of the constable Matthew de Clare. This violent arrest created great excitement throughout England; and earl John, availing himself of the occasion, openly took up his brother's cause, and menacingly ordered the chancellor to set the archbishop at liberty. The chancellor did not venture to resist; and, becoming more daring, the earl of Mortain proceeded to London, convoked the great council of barons and bishops, and charged William de Longchamp before them with having enormously abused the power which the king had confided to him. William had displeased so many persons, that his accuser was sure of a favourable audience. The assembly of barons cited him to appear before them; he refused, and, assembling troops, marched from Windsor, where he then was, to London, to prevent the barons from assembling a second time. But the earl's troops met him at the gates of the city, attacked and dispersed his escort, and forced him to throw himself, in great haste, into the Tower of London, where he remained close shut up, while the barons and bishops, assembled in parliament, deliberated on his fate.

The majority of them resolved to strike a decisive blow, and to remove the man to whom king Richard had confided the viceroyalty, and who, according to legal forms, could not be deposed without the express order of the sovereign. In this daring enterprise, the earl of Mortain and the Anglo-Norman barons resolved to involve the Saxon inhabitants of London, in order to secure, if it became necessary to fight, the aid of that great city's population. On the day fixed for their assembly, they rang the great alarm bell; and as the citizens issued from their houses, persons stationed in various places told them to go to Saint Paul's church. The traders and artisans went thither in crowds to see what was on foot; they were surprised to find assembled there the nobles of the land, the sons of the men of the conquest, with whom they had no other relations than those of villein and lord. Contrary to their usual practices, the barons and prelates gave a cordial reception to the citizens, and a sort of transient fraternity appeared, despite the difference of social condition, between the Normans and Saxons. The latter understood as much as they could of the harangues pronounced before them in the French language; and, the debate over, there was read a letter purporting to be from the king, dated at Messina, and setting forth that if the chancellor conducted himself ill in his office, he might be deposed, and the archbishop of Rouen substituted for him. This having been read, the votes of the whole assembly were taken without distinction of race; and the Norman heralds proclaimed, "that it had pleased John, earl of Mortain, the king's brother, all the bishops, earls, and barons of the kingdom, and the citizens of London, to depose from his office the chancellor, William de Longchamp."

Meantime the chancellor was close shut up in the Tower of London; he might have sustained a siege there; but, abandoning every thought of defence, he offered to capitulate. Egress was granted him, on condition of his surrendering to the archbishop of Rouen, his successor, the keys of all the king's castles. He was made to swear not to quit England until he had made this surrender, and his two brothers were imprisoned as hostages for his word. He withdrew to Canterbury, and after staying there some days, resolved to flee, preferring to leave his brothers in danger of their lives than to restore the castles, by the possession of which he hoped to regain all he had lost. He left the town on foot and disguised, having over his male attire a woman's petticoat and a cape with large sleeves; his head was covered with a veil of thick cloth, and he held a roll of cloth under his arm, and a measure in his hand. In this guise, that of the female English traders of the period, the chancellor went to the sea-coast, where he had to await for some time the vessel he had engaged to convey him abroad.

He sat down tranquilly on a stone, with his bundle on his knees; some passing fishermen's wives accosted him, asking the price of his cloth; but not knowing a word of English, the chancellor made no answer, which greatly surprised the women. They went on, however; but other women came up, saw the cloth, and examining it, asked the same question as their predecessors. The pretended trader continuing silent, the women repeated their question; at length, driven to extremity, the chancellor laughed aloud, thinking by such an answer to escape from his embarrassment. At this illtimed mirth the women thought they were addressing an idiot or a mad woman, and raising his veil for further examination, discovered the face of a dark-complexioned man, recently shaved. Their cries of surprise aroused the workmen of the port, who, delighted with an object of diversion, threw themselves on the disguised person, dragged him about by his clothes, threw him down, and amused themselves with his futile efforts to escape from them or to make them understand who he was. Having dragged him for some time over the stones and mud, the fishermen and sailors ended by shutting him up in a cellar, which he only quitted upon making himself known to the agents of the Norman authority.

Obliged to fulfil his engagements with the earl of Mortain and his partisans, the ex-chancellor gave up to them the keys of the castles, and thus obtained permission freely to leave England. On his arrival in France, he hastened to write word to king Richard that his brother John had seized upon all his fortresses, and would usurp his kingdom if he did not forthwith return. Other news, still more alarming, soon reached the king of England in Palestine. He learned that Philip of France, passing through Rome, had induced the pope to release him from the oath of peace he had sworn to Richard, and that, on his arrival at Fontainebleau, he had boasted that he would soon disturb the states of the king of England. Notwithstanding the distance which now separated him from Richard, king Philip still affected to fear some treachery or snare on his part. Once, on arriving at the castle of Pontoise for recreation, he suddenly appeared anxious, and hastily returned to Paris. He immediately assembled his barons, and showed them letters just arrived, he said, from beyond seas, and which warned him to be on his guard, for that the king of England had, from the east, sent hassassis or assassins to kill him.

Such was the name, then quite new in European languages, by which were designated certain Mahometans, fanatics in religion and patriotism, who thought to gain Paradise by devoting themselves to kill by surprise the enemies of their faith. It was generally believed that there existed in the defiles of Mount Libanus a whole tribe of these enthusiasts, subject to a chief called the "Old Man of the Mountain," and that the vassals of this mysterious personage joyfully ran to meet death at the first signal from their chief. The name of Haschischi, by which he was designated in Arabic, was derived from that of an intoxicating plant, of which they made frequent use to exalt or stupify themselves.

It will be readily understood, that the name of these men who poniarded people without the slightest warning of their attack, stabbed generals of armies in the very midst of their soldiers, and who, so they had struck their victim, themselves died laughing, necessarily inspired the western crusaders and pilgrims with great alarm. They brought back so vivid a memory of the terror they had felt at the mere word assassin, that this word soon passed into every mouth, and the most absurd tales of assassination readily found in Europe people disposed to credit them. This disposition existed, it would appear, in France, when king Philip assembled his barons in parliament at Paris. None of them expressed a doubt as to the king's danger; and Philip, whether the more to excite hatred among his vassals against the king of England, or to give himself greater security against his other enemies and against his subjects themselves, surrounded his person with extraordinary precautions. "Contrary to the custom of his ancestors," say the contemporary writers, "he was always escorted by armed men, and instituted, for more security, guards of his body, selected from among the men most devoted to him, and armed with great maces of iron or brass." It is mentioned, that some persons, who, with their previously accustomed familiarity, approached him too near, ran great risk of their lives. "This royal innovation astonished and singularly displeased many."

The ill effect produced by the institution of these bodyguards, then called sergents à masses, obliged king Philip again to convoke the assembly of the barons and bishops of France. He renewed before them his former imputations against the king of England, assuring them that it was he who had caused the marquis of Montferrat to be killed at Tyre, in broad daylight, by assassins in his pay. "Is it then astonishing," asked the king, "that I should take more care of myself than usual? nevertheless, if my precautions seem to you unbefitting or superfluous, say so, and I will discontinue them."

The assembly of course answered, that whatever the king thought fit to do for his personal safety was proper and just; the body-guards were maintained, and the institution existed many centuries after the belief in the mysterious power of the Old Man of the Mountain had disappeared from France. Another question addressed by king Philip to his barons was this: "Tell me, is it not fitting and lawful that I take prompt and full vengeance for the manifest injuries this traitor, Richard, has done me?" Upon this point the reply was still more unanimous, for the barons of France were all animated with the old spirit of national rancour against the Norman power.

Notwithstanding the distance which then separated him from France, king Richard was quickly informed of these matters, because, in the fervour of zeal excited in Europe against the followers of Mahomet, new pilgrims departed every day for the Holy Land. The deposition of the chancellor, and the occupation of the fortresses by earl John, had greatly disturbed the king of England, who foresaw that, sooner or later, his brother, following the example he himself had given, would unite his projects of ambition with the projects of hostility of the king of France. These fears troubled him to such a degree, that, despite the vow he had taken not to quit the Holy Land, so long as there remained an ass for him to eat, he concluded a truce of three years, three months, and three days, with the Saracens, and departed for the west.

Arrived off Sicily, he thought it might be dangerous for him to land in one of the ports of southern Gaul, because most of the seigneurs of Provence were relations of the marquis of Montferrat, and because the count of Toulouse, Raymond de Saint Gilles, suzerain of the maritime districts west of the Rhone, was his personal enemy. Apprehending some ambush on their part, instead of traversing the Mediterranean, he entered the Adriatic, having dismissed most of his suite in order to avoid recognition. His vessel was attacked by pirates, whose friendship, after a vigorous skirmish with them, he conciliated; and leaving his own vessel for one of theirs, was conveyed in it to a little port on the coast of Istria. He landed with a Norman baron, named Baldwin de Bethune, his chaplains maître Philip and maître Anselme, some Templars, and a few servants. It was necessary to obtain a passport from the seigneur of the province, who resided at Goritz, and who, by an unfortunate chance, was nearly related to the family of the marquis of Montferrat. The king sent one of his people to seek the safe conduct required, ordering him to present to the count of Goritz a ring, set with a large ruby, which he had bought in Palestine of a Pisan merchant. This ruby, already celebrated, was recognised by the count. "Who are they who send thee to ask this permission?" said he to the messenger. "Pilgrims returning from Jerusalem." "Their names?" "One is Baldwin de Bethune, and the other Hugh le Marchand, who offers you this ring." The count of Goritz, examining the ring attentively, remained for some time silent; he then said: "Thou sayest not true; his name is not Hugh; he is king Richard. But since he designed to honour me unknown with a gift, I will not arrest him; I return him his present, and leave him free to proceed on his way."

Surprised at this incident, which he had by no means anticipated, Richard immediately departed; no attempt was made to stay him. But the count of Goritz sent to inform his brother, the lord of a town at no great distance, that the king of England was in the country, and would pass through his lands. This brother had in his service a Norman knight, named Roger d'Argenton, whom he directed to visit every day all the inns where pilgrims lodged, and to see if he could not discover the king of England by his language, or any other token; promising him, if he succeeded in arresting him, the government of half his town. The Norman knight prosecuted his inquiries for several days, going from house to house, and at last discovered the king. Richard endeavoured to conceal who he was, but, driven to extremity by the Norman's questions, he was fain to avow himself. Hereupon, Roger, with tears, implored him to flee forthwith, offering him his best horse; he then returned to his lord, told him that the news of the king's arrival was a false report, and that he had not found him, but only Baldwin de Bethune, a countryman of his, who was returning from the great pilgrimage. The count, furious at having missed his aim, arrested Baldwin, and threw him into prison.

Meantime, king Richard was pursuing his flight on the German territory, his only companions being William de l'Etang, his intimate friend, and a valet, who spoke the Teutonic language, either from being an Englishman by birth, or because his inferior condition had permitted him to acquire the English language, at that time closely resembling the Saxon dialect of Germany, and altogether without French words, French expressions, or French constructions. Having travelled three days and three nights without taking any nourishment, almost without knowing whither they were going, they entered the province which in the Teutonic language was called Œster-reich, that is to say, country or the East. This name was a last reminiscence of the old empire of the Franks, of which this country had formed the eastern extremity. Œster-reich, or Autriche, as the French and Normans called it, was a dependent of the Germanic empire, and was governed by a lord who bore the title of here-zog, or duke; and, unfortunately, this duke, named Leotpolde, or Leopold, was the same whom Richard had mortally offended in Palestine by tearing down and dishonouring his banner. His residence was at Vienna on the Danube, where the king and his two companions arrived, exhausted with hunger and fatigue.

The servant who spoke English went to the exchange to convert gold besants into the money of the country. He made a great parade of his person and his gold, assuming an air of importance and the manners of a courtier. The citizens, conceiving suspicions, took him before their magistrate to ascertain who he was. He represented himself as the domestic of a rich merchant who was to arrive in three days, and was hereupon set at liberty. On his return to the king's lodging, he related his adventure, and advised him to depart at once, but Richard, desiring repose, remained. Meantime the news of his landing reached Austria; and duke Leopold, eager for revenge, and still more so to enrich himself by the ransom of such a prisoner, sent spies and soldiers in every direction in search of him. They traversed the country without discovering him; but one day the same servant who had once before been arrested, being in the market-place purchasing provisions, a pair of his master's richly-embroidered gloves, such as the nobles of the period wore with their court attire, were seen in his belt. He was again seized, and put to the torture to extract an avowal; he confessed the facts, and named the inn where king Richard was to be found. The house was immediately surrounded by the duke of Austria's troops, who, surprising the king, forced him to surrender. The duke treated him with respect, but shut him up in a prison, where chosen soldiers guarded him, with drawn swords, night and day.

As soon as the report of the king of England's arrest got abroad, the emperor or Cæsar of all Germany, Henry VI., summoned the duke of Austria, his vassal, to transfer the prisoner to him, alleging that an emperor alone ought to keep a king in prison. Duke Leopold submitted with seeming good grace to this singular reasoning, stipulating, however, for at least a portion of the ransom. The king of England was then removed from Vienna to one of the imperial fortresses on the banks of the Rhine; and the delighted emperor sent to the king of France a message, more agreeable to him, says an historian of the time, than a present of gold and jewels. Philip immediately wrote to the emperor, congratulating him on his prize, advising him to preserve it carefully, because, he said, there would be no peace in the world if such a firebrand got loose, and, lastly, offering to pay a sum equal to, or even exceeding, the ransom of the king of England, if the emperor would transfer his captive to him.

The emperor, as was the custom, submitted this proposition to the diet or general assembly of the lords and bishops of Germany. He set forth Philip's propositions, and justified the imprisonment of Richard by the pretended crime of murder committed on the marquis of Montferrat, the insult offered to the banner of the duke of Austria, and the truce of three years concluded with the Saracens. For these misdeeds, the king of England, he said, ought to be declared the capital enemy of the empire. The assembly decided that Richard should be tried by it for the offences imputed to him; but it refused to deliver Richard to the king of France. The latter did not await the prisoner's trial to send an express message to him, that he renounced him for his vassal, defied him, and declared war against him. At the same time he made to the earl of Mortain the same offers he had formerly made to Richard when exciting him against his father. He promised to guarantee to earl John the possession of Normandy, Anjou, and Aquitaine, and to aid him to obtain the crown of England; he only asked him in return to be faithfully his ally, and to marry the unfortunate Aliz. Without concluding any positive alliance with king Philip, John commenced intriguing with all the countries subject to his brother; and, under pretext that Richard was dead, or ought to be regarded as such, he demanded the oath of fealty from the public officers, and from the governors of the castles and towns.

The king of England was informed of these machinations by several Norman abbots, who obtained permission to visit him in his prison, and especially by his former chancellor, William de Longchamp, the personal enemy of the earl of Mortain. Richard received him as a friend persecuted in his service, and employed him in various negotiations. The day fixed for the king's trial arrived; he appeared as a prisoner before the Germanic diet assembled at Worms; to be absolved on every point, he had only to promise an hundred thousand marks of silver, and to acknowledge himself vassal of the emperor. This admission of vassalage, which was nothing more than a simple formality, derived importance in the eyes of the emperor from his pretensions to the universal domination of the Cæsars of Rome, whose heir he pretended to be. The feudal subjection of the kingdom of England to the German empire was not of a nature to have any protracted duration, yet its admission and declaration were made with all the pomp and ceremony required by the customs of the period. "King Richard," says a contemporary, "divested himself of the kingdom, and remitted it to the emperor, as to the universal suzerain, investing him with it by his hood, and the emperor returned it him, to hold it in fief, on the condition of an annual subsidy of five thousand pounds sterling, and invested him with it by a double cross of gold." After this ceremony, the emperor, bishops, and lords of Germany, promised by oath, upon their soul, that the king of England should be set at liberty as soon as he had paid an hundred thousand silver marks; and from that day Richard was less strictly confined.

Meantime, the earl of Mortain, pursuing his intrigues and machinations, solicited the justiciaries of England, the archbishop of Rouen, and the barons of Normandy, to swear fealty to him, and to acknowledge him as king. The majority refused; and the earl, knowing himself too weak to compel them to his wish, crossed over to France, and concluded a formal treaty with king Philip. He declared himself vassal and liegeman of this monarch for England and all the other states of his brother, swore to marry his sister, and to resign to him a considerable part of Normandy, Tours, Loches, Amboise, and Montrichard, whenever, by his aid, he should become king of England. Lastly, he subscribed this clause: "And if my brother Richard were to offer me peace, I would not accept it without the consent of my ally of France, even though my ally were to make peace on his own account with my said brother Richard."

Upon the conclusion of this treaty, king Philip passed the frontiers of Normandy with a numerous army, and earl John distributed gold among the Welsh tribes who were still free, in order to induce them to assist, by an invasion, the machinations of his partisans in England.

This people, oppressed by the Normans, joyfully placed their national hatred at the service of one of the two factions which dilacerated their enemy; but, incapable of great efforts beyond the little country where they so obstinately defended their independence, they were of little use to the adversaries of king Richard. Nor did these obtain much success elsewhere in England, so that earl John determined to take up his abode for awhile with the king of France, and to direct all his attention upon Normandy. But though thus freed from the scourge of war, England was none the happier, for she was subjected to enormous tributes, levied for the king's ransom. The royal collectors overran the country in every direction, making every class of men contribute, priests and laymen, Saxons and Normans. All the sums levied in the provinces were brought to London; it had been calculated that the total amount would constitute the sum required for the ransom; but an enormous deficiency was found, occasioned by the peculation of the collectors. This first collection accordingly being insufficient, the royal officers commenced another, covering, say the historians, under the plausible name of the king's ransom, their own shameful rapine.

Richard had been nearly two years in prison; he was tired of his captivity, and sent message after message to his officers and friends in England, and on the continent, urging them to deliver him by paying his ransom. He complained bitterly of being neglected by his people, and of their not doing for him what he would have done for them. He made his plaint in a song composed in the southern Romane language, an idiom he preferred to the less polished dialect of Normandy, Anjou, and France.

"I have many friends, but they give meagrely: shame to them, that for want of ransom, I have been a prisoner two winters."

"Let my men and my barons, English, Normans, Poitevins, and Gascons, know that no companion of mine, were he ever so poor, would I leave in prison for the sake of gold. I say not this in reproach; but I am still a prisoner!—"

While the second collection for the king's ransom was being made throughout England, officers of the emperor came to London, to receive, as part payment, the money which had been already got together. They tested the quality and verified the weight, and affixed their seals on the bags containing it, which were then conveyed by English sailors to Germany, at the risk and responsibility of the king of England. On receiving the money, the Cæsar of Germany sent one-third of it to the duke of Austria, as his share of the prize. A new diet was then assembled to decide on the fate of the prisoner, whose release was fixed for the third week after Christmas, on condition of his leaving a certain number of hostages as security for the payment of the balance remaining due.

King Richard consented to anything and everything, and the emperor, delighted with his facility, determined to make him a present in return. By a formal charter he granted him, to hold in fief, several provinces over which he himself had but a disputed pretension; the Viennois and part of Burgundy, and the towns and territories of Lyons, Arles, Marseilles, and Narbonne. "Now it should be known," says a contemporary, "that these territories given to the king by the emperor, contain five archbishoprics, and thirty-three bishoprics, but it must also be known that the said emperor has never been able to exercise any sort of authority over them, and the inhabitants have never acknowledged any lord nominated or presented by him."

When the king of France, and earl John, his ally, learned the resolution passed in the imperial diet, they feared they should not have time to execute their design before the king's release. They accordingly sent messengers in all haste to the emperor, offering him seventy thousand marks of silver, if he would prolong, if but for a year, the imprisonment of Richard, or if he preferred it, one thousand marks of silver for each extended month of captivity, or an hundred and fifty thousand marks, if he would transfer the prisoner to the custody of the king of France and the earl. Tempted by these brilliant offers, the emperor was inclined to break his word, but the members of the diet, who had sworn to keep it faithfully, opposed his views, and exercising the power vested in them, set the captive at liberty about the end of January 1194. Richard could not proceed either to France, or to Normandy, at that time invaded by the French; the safest course for him was to embark from some German port, and sail direct to England. But it was now the season of storms; he was necessitated to wait more than a month at Antwerp, and meantime the emperor was again tempted by avarice; the hope of doubling his profits overruled the fear of displeasing chiefs less powerful than himself, and whom, as lord paramount, he had a thousand ways of reducing to silence. He resolved a second time to seize the prisoner, whom he had allowed to depart; but this treacherous design becoming known, one of the hostages who had remained with the emperor found means to warn the king. Richard immediately embarked in the galiot of a Norman merchant, named Alain Tranchemer; and having thus escaped the soldiers sent to arrest him, landed safely at Sandwich.

Received with great demonstrations of joy, he found the majority of the Anglo-Norman earls and barons devoted to his cause. But just before, the great council or parliament of the kingdom had declared the earl of Mortain a public enemy, and had ordered that all his lands should be confiscated, and all his castles besieged. At the time of the king's arrival, this order was being executed, and, in all the churches, sentence of excommunication was being pronounced against the earl and his adherents, in the name of the archbishops and bishops, amid the ringing of bells and the glare of tapers. The news of the arrival of Cœur-de-Lion (so the Normans surnamed king

Richard,) terminated the resistance of the garrisons that still held for earl John. All surrendered, except that of Nottingham, which would not credit the report; the irritated king, prompt in his anger, marched to this town to besiege it in person, even before entering London.

His presence in the camp before Nottingham was announced to the garrison by an unwonted flourish of trumpets, horns, clarions, and other instruments of military music; but, deeming it a stratagem of the besiegers, they persevered in their resistance. The king, denouncing a terrible punishment upon them, assaulted the town and took it; but the garrison retired into the castle, one of the strongest that the Normans had built in England. Before battering the walls with his great guns and war-machines, Richard had a gibbet raised, high as a tall tree, and had hanged upon it, in sight of the garrison, several men who had been taken in the first assault. This spectacle seemed to the besiegers a more certain indication of the king's presence than any they had before observed, and they surrendered at discretion.

After his victory, king Richard, by way of recreation, made a pleasure journey into the greatest forest of England, which stretched from Nottingham to the centre of Yorkshire, over a space of several hundred miles; the Saxons called it Sire-Wode, a name changed, in the lapse of centuries, to that of Sherwood. "Never before in his life had he seen these forests," says a contemporary narrator, "and they pleased him greatly." On quitting a long captivity, the mind is ever vividly sensible to the charms of picturesque scenery; and, moreover, with this natural attraction was probably combined another, appealing still more powerfully, perhaps, to the adventurous spirit of Richard Cœur-de-Lion. Sherwood was at this time a forest formidable to the Normans; it was the dwelling of the last remains of the bands of armed Saxons who, still abnegating the conquest, persisted in withdrawing from the law of the foreigner. Everywhere hunted, pursued, tracked like wild beasts, it was here only that, favoured by the locality, they had been able to maintain themselves in any number, under a sort of military organization, which gave them a more respectable character than that of mere highwaymen.

At about the time that the hero of the Anglo-Norman baronage visited Sherwood forest, there lived in that forest a man who was the hero of the serfs, of the poor and of the low—in a word, of the Anglo-Saxon race. "At this time," says an ancient chronicler, "there arose among the disinherited, the most famous robber, Robert Hode, with his accomplices, whom the stolid vulgar celebrate in games and sports at their junketings, and whose history, sung by the minstrels, delights them more than any other." In these few words are comprised all our historical data as to the existence of the last Englishman who followed the example of Hereward; to find any traces of his life and character, it is to the old romances and popular ballads that we must of necessity resort. If we cannot place faith in all the singular and often contradictory incidents related in these poems, they are, at least, incontestable evidence of the ardent friendship of the English nation for the outlaw-chief whom they celebrate, and for his companions, who, instead of labouring for masters, "ranged the forest merry and free," as the old burthens express it.

It cannot be doubted that Robert, or, more commonly, Robin Hood, was of Saxon origin; his French Christian name proves nothing against this opinion, for with the second generation after the conquest, the influence of the Norman clergy had, in a great degree, superseded the former baptismal names of England by the names of saints and others used in Normandy. The name of Hood, or Hode, is Saxon, and the ballads most ancient in point of date, and consequently the most worthy of attention, place the ancestors of him who bore it in the class of peasants. Afterwards, when the recollection of the revolution effected by the conquest had become less vivid, the imagination of the rustic poets embellished their favourite personage with the pomp of grandeur and riches: they made him an earl, or at least the grandson of an earl, whose daughter, having been seduced, fled, and gave birth to the hero, in a wood. This theory formed the subject of a popular romance, full of interest and of graceful conceptions; but the supposition itself rests on no probable authority.

Whether or no Robin Hood was born, as the ballad relates—

* "Amang the leaves sae green,"

it was certainly in the woods that he passed his life, at the head of several hundred archers, formidable to the earls, viscounts, bishops, and rich abbots of England, but beloved by the farmers, labourers, widows, and poor people. These "merry men" granted peace and protection to all who were feeble and oppressed, shared with those who had nothing the spoils of those who fattened on other men's harvests, and, according to the old tradition, did good to the honest and industrious. Robin Hood was the boldest and most skilful archer of the band; and after him was cited Little John, his lieutenant and brother-in-arms, inseparable from him in danger and in pastime, and equally so in the old English ballads and sayings. Tradition also names several others of his companions—Mutch, the miller's son, old Scathlocke, and a monk, called Friar Tuck, who fought in frock and cowl, and whose only weapon was a heavy quarter-staff. They were all of a joyous humour, not seeking to enrich themselves, but simply to live on their booty, and distributing all they did not actually need themselves among the families dispossessed in the great pillage of the conquest. Though enemies of the rich and powerful, they did not slay those who fell into their hands, shedding blood only in their own defence. Their attacks fell chiefly on the agents of royal authority and on the governors of towns or provinces, whom the Normans called viscounts, and the English sheriffs.

* "But bend your bows, and strok your strings,

* Set the gallow-tree about;

* And Christ's curse on his head, said Robin,

* That spares the sheriff and the sergeant!"

The sheriff of Nottingham was the person against whom Robin Hood had the oftenest to contend, and who hunted him most closely, on horseback and on foot, setting a price on his head, and exciting his companions and friends to betray him. But none betrayed him, while many aided him to escape the dangers in which his daring often involved him.

"I would rather die," said an old woman to him one day, "I would rather die than not do all I might to save thee; for who fed and clothed me and mine, but thou and Little John?"

The astonishing adventures of this bandit chief of the twelfth century, his victories over the men of Norman race, his stratagems and his escapes, were long the only national history that a man of the people in England transmitted to his sons, having himself received it from his ancestors. Popular imagination adorned the person of Robin Hood with all the qualities and all the virtues of the middle ages. He is described as alike devout in church and brave in combat; and it is said of him that once within a church for the purpose of hearing the service, whatever danger presented itself, he would not depart until the close. This scrupulous devotion exposed him more than once to the danger of being taken by the sheriff and his men; but he always found means of effectual resistance, and instead of being taken by the sheriff himself, it would seem, from the old story, somewhat liable, indeed, to a suspicion of exaggeration, that he himself took prisoner the sheriff. Upon this theme, the English minstrels of the fourteenth century composed a long ballad, of which some verses merit quotation, if only as examples of the fresh and animated colouring given by a people to its poetry, at a time when a really popular literature exists.

* "In somer, when the shawes be sheyn,

* And leves be large and long,

* Hit is full mery in fayre forest

* To here the foulys song;

* To se the dere draw to the le,

* And leve their hillis hee,

* And shadow hem in the levis grene,

* Under the grenewode tre.

* Hit befel on Whitsontyde,

* Erly on a May mornyng,

* The son up feyre can spring, that day,

* And the birddis mery can sing.

* This is a mery morning, seid litull John,

* Be hym that dyed on tree,

* And moe mery man than I am on,

* Was not in Christante.

* Pluk up thi hert, my dere mayster,

* Litull John can say,

* And think it is a full fayre time,

* In a mornyng of May.

* The on thyng greves me, seyd Robyn

* And does my hert mych woo,

* That I may not no solem day

* To mas ne matyns go.

* Hit is a fourtnet and more, seyd Robyn,

* Sin I my Savyor see;

* To day will I to Notyngham, said Robyn,

* With the myght of Mylde Mary.

* * * * *

* Then Robyn goes to Notyngham,

* Hymselfe mornyng allone,

* * * * *

* He goes into Seinte Mary chyrche,

* And knelyd doun before the rode.

* * * * *

Robin Hood was not only renowned for his devotion to saints and to saints' days; he himself had, like the saints, his festival day, in which, religiously observed by the inhabitants of the villages and small towns of England, nothing was permitted but games and amusements. In the fifteenth century, this custom was still observed; and the sons of the Saxons and Normans took part in these popular diversions in common, without reflecting that they were a monument of the old hostility of their ancestors. On that day, the churches were deserted equally with the workshops; no saint, no preacher was more influential than Robin Hood; and this continued even after the Reformation had given a new impulse to religious zeal in England. We have this fact attested by an Anglican bishop of the sixteenth century, the celebrated and excellent Latimer. "I came once myselfe," says the bishop, in the sixth sermon before king Edward VI., "to a place, riding on a jorney homeward from London, and I sent worde over night into the toune that I wolde preche there in the morning, because it was a holy day, and methought it was an holy dayes worke. The church stode in my waye; and I tooke my horse and my company and went thither (I thought I should have found a great company in the churche), and when I came there, the churche dore was fast locked. I taried there half an hower and more; at last the keye was found, and one of the parishe comes to me and says: 'Sir, this is a busie daye with us, we cannot heare you; it is Robin Hoode's day. The parish are gone abroad togather for Robin Hoode; I pray you let (hender) them not.' " The bishop had assumed his ecclesiastical attire, but he was fain to lay it aside, and to continue his journey, giving place to archers dressed in green, who, in a theatre formed of branches, were enacting the parts of Robin Hood, Little John, and all their band.

Traces of this long-enduring memory, in which were buried even the recollection of the Norman invasion, subsist to the present day. In York, at the mouth of a small river, there is a bay which, in all modern maps, bears the name of Robin Hood's bay; and, not long ago, in the same county, near Pontefract, travellers were shown a spring of clear fresh water, called Robin Hood's well, at which they were invited to drink in honour of the famous archer. Throughout the seventeenth century, old ballads of Robin Hood, printed in gothic letters (a style of printing singularly liked by the lower classes of English), circulated in the country districts, by the medium of hawking pedlars, who sung them in a sort of recitative. Several complete collections of them were made for the use of town readers, one of which bore the pretty title of Robin Hood's Garland. These books, now become rare, interest only the erudite; and the history of the heroes of Sherwood, divested of its poetical decorations, is now scarce found but among children's tales.

None of the ballads that have been preserved relate the death of Robin Hood; the common tradition is that he perished in a nunnery, whither, one day, being ill, he had repaired for medical aid. He had to be bled, and the nun who performed this operation, having recognised Robin Hood, intentionally drew so much blood from him that he died. This story, which can neither be affirmed nor denied, is quite consistent with the manners of the twelfth century; many women, then, in the rich nunneries, studied medicine, and compounded remedies which they administered gratutiously to the poor. Further, in England since the conquest, the superiors of the nunneries and most of the nuns were of Norman extraction, as is proved by their statutes drawn up in old French; a circumstance that may, perhaps, explain how the chief of the Saxon bandits, who had been outlawed by royal ordinance, found enemies in the convent where he had sought assistance. After his death, the troop of which he was the chief and the soul disbanded; and his faithful companion, Little John, despairing of being able to hold his ground in England, and urged by a desire to prosecute his old war upon the Normans, went to Ireland, where he took part in the revolts of the natives. Thus was dissolved the last troop of English brigands that, having a political character, merit a place in history.

Between the refugees of the camp of Ely and the men of Sherwood, between Hereward and Robin Hood, there had been, especially in the north of England, a succession of partisan chiefs and outlaws, who were not without reputation, but of whom we know too little to admit of our considering them as historical personages. The names of several of them, such as Adam Bell, Clym of the Clough, or Clement of the Valley, and William Cloudesly, were long preserved in popular memory. The adventures of these three men, who cannot be separated from each other, any more than Robin Hood from Little John, are the subject of a long poem, composed in the eleventh century, and divided into three parts or cantos. Nothing positive can be said as to the authenticity of the facts there related, but they contain many original features calculated to present to the reader in a more striking light the idea which the English had formed of the moral character of those men, who, in the period of servitude, preferred the life of bandits to that of slaves.

Adam Bell, Clym of the Clough, and William Cloudesly, were, it would seem, natives of Cumberland. Having all three infringed the Norman forest laws, they were outlawed, and compelled to flee for their lives. United by the same fate, they swore brotherhood, according to the custom of the period, and went together to dwell in the forest of Inglewood, which the old romance calls Englishewood, between Carlisle and Penrith. Adam and Clement were not married; but William had a wife and children, whom he soon yearned to see. One day, he said to his two companions that he would go to Carlisle, and visit his wife and children. "Brother," answered they, "we counsel you not to do this:

* "If the justice may you take

* Your life were at an end."

William went despite this advice, and arrived at night in the town; but, recognised by an old woman whom he had once assisted, he was denounced to the judge and to the sheriff, who surrounded his house, took him, and rejoicing at this capture, had a new gibbet raised in the market-place to hang him. Fortunately, a little boy, a swineherd, who, while with his swine in the wood, had often seen William, and received alms and food from him, hastened to inform Adam and Clym of the fate of their adopted brother. The dangerous enterprise in which they engaged to save him is described with infinite animation by the old popular poet, whose description of the devotion of these men to each other is full of natural ease and truth:

* "William said to his brethren two,

* 'This day let us live and die;

* If ever you have need, as I have now

* The same shall you find by me.' "

In the combat, terminated by this unexpected deliverance, the three brothers-in-arms made great carnage of the royal officers and justice-men of Carlisle. They killed the sheriff, the judge, and the town-porter.

* "Many a man to the ground they threw,

* * * * * * * *

* Many a woman said—'Alas!' "

It is in a tone of pleasantry and a spirit of rejoicing that these numerous murders are related in the old song, the author of which manifests little goodwill to the agents of royal authority. His three heroes, however, end as the nation itself had ended, by growing weary of their resistance, and by coming to terms with the enemy. They proceed to London, to the king's palace, seeking a charter of peace. But even at the moment of making this act of submission, they retain their old character of pride and savage freedom:

* "Of no man would they ask no leave,

* But boldly went in thereat;

* They preced prestly unto the hall,

* Of no man have they dread . . . . "

If Robin Hood be the last chief of outlaws or Anglo-Saxon bandits that has enjoyed veritable popular celebrity, we are not thence to conclude that no man of the same race followed after him the same kind of life, in a spirit of political hostility to the government exercised by men of foreign race and language. The national struggle would continue under the form of brigandage, and the idea of freeman and of enemy to the foreign law, long remained associated together. But this had an end; and as the epoch of the conquest receded, as the English race, growing accustomed to the yoke, became attached by habit to that which it had tolerated from despair, brigandage gradually lost its patriotic sanction, and re-descended to its natural condition, that of an infamous profession. From that time forth the business of a bandit in the forests of England, without becoming less perilous, without requiring less individual courage and address, no longer produced heroes. There only remained in the opinion of the lower classes a great indulgence for the infractions of the game laws, and a marked sympathy for those who, from need or pride, braved these laws of the conquest. The life of the adventurous poacher, and in general the forest life, are affectionately celebrated in many comparatively modern songs and poems, all vaunting the independence enjoyed under the greenwood, in the good greenwood where there are no enemies but winter and rough weather, where—

* "All are mery and free,

* As happy as the day is long, as leaf on the tree."

King Richard, on his return to London, was crowned a second time with ceremonies that we have seen exactly reproduced in our days. After the rejoicings at this second coronation, he annulled at one stroke all the sales of domains that he had so freely made before departing for the crusade, alleging them to have been pledges which the holders were bound to restore. It was all in vain that the buyers presented their deeds, sealed with the great seal of the crown. The king, giving a mild form to this compulsory expropriation, said to them: "What pretext have you for retaining in your hands that which belongs to us? have you not amply repaid yourselves your advances out of the revenue of our domains? If so, you know that it is a sin to exercise usury towards the king, and that we have a bull from the pope prohibiting this under pain of excommunication. If upon a just account of what you have paid and what you have received, there should appear to be any balance due to you, we will pay it out of our own treasury, to leave you no subject of complaint."

No one had the courage to present such an account, and all was restored to the king without any compensation. He thus resumed possession of the castles, towns, offices, and domains that he had alienated; and this was the first benefit that the Norman race of England derived from the return of its chief, without whom the courtiers had declared it could not live, any more than a body without a head. As to the English race, after having been crushed with taxes for the deliverance of the king, it was crushed once more for that of the hostages whom Richard had left in Germany, and for the expenses of the war he had to maintain against the king of France.

It was not only in Normandy that Philip threatened to annihilate the power of his rival; he had leagued himself again with the barons of the north of Aquitaine; he had promised them aid and succours, and they, encouraged rather by his promises than by any actual assistance of his, had again attempted to establish their independence against the Anglo-Norman power. It was the passion of nationality and the desire to be the subject of no neighbouring king, of no man who was not of their own race and language, that had induced them to conclude the alliance with king Philip; but he, heeding not their patriotic sentiments, had wholly different views with reference to them. He aspired to extend his authority over the Gaulish provinces of the south, so as to become king of all Gaul, instead of being only king of France. Following the example of the Germanic chancery, which attributed to each successive emperor the actual possession of all the territories that his predecessors had governed and lost, the king of France and his council carried back, in idea, the boundaries of their legitimate dominion to the Pyrenees, where it was believed that Charlemagne had raised a cross to serve as a perpetual limit between France and Spain. "It is thither," said a poet of the period, a parasite of king Philip, "it is thither thou shouldst extend thy tents and thy territories, that thou mayest possess without reserve the domains of thy ancestors, that the stranger may no longer occupy a foot of land within our frontiers, and that the white dragon, with its venemous brood, may be extirpated from our gardens, as the Breton prophet promised us."

Thus the patriotic predictions put forth by the ancient Cambrian bards, to raise the courage of their nation, invaded by the Anglo-Saxons, passed, after the lapse of more than five hundred years, as prophecies in favour of the French against the Normans. This is, doubtless, a striking illustration of the capricious turns of human affairs; and another, not less remarkable, is, that the same provinces which the king of France alleged to be his, as the inheritance of Charlemagne, the emperor also claimed, in virtue of the rights of the same prince, who enjoyed the singular privilege of being regarded at once as French and as German. The cession of lands recently made by the Cæsar of Germany to king Richard was founded on this pretension. Besides the whole of Provence and part of Burgundy, imperial liberality, according to the ancient historians, had also granted him, over the county of Toulouse that right of perpetual suzerainty which the king of France at the same time asserted for himself. But, in reality, the counts of Toulouse enjoyed full political independence, and, according to the forms of the age, were free of their homage.

On the eve of opening the campaign against the king of France, Richard thought it necessary to operate upon public opinion, by relieving himself, in a striking manner, from the reproach of the murder of the marquis of Montferrat. He produced a forged autograph letter of the Old Man of the Mountain, written in Hebrew, Greek, and Latin characters, and containing the following passages:

"To Leopold, duke of Austria, and to all the princes and peoples of the Christian faith, greeting. Seeing that several kings in foreign lands impute the death of the marquis to Richard, king and lord of England, I swear, by the God who reigns eternally, and by the law which we obey, that king Richard had no share in that murder. Know that we have given these presents in our house and castle of Messiac, the middle of September, and have sealed them with our seal, the year 1505 after Alexander."

This singular despatch was officially published by William de Longchamp, who had again become chancellor of England, and sent to the foreign princes and to the monks who were known to occupy themselves in drawing up the chronicles of the time. Its manifest falsity was not remarked in an age when historical criticism and the knowledge of Eastern manners had slight prevalence in Europe. It even weakened, it would seem, the moral effect of the imputations of the king of France among his own vassals, and encouraged those of the king of England to fight more determinedly in a cause which they now thought the good cause; for there was at this period much superstition on this point. As soon as the two armies approached each other in Normandy, the army of France, which hitherto had ever taken the lead, began to retrograde. Earl John lost all courage as soon as he saw the chances of war becoming uncertain, and he resolved to betray his allies in order to regain his brother's favour. This treason was accompanied by atrocious circumstances—by the massacre of a great number of French knights whom the earl had invited to an entertainment. But notwithstanding all his vast demonstrations of repentance and friendship, Richard, who remembered that he had more than once acted a similar part towards their father, Henry II., placed no reliance in him, and, to use the words of the contemporary historians, gave him neither lands, nor towns, nor castles.

King Philip, successively driven from all the towns of Normandy that he had occupied, was soon fain to conclude a truce, which allowed Richard to carry his arms southward, against the insurgents of Aquitaine. At their head were the viscount of Limoges and the count of Perigord, whom king Richard summoned to surrender up their castles. "We hold thy menaces as nought," they answered: "thou hast returned far too proud, and we will render thee, despite thyself, humble, courteous, and frank, and will chastise thee by warring against thee." To render this reply more than a mere gasconade, it was necessary that peace should again be broken between the two kings; for the insurgents were by no means able to resist the forces of Richard, unless Philip kept at least a portion of those forces engaged. It was the famous Bertrand de Born, who, pursuing his political system, employed himself in rekindling war between the two enemies of his country. By his secret intrigues and his satirical verses, he determined the king of France to violate the truce he had just sworn; and, this time, the field of battle was Saintonge instead of Normandy. The first encounter of the two kings, at the head of their troops, took place at Mirambeau. They were only separated by a rivulet, on the banks of which each had respectively pitched his camp. The king of France had with him French, Burgundians, Flemings, and men of Champagne and of Berri; the king of England, Normans, English, Angevins, Tourainese, Manceaux, and men of Saintonge.

Whilst the two hostile armies were thus in presence of each other, both armed, several times, for the purpose of beginning the fight; but the archbishops, bishops, abbots, and other ecclesiastics, who had met together to labour for the re-establishment of peace, went from one camp to the other, intreating the kings to postpone the battle, and proposing arrangements which they deemed calculated to terminate the war. King Philip was the most difficult to persuade and the most exacting in his demands; he was resolved to fight, he said, unless Richard made him the oath of vassalage for Normandy, Guienne, and Poitou. This was his final resolve; as soon as it was repeated to Richard, the English monarch vaulted on his horse, placed his helmet on his head, gave the signal to advance and to sound trumpet, and unfurled his banner to cross the water. "Now, this confidence was given him," says an old history in the Provençal language, "by the circumstance that the Champagnese had secretly promised him that they would not come to blows with his men, by reason of the great quantity of sterlings he had distributed among them.

On their side, king Philip and all his people mounted their horses, and armed, with the exception of the Champagnese, who did not put on their helmets. This was the sign of their defection, and it intimidated the king of France, who had in no way anticipated it. This alarm changed all his views; and immediately sending for the bishops and ecclesiastics who had before intreated him in vain, he begged them to go, and say to Richard, that he declared him free from all vassalage, if he would conclude a peace. The king of England was already in full march, when the prelates and monks met him, carrying crucifixes in their arms, weeping, and conjuring him to have mercy on so many brave men, who, on both sides, would perish if a battle took place. They undertook that the king of France should comply with all his demands, and should immediately withdraw to his own territory. Peace was granted, the two kings swore a truce of ten years and dismissed their troops, no longer wishing to occupy themselves with arms, says an old chronicle, but only with the chase, with games, and with maltreating their men.

The evil that king Philip could do to his Frenchmen was slight in comparison with that which Richard now inflicted upon the Aquitans, and more especially upon those who had revolted against him. "This peace was a great affliction to them," says the same narrator; "and especially to Bertrand de Born, who was more chagrined thereat than any other person, for he delighted only in war, and above all in war between the two kings." He had once more recourse to his usual device of biting satire against the most irritable of the two rivals. He circulated poems in which he said that the French and Burgundians had exchanged honour for base crouching, and that king Philip was all hot for war before he had put on his armour, but that, as soon as he was armed, he lost courage. On their part, the other barons of Poitou and the Limousin, the same who had so fruitlessly made war upon king Richard, now excited that monarch to enter once more the field against the king of France, promising him their aid. Richard believed them, and, suddenly recommencing hostilities, devastated the provinces of France that bordered on his own.

King Philip, who would probably have been the first to recommence the war, had he been the first ready, complained of this violation of the sworn truce, and addressed himself to the bishops under whose auspices and guarantee it had been concluded. These again interposed, and obtained from the king of England his consent that a diplomatic conference should be held on the frontiers of Berri and Touraine. But the two kings, unable to agree upon any one point, began to abuse each other; and he of England gave the other the lie to his face, and called him a base renegade. "Whereat Bertrand de Born rejoiced," says his old biographer, "and composed a sirvente, in which he urged the king of France to commence the war with fire and blood, and reproached him with loving peace more than a monk. But despite all that Bertrand de Born could say in sirventes and couplets to king Philip, reminding him of the injury and shame that had been done him, he would not war against king Richard; but Richard warred against him, pillaged, took and burned his villages and his towns; at which all his barons, who loved not the peace, rejoiced, and Bertrand de Born composed another sirvente to confirm Richard in his purpose."

The destiny of Aquitaine to be incessantly balanced between two foreign powers, equally hostile to its independence, and yet by turns its allies, according to the circumstances of the warfare which divided them; this destiny, which afterwards became that of Italy, weighed at this period upon the whole of southern Gaul, comprising the mountainous country called Alvernhe in the Romane language of the south, and Auvergne in that of the north. This country, after having energetically resisted the invasion of the Franks, conquered by them, in common with the rest of the Gaulish territory, had been, for a time, comprehended in their conquest; it had then recovered its national freedom under the roi-faineans, the successors of Chlodowig; then devastated, and again conquered by the sons of Karle-Martel, it had become a province of the vast empire which they founded. Lastly, the dismemberment and total ruin of this empire had once more emancipated it; so that, in the twelfth century, the people of Auvergne were governed as freely as the civilization of the epoch admitted, by lords of their own race and language, who bore the title of counts, and who were also called dauphins (dalfins, dolphins), because a figure of this fish formed part of their coat-of-arms.

The dauphin of Auvergne acknowledged as suzerains the dukes of Aquitaine, perhaps from a reminiscence of the government of the Romans and of the subordination of the local magistrates of the empire to the provincial magistrates. As duke of Aquitaine, the king of England had received his oath of vassalage, according to the ancient custom, and the dauphin had exhibited no repugnance to render this purely nominal duty of submission. But it happened that after having, without much success, ravaged the dominions of the king of France, Richard, weary of the war, and desirous of concluding a truce more durable than the preceding, proposed to his rival to exchange with him the suzerainty of Auvergne for other political advantages. This proposition was accepted, and the king of England undertook to guarantee the cession he had made, or, in other words, to aid him in overcoming any objection on the part of the people of the country. This objection was soon manifested, the Auvergnats refusing to accept the king of France as their suzerain, first, because they had never had any such relations with him; and secondly, says an old history, because he was avaricious, a bad lord, and too near a neighbour. As soon as he had sent his officers to receive the homage of the count of Auvergne, who dared not at first refuse it, he purchased one of the strongest fortresses in the country, and garrisoned it; and shortly afterwards took from the count the town of Issoire, thus preparing the way for the conquest of the whole country, a conquest which he hoped to achieve without a war.

Richard perceived the projects of the king of France, but he took no steps to arrest them, foreseeing that Auvergne would one day lose patience, and relying upon the national hatred which the new lord was increasing, not only to regain the suzerainty, but to derive aid from it in the first war he should undertake against the rival of his ambition. And, accordingly, as soon as he deemed fit to break the truce, he sent word to the dauphin: "I know the great injuries the king of France has done you and your lands; and if you will, by revolting, lend me aid, I will support you, and will give you knights, cross-bowmen, and money, as much as you require." The count of Auvergne, crediting these promises, proclaimed the ban of national insurrection throughout his country, and commenced war against king Philip. But when Richard saw the struggle begun, he acted towards the Auvergnats as Louis, father of Philip, had acted towards the Poitevins; he formed a renewed truce with the king of France, and passed over into England, without in the smallest degree troubling himself as to the fate of the dauphin and of Auvergne. The French army entered that country, and, as the ancient chronicle expresses it, put it to fire and flame, seizing the fortified towns and the finest castles. Unable to resist such an enemy single-handed, the dauphin concluded a suspension of arms, during which he sent his cousin, count Gui, and ten of his knights to England, to remind king Richard of the promises he had made. Richard gave the count and his companions an ill reception, and sent them back without affording them men, arms, or money.

Ashamed and afflicted at having been thus deceived, and yielding of necessity to their fate, the Auvergnats made peace with the king of France, acknowledging his suzerainty over them, and again swearing to him the oath of homage. Shortly afterwards the truce between the two kings expired, and Philip immediately resumed fierce war upon the continental subjects of his rival. At this intelligence Richard proceeded to Normandy, whence he sent a message to the dauphin of Auvergne and count Gui, to the effect that the truce being broken between himself and the king of France, they ought, as loyal friends, to come to his aid, and fight for him. But they were not to be deceived a second time, and remained at peace with king Philip. Richard, hereupon, by way of avenging himself, composed, in the Provençal tongue, satirical couplets in which he said that, after having sworn fealty to him, the dauphin abandoned him in the hour of danger. The dauphin, equally ready with his pen, answered the king's verses in others characterized by more candour and dignity. "King," said he, "since you sing of me, you shall find me responsive. If ever I vowed an oath to you 'twas madness and folly on my part; I am not a crowned king, or a man of great riches: yet I can keep my own with my people, between Puy and Aubusson; and thank God I am neither a serf nor a Jew."

This last epigrammatic stroke seems allusive to the massacre and spoliation of the Jews which had taken place in England in the commencement of Richard's reign, and to the miserable condition of the natives of that country. However imperfect the state of society, in the twelfth century, in the southern provinces of Gaul, there was an enormous distance between its system and that of England, governed by foreigners. The difference of language, combining with that of condition, the haughtiness of the noble, all the greater that he had less means of entering into moral relation with his inferiors, that Norman insolence which, according to the old poet, increased with years, and the hostility of races, still vivid in the heart of the English, all this gave to the country an aspect somewhat similar to that of Greece under the rule of the Turks. There were Saxon families who, by an hereditary vow, had bound themselves, from father to son, to wear the beard long, as a memory of the old country and a token of disdain for the customs introduced by the conquest. But these families could do nothing, and the sons of the conquerors, not fearing them, allowed them to display in peace the mark of their descent, and the futile pride of a time which could never return.

In the year 1196, when king Richard was occupied in warring against the king of France, and his officers were levying money for the expenses of his campaigns and the payment of the balance of his ransom, the city of London was called upon to pay an extraordinary tax. The king's chancellor addressed the demand to the chiefs of the city, who, by a singular association of the two languages spoken in England, were called mayor and aldermen. These convoked, in the Guild-hall, or husting, as it was designated in the Saxon tongue, the principal citizens to deliberate, not as to granting the subsidy, but simply as to the proportions in which it should be paid by the citizens. In this assembly, composed for the most part of native English, there was a certain number of men of Norman, Angevin, or French race, whose ancestors, settling in England at the time of the conquest, had devoted themselves to commerce or trade. Either by reason of their foreign descent or of their riches, the citizens of this class formed in London a sort of ruling party; they governed the deliberations of the council, and often silenced the English, whom the habit of being oppressed rendered timid and circumspect.

But there was, at this time, in the class of natives, a man of very different character, a genuine old Saxon patriot, who let his beard grow, that he might in no way resemble the sons of the foreigners. His name was William, and he enjoyed great consideration in the city, on account of his zeal in defending, by every legal means, those of his fellow citizens who underwent injustice. The child of parents, whose industry and economy had secured him an independence, he had retired from business, and passed all his time in the study of jurisprudence. No Norman clerk surpassed him in the art of pleading in the French tongue, before a court of justice, and when he spoke English, his eloquence was vigorous and popular. He devoted his knowledge of the law and his power of language to save the poorer citizens from the embarrassments in which legal chicanery had involved them, and to protect them from the vexations of the rich, the most frequent of which was the unequal partition of the taxes. Sometimes the mayor and aldermen altogether exempted from the payment of taxes those who were best able to pay them, sometimes they called upon every citizen to contribute the same amount, without any regard to the difference of means, so that the heaviest burden fell upon the poor. These had often remonstrated, and William had pleaded their cause with more ardour than success. His efforts had rendered him dear to the citizens of lower condition, who named him the poor man's advocate; on the other hand, the Normans and their party surnamed him, ironically, the man with thebeard, and accused him of leading the multitude astray, by giving them a measureless desire for liberty and happiness.

This singular personage, the last representative of the hostility of the two races which the conquest had united on the same soil, appeared in his accustomed character at the common council of 1196. As mostly their habit, the leading citizens were for a distribution of the common charges that should throw only the smallest portion on themselves; William Longbeard alone, or almost alone, opposed them, and the dispute growing warm, they overwhelmed him with abuse, and accused him of rebellion and of treason to the king. "The traitors to the king," answered the Englishman, "are they who defraud his exchequer, by exempting themselves from paying what they owe him, and I myself will denounce them to him." He passed the sea, went to Richard's camp, and kneeling before him and raising his right hand, demanded from him peace and protection for the poor people of London. Richard listened to his plaint, said that he would do it right, and when the petitioner departed, thought no more of the matter, too much occupied with his great political affairs to descend to the details of a dispute between simple citizens.

But the Norman barons and prelates who filled the higher posts in the chancery and treasury took up the matter, and, from the instinct of nationality and aristocracy, warmly opposed the poor and their advocate. Hubert Gaultier, archbishop of Canterbury and grand justiciary of England, enraged that a Saxon should dare to denounce to the king men of Norman race, and apprehending a recurrence of the circumstance, ordered by edict every citizen of London to remain in the city, under penalty of being imprisoned as traitor to the king and kingdom. Several merchants who, despite the orders of the grand justiciary, went to Stamford fair, were arrested and imprisoned. These acts of violence caused a great fermentation in the city; and the poorer citizens, by an instinct natural to man in all times, formed an association for their mutual defence. William with the Long Beard was the soul and chief of this secret society, in which, say the contemporary historians, fifty-two thousand persons were engaged. They collected such arms as citizens, half serfs, could procure in the middle ages, iron-headed staves, axes, and iron crow-bars, wherewith to attack the fortified houses of the Normans, if they came to blows.

Urged by a natural desire to intercommunicate their sentiments and encourage each other, the poor of London assembled from time to time and held meetings in the open air, in the squares, and the market-places. At these tumultuous meetings William was the spokesman, and received applause which, perhaps, he was too fond of receiving, and which thus made him neglect the moment to act and to strike a decisive blow for the interests of those whom he sought to render formidable to their oppressors. A fragment of one of these harangues is given by a contemporary chronicler, who declares that he had it from the mouth of a person who was present. The speech, though its purpose was entirely political, turned, like the sermons of our days, upon a text from scripture, and this text was: "With joy shall ye draw water of the wells of salvation." William applied these words to himself: "It is I," he said, "who am the saviour of the poor; you, poor, who have felt how heavy is the hand of the rich, draw now from my well of water a salutary doctrine; and draw thence joyfully, because the hour of your relief is at hand. I shall separate the waters from the waters, that is to say, the men from the men; I will separate the people, humble and of good faith, from the proud and faithless; I will separate the elect from the reprobate, as light from darkness." Under this vague and mystic phraseology, the imagination of the hearers doubtless discerned sentiments and desires of a more precise nature; but the popular enthusiasm was not promptly turned to account; and the advocate of the poor allowed himself to be forestalled by the high Norman functionaries, who, assembling in parliament at London the bishops, earls, and barons, of the surrounding counties, cited the orator of the people to appear before this assembly.

William obeyed the summons, escorted by a great multitude who followed him, calling him the saviour and king of the poor. This unequivocal manifestation of immense popularity intimidated the barons of the parliament; employing artifice, they postponed the proceedings to a future sitting, which did not take place, and occupied themselves in working on the minds of the people by skilful emissaries. False promises and false alarms, aptly disseminated, calmed the public effervescence and discouraged the partisans of insurrection. The archbishop of Canterbury and the other justiciaries themselves convoked several meetings of the petty citizens of London; and discoursing to them, sometimes of the necessity of preserving order and peace, sometimes of the king's ample means of crushing sedition, they succeeded in spreading doubt and hesitation among the conspirators. Seizing this moment of weakness and vacillation, ever fatal to popular parties, they demanded, as hostages and guarantees of the public tranquillity, the children of a great many families of the middle and lower classes. The citizens had not sufficient resolution to oppose this demand; and the cause of power was gained, as soon as the hostages, taken from London, were imprisoned in various fortresses.

Notwithstanding the influence given them by the anxiety which prevailed in London as to the fate of the hostages, the justiciaries dared not publicly arrest the man whose destruction was contemplated in all these proceedings. They resolved to watch a moment when William should be from home alone, or with but few companions; two rich citizens, probably of Norman race, and one of whom was named Geoffroy, undertook this duty. Followed by armed men, they watched for several days all the movements of the Man with the Long-Beard; and one day, as he was quietly walking with nine friends, the two citizens approached him with an air of indifference, and, suddenly, Geoffroy laid hands on him, and gave the signal for the men-at-arms to advance. William's only weapon of defence was one of those long knives which, at that period, were worn in the belt; he drew it, and with one blow laid Geoffroy at his feet. The soldiers came up at the same moment, armed, from head to foot, in dagger-proof mail; but William and his nine companions, by dint of courage and address, got clear of them, and took refuge in the nearest church, dedicated to the Virgin, and called by the Normans the church of Saint-Mary de l'Arche. They closed and barricadoed the doors. Their armed pursuers endeavoured unavailingly to force an entrance; the grand justiciary, on learning the news, sent couriers to the adjacent castles for more troops, not relying, at this critical juncture, on the garrison of the Tower of London alone.

The report of these events caused great fermentation in the town: the people were sensible to the danger of a man who had so generously taken up their defence; but in general they exhibited more of sorrow than of anger. The sight of the soldiers marching into the city, and occupying the streets and market-places, and above all the conviction that, on the first outbreak, the hostages would be put to death, kept the citizens in their shops. It was in vain that the refugees awaited assistance, and that a few determined men exhorted their fellow citizens to march in arms to Saint Mary's church. The masses remained motionless as if struck with stupor.

Meanwhile, William and his friends prepared, as best they might, to sustain a siege in the tower, whither they had retired; repeatedly summoned to come forth, they pertinaciously refused to do so; and the archbishop of Canterbury, in order to force them from their post, had a quantity of wood collected, and set fire to the church. The heat and the smoke which soon filled the tower, compelled the besieged to descend, half suffocated. They were all taken, and as they were being led away bound, the son of the Geoffroy whom William had killed, approached him, and with a knife ripped open his stomach. Wounded as he was, they tied him to a horse's tail, and dragged him thus through the streets to the Tower, where he appeared before the archbishop, and, without any sort of trial, received sentence of death. The same horse dragged him in the same manner to the place of execution. He was hanged with his nine companions; "and thus," says an old historian, "perished William Longbeard, for having embraced the defence of the poor and of truth, if the cause makes the martyr, none may more justly than he be called a martyr."

This opinion was not that of one man only, but of all the people of London; who, though they had not had the energy to save their defender, at least wept for him after his death, and regarded as assassins the judges who had condemned him. The gibbet on which he had been hanged was carried away in the night as a relic, and those who could not procure any part of the wood, collected pieces of the earth in which it had stood. So many came for this earth, that in a short time a large pit was formed on the place of execution. People went there not only from the vicinity, but from all parts of the island, and no native Englishman failed to fulfil this patriotic pilgrimage when his affairs called him to London.

Ere long, popular imagination attributed the gift of miracles to this new martyr in the cause of resistance to foreign domination; his miracles were preached, as those of Waltheof had been, by a priest of Saxon origin; but the new preacher shared the fate of the former, and it was no less dangerous now to believe in the sanctity of Him with the Long Beard than it had been, an hundred and twenty years before, to believe in that of the last Anglo-Saxon chief. The grand justiciary Hubert sent soldiers to disperse with their lances the crowd who assembled to insult him, as he said, by bestowing such honours on the memory of an executed malefactor. But the English were not disheartened; driven away in the day, they returned at night to pray; soldiers were placed in ambush, and seized a great number of men and women, who were publicly whipped, and then imprisoned. At length, a permanent guard, posted on the spot which the English persisted in regarding as hallowed, prevented all access to it, the only measure that could discourage the popular enthusiasm, which then by degrees died away.

Here should properly terminate the narrative of the national struggle which followed the conquest of England by the Normans; for the execution of William Longbeard is the last fact which the original authors positively connect with the conquest. That there were, at subsequent periods, other events impressed with the same character, and that William was not the last of the Saxons, are indubitable propositions, but the inexactitude of the chronicles, and the loss of ancient documents, leave us without any proofs on this subject, and reduce us, all at once, to inductions and conjectures. The main task of the conscientious narrator, therefore, ends at this point; and there only remains for him to present, in a summary form, the ulterior destiny of the persons whom he has brought upon the stage, so that the reader may not remain in suspense.

And by the word personages, it is neither Richard, king of England, nor Philip, king of France, nor John, earl of Mortain, that is to be understood; but the great masses of men and the various populations who have simultaneously or successively figured in the preceding pages. For the essential object of this history is to contemplate the destiny of peoples, and not that of certain celebrated men; to relate the adventures of social, and not those of individual life. Human sympathy may attach itself to entire populations, as to beings endowed with sentiment, whose existence, longer than our own, is filled with the same alternations of sorrow and of joy, of hope and of despair. Considered in this light, the history of the past assumes somewhat of the interest which is felt in the present; for the collective beings of whom it treats have not ceased to live and to feel; they are the same who still suffer or hope under our own eyes. This is its most attractive feature; this it is that sweetens severe and arid study; that, in a word, would confer some value upon this work, if the author had succeeded in communicating to his readers those emotions which he himself experienced while seeking in old books names now obscure and misfortunes now forgotten.

CONCLUSION.

I. THE CONTINENTAL NORMANS AND BRETONS; THE ANGEVINS AND THE POPULATIONS OF SOUTHERN GAUL.

Birth of Arthur, duke of Brittany—Insurrection of Anjou and Maine—Policy of the king of France—Death of Arthur—Indignation of the Bretons—Invasion of Normandy—Taking of Ronen—Repentance of the Bretons—The Poitevins resist the king of France—Complete submission of Normandy—Project of a new invasion of England—Entrance of the English into Normandy—Guienne remains to the king of England—Heresy of the Toulousans and Albigenses—Crusade against the Albigenses—Additional aggrandizement of the kingdom of France—Charles of Anjou becomes count of Provence—Discontent and regrets of the Provençals—Insurrection of the cities of Provence—Termination of Provençal nationality—Limits of the kingdom of France—Character of the Basque population—Political condition of the Basques—Policy of the counts de Foix—Policy of the barons of Gascony—They pass alternately from one king to another—Confederation of the Armagnacs—The Gascons join the king of France—Conquest of Guienne by the French—Revolt of Bordeaux—Second conquest of Bordeaux—Patriotic efforts of the Armagnacs—Guienne and Gascony become parts of France.

Towards the end of the reign of Henry II., and some months after the death of his second son, Geoffroy, earl or duke of Brittany, there occurred an event of little importance in itself, but which became the cause, or at least the occasion, of great political revolutions; the widow of count Geoffroy, Constance, a woman of Breton race, gave birth to a son, whom his paternal grandfather, the king of England, wished to baptize in the name of Henry. But the Bretons, who surrounded the mother, were all opposed to the idea that the child, who would one day become their chief, should receive a foreign name. He was, by acclamation, called Arthur, and was baptized in this name, as popular with them as with the Welsh. The king of England took umbrage at this act of national will, and not venturing to remove Arthur from the Bretons, he compulsorily married the mother to one of his officers, Ranouf, earl of Chester, whom he made duke of Brittany, to the prejudice of his own grandson, now an object of suspicion in his eyes because the Breton nation loved him. But this nation, shortly after, expelled Ranouf of Chester, and proclaimed the son of Constance, still a mere boy, their chief.

This second act of national will, more serious than the first, involved the Bretons in a war with king Richard, successor to Henry II. While they were fighting for their own cause and that of young Arthur, the boy himself, directed by his mother, separated from them, and sometimes passed over to the king of England, his uncle, and sometimes to the French king, who entertained, in reference to the Bretons, similar views with those of the king of England. The ambitious projects of the king of France were assisted in Brittany, as in nearly all the western provinces of Gaul, by the general weariness of Anglo-Norman domination. Not only the Poitevins, who had for fifty years past been in continual revolt, but the Manceaux, the Tourangeaux, and even the Angevins, to whom their own counts, since they had become kings of England, had been almost entire strangers, also aspired to a great change. Without themselves desiring anything beyond an administration more devoted to their national interests, they met the policy of the king of France half way, and most imprudently aided him, in the hope of his aiding them, against the king of England.

Of all the continental provinces subject to the Normans, Guienne alone, at this time, exhibited no decided repugnance towards them, because the daughter of its ancient national chiefs, Eleanor, widow of Henry II. still lived, and tempered by her influence the harshness of the foreign government. Almost immediately after the death, by a cross-bow shot, of king Richard in Limousin, the revolution, which had been preparing some time, but which the fear of his military activity had kept in check, broke out. His brother John was recognised without opposition, king of England, and duke of Normandy and Aquitaine. But Anjou, Maine, and Touraine, separated themselves simultaneously from the Norman cause, proclaiming the young duke of Brittany their lord. The Poitevins imitated this defection, and formed, with their neighbours of the north and west, a league offensive and defensive. At the head of this league figured the Breton people, unfortunately represented by a mere boy and a woman, who, fearing to fall into the hands of the English king, gave up to the king of France, Philip II., all that the popular courage had recovered from the Anglo-Normans in the various confederate countries, and recognised his suzerainty over Anjou, Maine, and Brittany. Philip, whom the French surnamed Augustus, dismantled the towns and razed the fortresses which his new vassals had opened to him. When young Arthur, his liegeman and voluntary prisoner, addressed to him, on behalf of the people who had intrusted themselves to him, some remonstrances upon his conduct: "Am I not at liberty," said the king, "to do as I please in my own lands?"

Arthur soon perceived the fault he had committed in confiding himself to the mercy of one of the two kings, to escape from the other. He fled from Paris, and not knowing whither to go, delivered himself up to king John, his uncle, who, receiving him with infinite endearments, was about to imprison him, when the young duke, warned of his purpose, returned to the French king. The latter already despaired of being able to retain his new provinces, against at once the will of the inhabitants and of the king of England; he thought it better, therefore, to make with the latter an advantageous peace, and to obtain it, sacrificed his guest and protégé, whom he obliged to do homage to king John for Anjou, Maine, and Brittany. Philip, in return for these good offices, obtained peace, thirty thousand marks of gold, many towns, and the promise that, if John died without heirs, he should inherit all his possessions on the continent. In virtue of this treaty, the French garrisons of Anjou and Maine were replaced by Norman troops and by Brabançons in the pay of the king of England.

While Philip-Augustus was despoiling the young Arthur of his heritage, he was educating him at his court with his own children, and conciliating him in order to meet the contingency of a new rupture with king John. This rupture soon happened, on the occasion of a general insurrection of the Poitevins, under the direction of Hugh le Brun, count de La Marche, whom the king of England had deprived of his betrothed bride. All the barons of Poitou and those of a portion of Limousin confederated together, and when the king of France saw them compromised, hoping to profit by whatever they might venture to do, he suddenly broke the peace, and declared for them, on condition that they would take the oath of faith and homage to him. He forthwith produced Arthur on the political scene, gave him in marriage his daughter Marie, aged five years, had him proclaimed earl of the Bretons, Angevins, and Poitevins, and sent him at the head of an army to conquer the towns of Poitou, which still held out for the king of England.

The Bretons made alliance with the insurgent Poitevins, and promised to send them five hundred horse and four thousand foot. Awaiting this reinforcement, the new earl of Poitou laid siege to the town of Mirebeau, a few leagues from Poitiers, where, by a chance that proved fatal to the besiegers, the widow of Henry II. happened to be. The town was taken without much resistance, but Eleanor of Aquitaine retired into the castle, which was very strong, while Arthur and the Poitevins occupied the town. They were in the greatest security, when king John, urged by the desire of releasing his mother, appeared, after a rapid march, suddenly at the gates of Mirebeau, and made Arthur prisoner, with most of the chiefs of the insurrection. He took them into Normandy, and soon afterwards Arthur disappeared without any one knowing in what manner he had perished. Among the Normans, who had no feeling of national hatred or repugnance towards the king of England, it was said that the boy had died of sickness in the castle of Rouen, or, according to others, that he had killed himself in endeavouring to make his escape over the walls of the town. The French, animated by the spirit of political rivalry, affirmed that king John had poniarded his nephew with his own hand, one day that he was passing the Seine with him in a boat. The Bretons, who had centred all their hopes of liberty in young Arthur, adopted much the same story, but changed the scene of action, which they placed at Cherbourg, on the sea shore. The death of Arthur, however it happened, occasioned a great sensation, more especially in Brittany, where it was regarded as a national calamity. The same ardent imagination that had made the Bretons believe their future destiny bound up with that of the boy, filled them with an exaggerated affection for the king of France, because he was the enemy of Arthur's murderer. It was he whom they called upon to take vengeance for the deed, promising to aid him with all their power in any hostilities he might undertake against the king of England. Never king of France had so favourable an occasion for making himself master of those Bretons who were so attached to their independence. Philip, as suzerain, received the plaint of the lords and bishops of Brittany as to the murder of their young duke, and cited the king of England, his vassal for Normandy, to appear before the court of the barons of France, who now began to be called pairs (peers), a name borrowed from the romances on the life of Charlemagne. King John, as was expected, did not appear before the peers, and was accordingly condemned by them. All the lands he held of the kingdom of France were declared forfeit, and the Bretons were invited to take up arms to secure the execution of this sentence, which would only be effective in being followed up by a conquest.

The conquest was made, not by the power alone of the king of France, or by the authority of the decree of his peers, but by the co-operation, the more energetic that it was voluntary, of the surrounding populations, hostile to the Normans. Philip-Augustus did but appear on the frontier of Poitou, and an universal insurrection threw open to him well nigh every fortress; and when he returned to attack Normandy, the Bretons had already invaded and occupied a great portion of it. They took by assault Mont Saint-Michel, seized upon Avranches, and burned all the villages between that town and Caen. The report of their ravages, and the terror they inspired, contributed greatly to the success of the king of France, who, with the Manceaux and the Angevins, advancing from the east, took Andelys, Evreux, Domfront, and Lisieux, and at Caen formed his junction with the Breton army.

It was the first time that Normandy had been so simultaneously attacked by all the populations which surrounded her, south, east, and north; and it was also the first time that she had had a chief so indolent and so incompetent as king John. He hunted or amused himself while Philip and his allies were taking, one after another, all the towns and fortresses of the country; in less than a year he had none left him but Rouen, Verneuil, and Château-Gaillard. The people of Normandy made great but fruitless efforts to drive back the invaders; and at length only yielded from want of succours, and because their brothers in origin, the Normans of England, secured by the ocean, were in no way anxious to relieve them from a danger which did not threaten themselves. Moreover, finding themselves, as the result of their conquest, raised above the popular condition, they had little sympathy with the burgesses and peasants on the other side of the water, though descended from the same ancestors with themselves.

The citizens of Rouen suffered all the extremities of famine before they thought of capitulating; and when their provisions entirely failed them, they concluded a truce of thirty days with the king of France, at the expiration of which they were to surrender, if they did not meantime receive succours. In the interval, they sent some of their people to England to inform king John of the extremity to which they were reduced. The envoys found the king playing at chess; he did not quit his game, or answer them until he had finished it, and then merely said: "I have no means of assisting you within the period named, so do the best you can." The town of Rouen surrendered; the two places that still resisted followed the example, and the conquest of the whole country was established. This conquest, less severe upon the Normans than that of England had been upon the Saxons, was still not without its humiliation and suffering. The French razed the walls of a great many towns, and compelled the citizens of Rouen to demolish, at their own expense, their old fortifications, and to build a new castle in a place more convenient for the conquerors.

The national vanity of the Bretons was, no doubt, flattered, when they saw their ancient enemies, those who had struck the first blows on their national independence, subjugated, in their turn, by a foreign power. But this miserable satisfaction was all the fruit they derived from the victories they had won for the king of France. Moreover, in contributing to place their neighbours under the yoke, they had placed themselves under it, it becoming impossible for them to evade the domination of a king, who was environing them on every side, and combining with his own forces all those of Normandy. The constraint of French supremacy grew more and more intolerable to them; they attempted several times, but in vain, to renew their alliance with the king of England. To drown for awhile the thought of their own lost liberty, they, with a sort of insane fury, aided the kings of France entirely to destroy that of the populations along the Loire. They laboured at the aggrandizement of the French monarchy, and, at the same time, managed to maintain, to some extent, the remains of their ancient rights against the administrative invasions of that now powerful monarchy. Of the populations of Gaul, the Breton was, perhaps, at all times, that which manifested, in the highest degree, the need of political action. This innate disposition is far from being extinct among them, as is attested by the active part they have taken, in one way and another, in recent revolutions.

After having co-operated with the Bretons in the downfal of Normandy, the Angevins lost, as a result of this event, every relic of national existence, and the Manceaux never regained the independence of which the Normans had deprived them. The earls of Anjou were replaced by seneschals of the king of France, and the domination of this king was extended beyond the Loire, as far as Poitou. The rich Poitevins were not permitted to marry their daughters to any but French husbands. Under this yoke, novel to them, they repented of having repudiated the patronage of the king of England, and commenced negotiations with him, in which the malcontents of Anjou and Maine took part. A general insurrection was preparing in these three provinces, when the celebrated battle of Bovines, in assuring the fortunes of the kingdom of France, intimidated the conspirators. The Poitevins alone adhered to their resolution, and rose against king Philip, under the same chiefs who had, with him and for him, fought against king John. But Philip soon crushed them, with the aid of those who had feared to oppose him, of the Angevins, the Manceaux, the Tourangeaux, and the Bretons, and he carried his conquests southward as far as Rochelle. Thus these unhappy populations, from the absence of mutual affection and good understanding, fell, one after the other, under the yoke, and the overthrow of the Norman power on the continent, destroying the sort of equilibrium by means of which the southern countries had remained independent, the movement began by which, sooner or later, but infallibly, the whole of Gaul was to become French.

The restoration of Normandy to the kings of England could alone arrest this impulsion of things; but the incompetence of king John and the ability of Philip-Augustus, prevented anything of the kind from taking place, notwithstanding the discontent of the country. "Although the yoke of the king was light," says a poet of the thirteenth century, "Neustria long chafed at being subject to it; and yet, wishing well to those who wished him ill, he did not abolish their ancient laws, or give them reason to complain of being troubled with foreign regulations." No revolt of any importance took place in Normandy against the French. The popular discontent exhaled in individual murmurings, in regrets for past times, and especially for "Richard the Lion-hearted, whom no Frenchman had ever equalled," said the Norman soldiers, even in the camp of the king of France. The political nullity into which this nation, so renowned for its courage and its lofty pride, suddenly fell, may be attributed, perhaps, to that very pride, which forbad it to seek aid from its former subjects of Brittany, or to treat with them for an offensive league against the common oppressor. Further, the hope which the Normans had in the population that governed England, and the ancient sympathy of relationship between them and that population of gentlemen, would rapidly become extinct. When the two countries had ceased to be united under the same sceptre, the only inhabitants of England with whom the people of Normandy had frequent relations were merchants, men of English race, speaking a language foreign to the Normans, who, besides, nourished a hostile sentiment towards them, that of commercial rivalry. The ancient ties could not, therefore, fail to break between England and Normandy, while every day fresh bands were formed between the latter country and France, where the mass of the people spoke the same language with the Normans, and bore all the signs of a common origin, for every vestige of the Danish race had long ceased to exist in Normandy.

All these causes led to the result that, in less than a century after their conquest by Philip Augustus, the Normans, without scruple, nay, with ardour, espoused the enmity of the kings of France to England. In the year 1240, some of them formed an association with the Bretons for the purpose of privateering against English vessels. In each war that afterwards arose between the two countries, fleets of piratical vessels from Normandy essayed descents on the southern coast of England, for the purposes of devastation and pillage. The town of Dieppe was especially famous for these armaments. At length, when the great quarrel of succession, which occupied the whole of the fourteenth century, broke out between Philip V. and Edward III., the Normans conceived a project involving no less than a new conquest of England, a conquest as absolute, and perhaps more methodical than that of William the Bastard. The crown and all the public domains were adjudged beforehand to the chief of the expedition. All the lands of the barons and nobles of England were to belong to titled personages, the property of the commoners to the towns, and that of the churches to the clergy of Normandy.

This project, which, after three centuries of possession, was to reduce the conquerors of England to the state in which they themselves had placed the English in race, was drawn up with the utmost detail, and presented to king Philip de Valois at his castle of Vincennes, by the deputies of the Norman nation. They requested permission to place his son, their duke, at the head of the enterprise, and offered to defray the whole expense, requiring from the king only the aid of an ally, in case of reverses. The agreement was signed, sealed, and deposited at Caen, but circumstances, which the history of the period does not detail, retarded the execution. No progress was yet made in it when, in the year 1346, the king of England landed at Cape La Hogue, to take possession of the country which he called his hereditary domain. The Normans, attacked unexpectedly, no more resisted the English army, than the Anglo-Normans, perhaps, would have resisted their invaders, had the projected expedition taken place. The towns were closed, the bridges cut down, the roads broken up, but nothing stayed the march of that army, whose leading chiefs, the king included, spoke no other language than French with the Norman accent.

Notwithstanding this conformity of language, no national sympathy was aroused in their favour, and the towns which opened their gates only did so from necessity. In a short time, they took Barfleur, Carentan and Saint-Lo. In the official reports, drawn up in the French language, which they sent to England, they compared these towns in size and wealth to Sandwich, Leicester, and Lincoln, to which they still gave the name of Nicole. At Caen, where they visited, with great ceremony, the tomb of William the Conqueror, the author of their ancestors' fortunes, they found, among the town charters, the original of the treaty concluded between the Normans and the king of France for a new conquest, at which they were so enraged, that they pillaged and massacred the inhabitants. Then, still pillaging, they directed their course towards the ancient frontier of France, to Poissy, which they entered; then they went to Picardy, where between them and the French was fought the famous battle of Crécy.

The plan of invasion found at Caen was immediately forwarded to England, and publicly read in all the towns, in order to exasperate the popular mind against the king and against the French, from whom the Normans were now no longer distinguished. At London, the archbishop of Canterbury read this document after service, in front of the cross in St. Paul's church-yard. As it was drawn up in the French language, all the nobles present could understand it, and it was then translated into English for the people of low condition. This and the other means employed to interest the English in the quarrel of their king were not without effect upon them. The ambitious passions of the master, in the minds of the subjects assumed the form of a blind hatred to all the people of France, who, on their part, amply returned hate for hate. There was but one class of men in the two countries which escaped this frenzy, that of the poor fishermen of either shore, who, during the utmost fury of the wars, never did each other harm; "never warring," says Froissart, "but rather aiding each other; buying and selling upon the sea, one from the other, when either had had better fishing than the other."

By a singular destiny, while Normandy, the native land of the kings and nobles of England, became a country hostile to them, Aquitaine, from the sea of Rochelle to the Pyrenees, remained subjected to their authority, without apparent repugnance. We have seen how this country had been retained under the Anglo-Norman domination, by the influence of the duchess Eleanor, the widow of Henry II. After the death of this princess, the Aquitans preserved their faith to her grandson, from fear of falling under the lordship of the king of France, who, master of Poitou, had become their immediate neighbour. Pursuing a policy observed in the middle ages, they preferred, independently of all other considerations, to have as seigneur a king whose states lay at a distance, and for this reason, that generally the remote suzerain allowed the country to govern itself according to its local laws, and by men born within it, whereas a contiguous prince seldom permitted this arrangement.

The royal power preserved in south-west Gaul, would, perhaps, have long served as a fulcrum for the still independent populations of the south against the king of France, had not an unexpected event suddenly destroyed all the strength of the country between the Mediterranean, the Rhone, and the Garonne. The county of Toulouse, and the great lordships depending on it in the thirteenth century, by alliance or vassalage, far surpassed in civilization all the other parts of the ancient Gaulish territory. A great commerce was carried on thence with the ports of the east; its towns had the same form of municipal constitution, the same liberty, with the great Italian communes, which they imitated even in external appearance. Every rich citizen built himself a house, flanked with towers, and every citizen's son became a knight if he chose, and jousted at tournaments with the noblest.

This tendency to equality, which gave great umbrage to the noblesse of France, Burgundy, and Germany, opening a free communication among all classes, communicated to the minds of those who dwelt on the European coasts of the Mediterranean an activity which they exercised in every species of modern culture. They possessed the most elegant literature of all Europe, and their written idiom was classic in Italy and in Spain. With them Christianity, fervent and even enthusiastic,—for they were of an impassioned nature,—did not consist in a passive submission to the doctrine and observances of the Romish church. Without revolting against that church, without being sensible of the exact degree of their dissent from her, they had, in the course of the thirteenth century, adopted new opinions, singularly combined with old dogmas opposed to the Catholic dogma.

The church, alarmed at the extension and increase of the heresy of the southern Gauls, at first employed the resources of her powerful organization to stay its progress. But it was in vain that the pontifical couriers brought to Alby, Toulouse, and Narbonne, bulls of excommunication and anathema against the enemies of the Roman faith. Heterodoxy had gained upon even the ministers of the churches whence these bulls were to be fulminated, and the bishops themselves, though more firm in the Catholic discipline, being powerless, did not know how to decide, and at length underwent the influence of the universal example. It seemed clear that this great schism, in which all classes and ranks of society participated, could only be extinguished by a blow struck on the population, in a mass, by a war of invasion, which should destroy the social order whence had emanated its independence of spirit and its precocious civilization. This was what pope Innocent III. undertook, in the first years of the thirteenth century. Abusing the example of the crusades against the Saracens, he had one preached against the inhabitants of the county of

Toulouse and of the diocese of Alby, and published throughout Europe, that whoever would arm, to war against them, should obtain the remission of his sins and a share in the property of the heretics.

Unfortunately, the times were favourable to this crusade of Christians against Christians. The conquests of the king of France in Normandy, Anjou, and Aquitaine, had caused in these various countries the ruin or banishment of many men, and thus augmented the number of chevaliers sans avoir, of "knights with nothing," and of reckless fortune-hunters. The pilgrimage against the Albigeois (for so the war was designated) promised less risk, and a more certain profit, than the crusade against the Arabs, and accordingly the army of the new pilgrims soon numbered fifty thousand men of every rank and nation, but especially French and Flemings. The king of France sent fifteen thousand soldiers, and the king of England allowed a body of troops to be enrolled in Guienne, under the command of the archbishop of Bordeaux.

It would exceed our limits to recount in detail all the barbarities of the crusaders at the sacking of Beziers, Carcassonne, Narbonne, and other towns, laid under the ban of the church; to say how the inhabitants were massacred without distinction of age or sex, of catholic or heretic. "Poor towns," exclaims a poet, an eye-witness of these calamities, "how have I formerly seen you, and how see I you now." From the Garonne to the Mediterranean, the whole country was devastated and subjugated; and the chief of the conquering army, Simon de Montfort, not venturing to retain for himself such vast domains, did homage for them to the king of France.

As the crusaders, whose numbers increased every day, made new conquests, the suzerainty of this king extended more and more over the south of Gaul. The county of Toulouse, and the territories of Agen, Carcassonne, and Beziers, after three centuries of independence, were thus again attached to the kingdom which had formerly possessed them. A treaty, concluded in a moment of distress, between the heir of Simon de Montfort and the successor of Philip-Augustus, soon converted this feudal supremacy into direct sovereignty. Fully to secure this immense acquisition, Louis VIII. raised an army, assumed the cross, and proceeded to the south. He passed, not without resistance, the Rhone at the bridge of Avignon, took Beaucaire and Nîmes, which he united under the authority of a seneschal, placed also a seneschal at Carcassonne, and marched upon Toulouse, whose inhabitants then were in full revolt against the crusaders and against himself.

Hatred of the French name was the national passion of the new subjects of the king of France; that name never issued from their mouths unless accompanied by some injurious epithet. The troubadours in their sirventes called upon the son of the count of Toulouse to come with the aid of the king of Aragon, and reconquer his heritage, making a bridge of French corses. During the minority which followed the death of king Louis VIII., an extensive conspiracy was formed from the Vienne to the foot of the Pyrenees, having for its object to drive back the French within their ancient limits. The chiefs of the valleys through which the Arriege flows, and where the Adour takes its source, the counties of Foix and Cominges, formed an alliance with the count de Marche and the castellans of Poitou. The king of England, too, on this occasion, did not hesitate to take a decisive part, since it was no longer a pilgrimage against heresy that was to be opposed, but the political power of the king of France. The attempt, however, had little success; the catholic clergy, zealous for French dominion, terrified the confederates by threatening them with a new crusade, and repressed the movements of the Toulousans by means of the terrible police then instituted under the name of Inquisition. Weary of a hopeless struggle, the heir of the ancient counts of Toulouse made a definitive peace with king Louis IX., ceding to him all his rights, by a treaty far from voluntary. The king gave the county of Toulouse to his brother Alphonse, already count of Poitou by a similar title, and equally against the will of the country.

Notwithstanding these accessions, the kingdom of France had not yet, on the southern side, attained the limits whither aspired the ambition of its kings, nourished by the popular traditions of the reign of Charlemagne. The banner of the gold fleur-de-lys was not yet planted on the Pyrenees, and the chiefs of the populations which inhabited the foot or the slopes of those mountains were still free to give their homage to whom they pleased. Some, it is true, offered it to the king of France; but others, and these the greater number, were faithful to the kings of Aragon or Castile, or to the king of England; and others, again, remained without any suzerain at all, holding of God alone.

While one of the brothers of Louis IX. ruled the counties of Toulouse and Poitou, the other, named Charles, was count of Anjou and Maine. Never had the family of any French king combined such power, for we must not mistake the kings of the Franks for kings of France. The limits of this kingdom, formerly bounded by the Loire, already extended, in the middle of the thirteenth century, to the Mediterranean; on the south-west, it bordered upon the possessions of the king of England in Guienne, and on the south-east, upon the independent territory which bore the old name of Provence, (Provincia.) About this time, the count of Provence, Rémond Beranger, died, leaving an only daughter, called Beatrix, under the guardianship of some relations. The guardians, masters of the girl and of the county, offered the king of France to give both the one and the other to his brother, Charles d'Anjou; and the king, having agreed to the proposed conditions, sent troops into Provence, which entered it as friends. Charles d'Anjou proceeded thither soon afterwards, and Beatrix was married to him, without having been much consulted on the subject. As for the people of the country, their aversion to a foreign count, and especially to one of French race, was unequivocal. They had before them the example of what their neighbours on the other side of the Rhone suffered under the government of the French. "Instead of a brave lord," says a contemporary poet, "the Provençals are to have a master; they may no longer build towers or castles, they will no longer dare to bear lance or shield before the French. May they die rather than be reduced to such a condition!"

These fears were soon realized. All Provence was filled with foreign officers, who, treating the natives as subjects by conquest, levied enormous imposts, confiscated estates, and imprisoned and put to death their owners without trial and without sentence. At first, these excesses of power met with little resistance, because the clergy, making itself, in the words of an old poet, a whetstone for the swords of the French, upheld their domination by the terrible menace of a crusade. The troubadours, accustomed to serve in the south as organs of the patriotic interest, undertook the dangerous task of arousing the people, and shaming them out of their disgraceful endurance. One of them, playing on the name of his country, said that it ought no longer to be called Proensa (the land of the preux), but Faillensa (the land of the failers), because it allowed a foreign domination to replace its national government. Other poets, in their verses, addressed the king of Aragon, the former suzerain of Provence, inviting him to come and expel the usurpers from his lands. Others, again, urged the king of England to head an offensive league against the

French; their object being war, by means of which they might effect their enfranchisement. "Why is not the game commenced," they said, "in which many a helm will be split, many a hauberk pierced?"

Things were at this point, when the king of France, departing for the crusade in Egypt, took his brother, Charles d'Anjou, with him. News soon came that the two brothers had been made prisoners by the Saracens, and hereupon there was universal joy in Provence. It was said that God had worked this miracle to save the liberty of the country. The towns of Aix, Arles, Avignon, and Marseilles, which enjoyed an almost republican organization, made open preparations for war, repairing their fortifications, collecting provisions and arms; but the imprisonment of Charles d'Anjou was not of long duration. On his return, he began by devastating the whole district of Arles, in order to intimidate the citizens; he then blockaded them so long with a numerous army, that after enduring infinite sufferings they were fain to surrender. Such was the end of this great commune, as free in its days of prosperity as those which then flourished in Italy. Avignon, whose municipal constitution resembled that or Arles, opened its gates on the approach of Alphonse, count of Toulouse and Poitiers, who came to aid his brother in subjecting the Provençaux.

At Marseilles, the inhabitants of all ranks took up arms, and putting out to sea, attacked the count's fleet. But the coolness between the higher burghers and the country seigneurs and castellans produced fatal dissensions. The Marseillese were ill supported by this class of men, many of whom thought it more knightly to serve under the banner of the foreigner than to make common cause with the friends of national independence. Reduced to their own resources, the latter obtained a favourable capitulation, which, however, the count's French agents soon violated without scruple. Their tyranny and their exactions became so insupportable, that, despite the danger, a revolt was formed against them, in which they were all seized by the people, who, however, contented themselves with imprisoning them. The insurgents took possession of the chateau Saint-Marcel, shut the gates of the city, and sustained a second siege, during which the people of Montpellier, though long enemies of the Marseillese from commercial rivalry, profited by the last moments of their own independence to succour Marseilles against the conquerors of southern Gaul. Notwithstanding this assistance, the town, attacked by superior forces, was obliged to yield. All the stores in its public arsenals were removed, and the citizens were disarmed. A knight, named Boniface de Castellane, at once warrior and poet, who, by his sirventes, had excited the insurrection of the Marseillese, and had then fought in their ranks, was, according to some historians, taken and beheaded. The castellans and seigneurs who had abandoned the cause of the towns, were treated by the count almost as harshly as those who had adhered to it. He used every means to depress and impoverish them, his authority being strengthened by the public misery and terror.

The Provençals never recovered their ancient municipal liberty, or the high civilization and riches which had resulted from it. But, very singularly, after two centuries, the extinction of the house of the counts of Anjou, under which they had preserved at least a shadow of nationality, by an administration distinct from that of France, occasioned them almost as much grief as had the accession of that house. To fall under the immediate authority of the kings of France, after having been governed by counts, appeared to the people of Provence, about the close of the fifteenth century, a new national calamity. It was this popular feeling, rather than the personal qualities of René, surnamed the Good, which occasioned the long memory of him retained by the Provençals, and the exaggerated idea of public prosperity which tradition still connects with his reign.

Thus were annexed to the kingdom of France all the provinces of ancient Gaul situate right and left of the Rhône, except Guienne and the valleys at the foot of the Pyrenees. The old civilization of these provinces received a mortal blow in their compulsory reunion with countries far less advanced in intellectual culture, in industry, and in manners. The most disastrous epoch in the history of the peoples of southern France is that at which they became French, when the king, whom their ancestors used to call the king of Paris, began to term them his subjects of the langue d'oc, in contradistinction to the old French of Outre-Loire, who spoke the langue d'oui. From that time the classic poetry of the south, and even the language consecrated to it, disappeared from Languedoc, Poitou, Limousin, Auvergne, and Provence. Local dialects, inelegant and incorrect, prevailed in every direction, and soon replaced the literary idiom, the beautiful language of the troubadours.

The jurisdiction of the first seneschals of the kings of France in Languedoc, bounded on the west by that of the officers of the king of England in Aquitaine, only reached southward as far as the valleys which announce the vicinity of the great chain of the Pyrenees. It was here that the conquest of the crusaders against the Albigenses had stopped, because the profit of a war in a mountainous country, bristling with castles, built on the rocks like eagles' nests, did not seem at all equivalent to the dangers it would involve. Thus, on the southern frontier of the possessions of the two kings there remained a free territory, extending from one sea to the other, and which, extremely narrow at its eastern and western extremities, reached towards its centre the confluence of the Aveyron and the Garonne.

The inhabitants of this territory were divided into lordships under different titles, as all the south had been before the French conquest; and these various populations, with one sole exception, presented the signs of a common origin in their language and character. This race of men, more ancient than the Celtic races of Gaul, had probably been driven back to the mountains by a foreign invasion, and, together with the western part of the Gaulish Pyrenees, they also occupied the Spanish side of these mountains. The name they gave themselves in their own language—a language differing from all the known tongues—was Escualdun, in the plural Escualdunac. Instead of this name, the Romans had employed, we know not for what reason, those of Vaques, Vasques, or Vascones, which have been retained, with certain variations of orthography, in the neo-Latin languages of Spain and Gaul. The Vasques or Basques never wholly underwent the yoke of the Roman administration which ruled all their neighbours, or, like the latter, quitted their language for the Latin tongue, or any of its modifications. They, in like manner, resisted the invasions of the Germanic peoples; and neither the Goths nor the Franks had succeeded in annexing them at all permanently to their empire. When the Franks had occupied all the large cities of the two Aquitaines, the western mountaineers became the centre and fulcrum of the frequent rebellions of the inhabitants of the plain. The Basques were thus allied against the Frank kings of the first and second race, with the Gallo-Romans, whom they disliked and whom they were accustomed to pillage in the intervals of these alliances. It was this often renewed confederation which gave the name of Vasconie or Gascony to the portion of Aquitaine situated between the mountains and the Garonne; and the difference of termination in the nominative and oblique cases of the same Latin word occasioned the distinction of Basques and of Vascons or Gascons.

In placing themselves at the head of the great league of the natives of southern Gaul against the conquerors of the North, the only object of the Basques appears to have been their own independence, or the material profits of war, and by no means the establishment of their political sway in the plains, or the foundation of a new state; whether from excessive love of their native land, and contempt for foreign countries, or from a peculiar idiosyncrasy, ambition and the desire for renown were never their dominant passions. While with the aid of the insurgents, with whom they had so powerfully co-operated, there were formed, for the noble families of Aquitaine, the counties of Foix, Comminges, Bearn, Guienne, and Toulouse, they, as little seeking to be masters as consenting to be slaves, remained a people, a free people in their mountains and their valleys. They carried political indifference so far as to allow themselves to be nominally comprised in the territory of the count of Bearn, and in that of the king of Navarre, men of foreign race, whom they allowed to style themselves seigneurs of the Basques, on the understanding that this lordship should be in no way or degree real or effective.

It was under this aspect that they appeared in the thirteenth century, interfering, as a nation, in the affairs of none of the surrounding countries; divided into two different suzerainties, from habit, from indifference, not from constraint, and making no attempt to form a junction as one people. The only thing that seemed nationally to interest them, was the maintenance of their hereditary customs and laws decreed in their cantonal assemblies, which they called Bilsâr. No passion, either of friendship or of hate, induced them to take part in the wars of foreigners; but if offered good pay, they were ready, individually, to enrol themselves under any banner, no matter whose or in what cause. The Basques, in common with the Navarrese and the inhabitants of the eastern Pyrenees, had, at this time, the same high reputation as light troops that the Brabançons had as heavy infantry. Their agility, their familiarity with rugged paths, an instinctive sharpness of wit and aptitude for stratagem, arising to a certain extent from their life of mountain hunter and shepherd, rendered them excellently suited for sudden attacks, for ambuscades, for night surprises, for forced marches in bad weather and over bad roads.

Three cantons only of the Basque country, Labour, the Valley of Soule, and Lower-Navarre, were in the ancient territory of Gaul: the rest formed part of Spain. The city of Bayonne, dependent on the duchy of Guienne, marked on the sea-coast the extreme limit of the Romane tongue, perhaps advanced somewhat more northwards in anterior centuries. At the gates of Bayonne commenced the territory of the count or viscount of Bearn, the most powerful seigneur in those parts, and whose policy generally influenced that of all the surrounding lords. He recognised no suzerain in any fixed and permanent manner, unless, perhaps, the king of Aragon, whose family was allied with his own. As to the king of England, of whom he held some fiefs near Bayonne, he by no means deemed himself at his disposal, and only swore him fealty and homage in consideration of a large sum. It was at a cheaper rate, but still for money, that this king obtained the homage of the less powerful lords of Bigorre, Comminges, of the three valleys, and of Gascony proper. They more than once, in the thirteenth century, made war, in his pay, against the king of France; but on the first indication of lofty assumption, on the first act of tyranny of their adopted suzerain, the Gascon chiefs would forthwith abandon him, and ally with his rival, or themselves form a league against him. This league, often renewed, maintained a correspondence with Guienne, for the purpose of exciting insurrection there, and its success in this way, at different epochs, would seem to indicate a prevalent desire to unite all south-western Gaul in an independent state. This notion was peculiarly agreeable to the upper classes and to the rich burghers of the towns of Guienne; but the lower orders clung to the English domination, under the persuasion that there would be no market for the wines of the country, if the English merchants ceased to trade with them.

Towards the commencement of the fourteenth century, a treaty of alliance and of marriage united in perpetuity in the same person the two lordships of Foix and Bearn, and thus founded a considerable power upon the common frontier of the kings of France and England. In the long war which, shortly after, broke out between these two kings, the first made great efforts to bring over the count of Foix to his side, and to induce him to act, in the conquest he meditated in Guienne, the part that the Bretons, the Angevins, and the Mançeaux had formerly played in that of Normandy. The count was gained by the promise, made in advance, of the towns of Dax and Bayonne; but as the expedition then undertaken did not succeed, all alliance was soon broken between the kingdom of France and the counts of Foix. Resuming their ancient position of complete political independence, the chiefs of this small state remained, as in observation, between the two rival powers, each of which made every effort to bring them to a declaration. Once, in the middle of the fourteenth century, the king of France sent Louis de Sancerre, one of his marshals, to count Gaston de Foix, to say that he had a great desire to come and see him. "He will be welcome," answered the count, "I shall be happy to receive him."—"But, sir," said the marshal, "it is the king's intention on his arrival to ascertain, clearly and distinctly, whom you will back, French or English; for you have ever maintained reserve in the war, arming at no request and at no command that you have received." "Messire Louis," replied the count, "if I have abstained from arming, I had good reason and warranty therein; for the war between the kings of France and England concerns not me. I hold my country of Béarn of God, my sword, and my birthright; and I am in no way called upon to place myself in the servitude or in the enmity of either the one or the other king."

"Such is the nature of the Gascons," adds the old historian who relates this anecdote. "They are unstable, and never faithful to one lord for thirty years together." Throughout the war between the kings of England and France, the reproach of fickleness, ingratitude, and perfidy was alternately applied by the two kings to the lords who desired to remain free and neutral, and whom each was intent upon securing for himself. The pettiest castellan in Gascony was courted by messages and by letters sealed with the great seal of France or of England. Hence the importance attained, towards the fifteenth century, by persons of whom little had been heard before, as the sires d'Albret, d'Armagnac, and many others far less powerful, such as the sires de Durfort, de Duras, and de Fezensac. To secure the alliance of the seigneur d'Albret, the chief of a little territory of heath and furze, the king of France, Charles V., gave him in marriage his sister, Isabelle de Bourbon. The sire d'Albret came to Paris, where he was received and fêted in the palace of his brother-in-law; but in the midst of this cordial reception, he could not help saying to his friends: "I will remain French, since I have promised it; but, by God, I had a better life, both I and my people, when we fought for the king of England." About the same time, the sires de Durfort and de Rosan, made prisoners by the French in a battle, were both released without ransom, on condition, says a contemporary, that they would turn French, and promise, on their faith and honour, for ever to remain good Frenchmen, they and theirs. They swore it; but, on their return, they answered the first person who asked them the news: "Ah! sire, by constraint and menace of death, they made us become French; but we tell you, that in taking this oath, in our hearts we still kept faith to our natural lord, the king of England; and whatever we said or did, we will never be French."

The value set by such powerful kings on the friendship of a few barons, arose more especially from the influence which these barons, according to the party they adopted, could and did exercise over the castellans and knights of the duchy or Guienne, a great number of whom were related to them by marriage. Moreover, the Aquitans had, in general, more intimate relations with them than with the officers of the king of England, who could not speak the language of the country, or spoke it ill, and whose Anglo-Norman stateliness was altogether discordant with the vivacity and ease of the southerns. Accordingly, whenever one of the Gascon lords embraced the French party, a greater or less number of knights and squires of Aquitaine joined with him the army of the king of France. The various operation of this influence occasioned, during the whole of the fourteenth century and half of the fifteenth, constant movement among the noble population of the castles of Guienne; but far less among the bourgeoisie. This class of men adhered to the sovereignty of the king of England from the then prevalent idea that the sway of the other king would infallibly destroy all municipal liberty. The rapid decline of the communes of Languedoc, since they had become French, so deeply fixed this opinion in the minds of the Aquitans, that it made them quite superstitious on the subject. When the king of England, Edward III., assumed the title of king of France, they were alarmed, as though the mere title added to his name would altogether change his conduct towards them. Their apprehensions were so great, that, to dissipate them, king Edward thought it necessary to address to all the towns of Aquitaine a letter in which was the following passage: "We promise, in good faith, that, notwithstanding our taking possession of the kingdom of France, appertaining to us, we will not deprive you, in any manner, of your liberties, privileges, customs, jurisdictions, or other rights whatsoever, but will leave you in full enjoyment thereof, as heretofore, without any infringement by us or by our officers."

In the first years of the fifteenth century, the count d'Armagnac, who had for some time past been, with the sire d'Albret, at the head of a league formed among all the petty lords of Gascony, for the purpose of maintaining their independence, by relying, according to circumstances, on France or on England, formed an alliance with one of the two parties who, under the names of Orleans and Burgundy, then disputed the government of France. He engaged thus in a foreign quarrel, and brought his confederates into it, less, perhaps, from political motives than from personal interest; for one of his daughters had married the duke of Orleans, chief of the party of that name. Once mixed up with the intrigues and disputes which divided France, the Gascons, with the impetuosity of their southern temperament, displayed so great an activity, that the Orleans party soon changed its name to that of Armagnac, and the only party distinctions in the kingdom became those of Burgundians and Armagnacs. Notwithstanding the generality of this distinction, there were no true Armagnacs but those of the south, and these, enveloped as it were in a faction more numerous than themselves, forgot in their passionate partisanship the cause which had first made them league together, the independence of their native land. The interests of their country ceased to be the sole object of their policy; they no longer freely changed their suzerain and their allies, but blindly followed all the movements of a foreign faction.

Under the reign of Charles VII., this faction involved them more deeply than they had ever before been involved in alliance with the king of France against England. After the astonishing victories which signalized the deliverance of the country invaded by the English, when, to complete this great reaction, it was resolved to expel them from the continent, and to deprive them of Guienne, the friends of the count of Armagnac all employed their utmost energies in urging la fortune de la France to this final goal. Their example induced those of the Gascon lords, who still held for the king of England, to desert him for king Charles. Of this number was the count de Foix; and this petty prince, who, a few years before, had promised the former of the two kings to conquer Languedoc for him, now undertook to superintend for the other that of the whole duchy of Aquitaine.

A sort of superstitious terror, arising from the rapidity of the French triumphs, and the part played in them by the celebrated Maid of Orleans, now reigned in this country. It was believed that the cause of the king of France was favoured by Heaven, and when the count de Penthievre, chief of the French army, and the counts de Foix and d'Armagnac, entered on three sides the country of Guienne, they did not experience, either from the inhabitants or from the English, anything like the resistance formerly opposed to them. The English, despairing of their cause, gradually retreated to the sea; but the citizens of Bordeaux, more earnest for their municipal liberty than the English army for the dominion of its king on the continent, endured a siege of several months, nor did they capitulate at last, but on the express condition that they should be for ever exempt from taxes, subsidies, and forced loans. The city of Bayonne was the last to surrender to the count de Foix, who besieged it with an army of Bearnese and Basques, the former of whom followed him to the war because he was their seigneur, and the latter, because they hoped to enrich themselves. Neither of these two populations was in any degree interested in the cause of France; and while the Bearnese soldiers fought for king Charles, the Bearnese people looked upon the French as dangerous foreigners, and guarded their frontier against them. Once, during the siege of Saint-Sever, a French column, whether from mistake or in order to shorten its journey, entered the Bearnese territory; on the news of its march the tocsin rang in the villages, the peasants assembled in arms, and there took place between them and the troops of the king of France an engagement celebrated in the annals of the country, as the battle of Mesplede.

The French seneschal of Guienne, who filled at Bordeaux the place of the English officer bearing the same title, did not take, before the assembled people, the ancient oath his predecessors had been accustomed to take at their installation, when they swore, in the Bordelaise tongue, to preserve to all people of the town and the country, lors franquessas, vrivileges et libertats, establimens, fors, coustumas, usages, et observences. Notwithstanding the capitulation of most of the towns, the duchy of Guienne was treated as a conquered territory; and this state of things, to which the Bordelais were not accustomed, so chafed them, that, less than a year after the conquest, they conspired with several castellans of the country to drive out the French with the aid of the king of England. Deputies from the town repaired to London and treated with Henry VI., who accepted their offers, and despatched four or five thousand men under John Talbot, the famous captain of the age.

The English having landed at the peninsula of Medoc, advanced without any resistance, because the main body of the French army had withdrawn, leaving only garrisons in the towns. On the news of this debarkation, there was great discussion at Bordeaux, not as to whether they should again become English, but as to the manner in which they should treat the officers and soldiers of the king of France. Some wished them to be allowed to depart without impediment or injury, others that full vengeance should be inflicted on them. During the discussion, the English troops arrived before Bordeaux, some citizens opened one of the gates, and most of the French who remained in the town became prisoners of war. The king of France sent, in all haste, six hundred lances and a number of archers, to reinforce the garrisons of the towns; but before these succours arrived at their destination, the army of Talbot, now joined by all the barons of the Bordelais, and four thousand men from England, reconquered nearly all the fortresses.

Meantime king Charles VII. came in person, with a numerous army, to the frontiers of Guienne. He at first endeavoured to open a correspondence with the people, but he did not succeed; no one gave his co-operation in effecting the restoration of the royal government. Finding himself thus reduced to depend wholly on force, he took several towns by assault, and beheaded, as traitors, all the men of the country who were found with arms in their hands. The counts de Foix and d'Albret, and the other seigneurs of Gascony, gave him, in this campaign, the same aid as in the former; they reconquered southern Guienne, while the French army fought with the English, near Castillon, a decisive battle, in which John Talbot and his son were killed. This victory opened the road to Bordeaux for the army of the king and that of the confederate lords. They formed a junction at a short distance from the town, which they sought to starve into surrender by devastating its territory; and, at the same time, a fleet of Poitevin, Breton, and Flemish vessels, entered the Gironde. The English, who formed the majority of the garrison of Bordeaux, seeing the town invested on all sides, demanded to capitulate, and constrained the citizens to follow their example. They obtained permission to embark and to take with them all those citizens who desired to accompany them; so great a number departed in this way, that for many years Bordeaux was without population and without commerce.

In the terms of the capitulation, twenty persons only were to be banished for having conspired against the French. Among the number, were the sires de l'Esparre and de Duras; their property, and that of all the other suspected persons, served to recompense the conquerors. The king withdrew to Tours; but he left strong garrisons in all the towns, resolved, says a contemporary, to hold the rod over the heads of the people. And to reduce, says the same historian, the town of Bordeaux to more complete subjection than before, the French built two citadels there, the château Trompette, and the fort de Hâ. During the progress of these works, the French arrested the sire de l'Esparre, who had broken his ban; he was taken to Poitiers, where he was condemned to death, beheaded, and cut into six pieces, which were exposed in different places.

Long after this last conquest of Guienne, many of its inhabitants regretted the government of the English, and watched occasion to resume correspondence with England. Although they did not succeed in these intrigues, the effect of them was feared, and ordinances of the king of France forbad any Englishman to reside at Bordeaux. The English vessels were to leave their guns and other arms, with their powder, at Blaye; and the English merchants could not enter any house in the town, or go into the country to taste or buy wines, unless accompanied by armed men and officers appointed expressly to watch their actions and words. At a later period, these officers, useless in their former capacity, became sworn interpreters.

Despite its regrets, the province of Guienne remained French; and the kingdom of France, extending to Bayonne, weighed, without counterpoise, upon the free territory of Gascony. The lords of the country at the foot of the Pyrenees soon felt that they had gone too far in their affection for the French monarchy. They repented, but too late, for it was no longer possible for them to struggle against that monarchy, now comprehending the whole extent of Gaul, with the exception of their petty country. Yet the majority of them courageously adventured upon the unequal contest; they sought a fulcrum in the revolt of the high noblesse of France against the successor of Charles VII., and engaged in the league which was then called le bien public. The peace which the French leaguers made soon after with Louis XI., for money and offices, did not satisfy the southerns, whose views in this patriotic war had been wholly different. Frustrated in their hopes, the counts d'Armagnac, de Foix, d'Albret, d'Astarac, and de Castres, addressed themselves to the king of England, inviting him to make a descent on Guienne, and promising to march to his aid with fifteen thousand fighting men, to transfer to him all the towns of Gascony, and even to secure for him Toulouse. But English policy was no longer favourable to wars on the continent, and the offer of the Gascons was refused. In their conviction that their ancient liberty was for ever gone, did not the province of Aquitaine once more become a separate state, several of them intrigued to induce the brother of the king of France, Charles, duke de Guienne, to declare himself independent. But the duke died of poison, as soon as Louis XI. perceived that he listened to these suggestions; and a French army besieged in Lectoure count John d'Armagnac, the most active partisan of the cause of Gascony. The town was taken by assault, and given over to fire and blood; the count perished in the massacre; and his wife, who was within two months of her confinement, was forced, by the French officers, to take a draught which was to procure abortion, but which caused her death in two days. A member of the family of Albret, made prisoner in this war, was beheaded at Tours; and, shortly after, a bastard of Armagnac, who attempted to restore the fortunes of his country, and succeeded in taking several places, was also captured and put to death. Lastly, James d'Armagnac, duke de Nemours, who entertained, or was supposed to entertain, similar designs, was beheaded at Paris, at the Piliers des Halles, and his children were placed under the scaffold during their father's execution.

This terrible example was not lost upon the barons of Gascony; and although many men of that country turned their eyes to the other side of the ocean; although they long hoped the return, with English succours, of Gaillard de Durfort, sire de Duras, and the other Gascons or Aquitans who had sought refuge in England, no one dared undertake that which the Armagnacs had undertaken. The count de Foix, the most powerful lord of the Pyrenees, abandoned all idea of any other conduct towards the kings of France than that of a loyal servant, gallant at their court, brave in their camps, devoted to them in life and death. Most of the chiefs of these countries and the nobles of Guienne pursued the same policy; incapacitated from doing aught of themselves, they intrigued for the titles and offices which the king of France bestowed on his favourites. Many obtained these, and even supplanted the native French in the good graces of their own kings. They owed this advantage, rather brilliant than solid, to their natural shrewdness, and an aptitude for business, the result of their long and arduous efforts to maintain their national independence against the ambition of the neighbouring kings.

II.THE INHABITANTS OF WALES.

Wars of the Welsh against the Anglo-Normans—Complete submission of Wales—Persecution of the Welsh bards—Welsh refugees in France—Yvain of Wales—Free companies—The chevalier Rufin—Promises of the king of France to the Welsh—Insuriection of Owen Glendowr—Panic terror of the English soldiers—Landing of the French in Wales—March and retreat of the French—Termination of the insurrection of the Welsh—Wars of the succession in England—Enterprise of Henry Tudor—The Welsh under Henry VII., Henry VIII., Elizabeth, and the Stuarts—Actual state of the Welsh population—Turn of mind and character of the Welsh nation—Differences of idiom in Wales—Language of Cornwall.

The reproach of fickleness and perfidy, so long lavished on the free populations of southern Gaul by their national enemies, the French and the Anglo-Normans, was constantly applied by the latter to the natives of Cambria. And, indeed, if it were perfidy not to recognise any right of conquest, and to make incessant efforts to shake off the foreign yoke, the Welsh were certainly the most faithless of all nations; for their resistance to the Normans, by force and by stratagem, was as pertinacious as had been that of their ancestors against the Anglo-Saxons. They carried on a perpetual war of skirmishes and ambuscades, intrenching themselves in the forests and marshes, and seldom risking an engagement on level ground with horsemen armed at all points. The wet and rainy season was that in which the Cambrians were invincible; they then sent away their wives and children, drove their flocks into the mountains, broke down the bridges, let loose the ponds, and beheld with delight the brilliant cavalry of their enemies sinking in the waters and mud of their marshes. In general the first engagements were in their favour, but in the long run force gained the victory, and a fresh portion of Wales was conquered.

The chiefs of the victorious army took hostages, disarmed the inhabitants, and forced them to swear obedience to the king and justiciaries of England; this compulsory oath was speedily violated, and the Welsh insurgents would besiege the castles of the foreign barons and judges. On the news of this resumption of hostilities, the hostages, imprisoned in England in the royal fortresses, were generally put to death, and sometimes the king himself had them executed in his presence. John, son of Henry II., had twenty-eight, all under age, hanged in one day, before he sat down to breakfast.

Such were the scenes presented by the struggle of the Welsh against the Anglo-Normans, up to the period when king Edward, the first of that name since the conquest, passed the lofty mountains of North Cambria, which no king of England before him had crossed. The highest summit of these mountains, called in Welsh Craigeiri, or the snowy peak, and in English Snowdon, was considered sacred to poetry, and it was believed that whoever slept there awoke inspired. This last bulwark of Cambrian independence was not forced by English troops, but by an army from Guienne, composed for the most part of Basque mercenaries. Trained in their own mountains to military tactics almost identical with those of the Welsh, they were more adapted to surmount the difficulties of the country than the heavy cavalry and regular infantry who had hitherto been employed in the service.

In this great defeat perished a man whom his countrymen, in their old spirit of patriotic supersition, had regarded as predestined to restore the ancient British liberty. This was Llewellyn ap Griffith, chief of North Wales, who had gained more victories over the English than any of his predecessors. There existed an old prediction, that a prince of Wales would be crowned at

London; mockingly to accomplish this prophecy, king Edward had the head of Llewellyn, crowned with a wreath of ivy, stuck on a pike on the topmost turret of the Tower of London. David, brother of this unfortunate prince, attempted to resume the war; but, taken alive by the English troops, he was hanged and quartered, and his head was placed beside that of his brother on the battlements of the Tower, where the rain and the wind bleached them together.

It is said, that after his victory, Edward I. assembled the leaders of the conquered people, and announced to them that, out of regard to their spirit of nationality, he would give them a chief, born in their own country, and who had never spoken a single word either of French or English. All were full of joy at this, and sent forth loud acclamations. "Well then," said the king, "you shall have for a chief and prince, my son, Edward, just born at Caernarvon, and whom I here name Edward of Caernarvon." Hence the custom of giving the title of prince of Wales to the eldest sons of the kings of England.

Edward I. erected a great number of fortresses on the coasts, that he might at all times forward troops by sea; and cut down the forests of the interior, which might serve as a refuge for the partisan bands. If it be not true that he ordered the massacre of all the Welsh bards, he it was, at all events, who commenced the system of political persecution, of which this class of men were constantly the object on the part of the kings of England. The principal bards had perished in great numbers in the insurrectionary battles; the survivors, deprived of their protectors, after the downfal of the rich men of the country, and compelled to sing their verses, from town to town, were placed within the category of men without ostensible means of living, by the Anglo-Norman justiciaries. "Let no minstrels, bards, rhymers, or other Welsh vagabonds, be henceforth permitted to overrun the country as heretofore," said their ordinances. No native Welshman could, under the same ordinances, occupy the smallest public post in his native country; to be viscount, seneschal, chancellor, judge, constable of a castle, registrar, forester, etc., it was essential to have been born in England, or in some other foreign country. The towns and castles were occupied by foreign garrisons, and the natives were taxed arbitrarily, or, as the royal decrees expressed it, at the discretion of their lords, to supply maintenance for the garrisons of the said castles.

Many, forced by the conquest to expatriate themselves, passed into France, where they were well received; this emigration continued during the whole of the fourteenth century, and it is from these refugees that descend the French families that bear the now common name of Gallois or Le Gallois. The most considerable of those who proceeded thither in the reign of Philip VI. was a young man named Owen, whom the king retained in his palace, and brought up among the pages of his chamber. This Owen was of the family of Llewellyn, probably his great nephew, perhaps his grandson; and the French, who regarded him as the legitimate heir of the principality of Wales, called him Evain or Yvain of Wales. After the death of Philip de Valois, the young exile continued to reside at the court of France, greatly beloved by king John, by whose side he fought at the fatal battle of Poitiers. Afterwards, in the reign of Charles V., war recommencing against the English, Owen was entrusted with various military commands, and, among others, with a descent upon Guernsey, which had been English since the conquest of England by the Normans. Although a simple squire, he had more than once knights of renown under his orders; his company, as it was then called, consisted of an hundred men-at-arms, at whose head he made several campaigns in Limousin, in Perigord, and in Saintonge, against the captains of the king of

England. One of his relations, John Win or Wynne, celebrated for his graceful deportment, and who was surnamed le poursuivant d'amours, served with him in this war, having, in like manner, under his banner a small troop of Welsh exiles.

The grand-nephew of Llewellyn nourished in exile the thought of freeing his country from English domination, and of recovering, as he himself says in a charter, the inheritance of the kings of Wales, his predecessors. He received from king Charles V. assistance in money, munitions, and vessels; but notwithstanding this support, his ambition and his courage, he never revisited Cambria, and only encountered the English on foreign fields. He followed Duguesclin into Spain, where, for two years, the kings of France and of England waged war in the name of the rivalry of two pretenders to the throne of Castile, Peter the Cruel and Henry de Transtamare.

In one of the combats fought in this war, the earl of Pembroke and other English knights of Norman origin, were taken prisoners by the French, and, as they were being conducted to Santander, Owen went to see them, and, addressing the earl in French, said: "Come you, sir earl, to this country to do me homage for the lands you hold in the principality of Wales, of which I am heir, and which your king takes from me contrary to all right?" The earl of Pembroke was astonished to hear a man, whom he did not know, address him in this manner: "Who are you," asked he, "that speak to me thus?" "I am Owen, son of the prince of Wales, whom your king of England slew, disinheriting me; but, when I can, with the aid of God and of my dear lord, the king of France, I will apply a remedy; and know, that were it place and time for me to combat you, I would prove upon you that you and your fathers, and those of the earl of Hereford, have done me and mine treason and wrong." Hereupon one of the earl of Pembroke's knights, named Thomas Saint-Aubin, advanced to the Welshman and said: "Yvain, if you seek to maintain that in my lord, or his father, there has been or is any treason, or that he owes you homage, or anything else, throw down your glove, and you will soon find one to take it up." "You are a prisoner," answered the Welshman; "I cannot in honour challenge you now, for you are not your own man, but belong to those who have taken you; when you are free, I will speak further to you on the subject, and the thing shall not remain where it is." The dispute, however, had no result, for before the earl of Pembroke and Thomas Saint-Aubin had regained their liberty, Yvain of Wales died of a stiletto stab administered by a countryman of his, in whom he placed full confidence, but who had sold himself to the king of England. This murder was committed in the year 1378, near the town of Mortagne in Saintonge, then besieged by the French. The assassin effected his escape, and went into Guienne, where he was well received by the seneschal of Landes and the other English commanders.

Very few Cambrians consented to serve the ruler of their country; and they who came to the wars of France, under the standard of Edward III., did so on compulsion, and against their will. The Welsh who were levied, en masse, to form bodies of light infantry, brought with them into the king of England's armies their national enmity to the English, and often quarrelled and came to blows with them; often, too, they deserted to the French with arms and baggage, or spread over the country to live as free companies. This was a profession much in vogue at this time, and in which the Cambrians excelled, from their long habit of guerilla warfare in their forests and mountains. Thus, one of these great companies, which at this period rendered themselves so celebrated and so terrible, was under the orders of a Welshman, who was called in France the chevalier Rufin, but whose real name was probably Riewan. This captain, under whom adventurers of all nations had assembled, had adopted, as his district of pillage, the country between the Loire and the Seine, from the frontiers of Burgundy to those of Normandy. His head-quarters were sometimes near Orleans, sometimes near Chartres: he put to ransom or occupied the little towns and the castles, and was so dreaded, that his men went in scattered troops of twenty, thirty, or forty, and none dared attack them.

In the second half of the fourteenth century, when the kings of France and England were mutually exhausting every means of injuring each other, the former, who had learned to comprehend the national spirit of the Cambrians, sought to turn to account the patriotism of this petty nation, whose existence was scarcely suspected by his predecessors of the twelfth century. More than once his emissaries proceeded to north and south Wales, promising the natives the aid and protection of France, if they would rise against the English power. These agents spread themselves over the country, most of them attired as mendicant monks, a body greatly respected at this period, and whose habit was least liable to suspicion from the circumstance that it was worn by men of every nation, who made it a means of support. But the Anglo-Norman authority detected these manœuvres, and on several occasions expelled all foreigners from Wales, priests, laymen, and more especially the itinerant monks. It also prohibited the native Welsh from holding, upon any tenure whatever, any lands on the English territory. The long expected insurrection was to commence on the arrival of a French fleet in sight of the Welsh coast; for several years this fleet was expected by the Cambrians and by the English with very different feelings. Many proclamations of king Edward III. and Richard II. have this preamble: "Whereas our enemies of France propose to land in our principality of Wales—"followed by orders to all the Anglo-Norman lords of the country and marches of Wales, without delay, to garrison and provision their castles and fortresses, and to the justiciaries to seize and imprison, in safe custody, all men suspected of corresponding with the enemy.

The preparations of France for a descent upon Wales, were less considerable and less prompt than the king of England feared, and the Cambrians hoped. A rumour of it spread in the year 1369, and there was then formed a project of restoring the family of Llewellyn in the person of the unfortunate Yvain of Wales; but this pretender to the crown of Cambria died; and the century passed away without any real effort. In making great promises to the Welsh, France had no other design than that of exciting an insurrection which would create a diversion of part of the forces of England; and, on their side, the Welsh, unwilling rashly to hazard a movement, awaited the arrival of the promised succours ere they would revolt. At length, weary of the delay, and impatient to recover their national independence, they put themselves in motion, taking the chance of being supported. The immediate occasion of the insurrection was a casual circumstance, of little importance in itself.

Towards the end of the year 1400, a noble Welshman, who, from an ambition to shine, had repaired to the court of England, where he was well received, offended king Henry IV. and was compelled to quit London. Partly from personal resentment and the embarrassment of his position, partly from an impulse of patriotism, he resolved to place himself at the head of a movement which all his countrymen desired, but which no one had ventured to commence. He descended from an ancient chief of the country, and was called Owen Glendowr, a name which, at the court of England, in order to give it a Norman aspect, had been converted into Glendordy. As soon as Owen had raised the ancient standard of the Kymrys, in the recently conquered portion of Wales, the most considerable men of these districts collected around him. Among others, there were several members of a powerful family, named Ab Tudowr, or son of Tudowr, who counted among their ancestors one Ednyfed Vychan, who, desirous of having armorial bearings, like the barons of England, had emblazoned on his escutcheon three severed Norman heads. On the report of this national movement, the scattered remnant of the Welsh bards became animated with a new enthusiasm, and announced Owen Glendowr as the man who was to accomplish the ancient predictions, and to restore the crown of Britain to the Kymrys. Several poems, composed on the occasion, have come down to us. They produced such an effect, that, in a great assembly of the insurgents, Owen Glendowr was solemnly proclaimed and inaugurated chief and prince of all Cambria. He sent messengers into South Wales to diffuse the insurrection, while the king of England, Henry IV., ordered all his loyal subjects of Wales, French, Flemish, English, and Welsh, to arm against Owen de Glendordy, self-styled prince of Wales, guilty of high treason to the royal majesty of England.

The first engagements were favourable to the insurgents. They defeated the English militia of Herefordshire, and the Flemings of Ross and Pembrokeshire. They were about to cross the English frontier when king Henry, in person, advanced against them with considerable forces. He obliged them to retreat; but he had scarcely set foot on the Welsh territory, than incessant rains, flooding the roads, and swelling the rivers, prevented his further advance, and compelled him to encamp his army for several months in unhealthy places, where they suffered at once from sickness and hunger. The soldiers, whose imaginations were excited by fatigue and inaction, recalled to mind with terror old popular legends as to the sorceries of the Welsh, and believed the bad weather they suffered to be the work of supernatural powers, obedient to Owen Glendowr. Seized with a sort of panic terror, they refused to march further against a man who had the tempest at his disposal. This opinion gained ground among the people in England; but all Owen's magic consisted in his indefatigable activity, and in his great ability. There was at this period, among the Anglo-Norman aristocracy, a party of malcontents who desired to dethrone king Henry IV. At their head were Henry Percy, son of the earl of Northumberland, a family most powerful in the country ever since the conquest, and Thomas Percy, his brother, earl of Worcester; with these the new prince of Wales established a correspondence, and the alliance they concluded attached for a moment to the cause of Welsh independence all the northern marches of Wales, between the Dee and the Severn, and more especially of the county of Chester, whose inhabitants, of pure English race, were naturally less hostile to the Cambrians than were the Normans and Flemings established in the south. But the complete defeat of the two Percys, in a battle fought near Shrewsbury, dissolved the friendly relations of the Welsh insurgents with their neighbours of English race, and left them no other resources than their own strength and their hope in the aid of the king of France.

This king, Charles VI., who had not yet entirely fallen into imbecility, seeing the Cambrians at open hostility with the king of England, resolved to fulfil towards them his promises and those of his predecessors. He concluded with Owen Glendowr a treaty, the first article of which ran thus: "Charles, by the grace of God, king of France; and Owen, by the same grace, prince of Wales; will be united, confederated and bound to each other by the ties of true alliance, true friendship, and good and solid union, especially against Henry of Lancaster, the enemy of the said lords, king and prince, and against all his aiders and abettors."

Many Welshmen proceeded to France to accompany the troops which king Charles was to send, and many of them were taken in various landings which the French first attempted on the coast of England, preferring to enrich themselves with the pillage of some great town or sea-port, than to make war in the poor country of Wales, among mountains and marshes.

At length, however, a large fleet sailed from Brest to aid the Cambrians; it carried six hundred men-at-arms, and eighteen hundred foot soldiers, commanded by John de Rieux, marshal of France, and John de Hangest, grand-marshal of the cross-bowmen. They landed at Milford in Pembrokeshire, and seized upon that town and upon Haverford, both founded, as their names indicate, by the Flemings, who in the reign of Henry I. had taken possession of and occupied the country. The French then proceeded eastward, and, at the first purely Welsh town they reached, found ten thousand insurgents, commanded by a chief whom the historians of the time do not name. The combined forces then marched to Caermarthen, and thence to Llandovery, and thence towards Worcester, attacking and destroying on their way the castles of the Anglo-Norman barons and knights. Some miles from Worcester, a strong English army met them, but instead of offering them battle, it took up a position, and entrenched itself in the hills. The French and Welsh followed the example, and the two hostile bodies remained thus for a week in presence of each other, separated by a deep valley. Every day both armies formed into battle array to commence the attack, but nothing actually took place beyond some skirmishing, in which a few hundred men were killed.

The French and Welsh army soon suffered from want of provisions, the English occupying the plain around their encampments. Acting upon their usual tactics, the Welsh threw themselves by night on the baggage of the enemy, and, carrying off most of their provisions, necessitated the retreat of the English army, which, it would appear, was resolved not to commence the fight. The French men-at-arms, little accustomed to a dearth of food, and whose heavy armour and extensive baggage rendered incommodious and disagreeable to them warfare in a poor and mountainous country, grew weary of the enterprise, in which there was much obscure danger, and little renown to be acquired by brilliant feats of arms. Leaving therefore the Cambrians to contend with their national enemies, they quitted Wales, and landed at Saint Pol-de-Leon, relating that they had made a campaign, which in the memory of man no king of France had ventured to undertake, and had ravaged more than sixty leagues of country in the territories of the king of England, glorying only in the injury done to the English, and not at all in the aid they had given the Welsh, in whom, for themselves, no one in France took any interest.

The insurgents of south Wales were defeated, for the first time, in 1407, on the banks of the Usk, by an English army under the command of Henry, son of king Henry IV., who, bearing in England the title of prince of Wales, was charged with the conduct of the war against the chief elected by the Welsh. A letter which he wrote to his father, announcing this victory, is preserved among the ancient public acts of England. It is in French, the language of the Anglo-Norman aristocracy, but in a French somewhat differing in orthography, grammar, and, as far as we can judge, in pronunciation, from the language of the court of France at the same period. It would appear that, with the accent of Normandy, retained in England by the men of Norman descent, another accent had gradually combined, differing from all the dialects of the French language, and which the sons of the Normans had contracted by hearing English spoken around them, and by themselves speaking the Anglo-French jargon, which was the medium of their communications with the lower classes. This, at least, may be inferred from reading the following passages, taken promiscuously from the letter of the son of Henry IV., "Mon tres-redoutè et três soverein seigneur et peire . . . le onzieme jour de cest present moys de Mars, vos rebelx des parties de Glamorgan, Uske, Netherwent et Overwent, feurent assemblez à la nombre de oyt mille gentz . . . A eux assemblerent vos foialx et vaillants chivalers . . . vos gentz avoient le champe; nientmeins . ."

The fortune of the Welsh insurgents constantly declined after their first defeat, although ten years elapsed between that defeat and the entire subjection of the country. Perhaps, also, their hope of the aid of the French, a hope continually deceived but still fondly cherished, caused them a kind of discouragement never felt by their ancestors, who relied only on themselves. Owen Glendowr, the last person invested with the title of prince of Wales by the election of the Welsh people, survived the ruin of his party, and died in obscurity. His son Meredith capitulated, went to England, and received his pardon from the king. The other chiefs of the insurrection were also pardoned, and several of them even obtained posts at the court of London, in order that they might not return to Wales, which, indeed, had ceased to be inhabitable by the Welsh, from the increased vexations of the agents of English authority. Among these Cambrians, exiles by necessity or ambition, was a member of the family of the sons of Tudowr, named Owen ap Meredith ap Tudowr, who, during the reign of Henry V., lived with him as groom of his chamber, and was very much in grace with the king, who granted him many favours, and deigned to address him as nostre chìer et foyal. His manners and handsome form made a vivid impression on queen Catherine of France, who, becoming widow of Henry V., secretly married Owen ap Tudowr or Oven Tudor, as he was called in England. He had by her two sons, Jasper and Edmund, the second of whom, on attaining manhood, married Margaret, daughter of John de Beaufort, earl of Somerset, issue of the royal family of Plantagenet.

It was at this period that the branches of this family were slaughtering each other in a dispute for the possession of the crown conquered by William the Bastard. The right of hereditary succession had by degrees prevailed over the election retained, though imperfectly, in the first periods following the conquest. Instead of interfering to adjudge the crown to the most worthy to wear it, the Anglo-Norman aristocracy contented themselves with examining which of the pretenders approached nearest by his lineage to the original stock of the Conqueror. All was decided by the comparison of those genealogical trees of which the Norman families were so proud, and which from their form were called pé de gru, or crane's foot, in modern English, pedigree. The order of hereditary succession was tolerably peaceful so long as the direct line of descendants of Henry II. endured; but when the inheritance passed to the collateral branches, numerous pretenders on the score of hereditary right arose, and there were more factions, troubles, and discords, than the practice of election had ever occasioned. Then broke out the most hideous of civil wars, that of relations against relations, of grown men against children in the cradle. For several generations, two numerous families were killing each other, either in pitched battles or by assassination, to maintain their legitimacy, without either of the two being able to destroy the other, some member of which always started up to combat and dethrone his rival, and reign until he himself was dethroned. There perished in these quarrels, according to the historians of the time, sixty or eighty princes of the royal house, nearly all young, for the life of the males was brief in these families. The women, who lived longer, had time to see their sons massacred by their nephews, and the latter by other nephews or uncles, themselves speedily assassinated by some equally near relation.

In the reign of Richard III., of the house of York, who owed the crown to several assassinations, a son of Edmund Tudor and Margaret Beaufort, named Henry, was in France, whither he had been obliged to fly as an antagonist of the York party. Weary of living in exile, and relying on the universal hatred excited by king Richard, he resolved to try his fortune in England, as a claimant of the crown, in right of his mother, a descendant of Edward III. Having neither cross nor pile, as an old historian expresses it, he applied to the king of France, Louis XI., who gave him some money, with which he hired three thousand men in Normandy and Brittany. He sailed from Harfleur, and, after a passage of six days, landed in Wales, the country of his paternal ancestors. On landing, he unfurled a red flag, the ancient standard of the Cambrians, as though his project were to raise the nation, and render it independent of the English. This enthusiastic people, over whom the power of emblems was ever very great, without examining whether the quarrel between Henry Tudor and Richard III. was not wholly foreign to them, ranged themselves, by a sort of instinct, around their old standard.

The red flag was planted on Snowdon, which the pretender assigned as a rendezvous for those Welsh who had promised to arm in his cause. Not one failed on the appointed day. Even the bards, resuming their ancient spirit, sang and prophesied, in the style of other days, the victory of the Kymrys over the Saxon and Norman enemy. But the matter in hand was by no means the release of the Cambrians from the yoke of the foreigner; all the fruit of the victory for them was to place a man with a little Welsh blood in his veins on the throne of the conquerors of Wales. When Henry Tudor arrived on the frontiers of England, he found a reinforcement of several thousand men brought to him by sir Thomas Boucher, a Norman by name and origin; other gentlemen of the western counties came with their vassals and yeomen to join the army of the pretender. He penetrated into the English territory without encountering any obstacle, as far as Bosworth in Leicestershire, where he gave battle to Richard III., defeated him, killed him, and was crowned in his stead under the title of Henry VII.

Henry VII. placed in his armorial bearings the Cambrian dragon beside the three lions of Normandy. He created a new office of poursuivant-at-arms, under the name of rouge-dragon, and, with the aid of the authentic or fabulous archives of Wales, traced his genealogy back to Cadwallader, the last king of all Britain, and, through him, up to Brutus, son of Æneas, the pretended father of the Britons. But to these acts of personal vanity was limited the gratitude of the king to the people whose devotion had procured him victory and the crown. His son, Henry VIII., while he allowed the Welsh, whom Henry VII. had ennobled for services rendered to his person, to retain the Norman titles of earls, barons, and baronets, treated, like his predecessors, the mass of the people as a conquered nation, at once feared and disliked, and undertook to destroy the ancient customs of the Cambrians, the remnant of their social state, and even their language.

When the religious supremacy of the pope had been abolished in England, the Welsh, whom the Roman church had never aided in their attempts to maintain their national independence, adopted, without repugnance, the religious changes decreed by the English government. But this government, which gave every encouragement to the translation of the Bible, did not have it translated into Welsh; on the contrary, some natives of that country, zealous for the Reformation, having, at their own expense, published a Welsh version of the Scriptures, far from praising them, as would have been done in England, the authorities ordered the destruction of all the copies, which were taken for this purpose from the churches, and publicly burnt. English authority, at about the same time, attacked the historical manuscripts and documents, then more numerous in Wales than in any other country of Europe. The high families who possessed archives began to keep them secret, either as a mode of paying court to England, or to preserve them from destruction. Some of these families even incurred disfavour for communicating curious information to the learned men, who, towards the close of the sixteenth century, made researches into the antiquities of Wales. An estimable writer, Edward Lhuyd, author of British Archaiology, experienced infinite mortification on account of the publication of his book. This class of learning and research became matter of suspicion in the eyes of authority, and he who to prosecute it went to reside in Wales, was doubly an object of distrust. One antiquarian was actually subjected to public prosecution for an offence of this sort, in the reign of Elizabeth, the last descendant of Henry Tudor.

The Scottish family of the Stuarts showed quite as little good will to the Welsh nation; and yet, when the English rose against this family, the majority of the Welsh enrolled themselves on its side, from a sort of national opposition to the feelings of the English people. Perhaps, too, they hoped to effect some degree of freedom for themselves, amid the troubles of England, and by a compact with the royal family, whom they supported against the English. Things, however, turned out otherwise; royalty succumbed, and Wales, as being royalist, had to endure still greater oppression than before. Since that time the Welsh have tranquilly participated in all the political changes occurring in England, no longer rebelling, but still not forgetting the grounds upon which they might to themselves justify rebellion. "We will bear in mind," says one of their writers, "that the lordships and best lands of the country are in the hands of men of foreign race, who have taken them by violence from the ancient legitimate proprietors, whose names and real heirs are well known to us."

In general, the possessors of great domains and lordships in Wales were, up to a recent date, and probably still are, to a certain extent, harder than those in England towards their farmers and peasants; a fact, no doubt, attributable to the comparative novelty of the conquest of the Welsh provinces, not accomplished until about the fourteenth century, so that the nobles there are much newer-comers, and to the further circumstance that the tongue of the natives has always remained distinct from that of the conquerors. The species of national hostility between the seigneurs and the peasants has extended the emigration of the poorer Welsh families to the United States of America. There these descendants of the ancient Kymrys have lost their manners and their language, and have forgotten, in the bosom of the most complete liberty that civilized man can enjoy, the vain dreams of British independence. Those who have remained in the land of their ancestors retain, amidst the poverty or mediocrity of fortune which has ever been their lot, a character of haughty pride, the offspring of great recollections and long hopes, always deceived, but never abandoned. They stand with erect front before the powerful and rich of England and of their own country, "and think themselves a better and nobler race," said a Welshman of the last century, "than this nobility of yesterday, the issue of bastards, of adventurers, and of assassins."

Such is the national spirit of the most energetic among the present Cambrians, and they carry it, sometimes, to such a point, that the English designate them Red-hot Welshmen. Since the revolution of America and of France, this spirit is combined in them with all the grand ideas of natural and social liberty that those revolutions have everywhere aroused. But, whilst ardently desiring the progress of high modern civilization, the enlightened inhabitants of Wales have not lost their ancient passion for their national history, language, and literature. The wealthy among them have formed associations for the publication of their numerous collections of historical documents, and with the view of reanimating, if possible, the cultivation of the old poetic talent of the bards. These societies have established annual poetical and musical meetings, for the two arts ever go hand in hand in Wales; and out of, perhaps, a somewhat superstitious respect for ancient customs, the literary and philosophical assemblies of the new bards are held in the open air, on the hills. At the time when the French revolution still made the English government tremble, these meetings, always very numerous, were forbidden by authority, on account of the democratic principles which prevailed at them. Now they are perfectly free, and there is every year awarded by them the prize of poetical inspiration, a faculty which the Cambrian language expresses in one word, Awen.

The Awen is now found principally among the northern Welsh, the last who maintained their ancient social state against the invasion of the Anglo-Normans. It is also among them that the native language is spoken with the greatest purity, and over the largest extent of country. In the southern counties, earlier conquered, the Welsh dialect is mixed up with French and English idioms. There are, indeed, entire districts whence it has completely disappeared; and often a brook or bridle-path marks the separation of the two languages, of, on the one side, corrupt Cambrian, on the other, a barbarous English, spoken by the mixed posterity of the Flemish, Norman, and Saxon soldiers who conquered the country in the twelfth century. These men, although, for the most part, of the same condition with the conquered population, have retained a sort of hereditary disdain for it. They affect, for example, not to know the name of a single individual inhabiting the part of the hundred or parish in which Welsh is spoken. "I don't know the man," is the reply; "I believe there's some such person lives somewhere in Welshland."

Such is the actual state of that population and that language, for which the bards of the sixth century daringly predicted eternity of duration: their prediction, however, will not, at all events, be falsified in our days. The Cambrian idiom is still spoken by a sufficiently extensive population to render its future extinction very difficult to foresee. It has survived all the other dialects of the ancient British language; for that of the natives of Cornwall came within the category of a dead language towards the close of the last century. It is true that since the tenth century, when it was driven by the Anglo-Saxons beyond the river Tamer, the population of Cornwall has never played any political part. At the time of the Norman conquest, it supported the English of the adjacent counties in their resistance to the foreigners, but, conquered with them, it participated in all the phases of their subsequent fate. As it gradually mingled more and more closely with the populations of English race, its original language lost ground from north to south, so that, an hundred years ago, there were only a few villages at the extremity of the promontory, where the ancient idiom of the country was still spoken. In 1776, some travellers questioned, on this subject, an old fisherman in one of these villages, who answered: "I only know four or five persons who speak British, and they are old people like myself, from sixty to eighty years of age; the young people don't know a word of it."

Thus the eighteenth century beheld the end of the language of Cornwall, which now exists only in a few books. It differs in a remarkable manner from the Welsh dialect, and had probably been spoken in the ancient times by all the British tribes of the south and east, by the men whom the old annals call Loëgrwys, who, before they joined the Kymrys in Britain, dwelt, for a longer or shorter period, in the southwest of Gaul.

III.THE SCOTS.

Prophecy of Merlin—Nine pretenders to the throne of Scotland—Invasion of Edward I.— William Wallace—Robert Bruce—Enfranchisement of Scotland—Character of the people of the border—Social condition of the Scots—Establishment of the Reformation—English puritans— Scottish covenanters—Alliance between the two nations—Civil war in England— Misunderstanding between the two nations—Charles II. proclaimed king in Scotland—Oliver Cromwell enters Scotland—Measures taken against the Scots—Restoration of Charles II.— Persecution of the Presbyterians—Their insurrection—Battle of Bothwell-bridge—Expulsion of the Stuarts—Sympathy of the Scots for the martyrs—National character and spirit of the Scots— Present condition of the Gaelic population.

In the year 1174, William, king of Scotland, invaded the north of England; but he was conquered and taken prisoner by the Anglo-Norman barons, and his defeat was regarded as a miraculous effect of the pilgrimage that king Henry II. had made to the tomb of Thomas Beket. Those who took him prisoner, shut him up in the castle of Richmont, now Richmond, in Yorkshire, built, in the time of the conquest, by the Breton, Alain Fergan. This circumstance, again, was regarded as a fulfilment of a prophecy of Merlin, conceived in these terms: "He shall be bridled with a bit, forged on the shores of the Armorican gulf." And what is still stranger, is that the same prophecy had, a few months before, been applied to Henry II. when closely pressed by the Breton auxiliaries of his sons. The king of Scotland, removed from Richmond to Falaise, only quitted his prison on renewing the oath of homage which his predecessors had sworn to the Norman kings, and then broken. This act of enforced submission gave the king of England very little influence over the affairs of Scotland, so long as there were no intestine divisions, that is to say, during the hundred and twenty years which elapsed, up to the death of Alexander the Third.

Royalty among the Scots had never been purely elective, for their whole social order was founded on the principle of family; but, on the other hand, hereditary royalty had never any fixed rules: and the brother was often preferred to the grandson, and even to the son of the late king. Alexander III. left neither son nor brother, but cousins in great number, most of them of Norman or French origin, by the father's side, and bearing French names, such as Jean Bailleul, Robert de Brus, Jean Comine, Jean d'Eaucy, Nicolas de Solles, &c. There were nine pretenders to the crown on various titles. Unable to agree among themselves, and feeling the necessity of terminating the dispute peaceably, they submitted it to Edward I., king of England, as to their suzerain lord. King Edward declared for him who had the best title, according to hereditary right by primogeniture: this was John Bailleul or Baliol, as the Scotch spelt it. He was crowned, but the king of England, taking advantage of the deference which the Scots had just exhibited to him, resolved to render practical that suzerainty over them which hitherto had been purely honorary.

The king of Scotland, in order to secure support against the intrigues of his competitors, lent himself at first to the views of the king of England; he gave to Englishmen most of the offices and dignities of the kingdom, and repaired to the court of his suzerain, to do him homage and receive his orders. Encouraged by this condescension of the king his protégé, Edward went the length of demanding from him, as pledges of his fealty and allegiance, the fortresses of Berwick, Edinburgh, and Roxburgh, the strongest in all Scotland. But so decided a national opposition arose against this demand, that John Baliol was fain to reject it, and to refuse the English troops admission to his fortresses. Hereupon Edward summoned him to Westminster, to answer for the refusal; but, instead of obeying the summons, Baliol solemnly renounced his homage and faith as vassal. On hearing this, the king of England exclaimed, in his Norman-French: "Ah! le fol felon telle folie fait! s'il ne veint à nous, nous veindrons à ly!"

Edward I. set out for Scotland with all his chivalry of England and Aquitaine; with English archers so skilful that they seldom threw away one of their twelve arrows, and were wont to say, jestingly, that they had twelve Scots in their pouch; and, lastly, with a body of light-armed Welsh, who more often fought with the English than with the enemy, pillaged them whenever any opportunity occurred, and most frequently remained neuter in action. Notwithstanding the courage and patriotic energy of the Scots, the progress of the war was unfavourable to them. Their king did not support them heartily, and was ever desirous of making the amend to Edward for the resistance he had undertaken, as he said, through ill and false counsel. Moreover, there were at this time, in Scotland, neither well-fortified towns, nor fortresses, such as those the Normans had built in England. The seigneural habitations were not donjons, surrounded by a triple wall, but small square towers, with a simple ditch, when not situated on the edge of some natural ravine. King Edward accordingly penetrated without difficulty into the lowlands of Scotland, took possession of all the towns, placed garrisons in them, and removed to London the famous stone on which the kings of the country were crowned. Such of the Scots as would not submit to foreign sway, took refuge in the northern and western mountains, and in the forests which adjoined them.

From one of these retreats issued the famous patriot, William Walleys or Wallace, who for seven years made war upon the English, at first as a guerilla-chief, and then at the head of an army. The conquerors called him a highway robber, a murderer, an incendiary; and when they took him, hanged him at London, and stuck his head on a pike on the loftiest pinnacle of the Tower. The inhabitants of the conquered portion of Scotland suffered to the utmost extent the evils that follow upon a conquest; they had foreign governors, bailiffs, and sheriffs. "These English," says a contemporary poet, "were all avaricious and debauched; haughty and contemptuous; they insulted our wives and daughters; good, worthy, and honoured knights were put to death by the cord. Ah! freedom is a noble thing!"

This feeling, deeply impressed in the heart of the Scots, soon rallied them round another chief— Robert de Brus, or Bruce, one of the former competitors of John Baliol. Bruce was crowned king in the abbey of Scone, at a time when there was scarce a town, from the Tweed to the Orcades, that was not in the power of the English. Without an army and without treasure, he, like Wallace, took up his quarters in the forests and mountains, whither he was pursued by his enemies, with horse and foot, and dogs trained to hunt man, like game, by the scent. No one in the kingdom, says Froissart, dared lodge him, in castle or in fortress. Hunted like a wild beast, he went from mountain to mountain, from lake to lake, living on the produce of the chase and of fishing, until he reached the Mull of Cantyre, whence he gained the small island of Rachin or Rath Erin, lying near the coast of Ireland.

There he planted his royal standard as proudly as though he had been at Edinburgh, sent messengers into Ireland, and obtained some succours from the native Irish, on the ground of the ancient fraternity of the two nations, and of the common hatred they bore of the Anglo-Normans. He then sent messengers to the Hebrides, and along the whole western coast, soliciting the support of the Gaelic chiefs of those districts, who, in their wild independence, were very indifferent as to what became of the population of the lowlands of Scotland, which they called Saxon alike with that of England, and for which they had scarce more affection. All the clans, however, with one exception, promised him their faith and assistance. The chiefs and barons of the lowlands, of English, Norman, or Scottish race, formed among themselves compacts of alliance and fraternity-in-arms, in life and death, for king Robert and Scotland, against any man, French, English, or Scot. Probably, by the first of these names, they meant the king and all the lords of England, who at that time spoke among themselves no other language than French; for the French, the continental French, were warm friends of the patriots of Scotland.

Robert Bruce appointed as the rendezvous of his partisans a spot near the place where the western chain of mountains rises; and here was fought the decisive battle of Bannockburn. The Scotch were victorious; and their enemies, weakened by this great defeat, found themselves successively driven from all the fortified towns, and compelled to repass the Tweed in disorder, pursued in their turn by all the people of the southern lowlands, and especially by the men of the border, a population very formidable for an army in retreat.

The limits of England and Scotland were never well determined towards the west, where the country is mountainous and intersected in every direction by infinite valleys and small streams. The inhabitants of a large extent of this district were, properly speaking, neither Scots nor English, and the only national name by which they were known was that of Borderers, that is to say, people of the border or frontier. They were an aggregation of all the races of men that had come into Britain: of Britons, expelled by Anglo-Saxons; of Saxons, expelled by Normans; of Anglo-Normans or Scots banished for felonies or other crimes. This population was divided into great families, like the Celtic clans, but the names of these clans or families were, for the most part, English or French. The language of all the inhabitants was the Anglo-Danish dialect of the south of Scotland and the north of England. The chiefs and vassals lived familiarly together, the former in his embattled house, surrounded by rude palisades, and having the bed of some torrent for a moat; the latter in huts built around it. All followed the trade of marauders, their food being oxen and sheep, stolen from the inhabitants of the neighbouring plains. They made their expeditions on horseback, armed with a long lance, and having for defensive armour a quilted doublet, on which were sewn, as regularly as might be, plates of iron or brass.

Though divided, administratively, into two distinct nations, and, according to the territory they occupied, subjects or Scotland or of England, they nevertheless regarded the kings of these two countries as foreigners, and were by turns Scots, when they purposed forage in England, and English, when a descent was to be made upon Scotland. They seldom fought among themselves, but in personal quarrels. As to their robberies, they exercised them without mercy, but at the same time without cruelty, as a profession having its rules and its points of honour. The richer of them assumed armorial bearings, a fashion which the Normans had introduced into England and Scotland. Their arms, which are still worn by several families of the country, are nearly all allusive to the manner of life of the ancient borderers. Generally, the field of the escutcheon is the sky with moon and stars, to signify, that the best time for the borderers was the night; the mottoes, in English or Latin, are equally significant; for example:—Watch weel—Sleep not for I watch—Ye shall want ere I want, and so on.

Scotland, restored to freedom, gave the name of saviour to Robert Bruce, a man of Norman origin, and whose ancestors, in the time of the conquest of England, had usurped, upon the Scottish territory, the town and valley of Annan. The ancient kings of Scotland had confirmed to them, by charters, possession of this domain, where the ruins of their castle are still visible. Of all the countries of Europe, Scotland is that wherein the mixture of the races has been most easily effected, and where it has left the fewest traces in the respective situation of the different classes of inhabitants. There were never villeins or peasant serfs in this country, as in England and in France, and the antiquarians have observed that the ancient acts of Scotland offer no example of the sale of the man with the land; that in none are found this form, so usual elsewhere: "With the buildings, and all the chattels, labourers, beasts, ploughs, &c." From time immemorial, the burghers of the principal towns have sat in the great council of the kings of Scotland, beside the warriors of high rank, who styled themselves, in the Norman manner, knights, barons, earls, and marquises, or retained the ancient Anglo-Danish titles of thanes and lairds. When it became necessary to defend the country, the various trades' companies marched under their own banners, led by their burgmaster. They had their honour to maintain on the field of battle, and their share of glory to win. Old popular ballads, still sung, not long since, in the southern districts of Scotland, celebrate the bravery of the shoemakers of Selkirk at the famous battle of Flodden, fought and lost, in 1513, by James IV. of Scotland.

National opposition, or the natural reaction of the spirit of liberty against power, followed, in Scotland, the course it must ever follow in countries where the nation is not divided into two races of men, separated one from the other by a state of hereditary hostility; it was constantly and almost solely directed against the kings. In civil wars there were but two parties, that of the government and that of the body of the governed, and not, as elsewhere, three parties—royalty, the nobles, and the people. The military and opulent class never joined the kings against the people, and the people had seldom occasion to favour the royal power out of hatred to that of the nobles. In times of trouble, the struggle was between the king and his courtiers on one side, and on the other, all the orders of the nation leagued together. It is true that the active and turbulent barons and nobles of Scotland always prominently figured in political commotions, and that, to adopt the expression of one of them, they "belled the cat;" but their frequent acts of violence against the king's favourites and against the kings themselves, were rarely unpopular.

Towards the middle of the sixteenth century, a new bond strengthened this kind of political alliance between the nobles and bourgeoisie of Scotland; they embraced, together, and as it were with one impulse, the most extreme opinions of religious reformation, those of Calvin. The whole population of the south and east, speaking the same language and having the same views and the same civilization, co-operated in this revolution. It was only the mountain clans and a few lords of the northern lowlands that adhered to the catholic religion, the former from a spirit of innate hostility to the lowlanders, the latter from individual conviction rather than from any esprit de corps. Even the bishops did not oppose any very vigorous resistance to the partisans of the Reformation; the only formidable opposition they met with was from the court, early impressed with the fear that religious might lead to political changes; but the innovators were triumphant in the struggle; they got possession of king James VI., still a child, and brought him up in the new doctrines.

His mother, the unfortunate Mary Stuart, ruined herself by her ignorance of the national character of the Scots; it was after a battle fought against the presbyterian reformers that she passed into England, where she perished on a scaffold. After her death, and while her son still lived in Scotland, professing, in the new spirit of his nation, the presbyterian creed in all its rigour, the line of the Tudor kings of England became extinct in the person of Elizabeth, grand-daughter of Henry VII. James, a descendant of Henry VII. on the female side, was thus the next heir to the Tudors. He came to London, where he was readily acknowledged, and assumed the title of king of Great Britain, uniting under their ancient name his two kingdoms of England and Scotland. It is from him dates the royal arms of Britain, the three lions passant of Normandy, the lion rampant of Scotland, and the harp of Ireland; and the British standard, whereon the white cross of Saint Andrew combines with the red cross of Saint George.

King James, the first of that name in England, found opinion, in reference to the religious reformation, very different in his new kingdom from what it was in Scotland. There was not among the English any generally established opinion as to religious belief. They differed on this point according as they belonged to the higher or to the lower classes of the nation, with whom the ancient hostility of the two races seemed to re-appear under new forms. Though time and the intermingling of blood had greatly abated this primitive hatred, there still lurked in men's hearts a confused sentiment of mutual dislike and distrust. The aristocracy were strongly in favour of the modified reformation, instituted fifty years before by Henry VIII., a reformation which, simply substituting the king for the pope, as head of the Anglican church, retained for episcopacy its ancient importance. The bourgeoisie, on the contrary, inclined to the complete reformation established by the Scots, whose worship, free from bishops, was independent of all civil authority. The partisans of this opinion formed a sect, persecuted by the government, but in whom persecution did but increase their enthusiasm; they were excessively strict, even upon the smallest points, which procured for them the name of precisians or puritans. The nickname, Round-heads, by which they were ludicrously designated, was derived from their wearing their hair short and without any curl, a custom quite contrary to the fashion then followed by the gentlemen and courtiers.

The presbyterians of England had flattered themselves with the hope that they were about to see their belief reign in the person of a presbyterian king; but the triumph of this religious creed being bound up with that of the popular interest over the aristocratic interest, the king, whoever he might be, could not sanction it. The episcopal church, accordingly, was sustained under James I., as under Elizabeth, by rigorous measures against the adversaries of that church; nay more, from the habit of dwelling upon the political dangers of puritanism in England, the king formed the project of destroying it even in Scotland, where it had become the state religion, and he entered, for this purpose, into an open struggle, not only with the middle and lower classes, but with the entire nation. It was a difficult enterprise, and he made little progress in it, bequeathing it, with the crown, to his son Charles I.

Charles, extending and systematizing his father's views, resolved to approximate the Anglican worship to the forms of catholicism, and to impose this worship, so reformed, upon the two kingdoms of England and Scotland. He thus displeased the episcopalians and the aristocratic classes of England, whilst he raised against him the whole Scottish nation. Nobles, priests, and burgesses, entering into open rebellion, assembled spontaneously at Edinburgh, and signed there, under the name of Covenant, an act of national union, for the defence of the presbyterian religion. The king levied an army, and made preparations for a war with Scotland; and on their side the Scots raised national regiments, whose hats bore this device: "For Christ's crown and covenant." Men of every rank hastened to enrol themselves in this militia, and the ministers of religion pronounced from the pulpits malediction upon every man, horse, and lance that should side with the king against the defenders of the national faith. The resistance of the Scots was entirely approved in England, where discontent against king Charles became general on account of his religious innovations and his attempts to govern in an absolute manner, without the concurrence of the assembly which, under the name of parliament, had never ceased to exist since the conquest.

The burgesses of England, who had at first only appeared in this assembly as men summoned before the king and barons to receive their demands for money and to comply with them, had become, by a gradual revolution, an integral part of the parliament. In connexion with a certain number of petty feudatories, called knights of the shire, they formed, under the name of house of commons, a section of the great national council; in the other house, that of the lords, sat the titled men, the earls, marquises, barons, and Anglican bishops. This chamber, like the other, opposed the projects of Charles I.; but there was this difference between the two houses, that the lords aimed only at maintaining the established religion and the ancient privileges of parliament, while of the commons, the majority aspired to the establishment of presbyterianism and a diminution of the royal authority.

This desire for reform, moderate enough as regarded political order, was supported out of doors by something more vehement than itself, the old instinct of popular hatred to the noble families, proprietors of nearly the entire soil of the country. The inferior classes felt the vague want of some great change; their present position was intolerable to them, but not clearly perceiving what would improve it, they attached themselves to the most extreme political opinions, as in religion to the most rigid and gloomy puritanism. It was thus that the habitual language of the sect, which sought all in the Bible, became that also of the ultras in politics. This party, placing themselves ideally in the position of the Jews amidst their enemies, gave to their opponents the names of Philistines and of sons of Belial. They borrowed from the Psalms and the prophets the threats they sent forth against the lords and bishops, threatening, in the words of the Scripture, to take up "the two-edged sword, and to bind their nobles with fetters of iron."

Charles I. had great difficulty in collecting men and money for the war against the Scots. The city of London refused him a loan of 300,000l., and the soldiers openly declared that they would not risk their lives merely to support the pride of the bishops. During the delays occasioned by these difficulties, the Scots, commencing the attack, invaded England and advanced to the Tyne, preceded by a manifesto in which they declared themselves brothers and friends of the English people, and called down upon themselves maledictions from on high, if they in the slightest degree injured the country or individuals. No resistance was offered them but by the royal army, which they completely defeated near Newcastle. After this victory, the generals of the Scottish army excused themselves, in proclamations addressed to the English nation, for the violence of the measures they had been obliged to adopt in the defence of their rights, and expressed the hope that their success might aid that nation in vindicating its own menaced liberties. The commons replied by voting thanks and a money-aid to the Scots; and several envoys left London to conclude a treaty of alliance and friendship between the two nations at Edinburgh.

This compact was signed in 1642, and, the same year, the English parliament, and especially the house of commons, entered into an open struggle with royal power. By degrees, the opposition became centered in the latter chamber; for the great majority of the lords, seeing whither the dispute tended, had joined the king. The lower house voted itself the sole national representation, and invested with all the rights of parliament; and while the borough members and the petty landed proprietors, thus seized upon the legislative power, the people out of doors armed spontaneously, and took possession of all the royal arsenals. On the other hand, the king, preparing for war, planted his standard with the three lions of Normandy, on the keep of Nottingham castle. All the old castles, built by the Normans or their posterity, were closed, provisioned, furnished with artillery, and war to the death began between the sons of the seigneurs and the sons of the villains of the middle ages.

In this struggle, the Scots powerfully aided the parliament of England, which, as a first step, abolished episcopacy and established the presbyterian religion. This community of worship was the basis of a new treaty or covenant between the two peoples; they became security, one for the other, for the defence of Christianity without bishops; but though this alliance was concluded in good faith, it had neither the same meaning nor the same object with the two nations. The civil war was for the Scots a religious quarrel with Charles Stuart, their countryman and national king; it would, accordingly, end for them the moment the king should acknowledge the legal existence of the presbyterian worship in England as in Scotland. With the English, on the contrary, there was an instinct of revolution, going much beyond the mere desire to reform the episcopal church. This difference in the two nations, the necessary result of their different situation, and for some time not manifest to either, was of a nature to produce discord between them as soon as it became known, which soon occurred.

At the battle of Naseby, in Northamptonshire, the royal army was completely routed, and the king himself, his retreat cut off, yielded himself voluntarily to the Scots, his countrymen, choosing to be their prisoner rather than that of the parliamentarians. The Scots transferred him to their allies, not with the intention of destroying him, but that these might oblige him to conclude a treaty advantageous to both parties. Discussions of a very different nature now arose in the English army: the point was no longer the historical question of the origin of royal and seigneural power, for as to these time had effaced all the data: ardent minds became enthusiastically impressed with the idea of substituting for the ancient form of government an order of things founded on abstract justice and absolute right. They thought they saw the prediction of this order of things in the famous epoch of a thousand years, announced by the Apocalypse, and, in their favourite phraseology, they called it the reign of Christ. These enthusiasts, in like manner, relied upon a passage in the Holy Scriptures to justify their bringing Charles I. to trial and judgment, saying that the blood shed in the civil war ought to fall upon his head, so that the people might be absolved.

During these discussions, the groundwork of which was most grave, though the form was fantastic, the parties who had latest entered upon the struggle against royalty, the lower populace and the ultra-reformers in religion, gained ground, and ejected from the revolution those who had commenced it, the landed proprietors and rich citizens, Anglicans or presbyterians. Under the name of independents, there arose by degrees a new sect, which, rejecting even the authority of ordinary priests, invested every one of the faithful with sacerdotal functions. The progress of this sect greatly alarmed the Scots; they represented that in going beyond the religious reformation, such as they had established it by common accord, the English were violating the solemn act of union concluded between the two peoples. This was the commencement of a misunderstanding which attained the highest point when the independents, having seized upon the king's person, imprisoned him, and made him appear as a criminal before a high court of justice.

Seventy judges, selected from the house of commons, the parliamentary army, and the citizens of London, pronounced sentence of death on Charles Stuart, and the abolition of royalty. Some acted from a deep conviction of the king's guilt; others conscientiously desired the establishment of an entirely new social order; others, again, actuated by ambition alone, aspired to the usurpation of the sovereign authority. The death of Charles I. put an end to the reign of the presbyterians in England, and to the alliance of the English with the Scots. The latter, judging of the social condition of the English by their own, could not comprehend what had taken place; they deemed themselves unworthily betrayed by their former friends; and combining with this mortification a secret national affection for the Stuarts, their countrymen, they renewed amicable relations with this family, the instant that the English so violently cast it off. While, at London, all the royal statues were being thrown down, and on their pedestals there was inscribed: The last of the kings has passed away,—Charles, son of Charles I., was proclaimed king in the capital of Scotland.

This proclamation did not imply, on the part of the Scots, any abandonment of the reforms they had achieved and defended, sword in hand. When the commissioners from Scotland waited, at Breda, on Charles II., who had already assumed, of his own motion, the title of king of Great Britain, they signified to him the rigorous conditions on which the parliament of Edinburgh consented to ratify this title; these were the adhesion of the king to the first covenant signed against his father, and the perpetual abolition of episcopacy. Charles II., at first, made only evasive answers, in order to gain time for a stroke which he hoped would make him king without conditions. James Graham, marquis of Montrose, at first a zealous covenanter, and then a partisan of Charles I., was charged with this enterprise. He landed in the north of Scotland, with a handful of adventurers collected on the continent, and addressing himself to the chiefs of the mountain and island clans, he proposed to them a war at once national and religious against the presbyterians of the lowlands. The highlanders, who once already in the year 1645 had risen under the command of Montrose against the authority of the covenanters, and had been completely defeated, showed little inclination for a new attack; only a few ill-organized bands descended into the lowlands, around a flag on which was painted the decapitated body of Charles I. They were routed: Montrose himself was taken, tried as a traitor, condemned to death, and executed at Edinburgh. Hereupon Charles II., hopeless of regaining absolute royalty, condescended to that offered him by the Scottish commissioners, signed the covenant, swore to observe it inviolably, and entered Edinburgh as king, beneath the quartered limbs of the unfortunate Montrose, suspended from the gates of the town.

While acknowledging the rights of Charles II., the Scots did not propose to aid him in reconquering royalty in England. They separated their national affairs from those of their neighbours, and only contemplated the securing to the son of Charles I. the title of king of Scotland. But the party which in England had seized upon the revolution, grew alarmed at seeing the heir of him whom they called the last of the kings established over a portion of Great Britain. Fearing an hostile attempt on his part, the independents resolved to anticipate it. General Fairfax, a rigid presbyterian, was charged with the command of the army raised to invade Scotland; but refusing to serve against a nation which, he said, had helped the good work for which he had first drawn the sword, he sent in his resignation to the house of commons. The soldiers themselves manifested no inclination to fight men whom they had so long styled our brethren of Scotland.

The successor of Fairfax, Oliver Cromwell, a man of rare political and military activity, overcame this hesitation by persuasion or violence, marched to the north, defeated the Scots and their king at Dunbar, and occupied Edinburgh. He called upon the people of Scotland to renounce Charles II., but the Scots refused to abandon in danger him whom they had involved in danger, and patiently endured the oppressions inflicted by the English army in all directions. Charles II. was far from rendering them devotion for devotion; in the extremity of Scotland's misfortunes, deserting the presbyterians, he surrounded himself with old partisans of episcopacy, with highland chiefs, who gave the name of Saxons, Sassenachs, to their neighbours of a different religion, and debauched young nobles, to whom he said, in his orgies, that the religion of the Roundheads was not worthy of a gentleman. With the aid of the adventurers whom he assembled around him, he attempted an invasion of the western coast of England, while the English army occupied the east of Scotland. There were still in Cumberland and Lancashire many catholic families who, on his approach, took up arms for him. He hoped to raise Wales, and turn to profit the national enmity of the Cambrians to the English, but his troops were completely beaten near Worcester; and he himself fled in disguise, through many dangers, to the western coast, whence he sailed for France, leaving the Scots under the weight of the misfortunes which his coronation and his invasion of England had brought upon them.

These misfortunes were overwhelming; viewed with distrust, as a place of landing and of encampment for the enemies of the revolution, Scotland was treated as a conquered province. On the slightest appearance of revolt or opposition, her leading men were imprisoned or put to death; the thirty Scottish members, who had seats in the great council of the commonwealth of England, far from affording their fellow-citizens aid and succour, became the instruments of the foreign tyranny. Oliver Cromwell governed the Scots despotically up to the moment when, under the name of Protector, he obtained an unlimited authority over the whole of Great Britain; general George Monk, who succeeded him in Scotland, pursued a line of conduct equally harsh and cruel. Such was the state of things when, in the year 1660, after the death of the Protector and the deposition of his son, Richard Cromwell, Monk, suddenly changing sides, conspired against the republic and for the re-establishment of royalty.

The joy caused by the restoration of the Stuarts was universal in Scotland; it was not, as in England, caused simply by the sort of discouragement and political scepticism into which the ill success of the revolution had thrown men, but by a sentiment of real affection for a man whom the Scots regarded almost as the king of their choice. The return of Charles II. was not connected, in their country, with the re-establishment of an ancient social order, oppressive and unpopular; this great event appeared to their eyes, a personal restoration, as it were. They hoped that things would return to the point in which they were before the invasion of Cromwell's army, and that the covenant, then sworn by Charles II., would be the rule of his government. They attributed the king's former distaste for the rigidness of presbyterian discipline to youthful errors, which age and misfortune must have corrected.

But the son of Charles I. nourished in his bosom all the hatred of his grandfather and of his father against puritanism, and he felt no personal gratitude to the Scots for the gift of a kingdom which, in his opinion, was his by right of inheritance. Thinking himself, then, free from all obligation towards them, he had the covenant torn to pieces in the marketplace at Edinburgh, and bishops, sent from England, were paraded in triumph by royal officers along the streets. They required from all the ministers of worship the oath of obedience to their orders, the abjuration of the covenant, and the recognition of the absolute authority of the king in ecclesiastical matters. They who refused to take the oath were declared seditious rebels, and were violently expelled from their livings and churches, which were given to new comers, for the most part Englishmen, ignorant and of ill life. These proceeded to celebrate the services and to preach sermons, but none came to hear them, and the churches were deserted.

The faithful, zealous in their national cause, assembled every Sunday in the bye-places and mountains, which served as refuge for the persecuted ministers; a severe law was issued against these peaceful meetings, to which the agents of authority gave the name of conventicles. Troops were quartered upon the villages whose inhabitants did not frequent their church, and many persons, suspected or convicted of having attended conventicles, were imprisoned, and even publicly whipped. These acts of severity took place principally in the south-western districts, whose population was more disposed to resistance, either from the nature of the country, covered with hills and ravines, or from a remnant of the enthusiastic and pertinacious character of the British race, from which most of them were descended. It was in these districts that the presbyterians began to meet in arms at their secret assemblies, and that whole families, quitting their houses, went to live among the rocks and marshes, in order freely to hear the exhortations of their proscribed priests, and to satisfy the requirements of their conscience.

The constantly increasing severity of the measures against the conventicles, soon occasioned an open insurrection, in which figured as chiefs many rich and influential men of the country. The movement did not extend to the eastern provinces, because the forces of the government, and the terror they inspired, augmented the nearer the vicinity to the capital. The presbyterian army was defeated on the Pentland Hills by the regular troops, who had orders to kill the prisoners, and to pursue the fugitives with enormous bloodhounds. After the victory, every family in Ayrshire and Galloway was required to swear an oath not to attend the presbyterian assemblies, and not to give food or refuge to a wandering minister or contumacious presbyterian. Upon the refusal of many persons, all the inhabitants in a body were declared rebels and enemies to the king; and pardons not filled up were distributed for any murders that might be committed upon them.

These atrocities were at length crowned by a measure more monstrous than all. The northern highland clans were authorized to descend into the plain and to commit there all the devastation which their old instinct of national hatred against the inhabitants should suggest to them. For several months eight thousand highlanders overran Ayrshire and the neighbouring counties, pillaging and killing at will. A regiment of dragoons was sent from Edinburgh to assist and protect them in their expedition. When it was thought that they had produced the desired effect, an order sealed with the great seal sent them back to their mountains, and the dragoons remained by themselves to secure the entire submission of the country. But the evils inflicted upon the presbyterians had augmented their fanaticism by reducing them to despair; some of the most exasperated meeting on the road archbishop Sharp, whom Charles II. had named primate of Scotland, dragged him from his carriage, and killed him in his daughter's arms.

This crime of a few men was avenged upon the whole country by redoubled vexations and a host of executions. A second rebellion arose, more general and more formidable than the first. The presbyterian army, this time commanded by old soldiers, many of noble family, comprehended several cavalry regiments, composed of landed proprietors and rich farmers, but it was without artillery or ammunition. Every regiment had a blue flag, the favourite colour of the covenanters. Troops of women and children, following the army to the field of battle, excited the men by their cries. Sometimes, after having marched and fought a whole day, without eating or drinking, they would range in a circle round their ministers, and listen with enwrapt attention to a sermon of several hours' duration, before they thought of seeking provisions or of taking repose.

Such was the army which, a few miles from Glasgow, routed the regiment of guards, the best cavalry of all Scotland, occupied the town, and forced a body of ten thousand men to fall back upon Edinburgh. The alarm it caused the government was such that considerable forces were sent in all haste from London, commanded by the duke of Monmouth, natural son of Charles II., a man of gentle disposition, and inclined to moderate principles, with whom were joined two lieutenants of a very different character: general Thomas Dalziel, and Graham of Claverhouse, who, neutralizing the conciliatory tendencies of Monmouth, obliged him to give battle to the insurgents near the little town of Hamilton, south of Glasgow. The Clyde, whose stream is very deep in this spot, was crossed by a long and narrow stone bridge, called Bothwell Bridge, which the presbyterians occupied. They were driven from this position by the artillery that fired upon them from the bank of the river, and by a charge of cavalry upon the Bridge. Their defeat was complete, and the English army entered Edinburgh, carrying on their pikes severed heads and hands, and bringing, tied two and two upon carts, the chiefs of the presbyterian army, and the ministers whom they had taken prisoners, who underwent with the greatest firmness torture and death, bearing testimony unto death, as they expressed it, to the truth of their national faith.

The presbyterian party could not recover their defeat of Bothwell Bridge, and the mass of the Scots, renouncing the covenant, in the defence of which so much blood had been spilt, submitted to a kind of modified episcopacy, and acknowledged the authority of the king in ecclesiastical matters. But grief at having lost a cause that had been national for a century and a half, and the memory of the battle which had destroyed all hope of ever seeing it triumph, long survived in Scotland. Old ballads, still sung in the villages at the close of the last century, speak of Bothwell Bridge, and of the brave men who died there, with touching expressions of sympathy and enthusiasm. Even at the present day the peasants take off their caps when they pass the blackened stones that here and there, upon the hills and moors, mark the graves of the puritans of the eighteenth century.

As the enthusiasm and energy of the Scottish presbyterians gradually lessened, the government became less distrustful and less cruel towards them. James, duke of York, who, in the reign of his brother, Charles II., had, for pastime, witnessed the infliction of the torture upon refractory ministers, exercised no severity against them after he became king; and his endeavours to substitute catholicism for protestantism were far from exciting so much hostility in Scotland as in England. The presbyterians forgave him his love of popery, in consideration of the hatred he displayed to the episcopalians, their latest persecutors. When a conspiracy, led by the bishops and nobles of England, called in William of Orange and expelled James II., the Scottish people exhibited little enthusiasm for this revolution, lauded as so glorious on the other side of the Tweed; they even hesitated to concur in it, and their adhesion was rather the work of the members of government assembled at Edinburgh, than a genuine act of national assent. Yet the authors of the revolution of 1688 made to Scotland, in matters of religion, concessions which they had not made to England, where the intolerant laws of the Stuarts were maintained in all their rigour. On the other hand, the few obstinate enthusiasts who, under the name of Cameronians, endeavoured, in the beginning of the eighteenth century, to rekindle the half extinct flame of puritanism, were violently persecuted, and bore testimony, by the whip and pillory, on the market-place of Edinburgh. After their time, this austere and impassioned belief, which had combined into one sect the whole populations of the Scottish lowlands, was gradually concentrated in a few isolated families, distinguished from the rest by a more strict observance of the practices of their worship, a more rigid probity, or a greater affectation of it, and the habit of employing the words of the Scriptures on every occasion.

Notwithstanding the evils which the Stuarts had inflicted upon Scotland ever since they had filled the throne of England, the Scots preserved a sort of sympathy for this family, independent, in the minds of numbers, of all political or religious opinions. An instinctive aversion to the new dynasty was felt concurrently, though in unequal degree, by highlanders and by lowlanders. The former threw into it all the ardour of their ancient hatred to the people of England; among the latter, differences of social position, of connexion with the existing government, of religious belief or personal character, produced different shades of zeal in the cause of the heirs of James II. The Jacobite insurrection of 1715, and that of 1745, on the landing of the son of the Pretender, both commenced in the highlands: the second found in the towns of the south and east partisans enough to create a belief that the Celtic and Teutonic races of Scotland, hitherto enemies to each other, were about to become one nation. After the victory of the English government, its first care was to destroy the immemorial organization of the Gallic clans. It executed many chiefs of these clans on the scaffold; it removed others from the country, in order to suspend the exercise of their patriarchal authority; it constructed military roads over moor and mountain, and enrolled a great number of highlanders among the regular troops serving on the continent. As a sort of compromise with the tenacity of the Gael to their ancient customs, they were allowed to combine, in a singular manner, a portion of their national costume with the English uniform, and to retain the bagpipes, their favourite instrument.

When the Scots lost their religious and political enthusiasm, they directed to the cultivation of literature, the imaginative faculties which seem in them a last trace of their Celtic origin as Gauls or as Britons. Scotland is perhaps the only country of Europe where knowledge is really a popular acquirement, and where men of every class love to learn for learning's sake, without any practical motive, or any view to change their condition. Since the final union of that country with England, its ancient Anglo-Danish dialect, ceasing to be cultivated, has been replaced by English as the literary language. But, notwithstanding the disadvantage experienced by every writer who employs in his works an idiom different from that of his habitual conversation, the number of distinguished authors of every class, since the middle of the last century, has been far greater in Scotland than in England, taking into account the difference of population of the two countries. It is more especially in historical composition and in narrative that the Scots excel; and we may consider this peculiar aptitude as one of the characteristic indications of their original descent; for the Irish and the Welsh are the two nations who have at greatest length and most agreeably drawn up their ancient annals.

Civilization, which makes rapid progress among all the branches of the Scottish population, has now penetrated beyond the lowland towns into the highlands. Perhaps, however, in seeking to propagate it there, the means adopted of late years have been too violent, have been more calculated to effect the destruction than the amelioration of the Gaelic race. Converting their patriarchal supremacy into seigneural rights of property over all the land occupied by their clans, the heirs of the ancient chiefs, the English law in their hands, have expelled from their habitations hundreds of families to whom this law was absolutely unknown. In place of the dispossessed clans, they have established immense flocks and a few agriculturists from other parts, enlightened, industrious persons, capable of carrying into execution the most judicious plans of cultivation. The great agricultural progress of Rosshire and Sutherlandshire is greatly vaunted; but if such an example be followed, the race of the most ancient inhabitants of Britain, after having preserved itself for so many centuries and among so many enemies, will disappear, without leaving any other trace than a vicious English pronunciation in the places where its language used to be spoken.

IV. THE NATIVE IRISH AND THE ANGLO-NORMAN IRISH.

Effect of the conquest in Ireland—Degeneration of the Anglo-Irish—Tenacity of the natives—Invasion of Edward Bruce—Reform and civilization of Ireland—Influence of the Irish bards—Common hatred to England—Catholicism of the Irish—Entire completion of the territorial conquest—Religious and patriotic insurrections—Alliance of the Irish with Charles I.—Invasion of Ireland by Cromwell—Attitude of the Irish on the restoration of the Stuarts—Invasion of William III—Political association of the Irish—White Boys—Hearts of Oak—Right Boys—Volunteers—Patriotic views of the Volunteers—Their provincial assemblies—Peep-o'-day Boys—Defenders—The United Irishmen—Influence of the French revolution—The Orangemen—Organization of the United Irishmen—Succours from France—First symptoms of insurrection—Rise of the United Irishmen—Irish republic—Attack upon Dublin—Defeat of the United Irishmen—Rise of the Presbyterians—Landing of the French in Ireland—Their defeat—Termination of the rebellion—The Union.

The conquest of Ireland by the Anglo-Normans is perhaps the only conquest where, after the first disasters, the slow and imperceptible course of events has not brought about a gradual amelioration in the state of the conquered people. Without having ever enfranchised themselves from the foreign domination, the descendants of the Anglo-Saxons have still made great progress in prosperity and civilization. But the native Irish, though apparently placed in a similar position, have been constantly declining for the last five centuries; and yet that population is gifted by nature with great vivacity of mind and a remarkable aptitude for every class of intellectual labour. Although the soil of Ireland is fertile and adapted for cultivation, its fecundity has been alike unprofitable to the conquerors and to their subjects; so that notwithstanding the extent of their domains, the posterity of the Normans has become gradually impoverished, in common with that of the Irish. This singular and mournful destiny, which weighs almost equally on the old and on the new inhabitants of Erin, has for its cause the vicinity of England, and the influence which her government has exercised, ever since the conquest, over the internal affairs of that island.

This influence has always manifested itself at a time and in a manner to disturb the course of amicable relations which time and the custom of living together were tending to establish between the Anglo-Irish and the Irish by race. The intervention of the kings of England, whatever its ostensible aim, has always had the effect of keeping up the primitive separation and hostility. In times of war, they assisted the men of Anglo-Norman race; when the latter had compelled the natives to tranquillity, the kings, jealous of their power, and fearing a political separation, studied in every mode to injure and weaken them. Thus it became impossible that the struggle between the two populations should ever terminate, whether by the victory of the one or of the other, or by their complete fusion. This fusion, a rapid one had it taken place, would have presented a phenomenon which has not been met with elsewhere. Attracted by the gentleness of character and sociability of the natives, their conquerors felt an irresistible tendency to assimilate with the conquered, to adopt their manners, their language, and even their dress. The Anglo-Normans became Irish; they exchanged their feudal titles of earl and baron for patronymic surnames; the Dubourgs called themselves Mac-William-Bourg; the De Veres, Mac-Swine; the Delangles, Mac-Costilagh; the Fitz-Urses, Mac-Mahon; and the Fitz-Geraulds, Mac-Gheroit. They acquired a taste for Irish song and poetry, they invited the bards to their tables, and entrusted their children to women of the country. The Normans of England, so haughty towards the Saxons termed this degeneration.

To check the degeneration, and maintain entire the ancient manners of the Anglo-Irish, the kings and parliament of England made many laws, most of them very severe. Every Norman or Englishman by race, who married an Irishwoman, or wore the Irish dress, was treated as an Irishman—that is to say, as a serf in body and goods. Royal ordinances were published, regulating the cut of the hair and beard in Ireland, the number of ells of stuff that were to go to a dress, and the colour of the stuff. Every merchant of English race who traded with the Irish was punished by the confiscation of his merchandise; and every Irishman found travelling in the part of the island inhabited by the Anglo-Normans, especially if he were a bard, was considered and treated as a spy. Every lord, suspected of liking the Irish, became, for that sole offence, the mark of political persecution; and, if he were rich and powerful, he was accused of seeking to become king of Ireland, or, at least, of a desire to separate that kingdom from the crown of England. The great council of barons and knights of Ireland, who, like those of England, assembled every year in parliament, was regarded with almost as much scorn and hatred as were the national assemblies held by the native Irish on the hills. Every sort of freedom was refused to the parliament of Ireland: it could not assemble until the king sanctioned the purposes of its convocation, and even then it only passed laws sent ready drawn up from England. At the same time, the English government employed all its means of action upon the native Irish, to make them renounce their national customs and their ancient social order. It caused the archbishops, nearly all of them men from England, to declare that the ancient laws of the country, those which had governed Ireland in the ages when she was called the Island of the Saints, were abominable to God. Every Irishman convicted of having submitted any case to judges of his nation, was excommunicated, and ranked among those whom the ordinances of England called les irreys anemis nostre seigneur le rey.

To counteract the efforts made by the English government to destroy their ancient manners, the Irish applied themselves with obstinate pertinacity to maintain them. They manifested a violent aversion to the polish and refinement of the Anglo-Norman manners: "Ne faisant compte," says the historian Froissart, "de nulle jolivetè, et ne volant avoir aucune connoissance de gentillesse, mais demeurer en eur rudesse première." This rudesse was only external, for the Irish, when they chose, could live with foreigners and gain their affection, especially if they were enemies to the English. They concluded against the latter political alliances with several of the continental kings; and when, in the fourteenth century, the Scot, Robert Bruce, was named king by his countrymen, bodies of Irish volunteers crossed the sea to support him. After the entire enfranchisement of Scotland, Edward Bruce, brother of Robert, made a descent upon the north of Ireland, to aid the natives to regain their country, and the Anglo-Norman degenerates, to take vengeance for the vexations inflicted on them by their king. In fact, several of the latter, and among others, the Lacys, joined the Scottish army, which, in its march southwards, sacked several towns and dismantled many castles built by the sons of the companions of John de Courcy, the first conqueror of Ulster. Several families, who possessed great domains in those parts, such as the Audelys, the Talbots, the Touchets, the Chamberlains, the Mandevilles, and the Sauvages, all Normans by name and origin, were obliged to quit the country. On his arrival at Dundalk, Edward Bruce was elected and crowned king of Ireland, despite the excommunication pronounced by the pope against him, his aiders and abettors.

But his reign lasted only a year, and he was killed in a battle lost against considerable forces sent from England. The Scottish troops were recalled to their own country, and by degrees the Anglo-Normans regained their domination in Ireland, without, however, attaining their former limits towards the north. Most of Ulster remained Irish, and the few Norman families seen there after these events were poor, or had formed relations with the natives. By degrees, even the descendants of the conqueror, John de Courcy, degenerated. Notwithstanding the short duration and the little effect of the conquest of Edward Bruce, its recollection remained deeply imprinted on the mind of the Irish people. His name was applied to many places he had never visited, and many a castle, not built by him, was called Bruce Castle, as in Wales, and in the south of Scotland, many ruins bear the name of Arthur.

Things in Ireland resumed the same situation as before; the natives making no further conquests over the Anglo-Normans by their arms, did so by their manners, and the degeneration continued. The measures taken against this evil, consisting, for the most part, of laws as to the manner in which people should divert themselves and dress, and of prohibitions of the stuffs most common in the country, and consequently the least expensive, occasioned daily inconvenience and loss to the English population established in Ireland, whose resentment confirmed their attachment to the manners it was sought to compel them to quit, against their will and against the nature of things. As to the Irish by race, the action of the government upon them was limited in time of peace to the attracting to England their numerous chiefs and princes, and to the procuring for the king of England the guardianship and custody of their sons. It was considered a great achievement to give them a taste for the lordly pomp and aristocratic manners of the time: this was called first the reform, and then the civilization of Ireland.

But the habit of familiarity between persons of different conditions was so deeply rooted in this country, that the Anglo-Norman knights, charged with the education of the young heirs of the ancient kings of Erin, could never make them discontinue the custom of eating at the same table with their bards and followers, or from shaking hands with every one. Few of the Irish chieftains who, in the fifteenth and sixteenth centuries, obtained charters of Anglo-Norman nobility, and the titles of earl or baron, long retained these titles, foreign to their language, and having no relation to the history, manners, and social order of their nation. They became weary of bearing them, preferring to be called, as before, O'Neil or O'Brien, instead of earl of Thomond or of Tyrone. Even where they did not themselves adopt this course, public opinion often obliged them to renounce these signs of alliance with the enemies of their country; for public opinion had organs respected and feared by every Irishman.

These organs of popular praise or blame were the bards, poets, and musicians by profession, whose immemorial authority was founded on the passion of the Irish for poetry and song. They formed in Ireland a sort of constituted body, whose advice was sought in all important matters; and the duties of a good king, according to ancient political maxims, were to honour the bards and to conform to the laws. Ever since the invasion of the Anglo-Normans, the corporation of bards had taken part against them, and not a member of the body had ever belied his attachment to the ancient liberty of the country. The chief objects of praise in their verses were the enemies of the English government, and they pursued with their most biting satire all who had made peace with it, and had accepted any favour from it. Lastly, they boldly ranked above the princes and chiefs, friends to the kings of England, the rebels and bandits, who, from hatred to the foreign power, exercised armed robbery, and pillaged by night the houses of the Saxons. Under this name the natives comprised all the English or Normans who did not speak the Erse language, but, probably, a mixed dialect of French and old English. They accorded the name of Irish only to themselves and to those who had adopted their idiom, while in England the name of English was denied to the men of that nation established in Ireland, who were called Irois in the Norman language, and, in the English, Irse or Irisch, the only distinction between them and the genuine Irish being that the latter were called wild Irish.

The situation of the Anglo-Irish, detested by the natives around them, and despised by their countrymen across the Channel, was one of singular difficulty. Obliged to struggle against the action of the English government, and, at the same time, to resort to the support of that government against the attacks of the ancient population, they were, by turns, Irish against England, and English against the inhabitants of Gaelic race. This embarrassment could only be terminated by the rupture of the tie of dependence which bound them to England, and by the complete establishment of their domination over the natives. They simultaneously aimed at this double object; and, on their side, the natives also endeavoured to separate themselves from England, by recovering their lands and throwing off all authority not purely Irish. Thus, though the policy of the Irish by conquest and that of the Irish by race were naturally based upon mutual hostility, there was still a common point at which the views of these two classes of men concurred: the desire to restore to Ireland its independence as a state. These complex interests, which the natural course of things was ill calculated to bring to a simple order of relations, were complicated still more in the sixteenth century, by a revolution which added the seeds of religious dissension to the ancient elements of political hostility.

When king Henry VIII. had, for his own benefit, abolished the papal supremacy in England, the new religious reformation, established without difficulty over the eastern coast of Ireland, and in the towns where English was spoken, made little progress in the interior of the country. The native Irish, even when they understood English, were little inclined to hear sermons preached in that language; and, besides, the missionaries sent from England, acting upon the instructions they had received, enjoined it upon them as an article of faith to renounce their ancient usages, and to adopt the manners of the English. Their aversion to those manners, and to the government which sought to impose them, extended to the Reformation and to the reformers, whom they were accustomed to designate by the simple name of Saxons, Sassons. On the other hand, the Norman or English families, settled in places remote from the sea, and in some measure beyond the reach of authority, resisted the attempts made to persuade or force them to change their religion. They clung to catholicism, and this again knitted fresh ties of sympathy between them and the Irish. This change had also the effect of connecting with the general affairs of Europe, the quarrel of the native Irish against the sons of their invaders, a quarrel hitherto confined to the corner of land which it actually occupied. It became, thenceforward, a portion of the great contest between catholicism and protestantism; and the demands for foreign aid made by the population of Ireland, were no longer addressed merely to tribes of the same origin, peopling part of Scotland, but to the Catholic powers, to the pope, and to the kings of Spain and France.

The popes, more especially, those ancient enemies of Ireland, who had authorised its conquest by Henry II., and had excommunicated all the natives who armed against the English power, now became their firm allies, and were loved by them with all their soul, as they loved whatsoever gave them the hope of recovering their independence. But the court of Rome in the sixteenth and seventeenth centuries converted this unfortunate country into the focus of political intrigues, entirely foreign to its enfranchisement. By means of their apostolic nuncios, and more especially of the order of the Jesuits, who, on this occasion, displayed their wonted ability, the popes effected the formation in Ireland of a party of pure catholics, as hostile to the Irish of race, become protestants, as to the English themselves, and detesting the latter, not as usurpers, but as anti-papists. In the rebellions which afterwards broke out, this party played a part distinct from that of the Irish catholics who took up arms from simple motives of patriotism; it is easy to perceive this difference, even in the enterprises wherein these two classes of men acted together and in concert.

Under favour of the troubles resulting from religious contests, and the encouragement which the Catholic powers afforded to the insurgents of all parties, the old cause of the native Irish seemed to regain some force; their energy was aroused, and the bards sang that a new soul had descended upon Erin. But the enthusiasm created by religious dissensions had also communicated itself to the Anglo-Irish reformers, and even to the English, who, about the end of the sixteenth century, served in the wars of Ireland with more ardour than ever, as in a sort of protestant crusade. Their zeal furnished queen Elizabeth with more money and troops for these wars than any English monarch had obtained before her. Resuming with great means and vast activity the incomplete work of the conquest, Elizabeth recovered the northern provinces, and invaded the west, which had hitherto resisted. All this territory was divided into counties, like England, and governed by English, who, with a view, as they said, to civilise the wild Irish, made them perish by thousands of hunger and misery.

James I. pursued the work of this civilization by seizing a number of chiefs, and having them tried at London for past or present rebellion. According to the old Anglo-Norman law, they were condemned to lose their domains, as felons to their liege lord; and, under this name of domains, care was taken to comprise the whole extent of country occupied by the clans whom they ruled, seeing that in England the tenants of every lordship were only the farmers of the lord for longer or shorter terms. By means of this arbitrary assimilation of two orders of things entirely different, king James confiscated in Ireland whole districts, which he sold, in lots, to adventurers, as they were called. The dispossessed clans sought refuge in the mountains and forests, whence they soon issued in arms to attack the new English colonies; but they were repulsed by superior forces, and the province of Ulster, which had been the principal theatre of the war, was declared forfeit, and all titles of proprietorship within it declared null and void. They were not even allowed to remove their furniture; and a company of capitalists was established in London to effect the colonization of this district upon an uniform plan. They hired a number of Scottish labourers and artisans, who sailed from Galloway, and established themselves in Ireland, in the neighbourhood of Derry, which, under the name of Londonderry, became a manufacturing town. Other emigrants from the same nation passed in succession into the north of Ireland, and formed there a new population and a new religious party; for they were zealous presbyterians, and, in point of creed, equally hostile to the Anglicans and to the catholics.

The troubles arising in England at the beginning of the reign of Charles I., again encouraged the party of old Ireland and of the Irish papists; at first, because the struggle in which the government was engaged with the English people, lessened its means of action externally, and, afterwards, because the king's marked inclination for catholicism seemed to promise the catholics his support, or, at least, his sanction. The purely religious faction, under the command of an Anglo-Irishman, George Moor, was the first to rise up against what it called the tyranny of the heretics. It obtained little success, so long as that portion of the people which nourished political hatred against the English remained quiet, or did not assist it; but as soon as the native Irish, led by Phelim O'Connor, took part in the civil war, that war was pushed forward more vigorously, and had for its object, not the triumph of the catholics, but the extirpation of all the foreign colonists, of ancient or of recent date. The presbyterian colonists of Ulster and the Anglican inhabitants of the western provinces were attacked in their houses, amid cries of Erin go Bragh! (Hurrah for Ireland!) and it is calculated that forty thousand persons perished at this time, in various ways.

The news of this massacre produced a great impression in England, and although the victory obtained by the men of Irish race was in reality a great blow to the power of the king, the parliament accused him of having promoted the slaughter of the protestants. He warmly vindicated himself from the accusation, and, to remove all suspicion, sent to Ireland troops that he would fain have retained in England for the maintenance of his authority. The parliament gave, by anticipation, the lands of the rebels to those who would furnish money for the expenses of the war. The English army gave no quarter to any Irishman, rejecting even the submission of those who offered to lay down their arms. Despair communicated fresh strength to the fanatics in religion or patriotism. Though their military resources were far inferior, they resisted the English, and even recovered from them the province of Ulster, whence they expelled many families of Scottish race. Become thus again masters of the greater part of Ireland, they formed a council of national administration, composed of bishops, ancient chiefs of tribes, feudal lords of Anglo-Norman origin, and deputies chosen in each county by the native population.

When the civil war broke out between the king and the parliament of England, the national assembly of the Irish carried on a correspondence with both these parties, offering to join that which should most amply recognise the independence of Ireland. Whatever may have been the diplomatic skill natural to the Irish, it was difficult to effect a formal union between them and the parliamentarians; for the latter were at this time animated with a fierce hatred to the papists; the king came to terms more easily and more promptly with the confederates. By a treaty signed at Glamorgan, they engaged to furnish him with ten thousand men; and, in return, he made concessions to them, which were almost equivalent to the abdication of his royalty, as far as Ireland was concerned. This union did not hold, but it was the king who first violated it, by substituting for it a private treaty with those of the Anglo-Irish who had espoused the quarrel of the royalists of England, at the head of whom was the duke of Ormond. The mass of the confederates, who, their object being a total separation, were not a whit more royalist than parliamentarian, were not comprehended in this alliance, and even the papist party was excluded from it, because political interests alone were contemplated. Under the conduct of the papal nuncio, this party formed a stricter alliance than ever with the native party, which recognised as its chief a man of the name of O'Neil; but the intrigues of the nuncio and the intolerance of the priests, who had obtained great influence over the unenlightened multitude, again embroiled the affairs of the Irish, by confounding the religious with the patriotic cause. A few of the stronger minded alone continued to view these two interests in a distinct manner; and, after the condemnation to death of Charles I., they opened negotiations with the founders of the republic, while the Anglicans and presbyterians of Ireland, joining the duke of Ormond, proclaimed Charles II.

The alarmed republicans despatched to Ireland their best captain, Oliver Cromwell, who, in the ardour of his zeal and the inflexibility of his policy, carried on against all parties a war of extermination, and even undertook to complete fully and finally the conquest of the island. After having distributed among his troops, who were in arrears of pay, the lands taken from the rebels, he renewed, upon a larger scale, the great expropriation executed by James I. Instead of expelling the Irish, house by house and village by village, which enabled them to collect in the neighbouring forests, the western province of Connaught was assigned as the sole habitation for all the natives and for the Anglo-Irish catholics. All such received orders to repair thither, within a given time, with their families and goods; and when they were assembled there, a cordon of troops was formed round them, and death was denounced upon any who should cross that line.

The vast extent of territory thus rendered vacant was sold by the government to a company of rich capitalists, who retailed it in lots to new colonists and speculators.

Thus arose in Ireland, beside the Irish of race, the old Anglo-Irish, and the Scotch presbyterians, a fourth population, distasteful to the former, both on account of its origin and of its recent establishment in the country. No serious discord took place between them so long as the republic of England remained powerful under the protectorate of Cromwell; but after his death, when the English government fell into anarchy, there was formed in Ireland, for the restoration of the Stuarts, a party composed, for the most part, of Anglo-Irish protestants or catholics, with a small minority of natives. The bulk of the latter, hostile by instinct to every enterprise tending to place the country under the power of an Englishman, far from giving their adhesion to the party of Charles II., openly opposed his being proclaimed king of Great Britain and Ireland. The dispute between the pure Irish and the royalists grew so warm, that both sides took up arms, and several engagements took place; but the friends of the Stuarts, comprising all the colonists, old and new, got the better of a population which the late government had disorganized and impoverished.

Charles II., who felt that his re-establishment was owing to the lassitude of parties, carefully avoiding whatever might revive them, made little change in Ireland. He resisted the demands made by the papists and the natives to resume possession of their property, occupied by the soldiers or the new colonists; but under the reign of his successor, James II., himself a catholic, the catholic party, aided by the royal authority, acquired great ascendancy in Ireland. All the civil and military offices were given to papists, and the king, who doubted the result of the struggle he was maintaining in England against public opinion, essayed to organize in Ireland a force capable of supporting him. It was in this island that, after his deposition, he sought refuge. He assembled at Dublin a parliament, composed of papists and native Irish. The latter, previous to any other discussion, called upon king James to recognise the entire independence of Ireland; the king refused, unwilling to abandon any of his ancient prerogatives, but offered, as a compromise, not to tolerate any other religion than catholicism. The Irish, inflexible in their purpose of political enfranchisement, answered by a message, that since he separated himself from their national cause, they would manage their affairs without him. It was amidst these dissensions that the new king of England, William III., landed in Ireland with considerable forces, and gained, over the two confederate parties of the old Irish and the papists, the decisive battle of the Boyne.

The conquest of Ireland by William III. was followed by confiscations and expropriations which planted in the island one more English colony, round which rallied the zealous protestants and all the friends of the revolution, who assumed the appellation of Orangemen. The entire administration of public affairs passed into their hands, and the catholics no longer filled any office; but the protestants who oppressed them, were themselves oppressed by the government of England, as, for five centuries past, the English established in Ireland had ever been. Their industry and commerce were cramped by prohibitive duties, and the Irish parliament was seldom permitted to assemble. Under queen Anne, this parliament was deprived of the few rights that remained to it; and, as if to extenuate the wrong in the eyes of the Anglicans, and to blind them to their own interest by flattering their religious animosities, the papists were fiercely persecuted. They were disqualified from holding landed property or farms on long terms, and even from bringing up their children at home. But community of suffering, though in a very unequal degree, united in one opposition the protestants and the Anglo-Irish catholics, or Irish by race, who formed a new party, entirely political, under the name of Patriots. They all agreed upon one point, the necessity of rendering Ireland independent of England; but the former desired this solely out of hatred to the government, and the latter out of hatred to the English nation, or, rather, to the English race. This is proved by satires, composed in the middle of the last century, against the sons of Erin who learned and spoke English.

The patriot party augmented by degrees, and, on several occasions, came to blows with the English party, on the report, true or false, that it was intended finally to suppress the parliament of Ireland. At about the same time, the great landed proprietors of the south and the east began to convert their arable lands into pasture, with a view to increase their revenues by the breeding of cattle. This agricultural change occasioned the expulsion of a great number of small farmers, the ruin of many poor families, and a great cessation of work for the labourers, who were mostly Irish by race, and catholics. The discharged labourers, and others who were without work, and who thought they had as much right as the lord himself to the lands on which, from time immemorial, they had fed their sheep, assembled in organized troops. Armed with guns, swords, and pistols, and preceded by bagpipes, they overran the country, breaking down the fences, levying contributions on the protestants, and enrolling the catholics in their association, assuming the title of White Boys, from the white shirt they all wore as a rallying token. Several persons of Irish origin, and of some fortune, joined this association, which, it would appear, was negotiating with the king of France and the son of the Pretender, Charles Edward, when the latter was defeated at Culloden. It is not precisely known what their political projects were; it is probable that they would have acted in concert with the French expedition, which was to be commanded by M. de Conflans; but when France renounced this plan, the efforts of the White Boys were confined to a petty warfare against the agents of the royal authority.

In the northern counties, another association was formed under the name of Hearts of Oak; its members, for mutual recognition, wore an oak branch in their hats: farmers, evicted on the expiration of their lease, also united and armed, under the name of Hearts of Steel; and, at last, a fourth society, still more closely knit together, appeared in the southern counties, under the name of Right Boys. All those who joined it, swore to pay no tithes to any priest, not even to catholics, and to obey the orders of no one, except those of a mysterious chief, called Captain Right. This oath was so strictly observed, that in many places the officers of the government could not, at any price, obtain men to execute the sentences pronounced upon Right Boys.

While the struggle between these various associations and the civil and military authority was occasioning infinite disorder and spoliation in the country, some landed proprietors and young men of rich protestant families formed, under the name of Volunteers, a counter-association for the sole purpose of maintaining the public peace; at their own expense they furnished themselves with horses and arms, and patrolled night and day the places where there was any disturbance. The rupture of England with her colonies of North America had just involved her in a declaration of war from France, Spain, and Holland. All the troops employed in Ireland were recalled, and this country remained exposed to the aggressions of these three powers, and of the privateers which infested the seas. The great Anglo-Irish proprietors making loud complaints on this subject to the ministry, the answer was, "Arm, and look to yourselves."

The rich class zealously availed themselves of this permission. The companies of volunteers previously formed, served as a model and nucleus for the organization of a body of national militia, which, under the same name, soon increased to the number of forty thousand men. As it was almost wholly composed of Anglo-Irish protestants, the government, so far from distrusting it, presented it with a large quantity of arms and ammunition. Those who conceived the original idea of this great military association, had no other object than the defence of the Irish soil against the enemies of England; but Ireland was so wretched, every class of men underwent there such vexations, that, as soon as the volunteers felt their power, they resolved to employ it in ameliorating, if possible, the condition of the country. A new spirit of patriotism was developed among them, embracing with equal kindliness all the inhabitants of the island, without distinction of race or of religion. The catholics who entered the association were eagerly received, and arms were given them, notwithstanding the old law which reserved the use of them to protestants alone. The Anglican soldiers gave the military salute, and presented arms to the chaplains of the catholic regiments; monks and ministers of the reformed church shook hands and mutually congratulated each other.

In every county the volunteers held political meetings, each of which sent deputies to form a central assembly, with full power to act as representing the Irish nation. This assembly, held in Dublin, passed various resolutions, all based on the principle that the English parliament had no right to make laws for Ireland, and that this right rested wholly in the Irish parliament. The government, entirely occupied with the war against the United States of America, and having no force capable of counterbalancing in Ireland the organization of the volunteers, acknowledged, in a bill passed in 1783, the legislative rights of the two Irish chambers. Further, the habeas corpus act, securing every English subject from illegal imprisonment, was, now for the first time, introduced into Ireland. But these enforced concessions were far from being made in good faith; and as soon as peace was concluded in 1784, the agents of the government began to suggest to the volunteers to dissolve as useless, and to order the disarming of the catholics, according to the laws. Several regiments declared that they would only lay down their arms with their lives, and the protestants, concurring in this declaration, announced that their subaltern-officers and arms should be at the service of any Irishman who wished to exercise himself in military evolutions.

This spirit of mutual toleration was considered extremely formidable by the English government, which accordingly employed itself in destroying it, and in reviving the old religious and national hatred. It effected this object to a certain extent, by impeding the political meetings, and clubs of the volunteers, and by intimidating or seducing many members of this society. The rich were the first to desert, as being, in general, more cautious and less ardent than people of inferior condition. Deprived of its ancient chiefs, the association fell into a sort of anarchy, and the influence of unenlightened men was soon apparent in the gradual abandonment of the great principle of nationality, which, for a moment, had effaced all party distinctions. Following up some personal disputes, the more fanatic protestants began, in various places, forcibly to disarm the papists; there was formed for this purpose, a society under the name of Peep-o'-day Boys, because it was generally at this hour they entered the houses of the catholics. The latter, as a security against their violence, formed, under the name of Defenders, a counter-association, which did not always confine itself to defensive measures, but attacked the protestants in reprisal; this association gradually numbered all the catholics who withdrew from the society of the volunteers, whose dissolution became complete in all the counties, except Dublin, where it was retained as a municipal police. The society of Peep-o'-day Boys having, as it would seem, no distinct political object, contented itself with partial aggressions upon its antagonists; but the Defenders, the majority of whom were of Irish race, were animated with the instinctive aversion of the natives of Ireland towards all foreign colonists. Whether from the recollection of a former alliance or from conformity of character and manners, the Irish by race had a greater inclination for the French than for any other nation; the leading Defenders, who, for the most part, were priests or monks, kept up a correspondence with the cabinet of Versailles, in the years which preceded the French revolution.

This revolution made a vivid impression on the more patriotic of the various sects of Irish. There was then at Dublin a Catholic committee, formed of rich persons and priests of that religion, who undertook to transmit to the government the complaints and demands of their co-religionists; hitherto they had limited themselves to humble petitions, accompanied with protestations of devotion and loyalty; but, suddenly changing their tone, the majority of the members of the catholic committee resolved that it was now time to demand, as a natural right, the abolition of the laws against catholicism, and to invite every catholic to arm in assertion of this right. At the same time, there was formed at Belfast, a locality occupied by the Scottish colonists introduced into Ireland under James I., a presbyterian club, whose special object it was to consider the political state of Ireland and the means of reforming it. The Dublin committee speedily proposed to this club an alliance founded on community of interest and opinion, and the presidents of the two assemblies, one of them a catholic priest, and the other a Calvinist minister, carried on a political correspondence. These amicable relations became the basis of a new association, that of the United Irishmen, whose object was a second time to rally all the inhabitants of the island in one party. Clubs of United Irishmen were established in many towns, and especially in those of the east and south, all organized on the same model, and governed by similar rules. The various parties, united in this new alliance, made mutual concessions: the catholics published an explanation of their doctrines, and a disavowal of all hostility to other Christian sects; the majority, at the same time, making a formal renunciation of all claims to the lands taken at different times from their ancestors.

Thus the mainspring of English domination in Ireland was broken by the reconciliation of all the classes of her population, and the government accordingly adopted vigorous measures against what it called, by a new word, the revolutionary spirit. The habeas corpus act was suspended, but the association of United Irishmen, nevertheless, continued to recruit its numbers in all the counties, and to carry on friendly communication with the nation which invited all others to become free like itself. The festival of the French Federation was celebrated at Dublin on the 14th July, 1790, and in the course of 1791 many addresses were sent from all parts of Ireland to the Constituent assembly. When the coalition at Pilnitz declared war against France, the United Irishmen of Belfast voted supplies of money to the French armies, and on learning the retreat of the duke of Brunswick, had public rejoicings in many towns. In general, the Irish patriots aimed at following and imitating the movements of the French revolution. They established a national guard, like that of France; and the soldiers of this body, clothed and armed by subscription, saluted each other by the name of citizen. In 1793, they all became republicans, in language and in principles: Anglicans, Calvinists, and papists, united in this; and the titular catholic archbishop of Dublin, in one of his pastoral letters, endeavoured to prove from the example of the Italian republics of the middle ages, that the catholics were the creators of modern democracy.

The ill success of the French revolution struck a heavy blow at the power of the United Irishmen, by diminishing their own confidence in the infallibility of their principles, and by giving a sort of authority to the accusations of their enemies. The English ministry seized the moment at which this hesitation of opinion was manifested, to make the catholics a concession, which it had hitherto denied them; it gave them the privilege of bringing up their children themselves, and of exercising some of their political rights: the object being to represent the Irish Union to the papists as needless for the future, and, if they continued to agitate, to render them odious to the other sects, in imputing to them the secret design of exterminating the protestants. The bands of Defenders, who still overran several counties, gave weight to these imputations; and the Anglicans of Connaught, more readily alarmed in consequence of their limited numbers amidst the native Irish, armed spontaneously in the year 1795, and formed associations under the title of Orangemen. Their political dogma was the rigorous maintenance of the order of things established by William III., and of all the oppressive laws made, since his reign, against the catholics and the men of Irish race. From the outset, they displayed a fanaticism which rendered them formidable to such of their neighbours as differed from them in religion or in origin; nearly fourteen hundred families emigrated, southward and eastward, to escape this new persecution.

Several acts of cruelty, committed by the Orangemen on the catholics, excited great hatred against them; and all the violence exercised by the military and civil agents of the government were laid to their charge; such as the torture inflicted on suspected persons, and the destruction of the printing presses. A man accused of being an Orangeman at once became the object of popular vengeance; and, as this accusation was vague, it was easy for evil-intentioned men to make use of it for the purpose of destroying whom they chose; every protestant had reason to fear incurring it. The bond of Irish union was greatly weakened by this mutual hatred and distrust of the two religious parties; to remedy the evil by a more concentrated organization, the public association was replaced by a secret society, based on an oath and passive obedience to chiefs whose names were only known by a few associates. The society was divided into sections, communicating with each other by means of superior committees, composed of deputies elected from among the body. There were district committees and provincial committees; and above these was a directory of five members, who regulated the whole union, which consisted of nearly an hundred thousand members. The superior and inferior chiefs formed a military hierarchy, with the ranks of lieutenant, captain, major, colonel, general, and general-in-chief. Every associate, who possessed the means, was to furnish himself, at his own expense, with fire-arms, powder, and ball; among the poorer members, pikes were distributed, made by subscription and in great numbers by members of the union. This new plan of organization was carried into execution in 1796, in Munster, Leinster, and Ulster; but Connaught was not so prompt, owing to the vigilance of the Orangemen, and the support they afforded to the agents of authority.

The men whom the Irish Union acknowledged as their superior chiefs were of various origin and religion: Arthur O'Connor, who, in the popular opinion, was descended from the last king of all Ireland; lord Edward Fitz-Gerald, whose name connected him with the old Norman family of the Fitz-Geraulds; father Quigley, an Irishman by birth, and a zealous papist; Theobald Wolf-Tone, a lawyer of English origin, professing the philosophical opinions of the eighteenth century. Priests of every religion were members of the society; in general, they filled the higher stations; but there was no jealousy among them, or even distrust of the sceptical doctrines of some of the associates. They urged their parishioners to read much and variously, and to form reading-clubs at the houses of the schoolmasters or in the barns. Sometimes ministers of one religion were seen preaching in the church of another; an auditory, composed half of catholics and half of Calvinists, would listen with earnest attention to the same sermon, and then receive at the church-door a distribution of philosophical tracts, such as the Age of Reason, by Thomas Paine, of which many copies were printed at Belfast.

This tendency to subject their particular habits or creed to the views and orders of the Union, was exhibited in the lower classes by a total abstinence from all strong liquors, an abstinence difficult to observe in a damp, cold climate. The Directory recommended it, in 1796, to all the members, in order that each might cease to pay to the English government the duty on spirits; and towards the close of the same year, they announced by printed circulars the approaching arrival of a French fleet. Fifteen thousand men, in fact, who left France under the command of general Hoche, arrived in Bantry bay, but a tempest, which dispersed their vessels, prevented their landing.

This unexpected incident, and the tardiness of the Executive Directory of France in preparing a second expedition, gave the English government leisure to labour actively at the destruction of the Irish Union; visits by day and by night were made more frequently than ever upon suspected persons. In houses where arms were supposed to be concealed, the occupants were forced to confession, by the application, if they refused to answer, of various kinds of torture; the most usual being to half hang them, to whip them until they were half flayed, and to tear off the hair and the skin with a pitch cap. The Irish, driven to extremity by these cruelties, resolved to begin the insurrection, without waiting for the arrival of the French; pikes were fabricated, and balls cast with renewed activity. The government saw what was going on; for the larger trees near the towns were cut down and taken away at night, the leaden spouts disappeared from every house, and the catholics frequented the churches and confessionals oftener than usual. But notwithstanding this accession of zeal, their good understanding with the protestants did not cease to exist; a man who, in the beginning of 1798, was executed at Carrickfergus, as an agent of the United Irishmen, was accompanied to the scaffold by a monk and two presbyterian ministers.

In this state of things, one of the delegates from Leinster to the Irish Union, not pressed by any imminent danger, or gained over by considerable offers, but suddenly seized with a sort of panic terror, denounced to a magistrate of Dublin, a partisan of the government, the place where the committee of which he was a member was to hold one of its sittings. Upon this information thirteen persons were seized, with papers compromising many others. Numerous arrests took place, and four days after, an assemblage of several thousand men, armed with pikes and muskets, collected some miles from Dublin, and marched upon the city.

This was the commencement of the insurrection of the United Irishmen, which, for a moment, extended over the whole country between Dublin and the Wicklow mountains, intercepting all communication between the capital and the southern provinces. The precautions of defence adopted at Dublin, where there was plenty of artillery, secured that city from the attack of the insurgents; but several other less considerable towns fell into their hands. The first engagement between them and the royal troops took place on the hill of Tara, where, in ancient times, the general assembly of the Irish used to be held. The battalions of United Irishmen had green flags, upon which was painted a harp, surmounted, in lieu of a crown, with a cap of liberty, and the English words, liberty or death, or the Irish motto, Erin go bragh. The catholic members bore with them to the fight absolutions signed by a priest, upon which was drawn a tree of liberty; in the pockets of many of the dead were found books of litanies, and translations of the republican songs of France.

The catholic priests, who nearly all held posts in the insurgent army, employed their influence to prevent the mal-treatment of those protestants, against whom, though not members of the Union, it had no political grievance. They saved many of these from falling victims to the fanaticism which animated the lower ranks of the army, and their constant cry was: "This is not a religious war." Whatever may have been their other excesses, the insurgents always respected women, which neither the Orangemen nor even the English officers did, notwithstanding their pretensions to honour and refinement. These soldiers, who made the murder of a single prisoner matter of bitter reproach against the rebels, handed over their own without scruple to the executioner, because they said, this was the law. There were whole counties in revolt, where not a single protestant was killed; but not one of the insurgents, taken in arms, obtained his life; so that the chiefs of the United Irishmen said emphatically: "We fight with the cord round our necks."

According to the instructions of the Irish Directory, the insurrection should have commenced on the same day and the same hour in every town; but the arrest of the leaders, in compelling the persons compromised to hasten their outbreak, destroyed the concert, which alone could assure success to this perilous enterprise. The movement was only from place to place, and the associates remote from Dublin, having time to reflect, suspended their active co-operation until the insurrection should have attained certain territorial limits. In a short time, it extended to Wexford, where a provisional government was installed, under the name of Executive Directory of the Irish Republic. The green flag was unfurled on the arsenals and public buildings, and a few small vessels were equipped as cruizers, under the flag of the insurgents. They formed an entrenched camp, which became their head-quarters, on Vinegar Hill, near Wexford. They had some artillery there; but, entirely without field-pieces, they were, in order to make their way into towns, compelled to dash in upon the enemy's cannon, a mode of fighting the most destructive of all, but which they practised with characteristic gaiety. At the assault upon Ross, in Cork, a piece of heavy cannon, planted at one of the gates, with its discharges of grape-shot, stayed the assailants. One of the insurgents rushed forward to the mouth of the piece, and thrusting his arm into it, shouted: "Forward, boys, I've stopped it!"

The insurgent chiefs, thinking that to take the capital would determine all the towns that still hesitated, made a desperate attack upon Dublin; it failed completely, and the failure was fatal to the Irish cause. Shortly after, a battle lost near Wicklow restored that town to the royal troops, and, from this time, discouragement and divisions took possession of the patriot ranks: they were accusing and repudiating their chiefs, while an English army was advancing, by forced marches, against the camp at Vinegar Hill. With the aid of its artillery, it drove out the insurgents, most of whom were armed only with pikes, and pursuing them in the direction of Wexford, obliged them to evacuate that town, where the new republic perished, after a month's existence. The Irish made a sort of regular retreat, from hill to hill, but as they had no cannon, they could not make a stand anywhere, and the want of provisions soon compelled them to disband. The prisoners were tortured to extract from them the names of their chiefs; but they denounced none but those who were already dead or prisoners. Thus terminated the eastern and southern insurrection, but, during its last moments, another broke out in the north, among the presbyterians of Scottish race.

This population, in general more enlightened than the catholics, were calmer and more deliberate in their proceedings. They waited for news of the southern revolt to be confirmed ere they would act. But the delay occasioned by this caution gave the government time to take its measures; and when the insurrection commenced with the attack upon Antrim, this town had been strengthened by an accession of infantry and cavalry, with cannon and howitzers. The presbyterians, joined by some catholics of English or Irish origin, made the attack on three sides, having no artillery but a six-pounder, in so bad a condition that it could only be fired twice, and another without a carriage, which they had hastily mounted on the trunk of a tree and two small cart-wheels. For a moment they were masters of the town and of a part of the English artillery; but fresh reinforcements from Belfast obliged them to retire, while fifteen hundred men, posted on the Derry road, intercepted the succours they expected from that quarter.

The insurrection broke out with more success in Down, where the Irish, after defeating the royal troops, formed, near Ballinahinch, a camp similar to that on Vinegar Hill. Here was fought a decisive battle, in which the insurgents were defeated, but not until they had approached the English cannon so closely as to touch them. The royal soldiers took Ballinahinch, and punished the town by burning it. Belfast, which had been, in some measure, the moral focus of the insurrection, remained in the hands of the government, and this circumstance produced upon the northern insurgents the same impression that the fruitless attack upon Dublin had made upon their northern brethren. Their discouragement was accompanied by the same symptoms of division: false or exaggerated reports of the cruelties committed by the catholics upon the protestants of the southern counties, alarmed the presbyterians, who thought themselves betrayed, and that the patriotic struggle in which they had engaged had degenerated into a war of religion; they accepted an amnesty, after which their principal leaders were tried and put to death.

The victory of the English government over the insurgents of Leinster and Ulster destroyed the Irish Union, and, in great measure, its spirit; men of different sect and origin had scarce anything further in common than their disgust at the existing state of things, and the hope of a French invasion. On the news of the late insurrections, the Executive Directory of France had, at length, yielded to the intreaties of the Irish agents, and granted them some troops, who landed in the west of Ireland a month after all was at an end in the north, east, and south. These succours consisted of about fifteen hundred men of the army of Italy and of that of the Rhine, commanded by general Humber. They entered Killala, a little town of Mayo, and after making all the English garrison prisoners, unfurled the green flag of the United Irishmen. The general, in his proclamations, promised a republican constitution under the protection of France, and invited all the people, without distinction of religion, to join him. But in this district, which had given birth to the first societies of Orangemen, the protestants were, in general, fanatic foes of the papists, and devoted to the government: few of them complied with the invitation of the French, the greater number hiding themselves or taking to flight. The catholics, on the contrary, came in great numbers, and despite all that was said at the time of the irreligion of the French, the priests did not hesitate to declare for them, and, with all their powers of persuasion, urged their parishioners to take up arms. Several of these ecclesiastics had been driven from France by the revolutionary persecutions, yet these were as ready as the rest to fraternize with the soldiers. One of them went so far as to offer his chapel for a guardhouse. New patriotic songs were composed in which the French words, ça ira, en avant! were mixed up in English verses, with old Irish burthens.

The French and their allies marched southwards. Entering Ballina, they found in the market-place a man hanging from a gibbet, for having distributed insurgent proclamations; all the soldiers, one after the other, gave the corpse the republican salute. The first encounter took place near Castlebar, where the English troops were completely defeated, and, in the following night, fires lighted on all the hills gave the signal of insurrection to the population between Castlebar and the sea. The plan of the French was to march as rapidly as possible upon Dublin, collecting on their way the Irish volunteers; but the discord which reigned between the protestants and the catholics of the west rendered the number of these volunteers much less than it would have been in the eastern provinces.

While general Humber's fifteen hundred men were advancing into the country, their position becoming hourly more difficult, from the non-extension, in a proportionate degree, of the insurrection, thirty thousand English troops were marching against them from different points. The general manœuvred for some time to prevent their junction, but, obliged to fight a decisive battle at Ballinamuck, he capitulated for himself and his men, without any stipulations in favour of the insurgents, who retreated alone to Killala, where they endeavoured to defend themselves. They could not maintain the post; the town was taken and plundered by the royal troops, who, after having massacred a great number of Irish, drove the remainder into the neighbouring mountains and forests. Some of them formed bands there, and carried on a sort of guerilla warfare; others, to escape judicial pursuit, lived in caverns which they never quitted, and whither their relations brought them food. Most of those who could not conceal themselves in this way were hanged or shot.

Amidst the disunion of the different Irish sects and parties, their old hatred to the English government continued to manifest itself by the assassination of its agents, in the places where the insurrection had manifested itself, and elsewhere by partial revolts, which broke out a year later. In general, all classes of the population had their eyes fixed upon France: at the victories of the French they rejoiced, at those of the English they mourned. Their hope was that France would not give peace to England, without stipulating expressly for the independence of Ireland: they retained this hope up to the treaty of Amiens. The publication of this treaty created universal dejection among them. Two months after the conclusion of the peace, many refused to credit it, and said, impatiently: "Is it possible that the French have become Orangemen?" The English ministry profited by the general depression to tighten the political bond between Ireland and England by the abolition of the ancient Irish parliament. Although this parliament had never done much good to the country, men of all parties clung to it as a last sign of national existence, and the project of uniting England and Ireland under one legislature displeased even those who had assisted the government against the insurgents of 1798. They combined their discontent with that of the people, and assembled to remonstrate; but their opposition extended no further.

There is now but one parliament for the three united kingdoms, and it is from this assembly, the immense majority of which are English, that Ireland awaits the measures and laws that are to pacify her. After many years of vain solicitations, after many menaces of insurrection, one of her numerous wounds has been healed, by the emancipation of the catholics, who may now exercise public functions and sit in the united parliament; but many other grave questions remain to be settled. The exorbitant privileges of the Anglican church, the changes violently operated in property by wholesale confiscations and spoliations, and lastly, beyond all the quarrels of race, of sect and of party, the supreme question, that of the national independence and the Repeal of the Union between Ireland and England; such are the causes whence, sooner or later, may again arise the sad scenes of 1798. Meantime, the misery of the lower population, hereditary hatred, and a permanent hostility to the agents of authority, multiply crime and outrage, and convert a fertile country, whose people are naturally sociable and intellectual, into the most uninhabitable spot in Europe.

V. THE ANGLO-NORMANS AND THE ENGLISH BY RACE.

Poitevin courtiers in England—Alliance between the Saxons and Normans—League of the barons against king John—Magna Charta—Expulsion of the foreigners—Louis of France called in by the Anglo-Norman barons—Retreat of the French—Return of the Poitevins—Second insurrection of the Anglo-Norman barons—Simon de Montfort—His popularity—Language of the Anglo-Norman aristocracy—State of the higher classes of England—Impressment of aitisans—Labourers—State of the land—Peasants or cottagers in England—Great fermentation among the peasants—Political writings circulated in the country districts—Insurrection of the peasants—The insurgents march upon London—Their first demand—Their conduct in London—Their interview with Richard II.—The insurgents quit London—Wat Tyler and John Ball—Murder of Wat Tyler—The king deceives the insurgents—Dispersion and terror of the insurgents—Alarm of the gentry throughout England—Proclamation of Richard II.—Termination of the peasants' insurrection—Things remain in their former state—Individual enfranchisements—Separation of the parliament into two chambers—Position of the commons in the parliament—French the language of the court and the nobility—French literature in England—Revival of English poetry—Character of the new English language—The Norman idiom becomes extinct in England—Dissolution of the Norman society—Remnant of the distinction between the two races.

After the conquest of Anjou and Poitou by king Philip-Augustus, many men of these two countries, and even those who had conspired against the Anglo-Norman domination, conspired against the French, and allied themselves with king John. This monarch gave them no efficacious aid; all he could do for those who had exposed themselves to persecution on the part of the king of France, by intriguing or taking up arms against him, was to give them an asylum and a welcome in England. Thither repaired, from necessity or from choice, a great number of these emigrants, intellectual, adroit, insinuating men, like all the southern Gauls, and better fitted to please a king than the Normans, generally more slow-witted and of less pliant temperament. The Poitevins, accordingly, speedily attained infinite favour at the court of England, and even supplanted the old aristocracy in the good graces of king John. He distributed among them all the offices and fiefs at his disposal, and even, under various pretexts, deprived several rich Normans of their posts in favour of these new comers. He married them to the heiresses who were under his wardship, according to the feudal law, and made them guardians of rich orphans under age.

The preference thus manifested by the king for foreigners, whose ever-increasing avidity drove him to greater exactions than all his predecessors had committed, and to usurp unprecedented powers over persons and property, indisposed all the Anglo-Normans towards him. The new courtiers, feeling the precariousness of their position, hastened to amass all they could, and made demand upon demand. In the exercise of their public functions, they were more eager for gain than had been any former functionaries; and, by their daily vexations, rendered themselves as odious to the Saxon citizens and serfs as they already were to the nobles of Norman origin. They levied on the domains the king had given them more aids and taxes than any lord had ever demanded, and exercised more rigorously the right of toll on the bridges and highroads, seizing the horses and goods of the merchants, and only paying them, says an old historian, in tallages and mockery. Thus they harassed, at once and almost equally, the two races of men who inhabited England, and who, since their violent approximation, had not as yet experienced any one suffering, or sympathy, or aversion, in common.

The hatred to the Poitevins and the other favourites of the king, brought together, for the first time, two classes of men, hitherto, as a general rule, standing apart from each other. Here we may date the birth of a new national spirit, common to all born on English soil. All, in fact, without distinction of origin, are termed natives, by the cotemporary authors, who, echoing the popular rumour, impute to king John the design of expelling, if not of exterminating the people of England, and giving their estates to foreigners. These exaggerated alarms were, perhaps, even more strongly felt by English burghers and farmers than by the lords and barons of Norman race, who yet were alone really interested in destroying the foreign influence, and in forcing king John to revert to his old friends and countrymen.

Thus, in the commencement of his reign, John was in a position closely resembling that of the Saxon king Edward, on his return from Normandy. He menaced the rich and noble of England, or, at least, gave them reason to think themselves menaced, with a sort of conquest, operated, without apparent violence, in favour of foreigners, whose presence wounded, at the same time, their national pride and their interests. Under these circumstances, the barons of England adopted against the courtiers from Poitou and Guienne, and against the king who preferred them to his old liegemen, the same course that the Anglo-Saxons had adopted against Edward and his Norman favourites—that of revolt and war. After having signified to John, as their ultimatum, a charter of Henry I., determining the limits of the royal prerogative, on his refusal to keep within the legal limits that his predecessors had recognised, the barons solemnly renounced their oath of fealty, and defied the king, the manner at this period of declaring mortal war. They elected for their chief, Robert Fitz-Walter, who took the title of Marshal of the army of God and of holy church, and acted, in this insurrection, the part played by the Saxon Godwin, in that of 1052.

Fear of the gradual operation, in favour of Poitevin priests, of the ecclesiastical deprivations with which the Norman conquest had, at one blow, struck the entire clergy of English race, and at the same time, a sort of patriotic enthusiasm, added the Anglo-Norman bishops and priests to the party of the barons against king John, though this king was then in high favour with the pope. He had renewed to the holy see the public profession of vassalage made by Henry II. after the murder of Thomas Beket; but this act of humility, far from being as useful to the cause of John as it had been to that of his father, only served to bring down upon him public contempt, and the reproaches even of the clergy, who felt themselves endangered in their dearest interests, the stability of their offices and possessions. Abandoned by the Anglo-Normans, king John had not, like Henry I., the art of raising in his favour the English by origin, who, besides, no longer constituted a national body capable of aiding, en masse, either party. The burghers and serfs immediately depending on the barons, were far more numerous than those of the king; and, as to the inhabitants of the great towns, though they enjoyed privileges and franchises granted by the royal power, yet a natural sympathy drew them to that side which comprehended the majority of their countrymen. The city of London declared itself for those who unfurled their banners against the foreign favourites, and the king suddenly found himself left with no other supporters of his cause, than men born out of England, Poitevins, Gascons, and Flemings, commanded by Savari de Mauléon, Geoffroy de Bouteville, and Gautier de Buck.

John, alarmed at seeing in his adversaries' ranks all the zealous asserters of the independence of the country, whether as sons of the conquerors or as native English, subscribed the conditions required by the revolted barons. The conference took place in a large meadow called Runnymede, between Staines and Windsor, where both armies encamped; the demands of the insurgents having been discussed, were drawn up in a charter, which John confirmed by his seal. The special object of this charter was to deprive the king of that branch of his power by means of which he had fostered and enriched men of foreign birth at the expense of the Anglo-Normans. The population of English race was not forgotten in the treaty of peace which its allies of the other race formed with the king. Repeatedly, during the civil war, the old popular demand for the good laws of king Edward had figured in the manifestoes, which claimed, in the name of the English barons, the maintenance of the feudal liberties; but it was not, as under Henry I., the Saxon laws which the charter of the Norman king guaranteed to the descendants of the Saxons. It would seem, on the contrary, that they who drew up this memorable act, desired formally to abolish the distinction between the two races, and to have in England merely various classes of one people, all, to the very lowest, entitled to justice and protection from the common law of the land.

The charter of king John, since called Magna Charta, secured the rights of liberty and property of the classes of

Magna Charta.

John, by the grace of God, King of England, Lord of Ireland, Duke of Normandy and Aquitaine, and Earl of Anjou, to the Archbishops, Bishops, Abbots, Earls, Barons, Justiciaries of the Forests, Sheriffs, Governors, and Officers, and to all Bailiffs, and others his faithful subjects, greeting. Know ye, that we, in the presence of God, and for the health of our soul, and the souls of all our ancestors and heirs, and to the honour of God and the exaltation of his Holy Church, and amendment of our Kingdom, by advice of our venerable Fathers, Stephen, Archbishop of Canterbury, Primate of all England and Cardinal of the Holy Roman Church, Henry, Archbishop of Dublin, William, Bishop of London, Peter of Winchester, Jocelin of Bath and Glastonbury,

Hugh of Lincoln, Walter of Worcester, William of Coventry, Benedict of Rochester, Bishops, and Master Pandulph, the Pope's Sub-Deacon and ancient Servant, Brother Aymeric, Master of the Temple in England, and the Noble Persons, William Marshall, Earl of Pembroke, William, Earl of Salisbury, William, Earl of Warren, William, Earl of Arundel, Alan de Galoway, Constable of Scotland, Warin Fitz Gerald, Peter Fitz Herbert, and Hubert de Burgh, Seneschal of Poitou, Hugh de Neville, Matthew Fitz Herbert, Thomas Basset, Alan Basset, Philip Albiney, Robert de Roppell, John Marshall, John Fitz Hugh, and others our liege men, have, in the first place, granted to God, and by this our present charter confirmed, for us and our heirs for ever:

Norman origin, and at the same time established the right of the classes of Saxon origin to enjoy the ancient customs so favourable to them. It guaranteed their municipal franchises to the city of London and to all the towns of the kingdom; it modified the royal and seigneural statute-labour on the repair of castles, roads, and bridges; it gave special protection to merchants and traders, and, in suits against peasants, it prohibited the seizure of their crops or agricultural implements.

The principal article, if not as to ultimate results, at least in reference to the interests of the moment, was that by which the king promised to send out of the kingdom all the foreigners whom he had invited or received, and all his foreign troops. This article seems to have been received with great joy by all the people of England, without distinction of origin; perhaps, indeed, the English by race attached higher importance to it than to all the rest. That hatred of foreign domination which for a century and a half past had vainly fermented in men's souls, impotent against the order of things established by the Norman conquest, was let loose against the new comers whom king John had enriched and laden with honours. From the moment in which their expulsion was legally pronounced, every Saxon lent his aid to execute the decree; the more noted foreigners were besieged in their houses, and upon their retreat their domains were pillaged. The peasants stopped on the roads all whom public report, right or wrong, indicated as foreigners. They called upon them to pronounce some English words, or, at all events, a sentence of the mixed language employed by the nobles in conversing with the inferior population; and when the suspected person was convicted of inability to speak either Saxon or Anglo-Norman, or to pronounce these languages with the accent of southern Gaul, he was maltreated, despoiled, and imprisoned without scruple, whether knight, priest, or monk. "It was a sad thing," says a contemporary author, "for the friends of the foreigners to see their confusion, and the ignominy with which they were overwhelmed."

After having, against his will, and in bad faith, signed the charter, king John retired to the Isle of Wight, to await in security the occasion to resume the war. He solicited of the pope and obtained a dispensation from the oath he had sworn to the barons, and the excommunication of those who remained in arms to enforce his observance of his word. But no bishop in England consenting to promulgate this sentence, it remained without effect. The king, with what money he had left, hired a fresh body of Brabançons, who found means to land on the southern coast, and who, by their skill and military discipline, gained at first some advantages over the irregular army of the confederate barons and burghers. Thereupon, the former, fearing to lose all the fruit of their victory, resolved, like the king, to obtain foreign aid: they addressed themselves to Philip-Augustus, and offered to give his son Louis the crown of England, if he would come to them at the head of a good army. The treaty was concluded; and young Louis arrived in England with forces enough to counterbalance those of king John.

The entire conformity of language which then existed between the French and the Anglo-Norman barons necessarily modified, with the latter, the distrust and dislike ever inspired by a foreign chief; but it was different with the mass of the people, who, in reference to language, had no more affinity with the French than with the Poitevins. This dissonance, combined with the spirit of jealousy which speedily manifested itself between the Normans and their auxiliaries, rendered the support of the king of France more prejudicial than useful to the barons. Germs of dissolution were beginning to develop themselves in this party, when king John died, laden with the hatred and contempt of the entire population of England, without distinction of race or condition, actuated by which, the historians of the period, ecclesiastics though they be, give king John no credit for his constant submission to the holy see: in the history of his life they spare him no injurious epithet; and, after relating his death, they compose or transcribe epitaphs, such as these: "Who weeps, or has wept, the death of king John? hell, with all its foulness, is sullied by the soul of John."

Louis, son of Philip-Augustus, assumed, by the consent of the barons, the title of king of England; but the French who accompanied him soon conducted themselves as in a conquered country. The greater the resistance of the English to their vexations, the more harsh and grasping did they become. The accusation, so fatal to king John, was made against Louis of France: it was said that, in concert with his father, he had formed the project of exterminating or banishing all the rich and noble of England, and of replacing them by foreigners. Aroused by national interests, all parties united in favour of prince Henry, son of John, and the French, left alone, or nearly so, accepted a capitulation which gave them their lives, on condition of their immediate departure.

The kingdom of England having thus reverted to an Anglo-Norman, the charter of John was confirmed, and another, called the Forest Charter, giving the right of the chace to

Charta forestæ.

Made at Westminster, 10th Feb., Anno 9 Hen. III. ad 1225, and confirmed Anno 28 Edw. I. ad 1299.

Edward, by the grace of God, King of England, Lord of Ireland, and Duke of Guyan, to all to whom these presents shall come, sendeth greeting. We have seen the Charter of the Lord Henry our father, sometime King of England, concerning the Forest, in these words:

"Henry, by the grace of God, King of England, Lord of Ireland, Duke of Normandy and of Guyan, &c. as in the beginning of the Great Charter. the possessors of estates, was granted by Henry III. to the men of Norman race. But ere many years had elapsed, the new king, son of a Poitevin woman, who had again married in her own country, sent for and welcomed his uterine brothers, and many other men, who came, as in the time of king John, to seek their fortune in England. Family affection, and the easy, agreeable humour of the new Poitevin emigrants, had the same influence upon Henry III. as upon his predecessor; the great offices of the court, and the civil, military and ecclesiastical dignities, were once more heaped upon men born abroad. After the Poitevins flocked in the Provençals, because king Henry had married a daughter of the count of Provence; and after them, came Savoyards, Piedmontese, and Italians, distant relations or protégés of the queen, all attracted by the hope of wealth and advancement. Most of them attained their object, and the alarm of a new invasion of foreigners spread as rapidly and excited as much indignation as in the preceding reign. In the public complaints on the subject, the terms formerly employed by the Saxon writers, after the conquest, were repeated; it was said that, to obtain favour and fortune in England, it was only necessary not to be English.

A Poitevin, named Pierre Desroches, the favourite minister and confident of the king, when he was called upon to observe the charter of king John and the laws of England, was wont to reply: "I am no Englishman, to know aught of these charters or these laws." The confederation of the barons and burghers was renewed in an assembly held in London, at which the principal citizens swore to will all that the barons should will, and to adhere firmly to their laws. Shortly afterwards, most of the bishops, earls, barons, and knights of England, having held a council at Oxford, leagued together for the execution of the charters and the expulsion of the foreigners, by a solemn treaty, drawn up in French, and containing the following passage: "We make known to all, that we have sworn upon the holy gospel, and are bound together by this oath, and promise in good faith that each and all of us will aid one another against all men; and if any go counter to this, we shall hold him our mortal foe."

Singularly enough, the army assembled on this occasion to destroy the foreign influence, was commanded by a foreigner, Simon de Montfort, a Frenchman by birth, and brother-in-law of the king. His father had acquired great military reputation and immense wealth in the crusades against the Albigenses, and he himself was not deficient either in talent or in political skill. As is almost ever the case with men who throw themselves into a party from which their interest and position would seem naturally to exclude them, he displayed more activity and determination in the struggle against Henry III. than the Norman Robert Fitz-Walter had shown in the first civil war. A stranger to the Anglo-Norman aristocracy, he seems to have had much less repugnance than they to fraternize with men of English descent; and it was he who, for the first time since the conquest, summoned the commons to deliberate on public affairs, with the bishops, barons, and knights of England.

War thus commenced once more between the men born on English soil, and the foreigners who held offices and lordships there. The Poitevins and the Provençals were those whose expulsion was most ardently pursued. It was more peculiarly against the near relations of the king and queen, such as Guillaume de Valence and Pierre de Savoie, that the hatred of all classes of the population was directed; for the native English embraced with renewed ardour the cause of the barons, and a singular monument of this alliance subsists in a popular ballad on the taking of Richard, the king's brother, and emperor elect of Germany. This ballad is the first historical document that exhibits the mixture of the Saxon and French languages, though the mixture, as yet, is but a sort of patchwork, and not a regular fusion, like that which later gave birth to modern English.

After several victories gained over the king's party, Simon de Montfort was killed in a battle, and the ancient patriotic superstition of the people was awakened in his favour. As an enemy to the foreigner, and, in the words of a contemporary, defender of the rights of legitimate property, he was honoured with the same title that popular gratitude had assigned to those who, in the time of the Norman invasion, sacrificed themselves in the defence of the country. Like them, Simon received the title of defender of the native people; it was denounced as false and wicked to call him traitor and rebel; and, in common with Thomas Beket, he was proclaimed saint and martyr. The leader of the army of the barons against Henry III. was the last man in whose favour was manifested this disposition to confound together the two enthusiasms of religion and of politics; a disposition peculiar to the English race, and which was not shared by the Anglo-Normans; for although Simon de Montfort had done far more for them than for the citizens and serfs of England, they did not sanction the beatification accorded him by the latter, and left the poor country people to visit alone the tomb of the new martyr, and seek miracles there. Such miracles were not wanting, as we learn from various legends; but as the aristocracy gave no encouragement to the popular superstition, the miracles were soon lost sight of.

Notwithstanding the esteem which Simon de Montfort had manifested towards the men of Saxon origin, an enormous distance still separated them from the sons of the Normans. The chief chaplain of the army of the barons, Robert Grosse-Tête, bishop of Lincoln, one of the most ardent promoters of the war against the king, reckoned but two languages in England, Latin for the learned, and French for the unlearned; it was in the latter tongue that, in his old age, he wrote books of piety for the use of the laity, neglecting altogether the English language and those who spoke it. The poets of the same period, even the English by birth, composed their verses in French when they sought honour and profit from them. It was only the singers of ballads and romances for the burghers and peasants, who used the pure English, or the mixed Anglo-French language, that was the ordinary means of communication between the higher and lower classes. This intermediate idiom, the gradual formation of which was a necessary result of the conquest, was at first current in the towns where the two races were more mingled together, and where the inequality of conditions was less than in the country. Here it insensibly replaced the Saxon tongue, which, now only spoken by the poorest and rudest classes of the nation, fell as much beneath the new Anglo-Norman idiom as this was beneath the French, the language of the court, of the baronage, and of all who had any pretensions to refinement of manners.

The rich citizens of the great towns, and more especially those of London, sought, from interest or vanity, by Frenchisizing their language more or less skilfully, to imitate the nobles and approach nearer to them; they thus early acquired the habit of saluting each other by the title of sire, and even of styling themselves barons.

The citizens of Dover, Romney, Sandwich, Hythe, and Hastings, towns of extensive commerce, which were then, as they still are, called the cinque ports, or the five ports of England par excellence, assumed, in imitation of the Londoners, the title of Norman nobility, using it corporately in their municipal acts, and individually in their private relations. But the genuine Norman barons considered this pretension outrecuidente. "It is enough to make one sick," they said, "to hear a villein call himself a baron." When the sons of the citizens arranged a tournament of their own, in some field of the suburbs, the seigneurs would send their valets and grooms to disperse them, with the intimation that skilled feats of arms did not appertain to rustics, and mealmen, and soap-sellers, such as they.

Despite this indignation of the sons of the conquerors at the resistless movement which tended to approximate to them the richest portion of the conquered population, this movement was sensibly manifested during the fourteenth century, in the towns upon which royal charters had conferred the right of substituting magistrates of their own election for the seigneural viscounts and bailiffs. In these corporate towns, the burghers, strong in their municipal organization, commanded far more respect than the inhabitants of the petty towns and hamlets, which remained immediately subject to royal authority; but a long time elapsed ere that authority paid to the citizens individually the same consideration and respect as to the body of which they were members. The magistrates of the city of London, under the reign of Edward III., admitted to the royal feasts, already participated in that respect for established authority which distinguished the Anglo-Norman race; but the same king who entertained, at the third table from his own, the lord mayor and aldermen, treated almost as a serf of the conquest every London citizen, who, neither knight nor squire, exercised any trade or mechanical art. If, for example, he desired to embellish his palace, or to signalize himself by decorating a church, instead of engaging the best painters of the city to come and work for a given sum, he issued to his master-architect an order in the following terms: "Know, that we have charged our friend, William of Walsingham, to take from our city of London as many painters as he shall need, to set them to work in our pay, and to keep them as long as they are needed; if any be refractory, let him be arrested and kept in one of our prisons, there to abide until further orders." Again, if the king conceived a fancy for music and singing after his dinner, he, in like manner, sent forth officers of his palace to bring before him the best players and singers they could find, in London or the suburbs, without any reference whatever to their own inclinations. And thus, too, on the eve of departure for the French wars, we find king Edward requiring from his chief engineer twelve hundred stoneballs for his war-machines, and authorising him to take stonemasons and other artisans, wherever he could find them, to labour in the quarries, under penalty of imprisonment.

Such was still, at the end of the fourteenth century, the condition of those whom several historians of the time call the villains of London: and as to the country villains, whom the Normans, Frenchisizing the old Saxon names, called bondes, cotiers, or cotagers, their personal sufferings were far greater than those of the burghers, and without any compensation; for they had no magistrates of their own choice, and among themselves there was no one to whom they gave the title of sire or lord. Unlike the inhabitants of the towns, their servitude was aggravated by the regularisation of their relations with the seigneurs of the manors to which they belonged; the ancient right of conquest was subdivided into a host of rights, less violent in appearance, but which involved the class of men subject to them in numberless shackles. Travellers of the fourteenth century express their astonishment at the multitude of serfs they saw in England, and at the extreme hardness of their condition in that country, compared with what it was on the continent, and even in France. The word bondage conveyed, at this period, the last degree of social misery; yet this word, to which the conquest had communicated such a meaning, was merely a simple derivative from the Anglo-Danish bond, which, before the invasion of the Normans, signified a free cultivator and father of a family living in the country; and it is in this sense that it was joined with the Saxon word hus, to indicate a head of a house, husbond, or husband, in modern English orthography.

Towards the year 1381, all those in England who were called bonds, that is to say, all the cultivators, were serfs of body and goods, obliged to pay heavy aids for the small portion of land which supported their family, and unable to quit this portion of land without the consent of the lords, whose tillage, gardening, and cartage of every kind, they were compelled to perform gratuitously. The lord might sell them with their house, their oxen, their tools, their children, and their posterity, as is thus expressed in the deeds: "Know that I have sold such a one, my naif (nativum meum), and all his progeny, born or to be born." Resentment of the misery caused by the oppression of the noble families, combined with an almost entire oblivion of the events which had elevated these families, whose members no longer distinguished themselves by the name of Normans, but by the term gentlemen, had led the peasants of England to contemplate the idea of the injustice of servitude in itself, independently of its historical origin.

In the southern counties, whose population was more numerous, and especially in Kent, the inhabitants of which had preserved a vague tradition of a treaty concluded between themselves and William the Conqueror for the maintenance of their ancient rights and liberties, great symptoms of popular agitation appeared in the commencement of the reign of Richard II. It was a time of excessive expense with the court and all the gentlemen, on account of the wars in France, which all attended at their own cost, and wherein each vied with the other in the magnificence of his train and his armour. The proprietors of the lordships and manors overwhelmed their farmers and serfs with taxes and exactions, alleging, for every fresh demand, the necessity of going to fight the French on their own ground, in order to prevent their making a descent upon England. But the peasants said: "We are taxed to aid the knights and squires of the country to defend their heritages; we are their slaves, the sheep from whom they shear the wool; all things considered, if England were conquered, we should lose much less than they."

These and similar thoughts, murmuringly exchanged on the road, when the serfs of the same or of neighbouring domains met each other on their return from labour, became, after awhile, the theme of earnest speeches, pronounced in a sort of clubs, where they collected in the evening. Some of the orators were priests, and they derived from the Bible their arguments against the social order of the period. "Good people," they said, "things may not go on in England, and shall not, until there be no more villains or gentlemen among us, but we be all equal, and the lords no more masters than we. Where is their greater worth, that they should hold us in serfage? We all come from the same father and mother, Adam and Eve. They are clothed in fine velvet and satin, lined with ermine and minever; they have meat, and spices, and good wines; we, the refuse of the straw, and for drink, water. They have ease and fine mansions, we pain and hard labour, the rain and the wind, in the open fields." Hereupon the whole assembly would exclaim tumultuously: "There shall be no more serfs; we will no longer be treated as beasts; if we work for the lords, it shall be for pay." These meetings, held in many parts of Kent and Essex, were secretly organized, and sent deputies into the neighbouring counties to seek the counsel and aid of men of the same class and opinion. A great association was thus formed for the purpose of forcing the gentlemen to renounce their privileges. A remarkable feature of the confederation is, that written pamphlets, in the form of letters, were circulated throughout the villages, recommending to the associates, in mysterious and proverbial terms, perseverance and discretion. These productions, several of which have been preserved by a contemporary author, are written in a purer English, that is to say, less mixed up with French, than are other pieces of the same period, destined for the amusement of the rich citizens. Except as facts, however, these pamphlets of the fourteenth century have nothing curious about them; the most significant of them is a letter addressed to the country people by a priest, named John Ball, which contains the following passages: "John Ball greeteth you all well, and doth give you to understand he hath rung your bell. Now right and might, will and skill; God speed every idle one; stand manfully together in truth and helping. If the end be well, then is all well." Notwithstanding the distance which then separated the condition of the peasants from that of the citizens, and more especially from that of the London citizens, the latter, it would appear, entered into close communication with the serfs of Essex, and even promised to open the gates of the city to them, and to admit them without opposition, if they would come in a body to make their demands to king Richard. This king had just entered his sixteenth year, and the peasants, full of simple good faith, and a conviction in the justice of their cause, imagined that he would enfranchise them all in a legal manner, without their needing to resort to violence. It was the constant theme of their conversations: "Let us go to the king, who is young, and show him our servitude; let us go together, and when he shall see us, he will grant us his grace of his own accord; if not, we will use other means." The association formed round London was rapidly extending, when an unforeseen incident, in compelling the associates to act before they had attained sufficient strength and organization, destroyed their hopes, and left to the progress of European civilization the gradual abolition of servitude in England.

In the year 1381, the necessities of the government, arising from the prosecution of the war and the luxury of the court, occasioned the levy of a poll-tax of twelvepence for every person, of whatever station, who had passed the age of fifteen. The collection of this tax not having produced as much as had been expected, commissioners were sent to inquire into the subject. In their examination of the noble and rich, they were courteous and considerate, but towards the lower classes they were excessively rigorous and insolent. In several villages of Essex, they went so far as an attempt to ascertain the age of young girls in an indecent manner. The indignation caused by these outrages created an insurrection, headed by a tiler, named Walter, or familiarly Wat, and surnamed, from his trade, Tyler. This movement created others, in Sussex, Bedfordshire, and Kent, of which the priest, John Ball, and one Jack Straw were appointed leaders. The three chiefs and their band, augmented on its march by all the labourers and serfs it met, proceeded towards London "to see the king," said the simpler among the insurgents, who expected everything from the mere interview. They marched, armed with iron-tipped staves, and rusty swords and axes, in disorder, but not furious, singing political songs, two verses of which have been preserved:

* When Adam delved and Eve span,

* Who was then the gentleman?

They plundered no one on their way, but, on the contrary, paid scrupulously for all they needed. The Kentish men went first to Canterbury to seize the archbishop, who was also chancellor of England; not finding him there, they continued their march, destroying the houses of the courtiers and those of the lawyers who had conducted suits brought against serfs by the nobles. They also carried off several persons whom they kept as hostages; among others a knight and his two sons; they halted on Blackheath, where they entrenched themselves in a kind of camp. They then proposed to the knight whom they had brought with them, to go as messenger from them to the king, who on the news of the insurrection had withdrawn to the Tower of London. The knight dared not refuse; taking a boat, he proceeded to the Tower, and kneeling before the king: "Most dread lord," he said, "deign to receive without displeasure the message I am fain to bring; for, dear lord, it is by force I come." "Deliver your message," answered the king; "I will hold you excused." "Sire, the commons of your kingdom intreat you to come and speak with them; they will see no one but yourself; have no fear for your safety, for they will do you no evil, and will always hold you their king; they will show you, they say, many things it is necessary for you to know, and which they have not charged me to tell you; but, dear lord, deign to give me an answer, that they may know I have been with you, for they hold my children as hostages." The king having consulted with his advisers, said "that if on the following morning the peasants would come as far as Rotherhithe, he would meet them, and speak with them." This answer greatly delighted them. They passed the night in the open air as well as they could, for they were nearly sixty thousand in number, and most of them fasted, for want of food.

Next day, the 12th of June, the king heard mass in the Tower; and then, despite the entreaties of the archbishop of Canterbury, who urged him not to compromise himself with shoeless vagabonds, he proceeded in a barge, accompanied by some knights, to the opposite shore, where about ten thousand men from the camp at Blackheath had collected. When they saw the barge approach, "they," says Froissart, "set up shouts and cries as if all the devils from hell had come in their company," which so terrified the king's escort that they intreated him not to land, and kept the barge at a distance from the bank. "What would you have?" said the king to the insurgents: "I am here to speak with you." "Land, and we will show you more readily what we would have." The earl of Salisbury, answering for the king, said: "Sirs, you are not in fit order for the king to come to you;" and the barge returned to the Tower. The insurgents went back to Blackheath, to tell their fellows what had occurred, and there was now but one cry among them: "To London, to London, let us march upon London."

They marched accordingly to London, destroying several manor-houses on their way, but without plundering them of anything: arrived at London-bridge, they found the gates closed; they demanded admission, and urged the keepers not to drive them to use violence. The mayor, William Walworth, a man of English origin, as his name indicates, wishing to ingratiate himself with the king and the gentry, was at first resolved to keep the gates shut, and to post armed men on the bridge to stop the peasants; but the citizens, especially those of the middle and lower classes, so decidedly opposed this project, that he was fain to renounce it. "Why," said they, "why are we not to admit these good folk? they are our people, and whatever they do is for us." The gate was opened, and the insurgents, over-running the city, distributed themselves among the houses in search of food, which every one readily gave them, from good will or from fear.

Those who were first satisfied, hastened to the palace of the duke of Lancaster, called the Savoy, and set fire to it, out of hatred to this lord, the king's uncle, who had recently taken an active part in the administration of public affairs. They burned all his valuable furniture, without appropriating a single article; and threw into the flames one of their party whom they detected carrying something away. Actuated by the same sentiment of political vengeance, unmixed with other passion, they put to death, with a fantastic mockery of judicial forms, several of the king's officers. They did no harm to men of the citizen and trading class, whatever their opinions, except to the Lombards and Flemings, who conducted the banks in London, under the protection of the court, and several of whom, as farmers of the taxes, had rendered themselves accomplices in the oppression of the poor. In the evening, they assembled in great numbers in Saint Catherine's-square, near the Tower, saying they would not leave the place until the king had granted them what they required; they passed the night here, from time to time sending forth loud shouts, which terrified the king and the lords in the Tower. The latter held counsel with the mayor of London as to the best course to be pursued in so pressing a danger: the mayor, who had deeply compromised himself with the insurgents, was for violent measures. He said nothing could be easier than to defeat, by a direct attack with regular forces, a set of people, running in disorder about the streets, and scarce one in ten of whom was well armed. His advice was not followed, the king preferring the counsel of those who said: "If you can appease these people by good words, it were best and most profitable; for if we begin a thing we cannot achieve, we shall never regain our ground."

In the morning, the insurgents who had passed the night in St. Catherine's-square, set themselves in motion, and declared that unless the king came to them forthwith, they would take the Tower by assault, and put to death all that were within it. The king sent word that if they would remove to Mile-end, he would meet them there without fail, and shortly after their departure he accordingly followed them, accompanied by his two brothers, by the earls of Salisbury, Warwick, and Oxford, and by several other barons. As soon as they had quitted the Tower, those insurgents who had remained in the city entered it by force, and running from chamber to chamber, seized the archbishop of Canterbury, the king's treasurer, and two other persons, whom they decapitated, and then stuck their heads upon pikes. The main body of the insurgents, numbering fifty thousand men, was assembled at Mile-end when the king arrived. At sight of the armed peasants, his two brothers and several barons were alarmed, and left him, but he, young as he was, boldly advanced, and addressing the rioters in the English tongue, said: "Good people, I am your king and sire; what want you? what would you have from me?" Those who were within hearing of what he said, answered: "We would have you free us for ever, us, our children, and our goods, so that we be no longer called serfs or held in serfage." "Be it so," said the king; "return to your houses, by villages, as you came, and only leave behind you two or three men of each place. I will have forthwith written, and sealed with my seal, letters which they shall carry with them, and which shall freely secure unto you all you ask, and I forgive you all you have done hitherto; but you must return every one of you to your houses, as I have said."

The simple people heard this speech of the young king with great joy, not imagining for a moment that he could deceive them; they promised to depart separately, and did so, quitting London by different roads. During the whole day, more than thirty clerks of the royal chancery were occupied in writing and sealing letters of enfranchisement and pardon, which they gave to the deputies of the insurgents, who departed immediately upon receiving them. These letters were in Latin, and ran thus:

"Know that, of our special grace, we have enfranchised all our lieges and subjects of the county of Kent, and of the other counties of the kingdom, and discharged and acquitted all and several of them from all bondage and serfage.

"And that, moreover, we have pardoned these said lieges and subjects their offences against us, in marching to and fro in various places, with armed men, archers, and others, as an armed force, with banners and pennons displayed."

The chiefs, and especially Wat Tyler and John Ball, more clear-sighted than the rest, had not the same confidence in the king's words and charter. They did all they could to stay the departure and dispersion of the men who had followed them, and succeeded in collecting several thousand men, with whom they remained in London, declaring that they would not quit it until they had obtained more explicit concessions, and securities for such concessions.

Their firmness produced its effect upon the lords of the court, who, not venturing as yet to employ force, advised the king to have an interview with the chiefs of the revolt in Smithfield. The peasants, having received this notification, repaired thither to await the king, who came, escorted by the mayor and aldermen of London, and by several courtiers and knights. He drew up his horse at a certain distance from the insurgents, and sent an officer to say that he was present, and that the leader who was to speak for them might advance. "That leader am I," answered Wat Tyler, and heedless of the danger to which he exposed himself, he ordered his men not to move hand or foot until he should give them a signal, and then rode boldly up to the king, approaching him so near that his horse's head touched the flank of Richard's steed. Without any obsequious forms, he proceeded explicitly to demand certain rights, the natural result of the enfranchisement of the people, namely, the right of buying and selling freely in towns and out of towns, and that right of hunting in all forests, parks, and commons, and of fishing in all waters, which the men of English race had lost at the conquest.

The king hesitated to reply; and, meantime, Wat Tyler, whether from impatience, or to show by his gestures that he was not intimidated, played with a short sword he had in his hand, and tossed it to and fro. The mayor of London, William Walworth, who rode beside the king, thinking that Wat Tyler menaced Richard, or simply carried away by passion, struck the insurgent a blow on the head with his mace, and knocked him from his horse. The king's suite surrounded him, to conceal for a moment what was passing; and a squire of Norman birth, named Philpot, dismounting, thrust his sword into Tyler's heart and killed him. The insurgents, perceiving that their chief was no longer on horseback, set themselves in motion, exclaiming: "They have slain our captain! let us kill them all!" And those who had bows, bent them to shoot upon the king and his train.

King Richard displayed extraordinary courage. He quitted his attendants, saying, "Remain, and let none follow me;" and then advanced alone towards the peasants, forming in battle array, whom he thus addressed: "My lieges, what are you doing? what want you? you have no other captain than I. Tyler was a traitor; I am your king, and will be your captain and guide; remain at peace, follow me into the fields, and I will give you what you ask."

Astonishment at this proceeding, and the impression ever produced on the masses by him who possesses the sovereign power, induced the main body of the insurgents to follow the king, as it were, by a mechanical instinct. While Richard withdrew, talking with them, the mayor hastened into the city, rung the alarm-bell, and had it cried through the streets: "They are killing the king! they are killing the king!" As the insurgents had quitted the city, the English and foreign gentlemen, and the rich citizens, who sided with the nobles, and who had remained in arms in their houses with their people, fearful of pillage, all came forth, and, several thousand in number, the majority being on horseback and completely armed, hastened towards the open fields about Islington, whither the insurgents were marching in disorder, expecting no attack. As soon as the king saw them approach, he galloped up to them, and joining their ranks, ordered an attack upon the peasants, who, taken by surprise and seized with a panic terror, fled in every direction, most of them throwing down their arms. Great carnage was made of them, and many of the fugitives, re-entering London, concealed themselves in the houses of their friends.

The armed men who, at so little risk, had routed them, returned in triumph, and the young king went to receive the felicitations of his mother, who said to him: "Hola, fair son, I have this day undergone much pain and fear for you!" "Certes, madam, I can well believe it," answered the king; "but you may now rejoice, and thank God, whom we may justly praise, seeing that I have this day recovered my kingdom of England and my inheritance which I had lost." Knights were made on this occasion, as in the great battles of the period, and the first whom Richard II. honoured with this distinction were the mayor Walworth and the squire Philpot, who had assassinated Wat Tyler. The same day, a proclamation was made, from street to street, in the king's name, ordering all who were not natives of London, or who had not lived there a complete year, to depart without delay; and setting forth that if any stranger was found therein the next morning, he should lose his head as a traitor to the king and kingdom. The insurgents who had not yet quitted the city, hereupon dispersed in every direction. John Ball and Jack Straw, knowing they should be seized if they showed themselves, remained in concealment, but they were soon discovered and taken before the royal officers, who had them beheaded and quartered. This intelligence spread around London, stayed in its march a second body of revolted serfs, who, advancing from the remoter counties, had been longer on their road; intimidated with the fate of their brethren, they turned back and dispersed.

Meantime, all the counties of England were in agitation. Around Norwich, the great landholders, gentlemen, and knights hid themselves; several earls and barons, assembled at Plymouth for an expedition to Portugal, fearing an attack from the peasants of the neighbourhood, went on board their ships, and although the weather was stormy, anchored out at sea. In the northern counties, ten thousand men rose, and the duke of Lancaster, who was then conducting a war on the borders of Scotland, hastened to conclude a truce with the Scots, and sought refuge in their country. But the turn of affairs in London soon revived the courage of the gentry in all parts; they took the field against the peasants, who were ill armed and without any place of retreat, while the assailants had their castles, wherein, the drawbridge once raised, they were secure. The royal chancery wrote, in great haste, to the castellans of cities, towns and boroughs, to guard well their fortresses, and let no one enter, under pain of death. At the same time it was everywhere announced that the king would enfranchise under his royal seal all serfs who remained quiet, which greatly diminished the excitement and energy of the people, and gave them less interest in their chiefs. The latter were arrested in various places, without much effort being made to save them: all were artisans for the most part, with no other surname than the appellation of their trade, as Thomas Baker, Jack Miller, Jack Carter, and so on.

The insurrection being completely at an end from the defeat of the insurgents, the imprisonment of the chiefs, and the relaxation of the moral bond which had united them, proclamation was made by sound of trumpet, in the towns and villages, in virtue of a letter addressed by the king to all his sheriffs, mayors and bailiffs of the kingdom, thus conceived:—

"Make proclamation, without delay, in every city, borough and market town, that all and every tenant, free or otherwise, do, without resistance, difficulty, or delay, the works, services, aids, and labour, to their lords due, according to ancient custom, and as they were wont to do before the late troubles in various counties of the kingdom;

"And rigorously prohibit them longer to delay the said services and works, or to demand, claim, or assert any liberty or privilege they did not enjoy before the said troubles.

"And whereas, at the instance and importunity of the insurgents, certain letters patent under our seal were granted to them, giving enfranchisement from all bondage and serfage to our lieges and subjects, as also, the pardon of the offences committed against us by the said lieges and subjects;

"And whereas the said letters were issued from our court, without due deliberation, and considering that the concession of the said letters manifestly tended to our great prejudice and to that of our crown, and to the expropriation of us, the prelates, lords, and barons of our realms, and of holy church;

"With the advice of our council, we, by these presents, revoke, cancel and annul the said letters, ordering further, that those who have in their possession our said charters of enfranchisement and pardon, remit and restore them to us and our council, by the fealty and allegiance they owe us, and under penalty of forfeiture of all they can forfeit to us."

Immediately after this proclamation, a body of horse traversed, in every direction, the counties inhabited by the insurgents who had obtained charters. A judge of the king's bench, Robert Tresilyan, accompanied the soldiers, and made a circuit with them of every village, publishing on his way, that all who had letters of enfranchisement and pardon must surrender them to him without delay, under penalty of military execution upon the entire body of the inhabitants. All the charters brought to him were torn and burned before the people; but, not content with these measures, he sought out the first promoters of the insurrection, and put them to death with terrible tortures, hanging some, four times over, at the corners of the town, and drawing others and throwing their entrails into the fire, while themselves yet breathed. After this, the archbishop, bishops, abbots, and barons of the kingdom, with two knights from each shire, and two burgesses from each borough town, were convoked in parliament, by letters from king Richard. The king set forth to this assembly, the grounds of his provisional revocation of the charters of enfranchisement, adding that it was for them to decide whether the peasants were to be freed or not.

"God forbid," answered the barons and knights, "we should subscribe to such charters. 'Twere better for us all to perish in one day; for of what use our lives, if we lose our heritages."

The act of parliament ratifying the measures already taken, was drawn up in French, having probably been discussed in that language. We do not know what share the deputies of the towns took in the debate, or even whether they were present at it; for although they were convoked, in the same form as the knights of the shire, they often assembled separately, or only remained in the common chamber during the discussion of the taxes to be imposed on merchandise and commerce. However, whatever may have been the part taken in the parliament of 1381, by the borough-members, the affection of the commoner class towards the cause of the insurgents is beyond a doubt. In many a place did they repeat the words of the Londoners: "These are our people, and whatever they do, is for us." All who, not being noble or gentle, censured the insurrection, were ill regarded by public opinion, and this opinion was so decided, that a contemporary poet, Gower, who had enriched himself by composing French verses for the court, deemed it an act of courage to publish a satire, in which the insurgents were ridiculed. He declares that this cause has numerous and important partisans, whose hatred may be dangerous, but that he will rather expose himself to the danger than abstain from speaking the truth. It will thus seem probable, that, if the rebellion, begun by peasants and shoeless vagabonds, had not been so soon quelled, persons of a higher class might have assumed the conduct of it, and, with better means of success, might have effected its object. Then indeed, ere long, as a contemporary historian expresses it, toute noblesse et gentillesse might have disappeared from England.

Instead of this, matters remained in the order established by the conquest, and the serfs, after their defeat, continued to be treated in the terms of the proclamation, which said to them, "Villains you were and are, and in bondage you shall remain."

Notwithstanding the failure of the open attempt they had made, at once to free themselves from servitude and to destroy the distinction of condition which had succeeded the distinction of race, the natural movement tending gradually to render this distinction less marked, still continued, and individual enfranchisements, which had commenced long before this period, became more frequent. The idea of the injustice of servitude in itself, and, whatever its origin, ancient or recent, the grand idea, that had formed the bond of the conspiracy of 1381, and to which the instinct of liberty had elevated the peasants before it reached the gentry, at length came upon the latter.

In the moments when reflection becomes calmer and more profound, when the voice of interest or avarice is hushed before that of reason, in moments of domestic sorrow, of sickness, and of the peril of death, the nobles repented of possessing serfs, as of a thing not agreeable to God, who had created all men in his own image. Numerous acts of enfranchisement, drawn up in the fourteenth and fifteenth centuries, have this preamble: "As God, in the beginning, made all men free by nature, and afterwards human laws placed certain men under the yoke of servitude, we hold it to be a pious and meritorious thing in the eyes of God to deliver such persons as are subject to us in villainage, and to enfranchise them entirely from such services. Know then, that we have emancipated and delivered from all yoke of servitude, so and so, our naïfs of such a manor, themselves, and their children, born and to be born."

These acts, very frequent in the period we have referred to, and of which we find no instance in preceding centuries, indicate the birth of a new public spirit opposed to the violent results of the conquest, and which appears to have been developed, at once among the sons of the Normans and among the English, at the epoch, when from the minds of both had disappeared every distinct tradition of the historical origin of their respective position. Thus the great insurrection of the villains in 1381, would seem the last term of the series of Saxon revolts, and the first of another order of political movements. The rebellions of the peasants which afterwards broke out, had not the same character of simplicity in their motives, or of precision in their object. The conviction of the absolute injustice of servitude, and of the unlawfulness of the seigneural power, was not their sole moving cause; passing interests or opinions had more or less share in them. Jack Cade, who in 1448 acted the same part as Wat Tyler in 1381, did not, like the latter, put himself forward as simply the representative of the rights of the commons against the gentlemen; but, connecting his cause and the popular cause with the aristocratic factions which then divided England, he represented himself to be a member of the royal family, unjustly excluded from the throne. The influence of this imposture upon the minds of the people in the northern counties and in that same county of Kent, which, seventy years before, had taken for its captains, tilers, bakers, and carters, proves that a rapid fusion had been taking place between the political interests of the different classes of the nation, and that a particular order of ideas and of sympathies was no longer connected, in a fixed manner, with a particular social condition.

At about the same period, and under the influence of the same circumstances, the parliament of England took the form under which it has become celebrated in modern times, permanently separating into two assemblies, the one composed of the high clergy, the earls and barons, convoked by special letters from the king; the other of the petty feudatories or knights of the shire, and the burgesses of the towns, elected by their peers. This new combination, which brought together the merchants, almost all of them of English origin, and the feudal tenants, Normans by birth, or accounted such from the possession of their fiefs and their military titles, was a great step towards the destruction of the ancient distinction by race, and the establishment of an order of things wherein all the families should be classed solely by their political importance and territorial wealth. Still, notwithstanding the sort of equality which the meeting of the burgesses and knights in a chamber of their own seemed to establish between these two classes of men, that which had been heretofore inferior retained for awhile the token of its inferiority. It was present at the debates on political matters, on peace and war, taking no part in them, or withdrew altogether during these discussions, coming in merely to vote the taxes and subsidies demanded by the king from personal property.

The assessment of these imposts had, in former times, been the sole reason for summoning the burgesses of English race to the presence of the Anglo-Norman kings; the richer among them, as among the Jews, were rather ordered than invited to appear before their lord. They received the command to attend the king at London, and met him where they could find him—in his palace, in the open street, or in the suburbs on a hunting party. But the barons and knights whom the king assembled to counsel him, and to discuss with him the affairs which regarded the community, or, as it was then termed, the cominalté of the kingdom, were received in a very different manner, were treated with all dignity and honour. They found at court everything prepared for their reception: courtoisie, entertainments, knightly display, and royal pomp. After the fêtes, they had with the king, what the old writers call grave conferences on the state of the country; whilst the business of the deputies of towns was limited to the giving their adhesion, as briefly as possible, to the taxes propounded by the barons of the exchequer.

The habit gradually adopted by the kings of convoking the villains of their cities and boroughs, no longer in an irregular, casual manner, according to the wants of the moment, but at fixed and periodical times, when they held their court three times a year, made but slight difference in the ancient practice, in other respects, of which the reader has observed a striking instance in the time of Henry II. The forms employed in reference to the burgesses became, it is true, less contemptuous, when they were no longer summoned merely before the king, but were convoked in full parliament, among the prelates, barons, and knights. Yet the object of their admission into this assembly, where they occupied the lowest benches, was still a simple vote of money; and the taxes demanded from them still exceeded those required from the clergy and landholders, even when the assessment was a general one. For example, when the knights granted a twentieth or fifteenth of their revenues, the grant made by the burgesses was a tenth or a seventh. This difference was always made, whether the deputies of towns assembled separately, in the place where parliament was held, whether they were convoked in another town, or whether they assembled with the knights of the shire, elected like themselves, while the high barons received their letters of summons personally from the king. The commons, accordingly, in the fifteenth century, were by no means eager to attend parliament, and the towns themselves, far from regarding their electoral privilege as a precious right, often solicited exemption from it. The collection of the public acts of England contains many petitions to this effect, with several royal charters in favour of particular towns, maliciously constrained, say these charters, to send men to parliament.

The business of the knights and that of the burgesses, seated in the same chamber, differed according to their origin and social condition. The field of political discussion was boundless for the former; for the latter, it was limited to questions of imposts on commerce, on imports and exports. But the extension attained in the fifteenth century by commercial and financial measures, naturally augmented the parliamentary importance of the burgesses; they acquired by degrees, in monetary matters, a greater participation in public affairs than the titled portion of the lower chamber or even than the upper house. This revolution, the result of the general progress of industry and commerce, soon produced another; it banished from the lower chamber, called the house of the commonalty or commons, the French language, which the burgesses understood and spoke very imperfectly.

French was still, in England, at the end of the fifteenth century, the official language of all the political bodies; the king, the bishops, judges, earls, and barons spoke it, and it was the tongue which the children of the nobles acquired from the cradle. Preserved for three centuries and a half amidst a people who spoke another tongue, the language of the English aristocracy had remained far behind the progress made, at this same period, by the French of the continent. There was something antiquated and incorrect about it, certain phrases peculiar to the provincial dialect of Normandy; and the manner of pronouncing it, as far as we can judge from the orthography of the old acts, greatly resembled the accent of Lower Normandy. Moreover, this accent, brought into England, had acquired in the course of time a certain tinge of Saxon pronunciation. The speech of the Anglo-Normans differed from that of Normandy, by a stronger articulation of particular syllables, and, more especially, of the final consonants.

One cause of the rapid decline of the French language and poetry in England, was the total separation of this country from Normandy, in consequence of the conquest of the latter by Philip Augustus. The emigration of the literary men and poets of the langue d'oui to the court of the Anglo-Norman kings, became, after this event, less easy and less frequent. No longer sustained by the example and imitation of those who came from the continent to teach them the new forms of the beau langage, the Norman poets resident in England lost, during the thirteenth century, much of their former grace and facility. The nobles and courtiers delighted in poetry, but disdaining themselves to write verse or compose books, the trouveres who sang in royal and noble halls were fain to seek pupils among the sons of the traders and inferior clergy of English origin, and speaking English in their ordinary conversation. It was naturally more or less a matter of effort with these men to express their ideas and feelings in another language than that of their infancy, and this effort at once impeded the perfection of their works, and rendered them less numerous. From the end of the thirteenth century, most of those who, whether in the towns or in the cloister, felt a taste and talent for literature, sought to treat in the English language, the historical or imaginative subjects that had hitherto been only clothed in the Norman language.

A great many attempts of this kind appeared in succession during the first half of the fourteenth century. Some poets of this epoch, those chiefly who enjoyed or sought the favour of the higher classes of society, composed French verses; others, contenting themselves with the approbation of the middle classes, wrote for them in their own language; others, combining the two languages in one poem, alternated them by couplets, and sometimes even by verses. Gradually the scarcity of good French books composed in England became such, that the higher orders were obliged to obtain from France the romances or tales in verse with which they beguiled the long evenings, and the ballads which enlivened their banquets and courtly entertainments. But the war of rivalry which at the same period arose between France and England, inspiring the nobles of the two nations with a mutual aversion, lessened for the Anglo-Normans the attraction of the literature imported from France, and constrained the gentlemen, tenaciously delicate on the point of national honour, to content themselves with the perusal of the works of native authors. Those, indeed, who resided at London, and frequented the court, were still enabled to satisfy their taste for the poetry and language of their ancestors; but the lords and knights who lived on their estates, were fain, under penalty of utter ennui, to give admission to English story-tellers and ballad-singers, hitherto disdained as only fit to amuse the burghers and villains.

These popular writers distinguished themselves from those who, at the same period, worked for the nobles, by an especial attachment to country people, farmers, millers, or innkeepers. The writers in the French tongue ordinarily treated this class of persons with supreme contempt, giving them no place whatever in their poetical narrations, whose personæ were all individuals of high degree, powerful barons and noble dames, damoiselles and gentle knights. The English poets, on the contrary, took for the subjects of their mery tales, plebeian adventures, such as those of Piers Ploughman, and historiettes, such as those we find occupying so large a space in the works of Chaucer. Another characteristic common to nearly all these poets, is a sort of national distaste for the language of the conquest:—

* "Right is that English, English understand,

* That was born in England,"

says one of them. Chaucer, one of the greatest wits of his time, slily contrasts the polished French of the court of France, with the antiquated and incorrect Anglo-Norman dialect, in drawing a portrait of an abbess of high degree:—

* "And French she spake, full fair and featously,

* After the school of Stratford atte Bow;

* For French of Paris was to her unknow."

Bad as it was, the French of the English nobles had, at least, the advantage of being spoken and pronounced in an uniform manner, while the new English language, composed of Norman and Saxon words, and idioms promiscuously put together, varied from one county to another, and even from town to town. This language, which took its commencement in England from the first years of the conquest, was successively augmented with all the French barbarisms used by the English, and all the Saxon barbarisms used by the Normans, in their endeavours to understand one another. Every person, according to his fancy or the degree of his knowledge of the two idioms, borrowed phrases from them, and arbitrarily joined together the first words that came into his head. It was a general aim with people to introduce into their conversation as much French as they could remember, by way of imitating the great, and appearing themselves distinguished personages. This mania, which, according to an author of the fourteenth century, had taken possession even of the peasants, rendered it difficult to write the English of the period in a way to be generally understood. Notwithstanding the merit of his poems, Chaucer expresses a fear that the multiplicity of the provincial dialects will prevent their being appreciated, out of London, and prays God grant that his book may be understood by all who read it.

Some years before this, a statute of Edward III. had, not ordered, as several historians say, but simply permitted causes to be pleaded in English before the civil tribunals. The constantly increasing multiplicity of commercial transactions and of suits arising out of them, had rendered this change more necessary under that reign than before, when parties to a suit, who did not understand French, were fain to remain in ignorance of the proceedings. But in the suits against gentlemen before the high court of parliament, which took cognizance of treason, or before the courts of chivalry, which decided affairs of honour, the ancient official language continued to be employed. And, further, the custom was retained in all the courts, of pronouncing sentence in French, and of drawing up the record in that language. In general, it was a habit with the lawyers, of every class, even while pleading in English, to introduce every moment French words and phrases, as Ah! sire, je vous jure; Ah! de par Dieu! A ce j'assente! and other exclamations, with which Chaucer never fails to interlard their discourse, when he introduces them in his works.

It was during the first half of the fifteenth century, that the English language, gradually coming more into favour as a literary language, ended by entirely superseding French, except with the great lords, who, ere they entirely abandoned the idiom of their ancestors, diverted themselves equally with works in both languages. The proof of the equality which the language of the commons had now attained, is furnished by the public acts, which from about the year 1400, are indifferently drawn up in French and in English. The first statute of the house of commons in the English language bears date 1425; we do not know whether the upper house retained beyond this period the idiom of the aristocracy and of the conquest, but, from the year 1450, we find no more French acts on the statute book of England. Some letters, however, written in French by the nobles, and a few French epitaphs, are posterior to this epoch. Certain passages of the historians prove also, that, towards the close of the fifteenth century, the kings of England and the lords of their court understood and spoke French perfectly well;" but this knowledge was now merely a personal accomplishment with them, and not a necessity. French was no longer the first language lisped by the children of the nobles; it simply became for them, in common with the ancient languages and the continental tongues, the object of voluntary study, and the complement to a good education.

Thus, about four centuries after the conquest of England by the Normans, disappeared the difference of language, which, in combination with the inequality of social condition, had marked the separation of the families descended from the one or the other race. This entire fusion of the two primitive idioms, a certain indication of the union of the races, was perhaps accelerated, in the fifteenth century, by the long and sanguinary civil war of the houses of York and Lancaster. In destroying a great number of noble families, in creating among them political hatred and hereditary rivalry, in obliging them to form party alliances with people of inferior condition, this war powerfully contributed to the dissolution of the aristocratic society which the conquest had founded. During well nigh a century, the mortality among the men who bore Norman names was immense, and their places were necessarily filled by their vassals, their servants, and the burghers of the other race. The numerous pretenders to the crown, and the kings created by one party and treated as usurpers by the other, in their earnestness to obtain friends, had no time to be nice in the choice, or to observe the old distinctions of birth and condition. The great territorial domains founded by the invasion, and perpetuated thus far in the Norman families, now passed into other hands, by confiscation or purchase, while the late possessors, expropriated or banished, sought a refuge and begged their bread in foreign courts, in France, in Burgundy, in Flanders, in all the countries whence their ancestors had departed for the conquest of England.

We may assign the reign of Henry VII. as the epoch when the distinction of ranks ceased to correspond with that of races, as the commencement of the society now existing in England. This society, composed of new elements, has still in great measure retained the forms of the old; the Norman titles remain, and, very singularly, the surnames of several extinct families have themselves become titles, conferred by letters patent of the king, with that of earl or baron. The successor of Henry VII. was the last king who prefixed to his ordinances the old form, "Henry, eighth of the name since the conquest;" but up to the present day the kings of England preserve the custom of employing the old Norman language, when they sanction or reject legislative bills: Le roy le veult; le roy s'advisera, le roy remercie ses loyaux subjects, accepte leur benevolence, et aynsi le veult. These forms, which seem, after the lapse of seven hundred years, to connect English royalty with its foreign origin, have yet, ever since the fifteenth century been heard, year after year, in the English parliament, without revolting the feelings of any one. It is the same with the genealogies and titles that carry back the existence of certain noble families to the invasion of William the Bastard, and the great territorial properties to the division made at that epoch.

No popular tradition relative to the division of the inhabitants of England into two hostile peoples existing, and the distinction between the two elements of which their present language is formed having disappeared, no political passions connect themselves with these now forgotten facts. Normans and Saxons exist only in history; and as the latter fill the less brilliant part, the mass of English readers, little versed in the national antiquities, willingly deceive themselves as to their origin, and regard the sixty thousand companions of William the Conqueror as the common ancestors of all the people of England. Thus a London shopkeeper and a Yorkshire farmer say: "our Norman ancestors," just as would a Percy, a Darcy, a Bagot, or a Byron. The Norman, Poitevin, or Gascon names are no longer exclusively, as in the fourteenth century, the tokens of rank, power, and great estates, and it were inconsistent with reason to apply to the present times the old verses quoted in the epigraph to this work. Yet a fact, certain in itself and readily verified, is, that of an equal number of family names, taken, on the one hand, from the class of nobles, of country squires, gentlemen, and, on the other, from the trading, artizan, and agricultural classes, the names of French aspect are found in far greater proportion among the former. Such is all that now remains of the ancient separation of the races, and only within this limit can we now repeat the words of the old chronicler of Gloucester:

Of the Normans be these high men, that be of this land,

No. I. Cruelties exercised by the Norman-Lords in their Castles.

Hi suencten suithe the wrecce men of the land mid castelweorces. Tha the castles waren maked. Tha fylden hi mid deoules and yuele men. Tha namen hi tha men the hi wenden that ani god hefden. bathe be nihtes and be dæies. carl-men and wimmen. and diden heom in prisun efter gold and syluer. And pined heom untellendlice pining. for ne wæren næure nan martyrs swa pined alse hi wæron. Me henged up bi the fet and smoked heome mid ful smoke. Me henged bi the thumbes other bi the hefed. and hengen bryniges on her fet. Me dide enotted strenges abuton here hæued and uurythen to that it gæde to the hærnes. Hi diden heom in quarterne thar nadres and snakes and pades wæron inne. and drapen heom swa. Sume hi diden in crucet hus. that is in an ceste that was scort and nareu. and undep. and dide scærpe stanes ther inne. and threngde the man thær inne. Tha hi bræcon alle the limes. In mani of the castles wæron lof and grim. that wæron sachenteges that twa other thre men hadden onoh to bæron onne. That was swa maced that is fæstned to an beom. And diden an scærp iren abuton tha mannes throte and his hals. that he ne mihte nowiderwardes ne sitten, ne lien. ne slepen. oc bæron al that iren. Mani thusen hi drapen mid hungær. I ne canne. and ne mai, tellen all the wundes. ne alle the pines. that hi diden wrecce men on this land. and that lastede tha xix. wintre wile Stephne was king. and æure it was uuerse and uuerse. Hi læiden gæildes on the tunes æureu wile. and clepeden it tenserie. Tha the wrecce men ne hadden nan more to given. Tha ræueden hi and brendon alle the tunes, that wel thu mihtes faren all a dæis fare sculdest thu neure finden man in tune sittende. ne land tiled. Tha was corn dære. and flec. and cæse. and butere. for nan ne wæs o the land. Wrecce men sturuen of hungær, sume jeden on ælmes the waren sum wile rice men. Sum flugen ut of lande. Wes næure gæt mare wreccehed on land. ne næure hethen men werse ne diden than hi diden. For oner sithon ne forbaren hi nouther circe ne circeiærd. oc nam al the god that thar inne was. and brenden sythen the circe hand altegædere. Ne hi ne forbaren biscopes land. ne abbotes. ne preostes. ac ræueden muneces. and clerekes. and æuric man other the ouer myhte. Gif twa men other thre coman ridend to an tun al the tunscipe flugæn for heom. wenden that hi wæron ræueres. The biscopes and lered men heom cursede æure oc was heom naht thar of. for hi wæron all for cursæd and for suoren and forloren. Was sæ me tilede. the erthe ne bar nan corn. For the land was all for don mild suilce dædes. And hi sæden openlice. that Crist slep. and his halechen. Suilc and mare thanne we cunnen sæin we tholenden xix. wintre for ure sinnes.

No. II. War Song of the Troubadour Bertrand de Born, Seigneur de Hautefort.

*

o Be m play lo douz temps de pascor

o Que fai fuelhas e flors venir;

o E play mi quant aug la baudor

o Del auzels que fan retentir

o Lor chan per lo boscatge;

o E play me quan vey sus els pratz

o Tendaz e pavallos fermatz;

o E plai m'en mon coratge

o Quan vey per campanhas rengatz

o Cavalliers ab cavals armatz.

*

o E play mi quan li corredor

o Fan las gens e'ls avers fugir;

o E plai me quan vey aprop lor

o Gran ren d'armatz ensems brugir;

o Et ai gran alegratge,

o Quan vey fortz castelbs assetjatz,

o E murs fondre e derocatz

o E vey l'ost pel ribatge

o Qu'es tot entorn claus de fossatz

o Ab lissas de fortz pals serratz.

*

o Atressi me play de bon senhor

o Quant es primiers à l'envazir.

o Ab caval armat, ses temor;

o C'aissi fai los sieus enardir

o Ab valen vassallatge;

o E quant el es el camp intratz,

o Quascus deu esser assermatz,

o E segr'el d'agradatge

o Quar nulhs hom non es ren presatz

o Tro qu'a manhs colps pres e donatz.

*

o Lansas e brans, elms de color,

o Escutz traucar e desguarnir

o Veyrem a l'intrar de l'estor,

o E manhs vassalhs ensems ferir

o Don anaran a ratge

o Cavalhs dels mortz e dels nafratz;

o E ja pus l'estorn er mesclatz,

o Negus hom d'aut paratge

o Non pens mas d'asclar caps e bratz,

o Que mais val mortz que vius sobratz.

*

o Ie us dic que tau no m'a a sabor

o Manjars ni buere ni dormii,

o Cum a quant aug cridar: A lor!

o D'ambas las partz; et aug agnir

*

o Cavals voitz per l'ombratge,

o Et aug cridar: Aidatz! Aidatz!

o E vei cazer per los fossatz

*

o Paucs e grans per l'erbatge,

o E vei los mortz que pels costatz

o An los tronsons outre passatz.

*

o Baros, metetz en gatge

o Castels e vilas et ciutatz,

o Enans q'usquecs no us guerreiatz.

*

o Papiol d'agradatge

o Ad Oc e No t'en vai viatz,

o Dic li que trop estan en patz

No. III. History of the Marriage of Gilbert Beket, Father of Archbishop Thomas; Fragment of a Life of the Archbishop, by a Contemporary.

Pater ejus (Thomæ) Gilbertus, cognomento Beket, civis Londoniensis, mater vero Matildis fuit, ambo generis et divitiarum splendore suis nequaquam concivibus inferiores. Quibus e regione morum ingenuitas et piæ conversationis innocentia, longe intelleximus, præminebant. Justitiæ quidem actibus insistebant, et sine crimine et querela, ut traditur, conversati sunt. Nunc autem in principio restat de ipsius patris et matris conjugio inserendum, ut exinde advertatur quanta cura et pietate a solis ortu usque ad occasum tam diversos genere et conditione congregavit in unum prædestinatio mirifica Salvatoris, de quorum sane felici progenie sponsam suam Ecclesiam per mundum universum prævidit sublimari et triumphaliter decorari.

Præfatus ergo Gilbertus, ætate juvenis, crucem Dominicam causa pœnitentiæ votivæ arripuit Jerosolimam iturus, quendam de familia sua Ricardum nomine secum assumens, ipso solo pro serviente contentus. Quo tandem prospere venientibus, inter christianos et gentiles insidiis habitis loca sancta orationis causa cum aliis introrsus quam licuit visitantes, pariter capti sunt et cathenati, atque in carcere cujusdam Admiraldi, præclari principis paganorum, detenti, ut singulis diebus victum laboribus impositis quodammodo compararent. Qui Gilbertus per annum integrum et dimidium in captivitate sclavorum more serviens, cum honoratior cæteris atque præstantior haberetur, in oculis Admiraldi præ omnibus gratiam et favorem invenit, in tantum quod frequenter coram eo, sed tamen in vinculis, ad mensam veniret, discumbentes visitaret, et invicem de terrarum notitiis ac gentium diversarum moribus et ritu conferrent. Multa eciam ob gratiam ipsius collata sunt suis beneficia concaptivis, procurante insimul privatim, in quantum licuit, filia ejusdem Admiraldi, puella admodum curialis et decora, unica patris sui, quæ utique miro affectu ipsum Gilbertum, prout patebit inferius, diligebat.

Quadam autem die, nacta oportunitate puella liberius cum eo loquendi, inquisivit ab eo de quanam terra et civitate extiterat oriundus, de fide eciam, de religione et conversatione Christianorum, et quæ forent credentium spes et seculorum præmia futurorum. Qui cum responderet quod Anglicus esset et Londoniarum incola civitatis, inquisitaque de fide, prout melius noverat, exposuisset, consequenter et ipsa ab eo sciscitavit, dicens: Num mortem libenter pro Deo tuo et fide Christi quam profiteris conservanda intrepide exciperes? Libentissime, inquit, pro Deo meo moriar. Quo audito, puella mox quasi ex virtute verbi tota mutata, profitetur se Christianam fieri ipsius ob causam, dummodo ipsam in conjugem accipere in sua fide sponderet. Tacuit attamen ille secum deliberans, adquiescere statim noluit, timens nimirum fallaciam mulieris, unde tergiversando de die in diem prorogavit, nolens cito precibus illius præstare consensum. Cumque puella vehementer affligeretur, et in dies ob dilationem, ut moris est mulierum, plus anxia efficeretur, Gilbertus interim cum suis concaptivis de fuga cogitans, post annum et dimidium, nocte quadam, diruptis cathenis a carcere aufugerunt, totumque noctis residuum, quousque fines Christianorum attigissent, conciti peregerunt. Mane autem facto, præpositus operum, more solito, ut eos ad opera mitteret consueta, a carcere fracto ipsos evasos vidisset, in manu valida eos insequitur, donec, Christianorum terminis obstantibus, omni spe jam fraudatus reverteretur non parum iratus. Puella vero hæc audiens memorata, ex illa hora de profectione sua et fuga post ipsos cogitavit. Cumque super hoc diebus ac noctibus mire cogitativa efficeretur, et in meditatione sua exardesceret cautius evadendi, nocte quadam, universis sompno depressis, sola, nullo sciente, assumpto secum modico quid ad viaticum necessario, ut expeditius iter ageret satis attemptando, multiplici se discrimini tradidit fugiendi, nichil curans de universis hæreditario jure sibi pertinentibus, sufficientiam sibi reputans divitiarum, si desiderium suum pro voto posset complere.

O mirandam nimis hujus mulieris tam audaciam quam amorem tanta difficilia et ardua præsumentis! Non hæsitavit, cum esset tam ingenti gloria paternæ possessionis nobilitanda, irrecupabiliter eadem carere. Non trepidavit fragilis et delicata paupertatem pœnalem subire, nec per tot terrarum spacia et naufragantis maris innumera periculorum genera dubitavit sola discurrere, dum unius hominis tam remoti et ignoti quæreret amorem. Cum etiam nec de vitâ ipsius vel inventione securitatem haberet, imo necdum secura de conjugio etsi quæsitum hominem reperiret. Proficiscens igitur paganismum prospere pertransivit, et cum quibusdam peregrinis et mercatoribus repatriantibus, qui linguam ejus noverant, versus Angliam navigabat. Cumque, transactis cunctis periculis ob iter obviantibus, Angliam applicuisset, atque a suis comitibus jam dissociata fuisset, nichil aliud interrogare pro itinere noverat nisi tantum Londonia, Londonia.

Quo tandem perveniente, quasi bestia erratica per plateas civitatis incedens, et obviantes quosque exploratoris more circumspiciens, derisu omnibus habebatur, et maxime pueris in eam intendentibus et per vicos incedentibus ob disparem ipsius habitum et linguam simul admirantibus. Contigit antem quod sic per plateas et vicos incedens, contra domum præfati Gilberti ubi manebat, in solempniori scilicet et frequentiori civitatis foro, ubi nunc in honore sancti Thomæ hospitalis domus constructa est, casu fortuito deveniret; in qua quidem ab introeuntibus divulgatum est, quod quædam juvencula mulier quasi idiota, pueris eam et aliis sequentibus et irridentibus, evagaret. Audiens autem Ricardus, serviens Gilberti superius memoratus, quasi ad spectaculum cum cæteris et ipse accurrit. Qui cum propius accedens eam agnosceret, statim cum summa festinatione ad dominum suum recurrit, narrans ei secreto hanc filiam Admiraldi esse, ad quam admirationis causa intuendam hominum copia confluebat. Quo audito, supra modum admirans nec credere valens, eo quod impossibile ut sic eveniret omnino videretur, dominus Ricardo non potuit fidem dare, donec ipso in juramento diutius persistente, minus incredulus aliquantulum redderetur.

Cogitans tandem causam adventus ipsius, arbitratus est tamen consultius ei alibi providendum quam eam secum in domo propria retinendam, jussit Ricardo ut ad quandam matronam viduam ei vicinam eam adduceret, quæ ipsam tanquam filiam suam in omnibus custodiret. Quem cum videret puella et eum agnosceret, mox quasi mortua cecidit, jaceus in extasi resupina. Cumque ab illa mentis alienatione expergefacta et ad se reversa resideret, ad dictam matronam Ricardus eam adduxit, sicut ejus dominus imperarat. Gilbertus de adventu puellæ secum pertractans, cœpit animus fluctuare per diversa, et cogitationes concipiens invicem repugnantes, incidit in mentem ejus episcopum Londoniensem consulendum adire apud sanctum Paulum, ubi illo tempore sex episcopi aderant super arduis regni negotiis vel ecclesiæ tractaturi. Quibus coram positus cum veritatem rer gestæ superius memoratæ per ordinem exponeret, mox cicestrensis episcopus præ cæteris propheticam prorumpens in vocem, indubitanter asseruit, hanc vocationem non humanam sed potius fuisse divinam, et necessario magnifici operis prolem edituram, cujus sanctitate et labore universalis ecclesia esset ad Christi gloriam sublimanda. Cæteris autem episcopis qui aderant in hanc sententiam concordantibus, ut idem Gilbertus pueilam, dummodo baptizari vellet, duceret in uxorem; addneta est statuta die in crastino, in ecclesia beati Pauli in doctorum episcoporum præsentia, ubi et baptisterium competenter extitit præparatum, in quo et illa debuerat baptizari.

Cumque interrogaretur in medio posita, prout mos ecclesiæ exigit, per sæpedictum Ricardum communem eorum interpretem, si vellet baptizari, respondit. "Hujus rei causa a valde remotis partibus huc adveni, dummodo Gilbertus michi voluerit in conjugio copulari." Baptizatur igitur puella, sex episcopis grandi cum solempnitate baptismi sacramentum agentibus, eo quod præclari sanguims esset fœmina, imo vocationis clarioris ex gratia admodum divina; Gilberto traditur mox ab episcopis in conjugem cum celebritate conjugali, de fide catholica prius breviter instructa. Quam cum ad propria duceret, prima nocte mutuæ in unum concordiæ, sanctum Thomam, futurum Cantuariensem archiepiscopum et martyrem, genuerunt.

No. IV. Old Ballad on the Captivity and Marriage of Gilbert Beket.

*

o In London was young Beichan born,

o He longed strange countries for to see;

o But he was taen by a savage moor,

o Who handled him right cruellie;

*

o For he viewed the fashions of that land,

o Their way of worship viewed he;

o But to Mahound, or Termagant,

o Would Beichan never bend a knee.

*

o So, in every shoulder they've putten a bore;

o In every bore they've putten a tree;

o And they have made him trail the wine

o And spices on his fair bodie.

*

o They've casten him in a dungeon deep,

o Where he could neither hear nor see

o For seven years they kept him there,

o Till he for hunger's like to die.

*

o This Moor he had but as daughter,

o Her name was called Susie Pye;

o And every day as she took the air,

o Near Beichan's prison she passed by.

*

o And bonny, meek, and mild was she,

o Though she was come of an ill kin;

o And oft she sigh'd, she knew not why,

o For him that lay the dungeon in.

*

o O so it fell, upon a day

o She heard voung Beichan sadly sing;

o And ay and ever in her ears

o The tones of hopeless sorrow ring.

*

o "My hounds they all go masterless;

o My hawks they fiee from tree to tree;

o My younger brother will heir my land;

o Fair England again I'll never see!"

*

o The doleful sound, from under ground,

o Died slowly on her listening ear;

o But let her listen ever so long,

o The never a word more could she hear.

*

o And all night long no rest she got,

o Young Beichan's song for thinking on;

o She's stown the keys from her father's head,

o And to the prison strong is gone.

*

o And she has open'd the prison doors,

o I wot she open'd two or three,

o Ere she could come young Beichan at,

o He was locked up so curiouslie.

*

o But when she came young Beichan before,

o Sore wonder'd he that may to see;

o He took her for some fair captive:

o "Fair lady, I pray, of what countrie?"

*

o "O, have ye any lands," she said,

o "Or castles in your own countrie,

o That ye could give to a lady fair,

o From prison strong to set you free.

*

o —"Near London town I have a hall,

o With other castles two or three;

o I'll give them all to the lady fair:

o That out of prison will set me free."

*

o "Give me the truth of your right hand,

o The truth of it give unto me,

o That for seven years ye'll no lady wed,

o Unless it be along with me."

*

o —"I'll give thee the truth of my right hand,

o The truth of it I'll freely gie,

o That for seven years I'll stay unwed,

o For the kindness thou dost show to me."

*

o And she has brib'd the proud warder

o Wi' mickle gold and white monie;

o She's gotten the keys of the prison strong,

o And she has set young Beichan free.

*

o She's gi'en him to eat the good spicecake,

o She's gi'en him to drink the blood redwine;

o She's bidden him sometimes think on her,

o That sae kindly freed him out of pine.

*

o She's broken a ring from her finger,

o And to Beichan half of it gave she:

o "Keep it, to mind you of that love

o The lady bore that set you free.

*

o "And set your foot on good ship-board,

o And haste ye back to your own countrie,

o And before that seven years have an end,

o Come back again, love, and marry me."

*

o But long ere seven years had an end,

o She long'd full sore her love to see;

o For ever a voice within her breast

o Said, "Beichan has broke his vow to thee."

o So she's set her foot on good ship-board,

o And turn'd her back on her own countrie.

*

o She sailed east, she sailed west,

o Till to fair England's shore she came

o Where a bonny shepherd she espied,

o Feeding his sheep upon the plain,

*

o "What news, what news, thou bonny shepherd?

o What news hast thou to tell to me?"

o —"Such news I hear ladie," he says,

o "The like was never in this countrie;

*

o "There is a wedding in yonder hall

o Has lasted these thirty days and three,

o Young Beichan will not bed with his bride

o For love of one that's yond the sea."

*

o She's put her hand in her pocket,

o Gi'en him the gold an' white monie:

o "Hae, take ye that, my bonny boy,

o For the good news thou tell'st to me."

*

o When she came to young Beichan's gate,

o She tirled softly, at the pin;

o So ready was the proud porter

o To open and let this lady in.

*

o "Is this young Beichan's hall," she said,

o "Or is that noble lord within?"

o "Yea, he's in the hall among them all,

o And this is the day o' his weddin."

*

o —"And has he wed anither love?

o And has he clean forgotten me?"

o And, sighin', said that gay ladie,

o "I wish I were in my own countrie."

*

o And she has taen her gay gold ring,

o That with her love she brake so free;

o Says, "Gie him that, ye proud porter,

o And bid the bridegroom speak to me."

*

o When the porter came his lord before,

o He kneeled down low on his knee.

o "What aileth thee, my proud porter,

o Thou art so full of courtesie?"

*

o —"I've been porter at your gates,

o It's thirty long years now and three;

o But there stands a lady at them now,

o The like o' her did I never see;

*

o "For on every finger she has a ring,

o And on her mid finger she has three;

o And as meickle gold aboon her brow

o As would buy an earldom to me."

*

o It's out then spok the bride's mother,

o Aye and an angry woman was shee;

o "Ye might have excepted our bonny bride;

o And twa or three of our companie."

*

o —"O hold your tongue, thou brid's mother,

o Of all your folly let me be;

o She's ten times fairer nor the bride,

o And all that's in your companie.

*

o "She begs one sheave of your white bread,

o But and a cup of your red wine;

o And to remember the lady's love,

o That last reliev'd you out of pine."

*

o —"O well-a day!" said Beichan then,

o "That I so soon have married thee!

o For it can be none but Susie Pye,

o That sailed the sea for love of me."

*

o And quickly hied he down the stari;

o Of fifteen steps he made but three;

o He's ta'en his bonny love in arms,

o And kist, and kist her tenderlie.

*

o —"O hae ye ta'en anither bride?

o And hae ye quite forgotten me?

o And hae ye quite forgotten her,

o That gave you life and libertie?"

*

o She looked o'er her left shoulder,

o To hide the tears stood in her e'e:

o "Now fare thee well, young Beichan," she says,

o "I'll try to think no more on thee."

*

o —"O never, never, Susie Pye,

o For surely this can never be;

o Nor ever shall I wed but her

o That's done and dree'd so much for me."

o Then out and spake the forenoon bride:

o "My lord, your love it changeth soon;

o This morning I was made your bride,

o And another chose ere it be noon."

*

o —"O hold thy tongue, thou forenoon bride;

o Ye're ne'er a whit the worse for me;

o And whan ye return to your own countrie,

o A double dower I'll send with thee."

*

o He's taen Susie Pye by the white hand.

o And gently led her up and down,

o And ay as he kist her red rosy lips,

o "Ye're welcome, jewel, to your own."

*

o He's taen her by the milk white hand,

o And led her to yon fountain stane;

o He's changed her name from Susie Pye,

o And he's call'd her his bonny love, lady Jane.

No. V. Particulars of the worldly Life of Thomas Becket, before his elevation to the

Bishopric, from William Fitzstephen, his Secretary.

Cancellarii domus et mensa communis erat omnibus cujuscunque ordinis indigentibus ad curiam vementibus, qui probi vel essent, vel esse viderentur. Nulla fere die comedebat absque comitibus et baronibus, quos ipsemet invitabat. Jusserat quaque die, novo stramine vel fœno in hieme, novis scirpis vel frondibus virentibus in æstate, sterni hospitium suum, ut militum multitudinem, quam scamna capere non poterant, area munda et læta reciperet; ne vestes eorum pretiosæ, vel pulcliræ eorum camisiæ, ex areæ sorde maculam contraherent. Vasis aureis et argenteis domus ejus renitebat, ferculis et potibus pretiosis abundabat, ut si quæ esculenta vel poculenta commendaret raritas, emptores ejus nulla eorum comparandorum repellere deberet caritas......

Cancellario, et regni Angliæ et regnorum vicinorum magnates liberos suos servituros mittebant, quos ipse honesta nutritura et doctrina instituit, et cingulo donatos militiæ, ad patres et propinquos cum honore remittebat, aliquos retinebat. Rex ipse dominus suus, filium suum, hæredem regni, ei nutriundum commendavit: quem ipse cum coætaneis sibi multis filns nobilium, et debita eorum omnium sequela, et magistris, et servitoribus propriis, quo dignum erat honore, secum habuit. . . .

Cancellario homagium infiniti nobiles et milites faciebant; quos ipse, salva fide domini regis, recipiebat, et ut suos patrocinio fovebat.

Transfretaturus interdum sex aut plures naves in sua habebat velificatione, nullumque qui transfretare vellet, remanere sinebat: appulsus gubernatores suos et nautas ad placitum eorum remunerabat. Nulla fere dies effluebat ei, qua non ipse aliqua magna largiretur donaria, equos, aves, vestimenta, auream vel argenteam supellectilem, vel monetam. Sic nimirum scriptum est: quidam erogant propria, et semper abundant: alii rapiunt aliena, et curtæ semper abest rei. Tantamque habebat cancellarius donandi gratiam, ut amor et deliciæ totius orbis latini reputaretur. Utcunque erat ætas, ita quemque facetus adoptabat......

Cancellarius regi clero, militiæ et populo erat acceptissimus, ob ipsius dotes virtutum, animi magnitudinem, meritorum insignia, quæ animo ejus inhæserant. Pertractatis seriis, colludebant rex et ipse, tanquam coætanei pueruli, in aula, in ecclesia, in concessu, in equitando. Una dierum coequitabant in strata Lundoniæ; stridebat deformis hiems: eminus aspexit rex venientem senem, pauperem, veste trita et tenui; et ait cancellario: Videsue illum?—Cancellarius: Video.—Rex. Quam pauper, quam debilis, quam nudus! Numquidne magna esset eleemosyna dare ei crassam et calidam capam?—Cancellarius: Ingens equidem; et ad hujusmodi animum et oculum, rex, habere deberes. Interea pauper adest; rex substitit, et cancellarius cum eo. Rex placide compellat pauperem, et quærit, si capam bonam vellet habere. Pauper, nesciens illos esse, putabat jocum non seria agi. Rex cancellario: Equidem tu hanc ingentem liabebis eleemosynam; et injectis ad capitiume jus manibus, capam, quam novam et optimam de scarlata et grysio indutus erat, rex cancellario auferre, ille retinere laborabat. Fit ibi motus et tumultus magnus: divites et milites, qui eos sequebantur, mirati accelerant scire quænam esset tam subita inter eos causa concertandi: non fuit, qui diceret: intentus erat uterque manibus suis, ut aliquando quasi casuri viderentur.

Aliquandiu reluctatus cancellarius, sustinuit regem vincere, capam sibi inclinato detrahere, et pauperi donare. Tunc primum rex sociis suis acta narrat: risus omnium ingens: fuerunt, qui cancellario capas et pallia sua porrigerent. Cum capa cancellarii pauper senex abit, præter spem locupletatus, lætatus et Deo gratias agens.

Aliquotiensque ad hospitium cancellarii rex comedebat, tum ludendi causa, tum gratia videndi quæ de ejus domo et mensa narrabantur. Rex veniebat aliquando equo admisso in hospitium cancellarii sedentis ad mensam: aliquando sagitta in manu, rediens venatu, vel iturus in nemus; aliquando bibebat, et viso cancellario recedebat; aliquando saliens ultra mensam, assidebat et comedebat. Magis unanimes et amici nunquam duo alii fuerunt temporibus christianis.

Fuit aliquando gravi tentus infirmitate cancellarius Rothomagi apud sanctum Gervasium. Venerunt eum duo reges simul videre, rex Francorum et rex Anglorum, dominus suus. Tandem dispositus ad sanitatem, et convalescens, una dierum sedit ad ludum scaccorum, indutus capa manicata. Intravit eum visitare Aschetinus, prior Leghcestriæ, veniens a curia regis, qui tunc erat in Gasconia; qui liberius eum allocutus, ausu familiaritatis, ait: Quld est hoc quod capa manicata utimini? Hæc vestis magis illorum est, qui accipitres portant: vos vero estis persona ecclesiastica, una singularitate, sed plures dignitate: Cantuariæ archidiaconus, decanus Hastingæ, præpositus Buverlaci, canonicus ibi et ibi; procurator etiam archiepiscopatus; et sicut rumor in curia frequens est, archiepiscopus eritis. Cancellarius respondit, inter cætera, ad verbum illud: Equidem tres tales pauperes agnosco in Anglia sacerdotes, quorum cujuslibet ad archiepiscopatum promotionem magis optarem quam meam: nam ego, si forte promoverer, ita dominum meum regem intus et in cute novi, necesse haberem, aut ipsius gratiam amittere, aut Domini Dei, quod absit, servitium postponere: quod et post ita contigit...

Quinquaginta duos clericos cancellarius in obsequio suo habebat: quorum plurimi in suo erant comitatu, curabant episcopatus et abbatias vacantes, aut ejus proprios honores ecclesiasticos.

Deliberavit quandoque rex Anglorum cum cancellario et aliis quibusdam regni sui magnatibus, petere a rege Francorum filiam ejus Margaretam matrimonio copulandam filio suo Henrico. Placuit consilium Hæc siquidem regum et magnorum virorum magna est confœderatio. Ad tantam petitionem tanto principi faciendam quis mittendus erat, nisi cancellarius? Eligitur: assentitur. Igitur cancellarius rem, personas et officium suum attendens, et se tantæ rei commetiens, juxta illud poeticum:

* "Metire quod audes: nuptialiter se instruit

* Qui nuptias mittitur conciliare futuras."

Parat ostendere et effundere luxus anglicani opulentiam, ut apud omnes et in omnibus honoretur persona mittentis in missi, et missi sua in se. Circiter ducentos in equis secum habuit de familia sua, milites, clericos, dapiferos, servientes, armigeros, nobilium filios, militantes ei, et armis omnes instructos. Omnes isti et omnis earum sequela, novo festivo fulgebant ornatu vestium, quisque pro modo suo. Habuit etiam viginti quatuor mutatori avestimentorum, omnia fere donanda, et in transmarinis relinquenda, et omnem elegantiam varii, grysii, et pellium peregrinarum, palliorum quoque et tapetum, quibus thalamus et lectus episcopi hospitio recepti ornabantur. Habuit secum canes, aves, omne genus quo reges utuntur et divites. Habuit in comitatu suo octo bigas curriles; unamquamque bigam quinque equi trahebant, dextrariis corpore et robore similes; quisque equus suum sibi deputatum habebat fortem juvenem nova tunica succinctum, euntem cum biga; ipsaque biga suum veredum et custodem. Duæ bigæ solam cervisiam trahebant, factam in aquæ decoctione ex adipe frumenti, in cadis ferratis, donandam Francis. Habebat cancellarii capella bigam suam; camera suam, expensa suam, coquina suam; portabant aliæ esculentorum et poculentorum aliquid; aliæ dorsalia tapeta, saccos cum vestibus nocturnis, sarcinas et impedimenta. Habuit duodecim summarios. Octo scrinia cancellarii continebant supellectilem, auream scilicet et argenteam, vasculos, cullulos, pateras, ciphos, cuppas, urceolas, pelves, salina, cochlearia. cultellas. parapsides. Aliæ coffræ et clitellæ cancellarii continebant monetam, æs plurimum cotidianis ejus impensis et donis sufficiens, et vestes ejus, et libros aliquot et hujusmodi. Unus summarius capellæ sacra vasa, et altaris ornamenta, et libros portabat, cæterorum præambulus. Quisque summariorum suum habebat agasonem, qualem et qualiter decuit instructum. Quæque etiam biga habebat canem alligatum vel supra vel subtus, magnum, fortem et terribilem, qui ursum vel leonem dormiturus videretur. Sed et supra quemque summarium erat vel simia caudata, vel humani simulator simius oris. In ingressu gallicanorum villarum et castrorum, primi veniebant garciones pedites quasi ducenti quinquagenta, gregatim euntes sex vel deni vel plures simul, aliquid lingua sua pro more patriæ suæ cantantes. Sequebantui aliquo intervallo canes copulati et leporarii in loris et laxis suis, cum concuratoribus et sequacibus suis. Post modicum stridebant ad lapides platearum illæ bigæ ferratæ, magnis coriis animalium consutis coopertæ. Sequebantur ad modicam distantiam summarii, agasonibus, positis genibus super clunes summariorum, equitantibus. Aliqui Franci, ab domibus sui segressi, ad tantum strepitum quærebant cujus esset familia. Aiunt illi, quod cancellarius regis Anglorum ad dominum regem Franciæ missus veniret. Dicunt Franci: Mirabilis est ipse rex Anglorum, cujus cancellarius talis et totus incedit. Sequuntur post summarios armigeri, militum portantes scuta, et trahentes dextrarios; inde alii armigeri; dehinc ephebi; deinde qui aves portabant; postea dapiferi, et magistri, et ministri domus cancellarii; deinde milites et clerici, omnes bini et bini equitantes, postremo, cancellarius, et aliqui familiares ejus circa eum.

Appulsus in transmarinis, statim præmiserat domino regi Francorum cancellarius mandans, quod ad eum veniret. Venit per castrum Medlenti. Rescripserat ei rex Francorum, quod occurreret ei Parisius, et qua die. Rex itaque volens cancellarium procurare; sicut nobilitatis et consuetudinis gallicanorum regum est, omnem mortalem ad curiam Franciæ venientem, quamdiu in curia fuerit, procurare, edicto Parisius dato prohibuerat, ne quis aliquid cancellario, vel suis emptoribus venderet. Quo præcognito, cancellarius præmiserat suos ad fora vicina, Lamaci, Corboili, Pontis Isarei, sancti Dionysn, qui sibi emerent panes, et carnes, et pisces, vina, et cibaria, in abundantia, mutato, suppressisque nominibus, habitu. Et cum Parisius domi Templi hospitium habitaturus ingrederetur, occurrerunt ei sui dicentes, quod hospitium omnibus bonis instructum ad moram triduanam inveniret, quaque die mille hominibus procurandis. Equidem in divitiis regis Salomonis legitur quot animalium carnes quotidianis ejus impensis sufficerent. Equidem una die, anguillarum unum solum ferculum cancellarii centum solidis sterlingorum emptum fuit. quod omni patriæ notum, etiam loco proverbii multo tempore multis in ore erat. De aliis ejus ferculis et impensis sileo. Ex hoc uno intelligi potest, quod mensa cancellarii sumptuosa et sufficiens fuit.

Qualiter eum dominus rex Francorum et nobiles illi Franci honoraverunt, qualiter ipse vicissim eos, et præterea qua comitate suscepit scholares Parisius et magistros scholarum et cives scholarium angligenarum creditores, dicere non sufficio. Legitur de Hannibale, quod, post interfectum Hasdrubalem, Romam nuncios miserit, dicens eis: Ite, et omnem mortalem explete pecunia. Idem forte legit et curavit cancellarius, omnem nobilem Francum, baronem militem, servitorem regis vel reginæ regis Francorum, magistros scholarum, scholares civium nobiliores, muneribus suis explebat. Omnia sua vasa aurea et argentea donavit, omnia mutatoria vestimentorum: illi pallium, illi capam griseam, illi pelliciam, illi pallefridum, illi dextrarium. Quid plura? Supra omnem hominem suam gratiam adeptus est, legatione sua feliciter functus est, propositum assecutus est; quod petiit ei concessum est. In reditu suo Wydonem de La Val, regis Angliæ impugnatorem, patriæ stratæque publicæ deprædatorem, cepit, et conjectum in vincula apud castrum Novi Fori incarceravit. Unde hoc modo se cancellarius Thomas in pacis studio et tempore habuit.

Quid de eo in bellicis negotiis occupato loquar? In exercitu et obsidione Tholosæ, ubi tota Anglia, Normannia, Aquitania, Andegavis, Britannia, Scotia, inpræsidium regis Angliæ, militarem manum et fortitudinem bellicam emisit, cancellarius de propria familia lectam manum militum septingentos milites habebat Et quidem si ejus paritum esset consilio, urbem Tholosam, et regem Franciæ, qui favore sororis comitissæ Constantiæ se immiserat, sed et improvide sine exercitu et manu forti, invasissent et cepissent, tantus erat regis Anglorum exercitus. Sed vana superstitione et reverentia rex tentus consilio aliorum, super urbem, in qua esset dominus suus rex Franciæ, irruere noluit: dicente in contrarium cancellario, quod personam domini rex Francorum ibi deposuisset, eo quod supra conventa hostem se ei opposuisset. Non multo post, vocata et congregata venit in urbem militia regis Francorum; et rex Angliæ cum rege Scotiæ et omni exercitu suo, inops voti et inefficax propositi, rediit, capta tamen prius urbe Cadurcio. et plurimis castris, in vicinia Tholosæ, quæ erant comitis Tholosæ, et suffraganeorum ejus, vel quæ comes Tholosæ regis Angliæ fautoribus prius abstulerat. Ad quæ omnia retinenda post reditum regis Angliæ, comitibus omnibus recusantibus, solus cancellarius cum sua familia, et solo Henrico de Essexia, constabullario et barone regis, remansit. Et postea tria castra munitissima, et quæ inexpugnabilia videbantur, ipsemet lorica indutus et galea, cum suis in manu forti cepit. Sed et Garunnam cum militari manu transiit supra hostes; confirmataque in regis obsequium tota illa provincia, gratiosus et honoratus rediit.

Postmodum autem in guerra regis Francorum et domini sui regis Anglorum in Marchia, ad communem terminum terrarum suarum inter Gisorcium et Triam et Curceles, cancellarius, præter propriæ familiæ septingentos equites, alios mille ducentos stipendarios milites, habebat quatuor millia servientium, per unam quadragenam. Et cuique militi, quaque die, dabantur ad equos et armigeros procuiandos tres solidi illius monetæ, ipsique milites omnes ad mensam cancellarii erant. Ipsemet clericus cum esset, cum valente milite Francorum Engelramno, de Triœ regione subditis equo calcaribus veniente armato, lancea demissa et equo admisso congressus, ipsum equo dejecit, et dextrarium lucrifecit. Et in toto regis Anglorum exercitu semper primi erant milites cancellarii, semper majora audebant, semper præclare faciebant, eo docente, ducente, eo hortante cavere eductui, canere receptui in lituis suis ductilibus, quos in exercitu suo proprios, sed universo hinc inde exercitur habebat notissimos. Undeipse hostis etiam et expugnator regis Francorum, et terræ ipsius in igne et gladio depopulator, in magnam pervenit gratiam ipsius regis Francorum et magnatum totius Galliæ, suffragantibus ei meritis fider præstantis et nobilitatis suæ notissimæ: quam gratiam postmodum tempore opportuno sibi rex exhibuit. Virtus quippe et in hoste laudatur.

No. VI. Letter of John of Salisbury to Becket, respecting the Views of the king of France, the earl of Flanders, and the court of Rome, concerning him.

Venerabili domino et pairi carissimo Thomæ, Dei gratia Cantuariensi archiepiscopo et Anglorum primati, suus Joannes Saresberiensis, salutem et felices ad vota successus. Ex quo partes attigi cismarinas, visus sum mihi sensisse lenioris auræ temperiem, et detumescentibus procellis tempestatum, cum gaudio miratus sum rerum ubique copiam, quietemque et lætitiam populorum. Egredientem vero de navi, servientes comitis Gisnensis ex mandato ejus, procurante Arnulpho, nepote ipsius, honorifice susceperunt; et mihi et meis domum et terram comitis pro vestra reverentia exponentes, liberum ab omni consuetudinis onere, perduxerunt fere ad Sanctum-Audomarum. Quo cum venissem, procurante quodam Marsilio monacho, qui apud Thilleham et Irulege morari consuevit, in domo Sancti-Bertini honestissime receptus sum, et patenter intellexi quod ecclesia illa ad honorem Cantuariensis ecclesiæ et vestrum exposita est; et si placet, tam comiti quam monachis, oblata vobis opportunitate, gratias referatis. Exinde cum venissem Atrebatum, comitem Philippum apud Exclusam castrum, a quo tyrannus Iprensis tam longa obsidione exclusus est, esse audivi. Illuc itaque divertens, Domino misericorditer iter meum in omnibus prosperante, non longe a strata publica obvium habui quem quærebam. Ut enim, more divitum, quos oblectat hoc nugandi genus, in avibus cœli luderet, fluvios, stagna, paludes et scaturigines fontium peragrans circuibat. Gavisus est se invenisse hominem a quo fideliter audiret Angliæ statum, et ego magis, quia eum mihi Deus obtulerat, ita ut sine multo viæ dispendio mandatum vestrum exsequerer. De rege et proceribus multa percunctatus est; sed ego temperavi responsum, ut me nec de mendacio conscientia reprehendat, nec temeritatem meam in his quæ ad regein spectant quisquam possit arguere. Vestias vero angustias audrens vobis compassus est, auxiliumque promittit, naves etenim procurabit, si hoc necessitas vestia exegerit, et ipse ante, ut opoitet, admoneatur. Si vero ad hoc vos tempestas impulerit, præmittite aut Philippum emptorem vestrum, qui et comitis auctoritate utatui, et cum nautis et vectoribus, prout expedierit, contiahat. Sic a comite recedens, die sequenti Noviomum veni.

Et nescio quo præpetis et inquietæ famæ præcomo calamitas Anglorum ecclesiarumque vexatio, quocumque veniebam, fuerat divulgata, ut ubi multa audirem gesta in conventu londoniensi et wintoniensi, quæ in Anglia nunquam audieram. Et quidem pleraque, ut fit, majora et pejora veris referebantur: ego autem hæc omnia quæ per ora populi volitabant studiosissime dissimulabam; sed nec simulanti prospera plene credebatur, nec adversa dissimulanti. Quodque miremini, comes suessionensis, ea die qua Noviomi eram, omnes articulos londoniensis, nescio conciliabuli aut dissiliabuli dicam, decano ita seriatim exposuit ac si interfuisset omnibus præsens, non modo his quæ in palatio gesta sunt, sed quæ secretissime ab his vel ab illis dicta sunt in conclavi. Nec facile crediderim quin ibi, sive de suis, sive de nostratibus, cautos exploratores habuerint Galli.

Decanus autem noviomensis. vir integerrimæ fidei, concussionem vestram non sine multo dolore audierat; et se ad vos recipiendum præparat, non modo sua omnia expositurus pro vobis, sed pro cantuariensi ecclesia, si oportuerit, se ipsuin positurus. Decreverat autem transire ad curiam; sed quia de statu vestro mœstus est et sollicitus, donec certioretur, domi exspectat. Ibi a quibusdam pro certo accepi regem Francorum esse Lauduni, et prope eum dominum remensem ejus exspectare colloquium. Eos ergo adire proposui, sed, propter guerras quas comes de Roceio et alii quidam proceres, adversus dominum remensem exercebant, a proposito revocatus, iter Parisius deflexi. Ubi cum viderem victualium copiam, lætitiam populi, reverentiam cleri, et totius ecclesiæ majestatem et gloriam, et varias occupationes philosophantium admiratus, velut illam scalam Jacob, cujus summitas cœlum tangebat, eratque via ascendentium et descendentium angelorum, lætæ peregrinationis urgente stimulo, coactus sum profiteri quod Vere Dominus est in loco isto, et ego nesciebam. Illud quoque poeticum ad mentem rediit:

"Felix exilium, cui locus iste datui."

Evolutis autem paucis diebus in conducendo hospitio et sarcinulis componendis, regem Francorum adii eique ex ordine exposur causam vestiam. Quid multa? Compatitur, promittit auxilium, et pro vobis se domino Papæ scripsisse asseruit, et iterum, si oportuerit, scripturum et acturum quod poterit, viva voce. Cum vero eum ex parte filiæ suæ, quam nuper sanam videram, quando a domina regina licentiam accepi, salutassem, respondit sibi gratissimum esse; si illa jam ab angelis accepta esset in paradiso. Cui cum ego subjungerem quia istud per misericordiam Dei quandoque eveniet, sed ante multis gentibus lætitiam dabit, respondit rex: "Hoc quidem Deo possibile est; sed longe verisimilius quod multorum futura sit causa malorum. Sed absit ab illa quod paternus præsagit animus! quia vix, inquit, spero ut ab ea possit aliquid boni esse." Regem nostrum Franci timent pariter et oderunt; sed tamen quoad illos quieto et alto somno dormire potest.

Et quia Remensem adire non potui, literas meas ad abbatem S. Remigii amicissimum mihi direxi, ut in hac parte suppleat vices meas. Cæterum mihi videtur esse consilium, ut per aliquem monachum Boxleïæ, aut alium nuncium fidelem, literas vestias cum aliquo munusculo transmittatis ad dominum remensem, contrahatisque cum eo familiaritatem, quia ille, quisquis sit in persona, magnus est in regno Francorum, et in ecclesia romana multum potest, tum pro rege, tum pro eminentia ecclesiæ suæ. Ad ecclesiam romanam nondum descendi, declinans quantum possum, ne suspicio probabilis contra me concipi debeat; et hoc ipsum, sicut ex literis domini pictaviensis accepi, domino Papæ et curiæ satis innotuit Receptis autem literis vestris, illico scripsi domino Henrico et Willelmo Papiensi, et satis explanavi in quantam perniciem ecclesiæ romanæ tendant hæc, si processum habuerint, quæ contra vos præsumantur. Distuli autem illuc ire, quia de transitu abbatis S. Augustini aut episcopi lexoviensis nihil certum erat: et si ad curiam venerint, nobis per magistrum Henricum, qui ibi moratur, cito poterit innotescere. Verum quid ibi tunc possimus non clare video. Contra vos enim faciunt multa, pauca pro vobis. Venient enim magni viri, divites in effusione pecuniæ, quam nunquam Roma contempsit, eruntque non modo sua, sed domini regis, quem curia in nullo audebit offendere, auctoritate fieti. Ad hæc muniti erunt privilegiis ecclesiæ romanæ, quæ in hujusmodi causis nunquam cuicumque episcopo detulit aut raro. Deinde dominus Papa in causa hac nobis semper est adversatus, et adhuc non cessat reprehendere quod fecit pro nobis cantuariensis ecclesiæ amator Adrianus, cujus mater apud vos algore torquetur et media. Nos humiles, inopes, immuniti, numquid poterimus verba dare Romanis? At illi pridem suum comicum audierunt, ut non emant spera pretio.

Sed scribitis ut tandem, si alia via non patuerit, promittamus ducentas marcas. At certe pars adversa, antequam frustretur, tracentas dabit aut quadringentas.

Nec, si muneribus certas, concedet Iolas.

Et ego respondeo pro Romanis, quod pro amore domini regis et reverentia nunciorum mallent plus recipere, quam sperare minus. Stant autem pro vobis, quod pro libertate ecclesiæ tribulamini; sed, honestatem causæ nostræ extenuantes, excusatores regis et æmuli vestri hoc temeritati quam libertati magis adscribere conabuntui. Et ut eis citius credatur, ipsi domino Papæ (quia venas hujus susurri jam audiit auris mea) dabunt spem veniendi in Angliam, dicentque regii filii dilatom coronationem, ut manu apostolica consecretur. Et sciatis ad hoc promptos esse Romanos. Jam enim quidam nobis insultant, dicentes dominum Papam ad cantuariensem ecclesiam accessurum, ut moveat candelabrum vestrum, ibique aliquandiu sedeat. Nec tamen credo quod dominus Papa istud adhuc conceperit; nam, ut audio, multam ejus pro constantia vestra habetis gratiam. Sed unum procul dubio scio, quia lexoviensis, si venerit, nihil asserere verebitur. Notus enim mihi est, et in talibus expertus sum ejus fallacias. De abbate quis dubitat? Postremo scripsit mihi episcopus pictavensis, quod adversus abbatem S. Augustim nihil potucrat impetrare, etsi plurimani dedisset operam. Ibimus tamen illuc auctore Deo, quoniam ita præcipitis, et quid possimus experiemur. Sed si frustra, nobis imputari non debet; quoniam, ut ait ethicus,

* Non est in medico semper reveletur ut æger.

* Interdum docta plus valet arte malum.

Cæterum an recte mecum agatis prudentia vestra dijudicet. Nostis enim, si placet reminisci, quoniam, quando recessi à vobis, hoc mihi dedistis consilium, ut Parisius morarer omnino scholasticus, nec ad ecclesiam romanam diverterem, ut vel sic declinarem suspiciones; nec approbastis etiam quod ducebam fratrem meum, eo quod sumptus magnos nos facere oporteret, possetque tolerabilius Exomæ morari. Ad quod cum ego responderem ea quæ fiatris mei occasione comes Reginaldus episcopo exoniensi objecerat, meum consilium approbastis. Sic ergo discessi, instructus a vobis ut Parisius sedem figerem, et me studerem omnino scholaribus conformare. Deus mihi testis est quod, quando recessi à vobis, duodecim denarios in toto mundo non habebam, nec aliquid, quod ego scirem ad usum meum. Vascula quidem habebam pauca fere quinque marcarum omnibus hospitii nostri sociis satis nota; et eram quidem, quod multi sciunt, alreno ære, sed meo onere, graviter pressus. Accepi ergo decem marcas mutuas; sed, antequam egrederer Cantuaria, in sarcinulis et instructione clientum tres earum expendi. Deinde per manum Willelmi, filii Pagani, liberalitatis vestræ septem marcas accepi, tres adhuc, ut jusseratis, accepturus: quod enim minus factum est, vobis nequaquam imputandum est.

Vemens ergo Parisius, juxta instructionem vestram, pro tempore, ut videtur, commodum conduxi hospitium et antequam illud ingrederer, duodecim fere libras expendi; neque enim introitum potui obtinere, nisi in annum totum pretio prærogato. Equos itaque distraxi, et me disposui ad residendum potius quam ad peregrinandum. Unde et imparatior sum ad circuitus quos præscribitis faciendos, qui non possunt sine sumptibus fieri, præsertim ab homine ecclesiasticum habente officium notitiamque multorum. Præterea regis indignationem gratis, conscientia teste, sustineo; et, si me nunciis ejus opposuero, gravius sustinebo. Unde milii, si placet, in talibus quæ æque commode possent per alios exerceri, magis parcere debetis. Et tamen, quantum expensæ permiserint undecumque Quæsitæ, quod jusseritis exsequar: vos autem videritis quid jubeatis. Et quia ecclesia romana est in ea conditione quam nostis, nihil mihi videretur consultius in mundanis, quam duabus rebus operam dare. Altera quidem est, ut eximatis vos utcumque a laqueis creditorum: altera, ut domini regis, quatenus secundum Deum fieri potest, quæratis gratiam. Deus mederi potest; sed ecclesia romana non feret opem, et, ut timeo, rex Francorum baculus arundineus est. Præterea, si placet, cum Gaufrido, nepote vestro, misericordiam faciatis. Tempus est enim: nam ex quo hospitium meum ingressus est, quantum perpendere potui, honeste se habet et literis operam dat et diligentiam; exhibuit eum dominus pictavensis antequam veniret, et primo dedit ei quinque marcas, deinde centum solidos Andegavensium. Unde, si placet, cum amicis episcopi pictavensis debetis benignius agere, et in collocanda filia Willelmi, filii Pagani, non debetis, si placet, aliquam exercuisse duritiam, saltem pro episcopi reverentia. Valete.

No. VII. Letter relative to the Intrigues of Henry II. at the Court of Rome, and the Mission of two Legates into France. (ad 1169.)

Amicus amico. Actiones gratiarum debitas parturit animus; sed, ut ait propheta, vires non habet parturiens; nam devotionis effectum suspendit hactenus persecutionis acerbitas. sed affectum quin in partum gratulationis erumpere gestiat, nulla vis potest aut poterit cohibere. Et quidem, Deo propitiante, jam in eum calculum Christi et ecclesiæ suæ causa perducta est, ut de cætero perichtari non possit, eo quod schismatis capita defecerunt, et Anglicanæ ecclesiæ malleus, comprehensus in operibus suis, de cætero cui innitatur invenire non valet. Ventum erat ad summum, ubi constat habitudines periculosas esse, cum ille qui, sollicitando tam curiam quam schismaticos, Fredericum videlicet et complices suos, videns se hac via non posse proficere adversus Dominum et adversus Christum ejus, trausmissa legatione confugit ad Italiæ civitates, promittens Mediolanensibus tria millia marcarum et murorum suorum validissimam reparationem, ut, cum aliis civitatibus quas corrumpere moliebatur, impetrarent a Papa et ecclesia romana dejectionem vel translationem cantuariensis archiepiscopi. Nam, ob eamdem causam Cremonensibus duo millia marcarum promiserat, Parmensibus mille, et totidem Bononiensibus. Domino vero Papæ obtulit, quia data pecunia liberaret eum ab exactionibus omnium Romanorum, et decem millia marcarum adjiceret, concedens etiam ut tam in ecclesia cantuariensi, quam in aliis vacantibus in Anglia, pastores ordinaret ad libitum. Sed quia fidem multa promissa levabant, et in precibus manifesta contrnebatur iniquitas, repulsam passus est; et, quod per se impetrare non poterat, regis Siculi viribus conatus est extorquere. Sed nec ille, licet ad hoc toto nisu syracusanus episcopus et Robertus, comes de Bassevilla, multiplicatis intercessoribus, laboraverint, exauditus est pro sua reverentia, vel potentia, vel gratia, quamvis eam in ecclesia romana plurimam habeat. Dimissi sunt ergo nuncii regis impotes voti, hoc solum impetrato, ut dominus Papa mitteret nuncios qui pacem procurarent, Gratianum scilicet subdiaconum, et magistrum Vivianum, Urbis-Veteris archidiaconum, qui munere advocationis fungi solet in curia. Eos tamen ante, præscripta forma pacis, sacramenti religione adstrinxit, quod præfinitos terminos non excederent, mandatis quoque adjiciens ut a regis sumptibus abstineant, nisi pace ecclesiæ impetrata, et ne ultra diem qui eis præstitus est, aliquam faciant moram. Forma autem pacis quæ archiepiscopo expressa est, nihil inhonestum continet vel quod ecclesiam dedeceat aut personam, nec auctoritatem ejus in aliquo minuit, quin libere, omni occasione et appellatione cessante, in ipsum regem, in regnum et personas regm, severitarem ecclesiasticam valeat exercere, prout sibi et ecclesiæ Dei expedire cognoverit. Consilium tamen amicorum virorumque sapientum est, ut dum pacis verba tractantur, mitius agat et multa dissimulet; postea, si (quod absit!) pax non processerit, gravius quasi resumptis viribus persecutores ecclesiæ prostraturus.

Spera ergo, dilecte mi, et quidquid interim audieris, non movearis, quia Deus in tuto posuit causam suam. Audies forte superbiam Moab, sed memineris quod superbia major est quam fortitudo ejus. Nam territi sunt in Sion peccatores, possedit timor hypocritas, qui, nisi revertantur a pravitate sua, expellentur et stare non poterunt. Jam enim securis ad radicem eorum posita est, et ventilabrum habet angelus in manu sua, ut grana discernat a paleis. Præfati nuncii ad regem profecti sunt, sed quid apud ipsum invenerint nondum nobis innotuit. Hoc tamen certum est quod se rex verbo et scripto obligavit ad exequendum consilium et mandatum domini Papæ, scriptumque ejus præ manibus est, a quo si resiherit, facile convincetur: sed nec sic credendum censuit ecclesia, antequam verborum fidem operum testimonio roboraret. Salutatus a te plurimum et affectuose te resalutat archiepiscopus, se ad amorem et honorem tuum exponens promptissima devotione.

No. VIII. Letter of Thomas Beket to Cardinal Albert, on the conduct of the Court of Rome towards him. (ad 1170.)

Thomas, cantuariensis archiepiscopus, Alberto cardinali. Utinam, dilecte mi, aures vestræ sint ad ora nostratum, et andiant illa quæ in ignominiam ecclesiæ romanæ cantitantur in compitis Ascalonis! Aliquid consolationis novissimi nuncii nostri videbantur a sede apostolica retulisse in literis domini Papæ; sed earum auctoritas evacuata est missis a latere literis ut in perniciem ecclesiæ Sathanas absolveretur. Soluti sunt enim apostolico mandato Londomensis et Saresberiensis episcopi, quorum alter incentor schismatis et totius malitiæ artifex ab initio dignoscitur exstitisse, et tam Saresberiensem quam omnes quos potuit in crimen inobedientiæ impegisse. Nescio quo pacto pars Domini semper mactatur in curia, ut Barrabas evadat et Christus occidatur. Auctoritate curiæ jam ni finem sexti anni proscriptio nostra et ecclesiæ calamitas protracta est. Condemnantur apud vos miseri exules, innocentes, nec ob aliud, ut ex conscientia loquar, nisi quia pauperes Christi sunt et imbecilles et a justitia. Dei recedere noluerunt; absolvuntur e regione sacrilegi et homicidæ, raptores impœnitentes, quos, mundo reclamante, nec a Petro, si præsideret, apud Deum absolvi posse, libera voce, Christo auctore, pronuncio. Ait enim in evangelio secundum Lucam: Si peccaverit in te frater tuus, increpa illum; et si pœnitentiam eqerit, dimitte illi. Et si septies in die peccaverit in te, et septies in die conversus fuerit ad te, dicens, Pœnitet me, dimitte illi. Numquid otiosa sunt verba Christi quibus ait, Si pœnitentiam egerit, si conversus confiteatur dicens, Pœnitet me? Nequaquam de otiositate verbi redditurus est in die judicii rationem, sed potius eos damnaturus qui, contra formam quam dedit, iniquos sine confessione et pœnitentia vanis absolutionibus justificare præsumunt, et vivificare animas quæ non vivunt. Certe, si res ablata reddi potest, et non redditur, non agitur pœnitentia, sed fingitur. Profecto Spiritus Sanctus, ut scriptum est, effugiet fictum: quoniam ipse veritas est, et non figmentum. Obliget se qui audet, nec venturi judicis formidet sententiam; raptores, sacrilegos, homicidas, perjuros, sanguinarios et schismaticos impœnitentes absolvat: ego quæ ecclesiæ Dei ablata sunt impœnitenti nunquam remittam. Nonne nostra, aut potius ecclesiæ spolia sunt quæ nuncii regis cardinalibus et curialibus larginntur et promittunt? Quæ iniquitas manifesta est, si illa quæ in ecclesiam Dei apud nos exercetur occulta est? Nos ecclesiæ libertatem tueri non possumus, quia sedes apostolica proscriptionem nostram jam iu finem sexti anni protraxit. Viderit Deus, et judicet; sed pro ea mori parati sumus. Insurgant qui voluerint cardinales; arment non modo regem Augliæ, sed totum, si possuet, orbem, in perniciem nostram: ego, Deo propitiante, nec in vita nec in morte ab ecclesiæ fidelitate recedam. Causam suam de cætero committo Deo, pro quo exulo proscriptus; ille medeatur ut novit expedire. Non est mihi ulterius propositum vexandi curiam: eam adeant qui prævalent in iniquitatibus suis, et, triumphata justitia et innocentia captivata, in confusionem ecclesiæ redeunt gloriosi. Utinam via romana non gratis peremisset tot miseros innocentes! Quis de cætero audebit illi regi resistere, quam ecclesia romana tot triumphis animavit et armavit exemplo pernicioso ad posteros? Valeat semper sanctitas vestra, nostri memor ante Deum.

No. IX. Letter from Thomas Beket's companions in exile to Cardinal Albert, on the injustice of the Court of Rome, and the conduct of the Cardinals towards them. (ad 1170.)

Sanctissimo domino et patri carissimo Alberto, Dei gratia S. R. E. presbytero cardinali, miseri Cantuarienses totum id modicum quod relictum est exulibus et proscriptis, sinceræ fidei et veræ dilectionis affectum. Quantum sit innocentis conscientiæ bonum nesciunt qui sinceritatem conscientiæ perdiderunt; nec veretur alienam funestis infestare consiliis, qui, semel relicta verecundia, in turpitudinis suæ defensionem præclaros viros desiderat habere consortes erroris. Utinam hæc domini Papæ sanctitas, cum ecclesiæ confusione et infamia curiæ, non esset in nostris experta periculis, eorumque saluti pariter et honestati repugnantia consilia sapientiæ et auctoritatis qua cunctis præminet vigore, ab initio reprobasset, qui persuadere ausi sunt ut innocentium proscriptionem per sex annos derisoriis dilationibus protelaret! Certe quisquis et quantuscumque fuerit ille consultor illico audisse debuerat: Vade retro, Sathana, quia non sapis ea quæ Dei sunt. Nec persuadebitur mundo quod suasores isti Deum saperent; sed potius pecuniam, quam immoderato avaritiæ ardore sitiunt, olfecerunt: ideoque, prædonibus et sacrilegis adherentes consensu, consiliis instruentes, armantes patrociniis, insurrexerunt in pauperes Christi. acceptantes munera, secuti retributiones. Nec possunt illorum latere nomina, quæ tum evidentia operis manifestat, tum relatio nunciorum partis adversæ, tum attestatio literarum quibus gloriantur apud regem Anglorum se pro eo stetisse viriliter, et quod illis tacentibus erat credibile, persuasisse domino Papæ ut præfati regis immanitatem in tanta patientia sustineret in quo timendum est ne seductus sanctus erraverit nimis, adeo ut, quod in ecclesiam Dei deliquit, etiam cum voluerit, nequeat emendare; sic solet Deus talia plerumque punire delicta, ut qui divinitus oblata gerendorum opportunitate non utitur, eadem illi in perpetuum auferatur. Scrutanti legem loquimur et scienti, qui quod dicitur sibi familiaribus clarum habet exemplis.

Etsi tamen (ut culpam suam, quam sic magis auget, purgare curia videatur) ut nuncios nostros retorquet quod ecclesiæ Dei de tam manifestis injuriis et damnis justitia non sit exhibita; ergo, quasi re bene gesta, consulunt ut sapientiores mittanius, ac si per se non sit patens injuria, damna sint vel pauca vel modica, sæpc non sit prædo commonitus, nunciis nostris illatæ non sint atrociores injuriæ, diu, immo nimis et ultra omnem modum et contra æquitatem non sit exspectata correctio. Non sunt in nobis, pater, sapientes ille quos quærunt, non potentes aut divites, quos semper contra ecclesiam Dei et nos habere locum videmus in curia, ut assidue redeant cum triumpho. Vix sustentamur aliena stipe, et fere, nisi nos gratia conservaret, ab ecclesia romana attriti, qui soli in orbe occiduo pro illa dimicamus, deserere cogimur causam Christi et ecclesiæ contemnere libertatem. Potuit ab initio in solum regem Anglorum et nostræ proscriptionis et deprædationis ecelesiæ culpa refundi, qui per se et satellites suos, sine miseratione ætatis et sexus, sine reverentia dignitatis aut ordinis, circiter quadringentos innocentes addixit exilio, cantuariensem cum omnibus possessionibus et bonis suis confiscavit ecclesiam, bona vacantium sedium occupans, non permisit in eis episcopos et abbates regulariter ordinari. Dici non potest quot animæ sine confirmationis sacramento excesserint: quot causæ cum ecclesiarum et injuste oppressorum dispendio expiraverint; quanta injustitia totam possedit Angliam; quanta perditioni animarum janua Sathanæ sit aperta, pastoribus ovium Christi aut in exilium actis, aut coactis obmutescere et silere a bonis, aut illectis ut præberent sub prætextu religionis et dispensationis arma iniquitatis peccato, et ipsos serpentes et antiqui serpentes membra perniciosis consiliis toxicarent.

Tantas et tam patentes Christi injurias sæpe, immo continue per sex annos, prosecuti sumus in auditoriis vestris, parati in ipsa malorum novitate, cum adhuc essetis Senonis et nuncii regis adessent, appellationes prosequi quæ vel a nobis vel contra nos fuerant institutæ. Non placuit ut audiremur tunc, quando nobis adhuc aliquid, etsi modicum, suberat facultatis, et amicis et adjutoribus nonnihil spei. Longum erit et vobis, ut timemus, tædiosum, si retexamus quoties nos obtulerimus ad agendum; nec placuit ut audiremur, et adversariis nostris, oppressoribus ecclesiæ, facta est, ut scitis, non prosequendæ appellationis indulgentia. Interim, si pater noster dominus cantuariensis vellet ablata remittere, et perniciosum compositionis ineundæ coætaneis et posteris præbere exemplum, pacem facere, vobis non interponentibus partes vestras, cum rege potuerat et redire in gratiam familiaritatis antiquæ. Sed absit hæc lues a mentibus nostris, ut pro quolibet temporali emolumento jugulemus animas nostras, insanabili plaga conscientias vulneremus, et nefando voluptatis aut avaritiæ mercimonio vendamus ecclesiæ libertatem, et posteros pravo corrumpamus exemplo! Faciant hoc, si volunt, alu, aut potius nullus faciat; quia nos ita instituti sumus a sanctis patribus qui cantuariensem ecclesiam rexerunt in laboribus multis, et tandem mercedem laborum receperunt a Domino. Idem qui auctor propositi, conscientiæ nostræ testis est Deus, quod dominus cantuariensis præelegit in exilio mori, quam perniciosam ecclesiæ et probrosam inire concordiam: et si hæc (quod absit!) attentaret, rarus est inter nos, si quis tamen, qui deinceps illius posset dominium aut consortium sustinere.

Nobiscum de pace ecclesiæ mediantibus amicis tractabatur, cum Joannes de Oxeneford Romam proficiscens, et manifesto multis justificatus perjurio rediit triumphator, et ab apostolica sede furenti, quasi per se non satis insaniret, cornua attulit peccatori. Ab ea die proscriptio nostra, quæ antea soli regi et suis poterat imputari, ecclesiam romanam dissimulatione vel consensu auctorem habuit, cum persecutori in malitia perduranti sit indulta dilatio, et quodammodo licentia præstita incubandi ecclesiis et torquendi innocentes; et nobis si quid solatii videbatui esse porrectum, statim e latere nunciis aut literis impediebatur, ne votivum aut debitum sortiretur effectum. Nobis etiam tacentibus, rerum eventus ita esse convincit. Ecce enim cum pax nostra, sicut multi noverunt, esset in januis, et ecclesia solatium, ut putabamus, efficax a sanctissimo patre romano pontifice accepisset, supervenientes nuncii regis abstulerunt pacem, et, absolutis excommunicatis nostris, etiam spem reconciliationis visi sunt præclusisse. Siquidem denunciaverunt iis et aliis adversariis nostris ut, si libuerit, sex annorum appellationes, quas toties prosecuti sumus et interdum obtinuimus, prosequantur in festo beati Lucæ, scituri quod nullum eis honoris, officii, beneficii aut famæ dispendium generabitur ex hoc quod tanto tempore excommunicati fuerunt. Namque in eo, maxime apud nostrates, justitia viget ecclesiastica, quod qui per annum excommunicationem sustinent, notari solent infamia. Sed ecce ab hujus novitatis exemplo et quasi apostolico privilegio quod continctur in literis, solutus est ecclesiasticus vigor. Quid ergo superest nisi ut nullius momenti sit apud provinciales sententia, quam sine omni pœna vident tam facile posse dissolvi?

Juraverunt tamen, ut dicitur, se staturos mandato domini papæ; sed præcipitur esse absconditum. Deus bone! quid rei est quod quæ contra ecclesiam fiunt, libenter prædicantur in foro ut trahi possint ad consequentiam; et si quid pro ecclesia fit, cujus exemplum possit esse laudabile et prodesse in posterum, illud apostolica sedes jubet abscondi? Cum ergo sic apud vos, prævalentibus fautoribus regis aut potius malitiæ aut pecuniæ amatoribus, causa Christi tractetur, cur a nobis exigitur ut mittamus nuncios sapientes, quasi vos ipsi non debueritis tam justam causam, tam manifestam, defendere, etiam tacentibus universis? At enim estis in mundi cardine constituti, ut liberetis pauperem a potente, ut justitiam decernatis et faciatis inter filios hominum. Nos sane viros honestos et literatos credebamus, quos via romana absorbuit: quæ tandem nobis utilitas in sanguine eorum? Numquid mittemus plures ut ipsi moriantur, ut innocentium minatur numerus vel annuletur, et tyrannus, illis extinctis, licenter dominetur ecclesiæ, nullo contradicente? Si appellationes prosequendæ sunt, quare, cum nascebantur aut nondum expiraverant, non sunt examinatæ? Satius enim fuerat nobis eas tunc expidiri aut saltem denunciari nobis, ut aliquid aliud negotii ageremus, quo vitam nostram possemus utcumque transigere, et causam suam Deo committeremus expediendam. Spoliati et nudi sumus: satis hactenus delusionibus hujusmodi fatigatis consultius esse credimus, ut vitam in orationibus quam in litibus finiamus, domesticis exemplis edocti, ne de cætero non modo opera et impensa nobis periclitetur, sed et anima. Christus, cui eam committimus, ecclesiæ suæ sit patronus et causæ.

Sed fortasse dicet aliquis, quoniam pro bono pacis et quæ præmisimus gesta sunt, et toties indulta dilatio et dispensandi ratio admissa est. Utique, si pax exspectatur a Deo, peccatis et his quæ contra legem fiunt procuranda non est; si a Deo futura non est, nec est ecclesiæ necessaria, nec alicui utilis. Bonorum nostrorum non indiget Deus, sed certe peccatorum nostrorum minus, ad expediendam justitiam et misericordiam suam: et fortasse tamdiu dilata est pax, quia non via Domini, sed humana procurabatur astutia. Excessimus modum; sed urget nos necessitas, quæ nec modo nec regulæ necessitate arctatur; et Spiritus Sanctus, qui in vobis est, persuadebit ut necessario excedentibus indulgeatis et compatiamini. In summa, pietatis vestræ genibus provoluti, supplicamus attentius ut hæc omnia intimetis domino papæ, et persuadeatis ei ne de cætero circumventoribus credat, qui, amore sordium allecti, ipsum conantur inducere, ut in læsione nostra animam suam perdat et causam Christi.

No. X. Letter of John of Salisbury on the Landing of Thomas Beket, and his reception in England. (ad 1170.)

Joannes Saresberiensis Petro abbati Sancti-Remigii. Mora mea rectissime poterat accusari, si non eam necessitas excusaret. Debueram enim, ex quo primum in Angliam pedem posui, nuncium remisisse, per quem vestra dilectio de alumnorum suorum statu posset certiorari; sed, quia mihi in ipso navis egressu nova et stupenda rerum facies occurrit, alium certiorare non potui, qui ex variis opinionibus et verbis hominum reddebar incertus. Nam, triduo antequam applicarem, omnia bona domini cantuariensis et suorum annotata fuerant, procuratoribus suis ab administratione summotis, et in portubus edicto publico inhibitum est sub interminatione exilii et proscriptionis, ne quis nostrorum, si forte Angliam vellet exire, transveheretur. Piissimi tamen officiales domini regis provida nimis cautela et perniciosa nobis circumspectione præcaverant, ut archiepiscopus et sui ab exilio redeuntes nihil prorsus aut minimum invenirent præter domos vacuas ex magna parte consumptas, et horrea demolita, et areas nudas, et hoc ad consolationem diuturnæ proscriptionis et emendationem sacrilegii perpetrati. Et cum pax nobis in festo beatæ Magdalenæ fuisset reformata, et serinissimus dominus noster rex filio suo novo regi literis patentibus præcepisset ut archiepiscopo et suis omnia restituerentur in integrum, prout fuerant tribus mensibus antequam Angliam egrederentur, omnes tamen redditus nomine ejus prærepti sunt, qui usque ad Natale Domini percipi potuerunt. Plures possessiones et ecclesias quas, ipso jure et ratione pacti conventi, restitui oportebat ecclesiæ cantuariensi, adhuc publicæ potestatis auctoritate occupant curiales. Ego inter cæteros una ecclesia privatus sum, quæ quadraginta marcas annuas solvebat antecessori meo. Contigit autem me triduo applicare ante octavas beati Martini, et in ipsis octavis erat Cantuariæ synodus celebranda, in qua me vices absentis archiepiscopi gerere oportebat. Cum itaque præter spem, et contra bonam opinionem et bonas promissiones domini regis, sic omnia turbata reperissem, ut de pace nostra et de reditu archiepiscopi desperaretur ab omnibus, et me tanquam in carcere positum cognovissem, vultu hilari et animo constanti Cantuariam petii, ubi a clero et populo cum magno honore et quasi angelus Domini receptus sum, fidelibus jam ex adventu meo meliora sperantibus, eo quod eis persuasum erat quod me nullo modo archiepiscopus præmisisset, si non esset in brevi secutuius. Inde, synodo celebrata, ad novum regem profectus sum et satis humane receptus, licet concustodes sui aliquid timoiis prætenderint, suspicantes pacem nobiscum non simpliciter factam esse, sed rancoris palam remissi firmius hærere radices. Quod etsi ex variis signis patenter adverterem, sie egi ac si omnia ad votum procedere arbitrarer. Festinanter inde ad matrem meam deflexi iter, quam jam altero languentem anno, et amodo jam diem Domini cum gaudio præstolantem, ex quo me vidit, vestris et sanctorum quibus cohabitatis orationibus precor attentius commendari. Receperat autem responsum a spiritu, se mortem non visuram, donec me et fratrem meum videret ab exilio redeuntes.

Interim illi veteres amicid omini cantuariensis et ecclesiasticæ libertatis propugnatores, dominus eboracensis, episcopus Londoniensis et complices eorum, consilium inierunt cum publicanis, legatione transmissa ad dominum regem, ne præfatum cantuariensem in Angliam redire pateretur, antequam renunciaret legationis officio, et restitueret ei universas literas quas emeruerat ab apostolica sede, et repromitteret se regni jura inviolabiliter servaturum, ut sub obtentu cautionis hujus ad observantiam consuetudinum arctaretur. Dicebant quod reditus ejus domino regi damnosus et probrosus futurus erat, nisi ista præcederent. Fecerant etiam de singulis vacantibus ecclesiis senas evocari personas, in quas de pastore eligendo universitatis arbitria conferrentur, ut electiones de ecclesia in aliud regnum et palatium protractæ celebrarentur ad nutum regis: ubi, si cantuariensis ob reverentiam canonum pro officii sui debito obloqueretur, regiam offenderet majestatem; si consentiret, reus esset in Deum, et convinceretur in constitutiones ecclesiasticas incidisse. Sæpe dictus autem cantuariensis ex mandato domini regis Rotomagum venerat, inde ex promisso liberandus ab obligatione creditorum, et cum honore in patriam remittendus. Sed fefellit eum opinio, Joanne de Oxeneford afferente literas domini regis, quibus rogabat et monebat ut sine mora rediret ad ecclesiam suam, et antedicti Joannis conductu et solatio in itinere frueretur. Paruit archiepiscopus, et in redeundo æmutorum per amicos machinamenta cognovit, qui jam ad mare profecti ventum commodum exspectabant, archiepiscopo nostro in opposito littore similiter exspectante. Ubi cum de transitu eorum et machinationibus certior fieret, conatus eorum via qua potuit elisit, mittens archiepiscopo eboracensi literas apostolicas, quibus ipse et dunelmensis episcopus propter usurpatam novi regis coronationem ab episcopali officio suspenduntur. Alias quoque porrexit nuncius Londoniensi et Saresberiensi episcopis, quibus in sententiam anathematis revocantur, et suspenduntur omnes episcopi qui præfatæ coronationi interfuerunt. Quo facto, prosperior aura spirans a Flandria dominum archiepiscopum in Angliam felici navigatione perduxit, venientemque ad portum cut Sandwicus nomen est, regii satellites exceperunt, custodiis per littora dispositis, ut creditur, ad nocendum, et armatis perstrepentibus: quos antefatus Joannes de Oxeneford cohibuit et compulit arma deponere, non tam, ut putatur, favore nostrorum, quam ne temeritas eorum dominum regem et liberos suos nota proditionis inureret. Exegerunt tamen ut alienigenæ qui cum archiepiscopo venerant, sacramentum præstarent de servanda fidelitate regi et regno. Nec apparebat quisquam alienigena præter Simonem, senonensem archidiaconum, qui ad præstandum juramentum facile fuisset inductus, si archiepiscopus permisisset: qui, exempli perniciem veritus, respondit bonis moribus hoc prorsus esse contrarium, ut inaudita barbarie compellantur hospites et peregrini ad hujus modi juramenta. Et fortasse satellites vim parassent, nisi eos compeseuisset tumultus popularis, verentes plebis impetum, quæ sic de recepto pastore gavisa est ac si de cœlo inter homines Christus ipse descenderet.

Cum vero se die sequenti Cantuariæ recepisset, venerunt ad eum alterius archiepiscopi et episcoporum suspensorum muncii, ad sedem apostolicam appellantes, licet eis indubitanter constaret quod summus Pontifex omnem appellandi præcluserit facultatem. Venerunt ex alio latere domini regis officiales, suo rogantes nomine et publica denunciantes auctoritate, ut archiepiscopus latam in archiepiscopum eboracensem et alios episcopos sententiam relaxaret, nisi regis et regni vellet decerni publicus nostis, ut qui novo regi coronam moliebatur auferre. Ad quod archiepiscopus respondit se nullo modo impugnare regiam dignitatem, sed potius vires, opes et gloriam pro viribus in Christo augmentaturum: hoc tamen nulla ratione impetrari posse, quin adversus præsumptores episcopos ecclesiæ suæ justitiam prosequatur. Illis autem instantibus acrius, adjecit quod pro honore domini regis, licet ei periculosum esset et vires ejus excederet, quia judex inferior superioris non potest relaxare sententiam, paratus erat duos episcopos absolvere, recepto ab eis prius, secundum morem ecclesiæ, juramento, quod domini papæ, qui eos vinxerat, mandatis obedirent. Officiales autem non permiserunt ut fieret, dicentes hujusmodi juramentum ab episcopis non debere præstari, quia regni consuetudines impugnabat. Replicavit ad hæc archiepiscopus quod, cum dominum papam modis omnibus antea sollicitasset ut eos absolveret a vinculo anathematis quo solius cantuariensis ecclesiæ auctoritate fuerant innodati, nonnisi præstito juramento solvi potuerunt. Quod si necessarium fuit ad unius episcopi sententiam dissolvendam, quæ longe inferior est edicto summi pontificis, luce clarius est quod sententia apostolica sine eo, præsertim a judice inferiori, solvi non debet. Ad hujusmodi et similes allegationes episcopi moti sunt, et sicut pro certo relatum est, ad archiepiscopi clementiam confugissent, nisi eos sæpe nominatus eboracensis seduxisset, dissuadens ne quidr ege facerent inconsulto, quem patronum habuerant in omnibus operibus suis.

Illis itaque cum indignatione properantibus ad dominum regem, noster archiepiscopus ad novum regem iter arripuit. Cum vero Londonias pervenisset, denunciavit ei rex junior ne progrederetur, nec civitates ejus aut castella intraret, sed reciperet se cum suis infra ambitum ecclesiæ suæ; et suis denunciatum est ne regni fines exeant, ne prodeant in publicum, sed, sicut se ipsos diligunt, caveant sibi. Qua denunciatione publicata, se et suos Cantuariæ recepit archiepiscopus, ibique salutare Dei cum multo discrimine præstolamur. Neque nobis via consolationis ant securitatis alia patet, quam ut vestris et sanctorum orationibus evadamus insidias eorum qui ecclesiæ sanguinem sitiunt, et quærunt ut de terra penitus avellamur, aut celerius pereamus in ipsa. Licet autem peraecutio gravissima sit, et ad archiepiscopum rarus de numero divitum et honoratorum visitator accedat, ipse tamen cunctis ad se venientibus pontificali gravitate jus reddit, deducta prorsus acceptione personarum ac munerum. Frater meus ad nostrum exoniensem, quem mihi nondum licuit visitare, profectus, lateri ejus adhæret in timore multo et jugi sollicitudine. Longum erit, et vereor ne tædium generet, si cunctas angustias nostias cœpero replicare; sed quæ desunt epistolæ supplebuntur officio portitoris. Sit itaque, si placet, miserationis vestræ sollicitare sanctum priorem et amicos Christi de Monte-Dei et Valle-Sancti-Petri, et abbates sanctorum Nicasii et Crispini, et alios sanctos familiares vestros, quatenus nobis apud altissimum suffragentur, ut eorum meritis salubriter liberemur, qui periclitamur ex nostris. Carissimos autem fratres nostros et dominos, qui beatissimo Remigio famulantur, vix sine gemitu et suspirus aut madore lacrymarum possum ad animum revocare, recolens me quondam instar paradisi feliciter incoluisse, dum illorum præsentia fruebar, et caritatis experiebar imaginem quæ in æterna vita speratur. Illos, quæso, diligentius sollicitate, ut alumnorum suorum meminerint in orationibus suis. Quam cito Deus prospera donabit, vobis currentium literarum ministerio, Christo propitiante, communicare non differam. Valeat semper et vigeat sanctitas vestra, et totius ecclesiæ prosperitas in bonis omnibus provehatur, et, si placet, pauperem sacerdotem Sancti-Cosmæ commendatum habeatis.

No. XI. Extract from a Letter of John of Salisbury, relative to the Murder of Thomas Beket. (ad 1171.)

Passurus autem in ecclesia, ut dictum est, coram altari Christi martyr, antequam feriretur, cum se audisset inquiri, militibus qui ad hoc venerant in turba clericorum et monachorum vociferantibus, Ubi est archiepiscopus? occurrit eis e gradu quem ex magna parte ascenderat, vultu intrepido dicens: Ecce ego: quid vultis? Cui unus funestorum militum in spiritu furoris intulit: Ut modo moriaris. Impossibile enim est ut ulterius vivas. Respondit autem archiepiscopus, non minori constantia verbi quam animi, quia (quod omnium martyrum pace ex animi mei sententia fidenter dixerim) nullus eorum videtur in passione isto fuisse constantior: Et ego pro Deo mori paratus sum, et pro assertione justitiæ et ecclesiæ libertate. Sed, si caput meum quæritis, prohibeo ex parte omnipotentis Dei et sub anathemate, ne cuiquam alii, sive monacho, saive laico, majori vel minori, in aliquo noceatis, sed sint immunes a pæna sicut extiterunt a causa. Non enim illis, sed mihi imputandum est si qui eorum causam laborantis ecclesiæ susceperunt. Mortem libenter amplector, dummodo ecclesia in effusione sanguinis mei pacem consequatur et libertatem.

Quis isto videtur in caritate ferventior, qui, dum se pro lege Dei persecutoribus offerebat, in id solum erat sollicitus ne proximi in aliquo læderentur? Verba ejus nonne Christum videntur exprimere in passione dicentem, Si mequæritis, sinite hos abire? His dictis, videns carnifices eductis gladiis, in modum orantis inclinavit caput, hæc novissima proferens verba: Deo, beatæ Mariæ, et sanctis hujus ecclesiæ patronis, et beato Dionysio, commendo me ipsum et ecclesiæ causam. Cætera quis sine suspiriis, singultibus et lacrymis referat? Singula persequi pietas non permittit, quæ carnifices immanissimi, Dei timore contempto, et tam fidei quam totius humanitatis immemores, commiserunt. Non enim suffecit eis sanguine sacerdotis et nece profanare ecclesiam et diem sanctissimum incestare, nisi, corona capitis quam sacri chrismatis unctio Deo dicaverat amputata, quod etiam dictu horribile est, funestis gladiis jam defuncti ejicerent cerebrum, et per pavimentum cum cruore et ossibus crudelissime spargerent, immaniores Christi crucifixoribus, qui ejus crura quem obiisse viderant, sicut adhuc viventium, non censuerunt esse frangenda. Sed in his omnibus cruciatibus invicti animi et admirandæ constantiæ martyr nec verbum protulit, nec clamorem emiset, nec edidit gemitum, nec brachium aut vestem opposuit ferienti; sed caput inclinatum, quod gladiis exposuerat, virtute admiranda, donec con summaretur, tenebat immobile, et tandem in terram procidens recto corpore, nec pedem movit aut manum.

Carnifices autem, non minus cupidi quam crudeles, inde tam in regiæ potestatis quam divinæ majestatis injuriam ad ecclesiæ palatium redeuntes, universam supellectilem et quidquid in scriniis aut chtellis archiepiscopi et suorum potuit inveniri, sive auro sive in argento, aut vestibus aut variis ornamentis, aut libris, aut privilegiis, aut aliis quibuscumque scriptis, aut equitaturis, insatiabili avaritia et stupendo ausu diripientes, ea ut libuit inter se diviserunt, imitatores eorum facti qui inter se Christi vestimenta partiti sunt, licet eos quodammodo præcedant in scelere; et ut pontifici jam per martyrium coronato hominum gratia aurferetur, omnia scripta quæ sacrilegus prædo surripuit ad regem in Normanniam transmissa sunt. Sed nutu divino contigit quod, quanto magis athletæ fortissimi gloriam offuscare nitebatur humana temeritas, tanto eam amplius Dominus illustraret ostentione virtutis et miraculorum manifestis indiciis: quod viri impii, qui eum insatiabiliter oderant, intuentes, inhibuerunt nomine publicæ potestatis ne miracula quæ fiebant quisquam publicare præsumeret. Cæterum, frustra quis obnubilare desiderat quod Deus clarificare disponit: eo enim amplius percrebuere miracula, quo videbantur impils studiosus occultanda. Homo videt in facie, solus Deus est qui renes sciutatur et corda. Nam, cum beati martyris corpus sepulturæ tradendum esset, et de more pontificalibus indueretur, quod admodum pauci familiares ejus noverant, inventum est cilicio pedunculis et vermibus referto involutum, ipsaque femoralia ejus interiora usque ad poplites cilicina (quod apud nostrates antea fuerat inauditum) reperta sunt. Exterior tamen habitus cæteris conformabatur, juxta sapientis edictum dicentis: Frons tua populo conveniat, intus omnia dissimilia sint.

Quis referat quos gemitus, quantos lacrymarum imbres sanctorum cœtus qui aderant in revelatione sic adumbratæ religionis emiserit? Nec tamen in his omnibus persecutorum quievit furor dicentium corpus proditoris inter sanctos pontifices non esse humandum, sed projiciendum in paludem viliorem vel suspendendum esse patibulo. Unde sancti viri qui aderant, vim sibi timentes inferii, eum in crypta, antequam satellites Sathanæ qui ad sacrilegia perpetranda convocati fuerant convenirent, ante altare sancti Joannis Baptistæ et sancti Augustini Anglorum apostoli in sarcophago marmoreo sepelierunt: ubi ad gloriam omnipotentis Dei per eum multa magna miracula fiunt, catervatim confluentibus populis ut videant in alus et sentiant in se potentiam et clementiam ejus qui semper in sanctis suis mirabilis et gloriosus est. Nam et in loco passionis ejus, et ubi ante majus altare pernoctavit humandus, et ubi tandem sepultus est, paralytici curantur, cæci vident, surdi audiunt, loquuntur muti, claudi ambulant, evadunt febricitantes, arrepti a dæmonio liberantur, et a variis morbis sanantur ægroti, blasphemi a dæmonio arrepti confunduntur, illo hæc et plura quæ referre perlongum est operante, qui solus est super omnia benedictus in sæcula, et eos præelegit esse gloriæ suæ consortes quos, per veritatem fidei, zelum justitiæ, confessionis virtutem et invictæ constantiæ perseverantiam, facturus erat de virtutis ac fidei adversariis triumphantes. Quæ profecto nulia ratione scribere præsumpsissem, nisi me super his fides oculata certissimum reddidisset.

Superest itaque ut vestra parvitatem nostram instruat eruditio, an citra romani pontificis auctoritatem tutum sit in missarum solemniis et aliis publicis orationibus eum in catalogo martyrum tanquam salutis præsidem invocare, an adhuc ei quem Deus tantis miraculorum clarificavit indiciis, quast alii defuncto orationes subventorias teneamur exsolvere. Timetur enim ne sic orandi instantia beati martyris injuria videatur, et incredulitatis prætendat imaginem post tot signorum exhibitionem nondum secura devotio. Jam super hoc consultus esset romanus Pontifex, nisa quia facultus transeundi adeo omnibus præclusa est, ut nullus ad navigium admittatur nisi literas regis ante poirexerit. Nobis tamen interim consultius esse videtur ut assistamus Domini voluntati, et quem ipse honorare dignatur ut martyrem, nos, sive cantemus, sive ploremus, ut martyrem veneremur. Nam fere in omnibus mundi paitibus Deus, non exspectata cujuscumque hominis auctoritate, potuit et consuevit clarificare quos voluit: quod sapienti non potest esse ambiguum, qui varias scripturas solerti indagatione diligentius perscrutatur.

No. XII. Narrative of the Murder of Thomas Beket, by Edward Grim, who was wounded while endeavouring to defend him.

Abierunt tum quidam magni viri ad regem, et sanctum martyrem detulerunt, ita ut rex gravissime commotus iteratis vocibus ita dixisse feratur: Inertes ac miseros homines enutrivi et erexi in regno meo, qui nec fidem servant domino suo, quem a plebeio quodam clerico tam probrose patiuntur illudi. Aderant ibi nobiles quatuor genere conspicui, et e familia regis. Ii hæc verba ex ore regis rapientes, secus ea, quam rex vellet, interpretati sunt: moxque in necem sancti viii conspirarunt, nescienteque rege, mare celerrime trajecerunt, rege, ubi id comperit, suspicante mali quippiam illos moliri, mittenteque nuncios, qui eos revocarent: sed illi jam longius antecesserant, quam ut possent revocari. Invito quidem rege cæsum ab illis fuisse archiepiscopum, vel inde satis liquet, quod ibi comperit crudelissimum facinus, inciedibili dolore et horrore correptus fuit. Voluerat ille vel in carcerem eum conjicere, aut alio modo coercere, ut a sententia illum deduceret. Sed illi homines nefarii postquam in Angliam venerunt, adjunctis sibi quibusdam ministris regis, quos archiepiscopus excommunicarat, et militum satellitumque coacta manu, mentiebantur se jussos a rege, tollere e medio archiepiscopum. Itaque die illo, qui sanctorum Innocentum festum sequitur, absoluto jam prandio, sese colligunt adversus virum pium et innocentem, qui jam in interiorem domum secesserat cum domesticis, de negotiis tractaturus. Soli autem quatuor cum uno satellite ingressi sunt, itumque illis obviam est honorifice, tanquam domesticis regis. Illi jubent dici archiepiscopo, velle se cum ipso regis nomine colloqui. Annuit vir sanctus, ut introducantur. Introducti diu sedent taciti et neque salutant, neque appellant archiepiscopum. Tacet etiam ipse aliquamdiu: postea salutat pacifice. Illi pro salutatione reddunt maledicta, adeoque in necem ejus ferebantur præcipites, ut nisi ostiarius clericos, quos vir sanctus exire jusserat, revocasset, hasta quadam, quæ illic stabat, illum confodere voluerint, uti postea confessi sunt.

Intro autem reversis clericis, qui primarius erat in his quatuor viris, ita ait: Rex controversiis omnibus consopitis, te ad tuam sedem remisit: tu maleficus bona compensans, eos, quorum opera filius regis coronatus est, a suo ministerio suspendisti, ministros regis anathemate percussisti, ut satis appareat, te filio regis, modo possis, coronam auferre constituisse. De his utrum coram rege purgare te velis, edicito. Ea enim causa nos huc missi sumus. Respondit vir sanctus: Testis est Deus, nunquam me filio regis coronam eripere voluisse, cui ego mallem tres alias adjungere cum regnis amplissimis, modo id recte atque ordine fieri possit. Neque vero ego suspendi a ministerio episcopos, sed dominus Papa id tecit, nec me decet absolvere, ut vos vultis, quos ille ligavit. Tum illi: Jubet, inquiunt, rex ut cum omnibus tuis e regno excedas. Contra archiepiscopus: Sed me deinceps, ait, Deo propitio, nemo inter ecclesiam meam et mare conspiciet. Non veni ut fugerem: hic me reperiet, si quis quæsierit. Illis objicientibus, quod animi furore percitus, ministros regis ex ecclesia turpiter ejecisset, vir sanctus cum multo spiritus fervore illis respondit: Quisquis ausus fuerit sanctæ romanæ sedis instituta, vel ecclesiæ Christi jura violare, nec ultro satisfecerit, non parcam, nec differam ecclesiastica censura coercere peccantem. Hac illi viri Dei constantia perculsi, propius accedunt, dicuntque ei: In capitis tui periculum hæc prolocutus es. At vir sanctus: Non me, inquit, terrent minæ vestiæ: nec gladii vestri promptiores sunt ad feriendum, quam ego ad martyrium obeundum Alium quærite, qui vos fugiat: me collocato pede pro Domino meo præliaturum comperietis. Illis cum clamore et contumeliis exeuntibus, vir Dei suos consolabatur, et, ut nobis visum est, qui præsentes adfuimus, ita sedebat imperterritus, ac si ad nuptias invitatus esset ab illis.

Mox revertuntur illi loricati, accinctique gladiis, et securibus armati. Fores autem clausæ erant, nec pulsantibus aperiebatur. Tum illi occultiore via per pomarium ad sepem ligneam divertunt, ferroque et magna vi sibi aditum parant. Eo horribili strepitu ministri et clerici pene omnes territi fugerunt. Hortantibus illis, qui remanserant, ut vir sanctus in ecclesiam se conferret, plane recusavit. Non enim tali casu fugiendum erat, sed dandum potius subditis exemplum ut mallet quisque feriri gladio, quam videri legis divinæ contemptum, et sacrorum canonum eversionem. Instabant vero monachi, aiebant indecorum esse a vespertinis laudibus, quæ tum celebrabantur, ipsum abesse. Ille vero non cessit, veritus se privatum iri optata martyrii corona, si in templum esset ingressus, cujus reverentia arceri possent a tanto scelere parricidæ illi. Sane postquam ab exilio reversus fuit, sic dixisse fertur, tanquam certus jam se per martyrium hinc emigratum: Habetis hic dilectum Deo ac vere martyrem Elphegum: alium quoque vobis sine mora divina miseratio providebit. Monachi autem cum eum permovere non possent, valde invitum asportarunt in ecciesiam: quam cum ingressi essent, quatuoi illi nobiles cursu rapidissimo secuti sunt cum Hugone subdiacono deploratæ nequitiæ, quem malum clericum appellabant. Volentes autem monachi obserare foies ecclesiæ, prohibiti sunt a sancto viro, qui tum præclare dicebat: Nos patiendo potius quam pugnando, ex hoste triumphabimus; neque eo huc venimus ut repugnemus sed ut patiamur. Adsunt mox sacrilegi carnifices exclamantque furibundi: Ubi est Thomas Beket, regis et regni proditor? Eo non respondente, majori contentione vociferantur: Ubi est archiepiscopus? Tum ille plane intrepidus et imperritus: Ecce adsum, inquit, non proditor regni, sed sacerdos. Paratus sum pro illo mori, qui me redemit sanguine suo. Absit, ut propter enses vestros aut fugiam, aut a justititia recedam. At illi: Absolve, inquiunt, quos excommunicasti et suspendisti a suo officio. Nulla, ait vii sanctus, ab illis exhibita est satisfactio, itaque non absolvam. Rursus illi: Nunc igitur morieris, et recipies pro meritis. Ego vero, ait sanctus martyr, pro Domino meo mori paratus sum, ut ecclesia meo sanguine pacem et libertatem assequatur. Præcipio autem ex parte omnipotentis Dei, ne quemquam ex meis lædatis. Mox illi, facto impetu, in eum irruunt, conanturque extra fores extrahere, illic eum aut jugulaturi, aut vinctum absportaturi, uti postea confessi sunt. Sed cum difficile posset eum loco moveri, et unum ex eis acrius insistentem a se removisset, is terribili incersus furore, ensem contra ejus verticem vibravit. Tum vero pius et sanctus vir cernens adesse horam, qua promissam percipierit martyrn coronam, cervicem instar orantis inclinavit, junctisque et sursum erectis manibus, Deo et sanctæ Mariæ beatoque martyri Dionysio suam et ecclesiæ causam commendavit. Vix ea prolocutum, nefandus vir, metuens ne populus eum eriperet ex manibus ipsorum, coronam capitis ejus, vulnere capiti inflicto, tanta vi amputavit, ut pariter secaret et præcideret bracchium isthæc referentis, qui solus, cunctis et monachis et clericis præ metu fugientibus, sancto martyri constanter adhæsit, et inter ulnas eum continuit, donec altera earum amputata est. Additus inde est alter ictus in sacrum corpus ejus, et ille mansit immotus, nihil se commovens. Tertio percussus, genua flexit, dicens submissa voce: Pro nomine Jesu et ecclesiæ defensione mori paratus sum. Tum vero tertius ex illis sacrilegis percussoribus, ita procumbenti grave inflixit vulnus, ut cum sanguine pariter e capite cerebrum in ejus faciem deflueret. Quartus interim abigebat supervenientes, ut cæteri possent in ea horrenda cæde liberins versari. Quinto loco accessitis, quem ante diximus, Hugo subdiaconus execrabilis, et posito pede in collum sanctissimi martyris, quod sine horrore dici non potest, cerebrum cum sanguine per pavimentum sparsit, aitque ad illos quatuor: Abeamus hinc: iste posthac non resurget.

In his omnibus incredibilem licebat sancti martyris videre constantiam, ut qui neque manum, neque vestem opponeret percussoribus illis, nec ulluin vel verbum, vel clamorem ederet, immo ne gemitum quidem, aut aliquam doloris significationem exprimeret: sed caput gladiis oblatum teneret immotum, donec cerebro cum sanguine erumpente, tanquam oraturus, corpus in terram, spiritum in sinum Abrahæ deposuit. Cæsus est vir pius a cruentissimis illis carnificibus tempore sacro et loco sacro, in ipsa domo Dei, quarto calendas januarii, anno Christi millesimo centesimo septuagesimo.

No. XIII. Letter from king Louis VII. to pope Alexander III., demanding vengeance against the murderers of Thomas Beket. (ad 1171.)

Domino et Patri sanctissimo Alexandro, Dei gratia summo Pontifici, Ludovicus, Francorum Rex, salutem et debitam reverentiam. Ab humanæ pietatis lege recedit filius qui matrem deturpat, neque Creatoris beneficii reminiscitur qui de sanctæ ecclesiæ illata turpitudine non tristatur. Unde specialius est condolendum, et novitatem doloris excitat inaudita novitas crudelitatis, quoniam in sanctum Dei insurgens malignitas, in pupillam Christi gladium infixit, et lucernam cantuariensis ecclesiæ non tam crudeliter quam turpiter jugulavit. Excitetur igitur exquisitæ genus justitiæ, denudetur gladius Petri in ultionem cantuariensis martyris, quia sanguis ejus pro universali clamat ecclesia, non tam sibi quam universæ ecclesiæ conquerens de vindicta. Et ecce ad tumultum agonistæ, ut relatum est nobis, divina in miraculis revelatur gloria et divinitus demonstratur, ubi humatus requiescit, pro cujus nomine decertavit. Latores vero præsentium, patre orbati, vestræ pietati seriem indicabunt. Testimonio itaque veritatis aurem mitissimam adhibite, et tam de isto negotio quam de aliis, ipsis tamquam nobis credite. Valeat pietas vestra.

No. XIV. Letter from Thibault, earl of Blois, to pope Alexander III., on the murder of Thomas Beket. (ad 1171.)

Reverendissimo domino suo et patri Alexandro, summo Pontifici, Theobaldus blesensis comes et regni Francorum procurator, salutem et debitam cum filiali subjectione reverentiam. Vestræ placuit majestati quod inter dominum cantuariensem archiepiscopum et regem Anglorum pax reformaretur et integra firmaretur concordia. Itaque, juxta vestri tenorem mandati, illum rex Angliæ vultu hilari, fronte læta et pacem spondente, et gratiam sibi referente, recepit. Huic paci et concordiæ adfui, et me præsente dominus cantuariensis apud regem de coronatione filii sui conquestus est, quem voto festinante et ardenti desiderio in culmen regiæ dignitatis fecerat promoveri. Hujus autem injuriæ reus sibi et male conscius rex Angliæ, juris et satisfactionis ipsi cantuariensi pignus dedit. Conquestus est etiam de ipsis qui, contra jus et decus cantuariensis ecclesiæ, novum regem in sedem regiam præsumpserunt intrudere, non zelo justitiæ, non ut Deo placerent, sed ut tyrannum placarent. De illis vero liberam et licentem rex ei concessit facultatem, ut ad vestræ et suæ potestatis arbitrium in eos sententiam promulgaret. Hæc siquidem vobis, vel juramento, vel quolibet alio libuerit modo, attestari paratus sum et sancire. Sic, itaque pace facta vir Dei nil metuens recessit, ut gladio jugulum subderet et cervicem exponeret ferienti. Passus est ergo martyrium agnus innocens, crastina sanctorum Innocentium die; effusus est sanguis justus, ubi nostræ viaticum salutis sanguis Christi solitus est immolari. Canes aulici, familiares et domestici regis Angliæ, se ministros regis præbuerunt, et nocentes sanguinem innocentem effuderunt. Hujus prodigii modum detestabilem vobis scripto plenius significarem, sed vereor ne mihi in odium adscribatur; et latores præsentium patenter et plenius rei ordinem evolent, et eorum relatione discetis quantus sit mœroris cumulus, quanta sit universæ ecclesiæ et matris cantuariensis calamitas. Hanc salvo pudore non potest dissimulare romana mater ecclesia. Quidquid emm in filiam præsumitur, nimirum redundat in parentem, nec sine matris injuria captivatur filia. Ad vos itaque clamat sanguis justi, et flagitat ultionem. Vobis ergo, Pater sanctissime, adsit et consulat Pater Omnipotens, qui filii sui cruorem mundo impendit, ut mundi noxas detergeret et deleret maculas peccatorum: ille vobis insinuet vindictæ voluntatem, et suggerat facultatem ut ecclesia, inauditi sceleris confusa magnitudine, districta hilarescat ultione. Valeat Sanctitas Vestra, et, sicut vos decet, facite.

No. XV. Letter in which the Bishop of Lisieux, on the part of all the Prelates of Normandy, relates to the Pope the conduct of Henry II. after the murder of Thomas Beket. (ad 1171.)

Alexandro papæ Ernulphus, lexoviensis episcopus, post mortem S. Thomæ. Cum, apud regem nostrum pariter congregati, de magnis ecclesiæ regnique negotiis tractaturi crederemur, subitus nos de domino cantuariensi rumor lamentabili mœrore perfudit, adeo ut in momento securitas in stuporem, et consultationes in suspiria verterentur. Per aliquos enim ab Anglis revertentes certa relatione didicimus quod quidam inimici ejus, crebris, ut aiebant, exacerbationibus ad iracundiam et amentiam provocati, temere in eum irruptione facta (quod sine dolore dicere non possumus nec debemus), personam ejus aggredi et trucidare crudeliter perstiterunt. Ad regis dcnique notitiam rumor infaustus quibusdam preferentibus penetravit, quoniam ei non licuit ignorare quod ad ejus vindictam jure potestatis et gladii videbatur specialius pertinere. Qui statim in primis nefandi sermonis initiis ad omnia lamentationum et miserationum genera conversus, regiam prorsus majestatem quasi cilicio immutans et cinere, multo fortius amicum exhibuit quam principem, stupens interdum, et post stuporem ad gemitus acriores et acerbiores amaritudines revoltus. Tribus fere diebus conclusus in cubiculo, nec cibum capere, nec consolatores admittere sustinuit; sed mœstitia perniciosiore voluntariam sibi perniciem indicere pertinaciter videbatur. Miserabilis erat malorum facies, et anxia vicissitudo dolorum: quoniam qui sacerdotem lamentabamur primitus, de regis salute consequenter cœpimus desperare, et in alterius nece miserabiliter utrumque credebamus interiisse. Porro, quærentibus amicis et episcopis maxime quid eum ad se redire non permitteret, respondit se metuere ne sceleris auctores et complices, veteris rancoris confidentia, impunitatem sibi criminis promisissent, licet ipse novas inimicitias recentibus injurus et frequentibus malefieiis compararet; arbitrari se nominis sui famam et gloriam maledictis æmulatorum respergi posse, et confingi id ex ejus conscientia processisse: sed omnipotentem Deum se testem invocare in animam suam, quod opus nefandum nec sua voluntate nec conscientia commissum est, nec artificio perquisitum, nisi forte in hoc delictum sit, quod adhuc minus diligere credebatur: super hoc quoque se judicio ecclesiæ prorsus exponere, et humiliter suscepturum quidquid in eo fuerit salubriter statuendum. Communicato igitur consilio, in hoc universorum consultatio conquievit, ut sedis apostolicæ sapientiam et auctoritatem consuleret, quam spiritu sapientiæ et potestatis plenitudine christiana fides prædicat abundantius redundare, et apud eam suam studeat innocentiam modis legitimis et canonicis approbare. Supplicamus ergo quatenus, secundum datum a Deo vobis spiritum consilii et fortitudinis, tanti sceleris auctoribus secundum facti immanitatem servitas vestra retribuat, et suam innocentiam regi pietas apostolica et in statu suo velit affectuosius conservare. Omnipotens Deus personam vestram ecclesiæ suæ per multa tempora conservet incolumem.

No. XVI. Letter from Henry II. to the Pope, on the subject of the Murder of Thomas Beket. (ad 1171.)

Alexandro, Dei gratia summo Pontifici, Henricus rex Anglorum, et dux Normannorum et Aquitanorum, et Comes Andegavorum, salutem et debitam devotionem. Ob reverentiam romanæ ecclesiæ et amorem vestrum, quem. Deo teste, fideliter quæsivi et constanter usque modo servavi. Thomæ cantuariensi archiepiscopo, juxta vestri formam mandati, pacem et possessionum suarum plenam restitutionem indulsi, et cum honesto commeatu in Angliam transfretare concessi. Ipse vero in ingressu suo non pacis lætitiam, sed iguem portavit et gladium, dum contra me de regno et corona proposuit quæstionem. Insuper meos servientes passim sine causa excommunicare aggressus est. Tantam igitur protervitatem hominis non ferentes, excommunicati et alii de Anglia irruerunt in eum, et, quod dicere sine dolore non valeo, occiderunt. Quia igitur iram quam contra illum dudum conceperam, timeo causam huic maleficio præstitisse, Deo teste, graviter sum turbatus. Et quia in hoc facto plus famæ meæ quam conscientiæ timeo, rogo serenitatem vestram ut in hoc articulo me salubris consilii medicamine foveatis.

No. XVII. Letter from Henry II. to the Pope, on the Subject of the Rebellion of his Sons. (ad 1173.)

Sanctissimo domino suo Alexandro, Dei gratia catholicæ ecclesiæ summo Pontifici, Henricus, rex Angliæ, dux Northmanniæ et Aquitaniæ, comes Andegavensis et Cenomanensis, salutem et devotæ subjectionis obsequium. In magnorum discriminum angustiis, ubi domestica concilia remedium non inveniunt, eorum suffragia implorantur quorum prudentiam in altioribus negotiis experientia diuturmor approbavit. Longe lateque divulgata est filiorum meorum malitia, quos ita in exitium patris spiritus iniquitatis armavit, ut gloriam reputent et triumphum patrem persequi, et filiales affectus in omnibus diffiteri, prævemente meorum exigentia delictorum. Ubi pleniorem voluptatem contulerat mihi Dominus, ibi gravius me flagellat; et quod sine lacrymis non dico, contra sanguinem meum et viscera mea cogor odium mortale concipere, et extraneos mihi quærere successores. Illud præterea sub silentio præterire non possum, quod amici mei recesserunt a me, et domestici mei quærunt animam meam. Sic enim familiarium meorum animos intoxicavit clandestina conjuratio, ut observantia proditoriæ conspirationis universa posthabeant. Malunt namque meis adhærere filiis contra me transfugæ et mendici, quam regnare mecum et in amplissimis dignitatibus præfulgere. Quoniam ergo vos extulit Deus in eminentiam officii pastoralis, ad dandam scientiam salutis plebi ejus, licet absens corpore, præsens tamen ammo me vestris advolvo genibus, consilium salutare deposcens. Vestræ jurisdictionis est regnum Angliæ, et quantum ad feudatarii juris obligationem, vobis duntaxat obnoxius teneor et astringor. Experiatui Anglia quid possit romanus pontifex; et quia materialibus armis non utitur, patrimonium beati Petri spirituali gladio tueatur. Contumeliam filiorum poteram armis rebellibus propulsare, sed patrem non possum exuere. Nam, et Jeremia teste, nudaverunt lamiæ mammas suas; lactaverunt catulos suos. Et licet errata eorum quasi mentis efferatæ me fecerint, retineo paternos affectus, et quamdam violentiam diligendi eos mihi conditio naturalis importat. Utinam saperent et intelligerent ac novissima providerent! Lactant filios meos domestici hostes, et occasione malignandi habita non desistunt, quousque redigatur virtus eorum in pulverem, et, converso capite in caudam, servi eorum dominentur eis, juxta verbum illud Salomonis: Servus astutus filio dominabitur imprudenti. Excitet ergo prudentiam vestram Spiritus consilii, ut convertatis corda filiorum ad patrem. Cor enim patris pro beneplacito vestro convertetur ad filios, et in fide illius per quem reges regnant, vestræ magnitudini promitto me dispositioni vestræ in omnibus pariturum. Vos ecclesiæ suæ, Pater sancte, diu Christus servet incolumem.

No. XVIII. Political Poems of Bertrand de Born, preceded by the Historical Notices given in the Manuscripts at the head of each of the Productions of this Troubadour.

Sirvente on the League formed against Richard, earl of Poitiers, by the Scigneurs of Ventadour, Combor, Ségur, Tarenne, Gordon, and the count of Périgord.

Bertrans de Born, en la Sazon qu'el avia guerra ab lo comte Richart, el fez si qu'el vescoms de Ventedorn, el vescoms de Comborn, el vescoms de Segur, so fo lo vescoms de Lemogas, e'l vescoms de Torena, se jureron ab lo comte de Peiregors et ab los borges d'aquellas encontradas et ab lo seingnor de Gordon et ab lo seingnor de Montfort, e si se sarreron ensems per qu'il se deffendesson dal com Richard que los volia deseretar, per so car il volion ben al rei jove son fraire, ab cui el se guerreiava, alqual el avia toltas las rendas de las caretas, de lasquals caretas lo reis joves prendia certa causa, si com lo paire l'o avia donat, e no'l laissava neus albergar segur en tota la soa terra. E per aquest sagramen que tich aquist aviam fait de guerreiar en Richart, Bertrans de Born si fez aquest sirventes:

*

o Pus Ventedorn e Comborn e Segur

o E Torena e Montfort e Guordon

o An fag acort ab Peiregor et jur,

o E li borges si claven d'eviron,

o M'es bon e belh huyemais qu'ieu m'entremeta

o D'un sirventes per elhs aconortar,

o Qu'ieu no vuelh ges sia mia Toleta,

o Per qu'ieu segurs non i pogues estar.

*

o A! Puiguillems, e Clarens, e Granolh,

o E Sanh Astier, molt avetz gran honor,

o Et ieu mezeis qui conoisser la m vol,

o Et a sobrier Engolesmes maior,

o Qu'en charretier que gurpis sa charreta

o Non a deniers ni no pren ses paor;

o Per qu'ab onor pretz mais pauca terreta

o Qu'un emperi tener à dezonor.

*

o Si'l rics vescoms qui es caps dels Guascos,

o A cui apen Bearns e Gavardans,

o E'n Vezias o vol e'n Bernardos,

o E'l Senher d'Ayx, e selh cui es Marsans,

o D'aquellia part aura 'l coms pro que fassa,

o Et eissamen aissi com el es pros,

o Ab sa gran ost que atrai et amassa,

o Venha s' en sai et ajoste s'ab nos.

*

o Si Talliaborcs, e Pons, e Lezinhans,

o E Malleons, e Taunais fos en pes,

o Et a Siurac fos vescoms vius e sans,

o Ja non creirai que non nos ajudes

o Selh de Toartz; pois lo coms lo menassa,

o Venha s'ab nos, e non sia ges vans,

o E demandem li tro que dreg non fassa

o Dels homes qu'el nos a traitz d'entr' els mans.

*

o Entre Peitau e la Ylha' n Bocart,

o E Mirabelh, et Laudun, e Chino,

o A Claraval an bastit, ses regart,

o Un belh caslar el mieg d'un plan cambo:

o Mas no vuelh ges lo sapcha ni lo veya.

o Lo joves reys, que no ill sabria bo,

o Mas paor ai, pus aitan fort blanqueya,

o Qu'el lo veira ben de Matafelo.

*

o Del rey Felip veirem be si panteya,

o O si segra los usatges Karlo;

*

o D'en Talhafer, pus so senher l'autreya

o D'Engolesme, et elh l'en a fag do;

*

o Quar non es bo de so que reys autreya.

o Quant a dig d'oc, que puyes digua de no.

Sirvente on the Reconciliation of Bertrand de Born with Richard, Son of King Henry II.

Al temps qu'en Richartz era coms de Peitieus, anz qu'el fos reis, Bertrans de Born si era sos enemics, per so qu'en Bertrans volia ben al rer jove que guerreiava adoncs ab en Richart qu era sos fraire. En Bertrans si avia fait virar contra'n Richart lo bon vescomte de Lemogas que avia nom n Aemars, e'l vescomte de Ventedorn, e'l vescomte de Gumel, e'l comte de Peiragors e son fraire, e'l comte d'Engoleime e sos dos fraires, e'l comte Raimon de Tolosa, e'l comte de Flandres, e'l comte de Barsolona, en Centoill d'Estarae, un comte de Gascoingna, en Gaston de Bearn, comte de Bigora, e'l comte de Digon, e tuich aquistz si l'abandoneron e feiron patz ses lui, e si s perjureron vas lui. En Aemais, lo vescoms de Lemogas, que plus l'era tengutz d'amor e de sagramen si l'abandonet et fetz patz ses lui; en Richartz cant saup que tuich aquist l'avion abandonat, el s'en venc denant Autalort ab la soa ost, e dis e juret que jamais no s'en partiria si'l no ill dava Autafort, e no venia a son comandamen. Bertrans, quant auzi so qu'en Richartz avia jurat, e sabia qu'el era abandonatz de totz aquestz que vos avetz auzit, si'l det lo castel, e si venc a son comandamen. E'l coms Richartz lo receup, perdonan li e baisan lo; et sapchatz que per una cobla qu'el fetz el sirventes locals comensa:

* Si' l coms m'es avinens

* E non avars,

Lo coms Richartz li perdonet son brau talan, e rendet li son castel Autafort e venc sos fin amic coral; e vai s'en en Bertrans e comensa a guerreiar n Aemar lo vescomte que l'avia desamparat, e'l comte de Peiregors; don Bertrans receup de grans dans, et el a lor fetz de grans mals. En

Richartz, quant fon devengutz reis passet outra mar, e'n Bertrans remas guerreian, don Bertrans fetz d'aquestas doas razos aquest sirventes:

*

o Ges no mi desconort,

o S'ieu ai perdut,

o Qu'ieu non chant e m deport,

o E non m'aiut

o Com cobres Autafort

o Qu'ieu ai rendut

o Al senhor de Niort,

o Car l'a volgut,

o E pois en merceian

o Li sui vengutz denan,

o E'l coms en perdonan

o M'a receubut baisan;

o Ges no i dei aver dan,

o Qui qu'en dises antan,

o Ni lausengier non blan.

*

o Vas mi son perjurat

o Trei palazi,

o E'l quatre vescomtat

o De Lemozi,

o E li dui penchenat

o Peiragorzi,

o E li trei comte fat

o Englomezi,

o E'n Sestols ab Gasto,

o Et tuit l'autre baro

o Que m feron plevizo,

o E lo coms de Dijo,

o E Raimons d'Avigno,

o Ab lo comte breto,

o Et anc uns no m tenc pro.

*

o Si 'l coms m'es avinens

o E non avars,

o Mout li serai valens,

o En sos afars,

o E fis com fins argens,

o Humils e cars;

o E' l coms sega lo sens

o Que fai la mars,

o Quan ren i chai de bo

o Vol ben qu'ab lieis s'esto,

o E so que no 'l te pro

o Gieta fois el sablo;

o Qu'aissi s tainh de baro

o Que fassa son perdo,

o E s'el tol que pois do.

*

o Ses pro tener amic

o Tenc per aital

o Com fas mon enemic

o Que no m fai mal;

o Qu'en un mostier antic

o De San Marsal

o Mi jureron mant ric

o Sobr' un missal;

o Tals mi plevie sa fe

o Non feses patz ses me,

o Qu'anc pois no m'en tenc re,

o Ni li sovenc de me,

o Ni 'll membret mas de se,

o Quant si mes a merce;

o E non estet ges be.

*

o Lo comte vueill pregar

o Que ma maiso

o Mi comant a gardar,

o O que la m do;

o Q'ades mi son avar

o Tut sist baro,

o Q'ab els non puose durar

o Ses contenso;

o Ara mi pot cobiar

o Lo coms ses mal estar,

o Et ieu vas lui tornar

o E servir et onrar;

o E non o volgui far,

o Tro c'al dezamparar

o Sui vengutz d'en Aimar.

*

o Ma bella Esmanda's gar

o Hueimais de sordeiar,

o Que ja per meilhurar

o Non la cal trebailhar;

o Qu'el mon non sai sa par

o De joi ni de parlar

o Ni de bell domneiar.

*

o Domna, ab cor avar

o De prometr' e de dar,

o Pois no m voletz colgar

o Donasses m'un baisar;

o Aissi m podes ric far

o E mor dan restaurar,

o Si dombres dieus mi gar.

*

o Papiol, mon chantar

o Vai a mi dons contar;

o Per amor d'en Aimar

o Mi lais de guerreiar.

Sirvente in which Bertrand de Born encourages Prince Henry to resume the War against his brother Richard.

En la sazos qu'el reis joves ac faita la patz ab son fraire Richart et el ac fenida la demanda gue il fazia de la terra, si com fo la volontat del rei Henric lor paire; e'l paire li dava certa livrason de deniers per vianda, e per so que besoigua l'era, e neguna terra non tenia ni possezia; ni negus hom a lui no venia per mantenemen ni per secors de guerra; en Bertrans de Born e tuit li autre baron que l'avian mantengut contra Richart foron molt dolen. E'l reis joves si s'en anet en Lombardia torneiar e solasar; e lesset totz aquestz baros en la gueria ab en Richart. En Richartz asega borcs e chastels, e pres terras, e derroca e ars e abrasa. E'l reis joves si sojornava, torniava e dormia e solasava; don en Bertrans si fetz aquest sirventes que comensa:

*

o D'un sirventes no m quam far longor ganda,

o Tal talent ai qu'ei digua e que l'espanda,

o Quar n'ai razon tan novella e tan granda

o Del jove rey qu'a fenit sa demanda

o Son frair Richart, pus sos pairs lo y comanda,

o Tant es forsatz!

o Pus en Enrics terra non te ni manda,

o Sia reys dels malvatz.

*

o Que malvatz fai quar aissi viu a randa,

o A livrazon, a comte et a guaranda;

o Reys coronatz, que d'autrui pren livranda,

o Mal sembla Arnaut lo marques de Bellanda

o N'il pros Guillem que conquis tor Miranda,

o Tan fon prezatz!

o Pus en Peitau lur mente e lur truanda,

o No y er mais tant amatz.

*

o Ja per dormir non er de Goberlanda,

o Reys dels Engles, ni non conquerra Yrlanda,

o Ni duex clamatz de la terra normanda,

o Ni tenra Angieus ni Monsaurelli ni Canda

o Ni de Peitieus non aura la miranda,

o Ni coms palatz

o Sai de Bordelh, ni dels Gascos part landa

o Senliers ni de Bazatz.

*

o Cosselh vuelh dar el so de n'Alamanda

o Lai a'n Richart, sitot non lo m demanda,

o Ja per son frair mais sos homes no blanda.

o No com fai elh, ans asetja e'ls aranda,

o Tolh lur castelhs e derroqu' et abranda

o Devez totz latz;

o E'l reys torn lai ab aiselhs de Guarlanda

o Et l'autre sos conhatz.

*

o Lo coms Jaufres cui es Breselianda

o Volgra fos primiers natz,

o Car es cortes, e fos en sa comanda

o Regismes e duguatz.

Lament of Bertrand de Born on the Death of Prince Henry.

Lo plainz qu'en Bertrans de Born fetz del rei jove non porta autra razon sinon qu'el reis joves era lo meiller del mon. En Bertrans li volia meills qu'a home del mon, e lo reis joves ad el meills qu'a home del mon; e plus lo crezia que home del mon; per que lo reis Enrics sos paire e'l coms Richartz sos fraire volian mal a'n Bertran. E per la valor qu'el reis joves avia, e per lo grand dol que fon a tota gen, el fetz lo plaing de lui que dis:

*

o Si tut li dol e'l plor e'l marrimen

o E las dolors e'l dans e'l caitivier

o Que hom argues en est segle dolen

o Fosson emsems, semblaran tut leugier

o Contra la mort del jove rei engles,

o Don reman pretz e jovent doloiros,

o E'l mon escurs e tenhs e tenebros,

o Sem de tot joi, plen de tristor et d'ira.

*

o Dolent e trist e plen de marrimen

o Son remanzut li cortes soudadier

o E'l ti obador e'l joglar avinen,

o Trop an agut en mort mortal guerier,

o Que tolt lor a lo joven rei engles

o Vas cui eran li plus lare cobeitos:

o Ja non er mais, ni non crezas que fos

o Va aquest dan el segle plors ni ira.

*

o Estenta mort, plena de marrimen,

o Vanar te pods, qu'el melhor cavalier

o As tolt al mon qu'anc fos de nulha gen!

o Quar non es res qu'a pretz aia mestier

o Que tot no fos el jove rei engles;

o E fora miels, s'a dieu plagues razos,

o Que visques el que mant autre envios

o Qu'anc no feron als pros mas dol et ira.

*

o D'aquest segle flac, plen de marrimen,

o S'amor s'en vai, son joi teinh mensongier,

o Que ren no i a que non torn en cozen

o Totz jorns veiretz que val mens huei que ier:

o Cascun se mir el jove rei engles

o Qu'era del mon lo plus valens dels pros,

o Ar es anatz son gen cor amoros,

o Dont es dolors e desconort et ira.

*

o Celui que plac per nostre marrimen

o Venir el mon, e nos trais d'encombrier,

o E receup mort a nostre salvamen,

o Co a senhor humils e dreiturier

o Clamen merce, qu'al jove rei engles

o Perdon, s'il platz, si com es vers perdos

o E'l fassa estar ab onratz companhos

o Lai on anc dol non ac ne i aura ira.

Narrative of the interview between Bertrand de Born and Henry II. after the capture of the Castle of Hautefort.

Lo reis Henrics d'Engleterra si tenia assis en Bertran de Born dedins Autafort, e'l combatia ab sos edeficis, que molt li volia gran mal, car el crezia que tota la guerra qu'el reis joves, son fillz, l'avia faicha qu'en Bertrans la il agues faita far; e per so era vengutz denant Autafort per lui desiritar. E'l reis d'Aragon venc en l'ost del rei Henric denant Antafort. E cant Bertrans o saub, si fo molt alegres qu'el reis d'Aragon era en l'ost, per so qu'el era sos amics especials. E'l reis d'Aragon si mandet sos messatges dins lo castel, qu'en Bertrans li mandet pan e vin e carn; et el si l'en mandet assatz; e per lo messatge per cui el mandet los presenz, el li mandet pregan qu'el fezes si qu'el fezes mudar los edificis e far traire en autra part, qu'el murs on il ferion era tot rotz. Et el, per gran aver del rei Henric, li dis tot so qu'en Bertrans l'avia mandat a dir. E'l reis Henrics si fes metre dels edificis en aquella part on saub qu'el murs era rotz, e fon lo murs per terra, e'l castels pres; e'n Bertrans ab tota sa gen fon menatz al pabaillon del rei Henric. E'l reis lo receup molt mal; e'l reis Henrics si'l dis: "Bertrans, Bertrans, vos avetz dig que anc la meitatz del vostre sen no vos besognet nulls temps, mas sapchatz qu'ara vos besogna ben totz.— Seingner, dis Bertrans, el es ben vers qu'eu o dissi, e dissi me ben vertat." E'l reis dis: "Eu cre ben qu'el vos sia aras faillitz.—Seingner, dis en Bertrans, ben m'es faillitz.—E com? dis lo reis.—Seingner, dis en Bertrans, lo jor qu'el valens joves reis, vostre fills mori, eu perdi lo sen e'l saher e la conoissensa." E'l reis quant auzi so qu'en Bertrans li dis en ploran dell fill, venc li granz dolors al cor de pietat et als oills, si que no s pot tener qu'el non pasmes de dolor. E quant el revenc do pasmazon, el crida e dis en ploran: "En Bertrans, en Bertrans, vos avetz ben drech, e es ben razos, si vos avetz perdut lo sen per mon fill, qu'el vos volia meils que ad home del mon; et eu per amor de lui vos quit la persona e l'aver e'l vostre castel, e vos ren la mia amor e la mia gracia, e vos don cinc cenz marcs d'argen per los dans que vos avetz receubutz." En Bertrans, si'l cazec als pes, referren li gracias e merces. E'l reis ab tota la soa ost s'en anet.

No. XIX. Sirvente of Richard Cœur-de-Lion on his Captivity.

*

o Ja nuls hom pres non dira sa razon

o Adrechament, si com hom dolens non;

o Mas per conort deu hom faire canson:

o Pre n'ay d'amis, mas paure son li don,

o Ancta lur es, si per ma rezenson

o Soi sai dos yvers pres.

*

o Or sapchon ben miey hom e miey baron,

o Angles, Norman, Peytavin et Gascon,

o Qu'ieu non ay ja si paure compagnon

o Qu'ieu laissasse, per aver, en preison,

o Non ho dic mia per nulla retraison,

o Mas anquar soi ie pres.

*

o Car sai eu ben per ver, certanament,

o Qn'hom mort ni pres n'a amic ni parent,

o E si m laissan per aur ni per argent,

o Mal m'es per mi, mas pieg m'es per ma gent,

o Qu apres ma mort n'auran reprochament,

o Si sai mi laisson pres.

*

o No m meravilh s'ieu ay lo cor dolent,

o Que mos senher met ma terra en turment;

o No li membra del nostre sagrament

o Que nos feimes el Sans cominalment;

o Ben sai de ver que gaire longament

o Non serai en sai pres.

*

o Suer comtessa, vostre pretz sobeiran

o Sal dieus, et gard la bella qu'ieu am tan,

o Ni per cui soi ja pres.

No. XX. The King's Disguise, and Friendship with Robin Hood.

*

o King Richard hearing of the pranks

o Of Robin Hood and his men,

o He much admir'd and more desir'd

o To see both him and them.

*

o Then with a dozen of his lords

o To Nottingham he rode:

o When he came there, he made good cheer,

o And took up his abode.

*

o He having staid there some time,

o But had no hopes to speed,

o He and his lords, with one accord,

o All put on monk's weeds.

*

o From Fountain abbey they did ride,

o Down to Barnsdale,

o Where Robin Hood prepared stood,

o All company to assail.

*

o The king was higher than the rest,

o And Robin thought he had

o An abbot been whom he had seen;

o To rob him he was glad.

*

o He took the king's horse by the head:

o —"Abbot," says he, "abide;

o I am bound to rue such knaves as you,

o That live in pomp and pride."

*

o —"But we are messengers from the king,"

o The king himself did say;

o "Near to this place, his royal grace

o To speak with thee does stay."

*

o —"God save the king," said Robin Hood,

o "And all that wish him well,

o He that does deny his sovereignty,

o I wish he was in hell."

*

o —"Thyself thou cursest," said the king,

o "For thou a traitor art."

o "Nay, but that you are his messenger,

o I swear you he in heart.

*

o "For I never yet hurt any man

o That honest is and true;

o But those who give their minds to live

o Upon other men's due.

*

o "For I never hurt the husbandman

o That use to till the ground;

o Nor spill their blood, that range the wood,

o To follow hawk or hound.

*

o "My chiefest spite to clergy is,

o Who in these days bear sway;

o With fryars and monks, with their fine sprunks

o I make my chiefest prey.

*

o "But I am very glad," says Robin Hood,

o "That I have met you here;

o Come, before we end, you shall, my friend,

o Taste of our green wood cheer."

*

o The king he then did marvel much,

o And so did all his men,

o They thought with fear, what kind of cheer

o Robin would provide for them.

*

o Robin took the king's horse by the head,

o And led him to the tent:

o —"Thou would not be so us'd," quoth he,

o "But that my king thee sent.

*

o "Nay, more than that," quoth Robin Hood,

o "For good king Richard's sake,

o If you had as much gold as ever I told,

o I would not one penny take."

*

o Then Robin set his horn to his mouth,

o And a loud blast he did blow,

o Till an hundred and ten of Robin Hood's men

o Came marching all of a row.

*

o And when they came bold Robin before,

o Each man did bend his knee;

o "O," thought the king, "'tis a gallant thing,

o And a seemly sight to see"

*

o Within himself the king did say:

o —"These men of Robin Hood's

o More humble be than mine to me;

o So the court may learn of the woods."

*

o So then they all to dinner went

o Upon a carpet green;

o Black, yellow, red, finely mingled,

o Most curious to be seen.

*

o Venison and fowls were plenty there,

o With fish out of the river:

o King Richard swore, on sea or shore,

o He never was feasted better.

*

o Then Robin takes a cann of ale;

o —"Come let us now begin;

o And every man shall have his cann;

o Here's a health unto the king."

*

o The king himself drank to the king,

o So round about it went;

o Two barrels of ale, both stout and stale,

o To pledge that health was spent.

*

o And after that a bowl of wine

o In his hand took Robin Hood:

o —"Until I die, I'll drink wine," said he,

o "While I live in the green wood."

*

o —"Bend all your bows," said Robin Hood,

o "And with the grey goose wing

o Such sport now show, as you would do

o In the presence of the king."

*

o They shewed such brave archery,

o By cleaving stick and wands,

o That the king did say, "Such men as they

o Live not in many lands."

*

o —"Well, Robin Hood," then says the king,

o "If I could thy pardon get,

o To serve the king in every thing,

o Wouldst thou thy mind firm set?"

*

o —"Yes, with all my heart," bold Robin said

o So they flung off their hoods;

o To serve the king in every thing,

o They swore they would spend their bloods.

*

o —"For a clergyman was first my bane,

o Which makes me hate them all;

o But if you'll be so kind to me,

o Love them again I shall."

*

o —"I am the king, thy sovereign king,

o That appears before you all."

o When Robin saw that it was he,

o Strait then he down did fall.

*

o —"Stand up again," then said the king,

o "I'll thee thy pardon give:

o Stand up, my friend; who can contend

o When I give leave to live?"

*

o So they are all gone to Nottingham

o All shouting as they came;

o But when the people them did see,

o They thought the king was slain.

*

o And for that cause the outlaws were come

o To rule all as they list;

o And for to shun, which way to run,

o The people did not wist.

*

o The plowman left the plow in the fields,

o The smith ran from his shop;

o Old folks also, that scarce could go,

o Over their sticks did hop.

*

o The king soon did let them understand

o He had been in the green wood,

o And from that day for evermore

o He'd forgiven Robin Hood.

*

o Then the people they did hear,

o And the truth was known;

o They all did sing, God save the king,

o Hang care, the town's our own.

*

o —"What's that Robin Hood?" then said the sheriff,

o "That varlet I do hate;

o Both me and mine he caused to dine,

o And serv'd all with one plate."

*

o —"Ho ho," said Robin Hood, "I know what you mean;

o Come take your gold again:

o Be friends with me, and I with thee,

o And so with every man.

*

o "Now, master sheriff, you are paid;

o And since you are beginner,

o As well as you, give me my due,

o For you ne'er paid for that dinner.

*

o "But if that it should please the king,

o So much your house to grace,

o To sup with you, for to speak true,

o Know you ne'er was base."

*

o The sheriff could not gainsay,

o For a trick was put upon him;

o A supper was drest, the king was a guest,

o But he thought 'twould have undone him.

*

o They are all gone to London court,

o Robin Hood with all his train;

o He once was there a noble peer,

o And now he's there again.

No. XXI. The Birth of Robin Hood.

*

o O Willie's large o' limb and lith,

o And come o' high degree;

o And he is gane to Earl Richard

o To serve for meat and fee.

*

o Earl Richard had but ae daughter,

o Fair as a lily flower;

o And they made up their love-contract

o Like proper paramour.

*

o It fell upon a simmer's nicht,

o Whan the leaves were fair and green,

o That Willie met his gay ladie

o Intil the wood alane.

*

o "O narrow is my gown, Willie,

o That wont to be sae wide:

o And gane is a' my fair colour,

o That wont to be my pride.

*

o "But gin my father should get word

o What's past between us twa,

o Before that he should eat or drink,

o He'd hang you o'er that wa.

*

o "But ye'll come to my bower, Willie,

o Just as the sun gaes down;

o And kep me in your arms twa,

o And latna me fa' down."

*

o O whan the sun was now gane down,

o He's gaen him till her bower;

o And there, by the lee licht o' the moon,

o Her windows he lookit o'er.

*

o Intil a robe o' red scarlet

o She lap, fearless o' harm;

o And Willie was large o' lith and limb,

o And keppit her in his arm.

*

o And they've gane to the gude green wood;

o And ere the night was deen,

o She's born to him a bonny young son,

o Amang the leaves sae green.

*

o When night was gane, and day was come,

o And the sun began to peep,

o Up and raise he earl Richard,

o Out o' his drowsy sleep.

*

o He's ca'd upon his merry young men,

o By ane, by twa, and by three:

o "O what's come o' my daughter dear,

o That she's nae come to me?

*

o "I dreamt a dreary dream last night,

o God grant it come to gude!

o I dreamt I saw my daughter dear

o Drown in the saut sea flood.

*

o "But gin my daughter be dead or sick,

o O yet be stown awa,

o I mak a vow, and I'll keep it true,

o I'll hang ye ane and a'."

*

o They sought her back, they sought her fore,

o They sought her up and down;

o They got her in the gude green wood

o Nursing her bonny young son.

*

o He took the bonny boy in his arms

o And kist him tenderlie;

o Says, "Though I would your father hang.

o Your mother's dear to me."

*

o He kist him o'er and o'er again;

o "My granson I thee claim;

o And Robin Hood in gude green wood,

o And that shall be your name."

*

o And mony ane sings o' grass, o' grass,

o And mony ane sings o' corn;

o And mony ane sings o' Robin Hood,

o Kens little whare he was born.

*

o It wasna in the ha', the ha',

o Nor in the painted bower;

o But it was in the gude green wood,

o Amang the lily flower.

No. XXII. Sirvente of Bertrand de Born to induce the Kings of France and England to go to War.

*

o Pus li baron son irat e lor peza

o D'aquesta patz qu'an faita li duy rey,

o Farar chanso tal que, quant er apreza,

o A quadaun sera tart que guerrey:

o E no m'es bel de rey qu'en patz estey

o Dezeretatz, e que perda son drey,

o Tro 'l demanda que fai ara conqueza.

*

o Ben an camjat honor per avoleza,

o Segon qu'aug dir, Berguonhon e Francey;

o A rey armat ho ten hom a flaqueza,

o Quant es an camp e vai penre plaidey,

o E fora mielhs, par la fe qu'ieu vos dey,

o Al rey Felip que mogues lo desrey

o Que plaideyar armat sobre la gleza.

*

o Ges aital patz no met reys en proeza

o Cum aquesta, ni autra no l'agrey,

o E non es dregz qu'om l'abais sa riqueza,

o Que Yssaudun a fag jurar ab sey

o Lo reys Henrics e mes en son destrey,

o E no s cug ges qu'a son home s' autrey,

o Si 'l fieu d'Angieu li merma una cresteza.

*

o Si 'l rey engles a fait don ni largueza

o Al rey Felip, dreg es qu'el l'en mercey,

o Qu'el fetz liurar la moneda engleza,

o Qu'en Fransa'n son carzit sac e correy;

o E non foron Angevin ni Mansey,

o Quar d'esterlins foro ill primier conrey

o Que descofiron la gent Campaneza.

*

o Lo sors Enrics dís paraula corteza,

o Quan son nebot vi tornar en esfrey,

o Que desarmatz volgr' aver la fin preza.

o Quan fon armatz no vole penre plaidey;

o E no semblet ges lo senhor d'Orley

o Que desarmatz fon de peior mercey

o Que quant el cap ac la ventalha meza.

*

o Ad ambedos ten hom ad avoleza

o Quar an fag plait don quecs de lor sordey;

o Cinc duguatz à la corona Francesa,

o E dels comtatz son a dire li trey;

o E de Niort pert la rend 'e l'espley,

o E Caercins reman sai a mercey,

o E Bretanha e la terra engolmeza.

*

o Vai, Papiol, mon sirventes adrey

o Mi portaras part Crespin e'l Valey

o Mon Izembart, en la terra d'Arteza.

o Et diguas li m qu'a tal domna sopley

o Que jurar pot marves sobre la ley

o Que 'l genser es del mon e 'l pus corteza.

No. XXIII. Another Sirvente of Bertrand de Born, to the same purpose.

*

o Al dous nou termini blanc

o Del pascor ver la elesta

o Don lo nous temps s'escontenta,

o Quan la sazos es plus genta

o E plus covinens e val mais,

o Et hom devria esser plus guais,

o E meiller sabor mi a jais.

*

o Per que m peza quar m' estanc

o Qu'ieu ades no vey la festa,

o Q'us sols jorns mi sembla trenta

o Per una promessa genta

o Don mi sors temors et esglais,

o E no vuelh sia mieus Doais

o Ses la sospeysso de Cambrais.

*

o Pustell' en son huelh o cranc

o Qui jamais l'en amonesta,

o Que ja malvestatz dolenta

o No 'l valra mession genta

o Ni sojorns ni estar ad ais,

o Tan cum guerr'e trebaill e fais:

o So sapcha 'l seinher de Roais.

*

o Guerra ses fuec et ses sanc

o De rei o de gran podesta,

o Q'us coms laidis ni desmenta,

o Non es ges paraula genta,

o Qu'el pueys si sojorn ni s'engrays,

o E membre li qu'om li retrais

o Qu'anc en escut lansa non frais.

*

o Et anc no 'l vi bras ni flanc

o Trencat, ni camba ni testa

o Ferit de playa dolenta;

o Ni en gran ost ni en genta

o No 'l vim a Roam ni en assais,

o E ja entro que el s'eslais

o Lo reys on pretz non es verais.

*

o Rey frances ie us tenc per franc,

o Pus a tort vos far hom questa,

o Ni de Gisort no s presenta

o Patz ni fis que us sia genta,

o Qu'ab lui es la guerr' e la pais;

o E jovens, que guerra non pais,

o Esdeve leu flacx e savais.

*

o Ges d'en Oc e No m plane,

o Qu'ieu sai ben qu'en lui no resta

o La guerra ni no s'alenta

o Qu'anc patz ni fis no 'lh fon genta,

o Ni hom plus voluntiers non trais,

o Ni non fes cochas ni assais

o Ab pauc de gent ni ab gran fais.

o Lo reys Felips ama la pais

o Plus qu'el bons hom de Carentrais.

o En Oc e No vol guerra mais

o Que no fai negus dels Alguais.

No. XXIV. Sirvente of the Dauphin of Auvergne on his Quarrel with the King of England.

*

o Reis, pus vos de mi chantatz,

o Trobat avetz chantador:

o Mas tan me faitz de paor,

o Per que m torn a vos forsatz,

o E plazentiers vos en son:

o Mas d'aitan vos ochaizon,

o S'ueymais laissatz vostre fieus,

o No m mandetz querrs los mieus.

*

o Qu'ieu no soy reis coronatz,

o Ni hom de tan gran ricor

o Que pues'c a mon for, senhor,

o Defendre mas heretatz;

o Mas vos, que li Turc felon

o Temion mais que leon,

o Reis e duex, e coms d'Angieus,

o Sufretz que Gisors es sieus!

*

o Anc no fuy vostre juratz

o E conoissi ma folor;

o Que tant caval milsoudor

o E tant esterlis pesatz

o Donetz mon consin Guion:

o So m dizon siey companhon

o Tos temps segran vostr' estrieus,

o Sol tant larc nos tenga dieus.

*

o Be m par, quam vos diziatz

o Qu'ieu soli' aver valor,

o Que m laysassetz ses honor,

o Pueys que bon me laysavatz;

o Pero dieus m'a fag tan bon

o Qu' entr' el Puey et Albusson

o Puesc remaner entr' els mieus,

o Qu'ieu no soi sers ni juzieus.

*

o Senher valens et honratz

o Que m'avetz donat alhor,

o Si no m sembles camjador,

o Ves vos m'en fora tornatz;

o Mas nostre reis de saison

o Rend Ussoir' e lais Usson;

o E'l cobrar es me mot lieus,

o Qu'ieu n'ai sai agut sos brieus.

*

o Qu'ieu soi mot entalentatz

o De vos e de vostr' amor;

o Qu'el coms, que us fes tan d'onor,

o D'Engolmes n'es gen pagatz;

o Que Tolvera e la mayson,

o A guiza de larc baron,

o Li donetz, qu'anc non fos grieus;

o So m'a comtat us romieus.

*

o Reis, hueymais me veiretz proa,

o Que tal dona m'en somon,

o Cui soi tan finamen sieus

o Que totz sos comans m'es lieus.

No. XXV. Treaty of Alliance between Lewellyn Ap-Griffith, King of North Wales, with the King of France, Philip-le-Hardi.

Excellentissimo domino suo Philippo, Dei gracia illustri Francorum regi, Loelinus princeps Norwallie, fidelis suus, salutem et tam devotum quam debitum fidelitatis et reverentie famulatum. Quid retribuam excellentie nobilitatis vestre pro singulari honore et dono impreciabili quo vos, rex Francorum, imo princeps regum terre, me, fidelem vestrum, non tam munifice quam magnifice prevenientes, litteras vestras sigillo aureo impressas, intestimomum federis regni Francorum et Norwallie principatus michi militi vestro delegastis? Quas ego in armarus ecclesiasticis tanquam sacrosanctas relliquias conservari facio, ut sint memoriale perpetuum et testimonium inviolabile quod ego et heredes mei, vobis vestiisque heredibus inseparabiliter adherentes, vestris amicis amici erimus et inimici inimicis. Id ipsum a vestra regia dignitate erga me et meos amicos regaliter observari modis omnibus expecto postulans et expeto. Quod ut inviolabiliter observetur, congregato procerum meorum concilio et communi cunctorum Wallie principum assensu, quos omues vobiscum et hujus federis amicicia colligavi, sigilli mei testimonio me vobis fidelem in perpetuum promitto; et sicut fideliter promitto, fidelius promissum adimplebo. Preterea ex quo vestre sublimitatis litteras suscepi, nec treugas nec pacem nec etiam colloquium aliquod cum Anglicis feci. Sed per Dei graciam, ego et omnes Wallie principes unanimiter confederati, inimicis nostris imo vestris viriliter restitimus, et a jugo tirannidis ipsorum magnam partem terre et castra munitissima, que ipsi per fraudes et dolos occupaverant, per auxilium Domini in manu forti recuperavimus, recuperata in domino Deo potenter possidemus; unde postulantes expetimus universi Wallie principes quod sine nobis nec treugas nec pacem cum Anglicis faciatis, scituri quod nos nullo pacto vel precio, nisi precognita voluntatis vestre benivolencia, eis aliquo pacis seu federis vinculo copulabimur.

Leg. Sigillum Loclin.

No. XXVI. List of the Company of Yvain of Wales.

La reveue de Yvain de Galles, escuier, d'un chevalier bachelier et de quatre vins dix et huit autres escuiers de sa chambre et compaignie, receue à Limoges le viii jour de septembre, l'an mil trois cens soixante et seize.

* Ledit Yvain.

* Messire Frisemen.

* Hovel Duy le pennonier.

* Jeuffroy Blouet.

* Morgant de David.

* Evignon de Hovel.

* Guiffin de Jorwrch.

* Kerbut de Cadogon.

* David de Lewelin.

* Ithet de Jorwerth.

* Jenen de Jorwerth.

* Madot de Guiffin.

* Vledin Vagan.

* Genan Vaglan de Genan.

* Hovel de Eignon.

* Kendut de Genan.

* Guiffin de Rees.

* Algont.

* David ap Da.

* Guiffin de David ap Gervrlin.

* Genan ad Madot Gervrlin.

* Thoelbaret ap Grano.

* Jenan Goch ap Gelerym.

* Guiffin ap Blewelin.

* Jenan Hardeloch.

* Madot Jenan.

* Guillerme que Benebien.

* Joquen ap Morbran.

* Jonan Vachan ap Baudi.

* Eignon ap Jorwrch.

* Robin Barch.

* Joquen Caly.

* Robin ap Bledin.

* Madot Maclor.

* Bonet Cloyt.

* Guillerm Goch.

* Simont Garin.

* Bonet Agnean.

* Hany Walice Mon.

* Gionio Vach.

* Ienan Leclerc.

* Ada Bach.

* Roes Wathan.

* Madot Bloyt.

* Willin Goth.

* Lewelin Brun.

* Morice Bath.

* Ienan Guillin ap Eguen.

* Morice Gogher.

* David Bougan.

* Eignon Bach.

* Jarwerth Bauger.

* Hovel Bath.

* Jenan Goth.

* Jenan Cloyt.

* David Bath Helquen.

* Blewelin ap Jowerth.

* Jenan ap David Bath.

* Gernil.

* David Mon.

* Jenan Bloyt.

* Guillerme Pennyes.

* Madot duy ap Greffin.

* Guillerme Karul Villion.

* Madot voel Grath.

* Jenques Metham.

* Jaquen Pollrys.

* Jaquin Lewelin.

* Holquen ap Onucaut.

* Janan Rilivlis.

* Petit David.

* Jenan ap Guiffin ap Rait.

* Willot Vennet.

* Rye Saint Pere.

* Roullin Bouteillier.

* Robin Ichel.

* Madin Duy.

* Porhours.

* Guillin Guenart.

* Guiffin Bouton.

* Jorwerth ap Grox ap David.

* Thomas Chambellains.

* Madot Brechinot.

* Tomlin Grain.

* Jehan Lourppe.

* David Grath.

* Guiffin ap Jollis.

* David Rencon.

* Wollot Rael.

* Eignon ap Jenan Amis.

* Grigy Voulhedit.

* Eignon ap David Sais.

* Waquen Achyd.

* Jenan Glvynllench.

* Morice Buellet.

* Bellin Lyn.

* Jenan ap Glvilquin.

* Guiffin ap Jenan ap Roger.

* Jouston.

* Joquen ap Guiffin.

No. XXVII. List of the Company of John Wynn.

La reveue de Jehan Win, dit Poursigant, escuier, et de quatre vins dix et neuf autres escuiers de sa compaignie faite à Bourcneuf le premier jour de may l'an mil ccc quatre vins et un.

* Le dit Jehan Win, dit Poursigant.

* Hovel Flint.

* Le grant Kinorit.

* Le grant Win.

* Ichel ap Ironeich.

* Hovel Da

* Morgan Davi.

* Gieffin Blevet.

* Lawelin ap Ironeich.

* Gruffin ap Remeich.

* Jouan Gruffin ap Ruit.

* Hovel ap Eignon.

* Le Petit Davi.

* Joaun Davi Bach.

* Philippe Viglan.

* Jouan ap Gruffin Philip.

* Jouan ap Gruffin Melin.

* Jouan Scolart.

* Lemerlin Gechc.

* Hochelin Win.

* Tegoret ap Grono.

* Gruffin Lewelin.

* Ruit ap Davi Loit.

* Moris Goth.

* Lewillin Bren.

* Moris le Petit.

* Davy ap Ada.

* Eignen Adavisez.

* Bledin Vaquan.

* Greffin ap Ris.

* Geffroy ap Ollo.

* Kinorit ap Jennier.

* Jolem ap Gruffin.

* Jouan ap Madot.

* Madot a Gruffin ap Ledin.

* Madot Breheignon.

* Ullecot Ameurit.

* Madot a Gruffin.

* Villecot Benoist.

* Davi Mairon.

* Richart Eigin.

* Jouan ap Guilinap Eignon.

* Jouan Brith de Livroc.

* Jouan Bath ap Lewelin.

* Jouan Bath ap Madot Aguillin.

* Ada Bath.

* Jouan ap Galtier.

* Drolem Sibin.

* Gieffroy ap Madot.

* Javelin Ponis.

* Jambrois Methan.

* Merudut Buelt.

* Jorweith Landoin.

* Hovel ap Jouan.

* Jomerech son frere.

* Robin Maledin.

* Gruffin Karergnon.

* Jouan loit Bicham.

* Bichart Bach.

* Thomas Win.

* Jouan Goth ap Guillin.

* Gruffin Du.

* Eignen ap Madot ap Eignon.

* Davi ap Lewelin ap Linorit.

* Davi Bangain.

* Beneich ap Jennier.

* Gruffin Breton.

* Davi Mon.

* Richard Saint Pere.

* Belin Win.

* Henrri Vanlismion.

* Davi Goch.

* Robin ap Hovel.

* Eignen Bach.

* Ironeich ap Gren ap Davi.

* Hollen ap Ontron.

* Poil Pheich.

* Jonan Guin Loich.

* Jolem ap Morbrun.

* Gienen Bach ap Ichan.

* Eignen ap Hovel.

* Jennier Ardelet.

* Gruffin ap Ichan ap Prochet.

* Robin Yehel.

* Madot ap Ris.

* Mado ap Tudor.

* Gigny Vehendit.

* Jennier ap Jalx Bach.

* Jaques Flour.

* Gnellerme Lemorit.

* Jennier Wehan ap Jennier.

* Janhin W . .

* Madot ap Hovel Bach.

* Petit Yvain.

* Davy ap Greffin.

* Madot Guan.

* Gieffroy.

* Yvain Vaquant.

* Thomelin Chambellan.

* Thomas Coill.

No. XXVIII. Receipt given by Robin-ap-Llwydin, and List of his Company.

Sachent tuit que je Robin ab Ledin, escuier du pays de Gales, confesse avoir eu et receu de Jehan Chanteprim, trésorier des guerres du Roy notre sire, la somme de quatre vins et dix frans en prest et paiement sur les gaiges de moy et huit escuiers de ma compaignie, destinez et à destiner ès guerres du dit seigneur, ès bastides de devant le chastel de Ventadour, du nombre de ii cents homes d'armes ordennés à estre illeuc soubz le gouvernement de monseigneur de Coucy, capitaine général ès pays d'Auvergne et de Guyenne; de laquelle some de iiiixx et x frans je me tiens pour content et bien paiez et en quicte le Roy nostre dit seigneur, son dit trésorier et touz autres à qui quittance en appartient. Donné soubz mon seel, ou moutier devant le dit chastel de Ventadour, le xie jour du moys d'aoust l'an mil iiiciiiixx et neuf.

La monstre ou reveue Robin ap Ledin, escuier, né du pais de Gales, et huit autres escuiers de sa compaignie du dit pais faicte à la Bastide du moustier devant le chastel de Ventador, le xie jour d'aoust l'an mil ccc iiiixx et neuf.

* Premièrement, ledit Robin ap Ledin.

* Yvain ap Gault.

* Anudrier Scot.

* Edouart ap Davy.

* Clolin Baron.

* Guillaume de la Foy.

* Jehan Gras.

* Geuffroy le Roux.

* Yoquin Amorgant.

No. XXIX. List of the Company of Edward-ap-Owen.

La monstre ou reveue Edouart ap Yvain, escuier, né du pais de Gales, et neuf autres escuiers de sa compaignie du dit pais, faicte à la bastide du moustier devant le chastel de Ventador, le xie jour d'aoust l'an mil ccc iiiixx et neuf.

* Premièrement, ledit Edouard ap Yvain.

* Bellin Klin.

* Davy Levi.

* Richart de Saint-Pre.

* Eygnon ap Davy Sais.

* Davy Mon.

* Yvain Cloyt.

* Yvonnet Duclary.

* Jehan le Gales.

* Proffin Borton.

Pierre Saguet, chevalier, maistre d'ostel de monsieur le duc de Berry, commis de par le Roy notre sire à veoir les monstres ou reveues des gens d'armes et arballetriers estans ès bastides de devant le chastel de Ventadour, pour cet présent moys d'aoust à Jehan Chanteprime, trésorier des guerres du dit seigneur ou à son lieutenant, salut. Nous vous envoyons attachée soubz nostre scel la monstre ou reveue Edouart ap Yvain, escuier, né du pays de Gales, et neuft autres escuiers de sa compagnie du dit pays, montez et armez souffissans pour servir le dit seigneur en ses guerres ès dictes bastides, du nombre de iic lances ordonnées estre illeuc soubz le gouvernement de monseigneur de Coucy, général capitaine de par ledit sire ou pays de Guienne, faicte à la bastide du moustier devant ledit chastel, le xie jour d'aoust l'an mil ccc iiiixx et neuf. Sy vous mandons que au dit escuier pour lui et les dictes gens d'armes vous faictes prest et payement pour ledit moys en la manière accoustumée. Donné soubz nostre scel l'an et le jour dessus dit.

No. XXX. List of the Company of Owen-ap Griffith, and receipt given him.

La monstre ou reveue Yvain Greffin, escuier, né du pais de Gales, et neuf autres escuiers de sa compaignie du dit pais, faicte à la bastide du moustier devant le chastel de Ventador, le xie jour d'aoust l'an mil ccc iiiixx. et neuf.

* Premièrement, ledit Yvain Greffin.

* Morgan Davy.

* Cegaret ap Grono.

* Yvain Bulrayt.

* Petit Riquert.

* Madot ap Hovre.

* Philippe Bathan.

* Berthelot Davy.

* Davy Goth.

* Bertran de Lisle.

Sachent tuit que je Yvain Greffin, escuier, du pays de Gales, confesse avoir receu de Jehan Chanteprime, trésorier des guerres du Roy nostre sire, la somme de cent frans en prest et paiement sur les gaiges de moy et neuf escuiers de ma compaignie du dit pays de Gales, destinez et à destiner ès guerres du dit seigneur ès bastides de devant le chastel de Ventadour, du nombre de iie hommes d'armes ordennés à estre illeue soubz le gouvernement de monseigneur de Coucy, capitaine général de par le dit sire au pays de Guienne; de laquelle somme de cent frans dessus dits je me tiens pour contens et bien payez et en quitte le Roy nostre sire, son dit trésorier et touz autres à qui quittance en appartient. Donné à la bastide du moutier de devant le dit chastel, soubz mon seel, le xie jour du dit moys d'aoust l'an mil iiic iiiixx et neuf.

Yvain Greffin.

No. XXXI. Agreement of Yvain de Galles with King Charles V. for a sum of 300,000 francs d'or, and Alliance made between them and their Subjects.

A tous ceulx qui ces lectres verront Evain de Gales, salut. Comme les roys d'Angleterre, qui ont esté ès temps passez, meuz de mauvaiz courage et de convoitise dampnée, à tort et sanz cause et par traisons appensées, aient occis ou fait occirre aucuns de mes prédecesseurs roys de Gales et yceulx mis hors et deboutez du dit royaume, et ycellui royaume par force et puissance appliquie à eulx et detenu et ycellui soubzmis avec les subgiez du pais à plusieurs servitutes, lequel est et doit estre et appartenir à moi par la succession et comme plus prochain de sanc et de lignage et en droicte ligne descendant d'iceulx mes prédecesseurs roys d'icellui royaume, et pour avoir secours et aide à recouvrer le dit royaume, qui est mon héritage, me soye transportez devers pluseurs roys, princes et seigneurs chrestiens, et leur aye declairié et monstré clerement le droit que je y ay, en leur requerant et suppliant humblement que à ce me voulsissent aydier, et derrainement me soies traiz devers mon très puissant et très redoubté seigneur Charles, par la grace de Dieu roy de France, dauphin de Viennoys, et lui ay monstré mon droit que j'ay ou dit royaume et fait les requestes et supplicacions dessus dictes, et ycellui seigneur ayent compassion de mon estat, actendu le grant tort que les diz roys d'Angleterre ont eu en leur temps envers mes diz prédecesseurs et encores a le roy d'Angleterre qui est à present envers moy, et considéré toute la matière de mon fait de sa benigne et accoustumée clémence, qui est le mirouer singulier et exemple entire les chrestiens de toute justice et de toute grace et miséricorde pour touz opprimez relever et conforter, m'ayt octroyé son ayde et confort de gens d'armes et de navire pour recouvrer le dit royaume, qui est mon droit héritage, comme dit est; sachent tuit que je, en recongnoissant la grant amour que mon dit seigneur le roy de France m'a monstrée et monstre par vray effect en ce fait, ou quel et pour le quel mectre sus a mis et exposé du sien trois cens mil francs d'or et plus, tant en gaiges de gens d'armes, d'archiers et d'arbalestriers comme en navire et en gaiges et despens de marigniers, en hernoiz et en autres fraiz, missions et despens pluseurs, la quele somme je ne lui puis pas présentement rendre, promet loyaument et par la foy de mon corps et jure aux sains Euvangiles de Dieu, touchées corporelment pour moy et pour mes hoirs et successeurs à tousjoursmaiz, que la dicte somme de troiz cens mil francs d'or je lui rendray et payeray entièrement ou à ses diz hoirs et successeurs ou ceulx qui auront cause d'eulx, ou à leur commandement à leur voulenté, sanz autre terme, et dès maintenant ay fait et accordé pour moy, pour mes hoirs et successeurs et pour tout mon pais et subgiez perpetuelment avec mon dit seigneur le roy de France, pour lui, pour ses hoirs et successeurs roys, pour tout son pais et ses subgiez bonnes et fermes amitiez, confédéracions et aliances, si que je les ayderay et conforteray de ma personne, de mes subgiez et pays, de tout mon povoir, loyaument, contre toutes personnes qui pevent vivre et mourir. En tesmoing de ce, j'ay seellé ces lectres de mon seel. Donne à Paris, le xe jour de May, l'an de grace mil ccc soixante douze.

No. XXXII. Letter from Owen Glendowr, Prince of Wales, to the King of France, Charles VI.

Addressed—Serenissimo et illustrissimo principi domino Karolo, Dei gracia Francorum regi.

Serenissime princeps, humili recommendacione premissa scire dignemini quod nacio mea per plures annos elapsos per rabiem barbarorum Saxonum suppeditata fuit. Unde ex quo ipsi regimen habebant, licet de facto super nos oportuit cum eis ambulare, sed nunc, serenissime princeps, ex innata vobis bonitate, me et subditos meos ad recognoscendum verum Christi vicarium luculenter et graciose multipliciter informastis; de qua quidem informacione vestre excellencie regracior toto corde; et quia prout ex hujusmodi informacione intellexi, dominus Benedictus, summus pontifex, omnibus viis possibilibus offert se ad unionem in ecclesia Dei faciendam. Confidens eciam in jure ejusdem et vobiscum, quantum michi est possibile concordare, intendens ipsum pro vero Christi vicario, pro me et subditis meis, per licteras meas patentes hac vice majestati vestre per latorem presentium presentandas recognosco. Et quia, excellentissime princeps, rabie barbarica, ut prefertur, hic regnante, ecclesia menevensis metropolitica violenter ecclesie Cantuariensi obedire coacta fuit et in subjectione hujusmodi adhuc de facto remanet, et alia quamplura inconveniencia per hujusmodi barbaros ecclesie Wallie illata extiterint, que pro majori parte in licteris meis patentibus, de quibus prefertur, plenius sunt inserta, super quorum expedicione penes dominum summum pontificem habenda, magestatem vestram actencius deprecor et exoro, ut, sicut nos a tenebris in lucem erigere dignati estis, similiter violenciam et oppressionem ecclesie et subditorum meorum extirpare et aufferre, prout bene potestis, velitis, et vestram excellentissimam magestatem in prosperitate votiva diu conservet filius Virginis gloriose. Scriptum apud Pennal, ultimo die Marcii.

Vester ad vota

Owynus, princeps Wallie

No. XXXIII. The Souters of Selkirk at the Battle of Flodden Field, A Scottish Ballad of the Sixteenth Century.

*

o Up wi' the souters of Selkirk,

o And down wi' the earl of Home;

o And up wi' a' the braw lads,

o That sew the single-soled shoon.

*

o Fye upon yellow and yellow,

o And fye upon yellow and green,

o But up wi' the true blue and scarlet,

o And up wi' the single-soled sheen.

*

o Up wi' the souters of Selkirk,

o For they are baith trusty and leal;

o And up wi' the men o' the Forest,

o And down wi' the Merse to the deil.

No. XXXIV. The Battle of Bothwell Bridge— a Scottish

*

o "O, billie, billie, bonny billie,

o Will ye go to the wood wi' me?

o We'll ca' our horse hame masterless,

o An' gar them trow slain men are we."

*

o "O no, O no!" says Earlstoun,

o "For that's the thing that mauna be;

o For I am sworn to Bothwell Hill,

o Where I maun either gae or die."

*

o So Earlstoun rose in the morning,

o An' mounted by the break o' day;

o An' he has joined our Scottish lads,

o As they were marching out the way.

*

o "Now, farewell, father, and farewell, mother,

o And fare ye weel, my sisters three;

o An' fare ye weel, my Earlstoun,

o For thee again I'll never see!"

*

o So they're awa' to Bothwell Hill,

o An' waly' they rode bonnily!

o When the duke o' Monmouth saw them comin',

o He went to view their company.

*

o Ye're welcome, lads," the Monmouth said,

o 'Ye're welcome, brave Scots lads, to me;

o And sae are you, brave Earlstoun,

o The foremost o' your company!

*

o 'But yield your weapons ane an' a';

o O yield your weapons, lads, to me;

o For gin ye'll yield your weapons up,

o Ye' se a' gae hame to your country."

*

o Out then spak a Lennox lad,

o And waly but he spoke bonnily

o "I winna yield my weapons up,

o To you nor nae man that I see."

*

o Then he set up the flag o' red,

o A' set about wi' bonny blue;

o "Since ye'll no cease, and be at peace,

o See that ye stand by ither true."

*

o They stell'd their cannons on the height,

o And showr'd their shot down in the howe;

o An' beat our Scots lads even down,

o Thick they lay slain on every knowe.

*

o As e'er you saw the rain down fa',

o Or yet the arrow frae the bow,

o Sae our Scottish lads fell even down,

o An' they lay slain on every knowe.

*

o "O hold your hand," the Monmouth cry'd.

o Gie quarters to yon men for me!"

o But wicked Claver'se swore an oath,

o His cornet's death revenged sud be.

*

o "O hold your hand," then Monmouth cry'd,

o "If onything you'll do for me;

o Hold up your hand, you cursed Græme,

o Else a rebel to our king ye'll be."

*

o Then wicked Claver'se turn'd about,

o I wot an angry man was he;

o And he has lifted up his hat,

o And cry'd, "God bless his majesty!"

*

o Then he's awa' to London town,

o Aye e'en as fast as he can dree;

o Fause witnesses he has wi' him ta'en,

o And ta'en Monmouth's head frae his body.

*

o Alang the brae, beyond the brig,

o Mony brave man lies cauld and still;

o But lang we'll mind, and sair we'll rue,

o The bloody battle of Bothwell Hill.

12434704R00390

Printed in Great Britain
by Amazon.co.uk, Ltd.,
Marston Gate.